HONDA CR-V/ODYSSEY 1995-00 REPAIR MANUAL

CHILTON'S

Covers all U.S. and Canadian models of Honda CR-V and Odyssey

by **David R. Back,** A.S.E., S.T.S.

CHILTON Automotive Books

PUBLISHED BY **HAYNES NORTH AMERICA.** Inc.

Manufactured in USA
© 2000 Haynes North America, Inc.
ISBN 0-8019-9313
Library of Congress Catalog Card No. 99-076319-X
2345678901 9876543210

Haynes Publishing Group
Sparkford Nr Yeovil
Somerset BA22 7JJ England

Haynes North America, Inc
861 Lawrence Drive
Newbury Park
California 91320 USA

ABCDE
FGHIJ
KLMNO

Contents

Contents

DRIVE TRAIN   7

SUSPENSION AND STEERING   8

BRAKES   9

BODY AND TRIM   10

TROUBLESHOOTING   11

GLOSSARY

MASTER INDEX

SAFETY NOTICE

Proper service and repair procedures are vital to the safe, reliable operation of all motor vehicles, as well as the personal safety of those performing repairs. This manual outlines procedures for servicing and repairing vehicles using safe, effective methods. The procedures contain many NOTES, CAUTIONS and WARNINGS which should be followed, along with standard procedures to eliminate the possibility of personal injury or improper service which could damage the vehicle or compromise its safety.

It is important to note that repair procedures and techniques, tools and parts for servicing motor vehicles, as well as the skill and experience of the individual performing the work vary widely. It is not possible to anticipate all of the conceivable ways or conditions under which vehicles may be serviced, or to provide cautions as to all possible hazards that may result. Standard and accepted safety precautions and equipment should be used when handling toxic or flammable fluids, and safety goggles or other protection should be used during cutting, grinding, chiseling, prying, or any other process that can cause material removal or projectiles.

Some procedures require the use of tools specially designed for a specific purpose. Before substituting another tool or procedure, you must be completely satisfied that neither your personal safety, nor the performance of the vehicle will be endangered.

Although information in this manual is based on industry sources and is complete as possible at the time of publication, the possibility exists that some car manufacturers made later changes which could not be included here. While striving for total accuracy, the authors or publishers cannot assume responsibility for any errors, changes or omissions that may occur in the compilation of this data.

PART NUMBERS

Part numbers listed in this reference are not recommendations by Haynes North America, Inc. for any product brand name. They are references that can be used with interchange manuals and aftermarket supplier catalogs to locate each brand supplier's discrete part number.

SPECIAL TOOLS

Special tools are recommended by the vehicle manufacturer to perform their specific job. Use has been kept to a minimum, but where absolutely necessary, they are referred to in the text by the part number of the tool manufacturer. These tools can be purchased, under the appropriate part number, from your local dealer or regional distributor, or an equivalent tool can be purchased locally from a tool supplier or parts outlet. Before substituting any tool for the one recommended, read the SAFETY NOTICE at the top of this page.

ACKNOWLEDGMENTS

The publisher expresses appreciation to Honda Motor Company, Ltd, for their generous assistance.

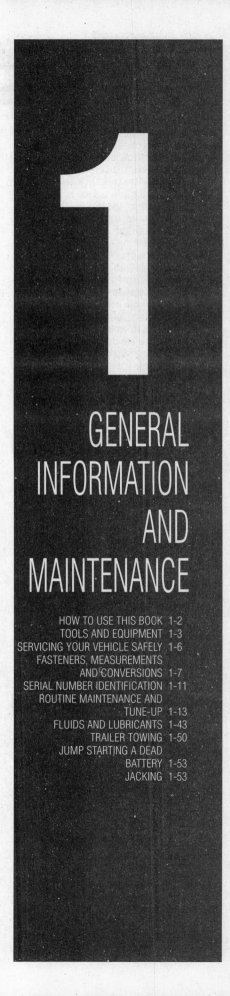

1

GENERAL INFORMATION AND MAINTENANCE

HOW TO USE THIS BOOK

Chilton's Total Car Care manual for the 1995–00 Honda Odyssey and 1997–00 Honda CR-V models is intended to help you learn more about the inner workings of your vehicle while saving you money on its upkeep and operation.

The beginning of the book will likely be referred to the most, since that is where you will find information for maintenance and tune-up. The other sections deal with the more complex systems of your vehicle. Operating systems from engine through brakes are covered to the extent that the average do-it-yourselfer becomes mechanically involved. This book will not explain such things as rebuilding a differential for the simple reason that the expertise required and the investment in special tools make this task uneconomical. It will, however, give you detailed instructions to help you change your own brake pads and shoes, replace spark plugs, and perform many more jobs that can save you money, give you personal satisfaction and help you avoid expensive problems.

A secondary purpose of this book is a reference for owners who want to understand their vehicle and/or their mechanics better. In this case, no tools at all are required.

Where to Begin

Before removing any bolts, read through the entire procedure. This will give you the overall view of what tools and supplies will be required. There is nothing more frustrating than having to walk to the bus stop on Monday morning because you were short one bolt on Sunday afternoon. So read ahead and plan ahead. Each operation should be approached logically and all procedures thoroughly understood before attempting any work.

All sections contain adjustments, maintenance, removal and installation procedures, and in some cases, repair or overhaul procedures. When repair is not considered practical, we tell you how to remove the part and then how to install the new or rebuilt replacement. In this way, you at least save labor costs. "Backyard" repair of some components is just not practical.

Avoiding Trouble

Many procedures in this book require you to "label and disconnect . . ." a group of lines, hoses or wires. Don't be lulled into thinking you can remember where everything goes—you won't. If you hook up vacuum or fuel lines incorrectly, the vehicle may run poorly, if at all. If you hook up electrical wiring incorrectly, you may instantly learn a very expensive lesson.

You don't need to know the official or engineering name for each hose or line. A piece of masking tape on the hose and a piece on its fitting will allow you to assign your own label such as the letter A or a short name. As long as you remember your own code, the lines can be reconnected by matching similar letters or names. Do remember that tape will dissolve in gasoline or other fluids; if a component is to be washed or cleaned, use another method of identification. A permanent felt-tipped marker or a metal scribe can be very handy for marking metal parts. Remove any tape or paper labels after assembly.

Maintenance or Repair?

It's necessary to mention the difference between maintenance and repair. Maintenance includes routine inspections, adjustments, and replacement of parts which show signs of normal wear. Maintenance compensates for wear or deterioration. Repair implies that something has broken or is not working. A need for repair is often caused by lack of maintenance. Example: draining and refilling the automatic transmission fluid is maintenance recommended by the manufacturer at specific mileage intervals. Failure to do this can shorten the life of the transmission/transaxle, requiring very expensive repairs. While no maintenance program can prevent items from breaking or wearing out, a general rule can be stated: MAINTENANCE IS CHEAPER THAN REPAIR.

Two basic mechanic's rules should be mentioned here. First, whenever the left side of the vehicle or engine is referred to, it is meant to specify the driver's side. Conversely, the right side of the vehicle means the passenger's side. Second, screws and bolts are removed by turning counterclockwise, and tightened by turning clockwise unless specifically noted.

Safety is always the most important rule. Constantly be aware of the dangers involved in working on an automobile and take the proper precautions. See the information in this section regarding SERVICING YOUR VEHICLE SAFELY and the SAFETY NOTICE on the acknowledgment page.

Avoiding the Most Common Mistakes

Pay attention to the instructions provided. There are 3 common mistakes in mechanical work:

1. Incorrect order of assembly, disassembly or adjustment. When taking something apart or putting it together, performing steps in the wrong order usually just costs you extra time; however, it CAN break something. Read the entire procedure before beginning disassembly. Perform everything in the order in which the instructions say you should, even if you can't immediately see a reason for it. When you're taking apart something that is very intricate, you might want to draw a picture of how it looks when assembled at one point in order to make sure you get everything back in its proper position. We will supply exploded views whenever possible. When making adjustments, perform them in the proper order. One adjustment possibly will affect another.

2. Overtorquing (or undertorquing). While it is more common for overtorquing to cause damage, undertorquing may allow a fastener to vibrate loose causing serious damage. Especially when dealing with aluminum parts, pay attention to torque specifications and utilize a torque wrench in assembly. If a torque figure is not available, remember that if you are using the right tool to perform the job, you will probably not have to strain yourself to get a fastener tight enough. The pitch of most threads is so slight that the tension you put on the wrench will be multiplied many times in actual force on what you are tightening. A good example of how critical torque is can be seen in the case of spark plug installation, especially where you are putting the plug into an aluminum cylinder head. Too little torque can fail to crush the gasket, causing leakage of combustion gases and consequent overheating of the plug and engine parts. Too much torque can damage the threads or distort the plug, changing the spark gap.

There are many commercial products available for ensuring that fasteners won't come loose, even if they are not torqued just right (a very common brand is Loctite®). If you're worried about getting something together tight enough to hold, but loose enough to avoid mechanical damage during assembly, one of these products might offer substantial insurance. Before choosing a threadlocking compound, read the label on the package and make sure the product is compatible with the materials, fluids, etc. involved.

3. Crossthreading. This occurs when a part such as a bolt is screwed into a nut or casting at the wrong angle and forced. Crossthreading is more likely to occur if access is difficult. It helps to clean and lubricate fasteners, then to start threading the bolt, spark plug, etc. with your fingers. If you encounter resistance, unscrew the part and start over again at a different angle until it can be inserted and turned several times without much effort. Keep in mind that many parts, especially spark plugs, have tapered threads, so that gentle turning will automatically bring the part you're threading to the proper angle. Don't put a wrench on the part until it's been tightened a couple of turns by hand. If you suddenly encounter resistance, and the part has not seated fully, don't force it. Pull it back out to make sure it's clean and threading properly.

Be sure to take your time and be patient, and always plan ahead. Allow yourself ample time to perform repairs and maintenance. You may find maintaining your car a satisfying and enjoyable experience.

TOOLS AND EQUIPMENT

▶ **See Figures 1 thru 15**

Naturally, without the proper tools and equipment it is impossible to properly service your vehicle. It would also be virtually impossible to catalog every tool that you would need to perform all of the operations in this book. Of course, it would be unwise for the amateur to rush out and buy an expensive set of tools on the theory that he/she may need one or more of them at some time.

The best approach is to proceed slowly, gathering a good quality set of those tools that are used most frequently. Don't be misled by the low cost of bargain tools. It is far better to spend a little more for better quality. Forged wrenches, 6 or 12-point sockets and fine tooth ratchets are by far preferable to their less expensive counterparts. As any good mechanic can tell you, there are few worse experiences than trying to work on a vehicle with bad tools. Your monetary savings will be far outweighed by frustration and mangled knuckles.

Begin accumulating those tools that are used most frequently: those associated with routine maintenance and tune-up. In addition to the normal assortment of screwdrivers and pliers, you should have the following tools:

- Wrenches/sockets and combination open end/box end wrenches in sizes from ⅛ –¾ in. or 3–19mm, as well as a ¹³⁄₁₆ in. or ⅝ in. spark plug socket (depending on plug type).

➡ **If possible, buy various length socket drive extensions. Universal-joint and wobble extensions can be extremely useful, but be careful when using them, as they can change the amount of torque applied to the socket.**

- Jackstands for support.
- Oil filter wrench.
- Spout or funnel for pouring fluids.
- Grease gun for chassis lubrication (unless your vehicle is not equipped with any grease fit-

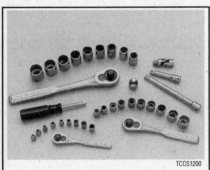

Fig. 1 All but the most basic procedures will require an assortment of ratchets and sockets

TCCS1200

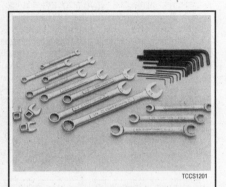

Fig. 2 In addition to ratchets, a good set of wrenches and hex keys will be necessary

TCCS1201

Fig. 3 A hydraulic floor jack and a set of jackstands are essential for lifting and supporting the vehicle

TCCS1202

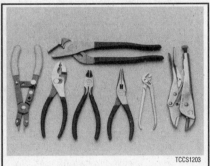

Fig. 4 An assortment of pliers, grippers and cutters will be handy for old rusted parts and stripped bolt heads

TCCS1203

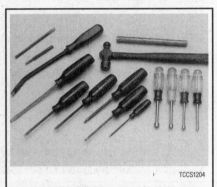

Fig. 5 Various drivers, chisels and prybars are great tools to have in your toolbox

TCCS1204

Fig. 6 Many repairs will require the use of a torque wrench to assure the components are properly fastened

TCCS1205

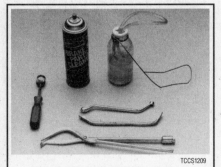

Fig. 7 Although not always necessary, using specialized brake tools will save time

TCCS1209

Fig. 8 A few inexpensive lubrication tools will make maintenance easier

TCCS1210

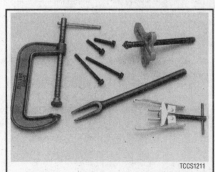

Fig. 9 Various pullers, clamps and separator tools are needed for many larger, more complicated repairs

TCCS1211

tings—for details, please refer to information on Fluids and Lubricants, later in this section).

• Hydrometer for checking the battery (unless equipped with a sealed, maintenance-free battery).
• A container for draining oil and other fluids.
• Rags for wiping up the inevitable mess.

In addition to the above items there are several others that are not absolutely necessary, but handy to have around. These include Oil Dry® (or an equivalent oil absorbent gravel—such as cat litter) and the usual supply of lubricants, antifreeze and fluids, although these can be purchased as needed. This is a basic list for routine maintenance, but only your personal needs and desire can accurately determine your list of tools.

After performing a few projects on the vehicle, you'll be amazed at the other tools and non-tools on your workbench. Some useful household items are: a large turkey baster or siphon, empty coffee cans and ice trays (to store parts), ball of twine, electrical tape for wiring, small rolls of colored tape for tagging lines or hoses, markers and pens, a note pad, golf tees (for plugging vacuum lines), metal coat hangers or a roll of mechanic's wire (to hold things out of the way), dental pick or similar long, pointed probe, a strong magnet, and a small mirror (to see into recesses and under manifolds).

A more advanced set of tools, suitable for tune-up work, can be drawn up easily. While the tools are slightly more sophisticated, they need not be outra-geously expensive. There are several inexpensive tach/dwell meters on the market that are every bit as good for the average mechanic as a professional model. Just be sure that it goes to a least 1200–1500 rpm on the tach scale and that it works on 4, 6 and 8-cylinder engines. The key to these purchases is to make them with an eye towards adaptability and wide range. A basic list of tune-up tools could include:

• Tach/dwell meter.
• Spark plug wrench and gapping tool.
• Feeler gauges for valve adjustment.
• Timing light.

The choice of a timing light should be made carefully. A light which works on the DC current supplied by the vehicle's battery is the best choice; it should have a xenon tube for brightness. On any vehicle with an electronic ignition system, a timing light with an inductive pickup that clamps around the No. 1 spark plug cable is preferred.

In addition to these basic tools, there are several other tools and gauges you may find useful. These include:

• Compression gauge. The screw-in type is slower to use, but eliminates the possibility of a faulty reading due to escaping pressure.
• Manifold vacuum gauge.
• 12V test light.
• A combination volt/ohmmeter
• Induction Ammeter. This is used for determin-ing whether or not there is current in a wire. These are handy for use if a wire is broken somewhere in a wiring harness.

As a final note, you will probably find a torque wrench necessary for all but the most basic work. The beam type models are perfectly adequate, although the newer click types (breakaway) are eas-ier to use. The click type torque wrenches tend to be more expensive. Also keep in mind that all types of torque wrenches should be periodically checked and/or recalibrated. You will have to decide for yourself which better fits your pocketbook, and pur-pose.

Special Tools

Normally, the use of special factory tools is avoided for repair procedures, since these are not readily available for the do-it-yourself mechanic. When it is possible to perform the job with more commonly available tools, it will be pointed out, but occasionally, a special tool was designed to perform a specific function and should be used. Before sub-stituting another tool, you should be convinced that neither your safety nor the performance of the vehicle will be compromised.

Special tools can usually be purchased from an automotive parts store or from your dealer. In some cases special tools may be available directly from the tool manufacturer.

TCCS1212

Fig. 10 A variety of tools and gauges should be used for spark plug gapping and installation

TCCX1P01

Fig. 11 Inductive type timing light

TCCX1P02

Fig. 12 A screw-in type compression gauge is recommended for compression testing

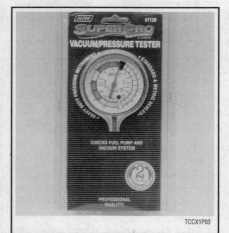

TCCX1P03

Fig. 13 A vacuum/pressure tester is neces-sary for many testing procedures

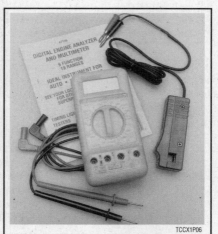

TCCX1P06

Fig. 14 Most modern automotive multime-ters incorporate many helpful features

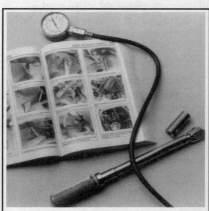

TCCS1213

Fig. 15 Proper information is vital, so always have a Chilton Total Car Care man-ual handy

DIAGNOSTIC TEST EQUIPMENT

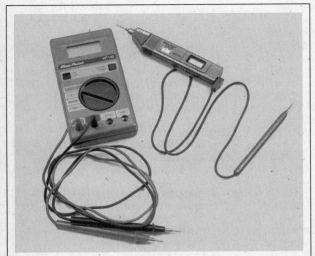

Digital multimeters come in a variety of styles and are a "must-have" for any serious home mechanic. Digital multimeters measure voltage (volts), resistance (ohms) and sometimes current (amperes). These versatile tools are used for checking all types of electrical or electronic components

Modern vehicles equipped with computer-controlled fuel, emission and ignition systems require modern electronic tools to diagnose problems. Many of these tools are designed solely for the professional mechanic and are too costly and difficult to use for the average do-it-yourselfer. However, various automotive aftermarket companies have introduced products that address the needs of the average home mechanic, providing sophisticated information at affordable cost. Consult your local auto parts store to determine what is available for your vehicle.

Trouble code tools allow the home mechanic to extract the "fault code" number from an on-board computer that has sensed a problem (usually indicated by a Check Engine light). Armed with this code, the home mechanic can focus attention on a suspect system or component

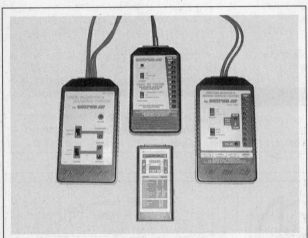

Sensor testers perform specific checks on many of the sensors and actuators used on today's computer-controlled vehicles. These testers can check sensors both on or off the vehicle, as well as test the accompanying electrical circuits

Hand-held scanners represent the most sophisticated of all do-it-yourself diagnostic tools. These tools do more than just access computer codes like the code readers above; they provide the user with an actual interface into the vehicle's computer. Comprehensive data on specific makes and models will come with the tool, either built-in or as a separate cartridge

SERVICING YOUR VEHICLE SAFELY

▶ **See Figures 16, 17, 18 and 19**

It is virtually impossible to anticipate all of the hazards involved with automotive maintenance and service, but care and common sense will prevent most accidents.

The rules of safety for mechanics range from "don't smoke around gasoline," to "use the proper tool(s) for the job." The trick to avoiding injuries is to develop safe work habits and to take every possible precaution.

Do's

• Do keep a fire extinguisher and first aid kit handy.

• Do wear safety glasses or goggles when cutting, drilling, grinding or prying, even if you have 20–20 vision. If you wear glasses for the sake of vision, wear safety goggles over your regular glasses.

• Do shield your eyes whenever you work around the battery. Batteries contain sulfuric acid. In case of contact with the eyes or skin, flush the area with water or a mixture of water and baking soda, then seek immediate medical attention.

• Do use safety stands (jackstands) for any undervehicle service. Jacks are for raising vehicles; jackstands are for making sure the vehicle stays

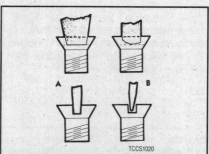

Fig. 16 Screwdrivers should be kept in good condition to prevent injury or damage which could result if the blade slips from the screw

raised until you want it to come down. Whenever the vehicle is raised, block the wheels remaining on the ground and set the parking brake.

• Do use adequate ventilation when working with any chemicals or hazardous materials. Like carbon monoxide, the asbestos dust resulting from some brake lining wear can be hazardous in sufficient quantities.

• Do disconnect the negative battery cable when working on the electrical system. The secondary ignition system contains EXTREMELY HIGH VOLTAGE. In some cases it can even exceed 50,000 volts.

• Do follow manufacturer's directions whenever working with potentially hazardous materials. Most chemicals and fluids are poisonous if taken internally.

• Do properly maintain your tools. Loose hammerheads, mushroomed punches and chisels, frayed or poorly grounded electrical cords, excessively worn screwdrivers, spread wrenches (open end), cracked sockets, slipping ratchets, or faulty droplight sockets can cause accidents.

• Likewise, keep your tools clean; a greasy wrench can slip off a bolt head, ruining the bolt and often harming your knuckles in the process.

• Do use the proper size and type of tool for the job at hand. Do select a wrench or socket that fits the nut or bolt. The wrench or socket should sit straight, not cocked.

• Do, when possible, pull on a wrench handle rather than push on it, and adjust your stance to prevent a fall.

• Do be sure that adjustable wrenches are tightly closed on the nut or bolt and pulled so that the force is on the side of the fixed jaw.

• Do strike squarely with a hammer; avoid glancing blows.

• Do set the parking brake and block the drive wheels if the work requires a running engine.

Don'ts

• Don't run the engine in a garage or anywhere else without proper ventilation—EVER! Carbon monoxide is poisonous; it takes a long time to leave the human body and you can build up a deadly

supply of it in your system by simply breathing in a little every day. You may not realize you are slowly poisoning yourself. Always use power vents, windows, fans and/or open the garage door.

• Don't work around moving parts while wearing loose clothing. Short sleeves are much safer than long, loose sleeves. Hard-toed shoes with neoprene soles protect your toes and give a better grip on slippery surfaces. Jewelry such as watches, fancy belt buckles, beads or body adornment of any kind is not safe working around a vehicle. Long hair should be tied back under a hat or cap.

• Don't use pockets for toolboxes. A fall or bump can drive a screwdriver deep into your body. Even a rag hanging from your back pocket can wrap around a spinning shaft or fan.

• Don't smoke when working around gasoline, cleaning solvent or other flammable material.

• Don't smoke when working around the battery. When the battery is being charged, it gives off explosive hydrogen gas.

• Don't use gasoline to wash your hands; there are excellent soaps available. Gasoline contains dangerous additives which can enter the body through a cut or through your pores. Gasoline also removes all the natural oils from the skin so that bone dry hands will suck up oil and grease.

• Don't service the air conditioning system unless you are equipped with the necessary tools and training. When liquid or compressed gas refrigerant is released to atmospheric pressure it will absorb heat from whatever it contacts. This will chill or freeze anything it touches.

• Don't use screwdrivers for anything other than driving screws! A screwdriver used as an prying tool can snap when you least expect it, causing injuries. At the very least, you'll ruin a good screwdriver.

• Don't use an emergency jack (that little ratchet, scissors, or pantograph jack supplied with the vehicle) for anything other than changing a flat! These jacks are only intended for emergency use out on the road; they are NOT designed as a maintenance tool. If you are serious about maintaining your vehicle yourself, invest in a hydraulic floor jack of at least a 1½ ton capacity, and at least two sturdy jackstands.

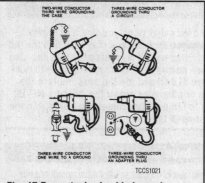

Fig. 17 Power tools should always be properly grounded

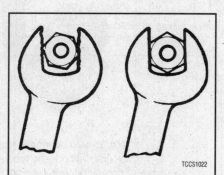

Fig. 18 Using the correct size wrench will help prevent the possibility of rounding off a nut

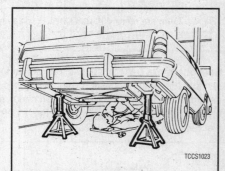

Fig. 19 NEVER work under a vehicle unless it is supported using safety stands (jackstands)

FASTENERS, MEASUREMENTS AND CONVERSIONS

Bolts, Nuts and Other Threaded Retainers

♦ See Figures 20, 21, 22 and 23

Although there are a great variety of fasteners found in the modern car or truck, the most com-monly used retainer is the threaded fastener (nuts, bolts, screws, studs, etc.). Most threaded retainers may be reused, provided that they are not damaged in use or during the repair. Some retainers (such as stretch bolts or torque prevailing nuts) are designed to deform when tightened or in use and should not be reinstalled.

Whenever possible, we will note any special retainers which should be replaced during a proce-dure. But you should always inspect the condition of a retainer when it is removed and replace any that show signs of damage. Check all threads for rust or corrosion which can increase the torque necessary to achieve the desired clamp load for which that fastener was originally selected. Additionally, be sure that the driver surface of the fastener has not been compromised by rounding or other damage. In some cases a driver surface may become only par-tially rounded, allowing the driver to catch in only one direction. In many of these occurrences, a fas-tener may be installed and tightened, but the driver would not be able to grip and loosen the fastener again. (This could lead to frustration down the line should that component ever need to be disassem-bled again).

If you must replace a fastener, whether due to design or damage, you must ALWAYS be sure to use the proper replacement. In all cases, a retainer of the same design, material and strength should be used. Markings on the heads of most bolts will help determine the proper strength of the fastener. The same material, thread and pitch must be selected to assure proper installation and safe operation of the vehicle afterwards.

Thread gauges are available to help measure a bolt or stud's thread. Most automotive and hardware stores keep gauges available to help you select the proper size. In a pinch, you can use another nut or bolt for a thread gauge. If the bolt you are replacing is not too badly damaged, you can select a match by finding another bolt which will thread in its place. If you find a nut which threads properly onto the damaged bolt, then use that nut to help select the replacement bolt. If however, the bolt you are replacing is so badly damaged (broken or drilled out) that its threads cannot be used as a gauge, you might start by looking for another bolt (from the same assembly or a similar location on your vehicle) which will thread into the damaged bolt's mounting. If so, the other bolt can be used to select a nut; the nut can then be used to select the replacement bolt.

In all cases, be absolutely sure you have selected the proper replacement. Don't be shy, you can always ask the store clerk for help.

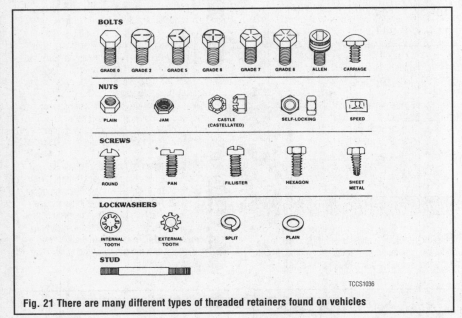

GRADE 0 · GRADE 2 · GRADE 5 · GRADE 6 · GRADE 7 · GRADE 8 · ALLEN · CARRIAGE

NUTS
PLAIN · JAM · CASTLE (CASTELLATED) · SELF-LOCKING · SPEED

SCREWS
ROUND · PAN · FILLISTER · HEXAGON · SHEET METAL

LOCKWASHERS
INTERNAL TOOTH · EXTERNAL TOOTH · SPLIT · PLAIN

STUD

TCCS1036

Fig. 21 There are many different types of threaded retainers found on vehicles

Fig. 20 figure:

POZIDRIVE · PHILLIPS RECESS · TORX® · CLUTCH RECESS

INDENTED HEXAGON · HEXAGON TRIMMED · HEXAGON WASHER HEAD

TCCS1037

Fig. 20 Here are a few of the most common screw/bolt driver styles

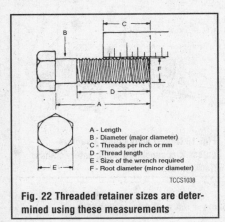

A - Length
B - Diameter (major diameter)
C - Threads per inch or mm
D - Thread length
E - Size of the wrench required
F - Root diameter (minor diameter)

TCCS1038

Fig. 22 Threaded retainer sizes are deter-mined using these measurements

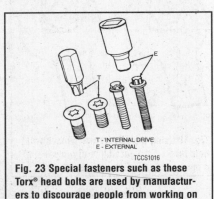

T - INTERNAL DRIVE
E - EXTERNAL

TCCS1016

Fig. 23 Special fasteners such as these Torx® head bolts are used by manufactur-ers to discourage people from working on vehicles without the proper tools

Torque

Torque is defined as the measurement of resis-tance to turning or rotating. It tends to twist a body about an axis of rotation. A common example of this would be tightening a threaded retainer such as a nut, bolt or screw. Measuring torque is one of the most common ways to help assure that a threaded retainer has been properly fastened.

When tightening a threaded fastener, torque is applied in three distinct areas, the head, the bearing surface and the clamp load. About 50 percent of the measured torque is used in overcoming bearing friction. This is the friction between the bearing surface of the bolt head, screw head or nut face and the base material or washer (the surface on which the fastener is rotating). Approximately 40 percent of the applied torque is used in overcoming thread friction. This leaves only about 10 percent of the applied torque to develop a useful clamp load (the force which holds a joint together). This means that friction can account for as much as 90 percent of the applied torque on a fastener.

TORQUE WRENCHES

♦ See Figures 24, 25 and 26

In most applications, a torque wrench can be used to assure proper installation of a fastener. Torque wrenches come in various designs and most automotive supply stores will carry a variety to suit your needs. A torque wrench should be used any time we supply a specific torque value for a fastener. A torque wrench can also be used if you are following the general guidelines in the accompanying charts. Keep in mind that because there is no worldwide standardization of fasteners, the charts are a general guideline and should be used with

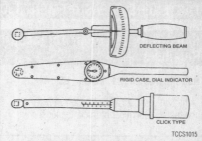

TCCS1015

Fig. 24 Various styles of torque wrenches are usually available at your local automotive supply store

	Mark		Class		Mark	Class
Hexagon head bolt	Bolt head No.	4—	4T	Stud bolt	No mark	4T
		5—	5T			
		6—	6T			
		7—	7T			
		8—	8T			
		9—	9T			
		10—	10T			
		11—	11T			
	No mark		4T			
Hexagon flange bolt w/ washer hexagon bolt	No mark		4T		Grooved	6T
Hexagon head bolt	Two protruding lines		5T			
Hexagon flange bolt w/ washer hexagon bolt	Two protruding lines		6T	Welded bolt		4T
Hexagon head bolt	Three protruding lines		7T			
Hexagon head bolt	Four protruding lines		8T			

TCCS1240

Fig. 25 Determining bolt strength of metric fasteners—NOTE: this is a typical bolt marking system, but there is not a worldwide standard

Class	Diameter mm	Pitch mm	Specified torque					
			Hexagon head bolt			Hexagon flange bolt		
			N·m	kgf·cm	ft·lbf	N·m	kgf·cm	ft·lbf
4T	6	1	5	55	48 in.·lbf	6	60	52 in.·lbf
	8	1.25	12.5	130	9	14	145	10
	10	1.25	26	260	19	29	290	21
	12	1.25	47	480	35	53	540	39
	14	1.5	74	760	55	84	850	61
	16	1.5	115	1,150	83	—	—	—
5T	6	1	6.5	65	56 in.·lbf	7.5	75	65 in.·lbf
	8	1.25	15.5	160	12	17.5	175	13
	10	1.25	32	330	24	36	360	26
	12	1.25	59	600	43	65	670	48
	14	1.5	91	930	67	100	1,050	76
	16	1.5	140	1,400	101	—	—	—
6T	6	1	8	80	69 in.·lbf	9	90	78 in.·lbf
	8	1.25	19	195	14	21	210	15
	10	1.25	39	400	29	44	440	32
	12	1.25	71	730	53	80	810	59
	14	1.5	110	1,100	80	125	1,250	90
	16	1.5	170	1,750	127	—	—	—
7T	6	1	10.5	110	8	12	120	9
	8	1.25	25	260	19	28	290	21
	10	1.25	52	530	38	58	590	43
	12	1.25	95	970	70	105	1,050	76
	14	1.5	145	1,500	108	165	1,700	123
	16	1.5	230	2,300	166	—	—	—
8T	8	1.25	29	300	22	33	330	24
	10	1.25	61	620	45	68	690	50
	12	1.25	110	1,100	80	120	1,250	90
9T	8	1.25	34	340	25	37	380	27
	10	1.25	70	710	51	78	790	57
	12	1.25	125	1,300	94	140	1,450	105
10T	8	1.25	38	390	28	42	430	31
	10	1.25	78	800	58	88	890	64
	12	1.25	140	1,450	105	155	1,600	116
11T	8	1.25	42	430	31	47	480	35
	10	1.25	87	890	64	97	990	72
	12	1.25	155	1,600	116	175	1,800	130

TCCS1241

Fig. 26 Typical bolt torques for metric fasteners—WARNING: use only as a guide

caution. Again, the general rule of "if you are using the right tool for the job, you should not have to strain to tighten a fastener" applies here.

Beam Type

♦ **See Figure 27**

The beam type torque wrench is one of the most popular types. It consists of a pointer attached to the head that runs the length of the flexible beam (shaft) to a scale located near the handle. As the wrench is pulled, the beam bends and the pointer indicates the torque using the scale.

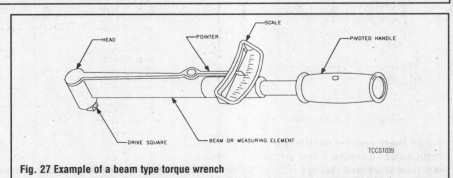

TCCS1039

Fig. 27 Example of a beam type torque wrench

Click (Breakaway) Type

♦ See Figure 28

Another popular design of torque wrench is the click type. To use the click type wrench you pre-adjust it to a torque setting. Once the torque is reached, the wrench has a reflex signaling feature that causes a momentary breakaway of the torque wrench body, sending an impulse to the operator's hand.

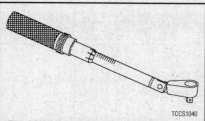

Fig. 28 A click type or breakaway torque wrench—note that this one has a pivoting head

Pivot Head Type

♦ See Figures 28 and 29

Some torque wrenches (usually of the click type) may be equipped with a pivot head which can allow it to be used in areas of limited access. BUT, it must be used properly. To hold a pivot head wrench, grasp the handle lightly, and as you pull on the handle, it should be floated on the pivot point. If the handle comes in contact with the yoke extension during the process of pulling, there is a very good chance the torque readings will be inaccurate because this could alter the wrench loading point. The design of the handle is usually such as to make it inconvenient to deliberately misuse the wrench.

➡ It should be mentioned that the use of any U-joint, wobble or extension will have an effect on the torque readings, no matter what type of wrench you are using. For the most accurate readings, install the socket directly on the wrench driver. If necessary, straight extensions (which hold a socket directly under the wrench driver) will have the least effect on the torque reading. Avoid any extension that alters the length of the wrench from the handle to the head/driving point (such as a crow's foot). U-joint or wobble extensions can greatly affect the readings; avoid their use at all times.

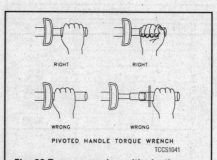

Fig. 29 Torque wrenches with pivoting heads must be grasped and used properly to prevent an incorrect reading

Rigid Case (Direct Reading)

♦ See Figure 30

A rigid case or direct reading torque wrench is equipped with a dial indicator to show torque values. One advantage of these wrenches is that they can be held at any position on the wrench without affecting accuracy. These wrenches are often preferred because they tend to be compact, easy to read and have a great degree of accuracy.

TORQUE ANGLE METERS

♦ See Figure 31

Because the frictional characteristics of each fastener or threaded hole will vary, clamp loads which are based strictly on torque will vary as well. In most applications, this variance is not significant enough to cause worry. But, in certain applications, a manu-

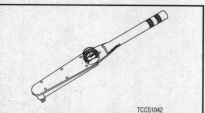

Fig. 30 The rigid case (direct reading) torque wrench uses a dial indicator to show torque

facturer's engineers may determine that more precise clamp loads are necessary (such is the case with many aluminum cylinder heads). In these cases, a torque angle method of installation would be specified. When installing fasteners which are torque angle tightened, a predetermined seating torque and standard torque wrench are usually used first to remove any compliance from the joint. The fastener is then tightened the specified additional portion of a turn measured in degrees. A torque angle gauge (mechanical protractor) is used for these applications.

Standard and Metric Measurements

♦ See Figure 32

Throughout this manual, specifications are given to help you determine the condition of various com-

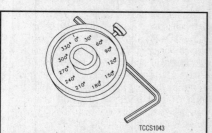

Fig. 31 Some specifications require the use of a torque angle meter (mechanical protractor)

CONVERSION FACTORS

LENGTH–DISTANCE

Inches (in.)	x 25.4	= Millimeters (mm)	x .0394	= Inches
Feet (ft.)	x .305	= Meters (m)	x 3.281	= Feet
Miles	x 1.609	= Kilometers (km)	x .0621	= Miles

VOLUME

Cubic Inches (in3)	x 16.387	= Cubic Centimeters	x .061	= in3
IMP Pints (IMP pt.)	x .568	= Liters (L)	x 1.76	= IMP pt.
IMP Quarts (IMP qt.)	x 1.137	= Liters (L)	x .88	= IMP qt.
IMP Gallons (IMP gal.)	x 4.546	= Liters (L)	x .22	= IMP gal.
IMP Quarts (IMP qt.)	x 1.201	= US Quarts (US qt.)	x .833	= IMP qt.
IMP Gallons (IMP gal.)	x 1.201	= US Gallons (US gal.)	x .833	= IMP gal.
Fl. Ounces	x 29.573	= Milliliters	x .034	= Ounces
US Pints (US pt.)	x .473	= Liters (L)	x 2.113	= Pints
US Quarts (US qt.)	x .946	= Liters (L)	x 1.057	= Quarts
US Gallons (US gal.)	x 3.785	= Liters (L)	x .264	= Gallons

MASS–WEIGHT

Ounces (oz.)	x 28.35	= Grams (g)	x .035	= Ounces
Pounds (lb.)	x .454	= Kilograms (kg)	x 2.205	= Pounds

PRESSURE

Pounds Per Sq. In. (psi)	x 6.895	= Kilopascals (kPa)	x .145	= psi
Inches of Mercury (Hg)	x .4912	= psi	x 2.036	= Hg
Inches of Mercury (Hg)	x 3.377	= Kilopascals (kPa)	x .2961	= Hg
Inches of Water (H_2O)	x .07355	= Inches of Mercury	x 13.783	= H_2O
Inches of Water (H_2O)	x .03613	= psi	x 27.684	= H_2O
Inches of Water (H_2O)	x .248	= Kilopascals (kPa)	x 4.026	= H_2O

TORQUE

Pounds-Force Inches (in-lb)	x .113	= Newton Meters (N·m)	x 8.85	= in-lb
Pounds-Force Feet (ft-lb)	x 1.356	= Newton Meters (N·m)	x .738	= ft-lb

VELOCITY

Miles Per Hour (MPH)	x 1.609	= Kilometers Per Hour (KPH)	x .621	= MPH

POWER

Horsepower (Hp)	x .745	= Kilowatts	x 1.34	= Horsepower

FUEL CONSUMPTION*

Miles Per Gallon IMP (MPG)	x .354	= Kilometers Per Liter (Km/L)	
Kilometers Per Liter (Km/L)	x 2.352	= IMP MPG	
Miles Per Gallon US (MPG)	x .425	= Kilometers Per Liter (Km/L)	
Kilometers Per Liter (Km/L)	x 2.352	= US MPG	

*It is common to covert from miles per gallon (mpg) to liters/100 kilometers (1/100 km), where mpg (IMP) x 1/100 km = 282 and mpg (US) x 1/100 km = 235.

TEMPERATURE

Degree Fahrenheit (°F)	= (°C x 1.8) + 32
Degree Celsius (°C)	= (°F − 32) x .56

Fig. 32 Standard and metric conversion factors chart

ponents on your vehicle, or to assist you in their installation. Some of the most common measurements include length (in. or cm/mm), torque (ft. lbs., inch lbs. or Nm) and pressure (psi, in. Hg, kPa or mm Hg). In most cases, we strive to provide the proper measurement as determined by the manufacturer's engineers.

Though, in some cases, that value may not be conveniently measured with what is available in your toolbox. Luckily, many of the measuring devices which are available today will have two scales so the Standard or Metric measurements may easily be taken. If any of the various measuring tools which are available to you do not contain the same scale as listed in the specifications, use the accompanying conversion factors to determine the proper value.

The conversion factor chart is used by taking the given specification and multiplying it by the necessary conversion factor. For instance, looking at the first line, if you have a measurement in inches such as "free-play should be 2 in." but your ruler reads only in millimeters, multiply 2 in. by the conversion factor of 25.4 to get the metric equivalent of 50.8mm. Likewise, if the specification was given only in a Metric measurement, for example in Newton Meters (Nm), then look at the center column first. If the measurement is 100 Nm, multiply it by the conversion factor of 0.738 to get 73.8 ft. lbs.

SERIAL NUMBER IDENTIFICATION

▶ See Figure 33

Vehicle

▶ See Figures 34 and 35

The Vehicle Identification Number (VIN) can be found in three locations. It is stamped into the body on the top, center portion of the firewall, on a stamped plate attached to the left front top of the dashboard, and on a label located on the driver's door jam near the door latch. The VIN on the dashboard is the easiest to see, as it is close to the windshield on the driver's side of the vehicle and visible by looking through the windshield near the tip of the left side wiper blade.

The 17-character label contains the following information:
- Digits 1, 2 and 3: Manufacturer, Make and Type of Vehicle
- Digits 4, 5 and 6: Line, Body and Engine Type
- Digit 7: Body and Transmission Type
- Digit 8: Vehicle Grade (Series)
- Digit 9: Check digit
- Digit 10: Vehicle model year
- Digit 11: Factory Code
- Digits 12 through 17: Serial Number

Engine

▶ See Figures 36 and 37

The installed engine type is part of the Line, Body, and Engine type three character code found in serial number positions 4, 5 and 6. This three-character code represents the basic body (or platform) type, and engine type installed for each particular model year. Sometimes this code will remain the

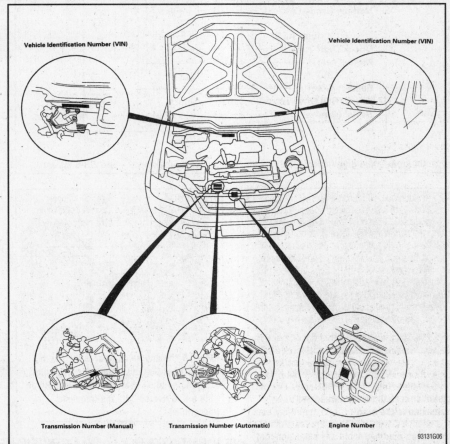

Fig. 33 Typical locations for Honda serial numbers. Knowing the VIN, Engine Number, and Transmission Number can be of great assistance when repairs and replacement parts are needed

VEHICLE IDENTIFICATION CHART

Engine Code						Model Year	
Code	Liters	Cu. In. (cc)	Cyl.	Fuel Sys.	Eng. Mfg.	Code	Year
B20B4	2.0	120 (1973)	4	SMFI	Honda	S	1995
B20Z2	2.0	120 (1973)	4	SMFI	Honda	T	1996
F22B6	2.2	132 (2156)	4	SMFI	Honda	V	1997
F23A7	2.3	137 (2254)	4	SMFI	Honda	W	1998
J35A1	3.5	212 (3471)	6	SMFI	Honda	X	1999
						Y	2000

SMFI - Sequential Multi-port Fuel Injection

93131C01

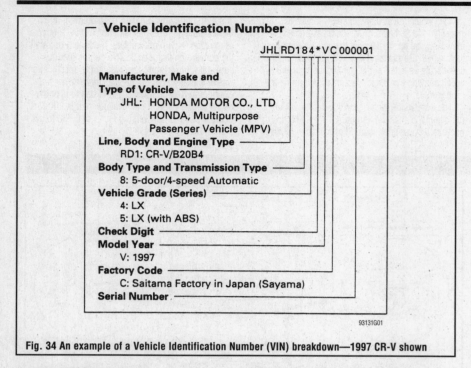

Vehicle Identification Number

JHLRD184*VC 000001

Manufacturer, Make and Type of Vehicle
JHL: HONDA MOTOR CO., LTD
HONDA, Multipurpose Passenger Vehicle (MPV)

Line, Body and Engine Type
RD1: CR-V/B20B4

Body Type and Transmission Type
8: 5-door/4-speed Automatic

Vehicle Grade (Series)
4: LX
5: LX (with ABS)

Check Digit

Model Year
V: 1997

Factory Code
C: Saitama Factory in Japan (Sayama)

Serial Number

93131G01

Fig. 34 An example of a Vehicle Identification Number (VIN) breakdown—1997 CR-V shown

93131P01

Fig. 35 To find the VIN, look through the left lower corner of the windshield. The number is stamped on a plate and attached to the dash

93131P12

Fig. 36 The engine number is the number on the right that is stamped directly onto the engine block. The VIN number plate on the left is riveted onto the transaxle assembly

same from one year to another although the installed engine type may change. Although the code describes which engine type is installed as original equipment for a particular model year, this code is not a portion of the five character engine type and serial number stamped on the engine block. The engine type and serial number are found near the front of the vehicle, stamped on the engine block where the transaxle housing and engine block join one another.

The engine type is a five-character code, which is followed by and separated from the engine serial number by a hyphen. This code is used the by the manufacturer to designate the engine type. The charts in this Total Car Care book use the engine type to provide engine specifications which may vary from engine to engine. Locate the engine code stamped in the engine block and determine the engine type before attempting to service the vehicle. It's a good idea to write the engine code and the engine type along with the complete VIN of the vehicle on the inside cover of this Total Car Care manual. Knowing the engine type and vehicle serial number will not only help with obtaining the correct service information, this information will assist the local parts vendors when shopping for replacement parts. Bring the manual along when shopping for parts. Having the manual handy could help to properly identify a needed part. If a part has to be ordered, it's far better to order it correctly the first time and/or avoid having a vehicle completely disassembled only to find out the part needed is not in stock. On rare occasions, a part may be backordered, meaning the part is temporarily unavailable. In a situation such as this, it may be wise to wait until the part is available before starting on the repair or maintenance about to be undertaken, if the vehicle can be operated in a safe and reliable manner.

Transaxle

▶ See Figure 38

The seventh position of the VIN represents the installed transaxle type and body type. This single digit represents the body (or platform) type, and transaxle type installed for each particular model

ENGINE IDENTIFICATION AND SPECIFICATIONS

Year	Model	Engine ID/VIN	Engine Displacement Liters (cc)	No. of Cyl.	Engine Type	Fuel System Type	Net Horsepower @ rpm	Net Torque @ rpm (ft. lbs.)	Bore x Stroke (in.)	Compression Ratio	Oil Pressure @ rpm
1995	Odyssey	F22B6	2.2 (2156)	4	SOHC	SMFI	140@5600	145@4500	3.35x3.74	8.8:1	50@3000
1996	Odyssey	F22B6	2.2 (2156)	4	SOHC	SMFI	140@5600	145@4500	3.35x3.74	8.8:1	50@3000
1997	CR-V	B20B4	2.0 (1973)	4	DOHC	SMFI	126@5400	133@4300	3.31X3.50	9.2:1	50@3000
	Odyssey	F22B6	2.2 (2156)	4	SOHC	SMFI	140@5600	145@4600	3.35x3.74	8.8:1	50@3000
1998	CR-V	B20B4	2.0 (1973)	4	DOHC	SMFI	126@5400	133@4300	3.31X3.50	9.2:1	50@3000
	Odyssey	F23A7	2.3 (2254)	4	SOHC	SMFI	150@5600	152@4700	3.39X3.82	9.3:1	50@3000
1999	CR-V	B20Z2	2.0 (1973)	4	DOHC	SMFI	146@6200	133@4500	3.31X3.50	9.6:1	50@3000
	Odyssey	J35A1	3.5 (3471)	6	SOHC	SMFI	210@5200	229@4300	3.50X3.66	9.4:1	71@3000
2000	CR-V	B20Z2	2.0 (1973)	4	DOHC	SMFI	146@6200	133@4500	3.31X3.50	9.6:1	50@3000
	Odyssey	J35A1	3.5 (3471)	6	SOHC	SMFI	210@5200	229@4300	3.50X3.66	9.4:1	71@3000

SMFI - Sequential Multi-port Fuel Injection
SOHC - Single Overhead Cam
DOHC - Double Overhead Cam

93131C02

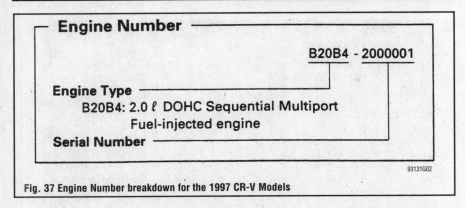

Fig. 37 Engine Number breakdown for the 1997 CR-V Models

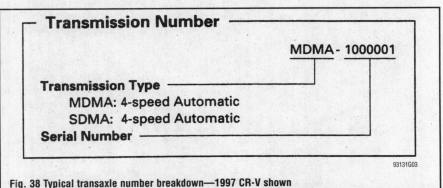

Fig. 38 Typical transaxle number breakdown—1997 CR-V shown

year. Sometimes this code will remain the same from one year to another and from one model to another, although the installed transaxle type could be different. Although the code describes which transaxle type is installed as original equipment for a particular model year, this code is not a portion of the four-character transaxle type and serial number stamped on the transaxle casing.

The transaxle type and serial numbers are stamped into the transaxle casing facing up and near the starter motor assembly. The transaxle type is a four-character code, which is followed by and separated from the transaxle serial number by a hyphen. This code is used the by the manufacturer to designate the transaxle type and the transaxle specifications may vary from transaxle to transaxle.

Vehicle Emission Control Information (VECI) Label

▶ See Figure 39

The Vehicle Emission Control Information (VECI) label is located on the underside of the hood on Honda CR-V and Odyssey models. This label is extremely important when performing maintenance, emissions inspection or ordering engine and engine management related parts.

Sometimes during production of the vehicle the manufacturer may institute updates that require a different component and/or specification. An example of this might be a change in the recommended spark plug and spark plug gap or

ignition timing and valve adjustment specifications.

The label also reflects the emissions group that is installed on the vehicle. There are 3 possible emission groups, and as a result, the emissions equipment installed on the vehicle and the related maintenance specifications could differ. The 3 possibilities are:

- 50ST (50 States)
- 49ST (49 States/Federal)
- CAL (California)

Another important emissions related notice is located directly below the VECI specifications. This notice pertains to the emissions test procedures that can be performed safely to the vehicle. Many states now perform a dynamic emissions inspection where the drive wheels are placed on a set of rollers. The emissions can be tested and a load applied to the driven wheels to simulate actual driving conditions. However on 4-Wheel Drive (4WD) vehicles, unless the inspection facility has specialized 4WD test equipment, this procedure cannot be performed and a static inspection must be substituted in lieu of a dynamic test.

If your vehicle is involved in a front end collision and the hood is replaced, make sure the repair shop either transfers or replaces the labels with the correct ones. The label part number will often appear on the label.

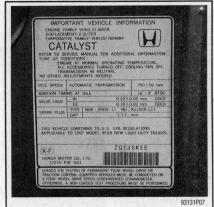

Fig. 39 The VECI label is located on the underside of the hood, and can reflect changes made during production

ROUTINE MAINTENANCE AND TUNE-UP

Proper maintenance and tune-up is the key to long and trouble-free vehicle life, and the work can yield its own rewards. Studies have shown that a properly tuned and maintained vehicle can achieve better gas mileage than an out-of-tune vehicle. As a conscientious owner and driver, set aside a Saturday morning, say once a month, to check or replace items which could cause major problems later. Keep your

own personal log to jot down which services you performed, how much the parts cost you, the date, and the exact odometer reading at the time. Keep all receipts for such items as engine oil and filters, so that they may be referred to in case of related problems or to determine operating expenses. As a do-it-yourselfer, these receipts are the only proof you have that the required maintenance was performed. In the event

of a warranty problem, these receipts will be invaluable.

The literature provided with your vehicle when it was originally delivered includes the factory recommended maintenance schedule. If you no longer have this literature, replacement copies are usually available from the dealer. A maintenance schedule is provided later in this section, in case you do not have the factory literature.

MAINTENANCE COMPONENT LOCATIONS—CR-V

1. Air filter
2. Battery
3. Coolant overflow tank
4. Upper radiator hose
5. Distributor cap and rotor
6. Fuel filter
7. Radiator cap
8. Engine oil fill cap
9. Spark plug wire
10. Positive Crankcase Ventilation (PCV) valve
11. Engine oil dipstick
12. Spark plugs
13. Brake master cylinder reservoir
14. Camshaft timing belt
15. Power steering belt
16. Power steering fluid reservoir
17. Washer fluid reservoir

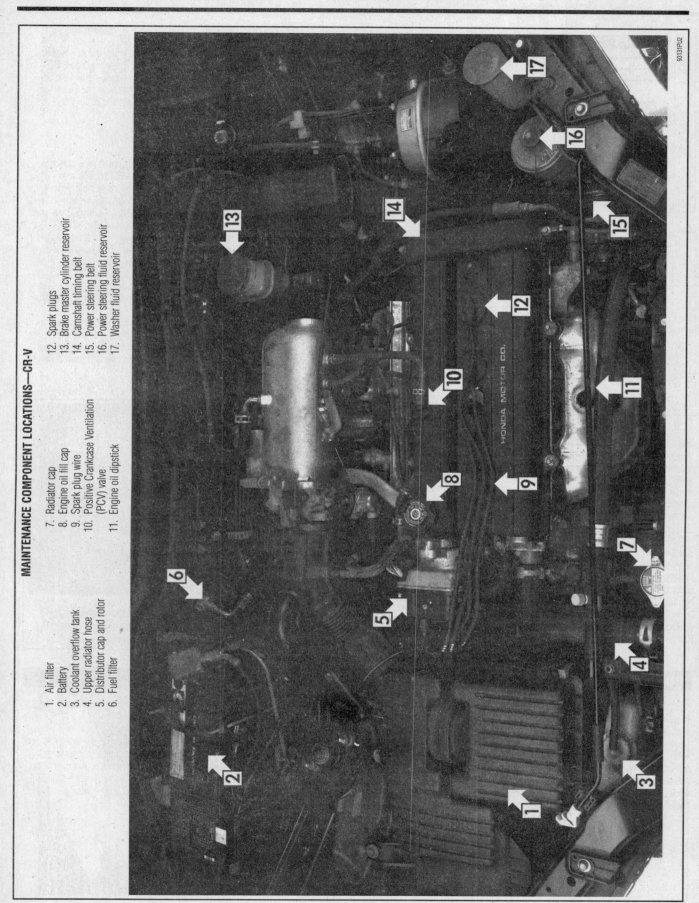

93131PU2

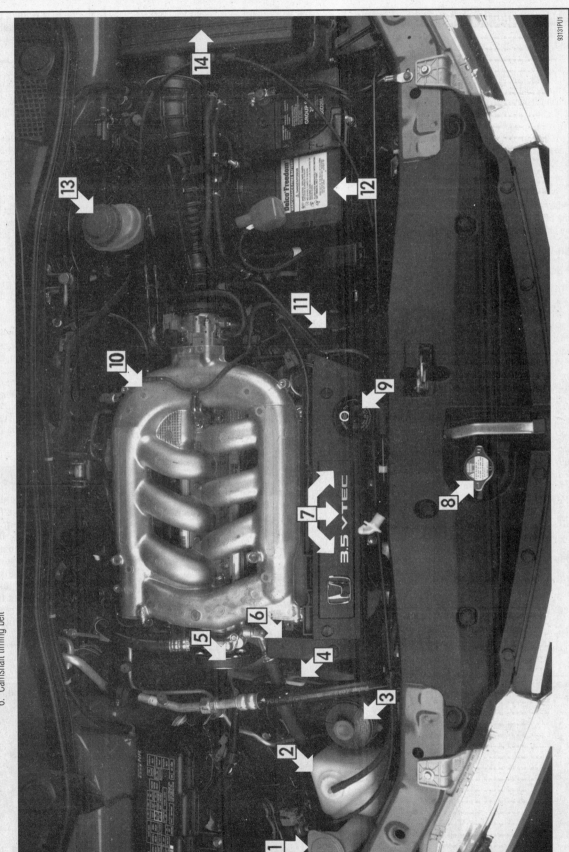

MAINTENANCE COMPONENT LOCATIONS—V6 ODYSSEY

1. Washer fluid reservoir
2. Coolant overflow tank
3. Power steering fluid reservoir
4. Engine oil dipstick
5. Power steering belt
6. Camshaft timing belt
7. Spark plugs
8. Radiator cap
9. Engine oil fill cap
10. Positive Crankcase Ventilation (PCV) valve
11. Upper radiator hose
12. Battery
13. Brake master cylinder reservoir
14. Air filter

Air Cleaner (Element)

REMOVAL & INSTALLATION

The air cleaner element on both the CR-V and Odyssey models is located in a plastic housing which is connected to the intake manifold via a flexible tubular air duct. The recommended normal replacement interval for the air filter is 30,000 miles (48,000 km) or 2 years, whichever occurs first. For Canadian vehicles or vehicles operated in severe conditions, the filter should be replaced every 15,000 miles (24,000 km) or every year, which ever occurs first.

➡**Per the manufacturer's recommendations, the air filter element should never be cleaned by blowing it off with compressed air.**

CR-V Models

▶ **See Figures 40, 41 and 42**

1. Release the spring loaded retainers from the upper air filter housing.
2. Release the upper air filter housing from the intake bellows, and lift the upper housing away from the air filter element and the lower air filter housing.
3. Cover the opening of the intake bellows to prevent debris from entering and then lift the air filter element away from the lower air filter housing.

To install:

4. Remove any debris found in the lower air filter housing and install a new air filter element into the housing with the open pleats facing downward, making sure the seal surrounding the air filter is fully seated.
5. Remove the cover used to protect the intake bellows and reinstall the air filter housing cover securely into the intake bellows. Seat the upper housing against the lower housing making sure the air filter seal is properly seated and fasten the two spring loaded retainers to secure the cover.

Odyssey Models

4-CYLINDER ENGINES

1. Remove the fasteners securing the air intake cover and remove the cover.
2. Loosen the battery hold down bracket and slide the bracket to access the upper air filter housing fasteners.

3. Loosen the upper air filter housing fasteners and remove the upper filter housing.

To install:

4. Remove any debris found in the lower air filter housing and install a new air filter element into the housing making sure the seal surrounding the air filter is fully seated.
5. Reinstall the air filter housing cover, seating the upper housing against the lower housing making sure the air filter seal is properly seated and tighten the housing fasteners in a criss-cross tightening sequence to secure the cover squarely.
6. Properly reposition the battery hold down bracket and tighten the fasteners to secure the battery.
7. Install the air intake cover.

V6 ENGINES

1. Obtain the radio security code and note the radio station presets.
2. Remove the cable guide clamp from the upper air filter housing.
3. Disconnect the negative battery cable.
4. Remove the plastic cover between the battery and the upper air filter housing.
5. Loosen the upper air filter housing fasteners and remove the upper filter housing.

To install:

6. Remove any debris found in the lower air filter housing and install a new air filter element into the housing making sure the seal surrounding the air filter is fully seated.
7. Reinstall the air filter housing cover, seating the upper housing against the lower housing making sure the air filter seal is properly seated and tighten the housing fasteners in a criss-cross tightening sequence to secure the cover squarely.
8. Install the plastic cover between the battery and the upper air filter housing.
9. Connect the negative battery cable.
10. Install the cable guide clamp to the upper air filter housing.
11. Enter the radio security code and the radio station presets.

Fuel Filter

✳✳ CAUTION

The fuel injection system remains under pressure after the engine has been turned

OFF. Properly relieve fuel pressure before disconnecting any fuel lines. Failure to do so may result in fire or personal injury.

The Honda CR-V and Odyssey models do not have a recommended replacement interval for the fuel filter. The manufacturer recommends inspecting the fuel system fuel lines, fittings and hoses at least once a year or every 15,000 miles (24,000 km), whichever occurs first, and more often if the vehicle is operated in severe conditions. If the fuel system pressure drops below specification, the filter should be replaced and the pressure rechecked before replacing the pump. Although the manufacturer does not have replacement intervals for the fuel filter, a restricted fuel filter can cause the fuel pump to work harder than necessary, reducing it's life expectancy and/or cause running problems. The pump operation may also become more noisy as well. For preventative maintenance purposes, replacing the filter every five years or during the 120,000 mile (192,000 km) maintenance interval could help to extend the life of the fuel pump. All of the fuel filters with exception of the V6 Odyssey models are located on the vehicle's firewall, in line with the fuel line feeding the engine's fuel rail. The fuel filter on the V6 Odyssey is located in the fuel tank and requires fuel pump removal to access. Fuel filters located on the firewall should be replaced if the fuel filter exhibits signs of seepage or corrosion. Always replace a fuel filter and its sealing washers if the fuel system has become contaminated, if the fuel system fuel pressure drops below specification prior to replacing the fuel pump, or whenever the fuel pump is replaced.

✳✳ CAUTION

Observe all applicable safety precautions when working around fuel. Whenever servicing the fuel system, always work in a well-ventilated area. Do not allow fuel spray or vapors to come in contact with a spark or open flame. Keep a dry chemical fire extinguisher near the work area. Always keep fuel in a container specifically designed for fuel storage; also, always properly seal fuel containers to avoid the possibility of fire or explosion.

Fig. 40 Release the air filter housing clips using a suitable flat bladed tool . . .

Fig. 41 . . . lift the upper air filter housing for access to the filter

Fig. 42 Once the top cover has been removed, the air filter can be removed from the lower housing

REMOVAL & INSTALLATION

CR-V and 4-Cylinder Odyssey Models

⟐ See Figures 43 and 44

> ❊❊ **CAUTION**
>
> **The fuel injection system remains under pressure after the engine has been turned OFF. Properly relieve fuel pressure before disconnecting any fuel lines. Failure to do so may result in fire or personal injury.**

➠The radio may contain a coded theft protection circuit. Always make note of the security code number and radio station presets before disconnecting the battery.

1. Disconnect the negative battery cable.
2. Remove the fuel filler cap.
3. Place a shop towel under the fuel filter to absorb leakage.

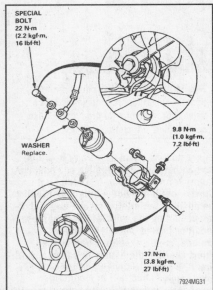

Fig. 43 Exploded view of the fuel line connections' mounting to the filter

Fig. 44 The CR-V fuel filter mounts on the passenger side of the firewall. Make sure to replace the two banjo bolt sealing washers when replacing the filter

4. Relieve the fuel system pressure by loosening the fuel line at the fuel filter.
5. Disconnect the fuel line from the filter. Due to the restricted location of the fuel filter, a flare nut wrench and socket may be needed to loosen the fuel filter fittings.
6. Use flare nut wrenches to loosen the fuel inlet line from the bottom of the filter.
7. Unbolt the fuel filter clamp from the vehicle's firewall. Remove the fuel filter.
   To install:

➠Always use new sealing washers when installing the fuel filter and reconnecting fuel lines. Replace any stripped banjo bolts.

8. Clean the fuel line fittings before installing the fuel filter.
9. Install the fuel filter and bracket. Connect the fuel inlet line to the filter and carefully tighten it to 27 ft. lbs. (37 Nm).
10. Connect the fuel line to the top of the filter with new sealing washers. Carefully tighten the service bolt to 16 ft. lbs. (22 Nm).
11. Install new sealing washers onto the fuel rail fitting. Then, tighten the fitting to 16 ft. lbs. (22 Nm).
12. Install the fuel filler cap.
13. Reconnect the negative battery cable.
14. Turn the ignition **ON**, but don't start the engine. Then, turn the ignition **OFF**. Repeat this step two or three times to pressurize the fuel system.
15. Check the fuel filter and fuel rail fittings for leakage.
16. Enter the radio security code and radio station presets.

V6 Odyssey Models

The fuel filter on the 3.5L Odyssey models is mounted on the fuel pump, which is located in the fuel tank. The fuel filter is **NOT** replaced during routine maintenance intervals on this model. The fuel filter should only be replaced when the fuel pressure drops below 41–48 psi (280–330 kPa) with the fuel pressure regulator vacuum hose disconnected and plugged and after making sure the fuel pump and fuel pressure regulator are not defective.

To remove the fuel pump to access the fuel filter refer to the procedures in Section 5.

PCV Valve

The Positive Crankcase Ventilation (PCV) valve is part of a system, which is designed to protect the atmosphere from harmful engine blow-by gas vapors. Blow-by gas from the crankcase, as well as fumes from crankcase oil, are diverted into the combustion chamber where they are burned during engine operation. Proper operation of this system is necessary for optimal engine performance, and decreases the amount of harmful vapors released into the atmosphere.

All Honda CR-V and Odyssey models are equipped with a Positive Crankcase Ventilation (PCV) system in which blow-by gas is returned to the combustion chamber through the air intake system.

The PCV valve should be checked according to the manufacturer's recommendations on 1995 2.2L Odyssey models every 60,000 miles (96,000 km) or 4 years, whichever occurs first. Although there is

not an official manufacturer's recommendation for the remaining model years, checking the PCV valve is a simple task, most professionals would recommend checking the valve during tune-ups. Two consequences of a failed PCV valve are the possibility of an intake vacuum leak which could cause erratic engine running conditions, or the inability of the crankcase to adequately vent combustion blow-by gasses causing potential oil leaks.

INSPECTION

⟐ See Figure 45

1. Check the PCV valve, hoses, and seal for leakage. Replace any component found to be leaking.
2. With the engine at operating temperature and idling, carefully pinch the hose between the PCV valve and the air intake system. When the hose is pinched closed, a clicking sound should be heard.
3. If a clicking sound is heard, the valve is operating properly. If no clicking noise is heard, replace the PCV valve mounting grommet and inspect the vacuum hose for a vacuum leak. Replace any part that is found to leak.

➠With the PCV valve removed, a rattling noise should be heard if the valve is shaken vigorously.

4. Pinch the PCV valve hose again. If a clicking sound is not present, replace the PCV valve.

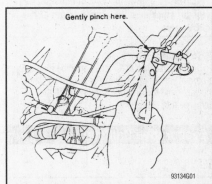

Fig. 45 To check the PCV valve, the engine should be idling and at normal operating temperature. Squeeze the PCV hose shut and listen for a clicking sound

REMOVAL & INSTALLATION

⟐ See Figures 46 thru 51

1. The PCV valve is mounted in a rubber grommet, which is seated in the intake manifold and has a hose connected to it from the crankcase breather chamber.
2. Before removing the valve, thoroughly clean the area surrounding the valve.
3. Remove the valve by carefully lifting the valve away from the sealing grommet and the manifold.
4. Once the valve is removed check for loose, disconnected or deteriorated lines or hoses and replace if necessary. Make sure the hoses are clean and free of debris. Clean them with a safe solvent, if necessary.

Fig. 46 To release the PCV valve vacuum hose clamp, squeeze the clamp together with pliers, then slide the clamp back

Fig. 47 This vacuum hose was stuck onto the plastic PCV valve spigot, so a cotter key removal tool was used to help release the hose

Fig. 48 While spraying the vacuum hose with a suitable penetrating fluid, the cotter key removal tool was carefully inserted and moved around the PCV valve spigot . . .

Fig. 49 . . . now, the vacuum hose is no longer stuck onto the plastic spigot of the PCV valve

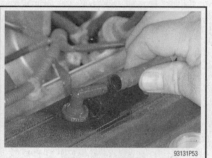

Fig. 50 Now that the hose has been loosened from the plastic spigot of the PCV valve, the hose can be easily removed from the valve

Fig. 51 If necessary, you can use a trim panel removal tool to remove the PCV valve, but remember to protect the valve cover with a soft cloth

To install:

5. To install the PCV valve, coat the mounting grommet with a light coating of engine oil, press the valve into the grommet, and reinstall the vacuum line and clamp.

Evaporative Canister

SERVICING

♦ See Figure 52

The charcoal canister is part of the Evaporative Emission Control System. This system is designed to prevent the gasoline vapors of the fuel tank and

Fig. 52 The canister is a black plastic container about the size of a coffee can and mounted onto the lower passenger side of the firewall on CR-V models

intake manifold from being discharged into the atmosphere. Vapor absorption is accomplished with a charcoal canister, which stores the vapors until they can be purged and burned in the combustion process. The charcoal canister is designed to absorb fuel vapors under certain conditions, and is a coffee can-sized cylinder located in the engine compartment.

➡ Because the evaporative canister temporarily stores and prevents unburned fuel vapors from entering the atmosphere, if when refueling, the vehicle's fuel tank is severely overfilled, it is possible to create a temporary condition of a raw fuel odor and possible sluggish performance until the vehicle is driven a distance of about 20 miles to purge the charcoal canister.

The canister does not require periodic replacement. However, you can check the canister and related hoses for cracks, splitting and other wear. Replace any components as necessary. For more information and component replacement, please refer to Section 4.

Battery

PRECAUTIONS

✳✳ CAUTION

Always use caution when working on or near the battery. Never allow any metal object such as a tool or jewelry to bridge the gap between the negative and positive battery terminals. Also, be careful not to allow a tool to provide a ground between the positive cable/terminal and any metal component on the vehicle. Either of these conditions could cause a battery to explode, create excessive heat in the object shorting the battery or cause a short circuit, leading to sparks and possible personal injury.

Do not smoke, have an open flame or create sparks near a battery. The gases contained in the battery are very explosive and, if ignited, could cause severe injury or death.

All batteries, regardless of type, should be carefully secured by a battery hold-down device. If this is not done, the battery terminals or casing may crack from stress applied to the battery during vehicle operation, or the battery could shift and short itself on another component or the body of the vehicle, or damage an electrical cable and cause the engine to stop running. A battery, which is not secured, may allow the acid to leak, and cause internal battery damage. The leaking corrosive acid can also eat away at paint and other components under the hood.

Always visually inspect the battery case for cracks, leakage and corrosion. A white corrosive substance on the battery case or on nearby components would indicate a leaking or cracked battery. If the battery is cracked, it should be replaced immediately.

When disconnecting a battery, on a negative ground system, ALWAYSdisconnect the negative (ground) cable first and then the positive battery cable. When connecting a battery on a negative ground system, always install the positive cable first, then the negative (ground) cable.

GENERAL MAINTENANCE

▶ See Figure 53

A battery that is not sealed must be checked periodically for electrolyte level. Water cannot be added to a sealed maintenance-free battery (though not all maintenance-free batteries are sealed); however, a sealed battery must also be checked for proper electrolyte level, as indicated by the color of the built-in hydrometer "eye."

Always keep the battery cables and terminals free of corrosion. Check these components at least once a year. Refer to the removal, installation and cleaning procedures outlined in this section.

Keep the top of the battery clean. A dirty or oily surface can actually conduct a small amount of an electrical current and may cause a battery that is not used for long periods of time to completely discharge. To clean a battery top, use a solution of baking soda and water, and then carefully flush this solution off with clear water. DO NOT allow any of the solution into the battery cell filler holes. Baking soda neutralizes battery acid and will de-activate a battery cell.

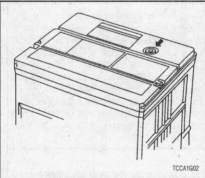

Fig. 53 A typical location for the built-in hydrometer on maintenance-free batteries

Batteries in vehicles which are not operated on a regular basis can fall victim to parasitic loads (small current drains which are constantly drawing current from the battery). Normal parasitic loads may drain a battery on a vehicle that is in storage and not used for 6–8 weeks. Vehicles that have additional accessories such as a cellular telephone, alarm system or other devices that increase parasitic load may discharge a battery more quickly. If the vehicle is to be stored for 6–8 weeks in a secure area and the alarm system, if present, is not necessary, the negative battery cable should be disconnected at the onset of storage to protect the battery charge.

Remember that constantly discharging and recharging will shorten battery life. Take care not to allow a battery to be needlessly discharged.

BATTERY FLUID

Check the battery electrolyte level at least once a month, or more often in hot weather or during periods of extended vehicle operation. On non-sealed batteries, the level can be checked either through the case on translucent batteries or by removing the cell caps on opaque-cased types. The electrolyte level in each cell should be kept filled to the split ring inside each cell, or the line marked on the outside of the case.

If the level is low, add only distilled water through the opening until the level is correct. Each cell is separate from the others, so each must be checked and filled individually. Distilled water should be used, because the chemicals and minerals found in most drinking water are harmful to the battery and could significantly shorten its life.

If water is added in freezing weather, the vehicle should be driven several miles to allow the water to mix with the electrolyte. Otherwise, the battery could freeze.

Although some maintenance-free batteries have removable cell caps for access to the electrolyte, the electrolyte condition and level on all sealed maintenance-free batteries must be checked using the built-in hydrometer "eye." The exact type of eye varies between battery manufacturers, but most apply a sticker to the battery itself explaining the possible readings. When in doubt, refer to the battery manufacturer's instructions to interpret battery condition using the built-in hydrometer.

➡**Although the readings from built-in hydrometers found in sealed batteries may vary, a green eye usually indicates a properly charged**

battery with sufficient fluid level. A dark eye is normally an indicator of a battery with sufficient fluid, but one that may be low in charge. In addition, a light or yellow eye is usually an indication that electrolyte supply has dropped below the necessary level for battery (and hydrometer) operation. In this last case, sealed batteries with an insufficient electrolyte level must usually be discarded.

If the battery electrolyte level seems to be constantly low even after being topped off on a periodic basis, check the charging system output for an over charging condition.

Checking the Specific Gravity

▶ See Figures 54, 55 and 56

A hydrometer is required to check the specific gravity on all batteries that are not maintenance-free. On batteries that are maintenance-free, the specific gravity is checked by observing the built-in hydrometer "eye" on the top of the battery case. Check with the battery's manufacturer for proper explanation of their built-in hydrometer readings.

Battery electrolyte contains sulfuric acid. If you should splash any on your skin or in your eyes, flush the affected area with plenty of clear water. If it lands in your eyes, get medical help immediately.

The fluid (sulfuric acid solution) contained in the battery cells reflects the condition of the battery. Because the cell plates must be kept submerged below the fluid level in order to operate, maintaining the fluid level is extremely important. The specific gravity of the acid is an indication of electrical charge, such that testing the fluid can be an aid in determining if the battery must be replaced. A battery in a vehicle with a properly operating charging system should require little maintenance, however careful periodic inspection should reveal problems before they cause a failure.

As stated earlier, the specific gravity of a battery's electrolyte level can be used as an indication of battery charge. At least once a year, check the specific gravity of the battery. It should be between 1.20 and 1.26 on a gravity scale. Most auto supply stores carry a variety of inexpensive battery testing hydrometers. These can be used on any non-sealed battery to test the specific gravity for each cell.

Fig. 54 On non-maintenance-free batteries, the fluid level can be checked through the case on translucent models; the cell caps must be removed on other models

Fig. 55 If the fluid level is low, add only distilled water through the opening until the level is correct

Fig. 56 Check the specific gravity of the battery's electrolyte with a hydrometer

The battery testing hydrometer has a squeeze bulb at one end and a nozzle at the other. Battery electrolyte is sucked into the hydrometer until the float is lifted from its seat. The specific gravity is then read by noting the position of the float. If gravity is low in one or more cells, the battery should be slowly charged and checked again to see if the specific gravity has increased. Generally, if after charging, the specific gravity between any two cells varies more than 50 points (0.50), the battery should be replaced, as it can no longer produce sufficient voltage to guarantee proper operation.

CABLES

▶ See Figures 57, 58, 59, 60 and 61

Once a year (or as necessary), the battery terminals and the cable clamps should be cleaned. Loosen the clamps and remove the cables, negative cable first. On batteries with posts on top, the use of a puller specially made for this purpose is recommended. These are inexpensive and available in most auto parts stores. Side terminal battery cables are secured with a small bolt.

Clean the cable clamps and the battery terminal with a wire brush, until all corrosion, grease, etc., is removed and the metal is shiny. It is especially important to clean the inside of the clamp thoroughly (an old knife is useful here), since a small deposit of foreign material or oxidation there will prevent a sound electrical connection and inhibit either starting or charging. Special tools are available for cleaning these parts, one type for conventional top post batteries and another type for side terminal batteries. It is also a good idea to apply some dielectric grease to the terminal, as this will aid in the prevention of corrosion.

After the clamps and terminals are clean, reinstall the cables, negative cable last; DO NOT hammer the clamps onto battery posts. Tighten the clamps securely, but do not distort them. Give the clamps and terminals a thin external coating of grease after installation, to retard corrosion.

Check the cables at the same time that the terminals are cleaned. If the cable insulation is cracked or broken, or if the ends are frayed, the cable should be replaced with a new cable of the same length and gauge.

CHARGING

A battery should be charged at a slow rate, usually about 10% of the rated capacity of the battery to keep the plates inside from getting too hot. However, if some maintenance-free batteries are allowed to discharge until they are almost "dead," they may have to be charged at a high rate to bring them back to "life." Always follow the charger manufacturer's instructions on charging the battery.

REPLACEMENT

When it becomes necessary to replace the battery, select one with sufficient cold cranking amps, with a rating equal to or greater than the battery originally installed. Deterioration and just plain aging of the battery cables, starter motor, and associated wires makes the battery's job more difficult in successive years. As the vehicle ages, the wiring becomes slightly less efficient causing an increase in electrical resistance. Because of this condition, when replacing the battery, it is suggested to choose a battery with a greater capacity.

Belts

▶ See Figures 62 and 63

Accessory drive belts used on the Honda CR-V and Odyssey include two basic types: the flat multi-ribbed V-belt and serpentine belt. The flat multi-ribbed V-belt actually resembles a serpentine belt, however, unlike a serpentine belt, only the ribbed inner surface of the belt makes contact with the components' pulleys. Rarely, does the back of a multi-ribbed belt ride against an idler or tensioner pulley.

Multi-ribbed V-belts typically operate one or two accessories per belt, whereas a single serpentine belt can often times drive multiple the accessories.

Fig. 57 Maintenance is performed with household items and with special tools like this post cleaner

Fig. 58 The underside of this special battery tool has a wire brush to clean post terminals

Fig. 59 Place the tool over the battery posts and twist to clean until the metal is shiny

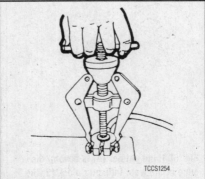

Fig. 60 A special tool is available to pull the clamp from the post

Fig. 61 The cable ends should be cleaned as well

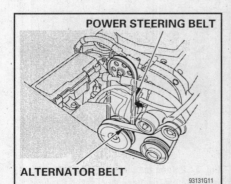

POWER STEERING BELT

ALTERNATOR BELT

Fig. 62 The V6 Odyssey models use both a multi-ribbed V-belt and a serpentine belt

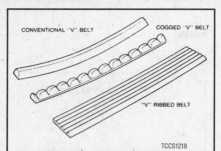

Fig. 63 These are 3 types of accessory drive belts found on vehicles today. The serpentine belt is very similar to the "V" multi-ribbed belt

The flat multi-ribbed V-belts used on both the CR-V and Odyssey models require periodic inspection and adjustment because the belts wear with age and are under tension and stretch over time. The serpentine belt is tensioned by a spring loaded tensioner assembly that keeps a constant tension on the belt at all times. As a serpentine belt wears and stretches over time, within a specified range, the tensioner automatically compensates for the wear and belt stretch.

➡The V6 Odyssey models use both a multi-ribbed V-belt and a serpentine belt. The multi-ribbed V-belt is used to drive the power steering pump. The serpentine belt is used to drive the alternator and the air conditioner compressor.

INSPECTION

◗ **See Figures 64, 65, 66, 67 and 68**

The maintenance intervals suggested by the manufacturer vary by time, operating conditions (normal or severe), and mileage. A good rule of thumb is to inspect the drive belts every 15,000 miles (24,000 km) or 12 months (whichever occurs first). On manually adjusted multi-ribbed V-belts, measure the belt tension at a point halfway between the pulleys by pulling or pressing on the belt with a known force and measuring how far the belt moves, referred to as the amount of deflection. Note that "deflection" is not free-play, but the ability of the belt, under actual tension, to stretch slightly and give. The specification for measuring belt tension includes the amount of force applied to the belt, and the amount of deflection (movement) the belt should have when the force is applied. The amount of deflection varies depending on whether the belt is new or used. Although the manufacturer markets a specific tool for measuring belt deflection, a fisherman's spring scale capable of measuring a 22 lb. (98 N) pull and a small ruler can be substituted for this tool.

Inspect the belts for the following signs of damage or wear: glazing, cracking, fraying, crumbling or missing chunks. A glazed belt will be slightly brittle and perfectly smooth from slipping, and may exhibit a screeching noise when the engine is suddenly accelerated or first started. A good belt will have a slight texture of fabric visible and the surface should be soft and flexible. Cracks will usually start at the inner edge of a belt and run outward. A belt that is fraying will have the fabric backing de-laminating itself from the belt. A belt that is crumbling or missing chunks will have missing pieces in the cross-section of the belt, some times these chunks will be stuck in the pulley groove and not easily seen. All worn or damaged drive belts should be replaced immediately. It is best to replace all drive belts at one time, as a preventive maintenance measure.

Although it is generally easier on a component to have the belt too loose than too tight, a loose belt may place a high impact load on a bearing due to the whipping or snapping action of the belt. A belt that is slightly loose may slip, especially when component loads are high. This slippage may be hard to identify. For example, the generator belt may run okay during the day, and then slip at night when headlights are turned on. Slipping belts wear quickly not only due to the direct effect of slippage but also because of the heat a slipping belt generates. Extreme slippage may even cause a belt to burn. A very smooth, glazed appearance on the belt's sides, as opposed to the obvious pattern of a fabric cover, indicates that the belt has been slipping.

Both multi-ribbed V-belts and serpentine belts can be checked for wear by inspecting the physical condition of the belt. To check belt stretch on multi-ribbed V-belts, look at the amount of adjustment that remains on the sliding portion of the adjustment bracket, or the threaded portion of the adjustment screw. If the adjustment range has is at its fully extended portion, the belt should be replaced.

Serpentine drive belts should be inspected for rib chunking (pieces of the ribs breaking off), severe glazing, frayed cords or other visible damage. Any belt which is missing sections of 2 or more adjacent ribs which are ½ in. (13mm) or longer must be replaced. You might want to note that serpentine belts do tend to form small cracks across the backing. If the only wear you find is in the form of one or more cracks are across the backing and NOT parallel to the ribs, the belt is still good and does not need to be replaced.

To check belt stretch on a serpentine belt, look at the range indicator on the tensioner assembly. The

Fig. 65 Deep cracks in a belt will cause flex, building up heat that will eventually lead to belt failure

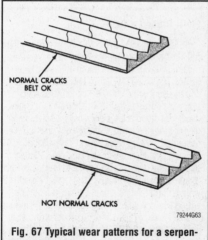

Fig. 67 Typical wear patterns for a serpentine drive belt

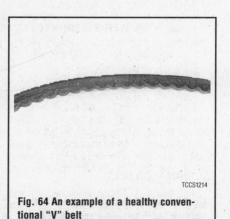

Fig. 64 An example of a healthy conventional "V" belt

Fig. 66 The cover of this belt is worn, exposing the critical reinforcing cords to excessive wear

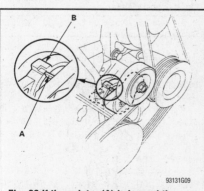

Fig. 68 If the pointer (A) is beyond the edge of the wear indicator block (B) the serpentine belt has stretched and should be replaced—3.5L Odyssey shown

tensioner arm has a pointer that is compared to a small rectangular reference block on the tensioner mounting bracket. If the tensioner pointer has reached or is beyond the edge of the inspection block, the belt has stretched beyond its wear limits and should be replaced.

CHECKING BELT TENSION

A damaged drive belt can cause problems should it give way while the vehicle is in operation. However, improper length belts (too short or long), as well as excessively worn belts, can also cause problems. Loose accessory drive belts can lead to poor engine cooling and diminished output from the alternator, air conditioning compressor or power steering pump. A belt that is too tight places a severe strain on the driven unit and can wear out bearings quickly.

✳✳ CAUTION

Always disable the power to the vehicle by disconnecting the negative battery cable before checking, replacing or adjusting the drive belts. Working with the drive belts requires placing tools, hands and fingers near areas of potential danger. In addition, the cooling fan could engage even with the ignition in the OFF position.

Multi-Ribbed V-Belts

To accurately check the belt tension of the multi-ribbed V-belts used on Honda products requires putting a known force on the belt midway between the longest straight distance between belt pulleys and measuring the belt's deflection. The specification varies depending on whether the belt is new or used. The manufacturer does have a belt tension gauge designed for this specific purpose, however a fisherman's spring scale capable of measuring 22 lbs. and a small ruler can be easily substituted. To use the fisherman's spring scale to pull on the belt requires that a small flat shaped hook be made to wrap around the belt and the small hook of the spring scale. A sturdy metal coat hanger is a good source for the needed hook. Use the spring scale to apply a force at a 90° angle to the belt via the metal hook and measure the amount of belt movement (deflection) with the ruler. To measure the belt deflection of a flat multi-ribbed V-belt proceed as follows:

1. Note the radio security code and disconnect the negative battery cable.
2. Inspect the belt and determine the longest straight distance between two of the pulleys.
3. Determine the center point of the belt between the two pulleys of the longest straight distance between the two pulleys.
4. Attach one end the hook made for the spring scale to the center point of the belt and the other end to the spring scale and pull the spring scale at a 90° angle from the belt just enough to remove any slack in the hook.
5. Using a small ruler, place the ruler at a 90° angle to the belt, with the base of the rule aligned with, but not touching the non-ribbed side of the belt.
6. While holding the ruler stationary, pull the spring scale at a 90° angle from the belt, until the

scale registers 22 lbs. while using the ruler to note the distance the belt has moved. This movement is the belt's deflection.

7. Compare the measurement with the specifications listed later in this section, to determine if the belt is properly adjusted.
8. Once the proper adjustment of the belt is achieved, remove the self-made hook, spring scale and ruler.
9. Reconnect the negative battery cable and enter the radio security code.

The following belt deflection information is a guide to proper belt adjustment and is measured while applying a 22 lb. force to the belt:

CR-V
- Air conditioner belt, new: ³⁄₁₆–¹⁄₄ in. (5.0–7.0mm)
- Air conditioner belt, used: ⁵⁄₁₆–³⁄₈ in. (7.5–10.5mm)
- Alternator belt, new: ³⁄₁₆–⁵⁄₁₆ in. (5.5–8.0mm)
- Alternator belt, used: ⁵⁄₁₆–⁷⁄₁₆ in. (8.5–11.5mm)
- Power steering belt, new: ⁵⁄₁₆–³⁄₈ in. (7.5–10.0mm)
- Power steering belt, used: ⁷⁄₁₆–⁹⁄₁₆ in. (11.0–14.5mm)

2.2L/2.3L Odyssey Models
- Air conditioner/alternator belt, new: ³⁄₁₆–¹⁄₄ in. (4.5–6.5mm)
- Air conditioner/alternator belt, used: ⁵⁄₁₆–³⁄₈ in. (8.0–10.5mm)
- Power steering belt, new: ⁷⁄₁₆–¹⁄₂ in. (11.0–12.5mm)
- Power steering belt, used: ¹⁄₂–⁵⁄₈ in. (13.0–16.0mm)

3.5L Odyssey Models
- Power steering belt, new: ⁵⁄₁₆–⁷⁄₁₆ in. (8.5–11.0mm)
- Power steering belt, used: ¹⁄₂–⁵⁄₈ in. (13.0–16.5mm)

➥The alternator and air conditioner belt on this model is driven by an automatically tensioned serpentine belt.

Serpentine Belts

▶ **See Figures 69 and 70**

The serpentine belt tension and tensioner can be checked but they cannot be adjusted. An automatic spring-loaded tensioner assembly is used with these belts to maintain proper adjustment at all times. The tensioner also serves as a wear indicator. When the belt is properly tensioned, the arrow on the tensioner arm must point within the small rectangular reference area on the tensioner's housing. If the arrow falls outside the range, either an improper belt has been installed or the belt has stretched beyond its wear limit. In either case, a new belt must be installed immediately to assure proper engine operation and to prevent possible accessory damage.

To check the serpentine belt tensioner assembly, look at the tension indicator on the tensioner assembly with the engine running. If the tensioner arm pointer moves excessively when the engine is running, the belt condition and the tensioner spring strength should be checked.

To check the tensioner spring strength proceed as follows:

1. Remove the serpentine belt. Refer to the procedure in this section for specific details.

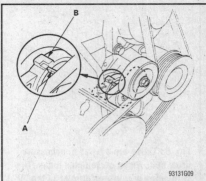

Fig. 69 If the pointer (A) is beyond the edge of the wear indicator block (B) the serpentine belt has stretched and the tension will be reduced—3.5L Odyssey models

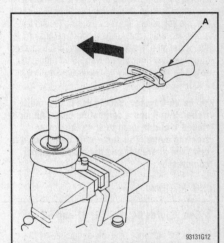

Fig. 70 With two 6mm bolts clamped in a suitable vise to hold the tensioner assembly, measure the amount of torque required to move the tensioner in a counterclockwise direction

2. Remove the mounting bolts that secure the tensioner assembly to the engine.
3. Place two 6 mm bolts through the tensioner assembly mounting holes and clamp the two bolts into a suitable vise. Do **not** clamp the tensioner assembly itself.
4. Using a beam type torque wrench, measure the amount of torque required to move the tensioner in a counterclockwise direction. If the torque required to move the tensioner is less than 17 ft. lbs. (23 Nm), replace the tensioner assembly.

ADJUSTMENT

Belt tension on multi-ribbed V-belts can be checked by applying a force on the belt at the center point of its longest straight span. The belt movement (deflection) is then measured to determine if the belt is properly tensioned. If the belt is loose, it will slip, whereas if the belt is too tight it will damage the bearings in the driven unit.

To tension a multi-ribbed V-belt there are generally three types of mounting and adjustment methods for the various components driven by the drive belt. These types of mounting and adjustment methods are as follows:

• A pivoting component without an adjuster. This method, referred to as pivoting type without adjuster, is designed such that the component is secured by at least 2 bolts. One of the bolts is a pivoting bolt and the other is the lockbolt. When both bolts are loosened so that the component may move, the component pivots on the pivoting bolt. The lockbolt passes through the component and a slotted bracket, so that when the lockbolt's nut is tightened the component is held in that position. The component must be moved by hand, or by carefully leveraging it with a properly placed object such as a hardwood handle or suitable prytool.

✳✳ CAUTION

Always disable the power to the vehicle by disconnecting the negative battery cable before checking, replacing or adjusting the drive belts. Working with the drive belts requires placing tools, hands and fingers near areas of potential danger. In addition, the cooling fan could engage even with the ignition in the OFF position.

• A pivoting component with an adjuster. This method of component mounting, referred to as pivoting type with adjuster, is designed such that the component is secured by at least 2 bolts, with one of the bolts serving as a pivoting bolt and the other a lockbolt. When the mounting bolts are loosened so that the component may move, the component is moved by turning an adjustment bolt. The adjuster is composed of a bracket attached to the component and a threaded adjusting bolt. After loosening the pivoting and lockbolts, the adjusting bolt can be tightened or loosened to increase or decrease the drive belt's tension. With this type of mounting, the component does not have to be held in a tensioned position while tightening the pivoting and lockbolts, because the adjusting bolt applies the tension to the belt.

• A stationary mounted component with an adjustable idler pulley. This type of component mounting is referred to as the stationary type, because, the component is mounted in a stationary position without the use of pivoting or lockbolts. The drive belt tension is adjusted by moving the position of an idler pulley.

➡When checking or adjusting the multi-ribbed V-belts, note that the belt deflection specification varies from component to component, and changes if the belt is new or used. Note, the amount of force applied to the belts when checking belt deflection is 22 lbs. (98 N), however the amount of deflection varies depending on belt type and whether new or used. Refer to the following information for each model to properly check and adjust the multi-ribbed drive belts.

CR-V

The CR-V models use 3 separate multi-ribbed V-belts to drive the alternator, air conditioner compressor and the power steering pump.

AIR CONDITIONER BELT

The air conditioner compressor is mounted to the engine and cannot be moved. The belt is tensioned by an idler pulley, which has two fasteners

securing it to the engine. When these fasteners are loosened, the idler pulley can be pivoted to loosen or tighten the belt and then secured in place by tightening the pivot and slotted adjustment plate fasteners.

To adjust:
1. Note the radio security code and disconnect the negative battery cable.
2. Loosen the pivot bolt of the idler pulley bracket, then loosen the locknut of the slotted adjusting mounting plate.
3. Turn the adjusting bolt to achieve the correct belt tension.
4. Tighten the pivot bolt of the idler pulley bracket, then tighten the locknut of the adjusting fastener.
5. Check the belt tension. If the belt tension is not within specification, repeat the previous procedure until the proper belt tension is achieved.
6. Reconnect the negative battery cable and enter the radio security code.

ALTERNATOR BELT

The alternator has two fasteners securing it to a bracket mounted on the engine. The upper locknut and fastener are installed through a slotted bracket and the lower fastener allows the alternator to pivot.

To adjust:
1. Note the radio security code and disconnect the negative battery cable.
2. Loosen the upper locknut and lower pivot nut.
3. Move the top most portion of the alternator assembly toward the engine to decrease the belt tension, or away from the engine to increase the belt tension.
4. Tighten the upper locknut, lower pivot bolt, and then check the belt tension. If the belt tension is not within specification, repeat the previous procedure until the proper belt tension is achieved.
5. Reconnect the negative battery cable and enter the radio security code.

POWER STEERING PUMP BELT

The power steering pump has two fasteners securing it to a bracket mounted on the engine. The lower locknut and fastener are installed through a slotted bracket and the upper fastener allows the pump to pivot.

To adjust:
1. Note the radio security code and disconnect the negative battery cable.
2. Loosen the upper pivot nut and lower locknut.
3. Move the pump by placing a ½ inch breaker bar into the square hole in the pump, near the upper pivot bolt. Move the assembly toward the engine to decrease the belt tension, or away from the engine to increase the belt tension.
4. Tighten the upper pivot bolt and lower locknut and then check the belt tension. If the belt tension is not within specification, repeat the previous procedures until the proper belt tension is achieved.
5. Reconnect the negative battery cable and enter the radio security code.

4-Cylinder Odyssey Models

The 2.2L/2.3L Odyssey models utilize two multi-ribbed V-belts. One belt is used to drive both the alternator and air conditioner compressor and a separate belt is used for the power steering pump.

ALTERNATOR BELT/AIR CONDITIONER BELT

The air conditioner compressor is mounted to the engine and cannot be moved, thus the belt is tensioned by moving the alternator which has two fasteners securing it to a bracket mounted on the engine. The lower locknut and fastener are installed through a slotted bracket and the upper fastener allows the alternator to pivot.

To adjust:
1. Note the radio security code and disconnect the negative battery cable.
2. Loosen the upper pivot nut and lower locknut.
3. Move the alternator by turning the adjustment bolt on the lower bracket. Turning the adjustment bolt clockwise increases the belt tension, conversely, turning the adjustment bolt counterclockwise will decrease the belt tension.
4. Tighten the upper pivot bolt and lower locknut and then check the belt tension. If the belt tension is not within specification, repeat the previous procedures until the proper belt tension is achieved.
5. Reconnect the negative battery cable and enter the radio security code.

POWER STEERING PUMP BELT

The power steering pump has two fasteners securing it to a bracket mounted on the engine. The upper locknut and fastener are installed through a slotted bracket and the lower fastener allows the pump to pivot.

To adjust:
1. Note the radio security code and disconnect the negative battery cable.
2. Loosen the upper locknut and lower pivot nut.
3. Move the pump by turning the adjustment bolt on the upper bracket. Turning the adjustment bolt clockwise increases the belt tension, conversely, turning the adjustment bolt counterclockwise will decrease the belt tension.
4. Tighten the upper locknut, lower pivot bolt, and then check the belt tension. If the belt tension is not within specification, repeat the previous procedures until the proper belt tension is achieved.
5. Reconnect the negative battery cable and enter the radio security code.

V6 Odyssey Models

The V6 Odyssey models utilize both a multi-ribbed V-belt and a serpentine belt. The serpentine belt is used to drive the alternator and air conditioner compressor and the multi-ribbed V-belt is used for the power steering pump.

ALTERNATOR BELT/AIR CONDITIONER BELT

The air conditioner compressor and alternator are both driven by a single serpentine belt and both units are mounted to the engine and cannot be moved, thus the belt is tensioned by a self adjusting tensioning pulley. No adjustment is possible, however the belt tension and tensioner assembly can be checked. For specific details refer to the information in this section.

POWER STEERING PUMP BELT

The power steering pump has two fasteners securing it to a bracket mounted on the engine. The right side locknut and fastener are installed through a slotted bracket and the left side fastener allows the pump to pivot.

To adjust:

1. Note the radio security code and disconnect the negative battery cable.

2. Loosen the right side locknut and left side pivot nut.

3. Move the pump by turning the adjustment nut on the right side bracket. Turning the adjustment nut clockwise increases the belt tension, conversely, turning the adjustment nut counterclockwise will decrease the belt tension.

4. Tighten the right side locknut and left side pivot bolt and then check the belt tension. If the belt tension is not within specification, repeat the previous procedures until the proper belt tension is achieved.

5. Reconnect the negative battery cable and enter the radio security code.

REMOVAL & INSTALLATION

If a belt must be replaced, the driven unit or idler pulley must be loosened and moved to its extreme loosest position, generally by moving it toward the center of the engine. After removing the old belt, check the pulleys for dirt or built-up material, which could affect belt contact. Carefully install the new belt, remembering that it is new and unused; it may appear to be just a little too small to fit over the pulley flanges. Fit the belt over the largest pulley (usually the crankshaft pulley at the bottom center of the engine) first, then work on the smaller one(s). Gentle pressure in the direction of rotation is helpful. Some belts run around a third, or idler pulley, which acts as an additional pivot in the belt's path. It may be possible to loosen the idler pulley as well as the main component, making the job much easier. Depending on which belt(s) being changed, it may be necessary to loosen or remove other interfering belts to access the being replaced.

✳✳ CAUTION

Always disable the power to the vehicle by disconnecting the negative battery cable before checking, replacing or adjusting the drive belts. Working with the drive belts requires placing tools, hands and fingers near areas of potential danger. In addition, the cooling fan could engage even with the ignition in the OFF position.

When buying replacement belts, remember that the fit is critical according to the length of the belt ("diameter") and the width of the belt. The belt shape should match the shape of the pulley exactly. Belts that are not an exact match can cause noise, slippage and premature failure.

After the new belt is installed, draw tension on it by moving the driven unit or idler pulley away from the engine and tighten its mounting bolts. This is sometimes a three or four-handed job; and an assistant could be helpful. Make sure that all the bolts that have been loosened are retightened and that any other loosened belts have the correct tension. A new belt can be expected to stretch a bit after installation, so be prepared to readjust the new belt, if needed, within the first two hundred miles of use.

CR-V

The CR-V uses separate drive belts for the air conditioner, alternator and the power steering pump.

The outermost belt of the three belts is the power steering belt, followed by the air conditioner belt, and lastly the alternator belt. Therefore to remove the air conditioner belt, requires power steering belt removal. To remove the alternator belt requires removal of both the power steering and air conditioner belts.

ALTERNATOR BELT

The alternator has two fasteners securing it to a bracket mounted on the engine. The upper locknut and fastener are installed through a slotted bracket and the lower fastener allows the alternator to pivot.

1. Note the radio security code and disconnect the negative battery cable.

2. Remove the power steering and air conditioner compressor belts.

3. Loosen the upper locknut and lower pivot nut.

4. Move the top most portion of the alternator assembly toward the engine to fully release the belt tension.

5. Remove the belt from the pulleys, one pulley at a time.

To install:

6. Install the belt around the pulleys, beginning with the largest pulley first.

7. Follow the adjustment procedure to correctly tension the belt.

8. Tighten the upper locknut, lower pivot bolt, and then check the belt tension. If the belt tension is not within specification, repeat the adjustment procedures until the proper belt tension is achieved.

9. Install the power steering and air conditioner compressor belts and tension correctly.

10. Reconnect the negative battery cable and enter the radio security code.

AIR CONDITIONER BELT

The air conditioner compressor is mounted to the engine and cannot be moved. The belt is tensioned by an idler pulley, which has two fasteners securing it to the engine. The locknut and fastener are installed through a slotted plate and allows the pulley to pivot.

1. Note the radio security code and disconnect the negative battery cable.

2. Remove the power steering belt.

3. Loosen the pivot bolt of the idler pulley bracket, then loosen the locknut of the adjusting bolt.

4. Turn the adjusting bolt fully counterclockwise to achieve the maximum amount of slack.

5. Remove the belt from the pulleys, one pulley at a time.

To install:

6. Install the belt around the pulleys, beginning with the largest pulley first.

7. Follow the adjustment procedure to correctly tension the belt.

8. Tighten the pivot bolt of the idler pulley bracket, then tighten the locknut of the adjusting bolt.

9. Check the belt tension. If the belt tension is not within specification, repeat the adjustment procedures until the proper belt tension is achieved.

10. Install and properly tension the power steering belt.

11. Reconnect the negative battery cable and enter the radio security code.

POWER STEERING PUMP BELT

The power steering pump has two fasteners securing it to a bracket mounted on the engine. The lower locknut and fastener are installed through a slotted bracket and the upper fastener allows the pump to pivot. To remove:

1. Note the radio security code and disconnect the negative battery cable.

2. Loosen the upper pivot nut and lower locknut.

3. Move the pump by placing a ½ inch breaker bar into the square hole in the pump, near the upper pivot bolt. Move the pump assembly toward the engine to decrease the belt tension.

4. Remove the belt from the pulleys, one pulley at a time.

To install:

5. Install the belt around the pulleys, beginning with the largest pulley first.

6. Follow the adjustment procedure to correctly tension the belt.

7. Tighten the upper pivot bolt and lower locknut and then check the belt tension. If the belt tension is not within specification, repeat the adjustment procedures until the proper belt tension is achieved.

8. Reconnect the negative battery cable and enter the radio security code.

4-Cylinder Odyssey Models

ALTERNATOR/AIR CONDITIONER BELT

The air conditioner compressor is mounted to the engine and cannot be moved, thus the belt is tensioned by moving the alternator which has two fasteners securing it to a bracket mounted on the engine. The lower locknut and fastener are installed through a slotted bracket and the upper fastener allows the alternator to pivot.

1. Note the radio security code and disconnect the negative battery cable.

2. Remove the power steering belt.

3. Loosen the upper pivot nut and lower locknut.

4. Move the alternator by turning the adjustment bolt on the lower bracket counterclockwise to decrease the belt tension.

5. Remove the belt from the pulleys, one pulley at a time.

To install:

6. Install the belt around the pulleys, beginning with the largest pulley first.

7. Follow the adjustment procedure to correctly tension the belt.

8. Tighten the upper pivot bolt and lower locknut and then check the belt tension. If the belt tension is not within specification, repeat the adjustment procedure until the proper belt tension is achieved.

9. Install and properly tension the power steering belt.

10. Reconnect the negative battery cable and enter the radio security code.

POWER STEERING PUMP BELT

The power steering pump has two fasteners securing it to a bracket mounted on the engine. The upper locknut and fastener are installed through a slotted bracket and the lower fastener allows the pump to pivot.

1. Note the radio security code and disconnect the negative battery cable.

2. Loosen the upper locknut and lower pivot nut.

3. Move the pump by turning the adjustment bolt on the upper bracket. Turn the adjustment bolt counterclockwise to release the belt tension.

4. Remove the belt from the pulleys, one pulley at a time.

To install:

5. Install the belt around the pulleys, beginning with the largest pulley first.

6. Follow the adjustment procedure to correctly tension the belt.

7. Tighten the upper locknut, lower pivot bolt, and then check the belt tension. If the belt tension is not within specification, repeat the adjustment procedure until the proper belt tension is achieved.

8. Reconnect the negative battery cable and enter the radio security code.

V6 Odyssey Models

POWER STEERING PUMP BELT

The power steering pump has two fasteners securing it to a bracket mounted on the engine. The right side locknut and fastener are installed through a slotted bracket and the left side fastener allows the pump to pivot.

1. Note the radio security code and disconnect the negative battery cable.

2. Loosen the right side locknut and left side pivot nut.

3. Move the pump by turning the adjustment nut on the right side bracket. Turn the adjustment nut counterclockwise to release the belt tension.

4. Remove the belt from the pulleys, one pulley at a time.

To install:

5. Install the belt around the pulleys, beginning with the largest pulley first.

6. Follow the adjustment procedure to correctly tension the belt.

7. Tighten the right side locknut and left side pivot bolt and then check the belt tension. If the belt tension is not within specification, repeat the adjustment procedure until the proper belt tension is achieved.

8. Reconnect the negative battery cable and enter the radio security code.

ALTERNATOR BELT/AIR CONDITIONER BELT

▶ See Figure 71

Because serpentine belts use a spring loaded tensioner for adjustment, belt replacement tends to be somewhat easier than it used to be on engines where accessories were pivoted and bolted in place for tension adjustment. All the belt replacement involves is to pivot the tensioner to loosen the belt, then slide the belt off the pulleys. The two most important points are to pay CLOSE attention to the proper belt routing (since serpentine belts tend to be "snaked" all different ways through the pulleys) and to make sure the V-ribs are properly seated in all the pulleys.

➡ Take a good look at the installed belt and make a note of the routing. Before removing the belt, make sure the routing matches that of the belt routing label or one of the diagrams in this book.

1. Note the radio presets and disconnect the negative battery cable.

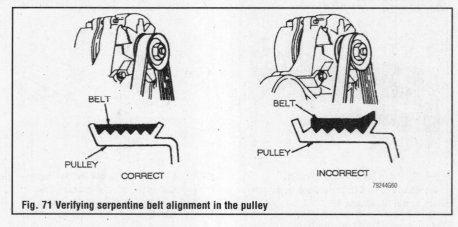

Fig. 71 Verifying serpentine belt alignment in the pulley

2. Remove the power steering belt.

3. Use the proper-sized socket and breaker bar (or a large handled wrench) on the tensioner idler pulley center bolt to pivot the tensioner away from the belt. This will loosen the belt sufficiently that it can be pulled off one or more of the pulleys. It is usually easiest to carefully pull the belt out from underneath the tensioner pulley itself.

4. Once the belt is off one of the pulleys, gently pivot the tensioner back into position. DO NOT allow the tensioner to snap back, as this could damage the tensioner's internal parts.

5. Remove the belt from the other pulleys and remove it from the engine.

To install:

6. Begin to route the belt over the pulleys, leaving whichever pulley the belt was first released from during removal for last.

7. Once the belt is mostly in place, carefully pivot the tensioner and position the belt over the final pulley. Carefully release the pressure on the tensioner and it to contact with the belt, making sure the belt is properly seated in the ribs. If not, release the tension and seat the belt.

8. Once the belt is installed, take another look at all the pulleys to double check the installation.

9. Install and properly tension the power steering belt.

10. Connect the negative battery cable, enter the radio presets, then start and run the engine to check belt operation.

11. Once the engine has reached normal operating temperature, turn the ignition OFF and check that the belt tensioner arrow is within the proper adjustment range.

Timing Belt

SERVICING

▶ See Figures 72 thru 78

Timing belts are typically only used on overhead camshaft engines. Timing belts are used to synchronize the crankshaft with the camshaft, at an exact 2 to 1 ratio, similar to a timing chain used on other overhead camshaft and overhead valve (pushrod) engines. Unlike a timing belt, a timing chain is not considered a maintenance item, as many timing chains can last the life of the engine without needing service or replacement. To maintain a constant 2 to 1 ratio, timing belts use raised teeth

to mesh with the crankshaft and camshaft sprockets to operate the valve train of an overhead camshaft engine.

✳✳ WARNING

Timing belt maintenance is extremely important! These models utilize an interference-type, non-free-wheeling engine. If the timing belt breaks, the valves in the cylinder head may strike the pistons, causing potentially serious (also time-consuming and expensive) engine damage.

The recommended replacement interval for the timing belt is under normal conditions every 84 months or 105,000 (168,000 km), miles whichever occurs first. For vehicles driven in severely hot (over 90°F or 32°C) or severely cold conditions (below -20°F or -29°C), the belt should be replaced every 60,000 miles (96,000 km), or every 84 months whichever occurs first. Refer to Section 3 for timing belt replacement procedures.

If the vehicle has been purchased used with an unknown service history, refer to the maintenance charts provided in this manual to compare the vehicle age and mileage to the recommended maintenance intervals.

Engines can be classified as either free-running or interference engines, depending on what would happen if the piston-to-valve timing were disrupted, which would occur should a timing belt fail. A free-running engine is designed with enough clearance between the pistons and valves to allow the crankshaft to continue to rotate (pistons still moving) while the camshaft stays in one position (several valves fully open). If no other engine related failure occurs, it is likely no further internal engine damage

Fig. 72 Never bend or twist a timing belt excessively, and do not allow solvents, antifreeze, gasoline, acid or oil to come into contact with the belt

Fig. 73 Clean the timing belt before inspection so that imperfections or defects are easier to recognize

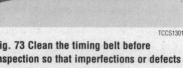

Fig. 76 Side wear from improper installation or a defective pulley plate

Rotating direction

Fig. 77 Worn teeth from excessive belt tension, camshaft or distributor not turning properly, or fluid leaking on the belt

Fig. 78 A comparison of two timing belts. The one on the left has been in service 60,000 miles, the one on the right 90,000 miles. Note how the belt on the right is beginning to separate and crack

will result. In an interference engine, should the timing belt fail, there is not enough clearance between the pistons and valves to allow the crankshaft to continue to rotate with the camshaft in one position, and the pistons will contact the valves causing internal damage. When this type of failure occurs, the engine will need to be disassembled

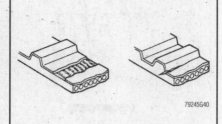

Fig. 74 Inspect the timing belt for damage, such as a broken or missing tooth, which may be due to a damaged pulley

and evaluated for repair or possibly replaced. Either choice is an expensive one, many times that of replacing the timing belt.

All of the Honda engines covered by this manual utilize timing belts to drive the camshaft from the crankshaft's turning motion and to maintain proper valve timing. In addition to the belt driven camshafts, the 4-cylinder Odyssey engines also have belt driven balance shafts. This belt is similar to the timing belt that drives the camshaft, though it is a separate belt and follows the same maintenance intervals as the camshaft drive belt.

The belt should be checked periodically to make sure it has not become damaged or worn. A severely worn belt may cause engine performance to drop dramatically, but a damaged belt (which could fail suddenly) may not give as much warning. In general, any time the engine timing cover(s) is (are) removed, inspect the belt for premature parting, severe cracks or missing teeth

❊❊ WARNING

Never allow antifreeze, oil or solvents to come into with a timing belt. If this occurs immediately wash the solution from the timing belt. Also, never excessive bend or twist the timing belt; this can damage the belt so that its lifetime is severely shortened.

Inspect both sides of the timing belt. Replace the belt with a new one if any of the following conditions exist:

- Hardening of the rubber—back side is glossy without resilience and leaves no indentation when pressed with a fingernail
- Cracks on the rubber backing
- Cracks or peeling of the canvas backing
- Cracks on rib root
- Cracks on belt sides
- Missing teeth or chunks of teeth
- Abnormal wear of belt sides—the sides are normal if they are sharp, as if cut by a knife.

Hoses

INSPECTION

♦ See Figures 79, 80, 81 and 82

The upper and lower radiator hoses, and the heater hoses, should be checked for deterioration, bulging, damage, leaks and loose hose clamps dur-

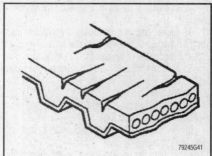

Fig. 75 Back surface worn or cracked from a possible overheated engine or interference with the belt cover

ing every oil change, or once a year, or every 15,000 miles (24,000 km) whichever occurs first. Because the engine's cooling system operates under moderate heat and pressure, a pinhole-sized leak could allow enough coolant to escape quickly enough to render the vehicle inoperable. Operating an engine low on coolant, even for a short period of time, could cause very expensive internal damage. It is also wise to check the hoses periodically in early spring and at the beginning of the fall or winter when performing other preventative maintenance. A quick visual inspection could discover a weakened hose, which could have failed, and left the vehicle stranded at the side of the road, if it had remained unrepaired.

Whenever checking the hoses, make sure the

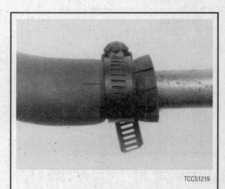

Fig. 79 The cracks developing along this hose are a result of age-related hardening

Fig. 80 A hose clamp that is too tight can cause older hoses to separate and tear on either side of the clamp

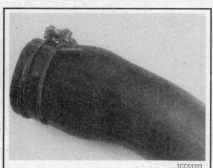

Fig. 81 A soft spongy hose (identifiable by the swollen section) will eventually burst and should be replaced

Fig. 82 Hoses are likely to deteriorate from the inside if the cooling system is not periodically flushed

engine and cooling system are cold. Visually inspect for cracking, rotting or collapsed hoses, and replace as necessary. Feel along the length of the hose. If a weak or swollen spot is noted when squeezing the hose wall, the hose should be replaced.

REMOVAL & INSTALLATION

✳✳ CAUTION

Never remove the radiator pressure cap from a hot engine, or when the engine is running, as personal injury from scalding, hot coolant or steam may result. The cooling system operates under moderate pressure as the engine temperature increases. Any attempt to remove the radiator pressure cap while the system is hot may cause the cap to be forced off by the cooling system pressure. Always wait until the engine has cooled before removing the pressure cap.

1. Before proceeding, make sure the engine is cool. Carefully feel the engine's valve cover, and upper and lower radiator hoses to ensure the engine and coolant temperature is cool enough to proceed.
2. Remove the radiator pressure cap.
3. Position a clean container under the radiator and/or engine draincock or plug, then open the drain and allow the cooling system to drain to an appropriate level. For most upper radiator hoses, only a small amount of coolant must be drained. To remove hoses positioned lower on the engine, such

as a lower radiator hose, the entire cooling system must be drained.

✳✳ CAUTION

When draining the coolant, keep in mind that small animals are attracted to ethylene glycol antifreeze. Because animals are attracted to the sweet odor and taste of engine coolant, they may attempt to drink any that is left in an uncovered container or in puddles on the ground. This will prove fatal in sufficient quantity. Always drain coolant into a sealable container. Coolant may be reused unless it is contaminated or several years old.

4. Loosen the hose clamps at each end of the hose requiring replacement. Clamps are usually either of the spring tension type (which require a pliers to squeeze the tabs and loosen) or of the screw tension type (which require screw or a hex driver to loosen). Slide the clamps back on the hose away from the connection once loosened.
5. Twist, pull and slide the hose off the fitting, taking care not to damage the neck of the component from which the hose is being removed.

➡If the hose is stuck at the connection, do not try to insert a screwdriver or other sharp tool under the hose end in an effort to free it, as the connection and/or hose may become damaged. Heater connections especially, may be easily damaged by such a procedure. Sometimes a cotter- key removal tool can be used with a suitable penetrating lubricant spray to loosen a hose if it must be reused. Make sure the tool is free of nicks and burrs that might damage the hose. If the hose is to be replaced, use a single-edged razor blade to carefully make a slice along the portion of the hose that is stuck on the connection, perpendicular to the end of the hose. Do not cut too deep to prevent damaging the connection. The hose can then be peeled from the connection and discarded.

6. Clean both hose mounting connections. Inspect the condition of the hose clamps and replace them, if necessary.
To install:
7. Dip the ends of the new hose into clean engine coolant to ease installation.
8. Slide the clamps over the replacement hose, then slide the hose ends over the connections into position.
9. Position and secure the clamps at least ¼ in. (6mm) from the ends of the hose. Make sure they are located on the connection beyond the raised bead of the connector.
10. Locate the air bleed valves and open the valves one full turn.
11. Close the radiator or engine drains and properly refill the cooling system with the clean drained engine coolant or a suitable mixture of ethylene glycol coolant and water.
12. Close the air bleed valve once the fluid flowing from the valve is free of any air bubbles.
13. If available, install a pressure tester and check for leaks. If a pressure tester is not available, run the engine until normal operating temperature is reached (allowing the system to naturally pressurize), then check for leaks.

14. Once the engine cools, open the radiator cap and recheck the fluid level and top off as necessary.

✳✳ CAUTION

If checking for leaks with the system at normal operating temperature, BE EXTREMELY CAREFUL not to touch any moving or hot engine parts. Once temperature has been reached, shut the engine OFF, and check for leaks around the hose fittings and connections that were removed or replaced.

CV-Boots

INSPECTION

▸ **See Figures 83 and 84**

The Constant Velocity (CV) boots should be checked for aging and damage each time the oil is changed and when performing maintenance service. These boots are found at the inner and outer ends of the front drive axles of the Honda Odyssey and at the inner and outer ends of the front and rear drive axles of the CR-V models. The boots are cone shaped and pleated, similar to an accordion. Because the axle must be able to rotate and turn at the same time, both ends of the drive axle are fitted with a CV-joint. The CV-boot is used to retain the grease used to lubricate the joint, and to prevent debris and contaminants from entering the joint. If

Fig. 83 CV-boots must be inspected periodically for damage

Fig. 84 A torn boot should be replaced immediately

the boots are punctured or split open, the centrifugal force of the spinning axle and CV-joint assembly will allow the grease to escape and the CV-joint will be permanently damaged. If the CV-boot is replaced before the CV-joint is damaged, the joint can be cleaned, repacked with grease, and reused. The cost of the CV-joint, is on average, about 5 to 10 times more expensive than just a boot. In some cases, the entire axle may have to be replaced. If a CV-boot failure occurs, replace the boot immediately. Signs of a CV-boot failure include the presence of heavy grease thrown around the inside of the front wheel(s) and on the brake caliper/drum. Thoroughly check the boots for missing clamps, tears and deterioration. The boot is far less expensive to replace than the joint it protects. Please refer to Section 7 for repair procedures.

Spark Plugs

♦ See Figure 85

A typical spark plug consists of a metal shell surrounding a ceramic insulator. A metal electrode extends downward through the center of the insulator and protrudes a small distance. Located at the end of the plug and attached to the side of the outer metal shell is the side electrode. The side electrode bends in at a 90° angle so that its tip is just past and parallel to the tip of the center electrode. The distance between these two electrodes (measured in thousandths of an inch or hundredths of a millimeter) is called the spark plug gap.

The spark plug does not produce a spark but instead provides a gap across which the current can arc. The ignition coil produces anywhere from 20,000 to 50,000 volts (depending on the type and application) which travels through the wires to the spark plugs. The current passes along the center electrode and jumps the gap to the side electrode, and in doing so, ignites the air/fuel mixture in the combustion chamber.

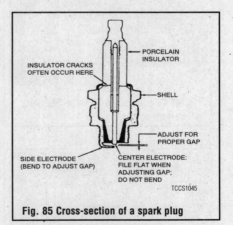

Fig. 85 Cross-section of a spark plug

SPARK PLUG HEAT RANGE

♦ See Figure 86

The spark plug heat range is the ability of the plug to dissipate heat. The deeper the insulator recedes into the body of the spark plug, the more heat the spark plug will retain and the hotter the plug will operate. If the amount the insulator recedes into the body of the spark plug is

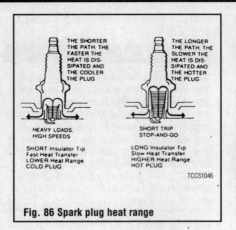

Fig. 86 Spark plug heat range

decreased, the less the plug will retain heat, and the cooler it will operate. A plug that absorbs little heat and remains too cool will quickly accumulate deposits of oil and carbon since it is not hot enough to burn them off. This causes carbon to build up on the porcelain insulator and the center electrode, creating an alternate path for the high energy electrical spark which eventually leads to spark plug fouling and consequently to misfiring.

A spark plug that absorbs too much heat will burn off deposits, however, due to the increased combustion temperature, the electrodes may also burn away more quickly and the excessive heat may cause pre-ignition or internal engine damage. Pre-ignition, also referred to as detonation, takes place when the combustion chamber gets hot enough to ignite the air/fuel mixture before the actual spark occurs. This early ignition may cause a "pinging", knocking or rattling noise during low speed acceleration or when operated under a heavy load condition, such as climbing a steep hill. Note that detonation can occur without being heard.

The general rule of thumb for choosing the correct heat range when selecting a spark plug is: consult the vehicle's owner's manual or a spark plug manufacturer's supply catalog for recommendations. If only one heat range of spark plug is listed, use the recommended plug, and note the recommended spark plug gap. If more than one heat range of spark plug is listed, depending on operating conditions, evaluate the type of driving the vehicle is most often subjected to. If the vehicle is used for extended high speed, long distance travel for long periods of time, in warm weather, use the colder plug of the recommend spark plugs. If, however, most of the driving is stop and go, or the vehicle is operated in extremely cold climates, use the hotter of the recommended spark plugs. Usually, original equipment plugs are a good compromise between the 2 styles of driving, and most vehicles rarely need to have their plugs differ from the factory-recommended heat range.

REMOVAL & INSTALLATION

♦ See Figure 87

The spark plug replacement intervals for the 1997–00 CR-V and the 4-cylinder Odyssey models is 2 years or 30,000 miles (48,000 km), whichever occurs first. The spark plug replacement intervals for the Odyssey models with the 3.5L V6 engine is 7 years or 105,000 miles (168,000 km), whichever occurs first. Refer to the maintenance interval chart

Fig. 87 Label each spark plug wire before disengaging and/or disconnecting them one at a time

located in the vehicle owner's manual or at the end of this section for additional items to be checked during the recommended maintenance services. During normal operation, The spark plug's gap increases as it wears. As the gap increases, the plug's ability to conduct a spark decreases, therefore the necessary voltage required to conduct a spark increases. The voltage required to jump the spark plug's gap at high engine speeds is about two to three times as much than at idle. The improved air/fuel ratio control of modern fuel injected engines combined with the higher voltage output of their ignition systems, will often allow an engine to run significantly longer on a set of spark plugs. However, the engine's efficiency most likely will drop as the spark plug gap widens and may decrease both fuel economy and power).

Before removing the spark plugs, label, or arrange the spark plug wires to ensure reinstalling them in the correct positions. On vehicles equipped with a distributor cap, mark the position of the spark plug wire for the number 1 cylinder. If for some reason the wires do become mismatched, the correct sequence can be easily determined by using the engine's firing order. The original equipment spark plug wires on Honda products are routed through well-organized guide clamps which can be removed from their mounting brackets while leaving the spark plug wires attached to the wire guides. Simply remove the spark plug wires from the spark plugs and move the wires aside as a unit. This will not only ensure the correct spark plug wire is reinstalled onto the correct cylinder, the guide clamps will also ensure correct routing of the wires. Because the spark plug wires conduct a high energy electrical current, the insulation of the wires must be kept clean and not allowed to rub against any object that may damage the insulation.

When removing the spark plugs, remove them one at a time in a logical order, noting which cylinder from which they were removed. A careful inspection of the spark plugs is one method of evaluating the engine's operating conditions. Spark plugs showing signs of a carbon build up or deposits around the center electrode, may be indications of an impending electrical or mechanical failure.

CR-V and 4-Cylinder Odyssey Models

♦ See Figures 88, 89, 90 and 91

1. Disconnect the negative battery cable, note the radio security code and, if the vehicle has been run recently, allow the engine to thoroughly cool.

2. Carefully remove the spark plug connectors from the spark plug by turning slightly while pulling. Do not use excessive force. If the connector seems to be stuck, turn the connector back and forth about a ¼ of a turn in each direction until the connector can be removed without excessive force.

3. Leaving the spark plug wires attached to the guide clamps, remove the clamps from the mounting brackets and place the spark plug wires safely aside as a unit.

➡Remove the spark plugs when the engine is cold, if possible, to prevent damage to the threads. If removal of the plugs is difficult,

Fig. 88 Rotate the plug wire cap ½ a turn and carefully pull upward. Using a suitable trim panel removal tool works well

Fig. 89 Inspect the plug wire boots and seals and make sure they are in good condition

Fig. 90 Be certain that the socket is squarely seated over the spark plug; otherwise, damage to the ceramic insulator could occur, making removal extremely difficult

Fig. 91 Depending on the tightness of the socket fit and the engine, carefully pull the spark plug out of the bore

apply a few drops of penetrating oil to the area around the base of the plug, and allowing it a few minutes to work.

4. Using a spark plug socket equipped with a rubber insert to properly hold the plug, turn the spark plug counterclockwise to loosen and remove the spark plug from the threaded hole in the cylinder head.

✳✳ WARNING

Avoid using a flexible extension on the spark plug socket. A flexible extension may allow a shear force to be applied to the plug. A shear force could break the plug off in the cylinder head, leading to costly repairs.

5. Inspect the spark plug boot, connectors, and wires for tears, damage, or deterioration. Make sure the plug wires and connectors are clean, and free of debris, such as engine oil. If a damaged boot, wire, or connector is found, the spark plug wire assembly must be replaced.

6. Using a wire feeler gauge, check and adjust the spark plug gap. When using a gauge, the proper size should pass between the electrodes with a slight drag. The next larger size should not be able to pass, while the next smaller size should pass freely.

7. Adjust the spark plug gap to 0.039–0.043 inches (1.0–1.1mm).

To install:

8. Apply a light coating of an anti-seize compound to the spark plug threads.

9. Carefully thread the plug into the threaded spark plug hole by hand. If resistance is felt before the plug is almost completely threaded, back the plug out and begin threading again. In small, hard to reach areas, a small piece of rubber hose pressed onto the spark plug can be used as a threading tool. The rubber hose will hold the plug and while twisting the end of the hose, the hose will be flexible enough to twist before allowing the plug to crossthread.

✳✳ WARNING

Do not use any excessive force when beginning to install the plugs. Always carefully thread the plug by hand or by using a rubber hose to prevent the possibility of crossthreading and damaging the cylinder head threads.

10. Carefully tighten the spark plug to 13 ft. lbs. (18 Nm).

11. Apply a small amount of silicone dielectric compound to the end of the spark plug lead or inside the spark plug boot to prevent sticking, then install the boot to the spark plug and push until it clicks into place. The click may be felt or heard, then gently pull back on the boot to assure proper contact.

12. Connect the negative battery cable and enter the radio security code.

V6 Odyssey Models

Beginning with model year 1999 the Odyssey models came equipped with a 3.5L V6 engine that uses a coil over plug ignition system. Each of the spark plugs has its own ignition coil which mounts directly above the spark plug and eliminates the need for a distributor, distributor cap, rotor and spark plug wires. Because the ignition coils are placed above the spark plugs, the coils must be removed before the spark plugs can be accessed.

1. Disconnect the negative battery cable, note the radio security code and, if the vehicle has been run recently, allow the engine to thoroughly cool.

2. Remove the trim covers located above the cylinder head covers.

3. Label the electrical terminals for each ignition coil, and detach the electrical connector from each ignition coil.

4. Remove the fasteners securing each ignition coil to the cylinder head cover, then remove the coils.

5. Using a spark plug socket equipped with a rubber insert to properly hold the plug, turn the spark plug counterclockwise to loosen and remove the spark plug from the threaded hole in the cylinder head.

✳✳ WARNING

Avoid using a flexible extension on the spark plug socket. A flexible extension may allow a shear force to be applied to the plug. A shear force could break the plug off in the cylinder head, leading to costly repairs.

6. Inspect each ignition coil for damage, or deterioration. Make sure the coils are clean, and free of debris, such as engine oil. If a damaged coil is found, it should be replaced.

✳✳ WARNING

The original equipment spark plugs installed in the 3.5L V6 engine are platinum tip spark plugs, and the plug gap must not be adjusted.

7. Using a wire feeler gauge, check, but **do not** adjust the spark plug gap. When using a gauge, the proper size should pass between the electrodes with a slight drag. The next larger size should not be able to pass, while the next smaller size should pass freely.

8. The spark plug gap should be 0.039–0.043 inches (1.0–1.1mm). If the spark plug gap exceeds 0.051 inches (1.3mm) replace the spark plug.

To install:

9. Apply a light coating of an anti-seize compound to the spark plug threads.

10. Carefully thread the plug into the threaded spark plug hole by hand. If resistance is felt before the plug is almost completely threaded, back the plug out and begin threading again. In tight, hard to reach areas, a small piece of rubber hose pressed onto the spark plug can be used as a threading tool. The rubber hose will hold the plug and while twisting the end of the hose, and the hose will be flexible enough to twist before allowing the plug to crossthread.

✳✳ WARNING

Do not use any excessive force when beginning to install the plugs. Always carefully thread the plug by hand or by using a rubber hose to prevent the possibility of crossthreading and damaging the cylinder head threads.

11. Carefully tighten the spark plug to 13 ft. lbs. (18 Nm).

12. Install the ignition coils, then attach the electrical connector to each ignition coil.

13. Install the trim covers onto the cylinder head covers.

14. Connect the negative battery cable and enter the radio security code.

INSPECTION & GAPPING

▶ **See Figures 92, 93, 94, 95 and 96**

Check the plugs for deposits and wear. Look carefully at the center electrode protrudes through the center of the porcelain. If the center electrode is eroded or rounded, replace the spark plugs. If the plugs are not going to be replaced, clean the plugs thoroughly. Remember that any kind of deposit will decrease the efficiency of the plug. Plugs can be cleaned on a spark plug-cleaning machine, which are sometimes found in service stations. These machines do a good job of cleaning the spark plug, although they tend to remove the protective anti-corrosive coating on the spark plug threads. They also cause the surface of porcelain around the center electrode to become slightly porous, allowing deposits to bond more easily to the porcelain. If a plug cleaner is used to clean the plugs, be sure the plug is thoroughly cleaned. The abrasive material used in the spark plug cleaners is very hard, and if allowed to enter the engine's combustion chamber, could cause internal damage. An acceptable job of cleaning the spark plug can be accomplished by using a stiff wire brush. Once the plugs are cleaned, the spark plug gap must be checked and reset to specification.

✳✳ WARNING

The original equipment spark plugs installed in the Odyssey 3.5L V-6 engine are platinum tip spark plugs, and the plug gap must not be adjusted.

Check spark plug gap before installation. Using a suitable spark plug gap gauge, check the spark plug gap. Make sure the L-shaped electrode connected to the body of the spark plug is parallel to the center electrode. If necessary, adjust the L-shaped electrode to attain the correct gap and

A **normally worn** spark plug should have light tan or gray deposits on the firing tip.

A **carbon fouled** plug, identified by soft, sooty, black deposits, may indicate an improperly tuned vehicle. Check the air cleaner, ignition components and engine control system.

This spark plug has been **left in the engine too long,** as evidenced by the extreme gap- Plugs with such an extreme gap can cause misfiring and stumbling accompanied by a noticeable lack of power.

An **oil fouled** spark plug indicates an engine with worn poston rings and/or bad valve seals allowing excessive oil to enter the chamber.

A **physically damaged** spark plug may be evidence of severe detonation in that cylinder. Watch that cylinder carefully between services, as a continued detonation will not only damage the plug, but could also damage the engine.

A **bridged or almost bridged** spark plug, identified by a build-up between the electrodes caused by excessive carbon or oil build-up on the plug.

TCCA1P40

Fig. 92 Inspect the spark plug to determine engine running conditions

TCCS1212
Fig. 93 A variety of tools and gauges are needed for spark plug service

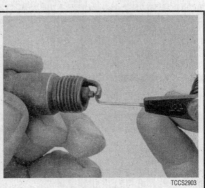
TCCS2903
Fig. 94 Checking the spark plug gap with a feeler gauge

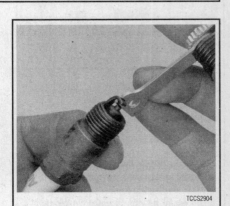
TCCS2904
Fig. 95 Adjusting the spark plug gap

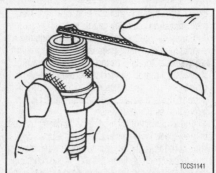

Fig. 96 If the standard plug is in good condition, the electrode may be filed flat—WARNING: do not file platinum plugs

Fig. 97 Checking individual plug wire resistance with a digital ohmmeter

proper alignment. Make sure to use the specified size wire gauge, which must pass between the electrodes with a slight drag and the next larger size should not be able to pass, while the next smaller size should pass freely. When adjusting a spark plug gap, always set the gap to the minimum specification to allow for electrode wear. Refer to the following information pertaining to spark plug gap.

On CR-V and 4-cylinder Odyssey models, adjust the spark plug gap to 0.039–0.043 inches (1.0–1.1mm). On Odysseys with the V6 engine, check, but **do not** adjust the spark plug gap. The spark plug gap should be 0.039–0.043 inches (1.0–1.1mm). If the spark plug gap exceeds 0.051inches (1.3mm), replace the spark plug.

➡**NEVER adjust the gap on a used platinum type spark plug.**

Always check the gap on new plugs as they are not always set correctly at the factory. Do not use a flat feeler gauge when measuring the gap because the reading may be inaccurate. A round-wire type gapping tool is the best tool for checking the plug gap. The correct gauge should pass through the electrode gap with a slight drag. If in doubt, try one size smaller and one larger. The smaller gauge should go through easily, while the larger one shouldn't go through at all. Wire gapping tools usually have a bending tool attached. Use this to adjust the side electrode until the proper clearance is obtained. Never attempt to bend the center electrode. Be careful not to bend the side electrode too far or too often as it may weaken and break off inside the engine, requiring removal of the cylinder head to retrieve it.

Spark Plug Wires

TESTING

CR-V and 4-Cylinder Odyssey Models

▶ **See Figure 97**

During every tune-up/inspection, visually check the spark plug cables for fluid contamination, burns, chaffing, cuts, or breaks in the insulation. Check the boots and the nipples on the ignition coil or distributor, if equipped. Replace any damaged wiring.

Every 60,000 miles (96,000 km) or 48 months, the resistance of the wires should be checked with

an ohmmeter. Wires with excessive resistance will cause misfiring, and may cause the engine to be difficult to start in damp weather. Ignition wire resistance should not be greater than 25 Kilo ohms.

To check resistance, remove the spark plug wire from the plug and ignition coil or distributor. Using an ohmmeter, measure the resistance of the wire by placing one lead of the ohmmeter at one end of the ignition wire, and the other ohmmeter lead at the other end of the ignition wire.

If the measured resistance is above the specifications, the ignition wire must be replaced.

REMOVAL & INSTALLATION

CR-V and 4-Cylinder Odyssey Models

➡**The spark plug wires must be routed and connected properly. If the wires must be completely disconnected from the spark plugs and/or from the distributor cap at the same time, label the wires to assure proper reconnection.**

When installing a new set of spark plug wires, replace the wires one at a time to avoid mixing them up. Start by replacing the longest cable first. Twist the boot of the spark plug wire ½ turn in each direction before pulling it off. Install the boot firmly over the spark plug. Route the wire exactly the same as the original. Insert the nipple firmly onto the tower of the distributor cap, if equipped. Use a silicone dielectric compound on the spark plug wire boots and distributor cap connectors prior to installation.

Distributor Cap and Rotor

REMOVAL & INSTALLATION

CR-V and 4-Cylinder Odyssey models

▶ **See Figures 98 thru 103**

1. Disconnect the negative battery cable.
2. If the distributor cap is to be replaced, mark the ignition wires for identification and remove them from the distributor cap.
3. Remove the two rear air filter housing bolts using a 10mm socket, extension and ratchet, and move the housing to the left to allow enough clearance to remove the distributor cap.
4. Completely loosen the distributor cap

mounting fasteners using an 8mm socket, extension and ratchet or a Phillips screwdriver.
5. Carefully remove the distributor cap taking care not to damage the cap seal and set aside.
6. Locate the threaded fastener that secures the ignition rotor to the shaft of the distributor, which is positioned opposite the rotor contact on the lower portion of the rotor, and remove the fastener.
7. Carefully lift the rotor off the distributor shaft.

➡**Inspect the distributor cap to housing seal for damage and/or cracks.**

To install:
8. Install the rotor onto the distributor shaft and tighten the rotor-mounting fastener.

Fig. 98 Number the spark plug wires to match the distributor cap before removal

Fig. 99 Loosen the distributor cap hold-down combination screws with a Phillips screwdriver

Fig. 100 You can also use a ¼ inch drive 8mm deep well socket and ratchet to loosen the distributor cap retainers

Fig. 101 Removing the two rear air filter housing bolts allows it to be moved slightly, and gives just enough room to remove the distributor cap—CR-V shown

Fig. 102 An inspection mirror is handy when trying to locate the rotor mounting screw on this CR-V distributor

Fig. 103 Remove the distributor rotor mounting screw before trying to lift off the rotor

9. Position the distributor cap seal on the distributor housing and position the distributor cap on the housing.

10. Install the distributor cap by tightening the mounting fasteners in a crisscross pattern. Use care to not over-tighten the fasteners.

11. Reconnect the spark plug wires, making sure to install them exactly in the same position from which they were removed.

12. Reconnect the negative battery cable and enter the radio security code.

INSPECTION

CR-V and 4-Cylinder Odyssey Models

1. Inspect the distributor cap for cracks and burned or worn electrodes. Inspect the center contact of the cap to make sure it will make a good connection with the rotor once installed. Replace the cap if it is cracked, or the contacts appear grooved, or if the center contact is worn.

2. Inspect the rotor for cracks and a worn or burned electrode. Replace the rotor if the contact surface is eroded or uneven.

3. Prior to reinstalling the distributor cap and rotor, thoroughly clean them with an electrical contact cleaner.

✶✶ WARNING

Because the distributor cap and rotor transmit a high-energy ignition voltage, avoid using any type of solvent, spray or lubricate on the inside or outside of the cap or on the rotor. When cleaning them, use only an electrical contact cleaner intended specifically for electrical circuits.

Ignition Timing

GENERAL INFORMATION

The ignition timing is a specification that is used to describe when a spark plug receives a high-energy voltage relative to the position of the piston. A piston that is at the top of its stroke is referred to as being at Top Dead Center (TDC). The piston in an internal combustion engine simply moves up and down in the cylinder bore of the engine block, and is attached to the crankshaft via the connecting rod. If the crankshaft is rotated one complete revolution, the piston will move two strokes, one downward stroke and one upward stroke. During the upward stroke of the piston, its position, relative to the top of its stroke is referred to as being Before Top Dead Center (BTDC). One complete revolution of the crankshaft is the equivalent to 360° of rotation. When a piston is at TDC, this position is referred to as the 0° position. If the crankshaft is rotated ½ a revolution, it has been rotated 180° and the piston would be at the bottom of its stroke.

Because the piston moves up or down as the crankshaft is rotated, the piston's location relative to TDC can be measured using the number of degrees of crankshaft rotation **before** the piston reaches TDC. The upward movement of the piston as it approaches TDC is referred to as Before Top Dead Center (BTDC). The ignition timing specifications provided by the manufacturer and used in this manual are provided in degrees Before Top Dead Center (°BTDC).

When the spark plug receives the high-energy voltage, the intensity of this voltage is enough that the voltage jumps the gap of the spark plug creating a spark. This spark is used to ignite the fuel air-mixture in the combustion chamber. As the fuel burns, it expands, creating energy and pressurizes the combustion chamber. This pressure presses on the top of the piston, pressing it downward on a power stroke, which transmits the energy through the connecting rod to the crankshaft.

For an engine to run properly and efficiently, the correct ignition timing is essential. If the ignition spark occurs too late during the piston's upward stroke, the ignition timing is referred to as being retarded. If the ignition spark occurs too early in the piston's upward stroke, the ignition timing is referred to as being advanced.

The engine's timing requirements change as the engine speed increases and as throttle position varies. The Honda products covered in this manual use an electronic ignition system, which monitors the engine's operating conditions, and changes the ignition timing accordingly. The 1997–00 CR-V's and 2.2L/2.3L Odyssey models use a distributor to provide the high-energy ignition voltage to the spark plugs. On these models, the ignition timing advance is controlled by the engine control units, however the idle speed ignition timing (base ignition timing) can be adjusted by placing the engine control unit in an adjust mode moving the distributor.

The 3.5L Odyssey models do not use a distributor. Each spark plug has its own ignition coil. This eliminates the need for a distributor, and the associated components, such as a distributor cap, rotor and ignition wires. The base ignition timing and ignition advance is controlled by the control unit. The ignition timing can be checked, but cannot be adjusted. If the ignition timing is found to be out of specification, the engine's ignition system must be fully checked. The control unit relies on input from sensors to determine the optimum ignition timing. If the ignition timing related sensors are found to be operating properly, the control unit must be replaced.

If the ignition timing is set too far advanced (BTDC), the ignition and expansion of the fuel in the cylinder will occur too soon and tend to force the piston down while it is still traveling up. This condition may causes engine detonation or ping. If the ignition timing is too far retarded After Top Dead Center, (ATDC), the piston will have already passed TDC and started on its way down when the fuel is ignited. This will cause the piston to be forced down for only a portion of its travel. This will result in poor engine performance and lack of power.

On vehicles with distributors, the ignition timing should be checked during a tune-up. Usually, once the timing is set it is not likely to change. On vehicles with distributorless ignition systems, the ignition timing can only be checked using expensive, specialized diagnostic equipment. Due to its cost and complexity, the use of such equipment is beyond the scope of this manual. The ignition timing on the distributorless ignition system cannot be adjusted and the system requires no maintenance aside from replacing spark plugs. The ignition timing will remain correct as long as the sensors and control unit function properly.

The ignition timing marks on both the CR-V and Odyssey are small notches located on the perimeter of the drive belt pulleys mounted on the engine's crankshaft. The engine cover above the pulleys has a pointer that is used to align with the timing notches. The CR-V and Odyssey 2.2L and 2.3L four cylinder engines run in a counterclockwise direction when facing the drive pulleys. Two of the notches in the crankshaft pulley are painted. The notch that is painted **white** is TDC, (0° mark). The notch that is painted **red** is the idle speed ignition timing mark.

On models where the crankshaft rotates in a counterclockwise direction, while facing the drive pulleys, the red idle speed ignition timing mark is located to the left of the white TDC mark. The painted red ignition timing notch also has notches on either side of it. These notches, on either side of the red notch, represent 2° increments. As long as the idle speed ignition timing occurs somewhere between these two notches, the ignition timing is within specification. For example, the idle speed ignition timing for the CR-V is 16°BTDC plus or minus 2°. The notches on either side of the red notch on the crankshaft pulley would indicate the following information. The notch to the right of the red notch would be 16° minus 2°, or 14°. The notch to the left of the red notch would be 16° plus 2°, or 18°. As long as the idle speed ignition timing for this example, occurs between these two marks (14°–18°), the idle speed ignition timing is considered to be within the recommended specification.

There are three basic types of timing lights available. The first is a simple neon bulb with two wire connections. One wire connects to the spark plug terminal and the other plugs into the end of the spark plug wire for the No. 1 cylinder, thus connecting the light in series with the spark plug. This type of light is dim and must be held very closely to the timing marks to be seen. Sometimes a dark corner has to be sought out to see the flash at all. This type of light is very inexpensive. The second type is powered by the vehicle's battery, by correctly connecting two alligator clips to the battery terminals. These timing lights are available with or without an inductive pickup. If the timing light does not have an inductive pickup, a wire must make physical contact with the ignition wire for the No. 1 spark plug. Using this type of arrangement usually requires the use of an adapter either at the spark plug or distributor cap connection. This tends to render this type of arrangement to be awkward, less convenient and time consuming to use.

A timing light with an inductive pickup is much easier to use. Simply connect the lead properly at the vehicle's battery and then clamp the inductive pickup around the ignition wire for the No. 1 spark plug. This type is a bit more expensive, but it provides a nice bright flash that can be easily seen, even in bright sunlight. It is easy to use, and the type most often seen in professional shops. The third type replaces the battery power source with 115-volt current. They work well, but are much less portable and convenient to use.

Some timing lights may have other features built into them, such as ignition advance checking devices, dwell meters, or tachometers. These are convenient, in that they reduce the tangle of wires under the hood, but may duplicate the functions of other tools and the features add to the expense of the tool. A timing light with an inductive pickup should always be used on Honda ignition systems when checking/adjusting ignition timing.

ADJUSTMENT

CR-V and 4-Cylinder Odyssey Models

▶ See Figures 104 and 105

➡No adjustment is possible for the 1999 and later Odyssey models equipped with the V6 engine.

1. If equipped with an automatic transaxle, place the shifter in Park or Neutral. If equipped with a manual transaxle place the shifter in Neutral. Make sure to apply the parking brake and block the drive wheels.

2. With the heater off and in the full cold position, start the engine and hold the engine speed at 3000 rpm, until the radiator fan comes on at least one time. To check the ignition timing, the engine must be at idle speed and at normal operating temperature. Make sure all electrical consumers (defroster, radio, air conditioning, lights, etc.,) are turned OFF.

3. Locate the blue plastic Service Check (SCS) Connector, as follows:

- CR-V models: centrally located under the passenger side of the dash. The connector's has two wires; one is brown and the other is black.
- Odyssey models with 4-cylinder engines: centrally located on the passenger side, under the dash. The connector has two wires; one is brown with a black tracer, and the other wire is red.

4. Connect the SCS service connector tool number 07PAZ-0010100 or equivalent to the service connector. A paper clip can be substituted for the tool by forming a "U" shaped bend in the paper

Fig. 104 The inductive lead of the timing light is placed around the No. 1 spark plug wire; and the light is aimed toward the marks on the crankshaft pulley

93131P72

Fig. 105 The red ignition timing mark on the crankshaft pulley is lined up with the pointer. The two small notches on either side of the red colored notch represent the plus (+) or minus (-) 2° increments. The white notch to the far right is Top Dead Center (TDC)

93131P69

clip and carefully inserting it into the back side of the SCS service connector terminals. The purpose of the tool is simply to connect the two wires together temporarily.

5. Connect a timing light to No. 1 ignition wire and point the light toward the pointer on the timing belt cover.

6. Check the idle speed and adjust if necessary.

7. The red mark on the crankshaft pulley should be aligned with the pointer on the timing belt cover.

➡The white mark on the crank pulley is Top Dead Center (TDC).

8. Adjust the ignition timing by loosening the distributor mounting bolts and rotating the distributor housing to adjust the timing. Set as follows:

- 1997–98 CR-V models: 14–18° at 700–800 rpm
- 1999–00 CR-V models: 14–18° at 680–780 rpm
- 2.2L/2.3L Odyssey 2.2L models: 13–17° at 650–750 rpm
- 1998 Odyssey 2.3L models: 10–14° at 650–750 rpm

9. Tighten the distributor bolts to 17 ft. lbs. (24 Nm) and recheck the timing.

10. Remove the SCS service connector or the substituted paper clip from the SCS service plug.

V6 Odyssey Models

These vehicles use a distributorless ignition system utilizing individual ignition coils for each spark plug, and the ignition timing cannot be adjusted. The ignition timing is controlled by the Powertrain Control Module (PCM) and automatically adjusts the ignition timing for optimum performance and efficiency based on the information communicated by a collection of input sensors. Because the ignition timing can only be checked for diagnostic purposes, and checking it requires the use of expensive, specialized diagnostic equipment, the use of such equipment is beyond the scope of this manual. The ignition timing on the distributorless ignition system cannot be adjusted, requires no maintenance aside from replacing spark plugs, and the ignition timing will remain correct as long as the sensors and control unit function properly.

Valve Lash

ADJUSTMENT

CR-V Models

▶ See Figures 106 thru 112

➡The radio may contain a coded anti-theft circuit. Obtain the security code before disconnecting the battery.

1. Disconnect the negative battery cable.

2. The valves should be checked and adjusted when the engine is cold. If the engine has been run, allow it to cool to below 100°F (38°C) before beginning adjustments.

3. The valves must be checked or adjusted for each cylinder with the cylinder in the TDC position of the compression stroke.

4. Remove the cylinder head cover and the upper timing belt cover.

5. Rotate the crankshaft in a counterclockwise direction and align the painted white notch Top Dead Center (TDC) mark on the crankshaft pulley with the pointer on the engine cover for the No. 1 cylinder compression stroke. The UP marks on the camshaft sprockets should be facing up and TDC marks of the camshaft sprockets should align with the pointers on the valve cover gasket surface of the cylinder head.

6. With the cylinder at TDC on the compression stroke, check the valve clearance by inserting the correct size feeler gauge between the rocker arm and the camshaft lobe of the valves for that cylinder.

7. To check the intake valves proceed as follows:

  a. Using a 0.003 in. (0.08mm) feeler gauge, see if the gauge will slide between the camshaft lobe and the rocker.

  b. If the 0.003 in. (0.08mm) feeler gauge does not fit between the rocker and the camshaft lobe, then adjust the valve. If the feeler gauge did fit, then try inserting a 0.006 in. (0.15mm) feeler gauge.

  c. If the 0.006 in. (0.15mm) feeler gauge can be inserted between the rocker and the camshaft lobe, then adjust the valve. If the feeler gauge cannot be inserted, then the valve adjustment for that valve is within the range specified.

8. The valve adjustment specification for the CR-V intake valve is 0.003–0.005 in. (0.08–0.12mm). To adjust an intake valve, proceed as follows:

  a. Loosen the locknut and turn the adjusting screw counterclockwise to loosen the adjustment.

  b. Insert a 0.004 in. (0.10mm) feeler gauge between the camshaft lobe and the rocker.

  c. Hold the locknut and turn the adjusting screw until a very light resistance is felt. The feeler gauge should be able to be moved with a slight amount of drag.

  d. While holding the adjustment screw in place, tighten the locknut and then recheck the clearance.

9. To check the exhaust valve clearance proceed as follows:

  a. Using a 0.006 in. (0.15mm) feeler gauge, see if the gauge will slide between the camshaft lobe and the rocker.

  b. If the 0.006 in. (0.15mm) feeler gauge does not fit between the rocker and the camshaft lobe, then adjust the valve. If the feeler gauge did fit, then try inserting a 0.009 in. (0.22mm) feeler gauge.

  c. If the 0.009 in. (0.22mm) feeler gauge can be inserted between the rocker and the camshaft lobe, then adjust the valve. If the feeler gauge cannot be inserted, then the valve adjustment for that valve is within the range specified.

10. The valve adjustment specification for the CR-V exhaust valve is 0.006–0.008 in. (0.16–0.20mm) To adjust an exhaust valve, proceed as follows:

  a. Loosen the locknut and turn the adjusting screw counterclockwise to loosen the adjustment.

  b. Insert a 0.007 in. (0.18mm) feeler gauge between the valve tip and the rocker.

  c. Hold the locknut and turn the adjusting screw until a very light resistance is felt. The feeler gauge should be able to be moved with a slight amount of drag.

  d. While holding the adjustment screw in place, tighten the locknut and then recheck the clearance.

11. Repeat the checking procedure for each valve and adjust the clearance for any valve found to be out of adjustment.

12. Once all of the valves for a cylinder have been checked, the crankshaft must be rotated counterclockwise to check the valves of another cylinder.

13. When rotating the crankshaft counterclockwise, the adjustment order is cylinder No. 1, cylinder No. 3, cylinder No. 4, cylinder No. 2.

14. Rotate the crankshaft counterclockwise 180° to bring the next cylinder to the TDC/compression position.

15. Refer to the following information to verify the cylinder to be checked is in the TDC/compression position:

- At TDC/compression for the No. 1 cylinder, the camshaft sprocket UP marks are pointed straight up, and the TDC marks align with the edge of the cylinder head.
- At TDC/compression for the No. 3 cylinder, the camshaft sprocket UP marks are both horizontal, pointed to the left.
- At TDC/compression for the No. 4 cylinder, the camshaft sprocket UP marks are pointed straight down, and the TDC marks align with the edge of the cylinder head.

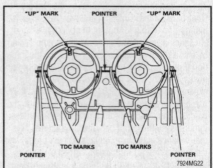

Fig. 106 Camshaft sprocket positioning for TDC/compression for the No. 1 cylinder—CR-V models

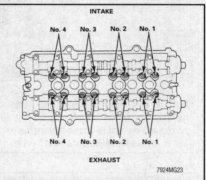

Fig. 107 Intake and exhaust valve identification—CR-V models

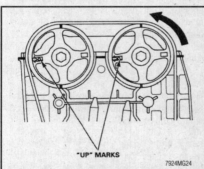

Fig. 108 Camshaft sprocket positioning for TDC/compression for the No. 3 cylinder—CR-V models

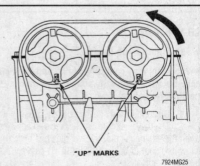

Fig. 109 Camshaft sprocket positioning for TDC/compression for the No. 4 cylinder—CR-V models

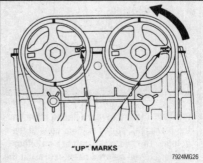

Fig. 110 Camshaft sprocket positioning for TDC/compression for the No. 2 cylinder—CR-V models

Fig. 111 The feeler gauge is placed between the camshaft lobe and the rocker on CR-V models

Fig. 112 A non-hardening gasket sealant should be applied to the every corner of the valve cover gasket. Make sure the gasket and cylinder head gasket surface are clean and dry before applying the sealant

- At TDC/compression for the No. 2 cylinder, the camshaft sprocket UP marks are both horizontal, pointed to the right.

16. After checking all of the valves for all of the cylinders, check, and if necessary, retighten the crankshaft pulley bolt in a clockwise direction to 130 ft. lbs. (177 Nm).

17. Thoroughly clean the cylinder head cover gasket and make sure it is fully seated into the head cover. Apply a liquid gasket sealant to the corners of the half circle portions of the gasket.

18. Install the cylinder head and timing belt covers, tightening the fasteners evenly to 86 inch pounds (9.8 Nm).

19. Reconnect the negative battery cable. Enter the radio security code.

Odyssey Models

4-CYLINDER ENGINES

◆ See Figures 113, 114, 115, 116 and 117

➡The radio may contain a coded anti-theft circuit. Obtain the security code before disconnecting the battery.

1. Disconnect the negative battery cable.
2. The valves should be checked and adjusted when the engine is cold. If the engine has been run, allow it to cool to below 100°F (38°C) before beginning adjustments.
3. The valves must be checked or adjusted for each cylinder with the cylinder in the TDC position of the compression stroke.

4. Remove the cylinder head cover and the upper timing belt cover.

5. Rotate the crankshaft in a counterclockwise direction until the painted white notch Top Dead Center (TDC) mark on the crankshaft pulley is aligned with the pointer on the engine cover, and the UP mark on the camshaft sprocket is facing up. The No. 1 cylinder is at TDC/compression stroke in this position.

6. With the cylinder at TDC on the compression stroke, check the valve clearance by inserting the correct size feeler gauge between the rocker and the valve tip of the valves for that cylinder.

7. Hold the rocker arm against the camshaft and use a feeler gauge to check the clearance at the valve stem; intake valve clearance should be 0.010 in. (0.26mm), exhaust valve clearance should be 0.012 in. (0.30mm). The service limit for both intake and exhaust valves is plus or minus 0.0008 in. (0.02mm).

8. To check the intake valves proceed as follows:

a. Using a 0.009 in. (0.24mm) feeler gauge, see if the gauge will slide between the valve tip and the rocker.

b. If the 0.009 in. (0.24mm) feeler gauge does not fit between the rocker and the valve tip, then adjust the valve. If the feeler gauge did fit, then try inserting a 0.011 in. (0.28mm) feeler gauge.

c. If the 0.011 in. (0.28mm) feeler gauge can be inserted between the rocker and the valve tip, then adjust the valve. If the feeler gauge cannot be inserted, then the valve adjustment for that valve is within the range specified.

9. The valve adjustment specification for the intake valve is 0.010 in. (0.26mm). To adjust an intake valve, proceed as follows:

a. Loosen the locknut and turn the adjusting screw counterclockwise to loosen the adjustment screw.

b. Hold the rocker arm against the camshaft and insert a 0.010 in. (0.26mm) feeler gauge between the rocker and the valve tip.

c. Hold the locknut and turn the adjusting screw until a very light resistance is felt. The feeler gauge should be able to be moved with a slight amount of drag.

d. While holding the adjustment screw in place, tighten the locknut and then recheck the clearance.

10. To check the exhaust valve clearance proceed as follows:

a. Using a 0.011 in. (0.28mm) feeler gauge, see if the gauge will slide between the valve tip and the rocker.

b. If the 0.011 in. (0.28mm) feeler gauge does not fit between the rocker and the valve tip, then adjust the valve. If the feeler gauge did fit, then try inserting a 0.013 in. (0.33mm) feeler gauge.

c. If the 0.013 in. (0.33mm) feeler gauge can be inserted between the rocker and the valve tip, then adjust the valve. If the feeler gauge cannot be inserted, then the valve adjustment for that valve is within the range specified.

11. The valve adjustment specification for the exhaust valve is 0.012 in. (0.30mm). To adjust an exhaust valve, proceed as follows:

a. Loosen the locknut and turn the adjusting screw counterclockwise to loosen the adjustment screw.

b. Hold the rocker arm against the camshaft and insert a 0.012 in. (0.30mm) feeler gauge between the rocker and the valve tip.

c. Hold the locknut and turn the adjusting screw until a very light resistance is felt. The feeler gauge should be able to be moved with a slight amount of drag.

d. While holding the adjustment screw in place, tighten the locknut and then recheck the clearance.

12. Repeat the checking procedure for each valve and adjust the clearance for any valve found to be out of adjustment.

13. Once all of the valves for a cylinder have been checked, the crankshaft must be rotated counterclockwise to check the valves of another cylinder.

14. When rotating the crankshaft counterclockwise, the adjustment order is cylinder No. 1, cylinder No. 3, cylinder No. 4, cylinder No. 2.

15. Rotate the crankshaft counterclockwise 180° to bring the next cylinder to the TDC/compression position.

16. Refer to the following information to verify the cylinder to be checked is in the TDC/compression position:

- At TDC/compression for the No. 1 cylinder, the camshaft sprocket UP mark should be pointed straight up, and the TDC marks align with the edge of the cylinder head.
- At TDC/compression for the No. 3 cylinder, the camshaft sprocket UP mark should be horizontal, and pointed to the left.

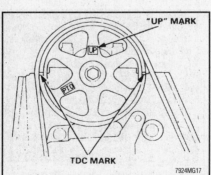

Fig. 113 Camshaft timing belt sprocket positioning for TDC/compression for the No. 1 cylinder—4-cylinder Odysseys

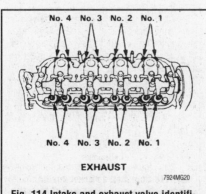

Fig. 114 Intake and exhaust valve identification—4-cylinder Odysseys

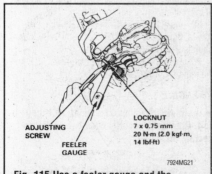

Fig. 115 Use a feeler gauge and the adjusting screw to change the valve lash, as shown—4-cylinder Odysseys

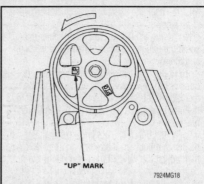

Fig. 116 Rotate the crankshaft until the camshaft sprocket is positioned as shown for TDC/compression for the No. 3 cylinder—4-cylinder Odysseys

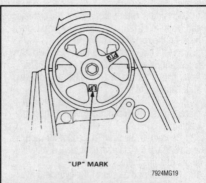

Fig. 117 TDC/compression for the No. 4 cylinder is achieved when the camshaft sprocket is positioned as shown—4-cylinder Odysseys

- At TDC/compression for the No. 4 cylinder, the camshaft sprocket UP mark should be pointed straight down, and the TDC mark should align with the edge of the cylinder head.
- At TDC/compression for the No. 2 cylinder, the camshaft sprocket UP mark should be horizontal, and pointed to the right.

17. After checking the valves, check and if necessary, retighten the crankshaft pulley bolt in a clockwise direction to 181 ft. lbs. (245 Nm).

18. Thoroughly clean the cylinder head cover gasket and make sure it is fully seated into the head cover. Apply a liquid gasket sealant to the corners of the half circle portions of the gasket.

19. Install the cylinder head and timing belt covers, tightening the fasteners evenly to 86 inch pounds (9.8 Nm).

20. Reconnect the negative battery cable. Enter the radio security code.

V6 ENGINE

➡ **The radio may contain a coded anti-theft circuit. Obtain the security code before disconnecting the battery.**

1. Disconnect the negative battery cable.
2. The valves should be adjusted when the engine is cold. If the engine has been run, allow it to cool to below 100°F (38°C) before beginning adjustments.

3. Label the vacuum hoses and remove the intake bellows assembly located near the battery from the throttle body.

4. Remove the two ignition coil trim covers and the intake manifold trim cover.

5. Disconnect the throttle and cruise control cables from the throttle body and place aside without bending severely or kinking.

6. Remove the brake booster vacuum hose and the crankcase breather hose.

7. Detach the engine wire harness connectors and harness clamps from the intake manifold.

8. Disconnect and plug the throttle body coolant hoses.

9. Remove the intake manifold.

10. Remove the cylinder head covers.

11. Remove the front upper timing belt cover.

12. Rotate the crankshaft in a clockwise direction and align the white Top Dead Center (TDC) mark on the crankshaft pulley with the pointer on the oil pump cover and make sure the **1** mark on the camshaft sprocket is up and aligned with the TDC pointer on the front cylinder head back cover.

13. Hold the No. 1 cylinder rocker arm against the camshaft and use a feeler gauge to check the clearance at the valve stem. Intake valve clearance should be 0.008–0.009 in. (0.20–0.24mm), exhaust valve clearance should be 0.011–0.013 in. (0.28–0.32mm).

14. Check the valve adjustment for cylinder No. 1, and adjust if necessary. To adjust:
- Loosen the locknut and turn the adjusting screw to adjust the clearance.
- Tighten the locknut to a torque of 14 ft. lbs. (20 Nm) and recheck the clearance.

15. Rotate the crankshaft clockwise until the pointer on the back cover of the front cylinder head aligns with the **4** mark on the camshaft sprocket.

16. Check the valve adjustment for cylinder No. 4, and adjust if necessary.

17. Rotate the crankshaft clockwise until the pointer on the back cover of the front cylinder head aligns with the **2** mark on the camshaft sprocket.

18. Check the valve adjustment for cylinder No. 2, and adjust if necessary.

19. Rotate the crankshaft clockwise until the pointer on the back cover of the front cylinder head aligns with the **5** mark on the camshaft sprocket.

20. Check the valve adjustment for cylinder No. 5, and adjust if necessary.

21. Rotate the crankshaft clockwise until the pointer on the back cover of the front cylinder head aligns with the **3** mark on the camshaft sprocket.

22. Check the valve adjustment for cylinder No. 3, and adjust if necessary.

23. Rotate the crankshaft clockwise until the pointer on the back cover of the front cylinder head aligns with the **6** mark on the camshaft sprocket.

24. Check the valve adjustment for cylinder No. 6, and adjust if necessary.

25. Install the front upper timing belt cover.

26. Install the cylinder head covers and torque the bolts to 104 inch lbs. (12 Nm).

27. Install the intake manifold, and torque the bolts to 16 ft. lbs. (22 Nm).

28. Connect and tighten the throttle body coolant hoses.

29. Attach the engine wire harness connectors and harness clamps for the intake manifold.

30. Install the brake booster vacuum hose and the crankcase breather hose.

31. Connect the throttle and cruise control cables to the throttle body.

32. Install the two ignition coil trim covers and the intake manifold trim cover.

33. Install the vacuum hoses and the intake bellows assembly to the throttle body.

34. After adjusting the valves, check and if necessary, tighten the crankshaft pulley bolt in a clockwise direction to 181 ft. lbs. (245 Nm).

35. Reconnect the negative battery cable. Enter the radio security code.

Idle Speed and Mixture Adjustment

Idle speed and mixture for all engines covered by this manual are electronically controlled by a computerized fuel injection system. The only adjustment possible is the warm idle engine speed. No other adjustments are possible.

Before setting the warm idle speed, the following items must be checked or verified:
- The MIL (Malfunction Indicator Light) light has not been on or flashing
- Ignition timing is within specification
- Spark plug condition is within specification
- Air cleaner condition is acceptable
- Positive Crankcase Ventilation (PCV) system is functioning properly

➡ **On Canadian vehicles, the parking brake must be applied before proceeding with any adjustments.**

1. Make sure the heater is in the full cold position and all electrical consumers are in the OFF position, such as headlights, defrosters, climate control fans, and other electrical accessories.

2. Start the engine and hold the engine speed to 3,000 rpm with the transmission in **Park** or **Neutral**, until the radiator cooling fan comes on, then let the engine idle.

3. Connect a tachometer or the Honda PGM Testing Assembly.

4. On CR-V's and 4-cylinder Odyssey models:
   a. Detach the round 2 pin electrical connector from the Idle Air Control (IAC) valve.

5. On 1998–00 Odyssey models, perform the following:
   a. Detach the 2 pin electrical connector for the Evaporative emissions purge control (EVAP) valve. Leave the Idle Air Control (IAC) valve connected.

6. If the engine stalls, restart pressing the accelerator, hold the engine speed at 1,000 rpm, and slowly release the gas pedal until the engine idles.

7. Check the idle speed making sure all electrical accessories are turned off, with the transmission in **Park** or **Neutral**.

8. The idle speed should be as follows:
   - CR-V: 430–530 rpm
   - 1995–97 Odyssey: 500–600 rpm
   - 1998 Odyssey: 650–750 rpm
   - 1990–00 Odyssey: 680–780 rpm

9. If the idle speed must be adjusted, do not turn the adjusting screw located at the top left of the throttle body inlet side more than ¼ of a turn a minute. Make sure no electrical accessories are operating when checking or adjusting the engine idle speed.

10. On CR-V's and 4-cylinder Odyssey models, perform the following:

ENGINE TUNE-UP SPECIFICATIONS

Year	Engine ID/VIN	Engine Displacement Liters (cc)	Spark Plug Gap (in.)	Ignition Timing (deg.) ② MT	AT	Fuel Pump (psi)	Idle Speed (rpm) MT	AT	Valve Clearance (in.) In.	Ex.
1995	F22B6	2.2 (2156)	0.039-0.043	—	13-17B	30-37	—	650-750	0.009-0.011	0.011-0.013
1996	F22B6	2.2 (2156)	0.039-0.043	—	13-17B	30-37	—	650-750	0.009-0.011	0.011-0.013
1997	B20B4	2.0 (1973)	0.039-0.043	—	14-18B	38-46	—	700-800	①	①
	F22B6	2.2 (2156)	0.039-0.043	—	13-17B	30-37	—	650-750	0.009-0.011	0.011-0.013
1998	B20B4	2.0 (1973)	0.039-0.043	14-18B	14-18B	38-46	700-800	700-800	①	①
	F23A7	2.3 (2254)	0.039-0.043	—	10-14B	38-46	—	650-750	0.009-0.011	0.011-0.013
1999	B20Z2	2.0 (1973)	0.039-0.043	14-18B	14-18B	38-46	680-780	680-780	①	①
	J35A1	3.5 (3471)	0.039-0.043	—	8-12B	32-40	—	680-780	0.008-0.009	0.011-0.013
2000	B20Z2	2.0 (1973)	0.039-0.043	14-18B	14-18B	38-46	680-780	680-780	①	①
	J35A1	3.5 (3471)	0.039-0.043	—	8-12B	32-40	—	680-780	0.008-0.009	0.011-0.013

NOTE: The Vehicle Emission Control Information label often reflects changes made during production and must be used if they differ from this chart.

NOTE: The fuel pressure readings are given with the vacuum hose connected to the regulator and the engine running

B - Before top dead center

① Measured between the rocker arm and the camshaft:

Intake: 0.003-0.005 in.

Exhaust: 0.006-0.008 in.

② Measured at warm idle speed in neutral or park

93131C03

a. Once the correct test procedure idle speed is attained, turn the ignition switch to the **OFF** position.

b. Attach the round 2 pin electrical connector to the Idle Air Control (IAC) valve.

c. Remove the BACK UP (RADIO) 7.5 Amp fuse located in the under-hood fuse/relay box for 10 seconds to reset the Powertrain Control Module (PCM).

11. On 1998–00 Odyssey models, perform the following:

a. Allow the engine to idle for 1 minute with the heater fan switch in the high position and the air conditioner running. Be sure to not make any adjustments while the air conditioner is operating.

b. Reconnect the 2 pin electrical connector for the Evaporative emissions purge control (EVAP) valve.

12. On CR-V's and 4-cylinder Odyssey models, recheck the ignition timing and reset as necessary.

Air Conditioning System

SYSTEM SERVICE & REPAIR

➡It is recommended that the A/C system be serviced by an EPA Section 609 certified automotive technician utilizing a refrigerant recovery/recycling machine.

The hands-on enthusiast should not service their vehicle's A/C system, unless certified, for many reasons, including legal concerns, personal injury, environmental damages and cost. Unless certified, the following are some of the reasons to consider why not to service a vehicle's A/C system.

According to the U.S. Clean Air Act, it is a federal crime to service or repair (involving the refrigerant) a Motor Vehicle Air Conditioning (MVAC) system for money without being EPA certified. It is also illegal to vent R-134a refrigerant into the atmosphere.

State and/or local laws may be stricter than the federal regulations. Check with the state and/or local authorities for further information. For further federal information on the legality of servicing an A/C system, call the EPA Stratospheric Ozone Hotline.

➡Federal law dictates that a fine of up to $25,000 may be levied on anyone convicted of venting refrigerant into the atmosphere. Additionally, the EPA may pay up to $10,000 for information or services leading to a criminal conviction for anyone found in violation of these laws.

When servicing an A/C system, there exists the risk of handling or coming in contact with refrigerant, which may result in skin or eye irritation, or frostbite. Although low in toxicity (due to chemical stability), inhalation of concentrated refrigerant fumes is dangerous and can result in death; cases of fatal cardiac arrhythmia have been reported in people accidentally subjected to high levels of refrigerant. Some early symptoms include loss of concentration and drowsiness.

In addition, refrigerants can decompose at high temperatures (near gas heaters or open flame), that may result in hydrofluoric acid, hydrochloric acid and phosgene (a fatal nerve gas).

R-134a refrigerant is a greenhouse gas which, if allowed to vent into the atmosphere, will contribute to global warming (the Greenhouse Effect).

It is usually more economically feasible to have a certified MVAC automotive technician perform A/C system service to a vehicle. Because it is illegal to service an A/C system without being certified and without using the proper equipment, the average hands-on enthusiast would have to purchase an expensive refrigerant recovery/recycling machine to service their own vehicle.

PREVENTIVE MAINTENANCE

Although the A/C system should not be serviced by anyone who is not certified in automotive A/C repair and servicing, the preventive maintenance can be practiced by a hands-on enthusiast. Several A/C system inspections can be performed to help maintain the efficiency of the vehicle's A/C system. For preventive maintenance, perform the following:

• The easiest and most important preventive maintenance for an A/C system is to be sure that it is used on a regular basis. Running the system for five minutes each month (no matter what the season) will help ensure that the seals and all internal components remain lubricated.

➡Some newer vehicles automatically operate the A/C system compressor whenever the windshield defroster is activated. When running, the compressor lubricates the A/C system components; therefore, on these systems, the A/C system would not need to be operated on a monthly basis.

• In order to prevent heater core freeze-up during A/C operation, it is necessary to maintain a proper antifreeze protection. Use a hand-held coolant tester (hydrometer) to periodically check the condition of the antifreeze in your engine's cooling system.

➡Antifreeze should be checked and replaced according the maintenance recommendations, and should not be used longer than the manufacturer specifies.

• For efficient operation of an air conditioned vehicle's cooling system, the radiator cap should have a holding pressure that meets manufacturer's specifications. A cap, which fails to hold adequate pressures, should be replaced.

• Any obstruction of or damage to the condenser assembly will restricts air flow, which is essential to efficient operation. It is, very important to keep this unit clean and in proper physical condition.

➥Bug screens, which are mounted in front of the condenser (unless they are original equipment), are regarded as obstructions.

• The evaporator drain tube expels the water, which accumulates on the bottom of the evaporator housing. If this tube is obstructed, the air conditioning performance can be compromised and condensation buildup can spill over onto the vehicle's floor.

SYSTEM INSPECTION

Although the A/C system should not be serviced by anyone who is not certified, preventive maintenance can be practiced and A/C system inspections can be performed to help maintain the efficiency of the vehicle's A/C system. For A/C system inspection, perform the following:

The easiest and often most important check for the air conditioning system consists of a visual inspection of the system components. A visual inspection can be performed on the following:

• Inspect the air conditioning system hoses and components for signs of refrigerant leaks

• Check the compressor clutch for excessive looseness

• Check the compressor drive belt tension and/or condition

• When the air conditioning is operating, make sure the drive belt is free of noise or slippage.

• Check the evaporator drain tube and clear if necessary

• Inspect the condenser, making sure it is free of debris, air blockage and the fins are straight and aligned

• Check for disconnected or broken wires, blown fuses, corroded electrical connections and poor wiring insulation.

• Check for kinks in hoses and lines. Check the system for leaks.

• Make sure the blower motor operates at all appropriate positions, then check for distribution of the air from all outlets with the blower on HIGH or MAX.

• Make sure the air passage selection lever is operating correctly. Start the engine and warm it to normal operating temperature, then make sure the temperature selection lever is operating correctly.

A refrigerant leak will usually appear as an oily residue at the leakage point in the system. The oily residue soon picks up dust or dirt particles from the surrounding air and appears greasy. Through time, this will build up and appear to be a heavy dirt impregnated grease.

➥Keep in mind that under conditions of high humidity, air discharged from the A/C vents may not feel as cold as expected, even if the system is working properly. This is because vaporized moisture in humid air retains heat more effectively than dry air, thereby making humid air more difficult to cool.

Windshield Wiper (Elements)

ELEMENT (REFILL) CARE & REPLACEMENT

▶ See Figures 118 thru 135

For maximum effectiveness and longest element life, the windshield and wiper blades should be kept clean. Dirt, tree sap, road tar and such will cause streaking, smearing and blade deterioration if left on the glass. It is advisable to wash the windshield carefully with a commercial glass cleaner at least once a month. Wipe off the rubber blades with the dampened rag afterwards. Do not attempt to move wipers across the windshield by hand; damage to the linkage, motor and drive mechanism will result.

Examine the wiper blade elements. If they are found to be cracked, broken or torn, they should be replaced immediately. Replacement intervals will vary with usage, although ozone deterioration usually limits element life to about one year. If the wiper pattern is smeared or streaked, or if the blade chatters across the glass, the elements should be replaced. It is easiest and most sensible to replace the elements in pairs.

Original equipment wiper refills are available from the dealer. To replace the original equipment wiper refill:

1. Remove the wiper blade assembly from the end of the wiper arm. Cover the end of the wiper

arm with a soft cloth and carefully lower the arm onto the windshield.

2. The wiper blade insert has two flat metal supports that fit into a groove on both sides of the insert. On one end of the insert, there is a tab in the groove that fits into a notch of the metal support to prevent the support from sliding out. Next to the notch for the metal support is a small rectangular hole. The wiper arm assembly has several, usually 4 small "C" shaped guide brackets referred to as yoke jaws that the wiper blade insert, along with the metal supports are slid into. The end yoke jaw is bent around the blade and into small rectangular holes on both sides of the wiper blade insert. Use a small screwdriver or needle nose pliers to carefully spread the yoke jaw and slide the wiper insert complete with the metal supports out of the wiper blade holder assembly.

3. Transfer the metal supports onto the new wiper insert and slide the insert through the yoke jaws of the wiper blade holder assembly. There are usually four jaws; be certain when installing that the refill is engaged in all of them.

4. Using a pair of pliers, carefully bend the end wiper arm yoke jaws around both sides of the blade and into the rectangular holes on both sides, making sure the blade is secure.

5. Carefully reinstall the wiper blade assembly back onto the wiper arm.

If the vehicle is equipped with aftermarket blades, there are several different brands and types of refills to that can be chosen. Aftermarket blades and arms rarely use the exact same type blade or refill as the original equipment. The following are some typical commercially available aftermarket blades, although not all of these may be available for your vehicle:

The Anco® type uses a release button that is pushed down to allow the refill to slide out of the yoke jaws. The new refill slides back into the frame and locks in place.

Some Trico® refills are removed by locating where the metal backing strip or the refill is wider. Insert a small screwdriver blade between the frame and metal backing strip. Then press down to release the refill from the retaining tab.

Other types of Trico® refills have two metal tabs which are unlocked by squeezing them together. The rubber filler can then be withdrawn from the frame jaws. A new refill is installed by inserting the refill into the front frame jaws and sliding it rear-

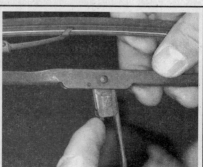

Fig. 118 To replace the original equipment wiper blade, first lift the wiper arm up and press the pivoting retainer to release the blade pivoting assembly

Fig. 119 While holding the retainer down, slide the blade holder assembly out of the wiper arm. Carefully lower the wiper arm downward and place a soft cloth between the arm and the windshield

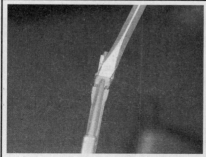

Fig. 120 Use a suitable flat-blade screwdriver to carefully wedge open the C-shaped retainer that is installed into the small rectangular hole at the end of the blade . . .

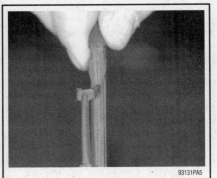

Fig. 121 . . . then lift the retainer out of the rectangular hole and slide the rubber blade along with the two metal supports out of blade holder assembly

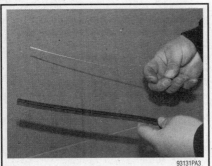

Fig. 122 Transfer the metal supports to the new blade. Make sure the bowed portion of both metal supports is installed such that ends are up when the center is touching a level surface

Fig. 123 With the metal supports installed into the upper groove of the new blade, slide the blade into the blade holder assembly . . .

Fig. 124 . . . then using a pair of slip joint pliers, gently squeeze the clip evenly back into the rectangular holes to lock the blade back into the blade holding assembly

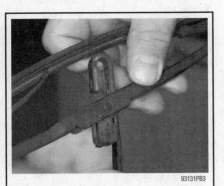

Fig. 125 Carefully lift the wiper arm off the windshield and slide the blade holder assembly back into the arm, then lower the wiper blade gently onto the windshield

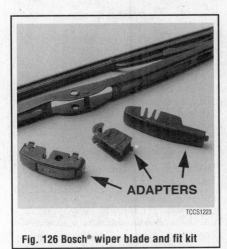

Fig. 126 Bosch® wiper blade and fit kit

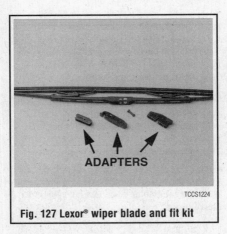

Fig. 127 Lexor® wiper blade and fit kit

Fig. 128 Pylon® wiper blade and adapter

Fig. 129 Trico® wiper blade and fit kit

ward to engage the remaining frame jaws. There are usually four jaws; be certain when installing that the refill is engaged in all of them. At the end of its travel, the tabs will lock into place on the front jaws of the wiper blade frame.

Another type of refill is made from polycarbonate. The refill has a simple locking device at one end which flexes downward out of the groove into which the jaws of the holder fit, allowing easy release. By sliding the new refill through all the

jaws and pushing through the slight resistance when it reaches the end of its travel, the refill will lock into position.

To replace the Tridon® refill, it is necessary to remove the wiper blade. This refill has a plastic backing strip with a notch about 1 in. (25mm) from the end. Hold the blade (frame) on a hard surface so that the frame is tightly bowed. Grip the tip of the backing strip and pull up while twisting counterclockwise. The backing strip will snap out of the

retaining tab. Do this for the remaining tabs until the refill is free of the blade. The length of these refills is molded into the end and they should be replaced with identical types.

Regardless of the type of refill used, be sure to follow the part manufacturer's instructions closely. Make sure that all of the frame jaws are engaged as the refill is pushed into place and locked. If the metal blade holder and frame are allowed to touch the glass during wiper operation, the glass will be scratched.

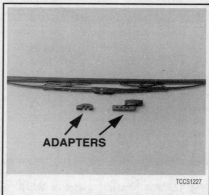

ADAPTERS

TCCS1227

Fig. 130 Tripledge® wiper blade and fit kit

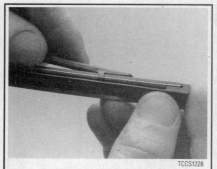

TCCS1228

Fig. 131 To remove and install a Lexor® wiper blade refill, slip out the old insert and slide in a new one

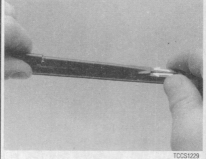

TCCS1229

Fig. 132 On Pylon® inserts, the clip at the end has to be removed prior to sliding the insert off

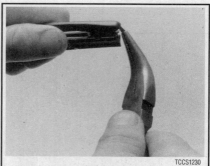

TCCS1230

Fig. 133 On Trico® wiper blades, the tab at the end of the blade must be turned up . . .

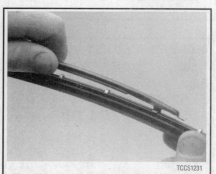

TCCS1231

Fig. 134 . . . then the insert can be removed. After installing the replacement insert, bend the tab back

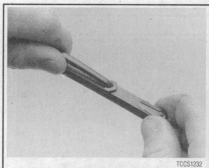

TCCS1232

Fig. 135 The Tripledge® wiper blade insert is removed and installed using a securing clip

Tires and Wheels

Common sense, good driving habits, and proper maintenance will afford maximum tire life. Fast starts, sudden stops and hard cornering causes premature tire wear and will shorten their useful life span. Make sure not to overload the vehicle or run with incorrect pressure in the tires. Both of these practices will increase tread wear.

➡**For optimum tire life, keep the tires properly inflated, rotate them often and have the wheel alignment checked periodically.**

Inspect the tires frequently. Be especially careful to watch for bubbles in the tread or sidewall, deep cuts or underinflation. Replace any tire with bubbles in the sidewall. If cuts are so deep that they penetrate to the cords, discard the tire. Any cut in the sidewall of a radial tire renders it unsafe. Also, look for uneven tread wear patterns that may indicate the front end is out of alignment, the shocks are worn, or that the tires are out of balance.

TIRE ROTATION

◗ **See Figures 136 and 137**

Tires must be rotated periodically to equalize wear patterns that vary with a tire's position on the vehicle. Tires will also wear in an uneven pattern as the front steering/suspension system wears to the point where the alignment should be reset.

Rotating the tires will ensure maximum life for the tires as a set. This avoids having to discard a

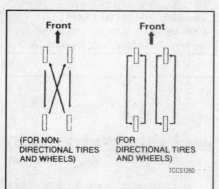

Front   **Front**

(FOR NON-DIRECTIONAL TIRES AND WHEELS)   (FOR DIRECTIONAL TIRES AND WHEELS)

TCCS1260

Fig. 136 Compact spare tires must NEVER be used in the rotation pattern

TCCS1234

Fig. 137 Unidirectional tires are identifiable by sidewall arrows and/or the word "rotation"

tire early due to wear on only part of the tread. Regular rotation is required to equalize wear.

When rotating "unidirectional tires," make sure that they always roll in the same direction. This means that a tire used on the left side of the vehicle must not be switched to the right side and vice-versa. Such tires should only be rotated front-to-rear or rear-to-front, while always remaining on the same side of the vehicle. These tires are marked on the sidewall as to the direction of rotation; observe the marks when reinstalling the tire(s).

Some styled or "mag" wheels may have different offsets front to rear. In these cases, the rear wheels must not be used up front and vice-versa. Furthermore, if these wheels are equipped with unidirectional tires, they cannot be rotated unless the tire is remounted for the proper direction of rotation.

➡**The compact or space-saver spare is strictly for emergency use. It must never be included in the tire rotation or placed on the vehicle for everyday use.**

TIRE DESIGN

◗ **See Figure 138**

For maximum satisfaction, tires should be installed in sets of four. Mixing of different types (radial, bias-belted, fiberglass belted) must be avoided. In most cases, the vehicle manufacturer has designated a type of tire on which the vehicle will perform best. Always consider using the same type of tire that the manufacturer recommends.

When radial tires are used, tire sizes and wheel diameters should be selected to maintain ground

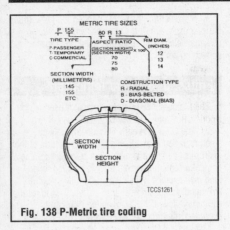

Fig. 138 P-Metric tire coding

clearance and tire load capacity equivalent to the original equipment tire. Radial tires should always be used in sets of four.

✳✳ CAUTION

Radial tires should never be used on only the front axle.

When selecting tires, pay attention to the original size as marked on the tire. Most tires are described using an industry size code sometimes referred to as P-Metric. This allows the exact identification of the tire specifications, regardless of the manufacturer. If selecting a different tire size or brand, remember to check the installed tire for any sign of interference with the body or suspension while the vehicle is stopping, turning sharply or heavily loaded.

Snow Tires

Good radial tires can be a big advantage in slippery weather, but in snow, a street radial tire does not have sufficient tread and tread depth to provide optimum traction and control. The small grooves of a street tire quickly pack with snow and the tire behaves much like a billiard ball on a marble floor. The more open, chunky tread of a snow tire will self-clean as the tire turns, providing much better grip on snow covered surfaces.

To satisfy municipalities requiring snow tires during weather emergencies, most snow tires carry either an M + S designation after the tire size stamped on the sidewall, or the designation "all-season." In general, no change in tire size is necessary when buying snow tires.

Most manufacturers strongly recommend the use of 4 snow tires on their vehicles for reasons of stability. If snow tires are fitted only to the drive wheels, the opposite end of the vehicle may become very unstable when braking or turning on slippery surfaces. This instability can lead to unpleasant endings if the driver can't counteract the slide in time.

Note that snow tires, whether 2 or 4, will affect vehicle handling in all non-snow situations. The stiffer, heavier snow tires will noticeably change the turning and braking characteristics of the vehicle. Once the snow tires are installed, it is important to re-learn the behavior of the vehicle and drive accordingly.

➡ **Consider buying extra wheels on which to mount the snow tires. Once done, the "snow wheels" can be conveniently installed and**

removed as needed. This eliminates the time to mount and remount tire onto the rims and potential damage to tires or wheels from seasonal removal and installation. Even if the vehicle has styled wheels, inexpensive steel wheels may be available. Although the look of the vehicle will change, the expensive wheels will be protected from salt, curb hits and pothole damage.

TIRE STORAGE

If they are mounted on wheels, store the tires at proper inflation pressure. All tires should be kept in a cool, dry place. If they are stored in the garage or basement, keep them away from appliances or heaters and do not let them stand on a concrete floor; set them on strips of wood, a mat or a large stack of newspaper. Keeping them away from direct moisture is of paramount importance. Tires should not be stored upright, but in a flat position.

INFLATION & INSPECTION

▶ **See Figures 139 thru 147**

The importance of proper tire inflation cannot be overemphasized. A tire uses air as part of its structure. It is designed around the supporting strength of the air at a specified pressure. For this reason, improper inflation drastically reduces the tire's ability to perform as intended. A tire will lose some air in day-to-day use; such that having to add a few pounds of air periodically is not necessarily a sign of a leaking tire.

Two items should be a permanent fixture in every glove compartment: an accurate tire pressure gauge and a tread depth gauge. Check the tire pressure (including the spare) regularly with a pocket type gauge. Too often, the gauge on the end of the air hose at the corner garage is not accurate because it suffers too much use and abuse. Always check tire pressure when the tires are cold, as pressure increases with temperature. If you must move the vehicle to check the tire inflation, do not drive more than a mile before checking. A cold tire is generally one that has not been driven for more than three hours and is not in direct sunlight.

A plate or sticker is normally provided somewhere in the vehicle (fuel filler door, driver door, post, hood, tailgate or trunk lid) which shows the proper pressure for the tires. Note that the recommended tire pressure will change based on vehicle load. Never counteract excessive pressure build-up by bleeding off air pressure (letting some air out). This will cause the tire to run hotter and wear quicker.

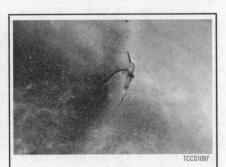

Fig. 139 Tires should be checked frequently for any sign of puncture or damage

✳✳ CAUTION

Never exceed the maximum tire pressure embossed on the tire! This is the pressure to be used when the tire is at maximum loading, but it is rarely the correct pressure for everyday driving. Consult the owner's manual or the tire pressure sticker for the correct tire pressure.

Once the correct tire pressure has been maintained for several weeks, the vehicle's braking and handling personality becomes more familiar and predictable. Slight adjustments in tire pressures can fine-tune these characteristics, but never run the tire with less or more pressure than what is recommended. Changing the cold tire pressure by more than 2 psi may completely change the handling characteristics of the vehicle. A slightly lower tire pressure provides a softer ride but also yields lower fuel mileage. A slightly higher tire pressure will give crisper dry road handling but can cause skidding on wet surfaces. Unless fully attuned to the vehicle,

Fig. 140 Tires with deep cuts, or cuts which show bulging, should be replaced immediately

- DRIVE WHEEL HEAVY ACCELERATION
- OVERINFLATION

- HARD CORNERING
- UNDERINFLATION
- LACK OF ROTATION

Fig. 141 Examples of inflation-related tire wear patterns

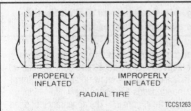

PROPERLY INFLATED IMPROPERLY INFLATED
RADIAL TIRE

Fig. 142 Radial tires have a characteristic sidewall bulge; don't try to measure pressure by looking at the tire. Use a quality air pressure gauge

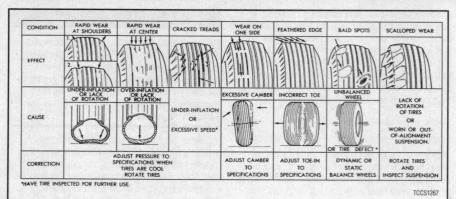

CONDITION	RAPID WEAR AT SHOULDERS	RAPID WEAR AT CENTER	CRACKED TREADS	WEAR ON ONE SIDE	FEATHERED EDGE	BALD SPOTS	SCALLOPED WEAR
EFFECT							
CAUSE	UNDER-INFLATION OR LACK OF ROTATION	OVER-INFLATION OR LACK OF ROTATION	UNDER-INFLATION OR EXCESSIVE SPEED*	EXCESSIVE CAMBER	INCORRECT TOE	UNBALANCED WHEEL OR TIRE DEFECT *	LACK OF ROTATION OF TIRES OR WORN OR OUT-OF-ALIGNMENT SUSPENSION.
CORRECTION	ADJUST PRESSURE TO SPECIFICATIONS WHEN TIRES ARE COOL ROTATE TIRES			ADJUST CAMBER TO SPECIFICATIONS	ADJUST TOE-IN TO SPECIFICATIONS	DYNAMIC OR STATIC BALANCE WHEELS	ROTATE TIRES AND INSPECT SUSPENSION

*HAVE TIRE INSPECTED FOR FURTHER USE.

TCCS1267

Fig. 143 Common tire wear patterns and causes

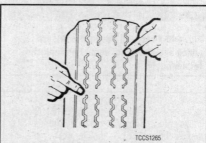

Fig. 144 A sticker showing recommended tire sizes and pressures is located on the inside of the driver's door

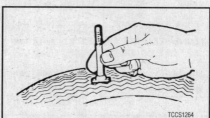

Fig. 145 Tread wear indicators will appear when the tire is worn

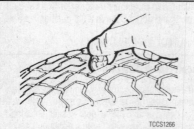

TCCS1266

Fig. 147 A penny works well for a quick check of tread depth

Fig. 146 Accurate tread depth indicators are inexpensive and handy

stick to the recommended inflation pressures.

All tires made since 1968 have built-in tread wear indicator bars that show up as ½ in. (13mm) wide smooth bands across the tire when ⅟₁₆ in. (1.5mm) of tread remains. The appearance of tread wear indicators means that the tires should be replaced. In fact, many states have laws prohibiting the use of tires with less than this amount of tread.

Tread depth can be checked with an inexpensive gauge or by using a Lincoln head penny. Slip the

Lincoln penny (with Lincoln's head upside-down) into several tread grooves. If the top of Lincoln's head is not visible in 2 adjacent grooves, the tire has less than ⅟₁₆ in. (1.5mm) tread left and should be replaced. Snow tires can be measured in the same manner by using the "tails" side of the Lincoln penny. If the top of the Lincoln memorial is not visible, it's time to replace the snow tire(s).

CARE OF SPECIAL WHEELS

If you have invested in magnesium, aluminum alloy or sport wheels, special precautions should be taken to make sure the investment is not wasted and that these special wheels look good for the life of the vehicle.

Special wheels are easily damaged and/or scratched. Occasionally check the rims for cracking, impact damage or air leaks. If any of these are found, replace the wheel. However, in order to prevent this type of damage and the costly replacement of a special wheel, observe the following precautions:

• Use extra care not to damage the wheels during removal, installation, balancing, etc. After removal of the wheels from the vehicle, place them on a mat or other protective surface. If they are to be stored for any length of time, support them on strips of wood. Never store tires and wheels upright; the tread may develop flat spots.

• When driving, watch for hazards; it doesn't take much to crack a wheel.

• When washing, use a mild soap or non-abrasive dish detergent (keeping in mind that detergent tends to remove wax). Avoid cleansers with abrasives or the use of hard brushes. There are many cleaners and polishes for special wheels.

• If possible, remove the wheels during the winter. Salt and sand used for snow removal can severely damage the finish of a wheel.

• Make certain the recommended lug nut torque is never exceeded or the wheel may crack. Never use snow chains on special wheels, as severe scratching will occur.

Emission Service Indicator

The Maintenance Required Indicator used on the Honda CR-V and Odyssey Models is one of two types. The CR-V and early Odyssey models use a small rectangular window in the lower portion of the instrument cluster that displays a colored flag. The flag color remains green until it is time for scheduled maintenance. When the 7,500 mile (12,000 km) maintenance interval approaches, the indicator will turn yellow. If 7,500 miles (12,000 km) is exceeded, the indicator will turn red.

Later model Odysseys use a Maintenance Required Indicator warning light located in the lower portion of the tachometer. Once reset, the warning light works as follows:

• During the first 6,000 miles (9,600 km), the light operates for two seconds when the ignition is switched **ON**.

• Between 6,000 miles (9,600 km) and 7,500 miles (12,000 km), the light operates for two seconds when the ignition is switched **ON**, and then flashes for 10 seconds.

• If 7,500 miles (12,000 km) is exceeded without having the scheduled maintenance performed and the light reset, the light remains on constantly.

RESETTING

Flag Type Maintenance Required Indicators

▶ See Figure 148

The indicator can be reset by inserting the ignition key into the slot below the indicator. This will extinguish the indicator for the next 7500 miles (12,000 km).

Warning Light Type Maintenance Required Indicators

1. Turn the ignition switch to the **OFF** position.
2. Press and hold the Select/Reset button on the instrument panel, then turn the ignition switch to the **ON** position and hold the button for about 10 seconds, until the light stops working.

93132P02

Fig. 148 Pressing the button in the slotted hole of the instrument panel will reset the maintenance indicator flag on CR-V and early Odyssey Models

FLUIDS AND LUBRICANTS

Fluid Disposal

Used fluids such as engine oils, transmission fluid, antifreeze and brake fluid are hazardous waste items and must be disposed of properly. Before draining any fluids, consult with the local authorities. In many areas, waste oil, coolant, etc. is being accepted as a part of recycling programs. A number of service stations and auto parts stores also accept waste fluids for recycling.

Be sure of the recycling center's policies before draining any fluids, as many will not accept different fluids that have been mixed together. Use care when using cleaning products such as carburetor cleaner and solvents. Many recycling facilities will not accept waste oil or used coolant if it contains even small amounts of toxic cleaning products.

Fuel and Engine Oil Recommendations

➡ **Some fuel additives contain chemicals that can damage the catalytic converter and/or oxygen sensor. Read all of the labels carefully before using any additive in the engine or fuel system.**

All Honda models are designed to run on unleaded fuel. The use of a leaded fuel in a car requiring unleaded fuel will permanently damage a catalytic converter and render it inoperative. A blocked converter will also increase exhaust backpressure to the point where engine output will be severely reduced. The minimum octane rating of the unleaded fuel being used must be at least 87, which usually means regular unleaded, but some high performance engines may require higher ratings. Fuel should be selected for the brand and octane that performs best with the engine. Judge a gasoline by its ability to prevent pinging, its engine starting capabilities (cold and hot) and general all weather performance.

As far as the octane rating is concerned, refer to the General Engine Specifications chart earlier in this section to find the vehicle's engine and its compression ratio. If the compression ratio is 9.0:1 or lower, a regular grade of unleaded gasoline can be used in most cases. If the compression ratio is higher than 9.0:1, use a premium grade of unleaded fuel.

The use of a fuel too low in octane (a measure of anti-knock quality) will result in spark knock or detonation. Since many factors such as altitude, terrain, air temperature and humidity affect operating efficiency, knocking may result although the recommended fuel is being used. If persistent knocking occurs, it may be necessary to switch to a higher grade of fuel. Continuous or heavy knocking may cause internal engine damage.

➡ **The engine's fuel requirement can change with time, mainly due to carbon build-up, which will, in turn, changes the compression ratio. If the engine pings, knocks or diesels (runs with the ignition OFF), switch to a higher grade of fuel. Sometimes, just changing brands will cure the problem. If it becomes necessary to retard the ignition timing from the specifications, don't change it more than a few degrees. Retarded timing will reduce power output and fuel mileage, in addition to making the engine run hotter.**

OIL

▶ **See Figures 149 and 150**

The Society Of Automotive Engineer (SAE) grade number indicates the viscosity of the engine oil and, thus, its ability to lubricate at a given temperature. The lower the SAE grade number, the lighter the oil; the lower the viscosity, the easier it is to crank the engine in cold weather. Oil viscosities should be chosen from those oils recommended for the lowest anticipated temperatures during the oil change interval. With the proper viscosity, the engine is assured of easy cold starting and sufficient engine protection.

Multi-viscosity oils (5W-30, 10W-30, etc.) offer the important advantage of being adaptable to temperature extremes. They allow easy starting at low temperatures, yet they give good protection at high speeds and engine temperatures. This is a decided advantage in changeable climates or in long distance driving.

The American Petroleum Institute (API) designation indicates the classification of engine oil used under certain given operating conditions. Only oil designated for Service SH, or the latest superseding oil grade, should be used. Oils of the SH type perform a variety of functions inside the engine in addition to their basic function as a lubricant. Through a balanced system of metallic detergents and polymeric dispersants, engine oil prevents the formation of high and low temperature deposits and keeps sludge and particles of dirt in suspension.

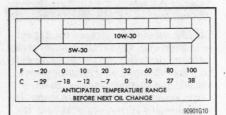

Fig. 149 Look for the API oil identification label when choosing your engine oil

Fig. 150 Recommended SAE engine oil viscosity grades for gasoline engines

Acids, particularly sulfuric acid, as well as other byproducts of combustion, are neutralized. Both the SAE grade number and the API designation can be found on the side of the oil bottle.

Synthetic Oils

There are excellent synthetic and fuel-efficient oils available that, under the right circumstances, can help provide better fuel mileage and better engine protection. However, these advantages come at a price, which can be significantly more than the price per quart of conventional motor oils.

Before pouring any synthetic oils into the car's engine, consider the condition of the engine and the type of driving that is done. It is also wise to check the vehicle manufacturer's position on synthetic oils.

Generally, it is best to avoid the use of synthetic oil in both brand new and older, high mileage engines. New engines require a proper break-in, and the synthetics are so slippery that they can impede this; most manufacturers recommend that you wait at least 5,000 miles (8,000 km) before switching to synthetic oil. Conversely, older engines, which have worn parts, tend to lose more oil; synthetics will slip past worn parts more readily than regular oil. If your car already leaks oil, (due to worn parts or bad seals/gaskets), it may leak more with a synthetic inside. Also, because synthetic oils have excellent cleaning abilities, putting a synthetic oil in a high mileage vehicle may flush away built up carbon particles which can be picked up by the oil pump and trapped in the oil filter, causing a loss of oil pressure and potential engine damage.

Consider the type of driving conditions most often encountered. If mostly on the highway at higher, steadier speeds, synthetic oil will reduce friction and probably help deliver increased fuel mileage. Under such ideal highway conditions, the oil change interval can be extended, as long as the oil filter can continue to operate effectively for the extended life of the oil. If the filter can't do its job for this extended period, dirt and sludge will build up in the engine's crankcase, sump, oil pump and lines, no matter what type of oil is used. If using synthetic oil in this manner, continue to change the oil filter at the recommended intervals.

Cars used under harder, stop-and-go, short hop circumstances should always be serviced more frequently; for these cars, the expense of using synthetic oil should be weighed against the long-term benefits of the oil. Because on average, 80% of an engine's wear occurs during a cold start up, the synthetic oil will help preserve the mechanical condition of the engine. However, the expense of frequent oil changes may offset the long-term benefits of using synthetic oil.

Engine

OIL LEVEL CHECK

▶ **See Figures 151, 152, 153 and 154**

Every time the vehicle is refueled, the engine oil should be checked, making sure the engine has fully warmed and the vehicle is parked on a level surface. Because it takes some time for the oil to drain back to the oil pan, wait a few minutes before checking the oil. When doing this at a fuel stop, first fill the fuel tank, then open the hood and check the oil, but don't get so carried away as to forget to pay for the fuel! Most station attendants won't accept forgetting as an excuse.

1. Make sure the car is parked on level ground.
2. When checking the oil level, it is best for the engine to be at normal operating temperature, however the engine should be stopped for about 5 minutes before checking. Checking the oil immediately after stopping the engine will lead to a false read-

Fig. 151 Locate the engine oil dipstick in the front center of the engine compartment

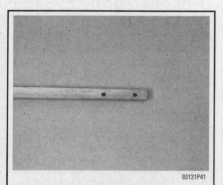

Fig. 152 The engine oil level should measure between the upper and lower dots

Fig. 153 Remove the oil filler cap from the top of the valve cover. Examine the condition of the cap and rubber seal; replace if worn or damaged

Fig. 154 Use a small funnel to avoid spillage, and pour in the proper amount of the correct viscosity engine oil

ing. Waiting a few minutes after turning off the engine allows the oil in the upper engine and cylinder head to drain back into the crankcase.

3. Open the hood and locate the dipstick, which will be in a guide tube located in the front of the engine compartment. Pull the dipstick from its tube, wipe it clean (using a clean, lint-free rag), look at the level marks, and then reinsert it.

4. Pull the dipstick out again and, holding it horizontally, read the oil level. The oil should be between the upper and lower dots on the dipstick. If the oil is below the lower dot, add oil of the proper viscosity through the screwed-in capped opening in the top of the valve cover. See the oil and fuel recommendations listed earlier in this section for the proper viscosity and rating of oil to use.

5. Insert the dipstick and check the oil level again after adding any oil. Approximately one quart of oil will raise the level from the lower dot mark to the upper dot mark. Be sure not to overfill the crankcase. Excess oil will generally be consumed at an accelerated rate and may cause problems. Overfilling the engine oil is much like overfilling a blender. Once running the liquid expands and needs somewhere to go and could force its way past a gasket or oil seal creating a leak or cause sluggish engine operation.

❈❈ WARNING

DO NOT overfill the crankcase. An overfilled crankcase may result in oil fouled spark plugs, oil leaks caused by oil seal failure, or engine damage due to oil foaming.

6. Close the hood.

OIL & FILTER CHANGE

▶ See Figures 155 thru 163

❈❈ CAUTION

The EPA warns that prolonged contact with used engine oil may cause a number of skin disorders, including cancer! Minimize exposure to used engine oil. Protective gloves should be worn when changing the oil. If hands or any other exposed skin is exposed to used engine oil wash them as soon as possible. Soap and water, or a waterless hand cleaner should be used.

The manufacturer's recommended oil change interval is 7,500 miles (12,000 km) or at least once a year under normal operating conditions and every 3,750 miles (6,000 km) or twice a year for vehicles driven in severe operating conditions. Because frequent oil changes help to prolong the life of an engine, it's a good idea to adopt an oil change interval of at least twice a year or every 3000–3500 miles (4800–5600 km) under normal conditions; and more frequently under severe conditions.

The following is a list of what the manufacturer considers severe use. If the vehicle meets any one of these conditions, the severe maintenance schedule should be followed.

• Vehicles operated in Canada or driven in extremely hot (over 90°F or 32°C) conditions
• Vehicles operated in long periods of stop and go driving or conditions requiring extensive idling
• Vehicles driven less than 5 miles (8 km) per trip or, in freezing temperatures driven less than 10 miles (16 km) per trip
• Vehicles driven with car top carriers, used for towing, driven in mountainous areas or on dusty, muddy, or de-iced roadways

Additionally, it is recommended that the oil filter be replaced EVERY time the oil is changed.

➡**Please be considerate of the environment. Dispose of waste oil properly by taking it to a service station, municipal facility or recycling center.**

1. Run the engine until it reaches normal operating temperature. Then turn the engine **OFF**.
2. Remove the oil filler cap.
3. Raise and safely support the front of the vehicle using jackstands.
4. Slide a drain pan of at least 5 quarts (4.7 liters) capacity under the oil pan. Wipe the drain plug and surrounding area clean using an old rag.
5. Loosen the drain plug using 17mm socket on a ratchet, or a suitable box wrench. Turn the plug out by hand, using a rag to shield fingers from the hot oil. Wear disposable latex gloves to protect the skin from exposure to the engine oil. Keep an inward pressure on the plug as it is unscrewed, then the oil won't escape past the threads and it can be removed without being burned by hot oil. Quickly withdraw the plug and move the hands out of the way, but be careful not to drop the plug into the drain pan, as fishing it out can be an unpleasant mess without the use of a magnet. Allow the oil to drain completely.
6. Examine the condition of the drain plug for thread damage or stretching. The manufacturer recommends replacing the aluminum drain plug crush washer with a new one every time the drain plug is removed.
7. Install the drain plug and new crush washer. Tighten the drain plug to:
   • Cast aluminum oil pans: 29 ft. lbs. (39 Nm)
   • Steel oil pans: 33 ft. lbs. (44 Nm)
8. Move the drain pan under the oil filter. Use an end cap-type tool to loosen the oil filter. Use disposable gloves to protect the skin from exposure to the used oil and cover the filter with a rag to minimize the risk of slinging engine oil, as the filter is unscrewed from the engine. Keep in mind that the filter holds about a quart of dirty, hot oil.

➡**Be careful when removing the oil filter, because the filter contains about 1 quart of hot, dirty oil.**

Fig. 155 After the drain pan is in the correct position, loosen the oil pan drain plug using a 17mm wrench. Avoid substituting a standard sized wrench, an adjustable wrench or pliers

Fig. 156 Remove the plug and allow the oil to drain until it stops dripping. Be careful not to drop the plug into the pan

Fig. 157 Examine the drain plug for wear or damage, and replace if necessary. The drain plug sealing washer should always be replaced

Fig. 158 An oil filter can usually be loosened with a variety of filter tools made specifically for that purpose . . .

Fig. 159 . . . however, due to the limited amount of available space, an end cap-type oil filter tool is a necessity on CR-V models

Fig. 160 During removal, always keep the opening of the filter straight up to prevent any of the old oil, still contained in the filter, from spilling

Fig. 161 Be sure to wipe the mounting surface of the filter adapter using a clean shop towel

Fig. 162 Before installing a new oil filter, lightly coat the rubber gasket with clean oil

Fig. 163 Pour some fresh oil into the new filter before installation to lubricate the engine quicker during initial start-up

9. Empty the old oil filter into the drain pan, then properly dispose of the filter.

10. Using a clean shop towel, wipe off the filter adapter on the engine block. Be sure the towel does not leave any lint, which could clog an oil passage.

11. Coat the rubber gasket and pour some fresh oil into the new filter before installation. This will lubricate the engine more quickly during the initial startup. Spin the filter onto the threaded fitting by hand until it contacts the mounting surface, then tighten it an additional ½–¾ turn. Do NOT overtighten the filter.

12. Carefully lower the vehicle.

13. Refill the crankcase with the correct amount of fresh engine oil. Please refer to the Capacities chart later in this section.

14. Install the oil filler cap.

15. Check the oil level on the dipstick. It is normal for the level to be a bit above the full mark until the engine is run and the new filter is filled with oil. Start the engine and allow it to idle for a few minutes.

※※ WARNING

Do not run the engine above idle speed until it has built up oil pressure, as indicated when the oil light goes out.

16. Shut off the engine and allow the oil to flow back to the crankcase for a minute, then recheck the oil level. Check around the filter and drain plug for any leaks, and correct as necessary.

When finished with the job, there are four or five

quarts of dirty oil and a used oil filter to be disposed. The best thing to do is to pour the oil into a sealable container, then, locate a service station or automotive parts store that will accept the used oil and oil filter.

➡ **Improperly disposing of used motor oil not only pollutes the environment, it violates federal law. Dispose of waste oil properly.**

Manual Transaxle

FLUID RECOMMENDATIONS

All Honda manual transaxles use the Honda Manual Transmission Fluid (MTF) as the original factory fill. This oil is similar to a 10W-30 or 10W-40 viscosity engine oil, and this oil can be substituted temporarily. However, the manufacturer recommends the use of their MTF when changing the fluid.

LEVEL CHECK

The transaxle fluid should be changed every 90,000 miles (144,000 km) or 6 years under normal driving conditions. In severe driving conditions the fluid should be changed every 30,000 miles (48,000 km) or every 2 years, whichever occurs first.

1. Make sure the vehicle is on a level surface. If the vehicle is raised, make sure the vehicle is safely supported and level.

➡ **Do not confuse the drain plug with the fill plug. The fill plug is in the mid section of the transaxle. The drain plug is near the bottom of the transaxle.**

2. The oil level is checked by removing the oil fill plug on the side of the transaxle. The transmission fluid should just meet the lower threads of the fill hole.

3. Remove the oil level check bolt from the side of the transaxle. If oil runs out, or if oil can be felt near the threaded fill hole opening reinstall and retighten the bolt to 33 ft. lbs. (45 Nm).

4. If the level needs to be topped off, pour oil in slowly until it begins to run out then, install and tighten the filler bolt to 33 ft. lbs. (45 Nm).

DRAIN & REFILL

▶ **See Figure 164**

1. Raise and safely support the vehicle, making sure it is level.
2. Place a fluid catch pan under the transaxle drain plug.
3. Remove the upper fill and lower drain plugs, and drain the fluid.
4. Using crush new washers, install the bottom plug tightening to 29 ft. lbs. (40 Nm). Refill the transaxle, until the oil is level with the upper filler plug hole, then the filler plug and tighten to 33 ft. lbs. (45 Nm).

➡ **The oil change capacity of the manual transaxle is 1.8 quarts (1.7 L)**

Fig. 164 With the transmission fill plug removed, the oil will drain from the drain hole much more quickly. Make sure to install both plugs with new sealing washers

Automatic Transaxle

FLUID RECOMMENDATIONS

The manufacturer recommends the use of Honda Premium Automatic Transmission Fluid (ATF) in their vehicles. The Dexron®III automatic transmission fluid can be substituted temporarily.

LEVEL CHECK

▶ **See Figures 165 and 166**

The first recommended transmission fluid change, under normal operating conditions, is 45,000 miles (72,000 km) or 3 years whichever occurs first. Thereafter, the interval is every 30,000 miles (48,000 km) or 2 years, whichever occurs first. For severe operating conditions, the interval is every 30,000 miles (48,000 km) or 2 years, whichever occurs first.

The level is checked with the vehicle on level ground and the engine hot, but not running. All models use a standard push in dipstick. Remove the dipstick and wipe it clean, reinstall it in position. Remove the dipstick and check the oil level on

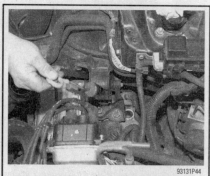

Fig. 165 The transaxle dipstick is found on the passenger's side of the engine compartment. The air filter housing assembly on this CR-V is removed, to fully expose the dipstick's location and oil fill hole

Fig. 166 Just the top ring of the transaxle dipstick is visible with the air filter housing lifted up. Removing the upper air filter housing and the ducting allows enough room for a funnel to be used on this CR-V

the stick. The level should be between the upper and lower marks on the dipstick.

1. If the fluid level is low, use a funnel to add the proper type and amount of transaxle fluid to bring it to the correct level as follows:
   - CR-V's and 4-cylinder Odyssey: through the dipstick tube.
   - V6 Odyssey: remove the hex head fill plug on the top of the transaxle near to the dipstick and add through the threaded hole.

➡ **It generally takes less than a pint to bring the fluid up to the proper level. DO NOT overfill the transaxle! If the fluid level is within specifications, simply push the dipstick back into the filler tube completely.**

✳✳ WARNING

To avoid getting any dirt or water in the transaxle, always make sure the dipstick is fully seated in the tube.

DRAIN & REFILL

▶ **See Figures 167 and 168**

1. Drive the vehicle to bring the transaxle fluid up to operating temperatures.
2. Raise and safely support the front of the vehicle.
3. Place a fluid catch pan under the transaxle.
4. Remove the drain plug, located on the bottom of the transaxle housing, and drain the transaxle.
5. Using a new washer, install the drain plug, and then tighten it to 36 ft. lbs. (49 Nm).
6. Using Honda Premium Automatic Transmission Fluid (ATF) or its temporary substitute, Dexron®III automatic transmission fluid, refill the transaxle using a suitable funnel as follows:
   - CR-V's and 4-cylinder Odyssey: through the dipstick tube.
   - V6 Odyssey: remove the hex head fill plug on the top of the transaxle near to the dipstick and add through the threaded hole.

➡ **DO NOT overfill the transaxle. Be sure that the quantity of fluid added is always slightly**

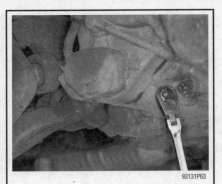

Fig. 167 The transaxle drain plug has a square ⅜ inch hole

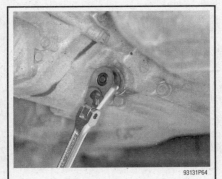

Fig. 168 Use a ⅜ inch drive ratchet to remove the drain plug

less than the specified quantity, due to the remaining fluid left in the transaxle housing recesses.

7. Start the engine and allow to idle for at least a minute. With the parking brake set and the brakes depressed, move the gear selector through each position, ending in the Park or Neutral position.

8. Check the fluid level and add just enough fluid to bring the level to ⅛ inch (3mm) below the ADD mark.

9. Allow the engine to fully warm up to normal operating temperature, then check the fluid level. The fluid level should be in the HOT range. If not, add the proper amount of fluid to bring it up to that level. If the fluid level is within specifications, simply push the dipstick back into the filler tube completely.

✳✳ WARNING

To avoid getting any dirt or water in the transaxle, always make sure the dipstick is fully seated in the tube.

Rear Differential

FLUID RECOMMENDATIONS

CR-V 4WD Models

The rear differential used in CR-V models with 4WD uses the fluid not only to lubricate the gears and bearings in the unit, it is also used as a

hydraulic fluid by the internal pump that engages the differential clutch pack. Using the correct lubricant is imperative, and failure to do so may result in poor performance and internal damage.

The manufacturer recommends using Honda CVT Fluid for this application, however for temporary use, a Dexron®III automatic transmission fluid can be substituted.

✳✳ WARNING

Failure to use the correct fluid may cause the unit to malfunction and may cause severe internal damage.

The fluid level should be checked during routine maintenance procedures or at least once a year. The fluid replacement intervals vary depending on the conditions and type of use (normal or severe) the vehicle receives. The fluid replacement intervals are as follows:
- Normal: Every 90,000 miles (144,000 km) or 6 years, whichever occurs first
- Severe: Every 60,000 miles (96,000 km) or 4 years, whichever occurs first

LEVEL CHECK

CR-V 4WD Models

▶ See Figure 169

The fluid level is checked by removing the hex head fill plug on the left side of the differential housing, near the axle. Do not confuse the level check plug with the drain plug located beneath the level check plug.

To check the fluid level:
1. Make sure the vehicle is level.
2. Place a small drain pan beneath the fluid level check plug and remove the plug.
3. If a small amount of fluid drips out of the fill plug, the fluid level is within specification. If no fluid is released, check the level to see if it meets the threaded hole of the fill plug. If the fluid meets the threads, the fluid level is within specification. If the fluid level is low, top off as necessary.
4. Once the fluid level has been verified or properly topped off, reinstall the check level plug and torque to 35 ft. lbs. (47 Nm).

Fig. 169 Making sure the vehicle is level, remove the rear differential fill plug to check the fluid level. The fluid should be filled until it is even with the lower threads of the fill hole

DRAIN & REFILL

CR-V 4WD Models

1. Make sure the vehicle is level.
2. Place a small drain pan beneath the fluid level drain plug.
3. Remove the hex head fluid level check/fill plug, and then remove the drain plug.
4. Allow the fluid to completely drain and then install the drain plug and torque to 35 ft. lbs. (47 Nm).
5. Using a funnel with a flexible spout, top off the differential using the recommended CVT fluid, or as a temporary substitute, use Dexron®III automatic transmission fluid. The fluid capacity for a fluid change is 1.1 quarts (1.0 L).
6. Top off the differential until a small amount of fluid drips out of the threaded fill plug. Once the fluid meets the threads, the fluid level is within specification.
7. Once the fluid level has been properly topped off, reinstall the check level/fill plug and torque to 35 ft. lbs. (47 Nm).

Cooling System

✳✳ CAUTION

Never remove the radiator cap under any conditions while the engine is hot! Failure to follow these instructions could result in damage to the cooling system, engine and/or personal injury. To avoid having scalding hot coolant or steam blow out of the radiator, use extreme care whenever removing the radiator cap. Wait until the engine has cooled, then wrap a thick cloth around the radiator cap and turn it slowly to the first stop. Step back while the pressure is released from the cooling system. When the pressure has been released, press down on the radiator cap (with the cloth still in position), then turn and remove the cap.

FLUID RECOMMENDATIONS

The first recommended cooling system fluid change is 45,000 miles (72,000 km) or 3 years whichever occurs first. Thereafter, the interval is every 30,000 miles (48,000 km) or 2 years, whichever occurs first. The cooling system should be inspected, flushed and refilled with fresh coolant during these maintenance intervals.

The manufacturer recommends using 50% Honda Antifreeze/Coolant mixed with 50% water. A high quality major-brand, non-silicate designed for use in aluminum engines can be substituted temporarily. Using distilled water instead of regular tap water to mix with the antifreeze will also help to keep the cooling system corrosion free, as some of the chemicals found in tap water may corrode aluminum. In addition, if the coolant is left in the system too long, it loses its ability to prevent rust and corrosion.

LEVEL CHECK

To check the coolant level, simply verify whether the coolant is up to the FULL line on the expansion tank. Add the proper mixture of coolant to the expansion tank if the level is low. Never add cold water or coolant to a hot engine as damage to both the cooling system and the engine could result.

CAUTION

Should it be necessary to remove the radiator cap, make sure the system has had time to cool, reducing the internal pressure.

The radiator cap should be removed only for cleaning or draining the system. The cooling system is under pressure when hot. Removing the radiator cap when the engine is warm or overheated will cause coolant to spill or be forced out, possibly causing serious burns. The system should be allowed to cool before attempting removal of the radiator cap or other cooling system components.

➡If any coolant spills on painted portions of the body, rinse it off immediately.

DRAIN & REFILL

See Figures 170, 171, 172 and 173

CAUTION

When draining the coolant, keep in mind that small animals and domestic pets are attracted by ethylene glycol antifreeze and may attempt to drink any that is left in an uncovered container or from puddles on the ground. This can be fatal if ingested in sufficient quantity. Always drain the coolant into a sealable container. Coolant should be reused until it becomes contaminated or several years old. To avoid injuries from scalding fluid and steam, DO NOT remove the radiator cap while the engine is running or if the engine or radiator is still hot.

1. Before draining the cooling system, place the heater's temperature selector to the full WARM position while the engine is running.
2. Turn the engine off before it gets hot and the system builds pressure.
3. Make sure the engine is still cool and the vehicle is parked on a level surface.

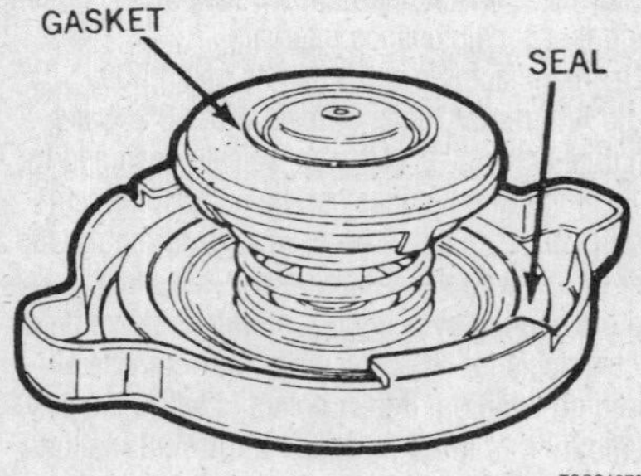

TCCS1079

Fig. 170 Always check the condition of the radiator cap gasket and seal. Place a light coating of coolant on the seal and gasket when installing

4. Remove and drain the reservoir recovery tank.
5. Place a fluid catch pan under the radiator. Turn the radiator draincock counterclockwise to open, then allow the coolant to drain.
6. Remove the radiator cap by performing the following:
   a. Slowly rotate the cap counterclockwise to the detent.
   b. If any residual pressure is present, WAIT until the hissing stops.

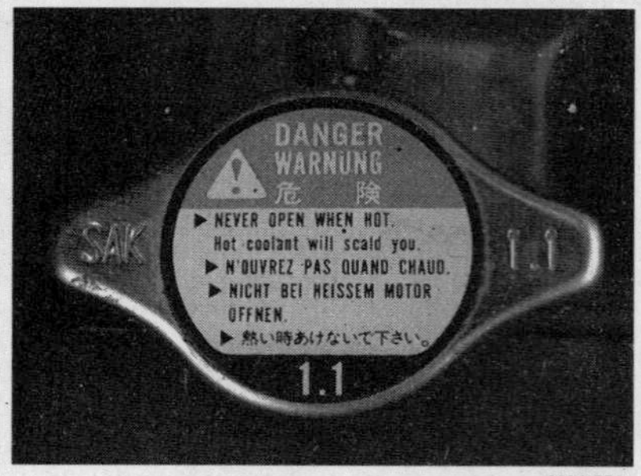

90941PB2

Fig. 171 The numbers "1.1" on the radiator cap indicate the rated holding pressure of the radiator cap measured in atmospheres. This cap is rated at 1.1 times atmospheric pressure (1.1 x 14.7) or 16 psi

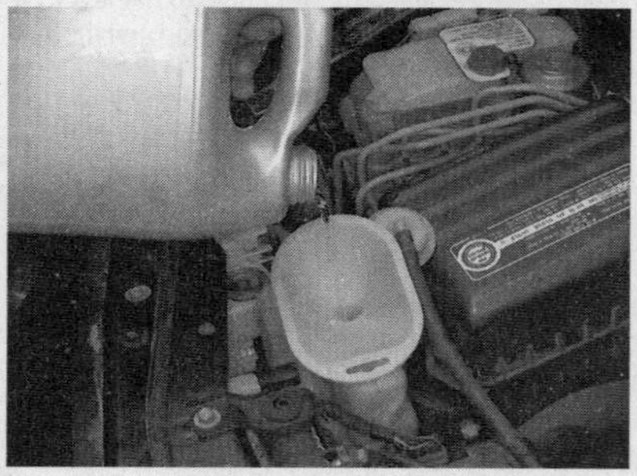

90941PC8

Fig. 172 Be sure to fill the radiator to the bottom of the filler neck with a 50/50 mixture of ethylene glycol (or other suitable) antifreeze and water. Always use a funnel to avoid spills

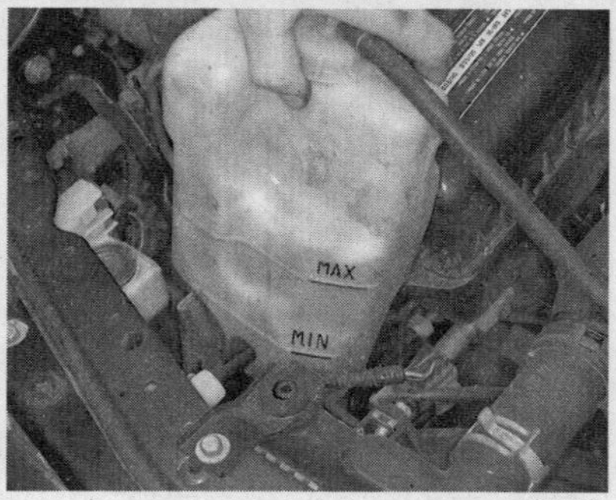

90941PC9

Fig. 173 Fill the coolant recovery tank to the proper level

   c. After the hissing noise has ceased, press down on the cap and continue rotating it counterclockwise to remove it.
7. Allow the coolant to drain completely from the vehicle.
8. Close the radiator draincock.

➡When filling the cooling system, be careful not to spill any coolant on the drive belts or alternator.

To refill:

9. Make sure the heater temperature is placed in the full hot position.
10. On 4-cylinder Odyssey models, open the bleed screw on the thermostat housing.
11. Install the reservoir recovery tank and using a 50/50 mixture of the recommended antifreeze and clean water, fill the cooling system reservoir tank to the FULL mark.

CAUTION

If any coolant is spilled on a painted surface, wipe it up immediately.

12. Begin filling the radiator with the 50/50 mixture of coolant. On 4-cylinder Odyssey models, watch for air being released from the open the bleed screw on the thermostat housing. Once coolant mixture begins to steadily flow through the bleeder, close the bleeder.
13. Continue to fill the radiator until the radiator is full.
14. Start the engine and allow the engine to run until the cooling fans operate two times, making sure to top off the system as the fluid level drops.
15. After the cooling fan has run for the second time, top off the system as necessary, then install the radiator cap.
16. Allow the engine to run and inspect the cooling system for leaks.

FLUSHING & CLEANING

1. Drain the cooling system, as described in the preceding drain and refill procedure.
2. Close the drain valve.

➡A flushing solution may be used. Ensure that it is safe for use with aluminum cooling system components, and follow the directions on the container.

3. If using a flushing solution, remove the thermostat, then reinstall the thermostat housing.
4. Add sufficient water to fill the system.
5. Start the engine and run it for a few minutes. Drain the system.
6. Allow the water to flow out of the radiator until it is clear.
7. Reconnect the heater hose.
8. Drain the cooling system.
9. Reinstall the thermostat.
10. Empty the coolant reservoir or surge tank and flush it.
11. Fill the cooling system, using the correct ratio of antifreeze and water, to the bottom of the filler neck. Fill the reservoir or surge tank to the FULL mark.
12. Install the radiator cap.

Brake Master Cylinder

FLUID RECOMMENDATIONS

Use only Honda®, or equivalent brake fluid meeting DOT 3 or DOT 4 specifications from a clean, sealed container. Using any other type of fluid may result in severe brake system damage. Avoid using any brake fluid which has been left open for several hours, or which had been initially opened more than 3 months prior to being used.

☀ WARNING

Brake fluid damages paint. It is also absorbs moisture from the air. Never leave a container or the master cylinder uncovered longer than necessary. All parts in contact with the brake fluid (master cylinder, hoses, plunger assemblies, etc.) must be kept clean, since any contamination of the brake fluid will adversely affect braking performance.

☀ CAUTION

When cleaning a brake component, make sure to use rubbing alcohol, or a suitable brake cleaner. Use of non-compatible cleaners will cause damage to brake seals and related components.

LEVEL CHECK

◆ See Figures 174 and 175

It should be obvious how important the brake system is to safe operation of your vehicle. The brake fluid is key to the proper operation of your vehicle. Low levels of fluid indicate a need for service (there may be a leak in the system or the brake pads may just be worn and in need of replacement). In any case, the brake fluid level should be inspected at least during every oil change, but more often is desirable. Every time you open the hood is a good time to glance at the master cylinder reservoir.

To check the fluid level, look on the side of the reservoir to see how high the fluid level is against the markings on the side of the reservoir. The level should be at the MAX mark. If not, remove the

Fig. 174 When checking the brake fluid level, it should be at the MAX line. Add the proper amount of fluid if necessary

Fig. 175 Pour in enough DOT 3 quality brake fluid to reach the MAX level. Be careful not to spill any brake fluid, as it can damage painted surfaces

reservoir cap, then add the proper amount of DOT 3 or DOT 4 brake fluid to bring the level up to MAX.

When making additions of brake fluid, use only fresh, uncontaminated brake fluid which meets or exceeds DOT 3 standards. Be careful not to spill any brake fluid on painted surfaces, as it will quickly eat the paint. Do not allow the brake fluid container or the master cylinder to remain open any longer than necessary; brake fluid absorbs moisture from the air, reducing the fluid's effectiveness and causing corrosion in the lines.

Clutch Master Cylinder

FLUID RECOMMENDATIONS

When adding or changing the fluid in the hydraulic clutch system, use a quality brake fluid conforming to DOT 3 OR DOT 4 specifications such as Honda® Brake Fluid, or equivalent. Never reuse old brake fluid.

LEVEL CHECK

◆ See Figure 176

The fluid in the clutch master cylinder is key to a smooth transition when in the friction zone of the clutch. The fluid condition can effect the clutch engagement while driving. Low levels of fluid indicate a need for service (there may be a leak in the system or the clutch pad lining may just be worn

Fig. 176 The clutch master cylinder reservoir looks very similar to the brake master, but is smaller, and holds much less fluid

and in need of replacement). The fluid level should be inspected during every oil change, however, more often is desirable. Every time the hood is raised is a good time to glance at the clutch master cylinder reservoir.

The fluid in the clutch master cylinder reservoir is more likely to become contaminated more quickly than the brake fluid in the brake master cylinder reservoir. When the clutch pedal is pressed, it is pressed completely to the floor during every gear change. Because of this, the seals in the clutch master and slave cylinders travel much further and more often than the brake master cylinder and wheel cylinder or caliper seals, which only travel far enough to achieve proper braking pressure.

To check the clutch master cylinder level:

1. Wipe the clutch master cylinder reservoir cap and the surrounding area clean with a shop towel.

2. Inspect the fluid in the reservoir, making sure the fluid level is between the MAX and MIN marks.

3. If required, remove the clutch master cylinder reservoir lid, then add fresh fluid to bring the level up to the MAX mark on the reservoir.

When making additions of fluid, use only fresh, uncontaminated brake fluid which meets DOT 3 or DOT 4 standards. Do not allow the brake fluid container or the master cylinder to remain open any longer than necessary; as brake fluid absorbs moisture from the air, reducing the fluid's effectiveness and causing corrosion in the lines.

☀ WARNING

Be careful to avoid spilling any brake fluid on painted surfaces, because the painted surface will become discolored or damaged.

4. Reinstall the lid onto the clutch master cylinder.

Power Steering Pump

FLUID RECOMMENDATIONS

Only genuine Honda® Power Steering fluid should be used when adding fluid. The manufacturer states that ATF or fluids manufactured for use in any other brand of vehicle by their manufacturers or independent suppliers are not compatible with the Honda power steering system.

☀ WARNING

The use of any other fluid may cause the seal failure, increased wear, and poor steering in cold weather.

LEVEL CHECK

◆ See Figures 177, 178 and 179

The fluid in the power steering reservoir should be checked every few weeks for indications of leaks or low fluid level. Check the fluid with the engine cold and the vehicle parked on a level spot. The level should be between the upper and lower marks. Fluid need not be added right away unless it has dropped almost to the lower mark. DO NOT overfill the reservoir.

Fig. 177 The fluid level is easily checked by looking at the reservoir

Fig. 178 To add fluid simply lift the reservoir top off . . .

Fig. 179 . . . then use a small funnel to avoid spillage, and add fluid until the fluid level is even with the upper level mark

When adding fluid, or making a complete fluid change, use only Honda Power Steering Fluid. NEVER add automatic transmission fluid. Failure to use the proper fluid may cause excessive wear, damage, and fluid leaks.

1. The power steering fluid reservoir has upper and lower level lines cast into the sides of the reservoir. The level is checked while the engine is cold and not running.

2. To top off the system, remove the cap and top off until the fluid level reaches the upper level fluid line, then reinstall the cap.

➡Be careful not to overfill, as this will cause fluid loss and seal damage. A large loss in fluid volume may indicate a problem, which should be inspected and repaired immediately.

Chassis Greasing

Inspect the chassis parts every 12 months or 15,000 miles (24,000 km). Look for signs of leakage, damaged, worn or deteriorating boots and seals.

The Honda vehicles covered in this manual are not equipped with grease fittings, and the suspension components that use grease are sealed units with lifetime lubrication.

Body Lubrication and Maintenance

The body mechanisms and linkages should be inspected, cleaned and lubricated, as necessary, to preserve correct operation and to avoid wear and corrosion. Before lubricating a component, make sure to wipe any dirt or grease from the surface with a suitable rag. If necessary, use a suitable cleaning solvent to clean off the surface. In addition, don't forget to wipe any excess lubricant off the component when finished.

To be sure the hood latch works properly, use white lithium grease to lubricate the latch, safety catch and hood hinges, as necessary. Apply Honda® or equivalent multi-purpose grease sparingly to all pivots and slide contact areas.

Use white lithium grease to lubricate the following components:

- Door hinges—hinge pin and pivot points
- Hood hinges—pivot points
- Trunk lid hinges—pivot points
- Door check mechanism
- Ashtray slides
- Parking brake moving parts
- Front seat tracks

Use multi-purpose grease to lubricate the following components:

- Throttle cable end at the throttle body
- Brake master cylinder pushrod
- Pedal linkage
- Battery terminals
- Fuel fill door latch mechanism
- Clutch master cylinder push rod
- Manual transmission shift lever pivots
- Manual transmission release fork

Wheel Bearings

All Honda vehicles are equipped with sealed hub and bearing assemblies. The hub and bearing assembly is non-serviceable. If the assembly is loose, worn or damaged, the complete unit must be replaced. Refer to Section 8 for hub and bearing removal and installation procedures.

TRAILER TOWING

General Recommendations

♦ **See Figures 180 thru 189**

The CR-V and 4-cylinder Odyssey models are designed primarily to carry passengers and their cargo, however the vehicle can be used to tow a trailer if the manufacturer's guidelines are observed.

The V6 Odyssey models have been designed to tow a trailer and carry passengers and their cargo. Not only is the basic body larger than previous Odyssey models, the V6 engine offers good pulling power, even when loaded. The manufacturer offers a trailer hitch assembly and a transmission cooler for this model, which can be purchased from a local dealership.

➡The CR-V and Odyssey models are equipped with a plug for trailer wiring. Complete ready to install wiring kits are available from aftermarket vendors such as Draw-Tite®, or the sub-harness can be purchased at the local Honda dealer. The trailer light plug is located as follows:

- CR-V models: On the left side cargo area behind the speaker

- 4-cylinder Odyssey models: Under the left rear light cover
- V6 Odyssey models: Behind the left side panel in the cargo area

It is important to remember that towing a trailer will place additional loads on the vehicle's engine, drive train, steering, braking and other systems. If using the vehicle for towing, follow the severe maintenance schedule to help offset the additional strain placed on the vehicle.

Local laws may require specific equipment such as trailer brakes or fender mounted mirrors. Check your local laws.

Fig. 180 Here's a Draw-Tite® trailer hitch, wiring kit and the basic tools needed for easy installation—CR-V kit shown

Fig. 181 This ready to install Draw-Tite® trailer hitch and wiring kit is comprised of the following components (from left to right) the wiring kit, trailer hitch, hitch pin, trailer ball and receiver

93131PC8

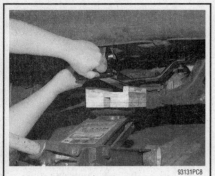

Fig. 182 To ease the installation of a trailer hitch use a floor jack to support the hitch and a block of wood to protect the finish

93131PC3

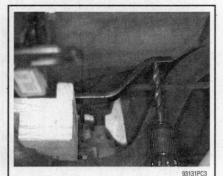

Fig. 183 Once the hitch is positioned properly, use the jack to hold the hitch securely while the mounting holes are drilled as necessary

93131PC1

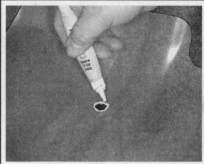

Fig. 184 If holes are drilled into the vehicle's body, paint the bare metal edges of the hole with touchup paint to help protect the body from rust and corrosion

93131PB9

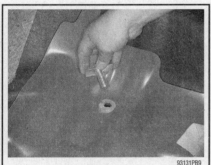

Fig. 185 Before installing the mounting bolts and support plate, apply a bead of silicone adhesive sealant or and an equivalent waterproof sealer around the drilled holes . . .

93131PB8

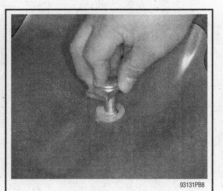

Fig. 186 . . . then lower the hitch enough to install the mounting bolt and support plate

93131PB7

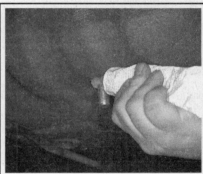

Fig. 187 Apply a bead of sealant around the mounting bolt where it protrudes through the underbody

93131PC4

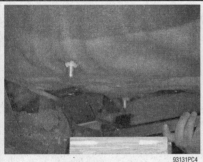

Fig. 188 Once the mounting bolts are in position and the sealant applied, use the jack to raise the hitch into place

⁂ CAUTION

Installing the trailer brakes to the vehicle's brake system lines can place an excessive load and cause a possible failure to the system. If the system fails when the brakes are needed, tragic consequences could result.

93131PB6

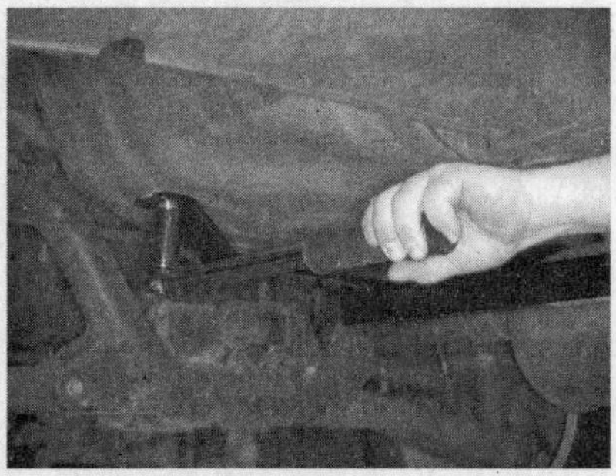

Fig. 189 Install the fasteners hand-tight, then tighten with a torque wrench to the manufacturer's specifications. The Draw-Tite® hitch for the CR-V is well made and was easy to install

Trailer Weight

The weight of the trailer is an important factor. The manufacturer provides very detailed information in their owner's manuals pertaining to trailer weight and vehicle occupant and cargo carrying capacity. The acceptable trailer weight that can be towed varies by model, the number of occupants, weight of their cargo, and on the V6 Odyssey models, whether a transmission cooler has been installed. Consult the following information for a general guideline for acceptable trailer weight.

⁂ WARNING

The manufacturer recommends that any trailer with a total weight more than 1,000 lbs. (450 kg) be equipped with its own electric or surge-type brakes. If electric brakes are chosen, they must be electronically operated. Any attempt to attach trailer brakes to the vehicle's hydraulic system will lower the braking effectiveness and create a potential hazard.

CR-V

- The combined weight of the vehicle, all occupants and their luggage and the trailer tongue weight cannot exceed the Gross Vehicle Weight Rating (GVWR) on the certification label located on the driver's door jamb
- The combined weight of the vehicle, all occupants and their luggage and the trailer tongue weight cannot exceed the Gross Axle Weight Rating (GAWR) on the certification label located on the driver's door jamb
- The total weight of the trailer, including every-

thing loaded on it must not exceed 1,000 lbs. (450 kg)

• The tongue weight of the trailer must not exceed (10% of the total trailer weight) 100 lbs. (45 kg)

2.2L/2.3L Odyssey models: (Information based on 4 passengers and a trailer equipped with brakes)

• The combined weight of the vehicle, all occupants and their luggage and the trailer tongue weight cannot exceed the Gross Vehicle Weight Rating (GVWR) on the certification label located on the driver's door jamb

• The combined weight of the vehicle, all occupants and their luggage and the trailer tongue weight cannot exceed the Gross Axle Weight Rating (GAWR) on the certification label located on the driver's door jamb

• The total weight of the trailer, including everything loaded on it must not exceed 1,300 lbs. (590 kg)

• The tongue weight of the trailer must not exceed (10% of the total trailer weight) 130 lbs. (59 kg)

3.5L Odyssey models: (Information based on 4 passengers and a trailer equipped with brakes)

• The combined weight of the vehicle, all occupants and their luggage and the trailer tongue weight cannot exceed the Gross Vehicle Weight Rating (GVWR) on the certification label located on the driver's door jamb

• The combined weight of the vehicle, all occupants and their luggage and the trailer tongue weight cannot exceed the Gross Axle Weight Rating (GAWR) on the certification label located on the driver's door jamb

Without the optional transmission cooler installed:

• The total weight of the trailer, including everything loaded on it must not exceed 1,700 lbs. (770 kg)

• The tongue weight of the trailer must not exceed (10% of the total trailer weight) 170 lbs. (77 kg)

• The total weight of the vehicle, including all occupants, cargo and the total weight of the loaded trailer must not exceed the Gross Combined Weight Rating (GCWR) of 6,660 lbs. (3,025 kg)

With optional transmission cooler installed:

• The total weight of the trailer, including everything loaded on it must not exceed 3,200 lbs. (1,450 kg)

• The tongue weight of the trailer must not exceed (10% of the total trailer weight) 320 lbs. (145 kg)

• The total weight of the vehicle, including all occupants, cargo and the total weight of the loaded trailer must not exceed the Gross Combined Weight Rating (GCWR) of 8,160 lbs. (3,700 kg)

A good weight-to-horsepower ratio is about 35:1, 35 lbs. of Gross Combined Weight (GCW) for every horsepower the engine develops. Multiply the engine's rated horsepower by 35 and subtract the weight of the vehicle, passengers and luggage. The

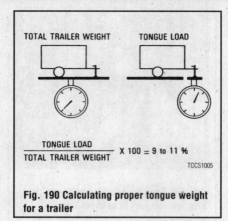

Fig. 190 Calculating proper tongue weight for a trailer

number remaining is the approximate ideal maximum weight you should tow, although a numerically higher axle ratio can help compensate for heavier weight.

Hitch (Tongue) Weight

▶ See Figure 190

Calculate the hitch weight in order to select a proper hitch. The weight of the hitch is usually 9–11% of the trailer gross weight and should be measured with the trailer loaded. Hitches fall into various categories: those that mount on the frame and rear bumper, the bolt-on type, or the weld-on distribution type used for larger trailers. Axle mounted or clamp-on bumper hitches should never be used.

Check the gross weight rating of the trailer. Tongue weight is usually figured as 10% of gross trailer weight. Therefore, a trailer with a maximum gross weight of 2000 lbs. will have a maximum tongue weight of 200 lbs. Class I trailers fall into this category. Class II trailers are those with a gross weight rating of 2000–3000 lbs., while Class III trailers fall into the 3500–6000 lbs. category. Class IV trailers are those over 6000 lbs. and are for use with fifth wheel trucks, only.

Once a suitable hitch has been selected, follow the manufacturer's installation instructions, exactly, especially when it comes to fastener torques. The hitch will be subjected to a lot of stress and good hitches are supplied with hardened bolts. Never substitute an inferior bolt for a hardened bolt.

Cooling

ENGINE

Overflow Tank

One of the most common, if not THE most common, problems associated with trailer towing is

engine overheating. If while driving the engine begins to overheat, pull over and allow enough time for the engine to cool.

Oil Cooler

Aftermarket engine oil coolers are helpful for prolonging engine oil life and reducing overall engine temperatures. Both of these factors increase engine life. While not absolutely necessary in towing Class I and some Class II trailers, they are recommended for heavier Class II and all Class III towing. Engine oil cooler systems usually consist of an adapter, screwed on in place of the oil filter, a remote filter mounting and a multi-tube, finned heat exchanger, which is mounted in front of the radiator or air conditioning condenser.

TRANSAXLE

An automatic transaxle is usually recommended for trailer towing. Modern automatics have proven reliable and, of course, easy to operate, in trailer towing. The increased load of a trailer, however, causes an increase in the temperature of the automatic transaxle fluid. Heat is the worst enemy of an automatic transaxle. As the temperature of the fluid increases, the life of the fluid decreases.

It is essential, therefore, to install an automatic transaxle cooler. The cooler, which consists of a multi-tube, finned heat exchanger, is usually installed in front of the radiator or air conditioning compressor, and hooked in-line with the transaxle cooler tank inlet line. Follow the cooler manufacturer's installation instructions.

Select a cooler of at least adequate capacity, based upon the combined gross weights of the vehicle and trailer.

Cooler manufacturers recommend using an aftermarket cooler in addition to and not instead of, the present cooling tank in your radiator. If using it in place of the radiator cooling tank, get a cooler at least two sizes larger than normally necessary.

➡**A transaxle cooler can, sometimes, cause slow or harsh shifting in the transaxle during cold weather, until the fluid has a chance to come up to normal operating temperature. Some coolers can be purchased with or retrofitted with a temperature bypass valve, which will allow fluid flow through the cooler only when the fluid has reached above a certain operating temperature.**

Handling a Trailer

Towing a trailer with ease and safety requires a certain amount of experience. It's a good idea to learn the feel of a trailer by practicing turning, stopping and backing in an open area such as an empty parking lot.

JUMP STARTING A DEAD BATTERY

▶ **See Figure 191**

Whenever a vehicle is jump started, precautions must be followed in order to prevent the possibility of personal injury. Remember that batteries contain a small amount of explosive hydrogen gas which is a by-product of battery charging. Sparks should always be avoided when working around batteries, especially when attaching jumper cables. To minimize the possibility of accidental sparks, follow the procedure carefully.

❊❊ CAUTION

NEVER hook up the batteries in a series circuit, or the entire electrical system will be severely damaged, including the starter!

Vehicles equipped with a diesel engine may utilize two 12 volt batteries. If so, the batteries are connected in a parallel circuit (positive terminal to positive terminal, negative terminal to negative terminal). Hooking the batteries up in parallel circuit increases battery cranking power without increasing total battery voltage output. Output remains at 12 volts. On the other hand, hooking two 12 volt batteries up in a series circuit (positive terminal to negative terminal, positive terminal to negative terminal) increases total battery output to 24 volts (12 volts plus 12 volts).

Regardless of whether the vehicle is equipped with a manual transaxle, push starting the vehicle IS NOT RECOMMENDED under any circumstance.

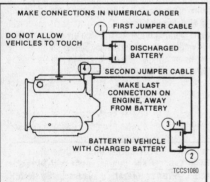

Fig. 191 Connect the jumper cables to the batteries and engine in the order shown

Jump Starting Precautions

- Be sure that both batteries are of the same voltage. Vehicles covered by this manual and most vehicles on the road today utilize a 12 volt charging system.
- Be sure that both batteries are of the same polarity (have the same terminal, in most cases NEGATIVE grounded).
- Be sure that the vehicles are not touching or a short could occur.
- On serviceable batteries, be sure the vent cap holes are not obstructed.
- Do not smoke or allow sparks anywhere near the batteries.
- In cold weather, make sure the battery electrolyte is not frozen. This can occur more readily in a battery that has been in a state of discharge.
- Do not allow the battery electrolyte to contact skin or clothing.

Jump Starting Procedure

1. Make sure that the voltages of the 2 batteries are the same. Most batteries and charging systems are of the 12 volt variety.
2. Pull the jumping vehicle (with the good battery) into a position so the jumper cables can reach the dead battery and that vehicle's engine. Make sure that the vehicles do NOT touch.
3. Place the transmissions/transaxles of both vehicles in **Neutral** (MT) or **P** (AT), as applicable, then firmly set their parking brakes.

➥ **If necessary for safety reasons, the hazard lights on both vehicles may be operated throughout the entire procedure without significantly increasing the difficulty of jumping the dead battery.**

4. Turn all lights and accessories OFF on both vehicles. Make sure the ignition switches on both vehicles are turned to the **OFF** position.
5. Cover the battery cell caps with a rag, but do not cover the terminals.
6. Make sure the terminals on both batteries are clean and free of corrosion or proper electrical connection will be impeded. If necessary, clean the battery terminals before proceeding.
7. Identify the positive (+) and negative (-) terminals on both batteries.
8. Connect the first jumper cable to the posi-

tive (+) terminal of the dead battery, then connect the other end of that cable to the positive (+) terminal of the booster (good) battery.
9. Connect one end of the other jumper cable to the negative (-) terminal on the booster battery and the final cable clamp to an engine bolt head, alternator bracket or other solid, metallic point on the engine with the dead battery. Try to pick a ground on the engine that is positioned away from the battery in order to minimize the possibility of the 2 clamps touching should one loosen during the procedure. DO NOT connect this clamp to the negative (-) terminal of the bad battery.

❊❊ CAUTION

Be very careful to keep the jumper cables away from moving parts (cooling fan, belts, etc.) on both engines.

10. Check to make sure that the cables are routed away from any moving parts, then start the donor vehicle's engine. Run the engine at moderate speed for several minutes to allow the dead battery a chance to receive some initial charge.
11. With the donor vehicle's engine still running at idle, try to start the vehicle with the dead battery. Crank the engine for no more than 15 seconds at a time and let the starter cool for at least 15 minutes between tries. If the vehicle does not start in 3 tries, it is likely that something else is also wrong or that the battery needs additional time to charge.
12. Once the vehicle is started, allow it to run at idle for a few seconds to make sure that it is operating properly.
13. Turn ON the headlights, heater blower and, if equipped, the rear defroster of both vehicles in order to reduce the severity of voltage spikes and subsequent risk of damage to the vehicles' electrical systems when the cables are disconnected. This step is especially important to any vehicle equipped with computer control modules.
14. Carefully disconnect the cables in the reverse order of connection. Start with the negative cable that is attached to the engine ground, then the negative cable on the donor battery. Disconnect the positive cable from the donor battery and finally, disconnect the positive cable from the formerly dead battery. Be careful when disconnecting the cables from the positive terminals not to allow the alligator clips to touch any metal on either vehicle or a short and sparks will occur.

JACKING

▶ **See Figures 192, 193, 194 and 195**

Your vehicle was supplied with a jack for emergency road repairs. This jack is fine for changing a flat tire or other short term procedures not requiring you to go beneath the vehicle. If it is used in an emergency, carefully follow the instructions provided either with the jack or in the owner's manual. Do not attempt to use the jack on any portions of the vehicle other than those specified by the vehicle manufacturer. Always block the diagonally opposite wheel when using a jack.

Never place the jack under the radiator, engine or transaxle components. Severe and expensive damage will result when the jack is raised. Additionally, never jack under the floorpan or bodywork; the metal will deform.

Whenever working under the vehicle, safely support it on jackstands or ramps. Never use cinder blocks or stacks of wood to support the vehicle, even if only going underneath the vehicle for a few minutes. Never crawl under the vehicle when it is supported only by a jack, whether the jack is the emergency tire changing jack or other floor jack.

➥ **Always position a block of wood or small rubber pad on top of the jack or jackstand to protect the lifting point's finish when lifting or supporting the vehicle.**

Small hydraulic, screw, or scissors jacks are satisfactory for raising the vehicle. Drive-on trestles or ramps are also a handy and safe way to both raise and support the vehicle. Be careful though, some ramps may be too steep to drive the vehicle onto without scraping the front bottom panels. Never support the vehicle beneath any

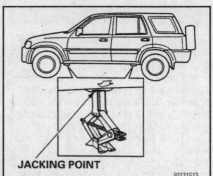

JACKING POINT

93131G13

Fig. 192 The jacking contact points shown here, as well as instructions for the manufacturer-supplied jack, are explained and illustrated in the owner's manual—CR-V shown

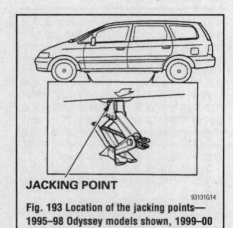

JACKING POINT

93131G14

Fig. 193 Location of the jacking points—1995–98 Odyssey models shown, 1999–00 similar

suspension member (unless specifically instructed to do so by a repair manual) or by an underbody panel.

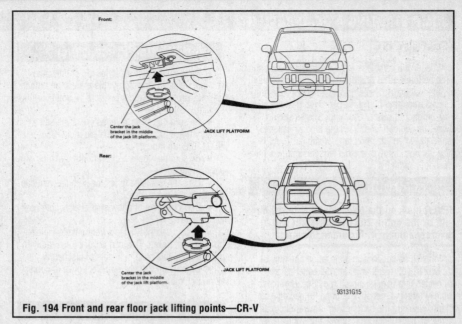

Front:

Center the jack bracket in the middle of the jack lift platform.

JACK LIFT PLATFORM

Rear:

Center the jack bracket in the middle of the jack lift platform.

JACK LIFT PLATFORM

93131G15

Fig. 194 Front and rear floor jack lifting points—CR-V

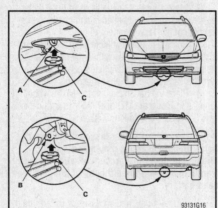

93131G16

Fig. 195 Floor jack lifting point locations—Odyssey

Jacking Precautions

The following safety points cannot be overemphasized:
- Always block the opposite wheel or wheels to keep the vehicle from rolling off the jack.
- When raising the front of the vehicle, firmly apply the parking brake.
- When the drive wheels are to remain on the ground, leave the vehicle in gear to help prevent it from rolling.
- Always use jackstands to support the vehicle when working underneath. Place the stands beneath the vehicle's jacking brackets. Before climbing underneath, rock the vehicle a bit to make sure it is firmly supported.

CAPACITIES

Year	Model	Engine ID/VIN	Engine Displacement Liters (cc)	Engine Oil with Filter (qts.)	Transmission (qts.) 4-Spd	5-Spd	Auto.	Transfer Case (pts.)	Drive Axle Front (pts.)	Rear (pts.)	Fuel Tank (gal.)	Cooling System (qts.)
1995	Odyssey	F22B6	2.2 (2156)	4.0	—	—	5.0	—	—	—	17.2	6.7
1996	Odyssey	F22B6	2.2 (2156)	4.0	—	—	5.0	—	—	—	17.2	6.7
1997	CR-V	B20B4	2.0 (1973)	4.0	—	—	①	②	—	2.2	15.3	4.1
	Odyssey	F22B6	2.2 (2156)	4.0	—	—	5.0	—	—	—	17.2	6.7
1998	CR-V	B20B4	2.0 (1973)	4.0	—	3.6	①	②	—	2.2	15.3	4.1
	Odyssey	F23A7	2.3 (2254)	4.5	—	—	5.8	—	—	—	17.2	6.7
1999	CR-V	B20Z2	2.0 (1973)	4.0	—	3.6	①	②	—	2.2	15.3	4.1
	Odyssey	J35A1	3.5 (3471)	4.6	—	—	6.2	—	—	—	20.0	7.0
2000	CR-V	B20Z2	2.0 (1973)	4.0	—	3.6	①	②	—	2.2	15.3	4.1
	Odyssey	J35A1	3.5 (3471)	4.6	—	—	6.2	—	—	—	20.0	7.0

NOTE: All capacities are approximate. Add fluid gradually and check to be sure a proper fluid level is obtained.

NOTE: Capacities given are service, not overhaul capacities

① 4WD: 6.2
 2WD: 5.8

② The transfer case fluid is shared with the transaxle assembly.

93131C06

MANUFACTURER RECOMMENDED NORMAL MAINTENANCE INTERVALS

VEHICLE MAINTENANCE INTERVALS ①

Service by time or mileage, whichever occurs first.		7.5	15	22.5	30	37.5	45	52.5	60	67.5	75	82.5	90	97.5	105	112.5	120
miles (x1000)		7.5	15	22.5	30	37.5	45	52.5	60	67.5	75	82.5	90	97.5	105	112.5	120
km (x1000)		12	24	36	48	60	72	84	96	108	120	132	144	156	168	180	192
months			12		24		36		48		60		72		84		96
Component	**Procedure**																
Engine oil and filter	Replace	✓	✓	✓	✓	✓	✓	✓	✓	✓	✓	✓	✓	✓	✓	✓	✓
Engine oil level	Inspect ②																
Coolant level	Inspect ②																
Air cleaner	Replace				✓				✓				✓				✓
Valve Adjustment:																	
All CRV engines	Adjust		③		③		③		③		③		③		✓		③
Odyssey 2.2L engine	Adjust		③		③		③		③		③		③		✓		③
Odyssey 2.3L engine	Adjust		✓		✓		✓		✓		✓		✓		✓		✓
Odyssey 3.5L engine	Adjust		③		③		③		③		③		③		✓		③
Spark plugs (except V6)	Replace				✓				✓				✓				✓
Spark plugs (V6)	Replace														✓		
Timing belt	Replace														✓		
Balance shaft belt ④	Replace														✓		
Water pump	Inspect														✓		
Drive belts	Inspect/Adjust				✓				✓				✓				✓
Idle speed	Inspect/Adjust								④						✓		
PCV Valve	Inspect								④								
Coolant	Replace						✓				✓				✓		
Transmission fluid	Replace						✓				✓				✓		
Rear differential fluid (CRV)	Replace												✓				
Front and rear brakes	Inspect	✓	✓	✓	✓	✓	✓	✓	✓	✓	✓	✓	✓	✓	✓	✓	✓
Brake fluid	Replace						✓						✓				
Parking brake	Inspect/Adjust		✓		✓		✓		✓		✓		✓		✓		✓
Air conditioner filter	Replace				✓				✓				✓				✓
Tires	Rotate	✓	✓	✓	✓	✓	✓	✓	✓	✓	✓	✓	✓	✓	✓	✓	✓
Tire pressure	Adjust ⑤																
Steering box	Inspect		✓		✓		✓		✓		✓		✓		✓		✓
Tie rod ends	Inspect		✓		✓		✓		✓		✓		✓		✓		✓
Steering boots	Inspect		✓		✓		✓		✓		✓		✓		✓		✓
Suspension	Inspect		✓		✓		✓		✓		✓		✓		✓		✓
Fluid levels and condition	Inspect		✓		✓		✓		✓		✓		✓		✓		✓
Cooling system connections and hoses	Inspect		✓		✓		✓		✓		✓		✓		✓		✓
Exhaust system	Inspect		✓		✓		✓		✓		✓		✓		✓		✓
CV joint boots	Inspect		✓		✓		✓		✓		✓		✓		✓		✓
Brake lines, fittings and ABS	Inspect		✓		✓		✓		✓		✓		✓		✓		✓
Fuel lines, fittings, and hoses	Inspect		✓		✓		✓		✓		✓		✓		✓		✓
Supplimental restraint	Inspect	Inspect supplemental restraint system (SRS) 10 years after date of production															

Perform maintenace at the same intervals for mileage beyond that on this chart

① Maintenance chart applies to vehicles driven in the continental United States under normal operating conditions.
Refer to the severe maintenance interval chart if operating conditions include any of the following:
Vehicles operated in Canada or driven in extremely hot (over 90°F or 32°C) conditions
Vehicles operated in long periods of stop and go driving or conditions requiring extensive idling
Vehicles driven less than 5 miles (8 km) per trip or, in freezing temperatures driven less than 10 miles (16 km) per trip
Vehicles driven with car top carriers, used for towing, driven in mountainous areas or on dusty, muddy, or de-iced roadways

② Check engine oil and coolant levels during each fuel fill up. Top off as necessary. Caution, never open the radiator cap when the engine is hot

③ Adjust only if valves are noisy

④ Odyssey models with 2.2L and 2.3L engines only

⑤ Check tire pressure and condition at least once a month

93131C04

MANUFACTURER RECOMMENDED SEVERE MAINTENANCE INTERVALS

VEHICLE MAINTENANCE INTERVALS ①

Service by time or mileage, whichever occurs first.	miles (x1000)	7.5	15	22.5	30	37.5	45	52.5	60	67.5	75	82.5	90	97.5	105	112.5	120
	km (x1000)	12	24	36	48	60	72	84	96	108	120	132	144	156	168	180	192
	months	6	12	18	24	30	36	42	48	54	60	66	72	78	84	90	96
Component	**Procedure**																
Engine oil and filter	Replace 6 mo. or 3,750 mi. ②	✓	✓	✓	✓	✓	✓	✓	✓	✓	✓	✓	✓	✓	✓	✓	✓
Engine oil level	Inspect ③																
Coolant level	Inspect ③			•													
Air cleaner	Replace		✓		✓		✓		✓		✓		✓		✓		✓
Valve Adjustment:																	
All CRV engines	Adjust		④		④		④		④		④		④		✓		④
Odyssey 2.2L engine	Adjust		④		④		④		④		④		④		✓		④
Odyssey 2.3L engine	Adjust		✓		✓		✓		✓		✓		✓		✓		✓
Odyssey 3.5L engine	Adjust		④		④		④		④		④		④		✓		④
Spark plugs (except V6)	Replace				✓				✓				✓				✓
Spark plugs (V6)	Replace														✓		
Timing belt	Replace								⑥						✓		
Balance shaft belt ⑤	Replace								⑥						✓		
Water pump	Inspect														✓		
Drive belts	Inspect/Adjust				✓				✓				✓				✓
Idle speed	Inspect/Adjust								⑤						✓		
PCV Valve	Inspect								⑤								
Coolant	Replace						✓				✓				✓		
Transmission fluid	Replace				✓				✓				✓				✓
Rear differential fluid (CRV)	Replace								✓								✓
Front and rear brakes	Inspect	✓	✓	✓	✓	✓	✓	✓	✓	✓	✓	✓	✓	✓	✓	✓	✓
Brake fluid	Replace						✓						✓				
Parking brake	Inspect/Adjust		✓		✓		✓		✓		✓		✓		✓		✓
Air conditioner filter	Replace		⑦		✓		⑦		✓		⑦		✓		⑦		✓
Antenna mast	Clean		✓		✓		✓		✓		✓		✓		✓		✓
hinges, locks, and latches	Lubricate		✓		✓		✓		✓		✓		✓		✓		✓
Tires	Inspect/Rotate	✓	✓	✓	✓	✓	✓	✓	✓	✓	✓	✓	✓	✓	✓	✓	✓
Tire pressure	Adjust ⑧																
Steering box	Inspect	✓	✓	✓	✓	✓	✓	✓	✓	✓	✓	✓	✓	✓	✓	✓	✓
Tie rod ends	Inspect	✓	✓	✓	✓	✓	✓	✓	✓	✓	✓	✓	✓	✓	✓	✓	✓
Steering boots	Inspect	✓	✓	✓	✓	✓	✓	✓	✓	✓	✓	✓	✓	✓	✓	✓	✓
Suspension	Inspect	✓	✓	✓	✓	✓	✓	✓	✓	✓	✓	✓	✓	✓	✓	✓	✓
Fluid levels and condition	Inspect		✓		✓		✓		✓		✓		✓		✓		✓
Cooling system connections and hoses	Inspect		✓		✓		✓		✓		✓		✓		✓		✓
Exhaust system	Inspect		✓		✓		✓		✓		✓		✓		✓		✓
CV joint boots	Inspect	✓	✓	✓	✓	✓	✓	✓	✓	✓	✓	✓	✓	✓	✓	✓	✓
Brake lines, fittings and ABS	Inspect		✓		✓		✓		✓		✓		✓		✓		✓
Fuel lines, fittings, and hoses	Inspect		✓		✓		✓		✓		✓		✓		✓		✓
Supplemental restraint	Inspect	Inspect supplemental restraint system (SRS) 10 years after date of production															

Perform maintenace at the same intervals for mileage beyond that on this chart

① Maintenance intervals for vehicles operated in severe conditions include any of the following:
  Vehicles operated in Canada or driven in extremely hot (over 90°F or 32°C) conditions
  Vehicles operated in long periods of stop and go driving or conditions requiring extensive idling
  Vehicles driven less than 5 miles (8 km) per trip or, in freezing temperatures driven less than 10 miles (16 km) per trip
  Vehicles driven with car top carriers, used for towing, driven in mountainous areas or on dusty, muddy, or de-iced roadways

② Replace engine oil and filter every 6 months or 3,750 miles, wichever occurs first

③ Check engine oil and coolant levels during each fuel fill up. Top off as necessary. Caution, never open the radiator cap when the engine is hot

④ Adjust only if valves are noisy

⑤ Odyssey 2.2L and 2.3L engines only

⑥ Replace at 60,000 miles or 100,000 km if driven in high temperatures (above 110°F or 43°C) or very low temperatures (below -20°F or -29°C)

⑦ Replace every 15,000 miles (24,000 km) if driven in conjested industrialized urban areas or if climate control air flow is reduced

⑧ Check tire pressure and condition at least once a month

93131C05

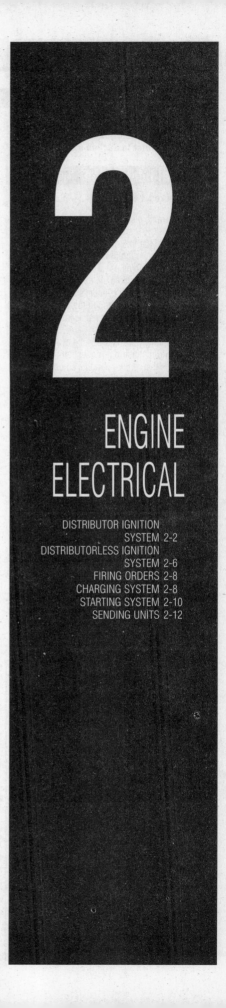

2

ENGINE
ELECTRICAL

DISTRIBUTOR IGNITION SYSTEM

➡ **For more information about understanding electricity and troubleshooting electrical circuits, please refer to Section 6 of this manual.**

General Information

◆ **See Figures 1 and 2**

The electronic distributor ignition systems used on the Honda CR-V and the 4-cylinder Odyssey models are similar to a distributor with the conventional breaker point ignition system found on earlier vehicles. Both systems use a distributor cap and ignition rotor to distribute the ignition spark from the ignition coil to each cylinder's spark plug in the correct order. They both require the cap and rotor to be inspected cleaned and/or replaced during periodic maintenance.

The main difference between the two systems is that the electronic distributor does not have any moving parts that require periodic adjustments, unlike breaker points, which require periodic rubbing block lubrication, adjustment and replacement. To advance the ignition timing relative to engine speed, the breaker point and the initial electronic ignition systems used a mechanical, centrifugal advance unit. The ignition timing would advance based solely on the engine's speed. Those systems worked well for their day, however to meet today's more stringent emission standards, an engine's operating efficiency must be optimized. To meet these standards, and optimize an engine's efficiency requires precise control of the ignition timing.

To achieve this level of efficiency, the ignition timing advance is controlled electronically by the Engine Control Module (ECM)/Powertrain Control Module (PCM). This allows the ignition timing to be adjusted electronically based on input from a collection of electronic sensors. This system allows the ignition timing advance to be adjusted and optimized instantly, for changes in engine speed, intake manifold airflow rate and the engine coolant temperature. Another electronic sensor was added

beginning with the 1999 CR-V models. This new sensor is the Knock Sensor (KS), which sets the ideal ignition timing for the octane rating of the gasoline being used.

Three of the sensors used to supply information to the ECM/PCM are located in the distributor housing of the CR-V and the 4-cylinder Odyssey models. These sensors are the Top Dead Center (TDC), Crankshaft Position (CKP), and Cylinder Position (CYP) sensors. The information these sensors supply to the ECM/PCM allows the control module to monitor the mechanical moving components of the engine. The CKP Sensor determines the timing for fuel injection and ignition for each cylinder and detects engine speed. The TDC Sensor determines ignition timing during start-up and when the crank angle is abnormal. The CYP Sensor detects the position of the No. 1 cylinder for sequential fuel injection to each cylinder

Each sensor is each triggered electronically by a reluctor. The reluctors are installed securely onto the distributor shaft, and rotate with the shaft. One reluctor that is pressed onto the distributor shaft looks very similar to a small straight cut gear. As the reluctor rotates with the distributor shaft, the teeth of the reluctor pass very closely to a small sensor, which is simply a small electric coil. As the teeth of the reluctor move toward the sensor, the electric field of the sensor is energized. As the teeth of the reluctor move past the sensor, the electric field of the sensor is collapsed causing an electric pulse that is sent from the sensor to the ECM/PCM control module. As each tooth of the reluctor passes the sensor, it causes an electrical pulse. For each complete revolution of the distributor shaft, the number of pulses generated per revolution, is equal to the number of teeth on the reluctor. The control module uses these electric pulses to gather information about the engine. The faster the engine spins, the faster the distributor spins, the faster the pulses are generated, which allows the control unit to know how fast the engine is spinning.

Reluctors vary is size and shape. Some reluctors look very similar to small gears, however their shape does vary. Another reluctor found in the distributor, has only one tooth, or raised edge. The shape of the reluctor is mostly rounded, with an oblong ramp leading up to a single raised edge. This reluctor operates just like the gear shaped reluctor, however, because it only has one raised edge to pass by the sensor, only one electric pulse is generated for each revolution of the distributor. The control module uses the single pulse of the CYP sensor to recognize the position of No. 1 cylinder for sequential fuel injection to each cylinder.

As the distributor shaft rotates with the attached reluctors, the electrical pulses for each sensor are used by the control module to track the mechanical moving components of the engine. This allows the control module to keep track of each phase of the four-stroke cycle for each cylinder. The Powertrain Control Module (PCM) can optimize the ignition timing and the amount of ignition advance for the engine's operating conditions (rpm, load and temperature).

The basic ignition timing information for the engine's operating conditions is stored in the memory of the PCM. This is why a jumper must be temporarily installed onto the Service Connector (SCS) when adjusting the idle speed ignition timing as described in the ignition timing adjustment procedure. Using the jumper allows the base ignition timing to be adjusted manually without the control module over riding the adjustment. Once the jumper is removed, the control module stores the base timing information into its memory.

As the PCM control module receives input from its sensors, it selects the optimal ignition timing and triggers the ignition coil by sending electric pulses. As with the reluctor collapsing the electrical field of the sensors, the PCM does much the same with the ignition coil. The electrical pulses from the PCM are used to trigger the ignition coil. To do this, the primary ignition current is momentarily cut off by the PCM. This allows the magnetic field of the ignition coil to collapse, creating a spark that the distributor passes on to the spark plugs via the rotor and spark plug wires.

The ignition coil is located within the distributor housing, eliminating the need for a high-tension wire from the ignition coil to the distributor cap. The only high-tension ignition wires used on this ignition system are the spark plug wires, which are connected to the distributor cap and the spark plugs.

Diagnosis and Testing

Prior to diagnosis or testing procedures, visually inspect the components of the ignition and engine control systems. Check for the following:
- Discharged battery or low alternator output
- Damaged, corroded, or loose electrical connections
- Damaged or worn electrical insulation
- Poor spark plug connections
- Ignition module multi-connector condition
- Blown fuses

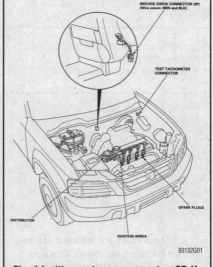

Fig. 1 Ignition system components—CR-V shown

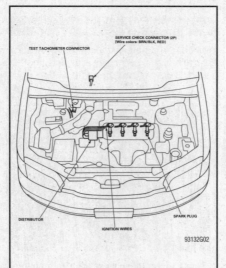

Fig. 2 Ignition system components— 1995–98 Odyssey shown

- Damaged or corroded ignition wires
- Excessively worn, defective, or damaged spark plugs
- Excessively worn or damaged distributor cap or rotor

Check the spark plug wires and boots for signs of poor insulation that could cause shorting or crossfiring. Make sure the battery is fully charged and that all accessories are off during diagnosis and testing. Make sure the idle speed is properly adjusted and within specification. Check all of the fuel injector electrical connections..

SECONDARY SPARK TEST

▶ **See Figures 3 and 4**

※ WARNING

When testing the ignition system for a high-energy spark, make sure the test equipment is sufficiently grounded. Failure to do so may cause severe and expensive internal component damage. When testing for an ignition, spark make sure the area is free of any flammable materials. Do not hold or place hands or fingers near the test equipment when checking for a high voltage spark.

Checking for a high-energy spark is easily performed using a spark tester (available at most automotive parts stores). Three types of spark testers are commonly available.

- The Neon Bulb type: This tool connects to the spark plug wire and flashes with each ignition pulse. This is easy to use as it lights up with each ignition pulse
- The Air Gap type: This tester is adjusted according to the spark plug gap specification for the engine. It is very useful because the gap can be adjusted to check the strength of the electrical spark and the color of the spark can be verified
- The Spark Plug simulator: This looks like a spark plug, and has a grounding alligator style clip on the side. This checker is easy to use, and the spark color can be monitored

The last two types of testers mentioned allow the user to not only detect the presence of spark, but also the intensity (orange/yellow is weak, blue is strong). To use these testers proceed as follows:

1. Disconnect a spark plug wire from the spark plug end.

2. Connect the plug wire to the spark tester and ground the tester to an appropriate location on the engine.

3. Crank the engine and check for spark at the tester.

4. If spark exists at the tester, the ignition system is functioning properly.

5. If all of the spark tests for all of the spark plug wires indicate irregular or weak spark, perform the following:

   a. Refer to the coil test.

   b. Carefully inspect the distributor cap and rotor for damage, corrosion or excessive wear.

   c. Inspect and test the ignition wires. Check the resistance of each spark plug wire. Refer to Section 1 for checking the resistance of the spark plug wires. If the wires are within specification, it will be necessary to diagnose the individual components of the ignition system.

6. If one or more, but not all of the tests indicate irregular, or weak spark:

   a. Inspect and test the ignition wire. Check the resistance of each spark plug wire. Refer to Section 1 for checking the resistance of the spark plug wires. If the wire is within specification, it will be necessary to diagnose the individual components of the ignition system.

   b. Carefully inspect the distributor cap and rotor for an internal short, damage, corrosion or excessive wear.

7. If spark does not exist, perform the following:

   a. Remove the distributor cap, detach all of the electrical connectors at the distributor, and ensure that the rotor is turning when the engine is cranked.

   b. Carefully inspect the distributor cap and rotor for damage, corrosion or excessive wear.

   c. Inspect and test the ignition wires. Check the resistance of each spark plug wire. Refer to Section 1 for checking the resistance of the spark plug wires. If the wire is within specification, it will be necessary to diagnose the individual components of the ignition system.

CYLINDER DROP TEST

▶ **See Figure 5**

※ WARNING

When performing a cylinder drop make sure the cylinder's high-tension lead for the cylinder being checked is sufficiently grounded. Failure to do so may cause severe and expensive internal component damage.

A cylinder drop test can be performed when an engine misfire is present. This test helps determine which cylinder is not contributing to the engine's power. The easiest way to perform this test is to remove and ground the plug wires one at a time for each cylinder with the engine running. A cylinder drop test can be performed when an engine misfire is present

1. Place the automatic transaxle in **P**, and the manual transaxle in **N** and engage the emergency brake. Then start the engine and allow the engine to reach a warm idle.

2. Using a spark plug wire-removing tool, preferably, the pliers type, carefully remove and ground the ignition wire from one of the cylinders.

※ WARNING

Make sure not to touch any part of the car that is metal. The secondary voltage from the ignition system is a high-energy spark, and although it is not deadly, the voltage is significant enough to cause a painful electrical shock.

3. The engine will sputter, run worse, and possibly nearly stall. If this happens reinstall the plug wire and move to the next cylinder. If the engine runs no differently, or the difference is minimal, shut the engine off and inspect the spark plug wire, spark plug, and if necessary, perform component diagnostics as covered in this section. Perform this test on all cylinders to verify which cylinders seem low on power.

Adjustments

The only adjustment possible on the CR-V and 2.2L/2.3L Odyssey ignition system is the base ignition timing. Please refer to Section 1 for information about setting the base ignition timing.

Ignition Coil

TESTING

1. Note the radio security code, then disconnect the negative battery cable.

2. Loosen the fasteners securing the distributor

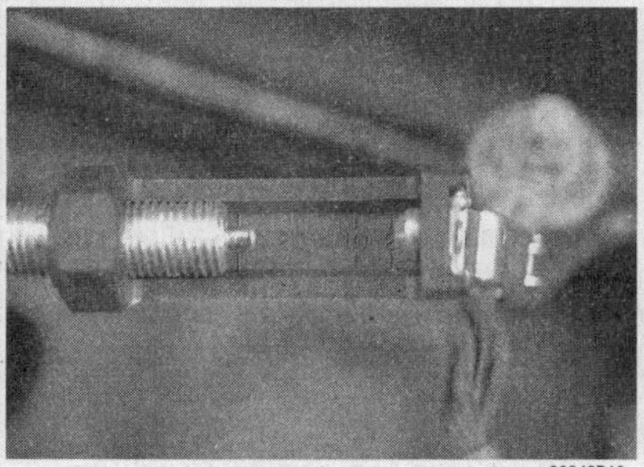

Fig. 3 This spark tester has an adjustable air-gap for measuring spark strength and testing different voltage ignition systems

90942P10

Fig. 4 To test for spark at the plug, ground the body to a known good ground such as this ground strap bolt

90942P08

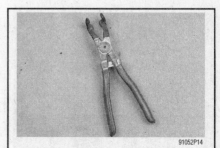

91052P14

Fig. 5 These pliers are insulated and help protect the user from shock. They also prevent the plug wires from being damaged

cap to the distributor housing, remove the cap with the wires attached and place safely aside and remove the distributor cap seal from the distributor body.

3. On models equipped with a protective cover under the distributor cap, locate the fastener that secures the ignition rotor to the distributor shaft. Note the position of the rotor for reinstallation, remove the fastener, the rotor and then the protective cover.

4. Locate the ignition coil that is secured by two fasteners onto the metal mounting posts. Remove the black/yellow wire from the terminal marked A (+) and white/blue wire from the terminal marked B (-).

➡**Resistance will vary with coil temperature. All specifications are measured at a temperature of 68°F (20°C)**

5. Measure the primary resistance between the A (+) and B (-) terminals using an ohmmeter, then compare with the following specifications:
- CR-V: 0.63–0.77 ohms
- 4-cylinder Odyssey models: 0.40–0.60 ohms

6. Measure the secondary resistance between the A (+) and the high-voltage output secondary winding terminal using an ohmmeter. Then, compare with the following specifications:
- CR-V: 12,800–19,200 ohms
- 4-cylinder Odyssey models: 22,400–33,600 ohms

➡**The Powertrain Control Module (PCM) idle memory must be reset after reconnecting the battery. Start the engine and hold it at 3000 rpm until the cooling fan comes on. Then**

allow the engine to idle for about five minutes with all accessories OFF and with the transaxle in Park or Neutral.

7. Reconnect the negative battery cable and enter the radio security code.

REMOVAL & INSTALLATION

➡ **See Figures 6 thru 12**

1. Disconnect the negative battery cable and note the radio security code.

2. Loosen the fasteners securing the distributor cap to the distributor housing, remove the cap with the wires attached and place safely aside and remove the distributor cap seal from the distributor body.

3. Locate the fastener that secures the ignition rotor to the distributor shaft, and note the position of the rotor for reinstallation, remove the fastener, the rotor and then, if equipped, the protective cover.

4. Locate the ignition coil that is secured by two fasteners onto the metal mounting posts. Remove the black/yellow wire from the terminal marked A (+) and white/blue wire from the terminal marked B (-).

5. Remove the two fasteners that secure the ignition coil to the distributor housing and remove the ignition coil.

To install:

6. Install the components in the reverse order of removal.

7. Connect the battery negative cable and enter the radio security code.

➡**The Powertrain Control Module (PCM) idle memory must be reset after reconnecting the**

battery. Start the engine and hold it at 3000 rpm until the cooling fan comes on. Then allow the engine to idle for about five minutes with all accessories OFF and with the transaxle in Park or Neutral.

Ignition Control Module

➡ **See Figure 13**

The Ignition Control Module (ICM) is located in the distributor housing near the ignition coil. To access the module, remove the distributor cap, rotor, and if equipped, the dust cover.

TESTING

Make sure to note the location where the wires are connected. Use a piece of paper and note the wire locations and connections, or carefully mark the wires before removing them. Failure to reinstall the wires correctly could cause expensive component failure.

CR-V Models

1. Loosen the fasteners securing the distributor cap to the distributor housing, remove the cap with the wires attached and place safely aside and remove the distributor cap seal from the distributor body.

2. Locate the fastener that secures the ignition rotor to the distributor shaft and note the position of the rotor for reinstallation, remove the fastener, the rotor and then, if equipped, the protective cover.

3. Locate the Ignition Control Module (ICM)

Fig. 6 To remove the ignition coil, first remove the distributor cap

Fig. 7 Locate the Phillips screw that secures the rotor to the distributor shaft and remove the screw . . .

Fig. 8 . . . then remove the rotor from the shaft

Fig. 9 Remove the plastic cover to expose the ignition coil

Fig. 10 Label and detach the coil electrical connections

Fig. 11 Remove the two Phillips screws that mount the coil to the distributor housing . . .

Fig. 12 . . . then remove the ignition coil from the housing

Fig. 13 The ICM is located in the distributor housing. The distributor cap, rotor and dust protector must be removed to gain access the module

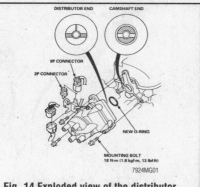

Fig. 14 Exploded view of the distributor mounting—Odyssey 4-cylinder models

which is near the ignition coil and mounted onto the distributor housing plate. To test proceed as follows:

4. Remove the yellow/green, black/yellow, white/blue wires, and the blue wires from the ICM

5. With the ignition switch ON, check for battery voltage between the black/yellow and ground. If voltage is present, proceed with testing. If no voltage is present check for an open circuit between the wire and the ignition switch.

6. With the ignition switch ON, check for battery voltage between the white/blue and ground. If voltage is present, go to the next step. If no voltage is present, check the ignition coil and the white/blue between the ICM and the coil.

7. Detach the electrical multi-connector at the Engine Control Module/Powertrain Control Module ECM/PCM and check for continuity on the yellow/green wire between the multi-connector and the yellow/green wire at the ICM. There should be continuity. If there is no continuity, check for an open circuit in the yellow/green wire circuit. Check for continuity between the yellow/green wire and ground. There should be no continuity. If there is continuity to ground, locate where the yellow/green wire is shorted to ground, and repair. Reconnect the ECM/PCM multi-connector.

8. On 1997–98 CR-V models, check for continuity between the ICM blue wire and the test tachometer connector located on the firewall, left of the brake booster. There should be continuity. If there is no continuity, check for an open circuit in the blue wire circuit. Check for continuity between the blue wire and ground. There should be no continuity. If there is continuity to ground, locate where the blue wire is shorted to ground, and repair.

9. If all the test conditions are passed, replace the ICM.

4-Cylinder Odyssey Models

To test the 2.2L/2.3L Odyssey models proceed as follows:
- 1995 vehicles: Remove the black/yellow, blue (1), yellow/green, and the blue (2) wires from the ICM
- 1996–97 vehicles: Remove the yellow/green, black/yellow, white/black, and the blue wires from the ICM
- 1998 vehicles: Remove the yellow/green, black/yellow, and white/black wires from the ICM

1. With the ignition switch ON, check for battery

voltage between the black/yellow and ground. If voltage is present, proceed with testing. If no voltage is present, check for an open circuit between the wire and the ignition switch.

2. With the ignition switch ON, check for battery voltage between the white/black (1996–98 models) or blue (2) (1995 model) and ground. If voltage is present, go to the next step. If no voltage is present, check the ignition coil and the white/black or blue (2) wire between the ICM and the coil.

3. Detach the electrical multi-connector at the Engine Control Module/Powertrain Control Module ECM/PCM and check for continuity on the yellow/green wire between the multi-connector and the yellow/green wire at the ICM. There should be continuity. If there is no continuity, check for an open circuit in the yellow/green wire circuit. Check for continuity between the yellow/green wire and ground. There should be no continuity. If there is continuity to ground, locate where the yellow/green wire is shorted to ground, and repair. Reconnect the ECM/PCM multi-connector.

4. On 1995 models, check for continuity between the ICM blue (1) wire and the Transmission Control Module (TCM). There should be continuity. If there is no continuity, check for an open circuit in the blue (1) wire circuit. Check for continuity between the blue (1) wire and ground. There should be no continuity. If there is continuity to ground, locate where the blue (1) wire is shorted to ground, and repair.

5. On 1996–97 models, check for continuity between the ICM blue wire and the test tachometer connector located on the right side firewall, behind the air intake bellows. There should be continuity. If there is no continuity, check for an open circuit in the blue wire circuit. Check for continuity between the blue wire and ground. There should be no continuity. If there is continuity to ground, locate where the blue wire is shorted to ground, and repair.

6. If all the test conditions are passed, replace the ICM.

REMOVAL & INSTALLATION

◗ See Figure 13

1. Note the radio security code, if equipped, then disconnect the negative battery cable.

2. Loosen the fasteners securing the distributor cap to the distributor housing, remove the cap with the wires attached and place safely aside and

remove the distributor cap seal from the distributor body.

3. Locate the fastener that secures the ignition rotor to the distributor shaft. Note the position of the rotor for reinstallation, remove the fastener, the rotor and, if equipped, the protective cover.

4. Locate the Ignition Control Module (ICM) which is near the ignition coil and mounted onto the distributor housing plate. Remove the following wires:
- CR-V: Remove the yellow/green, black/yellow, white/blue wires, and if equipped the blue wire from the ICM
- 4-cylinder Odyssey models: On 3-connector ICM's, remove the yellow/green, black/yellow, and white/black wires. On 4-connector ICM's, remove the three-wire harness containing the black/yellow, blue, and yellow/green wires, white/black or blue (1) and the separate blue (2) wire from the ICM

5. Remove the fasteners that secure the ICM to the distributor body, then remove the ICM.

6. Install the components in the reverse order of removal.

7. Connect the battery negative cable and enter the radio security code.

➡The Powertrain Control Module(PCM) idle memory must be reset after reconnecting the battery. Start the engine and hold it at 3000 rpm until the cooling fan comes on. Then allow the engine to idle for about five minutes with all accessories OFF and with the transaxle in Park or Neutral.

Distributor

REMOVAL & INSTALLATION

◗ See Figures 14, 15 and 16

➡The radio may contain a coded theft protection circuit. Always make note of the code before disconnecting the battery.

1. Disconnect the negative battery cable.

2. Access the crankshaft pulley bolt through the left side inner fender liner. Use a socket, long extension and a suitable ratchet to rotate the engine. Rotate the engine counterclockwise until the white Top Dead Center (TDC) mark on the pulley aligns with the pointer on the engine cover.

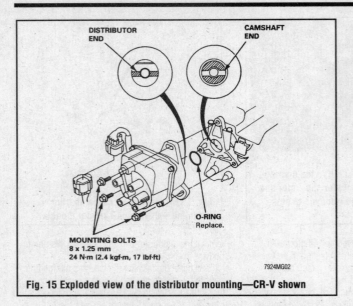

Fig. 15 Exploded view of the distributor mounting—CR-V shown

Fig. 16 The distributor keyway is offset and can only be installed in one direction

3. Label the ignition wires, but do not remove them.

4. Remove the distributor cap and note the location of the ignition rotor. If the ignition rotor is **not** pointing toward the terminal of the distributor cap for cylinder No. 1, rotate the crankshaft one complete revolution counterclockwise, and align the white (TDC) mark on the pulley with the pointer on the engine cover.

5. If the distributor is going to be reinstalled, make an alignment mark between the distributor housing and the cylinder head using a scribe or a chisel. Then, and using a scribe, felt tipped marker or touch up paint, make an alignment mark on the distributor housing for the rotor.

6. Uncouple the electrical connectors on the side of the distributor.

7. Remove the three distributor mounting bolts, then remove the distributor from the cylinder head.

To install:

➡If the camshaft or crankshaft has rotated during assembly, rotate the crankshaft counterclockwise until the white Top Dead Center (TDC) mark on the pulley aligns with the pointer on the engine cover. If the valve cover and upper timing cover have been removed, be sure the UP mark on the camshaft is facing up, and that the crankshaft TDC mark aligns with the pointer on the lower timing cover.

8. Coat a new O-ring with clean engine oil and install it onto the distributor shaft.

9. Install the distributor into the cylinder head. The offset lug on the distributor shaft will fit into the groove on the end of the camshaft in only one direction. If the distributor is being reinstalled, align the marks made during disassembly.

10. Install the three mounting bolts, only hand-tighten them at this time.

11. Couple the electrical connectors on the side of the distributor.

12. If removed, reconnect the ignition wires in the correct order.

13. Reconnect the negative battery cable.

➡The Powertrain Control Module(PCM) idle memory must be reset after reconnecting the battery. Start the engine and hold it at 3000 rpm until the cooling fan comes on. Then allow the engine to idle for about five minutes with all accessories OFF and with the transaxle in Park or Neutral.

14. Check and adjust the ignition timing. Refer to the ignition timing procedure outlined in Section 1.

15. Enter the radio security code.

Crankshaft Position Sensor

Refer to Electronic Engine Controls in Section 4 for information on servicing the Crankshaft Position (CKP) Sensor.

Cylinder Position Sensor

Refer to Electronic Engine Controls in Section 4 for information on servicing the Cylinder Position (CYP) Sensor.

Top Dead Center Position Sensor

Refer to Electronic Engine Controls in Section 4 for information on servicing the Top Dead Center (TDC) Sensor.

DISTRIBUTORLESS IGNITION SYSTEM

General Information

▸ **See Figure 17**

Beginning with model year 1999, the Odyssey models are equipped with a 3.5L V6 engine that uses a distributorless ignition system. The ignition timing and the ignition advance are both controlled by the Powertrain Control Module (PCM) to match the driving conditions. The PCM optimizes the ignition timing using input from a collection of sensors. The ignition timing can be checked for diagnostic purposes, although it cannot be adjusted. The distributorless ignition system uses one ignition coil per cylinder, unlike the distributor type system that uses one ignition coil for the entire system and uses the distributor to dispense the high-voltage ignition to the spark plugs.

The distributorless ignition system, which uses individual ignition coils, operates on the same principle as those on the distributor-equipped engines. However, instead of the distributor's rotation being used to trigger the ignition coil, the PCM controls the switching of the current through the primary windings for each of the individual ignition coils. When current to the ignition coil is stopped, a high voltage current flows directly from the ignition coil to the spark plug.

The PCM contains the memory for basic ignition timing for different engine speeds and manifold air-flow rates. The PCM also adjusts the ignition timing according to engine coolant temperature. The Cylinder Position (CKP) Sensor is used by the PCM to monitor the crankshaft speed. A misfire is detected by the PCM if the crankshaft speed fluctuates.

The following sensors are used by the PCM for ignition timing control:

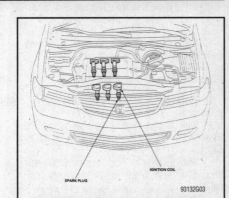

Fig. 17 Beginning in 1999, the Odyssey is equipped with a distributorless ignition system

• Top Dead Center (TDC) Sensors. These two sensors, TDC1 and TDC2, determine ignition timing during start up and when the crank angle is abnormal

• Cylinder Position (CKP) Sensor. This sensor detects engine speed

• Manifold Absolute Pressure (MAP) Sensor. This sensor detects the intake manifold air volume

• Engine Coolant Temperature (ECT) Sensor. This sensor monitors the engine coolant temperature

• Knock (KS) Sensor. Allows the PCM to adjust ignition timing for the octane rating of the gasoline being used

Diagnosis and Testing

The distributorless ignition system can be diagnosed and tested using a logical test sequence. The system can be broken down into three basic components. These components are the inputs (sensors), the processor (Powertrain Control Module) and the output components (ignition coils). Basic troubleshooting of the ignition system can be accomplished by testing the input and output components. These simple troubleshooting procedures can be used to help locate and diagnose most problems.

Diagnosing the PCM using basic tools and test equipment requires a process of elimination technique.

1. Check the operation of all input sensors. Please refer to Section 4 for additional information.

2. Check the wiring for all input sensors for continuity or a short to ground.

3. Check the ignition coils. Please refer to the following Ignition Coil Pack procedures for additional information.

4. Check the ignition coil wiring for continuity or a short to ground.

5. If the sensor inputs and the ignition coils are within specification, and the wiring is connected and functioning properly, the PCM could be faulty.

➡**The Powertrain Control Module (PCM) has a fault memory to monitor the operation of the system. The PCM has the ability to recognize a problem in the system, and can prioritize the problem. If the problem is severe enough, the Malfunction Indicator Light (MIL) can be turned on by the PCM to indicate the problem is compromising the efficient and optimal**

operation of the engine. The PCM uses its fault memory to store fault codes that can be accessed using specially designed test equipment which due to its cost and the training required to use this equipment is beyond the scope of this manual. This test equipment is used to read the stored faults, as well as erase the faults from the PCM memory once a repair is completed.

Adjustments

The programmed ignition system provides an adaptive, optimal ignition timing that is controlled the by the Powertrain Control Module (PCM), based on input sensor information. This system cannot be adjusted.

Ignition Coil Pack

TESTING

▶ **See Figures 18, 19 and 20**

1. Remove the cover for the ignition coil.

2. Tag and detach the electrical connectors from all 6 ignition coils.

3. Turn the ignition switch to the **ON** position and measure the voltage at the black/yellow wire for each connector. If voltage is present go to the next step. If voltage is not present, repair the open circuit in the wire between the ignition coil and fuse No. 11 in the left side under dash fuse panel.

4. Turn the ignition switch **OFF** and check for continuity between the black wire and ground. If ground is present, go to the next step. If ground is not present, repair the open circuit in the wire between the ignition coil and the body ground.

5. Unplug the 31-pin connector from the Powertrain Control Module (PCM). Hold the 31-pin multi-connector such that the wire connectors are visible, with the locking tab on top. The first row of connectors from left to right are numbered 1 through 10. On the second row, the number 11 slot is empty and the remaining connectors are numbered 12 through 22. The third row is numbered 23 though 31, with slot number 24 empty. Check the following wires from the provided pin location for continuity to ground. If there is not continuity go to the next step. If there is continu-

ity, repair the short in the wire between the PCM and the ignition coil.

• Blue, pin location No. 3 to ground
• Yellow/green, pin location No. 4 to ground
• Black/red, pin location No. 12
• Yellow, pin location No. 13 to ground
• Red, pin location No. 14
• White/blue, pin location No. 23 to ground

6. Reconnect the PCM multi-plug connector. With the ignition switch in the start position, check for voltage at the multi-plug connector for each ignition coil for the following wires: blue, yellow/green, black/red, yellow, red, and white/blue. If the measured voltage is 0.5 volts, replace the ignition coil. If no voltage is measured, repair the open circuit in the wire between the PCM and the ignition coil.

REMOVAL & INSTALLATION

1. Remove the ignition coil covers.

2. Remove the multi-plug wiring harness from the ignition coil.

3. Remove the ignition coil by removing the mounting bolts.

4. Remove the ignition coil.

5. Installation is the reverse of the removal procedure.

Ignition Module

➡**The Ignition Control Module (ICM) on the 3.5L V6 Odyssey models is incorporated into each individual ignition coil, and cannot be replaced separately from the ignition coil. If an ICM failure occurs, the ignition coil assembly must be replaced.**

Top Dead Center Sensors

Refer to Electronic Engine Controls in Section 4 for information on servicing the Top Dead Center (TDC) Sensors.

Cylinder Position Sensor

Refer to Electronic Engine Controls in Section 4 for information on servicing the Cylinder Position (CKP) Sensor.

IGNITION COIL 3P CONNECTOR

```
1
2   IG
3   (BLK/YEL)
```

Wire side of
female terminals

93132G04

Fig. 18 With the ignition switch ON, measure the voltage at the No. 3 terminal (black/yellow wire) of each ignition coil 3P connector

---

IGNITION COIL 3P CONNECTOR

```
1   GND
2   (BLK)
3
```

Wire side of
female terminals

93132G05

Fig. 19 With the ignition switch OFF, check for continuity between the No. 2 terminal (black wire) of each ignition coil 3P connector and ground

---

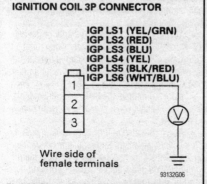

IGNITION COIL 3P CONNECTOR

IGP LS1 (YEL/GRN)
IGP LS2 (RED)
IGP LS3 (BLU)
IGP LS4 (YEL)
IGP LS5 (BLK/RED)
IGP LS6 (WHT/BLU)

```
1
2
3
```

Wire side of
female terminals

93132G06

Fig. 20 Place the ignition switch to the START position, then check for voltage at the No. 1 terminal of each ignition coil 3P connector

Manifold Absolute Pressure Sensor

Refer to Electronic Engine Controls in Section 4 for information on servicing the Manifold Absolute Pressure (MAP) Sensor.

Engine Coolant Temperature Sensor

Refer to Electronic Engine Controls in Section 4 for information on servicing the Engine Coolant Temperature (ECT) Sensor.

Knock Sensor

Refer to Electronic Engine Controls in Section 4 for information on servicing the Knock Sensor (KS).

FIRING ORDERS

◆ **See Figures 21, 22 and 23**

➥To avoid confusion, always tag the spark plug wires and, if equipped, the distributor cap before removal of the wires or distributor cap.

The distributors used on the CR-V and 2.2L/2.3L Odyssey models use an offset keyway on the dis-

tributor shaft where it mates with the end of the camshaft. This prevents the distributor from being installed incorrectly. Although the distributor is keyed, the spark plug wires must be installed onto the distributor cap in the correct order for the engine to run properly.

As long as the distributor housing has not

been moved or removed, the ignition timing will not be affected by the removal or replacement of the ignition wires, spark plugs, distributor cap or ignition rotor. If the distributor has been moved, or removed, the ignition timing must be checked and possibly reset as described in Section 1.

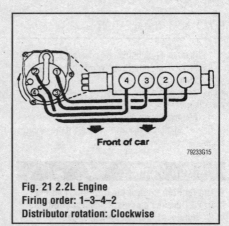

Fig. 21 2.2L Engine
Firing order: 1–3–4–2
Distributor rotation: Clockwise

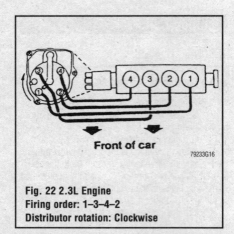

Fig. 22 2.3L Engine
Firing order: 1–3–4–2
Distributor rotation: Clockwise

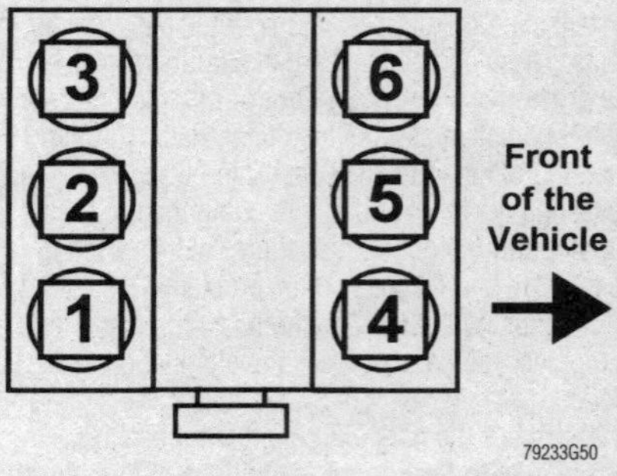

Fig. 23 3.5L V6 Engine
Firing order: 1–4–2–5–3–6
Distributorless ignition system

CHARGING SYSTEM

General Information

The charging system used on the Honda CR-V and Odyssey models is a 12 volt DC (Direct Current) negative (-) ground system. The system consists of an alternator with an internal voltage regulator, an alternator belt, a charging system light, an under-hood fuse/relay box with a built-in Electrical Load Detector (ELD) Unit, and a battery.

Alternator Precautions

Several precautions must be observed with alternator equipped vehicles to avoid damage to the unit.

• ALWAYS observe proper polarity of the battery connections. Use extreme care when jump starting the car. Reversing the battery connections may cause the battery to explode, or result in damage to the one-way rectifiers.
• ALWAYS remove the battery or, at least, disconnect the cables while charging to avoid damaging the alternator.
• ALWAYS match and/or consider the polarity of the battery, alternator and regulator before making any electrical connections within the system.
• ALWAYS disconnect the battery ground terminal while repairing or replacing any electrical components.
• NEVER use a fast battery charger to jump start a vehicle with a dead battery.
• NEVER attempt to polarize an alternator.

• NEVER use test lights of more than 12 volts when checking diode continuity.
• NEVER ground or short out the alternator or regulator terminals.
• NEVER separate the alternator on an open circuit. Make sure all connections within the circuit are clean and tight.
• NEVER use arc welding equipment on the car with the battery cable, PCM or alternator connected.
• NEVER operate the alternator with any of its or the battery's lead wires disconnected.
• NEVER subject the alternator to excessive heat or dampness (for instance, steam cleaning the engine).
• When utilizing a booster battery as a starting aid, always connect the positive to positive terminals and the negative terminal from the booster battery to a good engine ground on the vehicle being started.

Alternator

TESTING

Voltage Drop Test

➥These tests will show the amount of voltage drop across the alternator output wire from the alternator output (B+) terminal to the battery positive post. They will also show the amount of voltage drop from the ground (-) terminal on the alternator.

A voltmeter with a 0–18 volt DC scale should be used for these tests. By repositioning the voltmeter test leads, the point of high resistance (voltage drop) can easily be found. Test points on the alternator can be reached by either removing the air cleaner housing or below by raising the vehicle.

1. Before starting the test, make sure the battery is in good condition and is fully charged. Check the conditions of the battery cables.
2. Start the engine, let it warm up to normal operating temperatures, then turn the engine **OFF**.
3. Connect an engine tachometer, following the manufacturer's directions.
4. Make sure the parking brake is fully engaged.
5. Start the engine, then place the blower on HIGH, and turn on the high beam headlamps and interior lamps.
6. Bring the engine speed up to 2,400 rpm and hold it there.
7. To test the ground (-) circuitry, perform the following:
   a. Touch the negative lead of the voltmeter directly to the positive battery terminal.
   b. Touch the positive lead of the voltmeter to the B+ output terminal stud on the alternator (NOT the terminal mounting nut). The voltage should be no higher than 0.6 volts. If the voltage is higher than 0.6 volts, touch the test lead to the terminal mounting stud nut, and then to the wiring connector. If the voltage is now below 0.6 volts, look for dirty, loose or poor connections at

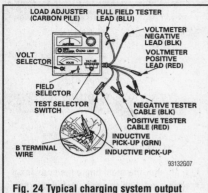

Fig. 24 Typical charging system output voltage test connections

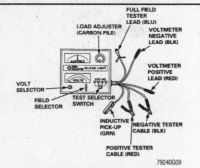

Fig. 25 VAT-40 charging system tester. Similar testers are available that perform as well

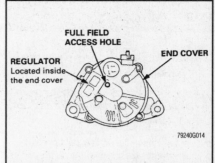

Fig. 26 A rear view of the alternator showing the regulator, end cover and full field access hole locations

this point. A voltage drop test may be performed at each ground (-) connection in the circuit to locate the excessive resistance.

8. To test the positive (+) circuitry, perform the following:

   a. Touch the positive lead of the voltmeter directly to the negative battery terminal.

   b. Touch the negative lead of the voltmeter to the ground terminal stud on the alternator case (NOT the terminal mounting nut). The voltage should be no higher than 0.3 volts. If the voltage is higher than 0.3 volts, touch the test lead to the terminal mounting stud nut, and then to the wiring connector. If the voltage is now below 0.3 volts, look for dirty, loose or poor connections at this point. A voltage drop test may be performed at each positive (+) connection in the circuit to locate the excessive resistance.

9. This test can also be performed between the alternator case and the engine. If the test voltage is higher than 0.3 volts, check for corrosion at the alternator mounting points or loose alternator mounting.

Output Voltage Test

▶ See Figures 24, 25 and 26

1. Before starting the test, make sure the battery is in good condition and is fully charged. Check the conditions of the battery cables.

2. Perform the voltage drop test to ensure clean and tight alternator/battery electrical connections.

3. Be sure the alternator drive belt is properly tensioned, as outlined in Section 1.

4. A volt/amp tester such as the VAT-40 or an equivalent, which is equipped with a battery load control (carbon pile rheostat), full field tester and an inductive-type pickup clamp (ammeter probe) is used for this test. Make sure to follows all directions supplied with the tester.

5. Start the engine and let it run until it reaches normal operating temperature.

6. Connect the VAT-40 or equivalent and turn the selector switch to position 1 (starting). Make sure all electrical accessories and lights are turned OFF.

7. Set the parking brake, place the transmission in Park or Neutral, and start the engine. Operate the throttle and hold the engine at 3,000 rpm with all accessories in the off position, until the radiator cooling fan comes on. Then allow the engine to idle for 15 seconds.

8. Raise the engine speed to 2,000 rpm and check the voltage. If the voltage is less than 15.1 volts, go to the next step. If the voltage is greater than 15.1 volts, replace the alternator.

9. Allow the engine to idle with all electrical accessories turned off. Turn the selector switch on the VAT-40 or equivalent to position 2 (charging).

10. Remove the inductive pick-up and zero the ammeter.

11. Place the inductive pick-up over the B terminal wire from the alternator, making sure the arrow points away from the alternator.

12. Raise the engine speed to 2,000 rpm and read the voltage. If the voltage is 13.5 volts or greater, go to the next step. If the voltage is below 13.5 volts, replace the alternator.

13. Apply a load with the VAT-40 or equivalent until the battery voltage drops to between 12–13.5 volts. If the amperage output is 75 amps or more, the charging system is good. If the amperage output is below 75 amps, go to the next step.

✳✳ WARNING

When performing the full field test, do not allow the voltage to exceed 18 volts as damage to the electrical system may occur.

14. Perform a full field test by attaching the full field probe from the VAT-40 or equivalent into the full field terminal inside the full field access hole on the back of the alternator. Hold the engine speed to 2,000 rpm, switch the field selector to the A (Ground) position, and check the amperage reading.

- CR-V models: If the amperage is 65 amps or more, replace the voltage regulator. If the amperage is less than 65 amps, replace the alternator.
- Odyssey models: If the amperage is 75 amps or more, replace the voltage regulator. If the amperage is less than 75 amps, replace the alternator.

REMOVAL & INSTALLATION

CR-V

▶ See Figure 27

1. Note the radio security code and the radio presets.

2. Disconnect the negative battery cable, then the positive.

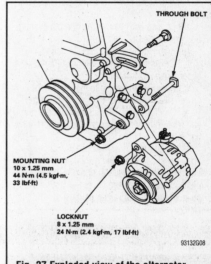

Fig. 27 Exploded view of the alternator mounting—CR-V shown

3. Detach the four prong connector and the white wire from the rear of the alternator.

4. Remove the alternator adjusting bolt.

5. Remove the locknut.

6. Remove the alternator belt.

7. Remove the alternator assembly.

8. Alternator installation is the reverse of the removal procedure.

9. Connect the positive battery cable, then the negative battery cable. Enter the radio security code and station presets.

✳✳ WARNING

Be sure to adjust the alternator belt to the proper tension or alternator bearing failure may occur.

Odyssey Models

4-CYLINDER ENGINES

▶ See Figure 28

1. Note the radio security code and the radio presets.

2. Disconnect the negative battery cable, then the positive.

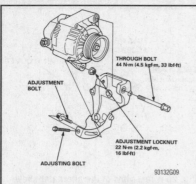

Fig. 28 Exploded view of the alternator mounting—4-cylinder Odyssey shown

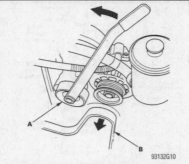

Fig. 29 Move the auto tensioner (A) to relieve the tension from the alternator belt (B), then remove belt

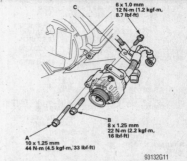

Fig. 30 After the mounting bolts and clamp are removed, you can remove the alternator

3. Remove the power steering pump as follows:

a. Loosen and remove the pump adjusting bolt, mounting bolt and nuts.

b. Remove the power steering belt.

c. Cover the alternator with a suitable, absorbent shop towel.

d. Remove the two bolts that secure the power steering pump outlet line to the pump.

e. Carefully remove the pipe from the pump, and while removing place the O-ring from the fitting aside.

f. Wrap the end of the hose with a clean shop towel and place the hose aside. Cover the hole in the power steering pump with a small piece of cloth, and then cover the cloth with a piece of duct tape or electrical tape to hold the cloth in place.

g. Carefully remove the power steering pump taking care not to spill fluid from the covered hole, and place the pump aside onto a thick shop towel away from the alternator.

4. Detach the four prong connector and the black wire from the rear of the alternator.

5. Remove the alternator adjusting bolt.

6. Remove the locknut.

7. Remove the alternator belt.

8. Remove the alternator assembly.

To install:

9. Install the alternator in the reverse order of removal.

10. Check and properly tension the alternator belt as outlined in Section 1.

11. Reinstall the power steering pump in the reverse order of removal, using a new O-ring for the power steering outlet hose fitting. If in an emergency, and the power steering hose O-ring must be re-used, coat the O-ring with a light film of power steering fluid before installing it.

✳✳ WARNING

Be sure to adjust the alternator belt and power steering belts to the proper tension or bearing failure may occur.

12. Connect the positive battery cable, then the negative battery cable. Enter the radio security code and station presets.

13. Start the engine and turn the steering wheel full left, full right and the full left. Check the power steering fluid level and top off as necessary using only Honda Power Steering Fluid.

✳✳ WARNING

Substituting another power steering fluid could cause damage to the power steering components.

V6 ENGINE

▶ See Figures 29 and 30

1. Note the radio security code and the radio presets.

2. Disconnect the negative battery cable, then the positive.

3. Move the auto tensioner to relieve tension on the serpentine drive belt and remove the belt.

4. Detach the four prong connector and the black wire from the rear of the alternator.

5. Remove the alternator mounting bolt, the bracket mounting bolt and the harness clamp from the alternator.

6. Remove the alternator assembly.

7. Alternator installation is the reverse of the removal procedure.

8. Connect the positive battery cable, then the negative battery cable. Enter the radio security code and station presets.

STARTING SYSTEM

Starter

TESTING

Testing Preparation

➥**The air temperature should be between 59–100°F before any testing.**

The starting system consists of an ignition switch, starter relay, neutral safety switch, wiring harness, battery, and a starter motor with an integral solenoid. These components form two separate circuits: a high amperage circuit that feeds the starter motor up to 300 or more amps, and a control circuit that operates on less than 20 amps.

Before commencing with the starting system diagnostics, verify:

- The battery top posts and terminals are clean.
- The alternator drive belt tension and condition is correct.

- The battery state-of-charge is correct.
- The battery cable connections at the starter and engine block are clean and free from corrosion.
- The wiring harness connectors and terminals are clean and free from corrosion.
- Proper circuit grounding.

Starter Feed Circuit

✳✳ CAUTION

The ignition system must be disabled to prevent engine start while performing the following tests.

1. Connect a volt-ampere tester (multimeter) to the battery terminals.

2. Disable the ignition system.

3. Verify that all lights and accessories are off, and the transaxle shift selector is in Park (automatic) or Neutral (manual). Set the parking brake.

4. Rotate and hold the ignition switch in the

START position. Observe the volt-ampere tester:

- If the voltage reads above 9.6 volts, and the amperage draw reads above 250 amps, go to the starter feed circuit resistance test (following this test).
- If the voltage reads 12.4 volts or greater and the amperage reads 0–10 amps, refer to the starter solenoid and relay tests.

✳✳ WARNING

Do not overheat the starter motor or draw the battery voltage below 9.6 volts during cranking operations.

5. After the starting system problems have been corrected, verify the battery state of charge and charge the battery if necessary. Disconnect all of the testing equipment and connect the ignition coil cable or ignition coil connector. Start the vehicle several times to assure the problem was corrected.

Starter Feed Circuit Resistance

▶ **See Figures 31 and 32**

Before proceeding with this test, refer to the battery tests and starter feed circuit test. The following test will require a voltmeter, which is capable of accuracy to 0.1 volt.

✳✳ CAUTION

The ignition system must be disabled to prevent engine start while performing the following tests.

1. Disable the ignition system.
2. With all wiring harnesses and components (except for the coils) properly connected, perform the following:

   a. Connect the negative (-) lead of the voltmeter to the negative battery post, and the positive (+) lead to the negative (-) battery cable clamp. Rotate and hold the ignition switch in the **START** position. Observe the voltmeter. If the voltage is detected, correct the poor contact between the cable clamp and post.

   b. Connect the positive (+) lead of the voltmeter to the positive battery post, and the negative (-) to the positive battery cable clamp. Rotate and hold the ignition switch key in the **START** position. Observe the voltmeter. If voltage is detected, correct the poor contact between the cable clamp and post.

   c. Connect the negative lead of the voltmeter to the negative (-) battery terminal, and positive

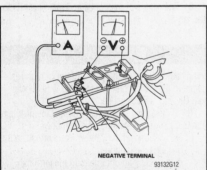

Fig. 31 Proper voltmeter and ammeter connections—CR-V shown, 1995–98 Odyssey similar

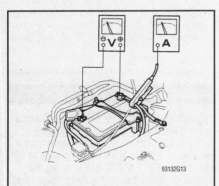

Fig. 32 The voltmeter and ammeter must be connected properly—1999–00 Odyssey

lead to the engine block near the battery cable attaching point. Rotate and hold the ignition switch in the **START** position. If the voltage reads above 0.2 volt, correct the poor contact at ground cable attaching point. If the voltage reading is still above 0.2 volt after correcting the poor contact, replace the negative ground cable with a new one.

3. Remove the heater shield. Refer to removal and installation procedures to gain access to the starter motor and solenoid connections. Perform the following steps:

   a. Connect the positive (+) voltmeter lead to the starter motor housing and the negative (-) lead to the negative battery terminal. Hold the ignition switch key in the **START** position. If the voltage reads above 0.2 volt, correct the poor starter to engine ground.

   b. Connect the positive (+) voltmeter lead to the positive battery terminal, and the negative lead to the battery cable terminal on the starter solenoid. Rotate and hold the ignition key in the **START** position. If the voltage reads above 0.2 volt, correct poor contact at the battery cable to the solenoid connection. If the reading is still above 0.2 volt after correcting the poor contacts, replace the positive battery cable with a new one.

   c. If the resistance tests did not detect feed circuit failures, refer to the starter solenoid test.

Starter Solenoid

ON VEHICLE TEST

▶ **See Figures 33, 34 and 35**

1. Before testing, assure the parking brake is set, the transmission is in Park (automatic) or Neutral (manual), and the battery is fully charged and in good condition.
2. Connect a voltmeter from the (S) terminal on the solenoid to ground. Turn the ignition switch to the **START** position and test for battery voltage. If battery voltage is not found, inspect the ignition switch circuit. If battery voltage is found, proceed to next step.
3. Connect an ohmmeter between the battery negative post and the starter solenoid mounting late (manual) or the ground terminal (automatic). Turn the ignition switch to the **START** position. The ohmmeter should read zero (0). If not, repair the faulty ground.
4. If both tests are performed and the solenoid still does not energize, replace the solenoid.

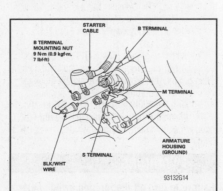

Fig. 33 Starter solenoid connector and terminal identification—CR-V shown

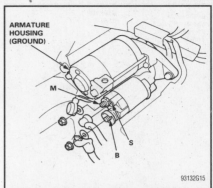

Fig. 34 Starter solenoid connector and terminal identification—1995–98 Odyssey shown

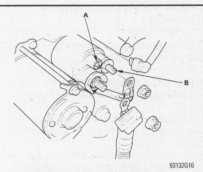

Fig. 35 Starter solenoid connector and terminal identification—1999–00 Odyssey shown

BENCH TEST

1. Note the radio security code and the radio presets.
2. Disconnect the battery negative cable then the positive cable.
3. Remove the starter from the vehicle.
4. Disconnect the field coil wire from the field coil terminal.
5. Check for continuity between the solenoid terminal and field coil terminal with a continuity tester. Continuity (resistance) should be present.
6. Check for continuity between the solenoid terminal and solenoid housing. Continuity should be detected. If continuity is detected, the solenoid is good.
7. If continuity is not detected in either test, the solenoid has an open circuit, is defective, and must be replaced.

Starter/Ground Cable Test

When performing these tests, it is important that the voltmeter be connected to the terminals, not the cables themselves.

Before testing, assure that the ignition control module (if equipped) is disconnected, the parking brake is set, the transmission is in Park (automatic) or Neutral (manual), and the battery is fully charged and in good condition.

1. Check voltage between the positive battery post and the center of the B + terminal on the starter solenoid stud.

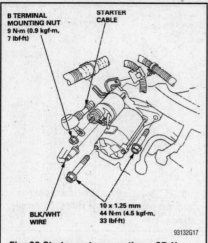

Fig. 36 Starter motor mounting—CR-V shown

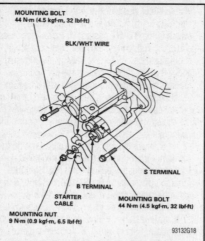

Fig. 37 View of the starter motor assembly—1995–98 Odyssey

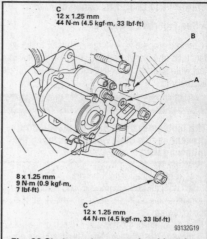

Fig. 38 Starter motor removal and installation—1999–00 Odyssey

2. Check voltage between the negative battery post and the engine block.

3. Disconnect the ignition coil wire from the distributor cap and connect a suitable jumper wire between the coil cable and a good body ground.

4. Have an assistant crank the engine and measure voltage again. Voltage drop should not exceed 0.5 volts.

5. If voltage drop is greater than 0.5 volts, clean metal surfaces. Apply a thick layer of silicone grease. Install a new cadmium plated bolt and star washer on the battery terminal and a new brass nut on the starter solenoid. Retest and replace cable not within specifications.

REMOVAL & INSTALLATION

▶ **See Figures 36, 37 and 38**

➡ **The factory sound system has a coded theft protection system. It is recommended that you know your reset code before you begin.**

1. Note the radio security code and the radio presets.

2. Disconnect the negative battery, then the positive battery cable.

3. On V6 engines, remove the automatic transmission cooler hose from the bracket on the starter motor.

4. Remove the starter cable from terminal B located on the back of the solenoid.

5. Remove the black/white wire from the S (solenoid) terminal.

6. Remove the two bolts that mount the starter the transaxle assembly, then remove the starter motor assembly.

7. Install in the reverse order of removal.

➡ **When installing the heavy gauge starter cable, make sure the crimped side of the terminal end is facing out.**

8. Enter the anti-theft code and radio presets for the radio.

SENDING UNITS

➡ **This section describes the operating principles of sending units, warning lights and gauges. Sensors that provide information to the Electronic Control Module (ECM) are covered in Section 4 of this manual.**

Instrument panels contain a number of indicating devices (gauges and warning lights). These devices are composed of two separate components. One is the sending unit, mounted on the engine or other remote part of the vehicle, and the other is the actual gauge or light in the instrument panel.

Several types of sending units exist, however most can be characterized as being either a pressure type or a resistance type. Pressure type sending units convert liquid pressure into an electrical signal that is sent to the gauge or warning light. Resistance type sending units are most often used to measure temperature and use variable resistance to control the current flow back to the indicating device. Both types of sending units are connected in series to the gauge or warning light by a wire. When the ignition is turned **ON**, current flows from the battery to the gauge or warning light and on to the sending unit.

Engine Coolant Temperature Sending Unit

The coolant temperature information is conveyed to the instrument panel, through the PCM, from the Engine Coolant Temperature (ECT) gauge sending unit. To test the gauge sending unit, first test the gauge operation to make sure the problem is not in the gauge or gauge wiring. To test the gauge operation, perform the following procedures.

TESTING

▶ **See Figures 39 and 40**

1. Check the following fuses for battery voltage before testing.
   • CR-V Models: Fuse No. 25 (7.5 amp)
   • 2.2L/2.3L Odyssey Models: Fuse No. 1 (10 amp)
   • 3.5L V6 Odyssey Models: Fuse No. 25 (7.5 amp)

2. With the ignition switch **OFF**, disconnect the yellow/green wire from the ECT gauge sending unit. Then ground it to a place on the engine block (or other known good ground) with a jumper wire.

3. Turn the ignition switch to the **ON** position.

4. Watch the Engine Coolant Temperature (ECT) gauge. It should start moving towards the hot ("H") mark.

✲✲ WARNING

Failure to turn off the ignition switch before it reaches the hot ("H") mark may lead to gauge failure.

5. If the pointer does not move at all or moves erratically, check for an open or point of high resistance in the yellow/green wire. If the wire checks out OK, replace the gauge.

6. If the above steps did not reveal the problem, the test the gauge sending unit as follows:
   a. Disconnect the yellow/green wire from the ECT gauge sending unit.
   b. Connect an ohmmeter to the terminal where the yellow/green wire was attached to the sending unit and a good known ground on the engine block.
   c. The ECT gauge sending unit resistance should be 137 ohms at a temperature of 133°F (56°C). If the engine is hot and has a temperature of 185–212°F (85–100°C) the ECT gauge sending unit resistance should be 30 ohms–46 ohms.

REMOVAL & INSTALLATION

✲✲ CAUTION

Engine coolant can spray out causing severe burns if the Engine Coolant Temperature (ECT) gauge sending unit is removed from a hot engine without allowing the engine to cool below 100°F (37°C) and draining the engine coolant into a sealable container first.

1. Allow the engine to cool below 100°F (37°C) before working on the cooling system.

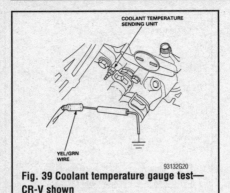

Fig. 39 Coolant temperature gauge test—CR-V shown

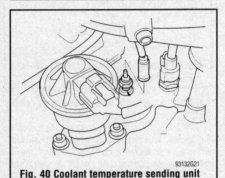

Fig. 40 Coolant temperature sending unit test—1999 Odyssey shown

2. Note the anti-theft code and radio presets for the radio.

3. Locate the Engine Coolant Temperature (ECT) gauge sending unit located near the thermostat housing on the engine.

4. Disconnect the negative battery cable.

5. Detach the ECT gauge sending unit electrical connection.

6. Drain the engine coolant into a sealable container.

7. Remove the ECT gauge sending unit using a pressure switch socket or box-end wrench.

To install:

8. Use a sensor safe liquid thread sealant to coat the threads before installation.

➡Using a tape type of sealant may electrically insulate the sensor not allowing the gauge to register.

9. Install the new sensor and tighten to 7 ft. lbs. (9 Nm) using a box-end wrench or sending unit pressure switch socket.

10. Refill the engine with a 50/50 solution of water and Honda approved or an equivalent coolant.

11. Reconnect the negative battery cable.

12. Enter the anti-theft code and radio presets for the radio.

13. Start the engine, allow it to reach operating temperature and check for leaks.

14. Bleed the cooling system to remove air as necessary.

Oil Pressure Sender

TESTING

The low oil pressure warning lamp will illuminate anytime the ignition switch is turned to the **ON**

position without the engine running. When the engine is running, the light also illuminates if the engine oil pressure drops below a safe oil pressure level. To test the system, perform the following:

If the oil pressure light does not work, perform the following:

1. Turn the ignition switch to the **ON** position.

2. If the lamp does not light, check for a broken or disconnected wire around the engine and oil pressure sending unit switch.

3. If the wire at the connector checks out OK, pull the connector loose from the switch and, with a jumper wire, ground the connector to the engine.

4. With the ignition switch turned to the **ON** position, check the warning lamp. If the lamp lights, make sure the oil pressure switch is properly grounded in the cylinder block, and if so replace the oil pressure switch. If the lamp still fails to light, check for a burned out lamp or disconnected socket in the instrument cluster.

To diagnose an oil pressure light that stays on, perform the following:

5. Check the engine oil level and top off as necessary. If the engine was 2 or more quarts low on oil, test start the engine after topping off the oil level and recheck the oil pressure light operation. If the light stays on, stop the engine immediately and go to the next step.

6. Disconnect the wire at the sending unit, then turn the ignition switch to the **ON** position. If the light remains on, check the wire from the sending unit to the gauge for being shorted to ground and repair as necessary. If the light goes out, turn the ignition switch **OFF** and go to the next step.

7. Replace the oil pressure sending switch with a known good switch.

8. Start the engine and check the oil pressure light operation. If the light stays on with the engine running, stop the engine immediately to avoid severe engine damage until the cause of the problem can be determined.

✳✳ WARNING

If the oil pressure light remains on while the engine is started, stop the engine immediately. Do not operate the engine until the cause of the problem can be determined. Operating an engine with low oil pressure will cause severe internal damage.

Possible causes for an oil pressure light to stay on are:
- Pinched or grounded sensor wire
- Defective oil pressure sending unit
- Restricted or severely leaking oil filter
- Excessive internal engine bearing clearance.
- Insufficient or severely contaminated engine oil
- Blocked oil pump pickup screen or severely worn oil pump

REMOVAL & INSTALLATION

▶ See Figure 41

1. Locate the oil pressure sending unit on the engine.

2. Note the anti-theft code and radio presets for the radio.

3. Disconnect the negative battery cable.

4. Disconnect the sending unit electrical harness.

5. Using a pressure switch socket, deep-well

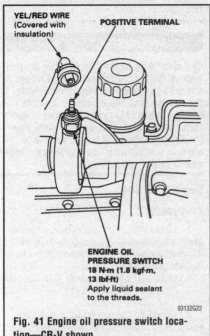

Fig. 41 Engine oil pressure switch location—CR-V shown

socket or wrench, loosen and remove the sending unit from the engine.

To install:

6. Apply a liquid thread sealant to the sending unit and install the sending unit in the engine and tighten securely.

7. Attach the electrical connector to the sending unit.

8. Check the engine oil level and top off as necessary.

9. Connect the negative battery cable.

10. Enter the anti-theft code and radio presets for the radio.

11. Start the engine, allow it to reach operating temperature and check for leaks.

12. Check for proper sending unit operation.

Cooling Fan Switch

The electric cooling fan switch is installed into a coolant passage of the engine near the thermostat housing and operates the radiator electric cooling fans when the coolant temperature reaches a specified temperature.

➡If the air conditioner is in proper working order, the engine cooling fans will operate when the air conditioner is turned on, regardless of the coolant temperature. When testing the electric cooling fan switch, make sure the air conditioner is OFF.

Below the specified temperature the switch is off (open), and at or above the specified temperature, the switch is on (closed), and completes a series circuit that triggers the cooling fan relay allowing the cooling fan to operate.

The CR-V models have one fan switch. The Odyssey models have two fan switches, switch A and switch B, that operate at different coolant temperatures to allow the cooling fans to operate at two different speeds, hi and low, depending on the engine's coolant temperature.

TESTING

Switch Installed

CR-V MODELS

1. Locate the cooling fan switch near the thermostat housing on the left side of engine behind the distributor assembly. The switch wire colors should be green and black.
2. Disconnect the wire terminal at the fan switch.
3. Allow the engine to reach a coolant temperature of 196–203°F (91–95°C).
4. Using a suitable ohmmeter or continuity tester check for continuity between the two fan switch terminals. The fan switch should have continuity (switch closed) at the above temperatures. The switch should have no continuity (switch open) when the temperature drops between 5–15°F (3–8°C) from the temperature that the switch first had continuity (switch closed).
5. If the switch does not operate within the range of the supplied information, allow the engine to cool below 100°F (37°C) and replace the switch.

4-CYLINDER ODYSSEY MODELS

The 4-cylinder Odyssey models have two electric cooling fan switches, switch A and switch B.
1. Locate the cooling fan switch near the thermostat housing as follows:
   a. Switch A: Left side of engine behind the distributor assembly, facing up. Switch wire colors green and black.
   b. Switch B: Left side of engine behind the distributor assembly, facing the firewall. Switch wire colors white/green and black.
2. Disconnect the electric wire terminal at the cooling fan switch to be tested.
3. Allow the engine to reach a coolant temperature of:
   a. Switch A: 196–203°F (91–95°C)
   b. Switch B: 217–228°F (103–109°C)
4. Using a suitable ohmmeter or continuity tester check for continuity between the two fan switch terminals. The fan switch should have continuity (switch closed) at the above temperatures.
5. The switch should have no continuity (switch open) when the temperature drops between:
   a. Switch A: When the temperature drops between 5–15°F (3–8°C) from the temperature that the switch had continuity (switch closed).
   b. Switch B: When the temperature drops between 7–16°F (4–9°C) from the temperature that the switch had continuity (switch closed).
6. If the switch does not operate within the range of the supplied information, allow the engine to cool below 100°F (37°C) and replace the switch.

V6 ODYSSEY MODELS

The V6 Odyssey models have two cooling fan switches, switch A and switch B.
1. Locate the cooling fan switch near the thermostat housing as follows:
   a. Switch A: Right side of engine facing the battery. The switch wire colors are green and black.
   b. Switch B: Left side of engine toward the front, facing the radiator. Switch wire colors blue/red and black.
2. Disconnect the electric wire terminal at the ECT cooling fan switch to be tested.
3. Allow the engine to reach a coolant temperature of:
   a. Switch A: 196–203°F (91–95°C).
   b. Switch B: 205–216°F (96–102°C).
4. Using a suitable ohmmeter or continuity tester check for continuity between the two fan switch terminals. The fan switch should have continuity (switch closed) at the above temperatures.
5. The switch should have no continuity (switch open) when the temperature drops as follows:
   a. Switch A: 5°F–15°F (3°C–8°C) from the temperature that the switch had continuity (switch closed).
   b. Switch B: 5°F–18°F (3°C–10°C) from the temperature that the switch had continuity (switch closed).
6. If the switch does not operate within the range of the supplied information, allow the engine to cool below 100°F (37°C) and replace the switch.

Switch Removed

▶ See Figure 42

Testing a radiator fan switch is not difficult, however to do so requires some basic equipment. To properly test the fan switch, the switch's probe must be submersed in coolant, only as far as the component's threads. The coolant must be heated and the temperature monitored. When the coolant reaches the specified temperature, the fan switch should be closed. Testing the switch requires the following equipment:
• A safe source of heat, such as a portable electric hot plate
• A container capable of being safely heated by a hot plate and handling heated coolant
• A thermometer safely capable of reading 228°F (109°C)
• A device to safely hold the switch such that only the coolant probe is submerged into the water
• An ohmmeter or continuity tester
1. Refer to the cooling fan switch removal and

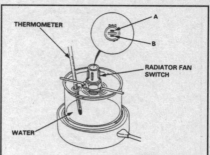

Operation	Temperature	Terminal A	B
SWITCH	ON	196 – 203°F (91 – 95°C)	○———○
	OFF	5 – 14°F (3 – 8°C) lower than the temperature when it goes on	

93132G23

Fig. 42 Cooling fan switch testing—switch removed from vehicle

installation warning and procedures and remove the switch.

Attach a 12 inch wiring sub-harness to the cooling fan switch to avoid having to probe the switch while in the heated coolant. Place the switch into a suitable holding device such that the coolant probe of the switch is submersed in a container of coolant. Make sure the container can be safely heated using a suitable source of heat such as a portable electric hot plate.
2. Using a suitable thermometer to measure the coolant temperature, heat the coolant until the specified temperature is attained.
3. When the specified coolant temperature is attained, using an ohmmeter or a continuity tester, check the continuity between the ends of the two-wire sub-harness attached to the terminals of the switch.

➡Refer to the information in this section for test temperatures and continuity results.

REMOVAL & INSTALLATION

The electric cooling fan switches are mounted into the engine cooling system passages.

1. Note the radio security code and radio station presets.
2. Disconnect the negative battery cable.
3. Drain the coolant from the radiator drain petcock into a suitable and sealable container.
4. Locate the fan switch, then disconnect the wire terminal from the fan switch.
5. Remove the switch using a sensor socket or box-end wrench.

To install:

6. Installation is the reverse of the removal procedure.
7. Reconnect the negative battery cable.
8. Top off coolant level and bleed cooling system as necessary.
9. Enter the radio security code and radio presets.

3

ENGINE AND ENGINE OVERHAUL

ENGINE MECHANICAL

Engine

REMOVAL & INSTALLATION

In the process of removing the engine, you will come across a number of steps which call for the removal of a separate component or system, such as "disconnect the exhaust system" or "remove the radiator." In most instances, a detailed removal procedure can be found elsewhere in this manual.

It is virtually impossible to list each individual wire and hose which must be disconnected, simply because so many different model and engine combinations have been manufactured. Careful observation and common sense are the best possible approaches to any repair procedure.

Removal and installation of the engine can be made easier if you follow these basic points:

• If you have to drain any of the fluids, use a suitable container.

• Always tag any wires or hoses and, if possible, the components they came from before disconnecting them.

• Because there are so many bolts and fasteners involved, store and label the retainers from components separately in muffin pans, jars or coffee cans. This will prevent confusion during installation.

• After unbolting the transmission or transaxle, always make sure it is properly supported.

• If it is necessary to disconnect the air conditioning system, have this service performed by a qualified technician using a recovery/recycling station. If the system does not have to be disconnected, unbolt the compressor and set it aside.

• When unbolting the engine mounts, always make sure the engine is properly supported. When removing the engine, make sure that any lifting devices are properly attached to the engine. It is recommended that if your engine is supplied with lifting hooks, your lifting apparatus be attached to them.

• Lift the engine from its compartment slowly, checking that no hoses, wires or other components are still connected.

• After the engine is clear of the compartment, place it on an engine stand or workbench.

• After the engine has been removed, you can perform a partial or full teardown of the engine using the procedures outlined in this manual.

CR-V

♦ See Figures 1, 2, 3 and 4

The engine and transaxle assembly are removed as a unit from the vehicle.

1. Note the radio security code and station presets.

2. Disconnect the negative and then the positive battery cables.

3. Raise the hood and mark the positions of the hinge plates with a felt-tipped marker. Protect the inner corners of the hood with shop towels or soft cardboard Remove the hood and place it out of the work area to avoid scratching the paint.

4. Remove the battery. Disconnect the ground cable from the battery tray. Unbolt and remove the battery tray and its support bracket.

5. Remove the front lower splash shield and guard bar. There are three types of fasteners securing these in place:

    a. The inner fender fasteners are two pieces. The inner button looking piece must be carefully pried out of the holder, then the holder can be removed.

    b. The guard bar and front center fasteners are attached with a 6mm bolt and are removed with a 10mm socket, on a 6 inch extension and a ratchet.

    c. The outer forward fasteners are Phillips head screws.

6. Relieve the fuel system pressure as outlined in Section 5.

7. Drain the cooling system into a sealable container.

8. Drain the engine oil and the automatic transmission fluid into a sealable container, but do not use the same container as used for the coolant. Reinstall the drain plugs using a new sealing washer.

9. Disconnect the upper and lower radiator hoses.

10. Remove the air cleaner housing and duct hose assembly.

11. Detach the engine cooling fan electrical connector, then remove the fan with the shroud by removing the bolts that attach it to the radiator.

12. Locate the engine wiring harness, throttle linkage, and all hoses or lines that attach to the engine or transmission and do the following:

13. Make a drawing and/or label the following

components for the routing and connection location:

• The engine wiring harness routing and connector location
• The fuel lines
• The throttle linkage
• The hoses that attach to the engine, including the cooling, fuel and vacuum hoses

14. Detach all the electrical connectors, fuel lines, throttle linkage and hoses from the engine. Make sure to label the connections as needed to aid installation.

15. If equipped with an automatic transaxle, place a drain pan below the transmission cooler lines, at the bottom of the radiator. Label and disconnect the transmission cooler lines from the radiator, and plug the fittings and the lines.

16. Remove the bolts that attach the radiator to the front inner fender support and remove the radiator.

17. Remove the accessory drive belts, as outlined in Section 1.

18. Remove the power steering mounting fasteners, and the hose guide clamps, but **do not** remove the hoses. Position it out of the way on a shop towel to avoid scratches, and secure it with suitable sturdy nylon type ties or mechanic's wire.

.19. If equipped with A/C, remove the compressor from the engine bracket assembly leaving the hoses attached. Position it out of the way on a shop towel to avoid scratches, and secure it with suitable sturdy nylon type ties or mechanic's wire.

20. On vehicles with manual transaxle, perform the following:

    a. Remove the slave cylinder and clutch hose bracket bolts and place the slave cylinder aside with the hoses attached, taking care not to bend the pipe.

    b. Remove the bolt that attaches the ground cable to the transaxle case.

    c. Remove the cotter keys and bolts securing the shift cable assembly to the shift linkage. Be sure to note that the location of the plastic washer should between the cable end and the steel washer.

➡**Be careful not to bend or kink the cable when removing it.**

21. Raise and safely support the vehicle.

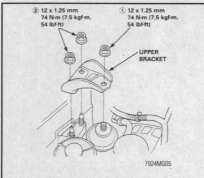

Fig. 1 Upper bracket tightening sequence—CR-V models

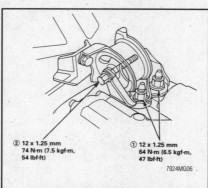

Fig. 2 Transition mount fastener tightening sequence and values—CR-V models

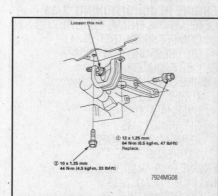

Fig. 3 Right front mount/bracket tightening sequence—CR-V models

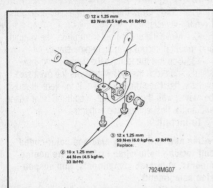

① 12 x 1.25 mm
83 N·m (8.5 kgf·m, 61 lbf·ft)

③ 12 x 1.25 mm
59 N·m (6.0 kgf·m, 43 lbf·ft)
Replace.

② 10 x 1.25 mm
44 N·m (4.5 kgf·m,
33 lbf·ft)

7924MG07

Fig. 4 Left front mount/bracket tightening sequence—CR-V models

22. Unplug electrical connection for the Heated Oxygen Sensor (HO2S) at the front pipe.

23. Remove the fasteners for the front exhaust pipe at the exhaust manifold and the exhaust pipe joint and remove the pipe. Use care to not damage the HO2S handling the pipe.

24. On vehicles with an automatic transmission:

  a. Remove the three bolts for the shift linkage cover.

  b. Remove the snap pin from the control pin and remove the cable.

  c. Remove the ground cable from the transmission housing.

➡ **Be careful not to bend or kink the cable when removing it.**

25. Remove the front wheels.

26. Remove the halfshafts. Refer to Section 7 for specific details on removal.

27. On models with Four Wheel Drive (4WD), perform the following:

  a. Make matchmarks on the output shaft flange and the driveshaft flange prior to removal for proper alignment when reinstalling.

  b. Remove the four bolts that attach the driveshaft to the transfer assembly and separate them.

28. Remove the A/C hose clamp bracket nut and bolt and remove the bracket.

29. Attach a hoist to the engine and take up the engine weight and do the following:

  a. Remove the left and right front engine mounts.

  b. Remove the rear mount bracket bolt.

  c. Remove the upper bracket from the mount on the left side near the cylinder head.

  d. Remove the upper transmission mount bracket, and then remove the mount.

➡ **Note that some engine mount pieces have arrows on them for proper assembly.**

30. Double-check that all cables, hoses, wiring harnesses, etc., are disconnected from the engine.

31. Lift the engine slowly from the engine compartment about 6 inches and recheck that all cables, hoses, wiring harnesses, etc., are disconnected from the engine.

32. Raise the engine from the vehicle.

To install:

➡ **Install the mounting nuts/bolts in the sequence presented. Failure to follow the sequence may cause excessive noise and vibration, and reduce bushing life.**

33. Slowly lower the engine into the engine compartment.

34. Install the rear mount bracket mounting bolt, but do not tighten it yet.

35. Install the mount and bracket. Tighten the bolts on the frame side to 47 ft. lbs. (64 Nm).

36. Install the upper bracket and tighten the nuts according to the accompanying illustration.

37. Tighten the nuts/bolts on the transmission mount in sequence as shown.

38. Tighten the rear mount bracket mounting bolt to 43 ft. lbs. (59 Nm).

39. Install and tighten the right and left front mounts/brackets according to the accompanying illustration.

40. Tighten the right front mount to 43 ft. lbs. (59 Nm).

41. The remainder of the installation of the engine/transaxle is the reverse order of the removal procedure.

42. Refill the engine with fresh oil.

43. Refill the transaxle with the recommended fluid.

The manual and automatic transaxles use two different types of fluid. To avoid severe internal damage, refer to Section 1 for the correct fluid type for the engine and transaxle assembly.

44. Start the engine and allow it to reach normal operating temperature.

45. Check all fluid levels and top off if necessary. Check for signs of fluid or fuel leaks.

46. Check the operation of the heater and air conditioner.

47. Enter the radio security code.

48. Road test the vehicle and check the transaxle shift points and the operation of all engine-driven accessories, such as power steering and air conditioning.

Odyssey

4-CYLINDER ENGINES

▶ **See Figure 5**

➡ **The engine and transaxle are removed from the vehicle as a unit. A hydraulic lift is helpful for this procedure since the front subframe must be removed for the engine/transaxle assembly to be lowered from the vehicle. If a hydraulic lift is not available, the vehicle must raised and safely supported to allow enough clearance for the engine to be removed from underneath the vehicle.**

1. Note the radio security code and station presets.

2. Disconnect the negative battery cable first and then disconnect the positive battery cable.

3. Raise the hood and mark the positions of the hinge plates with a felt-tipped marker. Remove the hood and move it out of the work area to avoid scratching the paint.

4. Loosen the throttle cable and cruise control cable locknuts. Remove both cables from their brackets and slip them out of their linkages.

5. Remove the intake air duct.

6. Remove the battery. Disconnect the ground cable from the battery tray. Unbolt and remove the battery tray and its support bracket.

7. Drain the engine oil, transaxle fluid, and engine coolant into separate, sealable containers.

Never open, service or drain the radiator or cooling system when hot; serious burns can occur from the steam and hot coolant. Also, when draining engine coolant, keep in mind that cats and dogs are attracted to ethylene glycol antifreeze and could drink any that is left in an uncovered container or in puddles on the ground. This will prove fatal in sufficient quantities. Always drain coolant into a sealable container. Coolant should be reused unless it is contaminated or is several years old.

8. Disconnect the battery cable from the fuse/relay box and ABS relay box.

9. Uncouple the three engine harness connectors located on the right side of the engine compartment.

10. Disconnect the brake booster vacuum hose and EVAP canister hose from the intake manifold plenum.

11. Relieve the fuel system pressure as outlined in Section 5.

12. Disconnect the fuel line and the return hose from the fuel rail. Clean up any spilled fuel.

13. Disconnect the three vacuum hoses from the left side of the intake manifold. Unclamp the power steering hose.

14. Uncouple the three engine harness connectors located on the left side of the engine compartment. Unplug the fuel injector resistor connector.

15. Loosen the power steering pump adjusting bolt and mount bolts. Slip the belt off its pulleys.

16. Unbolt and remove the power steering pump, but do not disconnect its hydraulic lines. Wire the pump away from the engine.

17. Disconnect the alternator. Loosen and remove the alternator belt.

18. Unbolt and remove the alternator and its mounting bracket.

19. Disconnect and remove the upper and lower radiator hoses.

20. Remove the radiator with both cooling fans attached to it.

21. Disconnect the heater hoses from the coolant pipe under the intake manifold.

22. Disconnect the two cooler lines from the front of the transaxle case. Plug the inlet lines on the transaxle case to prevent moisture contamination.

23. Unbolt the A/C compressor from the side of the engine block. **Do not** disconnect the A/C lines. Wire the compressor to the radiator support so it's out of the work area.

24. Attach a chain hoist to the lifting hooks on either side of the engine block.

25. Raise and safely support the vehicle. Take up the slack of the chain hoist.

26. Disconnect the Heated Oxygen (HO2S) sensor wiring harness. Leave the sensor installed in the exhaust pipe.

27. Separate the exhaust pipe from the catalytic converter and the exhaust manifold and remove it.

28. Matchmark the subframe center beam to the rear beam. Remove the two bolts, but don't remove the center beam at this point.

29. Remove the shift cable cover. Disconnect the shift cable from the control shaft and suspend it out of the way with wire.

30. Remove the splash shield and the front wheels.

31. Remove the damper fork flange bolts from the lower control arms. Unbolt the damper fork from the strut and remove it from the vehicle.

32. Use a ball joint removal tool to separate the lower control arms from the steering knuckles.

33. Use a prytool to detach the left and right halfshafts from the intermediate shaft and transaxle case. Tap the splined shafts out of the hubs using a plastic mallet. Move the halfshafts out of the way and wire them up. Tie plastic bags over the halfshaft ends to protect the boots and splined shafts.

34. Unbolt and remove the front engine mount bracket.

✳✳ WARNING

The next step involves the removal of the subframe front beam. Be sure the vehicle is securely supported. Take up any slack in the chain hoist to support the weight of the engine and transaxle assembly.

35. Support the subframe front beam with a transmission jack and a sturdy wood plank.

36. Unbolt the front beam with the center beam, front engine mount, radius rods, and lower control arms attached to it. Lower the front beam assembly from the vehicle.

37. Remove the through-bolt to separate the rear mount from its bracket.

38. Unbolt and remove the side engine mount.

39. Unbolt and remove the transaxle side mount.

40. Verify that all hoses, wires, and vacuum lines have been disconnected from the engine.

41. Slowly lower the engine/transaxle assembly from the vehicle.

42. Move the engine out from under the vehicle and mount it securely on an engine stand.

43. Support the front of the vehicle with jackstands and block the rear wheels, as the front suspension has been disassembled. If the vehicle must be moved with the engine out, install the front beam and all the suspension components.

To install:

➡**Use new self-locking nuts and color-coded self-locking bolts when installing the engine mounts, subframe components, and suspension components.**

44. Raise and safely support the vehicle.

45. Move the engine/transaxle assembly into position under the vehicle and attach a chain hoist to the engine lifting hooks.

46. Carefully lift the engine/transaxle assembly into position in the vehicle.

47. Install the side engine mount. Use a 6mm punch or similarly-sized tool to steady the mount. Install the nut and bolts. Tighten the bolt to 47 ft. lbs. (64 Nm), and remove the 6mm punch. Only hand-tighten the nut and bolt on the engine side of the mount.

48. Install the transaxle side mount. Use a 6mm punch or similarly-sized tool to steady the mount. Install and only hand-tighten the nuts. Install the bolt and tighten it to 47 ft. lbs. (64 Nm).

49. Connect the rear mount bracket and tighten its bolt to 47 ft. lbs. (64 Nm).

50. Install the front beam assembly. Install and only hand-tighten the new color-coded bolts.

51. Align the center beam and rear beam matchmarks. Install the two bolts and tighten them to 37 ft. lbs. (50 Nm).

52. Tighten the front beam bolts to 47 ft. lbs. (64 Nm).

53. Connect the lower control arms and stabilizer bar links. Be sure that all the stabilizer link spacers and washers are properly positioned. Only hand-tighten the fasteners at this time.

54. Install the front engine mount bracket and only hand-tighten the three bolts. Tighten the mount through-bolt to 47 ft. lbs. (64 Nm).

55. Tighten the side engine mount nut and bolt to 47 ft. lbs. (64 Nm) each.

56. Tighten each of the three transaxle side mount nuts to 28 ft. lbs. (38 Nm).

57. Tighten each of the three front engine mount bracket bolts to 28 ft. lbs. (38 Nm).

58. Install new set rings onto the inboard splined shaft of halfshaft. Install the halfshafts, making sure that each snaps securely into place.

59. Reconnect the lower control arm to the steering knuckle ball joint. Tighten the castle nut to 36–43 ft. lbs. (49–59 Nm). Then, tighten the nut only enough to install a new cotter pin.

60. Connect the shift cable linkage with a new lockwasher and tighten the bolt to 88 inch lbs. (10 Nm). Install the shift cable cover.

61. Install the exhaust pipe using new gaskets. Tighten the manifold nuts to 40 ft. lbs. (54 Nm). Tighten the converter flange nuts to 16 ft. lbs. (22 Nm). Tighten the bracket nuts to 13 ft. lbs. (18 Nm). Reconnect the O₂S sensor.

62. Move the A/C compressor back into position and tighten the bolts to 16 ft. lbs. (22 Nm).

63. Reconnect the transaxle cooler line hoses.

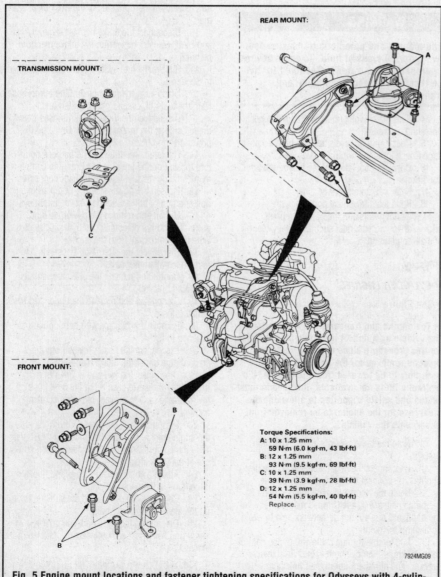

TRANSMISSION MOUNT:

REAR MOUNT:

FRONT MOUNT:

Torque Specifications:
A: 10 x 1.25 mm
   59 N·m (6.0 kgf·m, 43 lbf·ft)
B: 12 x 1.25 mm
   93 N·m (9.5 kgf·m, 69 lbf·ft)
C: 10 x 1.25 mm
   39 N·m (3.9 kgf·m, 28 lbf·ft)
D: 12 x 1.25 mm
   54 N·m (5.5 kgf·m, 40 lbf·ft)
   Replace.

7924MG09

Fig. 5 Engine mount locations and fastener tightening specifications for Odysseys with 4-cylinder engines

64. Install the front wheels and splash shield.

65. Lower the vehicle and remove the chain hoist.

66. With the vehicle on the ground, tighten the damper fork bolt to 47 ft. lbs. (64 Nm). Tighten the pinch bolt to 32 ft. lbs. (44 Nm). Tighten the control arm flange bolt to 40 ft. lbs. (50 Nm). Tighten the stabilizer bar linkage nut to 14 ft. lbs. (19 Nm).

67. Install the remaining components in the reverse order of removal. Please note the following important steps:

    a. Tighten the alternator bracket bolts to 36 ft. lbs. (49 Nm) and the alternator mounting bolts to 33 ft. lbs. (44 Nm). Adjust the tension of both belts.

    b. Tighten the power steering pump mounting nuts to 16 ft. lbs. (22 Nm), then adjust the belt tension.

68. Using a back-up wrench, tighten the fuel line fitting to 6 ft. lbs. (22 Nm), and the service bolt to 106 inch lbs. (12 Nm).

69. Refill the engine with fresh oil.

70. Refill the transaxle with the recommended fluid.

✲✲ WARNING

The manufacturer recommends using their automatic transaxle fluid. To avoid severe internal damage, refer to Section 1 for the correct fluid type for the engine and transaxle assembly.

71. Refill the radiator with a 50⁄50 mixture of a recommended fresh antifreeze and distilled water, and bleed the cooling system.

72. Fit the hood into position and loosely install the hinge bolts. Align the hinges with their matchmarks and tighten the bolts to 88 inch lbs. (10 Nm). Close the hood and check its alignment with the fenders, bumper, and windshield. Be sure the windshield washer fluid tube is connected.

73. Check the shift cable adjustment.

74. Start the engine and allow it to reach normal operating temperature.

75. Check all fluid levels and top off if necessary. Check for signs of fluid or fuel leaks.

76. Check the operation of the heater and air conditioner.

77. Check and adjust the front wheel alignment.

78. Enter the radio security code.

79. Road test the vehicle and check the transaxle shift points and the operation of all engine-driven accessories, such as power steering and air conditioning.

V6 ENGINE

▶ See Figures 6, 7, 8 and 9

➡The engine and transaxle are removed from the vehicle as a unit. A hydraulic lift is helpful for this procedure since the front subframe must be removed for the engine/transaxle assembly to be lowered from the vehicle. If a hydraulic lift is not available, the vehicle must raised and safely supported to allow enough clearance for the engine to be removed from underneath the vehicle.

1. Note the radio security code and station presets.

2. Disconnect the negative battery cable first and then disconnect the positive battery cable.

3. Raise the hood and mark the positions of the hinge plates with a felt-tipped marker. Remove the hood and move it out of the work area to avoid scratching the paint.

4. Remove emissions canister evaporative hose from the throttle body.

5. Disconnect both the vacuum hose and breather pipe from the intake air duct.

6. Remove the intake air duct from the intake manifold throttle body.

7. Remove the battery.

8. Disconnect the engine wire harness connectors located on the left side of the engine compartment.

9. Disconnect the ground cable from the battery tray, remove the relay bracket, and the wire harness clamp. Unbolt and remove the battery support tray.

10. Loosen the throttle cable and cruise control cable locknuts. Remove both cables from their brackets and slip them out of their linkages. Use care not to kink or bend the cables. Always replace a damaged cable.

✲✲ CAUTION

The fuel injection system remains under pressure after the engine has been turned OFF. Properly relieve fuel pressure before disconnecting any fuel lines. Failure to do so may result in fire or personal injury.

11. Relieve the residual fuel pressure in the fuel lines before removing. To relieve fuel line pressure remove the fuel filler cap, place a suitable rag or shop towel over the fuel pulsation damper and slowly loosen the fuel pulsation damper one complete turn using a suitable wrench. Always replace the sealing washers whenever the pulsation damper is removed or loosened.

12. Remove the fuel inlet and return hoses.

13. Remove the large and small diameter vacuum hoses from the brake booster.

14. Locate the Powertrain Control Module (PCM) found in the front passenger side foot well area and disconnect the drivetrain wire harness from the PCM control module at the connectors.

15. Locate the drivetrain wire harness in the engine compartment and remove all the wire harness clamps.

16. Loosen the drivetrain wire harness grommet mounting nuts on the firewall and turn the grommet counterclockwise to release the grommet and carefully pull out the grommet with the wire harness.

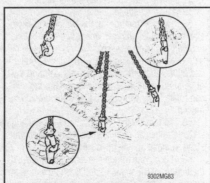

Fig. 6 The engine should be safely supported in three places before removing the lower subframe on V6 Odyssey engines

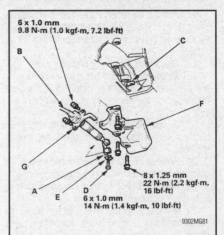

Fig. 7 Shifter cable, cover and bracket tightening torque. (A) Control lever (B) Shift cable (C) Control shaft (D) Lock bolt (E) Locking tab (F) cable cover (G) cable holder—V6 Odyssey

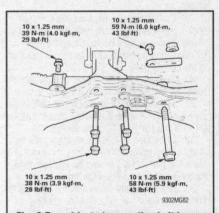

Fig. 8 Rear drivetrain mounting bolt location and tightening specifications—V6 Odyssey

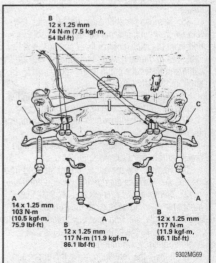

Fig. 9 Subframe fastener locations and tightening specifications—Odyssey V6 models

17. Remove the battery cable from the combination fuse and relay box located in the engine compartment, and remove all the harness clamps for the cable.

18. Disconnect the engine ground cable.

19. Move the alternator belt tensioner with a belt tensioner release arm or suitable tool to relieve the tension on the alternator belt, and remove the belt.

20. Loosen the power steering pump adjustment nut, and remove the adjustment locknut and mounting bolt.

21. Remove the pump drive belt and pump assembly without removing power steering hoses.

22. Remove the bolt that secures power steering hose guide clamp to the engine.

23. Remove the starter motor battery cable from the starter motor solenoid and disconnect the cable clamp.

24. Carefully loosen the radiator cap and remove the cap.

25. Raise the vehicle to a working height that will enable access to the vehicle underbody.

26. Remove the front road wheels.

27. Remove the front lower engine splash shield.

28. Drain the engine oil, transaxle fluid, and engine coolant into separate, sealable containers.

29. Disconnect the Heated Oxygen Sensor (HO2S) wiring harness. Leave the sensor installed in the exhaust pipe.

30. Separate the exhaust pipe from the catalytic converter and the exhaust manifolds and remove it.

31. Remove the damper fork flange bolts from the lower control arms. Unbolt the damper fork from the strut and remove it from the vehicle.

32. Disconnect both stabilizer lower links by using a 6mm hex type wrench to hold the end of the lower link ball socket threaded spindle and remove the mounting nut to release the link.

33. Use a ball joint removal tool to separate the lower control arm ball joint from the steering knuckle.

34. Use a suitable prytool to detach the left and right halfshafts from the intermediate shaft and transaxle case. Tie plastic bags over the exposed halfshaft ends to protect the boots and splined shafts.

35. Remove the shift cable holder bolts, then remove the cover. Disconnect the shift cable locking bolt from the cable control lever and suspend the cable out of the way without bending or kinking the cable and fasten the cable to the vehicle under body temporarily with wire.

36. Remove the power steering hose from the clamps securing the hose to the front subframe.

37. Remove the transmission mount lower front and rear nuts.

38. Remove the frame stiffener fasteners and brackets from the subframe.

39. Remove the remaining power steering hose clamps and harness clamps from the subframe.

40. Remove the fasteners and brackets that mount the steering gearbox to the front subframe and remove the steering gear box from the subframe.

41. Remove the bolts that secure the rear engine/transmission mount.

42. Lower the vehicle, remove the upper and lower radiator hoses, and water bypass hoses.

43. Disconnect both heater hoses from the engine.

44. Remove the automatic transmission cooler hoses from the transmission and plug the lines and the hoses to avoid contamination.

45. Attach a suitable engine chain hoist to the lifting hooks provided on the front and rear of the engine.

46. Remove the engine side mount bracket.

47. Remove the engine front mount bracket support nut.

✳✳ WARNING

The next step involves the removal of the subframe front beam. Be sure the vehicle is securely supported. Take up any slack in the chain hoist to support the weight of the engine and transaxle assembly during the subframe removal procedure.

48. Raise the vehicle to allow access to the vehicle's underbody.

49. With the vehicle raised and the vehicle safely supported, take up the slack of the chain hoist attached to the engine lifting brackets to secure the engine/transmission assembly during removal of the lower front subframe.

50. Draw alignment marks for side-to-side and front-to-rear alignment between the subframe and the mounting points on the vehicle to ensure proper subframe alignment during reassembly.

51. Remove the lower front subframe mounting bolts and carefully lower the subframe down and away from the vehicle.

52. Secure the steering gear box to the underbody of the vehicle by using a strong rope wrapped around the passenger side of the steering gear box, and attached to the vehicle securely.

53. Remove the air conditioner compressor mounting bolts from the engine, and remove the air compressor without removing the air conditioner high pressure hoses. Support the compressor in such a way that is safe, and does not allow the compressor to put tension on the hoses or fittings.

54. Check the engine/transmission assembly and verify that all the electrical wiring, vacuum, fuel and coolant hoses are completely disconnected.

55. Carefully and slowly lower the engine and transmission assembly about 6 inches and check again that all the electrical wiring, vacuum, fuel and coolant hoses are completely disconnected.

56. Lower the engine and transmission assembly all the way down.

57. Once the engine and transmission assembly is completely lowered, it can be removed from underneath the vehicle.

58. Support the front of the vehicle with jackstands and block the rear wheels, as the front suspension has been disassembled. If the vehicle must be moved with the engine out, install the subframe and all the suspension components. Support the drive axles so they are level with the ground and can rotate freely without binding while the vehicle is moved.

59. To remove the transmission from the engine so the engine can be placed on a suitable engine stand, remove the intermediate shaft.

60. Locate the torque converter cover plate at the bottom of the transmission housing and remove the cover plate.

61. Rotate the engine crankshaft pulley to access the eight torque converter drive plate bolts

from the bottom of the transmission housing and remove all eight drive plate bolts one at a time.

62. Remove the engine stiffener bolts, starter motor, and the transmission housing bolts.

63. Carefully separate the transmission from the engine, making sure the torque converter assembly remains in the transmission housing and is released from the engine drive plate. If the torque converter is stuck to the engine drive plate, pull it toward the transmission housing from the starter motor opening in the transmission housing.

To install:

➡ **Use new self-locking nuts and color-coded self-locking bolts when installing the engine mounts, subframe components, and suspension components.**

64. If the transmission has been removed from the engine, attach the transmission to the engine and torque the mounting bolts to 47 ft. lbs. (64 Nm).

65. Install the eight torque converter drive plate bolts one at a time and torque to 4 ft. lbs. (6 Nm), one half of the recommended torque of 8 ft. lbs. (12 Nm).

66. Using a crisscross tightening pattern, tighten the eight torque converter bolts to the recommended torque of 104 inch lbs. (12 Nm).

67. After tightening the torque converter bolts rotate the crankshaft in the direction of normal operation and ensure the crankshaft rotates freely.

68. Check the crankshaft pulley bolt torque as necessary. To check torque use a commercially available torque wrench and 3/4 in. (19mm) socket and hold the crankshaft pulley with a holder handle tool number 07JAB-001020A or equivalent, and a hollow offset holder attachment tool number 07MAB-PY3010A or equivalent and torque the bolt to 181 ft. lbs. (245 Nm).

69. Install the intermediate shaft using a new set ring and tighten the mounting bolts to 29 ft. lbs. (39 Nm).

70. Raise and safely support the vehicle.

71. Move the engine/transaxle assembly into position under the vehicle and attach a chain hoist to the engine lifting hooks.

72. Carefully lift the engine/transaxle assembly into position in the vehicle.

➡ **Install the mounting bolts and nuts in the sequence provided. Failure to follow the sequence could cause excessive vibration and noise, and could reduce bushing life.**

73. Install the air conditioner compressor and tighten the bolts to 16 ft. lbs. (22 Nm).

74. Install the front subframe taking care to align the reference marks made during disassembly and torque the bolts to the specifications provided in the illustration of the subframe mount locations and fastener tightening specifications.

75. Install the transmission lower front and rear mounts on the subframe and torque the nuts to 28 ft. lbs. (38 Nm).

76. Install the drive line rear mount on the subframe and tighten the bolts to 28 ft. lbs. (38 Nm).

77. Install the front mount bracket support nut and tighten the nut to 40 ft. lbs. (54 Nm).

78. Install the side engine mount bracket and torque the bracket mounting bolts to 33 ft. lbs. (44 Nm) and then tighten the bushing through bolt to 40 ft. lbs. (54 Nm).

79. Carefully remove the chain hoist from the engine.

80. Install the steering gearbox and mounting brackets and torque the mounting bolts to 29 ft. lbs. (39 Nm).

81. Install the power steering hose guide clamps, and harness clamp.

82. Install the frame stiffeners, then torque the nuts and bolts to 43 ft. lbs. (58 Nm).

83. Install the power steering hose support clamp bolt and install the hose into the remaining support clamps.

84. Install new spring clips on both inner axle splined shafts, and install the drive shafts making sure the clips "click" into place in the intermediate shaft and the differential.

85. Connect the lower ball joints and the stabilizer linkage.

86. Connect the damper forks.

87. Install the exhaust pipe using new gaskets and self locking nuts. Torque the exhaust manifold to exhaust pipe nuts to 40 ft. lbs. (54 Nm), install the exhaust pipe flange to the mating exhaust pipe mounting flange, and tighten the nuts to 25 ft. lbs. (33 Nm). Tighten the exhaust pipe hanger mounting bolt to 28 ft. lbs. (38 Nm).

88. Attach the HO_2S electrical connection.

89. Carefully and without kinking the cable, install the shift selector control cable on the shaft using a new lock tab washer. Tighten the mounting bolt to 10 ft. lbs. (14 Nm).

90. Install the shift cable cover tightening the bolts to 16 ft. lbs. (22 Nm).

91. Install the shift cable holder onto the cover and torque the bolts to 104 inch lbs. (12 Nm).

92. Install the front lower splash shield.

93. Install the front wheel and tire assemblies.

94. Carefully lower the vehicle.

95. Install the upper and lower radiator hoses and the water bypass hoses.

96. Install the heater hoses.

97. Install the transmission cooler hoses.

98. Install the starter motor cable and cable guide clamp.

99. Install the alternator drive belt, then loosely install the power steering pump and drive belt.

100. Adjust the power steering belt to a tension such that a 22 pound pull halfway between the two drive pulleys will allow the belt to move 0.51–0.65 in. (13.0–16.5mm).

101. Tighten the power steering pump mounting bolt and adjustment lock nut.

➡If a new belt is used set the deflection to 0.33–0.43 in. (8.5–11mm) and after the engine has run for five minutes readjust the new belt to the used belt specification.

102. Install the battery cable to the under hood combination fuse and relay box, and install all the cable harness clamps.

103. Route the engine PCM harness through the firewall, fasten all the harness clamps, install the grommet on the firewall and tighten the mounting nuts.

104. Attach the PCM connectors to the PCM control module.

105. Install the brake booster vacuum hoses.

106. Install the fuel return line and fuel feed hose using new sealing washers.

107. Install the cruise control and throttle cables.

108. Install the battery tray, ground cable, relay box bracket and wire harness clamp.

109. Attach the engine wire harness connections on the left side of the engine compartment.

110. Install the air intake duct, and connect the vacuum hose and breather pipe to the duct.

111. Install the control canister hose to the throttle body.

112. Install the battery and inspect the battery terminals. Clean the terminals if needed and install the positive battery cable first and then the negative battery cable.

113. Refill the engine oil, and refill the automatic transmission to the correct level using the recommended transmission fluid.

114. Refill the radiator with the proper mix of engine coolant with the heater valve open, and bleed the air from the cooling system.

115. Move the gear selector lever to each gear position and verify that the transmission gear position indicator follows the transmission gear position switch.

116. Inspect the vehicle for fluid leaks. Turn the ignition switch to the **RUN** position but do not attempt to start the engine. The fuel pump should operate for approximately two seconds and pressurize the fuel lines. Continue to turn the ignition switch **ON** and **OFF** two or three times without starting the engine. Recheck the vehicle for any fuel line leaks.

117. Fit the hood into position and loosely install the hinge bolts. Align the hinges with their matchmarks and tighten the bolts to 88 inch lbs. (10 Nm). Close the hood and check its alignment with the fenders, bumper, and windshield. Be sure the windshield washer fluid tube is connected.

118. Start the engine and allow it to reach normal operating temperature.

119. Check for proper adjustment of the cruise control and throttle cables once the engine has been started, reaches normal operating temperature, and is idling at the normal idle speed. The correct cable free play for the cruise control cable should be 0.13–0.17 in. (3.25–4.25mm). The throttle cable should have enough free play that the cable can be moved side to side ⅜–½inch (10–12mm) at the throttle linkage.

120. Check all fluid levels and top off if necessary. Check for signs of fluid or fuel leaks.

121. Check the operation of the heater and air conditioner.

122. Verify proper wheel alignment and adjust as needed.

123. Enter the radio security code and radio presets.

124. Road test the vehicle and check the transaxle shift points and the operation of all engine-driven accessories, such as power steering, heating, and air conditioning.

Rocker Arm (Cam/Valve) Cover

REMOVAL & INSTALLATION

CR-V and 4-Cylinder Odyssey Models

▸ See Figures 10 thru 15

1. Tag the spark plug wires, then remove the spark plug wires by twisting side to side and gently pulling.

2. Starting from the outside and working inward, using a 10mm wrench or socket with an extension and ratchet, remove the fasteners securing the valve cover to the cylinder head.

3. If equipped, remove all hoses and brackets.

4. Carefully lift the cover off the cylinder head. Use care to not lose the sealing grommets when lifting the cover. Place the cover upright in a clean, protected area. If the cover is stuck onto the cylin-

93133P23

Fig. 10 Using reference marks to note bracket locations during valve cover removal will speed reassembly, and make sure the brackets are reinstalled where they belong

93131P87

Fig. 11 A trim panel removal tool is very useful when removing the valve cover sealing grommets

93131P86

Fig. 12 Once the plug wires, EGR valve, fasteners and all of the grommets are removed, using a suitable prytool, carefully pry the valve cover up a little at a time on both sides until it is loose

Fig. 13 Squeeze the hose clamp to release the tension and slide it back, then carefully slide the breather hose off the nipple

Fig. 14 As a vehicle ages, the rubber seals and hoses tend to become brittle. Because this PCV valve is made of plastic, removing the hose is a safer alternative than trying to remove the valve

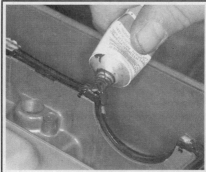

Fig. 15 Always apply a non-hardening gasket sealant to all of the right angle corners of the half-moon areas of the valve cover gasket during reassembly

der head, use a suitable prytool to carefully pry the cover upward at the corners. Move each corner no more than a ¹⁄₁₆ of an inch at a time.

To install:

5. Thoroughly clean and inspect the gasket surface of the cover and cylinder head. Rubbing alcohol or a suitable brake cleaner works well for this application.

❊❊ WARNING

Protect the eyes and exposed skin from contact with cleaning agents. Do not use near an open flame.

6. Inspect the rubber valve cover gasket, the sealing grommets, and the seal around the spark plug holes. If the gasket or seals are brittle, cracked or damaged, replace them. If the old gasket and seals are not worn or damaged they can be reused once cleaned.

To clean the valve cover gasket, perform the following:

- Place the gasket in a suitable, clear plastic bag.
- Spray a small amount of brake cleaner, or pour about 2 ounces of rubbing alcohol into the bag.
- Close the end of the bag and swish the cleaning fluid around, making certain the entire gasket has been thoroughly saturated. Do not leave the gasket in the bag for more than 5 minutes.
- Remove the gasket, and wipe clean with a paper towel or clean soft cloth.

7. Apply a liquid, non-hardening gasket sealant, such as Honda sealant part No. 08718-0001 or 08718-0003 to the valve cover side of the spark plug opening seals and press them into the valve cover.

8. Install the valve cover gasket securely into the groove in the valve cover.

9. Apply a ½ inch bead of sealant to the corners of the gasket, where the gasket meets the cylinder head and the camshaft journal cap.

10. Install the grommets if removed, and tighten the valve cover fasteners from the inside out evenly in three steps. Tighten the fasteners to 86 inch lbs. (9.8 Nm).

11. The remainder of the assembly procedure is the reverse of the removal sequence.

V6 Odyssey Models

The engine trim covers, upper timing belt cover, and intake manifold assembly must be removed to access the valve covers. The intake manifold gasket must be replaced once the manifold is removed.

1. Remove the intake manifold, as outlined in the intake manifold removal procedure in this section.

2. Label and detach the electrical connectors from the ignition coils.

3. Remove the ignition coil assemblies.

4. Starting from the outside, working inward, using a 10mm wrench or socket with an extension and ratchet, remove the fasteners securing the valve cover to the cylinder head.

5. Carefully lift the cover off the cylinder head. Use care to not loose the sealing grommets when lifting the cover. Place the cover upright in a clean, protected area. If the cover is stuck onto the cylinder head, using a suitable prytool carefully pry the cover upward at the corners. Move each corner no more than a ¹⁄₁₆ of an inch at a time.

To install:

6. Thoroughly clean and inspect the gasket surface of the cover and cylinder head. Rubbing alcohol or a suitable brake cleaner works well for this application.

❊❊ WARNING

Protect the eyes and exposed skin from contact with cleaning agents. Do not use near an open flame.

7. Inspect the rubber valve cover gasket, the sealing grommets, and the seal around the spark plug holes. If the gasket or seals are brittle, cracked or damaged, replace them. If the old gasket and seals are not worn or damaged they can be reused once cleaned.

To clean the valve cover gasket:

- Place the gasket in a suitable, clear plastic bag.
- Spray a small amount of brake cleaner, or pour about 2 ounces of rubbing alcohol into the bag.
- Close the end of the bag and swish the cleaning fluid around, making certain the entire gasket has been thoroughly saturated. Do not leave the gasket in the bag for more than 5 minutes.

- Remove the gasket, and wipe clean with a paper towel or clean soft cloth.

8. Apply a liquid, non-hardening gasket sealant, such as Honda sealant part No. 08718-0001 or 08718-0003 to the valve cover side of the spark plug opening seals and press them into the valve cover.

9. Install the valve cover gasket securely into the groove in the valve cover.

10. Install the grommets if removed, and tighten the valve cover fasteners from the inside out evenly in three steps. Tighten the fasteners to 86 inch lbs. (9.8 Nm).

11. The remainder of the assembly procedure is the reverse of the removal sequence.

➡The intake manifold gasket must be replaced and the tightening sequence must be followed, otherwise the engine running performance could be compromised.

Rocker Arm/Shafts

REMOVAL & INSTALLATION

CR-V

▶ **See Figures 16 thru 21**

➡On the CR-V, the rockers pivot on individual pedestals and do not use rocker shafts. The rockers are located underneath the camshafts, therefore the camshafts must be removed to access the rockers.

1. Note the radio security code and station presets.

2. Disconnect the negative battery cable.

3. Remove the cylinder head valve cover.

4. Rotate the crankshaft in direction of operation until both camshaft sprockets have the **UP** at the top, and the Top Dead Center (TDC) marks on the camshaft sprocket and crankshaft are aligned with the pointers.

5. Remove the camshaft timing belt. Refer to the timing belt procedure located in this section.

6. Mark the distributor location for reinstallation and remove the distributor.

7. Loosen the valve adjustment locknuts and adjustment screws.

Fig. 16 The CR-V valve rockers pivot on a pedestal and rest on the valve. The camshaft must be removed to replace the rockers

Fig. 17 The rocker is simply lifted out of place once the camshaft is removed

Fig. 18 Because the cams and rockers develop unique wear patterns over time, it is absolutely necessary to label and reassemble the parts in the exact location from which they were removed

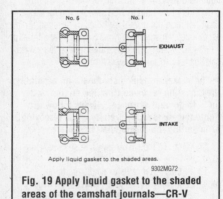

Fig. 19 Apply liquid gasket to the shaded areas of the camshaft journals—CR-V models

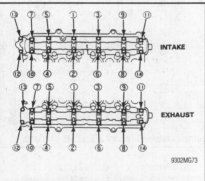

Fig. 20 Camshaft journal torque sequence—CR-V models

Fig. 21 When reassembling the rockers, always check and adjust the valves as necessary

8. Carefully loosen the camshaft journal bolts about ½ a turn at a time until the bolts are loose.

➡️Be sure to note or mark the location of all parts prior to disassembly. All parts must be installed in the exact location from which they were removed.

9. Remove the camshaft journals, camshaft, and rocker arms.

To install:

10. Verify the engine is at TDC by the TDC marks on the crankshaft pulley and the pointer. If the engine is not at TDC, slowly and carefully rotate the crankshaft pulley to align the TDC timing marks.

11. Install the rockers onto the pivots, and lubricate with fresh engine oil.

12. Lubricate the camshaft journals and mounting bolts with fresh engine oil.

13. Place the camshafts in the cylinder head in the correct order, with the **UP** marks at the top and the TDC marks aligned with the TDC pointers.

14. Carefully clean and dry the cylinder head mating surfaces for the camshaft holders and apply a thin layer of a suitable sealant to the outer edges of the number one and number six cam journals on both the intake and exhaust camshaft holders. Refer to the shaded areas of the illustration provided.

15. Replace the cylinder head plug located at the end of the exhaust camshaft.

16. Install the camshaft journals and torque the camshaft journal bolts evenly to 86 inch lbs. (9.8

Nm) following the torque sequence provided in the illustration.

17. Install the timing belt, as outlined in this section.

18. Adjust the valves to the correct clear-ances.

19. Inspect the valve cover gaskets and replace if damaged. Apply a suitable non-hardening sealant to all eight of the corners on the gasket.

20. Install the cylinder head valve cover.

21. Locate the reference mark on the distributor, install the distributor and align the marks.

22. Reconnect the battery ground cable.

23. Start the engine and check for fluid leaks.

24. Top off all fluid levels as necessary.

25. Check the ignition timing and reset if necessary, For specific details see Section 1.

26. Enter the radio security code.

Odyssey

4-CYLINDER ENGINES

▶ See Figures 22, 23 and 24

1. Note the radio security code and station presets.

2. Disconnect the negative battery cable.

3. Remove the valve cover and the upper timing belt cover.

4. Set the No. 1 cylinder to Top Dead Center (TDC) for the compression stroke. Verify that the TDC marks are correctly aligned. Once the engine is set in this position, it must not be disturbed.

5. Remove the distributor as an assembly.

6. Loosen the valve adjusting screws.

7. Cover the timing belt with a clean shop towel to protect it from engine oil. If the belt is contaminated with oil, it must be replaced.

8. Loosen, but DO NOT remove the camshaft holder bolts from their holes in the shaft assemblies. Unscrew the bolts two turns at a time in a crisscross pattern to prevent damaging the valves. camshaft, or rocker arm assembly.

➡️The rocker arms and shafts are an assembly; they must be removed from the engine as a unit. To prevent warpage, always follow the tightening sequence carefully when removing or installing the rocker shaft assembly.

9. Remove the rocker arm and shaft assemblies. Do not remove the camshaft holder bolts from the camshaft holder. The bolts keep the camshaft bearing caps, springs, and rocker arms in place on the shafts.

10. If the rocker arms or shafts are to be replaced, identify the parts as they are removed from the shafts to ensure reinstallation in the original location.

To install:

11. Verify that the engine is set to TDC/compression for the No. 1 cylinder. The camshaft keyway faces up when the engine is at TDC/compression.

12. Lubricate the camshaft journals and lobes with clean engine oil. Install a new camshaft seal if necessary.

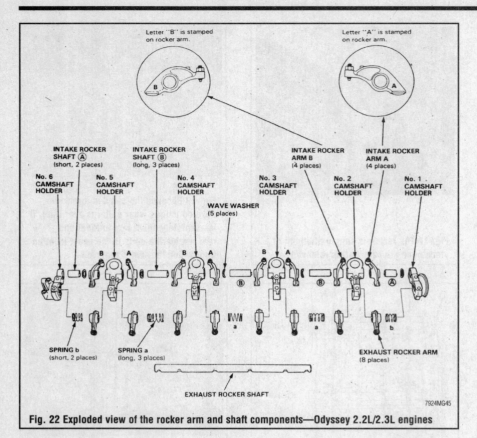

Fig. 22 Exploded view of the rocker arm and shaft components—Odyssey 2.2L/2.3L engines

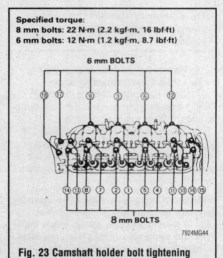

Specified torque:
8 mm bolts: 22 N·m (2.2 kgf·m, 16 lbf·ft)
6 mm bolts: 12 N·m (1.2 kgf·m, 8.7 lbf·ft)

Fig. 23 Camshaft holder bolt tightening sequence—Odyssey 2.2L/2.3L engines

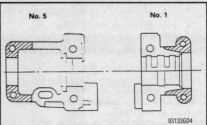

Fig. 24 Apply a suitable sealant to the shaded areas of the outer camshaft holders on Odyssey 2.2L/2.3L engines

13. If necessary, assemble the rocker arms, shafts, and camshaft bearing caps.

14. Apply sealant to the mating surfaces of the first and last camshaft bearing caps. Do not allow the sealant to cure before the rocker arm assembly is installed.

15. Set the rocker arm assembly in place and loosely install the bolts. Tighten each bolt two turns at a time in the proper sequence to ensure that the rockers do not bind on the valves. Tighten the 8mm rocker arm bolts to 16 ft. lbs. (22 Nm). Tighten the 6mm bolts to 104 inch lbs. (12 Nm).

16. Verify that the engine is at TDC/compression, and install the distributor.

17. Adjust the valves and tighten the locknuts to 14 ft. lbs. (20 Nm).

18. Install the valve cover and upper timing belt cover.

19. Reconnect the negative battery cable.

20. Check the ignition timing and adjust if necessary. See Section 1 for specific details. Tighten the distributor mounting bolts to 13 ft. lbs. (18 Nm).

V6 ENGINE

▶ See Figure 25

1. Note the radio security code and station presets.

2. Disconnect the negative battery cable.

3. Set the No. 1 cylinder to Top Dead Center (TDC) for the compression stroke. Verify that the TDC marks are correctly aligned. Once the engine is set in this position, it must not be disturbed.

4. Remove the evaporative hose from the throttle body, and the breather pipe and vacuum hose from the intake duct assembly.

5. Remove the intake duct assembly.

6. Remove the intake manifold and ignition coil covers.

7. Remove the throttle and cruise control cables.

8. Remove the brake booster vacuum hoses and the crankcase ventilation hose.

9. Remove the wire harness connections from the intake manifold electrical components.

10. Locate the intake manifold throttle body and remove the water bypass hoses and the breather hose.

11. Remove the intake manifold.

12. Remove the valve covers and the upper timing belt covers.

13. Verify that the TDC alignment marks line up on the camshaft sprockets.

14. Loosen the valve adjusting screws.

15. Cover the timing belt with a clean shop towel to protect it from engine oil. If the belt is contaminated with oil, it must be replaced.

16. Loosen, but DO NOT remove the rocker shaft holder bolts from their holes in the shaft assemblies. Unscrew the bolts two turns at a time in a crisscross pattern to prevent damaging the valves, camshaft, or rocker arm assembly.

➡The rocker arms and shafts are an assembly; they must be removed from the engine as a unit. To prevent warpage, always follow the tightening sequence carefully when removing or installing the rocker shaft assembly.

17. Remove the rocker arm and shaft assemblies.

18. If the rocker arms or shafts are to be replaced, identify the parts as they are removed from the shafts to ensure reinstallation in the original location.

To install:

19. Lubricate the camshaft lobes and rocker arms with clean engine oil.

20. If necessary, assemble the rocker arms, and shafts.

21. Set the rocker arm assembly in place and loosely install the bolts. Tighten each bolt two turns at a time in the proper sequence to ensure that the rockers do not bind on the valves. Torque the rocker arm bolts to 17 ft. lbs. (24 Nm) following the tightening sequence illustration.

22. Verify that the TDC alignment marks line up on the camshaft and crankshaft pulleys.

23. Adjust the valves and tighten the locknuts to 14 ft. lbs. (20 Nm).

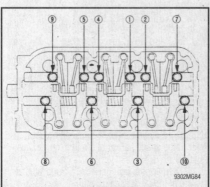

Fig. 25 Rocker shaft tightening sequence—V6 Odyssey

Fig. 26 A thermostat can be tested by placing it in a suitable container filled with water, and heating the water with a hot plate while monitoring the temperature with a thermometer

Fig. 27 The thermostat should open when the water reaches the correct temperature

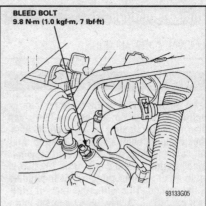

Fig. 28 The coolant bleed screw is located near the thermostat housing on Odysseys with 4-cylinder engines

24. Install the valve covers and the upper timing belt covers.

25. Install the intake manifold.

26. Tighten the bolts in a crisscross pattern from the inside out and torque to 16 ft. lbs. (22 Nm).

27. Locate the intake manifold throttle body and install the water bypass hoses and the breather hose.

28. Install the wire harness connections from the intake manifold electrical components.

29. Install the brake booster vacuum hoses and the crankcase ventilation hose.

30. Install the throttle and cruise control cables.

31. Install the intake manifold and ignition coil covers.

32. Install the intake duct assembly.

33. Install the evaporative hose to the throttle body, and the breather pipe and vacuum hose to the intake duct assembly.

34. Reconnect the negative battery cable.

35. Enter the security code for the radio.

36. Check and top off all fluid levels and check for any fluid leaks.

Thermostat

REMOVAL & INSTALLATION

▶ See Figures 26, 27, 28 and 29

❊❊ CAUTION

Never open, service or drain the radiator or cooling system when hot; serious burns can occur from the steam and hot coolant. Also, when draining engine coolant, keep in mind that cats and dogs are attracted to ethylene glycol antifreeze and could drink any that is left in an uncovered container or in puddles on the ground. This will prove fatal in sufficient quantities. Always drain coolant into a sealable container. Coolant should be reused unless it is contaminated or is several years old.

1. Note the radio security code and station presets.

2. Disconnect the negative battery cable.

3. Drain the engine coolant into a sealable container.

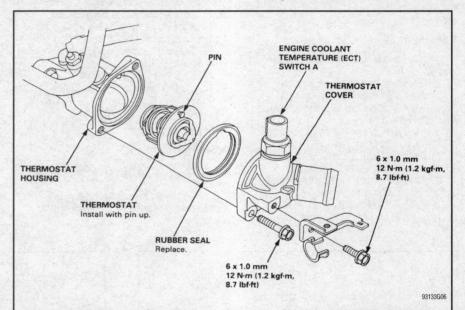

Fig. 29 Always install the thermostat with the small pin at the top. The rubber thermostat seal is installed around the thermostat

4. Remove the fasteners from the thermostat housing, then remove the thermostat.

To install:

5. Install the thermostat using a new seal. If the thermostat has a small bleed hole, make sure the bleed hole is on the top.

6. Apply an anti-seize compound to the threads of the fasteners.

7. Reassemble in the reverse order of disassembly.

8. Set the heater to the full hot position. Set the heater to the full hot position.

9. On Odyssey models with 4-cylinder engines, locate the coolant bleed valve near the thermostat housing and open the valve ½ turn.

10. Top off the cooling system and overflow reservoir with a 50/50 mixture of a recommended antifreeze and water solution.

and bleed the system to remove any air pockets as necessary. Simultaneously squeeze the upper and lower radiator hoses to help push any captured air pockets out of the system.

11. Inspect all coolant hoses and fittings to make sure they are properly installed and if previously opened, close the bleed valve.

12. Connect the negative battery cable.

13. Install the radiator cap loosely and start the engine. Allow the engine to run until the cooling fan has cycled two times, then turn the engine OFF and top off the cooling system as necessary.

14. Install the radiator cap and inspect for leaks.

15. Enter the radio security code.

❊❊ WARNING

The manufacturer does not recommend using a coolant concentration of greater than 60% antifreeze.

➡When mixing a 50/50 solution of antifreeze and water, using distilled water may help to keep the cooling system from building up mineral deposits and internal blockage.

Intake Manifold

REMOVAL & INSTALLATION

✳✳ CAUTION

Never open, service or drain the radiator or cooling system when hot; serious burns can occur from the steam and hot coolant. Also, when draining engine coolant, keep in mind that cats and dogs are attracted to ethylene glycol antifreeze and could drink any that is left in an uncovered container or in puddles on the ground. This will prove fatal in sufficient quantities. Always drain coolant into a sealable container. Coolant should be reused unless it is contaminated or is several years old.

CR-V

▶ See Figure 30

1. Note the radio security code and station presets.
2. Disconnect the negative battery cable.
3. Drain and recycle the engine coolant.
4. Properly relieve the fuel system pressure, as outlined in Section 5.
5. If equipped, disconnect the cruise control cable from the throttle linkage.
6. Detach all electrical connectors associated with the throttle body and intake manifold.
7. Remove the intake air hose, throttle cable, and coolant hoses from the throttle body.
8. Remove the two bolts and two nuts mounting the throttle body to the intake manifold.

9. Remove the two intake manifold support brackets.
10. Unbolt the intake manifold and remove it from the cylinder head. Inspect the manifold for cracks or damage to any of the gasket surfaces. Replace if a fault is found.

To install:

➡**Use new O-rings and gaskets when reassembling.**

11. Clean any old gasket material from the cylinder head, intake manifold, and throttle body.
12. Install a new manifold gasket. Place the manifold into position and support it.
13. Install the support brackets to the manifold. Tighten the bolt holding the brackets to the manifold to 17 ft. lbs. (24 Nm).
14. Starting at the center of the manifold, tighten the nuts in a crisscross pattern to 17 ft. lbs. (24 Nm). The tension must be even across the entire face of the manifold to prevent leaks.
15. Place the throttle body into position and tighten the nuts/bolts to 16 ft. lbs. (22 Nm).
16. The completion of installation is the reverse of the removal procedure.
17. Refill the engine with coolant.
18. Connect the negative battery cable.

Odyssey

4-CYLINDER ENGINES

▶ See Figure 31

1. Note the radio security code and station presets.
2. Disconnect the negative battery cable.
3. Drain the engine coolant into a sealable container.

4. Disconnect the cooling hoses from the intake manifold.
5. Label and disengage the vacuum hoses and electrical connectors on the manifold and throttle body. Unplug the connector from the Exhaust Gas Recirculation (EGR) valve. Position the wiring harnesses out of the way.
6. Disconnect the throttle cable from the throttle body.
7. Disconnect the cruise control cable from the throttle linkage. Unbolt the cable clamp from the valve cover and move the cable out of the way.
8. Relieve the fuel pressure, as outlined in Section 5.

✳✳ CAUTION

The fuel injection system remains under pressure after the engine has been turned-OFF. Properly relieve fuel pressure before disconnecting any fuel lines. Failure to do so may result in fire or personal injury.

9. Remove the fuel rail and fuel injectors. Refer to Section 5 for procedures.
10. Remove the thermostat housing mounting bolts. Gently pull and twist the thermostat housing to remove it from the intake manifold and the coolant connecting pipe. Discard the O-rings.
11. It may be necessary to remove the upper intake manifold chamber and throttle body assembly in order to access the nuts securing the manifold to the head.
12. Unbolt and remove the intake manifold support bracket. If necessary, raise and support the vehicle safely to reach the manifold support bracket.
13. Loosen the intake manifold nuts in a crisscross pattern starting at the edges and working toward the center of the manifold. Supporting the intake manifold, remove the nuts, then the manifold.

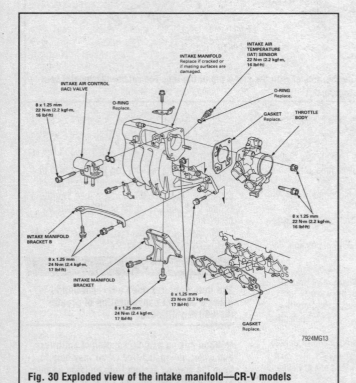

Fig. 30 Exploded view of the intake manifold—CR-V models

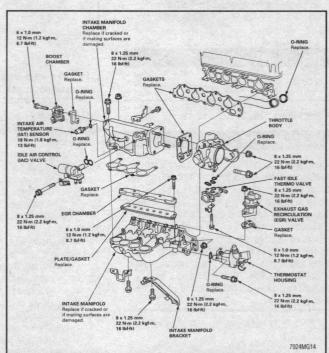

Fig. 31 Exploded view of the intake manifold and related components—4-cylinder Odyssey models

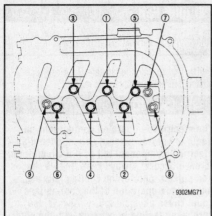

Fig. 32 Intake manifold tightening sequence—V6 Odyssey models

Fig. 33 Before accessing the exhaust manifold mounting fasteners, the heat shield must be removed

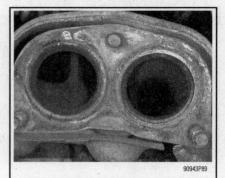

Fig. 34 The manifold studs for the exhaust pipe become rusty over time. Before disassembly, spray the studs with a penetrating lubricant. Use an anti-seize compound when assembling

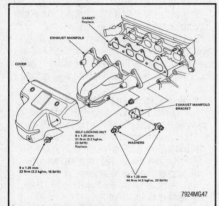

Fig. 35 An exploded view of a typical Honda exhaust manifold

14. Clean any old gasket material from the cylinder head and the intake manifold. Check and clean the chamber and mating surfaces on the cylinder head.

To install:

15. Install a new manifold gasket. Place the manifold into position and support it.

16. Install the support bracket to the manifold. Tighten the bolt holding the bracket to the manifold to 16 ft. lbs. (22 Nm).

17. Starting at the center of the manifold, tighten the nuts in a crisscross pattern to 16 ft. lbs. (22 Nm). The tension must be even across the entire face of the manifold to prevent leaks.

18. If the upper intake manifold chamber and throttle body assembly was removed, install it with a new gasket. Tighten the nuts and bolts to 16 ft. lbs. (22 Nm).

19. Install new O-rings onto the coolant connecting pipe and the thermostat housing. Install the housing to the coolant pipe and the intake manifold. Tighten the mounting bolts to 16 ft. lbs. (22 Nm).

20. Connect and adjust the throttle cable.

21. Install the fuel rail and injector assembly. Reconnect the fuel lines using new sealing washers.

22. Properly position the wiring harnesses and engage the electrical connectors.

23. Connect the cruise control cable and place it back into its clamp on the valve cover. Adjust the

cruise control cable so there is 0.18–0.22 in. (4.5–5.5mm) of free-play at the linkage.

24. Connect the vacuum hoses.

25. Fill and bleed the air from the cooling system.

26. Connect the negative battery cable and enter the radio security code.

27. Start the engine and check carefully for any fuel, coolant, or vacuum leaks. Check the manifold gasket areas carefully for any vacuum leaks.

V6 ENGINE

♦ See Figure 32

1. Note the radio security code and station presets.

2. Disconnect the battery ground cable.

3. Remove the evaporative hose from the throttle body, and the breather pipe and vacuum hose from the intake duct assembly.

4. Remove the intake duct assembly.

5. Remove the intake manifold and ignition coil covers.

6. Remove the throttle and cruise control cables.

7. Remove the brake booster vacuum hoses and the crankcase ventilation hose.

8. Remove the wire harness connections from the intake manifold electrical components.

9. Locate the intake manifold throttle body and remove the water bypass hoses and the breather hose.

10. Remove the intake manifold.

11. Clean any old gasket material from the cylinder head and the intake manifold. Check and clean the chamber and mating surfaces on the cylinder head.

To install:

12. Position a new gasket, then install the intake manifold.

13. Tighten the bolts as illustrated in a crisscross pattern from the inside out and torque to 16 ft. lbs. (22 Nm).

14. Locate the intake manifold throttle body and install the water bypass hoses and the breather hose.

15. Install the wire harness connections from the intake manifold electrical components.

16. Install the brake booster vacuum hoses and the crankcase ventilation hose.

17. Install the throttle and cruise control cables.

18. Install the intake manifold and ignition coil covers.

19. Install the intake duct assembly.

20. Install the evaporative hose to the throttle body, and the breather pipe and vacuum hose to the intake duct assembly.

21. Reconnect the negative battery cable.

22. Enter the security code for the radio.

23. Check and top off all fluid levels and check for any fluid leaks.

Exhaust Manifold

REMOVAL & INSTALLATION

♦ See Figures 33, 34 and 35

1. Note the radio security code and station presets.

2. Disconnect the negative battery cable, then raise and safely support the vehicle.

3. Remove the nuts attaching the front exhaust pipe to the exhaust manifold(s). Separate the pipe from the manifold(s) and discard the gasket. A long extension may be helpful for reaching the nuts.

On Odyssey models with the V6 engine, it may be necessary to remove the bolts from the front pipe exhaust hanger.

4. Remove the exhaust manifold heat shield(s).

5. On models equipped with a support bracket, remove the exhaust manifold bracket bolts and remove the bracket.

6. Loosen the exhaust manifold nuts in a crisscross pattern starting at the edges of the manifold(s) and working toward its center. Remove the nuts.

7. Remove the manifold(s) and discard the gaskets. Clean the manifold(s) and cylinder head mating surfaces.

To install:

8. Install a new exhaust manifold gasket onto the cylinder head(s). Place the manifold(s) into position and support it. Install the nuts snugly onto the studs.

9. On models equipped with a support bracket, install the support bracket below the manifold. Tighten the bracket mounting bolts to 33 ft. lbs. (44 Nm).

10. Starting with the inner or center nuts,

tighten the nuts in a crisscross pattern to 23 ft. lbs. (31 Nm). The tension must be even across the entire face of the manifold to prevent leaks.

11. Install the exhaust manifold heat shield(s) and tighten its bolts to 16 ft. lbs. (22 Nm).

On Odyssey models with the V6 engine, if the bolts for the front pipe exhaust hanger were removed, install the bolts and tighten to 28 ft. lbs. (38 Nm).

12. Connect the front exhaust pipe, using new gaskets and self-locking nuts. Tighten the exhaust pipe attaching nuts to 40 ft. lbs. (55 Nm).

13. Connect the negative battery cable and enter the radio security code.

14. Start the engine and check for exhaust leaks.

Radiator

REMOVAL & INSTALLATION

✳✳ CAUTION

Never open a radiator cap or cooling system when the coolant temperature is above 100°F (38°C). Avoid physical contact at all times, wear protective clothing and eye protection. Always drain coolant into a sealable container. If spillage occurs take care to clean the spill as quickly as possible.

CR-V and 4-Cylinder Odyssey Models

1. Drain the coolant into a sealable container by loosening the radiator drain plug.

2. Remove the upper and lower radiator hoses.

3. If equipped with an automatic transaxle, place a separate sealable drain container under the transaxle Automatic Transmission Fluid (ATF) cooling lines and disconnect, drain and plug the lines and radiator fittings.

4. Detach the electrical connectors for the radiator cooling fans.

5. Remove the two upper radiator support brackets and cushion assemblies.

6. Carefully lift the radiator upward and away from the vehicle.

7. Remove the fasteners that secure the cooling fans to the radiator.

To install:

8. Install the radiator in the reverse order of disassembly.

9. Once installed, on Odyssey models, open the bleed valve on the thermostat housing ½ a turn.

10. Set the heater to the full hot position.

11. Fill the cooling system with a 50/50 mixture of a suitable coolant and water and bleed the air out of the system as necessary. Alternately squeeze the upper and lower radiator hoses to help force out any trapped air pockets. On Odyssey models, close the bleed valve once a steady stream of coolant is visible.

➡ **When mixing a 50/50 solution of coolant and water, using distilled water instead of regular tap water may help prevent the cooling system from internal deposit build-up.**

12. With the radiator cap partially installed, start the engine, and allow the engine to run until the cooling fan runs two times. Turn the engine off and top up the cooling system and overflow reservoir as necessary.

13. Close the radiator cap, restart the engine and check for leaks.

V6 Odyssey Models

1. Note the anti-theft code for the radio and then disconnect the negative battery cable, then disconnect the positive battery cable and remove the battery.

2. Drain the coolant into a sealable container by loosening the radiator drain plug.

3. Remove the upper radiator trim cover by carefully prying out the two piece pressed in plastic fasteners.

4. Remove the wire harness holder next to the stamped Y-shaped support bracket located just behind the grill.

5. Remove the bolts that secure the stamped Y-shaped support bracket, and remove the bracket.

6. Disconnect the wire harness guides from the battery tray.

7. Remove the ground strap and the relay box bracket from the battery tray.

8. Remove the battery tray mounting bolts and remove the battery tray.

9. Remove the wire harness holders from the upper radiator support, and detach the electrical connectors for the cooling fan motors and air conditioning compressor clutch.

10. Remove the upper and lower radiator hoses.

11. Place a separate sealable drain container under the transaxle Automatic Transmission Fluid (ATF) cooling lines, then disconnect, drain and plug the lines and radiator fittings.

12. Remove the upper radiator support bracket/cushion and condenser bracket assembly.

13. Remove the upper cooling fan shroud mounting bolts, and loosen the lower bolts for both cooling fans, and remove the fan assemblies from the battery side of the vehicle.

14. Disconnect the coolant overflow reservoir hose from the radiator cap fitting.

15. Carefully lift the radiator upward and away from the vehicle.

16. If the radiator is being replaced, remove the metal ATF cooler line and transfer parts as needed.

To install:

17. Install the radiator, cooling fans, wires, brackets and battery support in the reverse order of disassembly.

18. Install the positive battery cable, then connect the negative battery cable.

19. Set the heater to the full hot position.

20. Fill the cooling system with a 50/50 mixture of a suitable coolant and water and bleed the air out of the system as necessary. Alternately squeeze the upper and lower radiator hoses to help force out any trapped air pockets.

➡ **When mixing a 50/50 solution of coolant and water, using distilled water instead of regular tap water may help prevent the cooling system from internal deposit build-up.**

21. With the radiator cap partially installed, start the engine, and allow the engine to run until the cooling fan runs two times. Turn the engine off and top up the cooling system and overflow reservoir as necessary.

22. Close the radiator cap, restart the engine and check for leaks.

23. Enter the radio security code.

Engine Fan

REMOVAL & INSTALLATION

The radiator cooling fans are electrically operated and mount directly to the radiator.

✳✳ CAUTION

The electrically operated cooling fans can begin to operate without notice, should an electrical component fail or if a circuit interference occurs. Always keep fingers, hands and objects clear of the cooling fans as unexpected operation of the cooling fans could cause physical injury. Always use care when testing or working with the cooling fans or related equipment.

1. Note the radio security code and disconnect the negative battery cable.

2. Detach the electrical connectors and wiring guide brackets for the cooling fans

3. If additional work space is needed, drain about 3 quarts of coolant from the radiator into a sealable container by loosening the radiator drain plug, then disconnect and plug the upper radiator hose.

4. On V6 Odyssey models:

a. Remove the positive battery cable and remove the battery.

b. Disconnect the wire harness guides from the battery tray.

c. Remove the ground strap and the relay box bracket from the battery tray.

d. Remove the battery tray mounting bolts and remove the battery tray.

e. Remove the wire harness holders from the upper radiator support, and disconnect the electrical connectors for the Air Conditioning compressor clutch.

5. Remove the fan shroud mounting bolts.

6. On CR-V and 4-cylinder Odyssey models, carefully remove the cooling fan assembly from the vehicle.

7. On V6 Odyssey models, carefully remove the cooling fans from the battery side of the vehicle.

To install:

8. The installation is in the reverse order of removal except for the following steps.

9. Top off and bleed the cooling system as necessary.

10. When connecting the battery cables, connect the positive battery cable first, then the negative cable.

11. Enter the radio security code.

12. Start the engine and check for coolant leaks and normal operation of the cooling fans.

TESTING

✳✳ CAUTION

The electrically operated cooling fans can begin to operate without notice, should an electrical component fail or if a circuit interference occurs. Always keep fingers, hands and objects clear of the cooling fans as unexpected operation of the cooling fans could cause physical injury. Always use

care when testing or working with the cooling fans or related equipment.

The electric cooling fans are electrically operated and controlled by two basic electrical circuits. One of the electrical circuits has a temperature sensor which triggers a relay to power the fans. The cooling fan will begin to operate once the coolant temperature reaches the designated temperature of the temperature sensor, which completes the circuit for the fan relay causing the fan to operate.

Possible failures in this circuit include the following:
- A failed relay
- A failed fan motor
- A blown or missing fuse
- A defective ignition switch
- A defective temperature sensor
- Damaged, shorted or disconnected wiring or electrical connector

Possible cooling system problems that could affect the cooling fan operation include:
- Coolant leaks
- Low coolant level
- A restricted radiator
- A failed head gasket
- A defective water pump
- A defective radiator cap
- Excessively contaminated coolant

The second electrical circuit that controls the cooling fans is the air conditioner circuit. When the air conditioning is used, the cooling fans automatically operate, regardless of the engine coolant temperature.

This can be a handy tidbit of information to know should the temperature sensor fail. If the air conditioner is turned on, the cooling fans should function if the A/C system is in proper working order.

Possible failures in this circuit include a faulty A/C switch as well as those items from the previous list.

Electric cooling fan circuit failures can be one of several types:
- The fans fail to operate, either completely or not within the designed temperature range
- The fans run continuously regardless of the coolant temperature with the A/C and ignition switch **OFF**
- The fans run continuously regardless of the coolant temperature only when the ignition switch is **ON** but with the A/C switch off

The danger of a cooling fan that fails to operate is an overheated engine. A cooling fan that runs all the time only when the ignition is **ON** never allows

the engine to fully warm up, and driveability and fuel economy may suffer. A cooling fan that runs all the time even when the ignition is switched **OFF**, never allows the engine to fully warm up, the driveability and fuel economy may suffer, and the battery will eventually discharge.

To test the cooling fans, proceed as follows:
1. Detach the electrical connector for the cooling fan. Consult the wiring schematics in Section 6 for the exact wire color for each fan. The black wire is ground and the colored, striped wire is positive.
2. Carefully connect a 30 amp fused jumper wire between the fan positive wire and the battery positive terminal.
3. Connect a jumper wire between the fan ground terminal and a known good chassis ground and the fan should operate. If the fan fails to operate, check the test circuit with a known good 12 Volt test light to make sure the jumper leads are functioning properly. If the circuit tests OK and the fan fails to function when connected to the jumper circuit, replace the fan. If the jumper circuit fuse blows, check for a shorted fan wire and test again. If the jumper circuit continues to blow the fuse the fan motor is internally shorted and must be replaced.

Water Pump

REMOVAL & INSTALLATION

▶ **See Figures 36, 37 and 38**

1. Note the radio security code and station presets.
2. Disconnect the negative battery cable.
3. Drain the coolant from the radiator, into a suitable container.
4. Remove the timing belt. Refer to the Timing Belt replacement in this section for specific details.
5. On Odyssey models with the V6 engine, remove the timing belt tensioner. Refer to the Timing Belt replacement in this section for specific details.
6. Remove the bolts that attach the pump to the cylinder block.
7. If available, locate the two 6.0 mm x 1.0 mm threaded holes opposite from one another on the outer perimeter of the water pump.

   a. Install by hand, two 6.0mm x 1.0mm bolts at least 1 in. (25mm) long, until resistance is felt.

   b. Simultaneously turn each bolt one turn at

a time until the water pump can be released from the engine block.
8. Remove the water pump.

To install:
9. Inspect and clean the O-ring mating surface on cylinder block.
10. Install a new O-ring on the water pump. Apply a non-hardening gasket sealant between the water pump O-ring and the pump to hold the O-ring in place during assembly.
11. Install the water pump onto the cylinder block and tighten the bolts to 106 inch lbs. (12 Nm).
12. On Odyssey models with the V6 engine, install the automatic timing belt tensioner, with the tensioner fully retracted using the special tool 14540-P8A-A01 or equivalent. Refer to the Timing Belt replacement in this section for specific details.
13. Install the timing belt.
14. On 4-cylinder Odyssey models, open the cooling system bleed bolt located on the thermostat housing.
15. Set the heater to the full hot position.
16. Refill the radiator with a coolant mixture containing 50% antifreeze. Use only antifreeze formulated to prevent the corrosion of aluminum parts. Fill the radiator with the coolant solution.
17. On 4-cylinder Odyssey models, fill with coolant until the bleed bolt is free of air bubbles. Then, tighten the bleed bolt to 88 inch lbs. (10 Nm).
18. Install the radiator cap loosely.
19. Reconnect the negative battery cable.
20. Run the engine until the cooling fans cycle two times.
21. Turn the engine OFF and top off the cooling system as necessary.
22. Install the radiator cap and check for coolant leaks. Be sure the cooling fan turns on.
23. Recheck the coolant level and add more if necessary.
24. Enter the radio security code.

Cylinder Head

REMOVAL & INSTALLATION

✳✳ WARNING

To avoid damaging the cylinder head, allow the coolant temperature to drop below 100°F (38°C) before removing the head bolts.

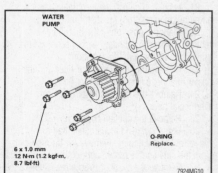

6 x 1.0 mm
12 N·m (1.2 kgf·m, 8.7 lbf·ft)

O-RING
Replace.

WATER PUMP

7924MG10

Fig. 36 Exploded view of the water pump mounting—be sure to replace the O-ring during assembly

93133P25

Fig. 37 If available, use the two 6.0 mm x 1.0 mm threaded holes on the water pump to release the pump from the engine block

93133P24

Fig. 38 Make sure the water pump O-ring is fully seated in the water pump. Using a non hardening gasket sealant will help to hold the seal in place during assembly

Read the procedures before starting to get a thorough understanding of the tools and equipment needed. Many of the components of the cylinder head are precision machined pieces that need to be thoroughly cleaned and inspected before reinstalling. For specific details on the basics of the cylinder head, refer to the ENGINE RECONDITIONING information located further along in this section.

CR-V

▶ **See Figure 39**

1. Note the radio security code and station presets.
2. Disconnect the negative battery cable.
3. Drain and recycle the engine coolant.
4. Remove the air cleaner and the air intake duct.
5. Remove the accessory drive belts.
6. Remove the power steering pump and its bracket.
7. Properly relieve the fuel system pressure, as outlined in Section 5.
8. Disengage all electrical connectors, fuel lines, throttle linkage and hoses from the engine associated with cylinder head removal. Label the connections as needed to aid installation.
9. Remove the spark plug caps, plug wires, and distributor from the cylinder head.
10. Use a jack with a cushioned pad to support the weight of the engine.
11. Remove the valve cover.
12. Remove the timing belt, camshaft sprocket and back cover.
13. Remove the exhaust header pipe from the manifold.
14. Remove the intake manifold mounting bolts and water bypass hose.
15. Remove the camshafts.
16. Remove the cylinder head bolts. To prevent warpage of the cylinder head, loosen the bolts⅓ of a turn in the reverse sequence of the cylinder head tightening sequence.
17. Remove the cylinder head.

To install:
18. Clean the cylinder head and block surface.
19. Clean the oil control orifice and install on the block. Be sure the dowel pins are properly located in the block.
20. Place the new head gasket on the engine block. Apply clean engine oil to the bolt threads and under the bolt heads.
21. Carefully mate the cylinder head to the engine block.

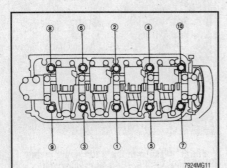

Fig. 39 Cylinder head bolt tightening sequence—all four cylinder engines

7924MG11

22. Tighten the cylinder head in two steps following the illustrated sequence:
   • Step 1: 22 ft. lbs. (29 Nm)
   • Step 2: 63 ft. lbs. (85 Nm)
23. Tighten the intake manifold bolts to 17 ft. lbs. (24 Nm).
24. Install the exhaust header pipe to the exhaust manifold.
25. Install the camshafts and the back cover.
26. Set the camshafts at Top Dead Center (TDC) for No. 1 piston, align the holes in the camshafts with the holes in the No. 1 camshaft holder and insert a 5mm pin punch into the holes.
27. Install the keys into the keyways on the camshafts and install the pulleys, then tighten the retaining bolts to 27 ft. lbs. (37 Nm).
28. Install the timing belt.
29. Adjust the valve clearance, as outlined in Section 1.
30. Install the valve cover and tighten the nuts to 86 inch lbs. (9.8 Nm).
31. Install the spark plug caps, plug wires, and distributor.
32. Install the air cleaner and the air intake duct.
33. Verify that all tubes, hoses and connectors are installed properly.
34. Connect and adjust the throttle cable. Connect and adjust the throttle control cable and the cruise control cable, if equipped.
35. Drain the engine oil into a sealable container. Install the drain plug with a new crush washer.
36. Refill the engine with clean oil.
37. Fill and bleed the air from the cooling system.
38. Connect the positive and the negative battery cables. Enter the radio security code.
39. Start the engine, checking carefully for any coolant, fuel, oil, or air leaks.
40. Check the ignition timing and adjust it if necessary, then tighten the distributor bolts to 13 ft. lbs. (18 Nm).

Odyssey

4-CYLINDER ENGINES

▶ **See Figures 39 and 40**

1. Note the radio security code and station presets.
2. Disconnect the negative and positive battery cables.
3. Remove the valve cover and the upper timing belt cover.
4. Turn the crankshaft to align the Top Dead Center (TDC) marks and set cylinder No. 1 to TDC/compression. The white mark on the crankshaft pulley should align with the pointer on the timing belt cover.
5. Drain the engine coolant into a sealable container.
6. Drain the engine oil into a suitable container.
7. Disconnect the throttle cable and throttle control cable from the throttle body. If equipped with cruise control, remove the cruise control cable.

➡ **Be careful not to bend the cable when removing it. Do not use pliers to remove the cable from the linkage. Always replace a kinked cable with a new one.**

8. Remove the intake air duct.
9. Disconnect and label the breather hose,

Positive Crankcase Ventilation (PCV) hose, and evaporative emissions (EVAP) control canister hose.
10. Relieve the fuel system pressure, as outlined in Section 5.

❉❉ CAUTION

The fuel injection system remains under pressure after the engine has been turned-OFF. Properly relieve fuel pressure before disconnecting any fuel lines. Failure to do so may result in fire or personal injury.

11. Disconnect the fuel feed and return hoses from the fuel rail.
12. Disconnect the vacuum hoses located near the fuel feed and return hoses.
13. Remove the brake booster vacuum hose from the intake manifold. Label and remove the other vacuum hoses from the intake manifold.
14. Remove the clamp holding the power steering hose to the strut tower.
15. Remove the wiring harness clamp and the ground cable from the intake manifold.
16. Remove the connector and the terminal from the alternator. Then, remove the engine wiring harness from the valve cover.
17. Remove the mounting bolts and drive belt from the power steering pump. Pull the pump away from the mounting bracket without disconnecting the hoses. Support the pump out of the way.
18. Loosen the adjusting and mounting bolts for the alternator and remove the drive belt.
19. Unclamp the engine wiring harness and bypass hose from the lower side of the intake manifold.
20. Label and detach the following engine wiring harness connectors:
   • Fuel injector connectors
   • Intake Air Temperature (IAT) sensor connector
   • Idle Air Control (IAC) valve connector
   • Throttle Position Sensor (TPS) connector
   • Manifold Absolute Pressure (MAP) sensor connector
   • Heated Oxygen Sensor (HO2S) connector
   • Engine Coolant Temperature (ECT) sensor connector
   • ECT switch connector
   • ECT gauge sending unit connector
   • Exhaust Gas Recirculation (EGR) valve lift sensor
   • CKP/TDC/CYP sensor connector
   • Ignition coil connector
21. Label and detach the electrical connectors and ignition wires from the distributor.
22. Mark the position of the distributor and remove it from the cylinder head. Disconnect the ignition coil wire from the distributor.
23. Remove the upper radiator hose and the heater inlet hose from the cylinder head.
24. Remove the lower radiator hose from the thermostat housing.
25. Remove the coolant bypass hoses.
26. Use a jack with a cushioned pad to support the weight of the engine. Remove the through-bolt from the side engine mount and remove the mount.
27. Remove the cylinder head cover. Replace the rubber seals if they're damaged or deteriorated.
28. Remove the timing belt covers and the timing belt.

29. Remove the camshaft sprocket and the back cover. Do not lose the sprocket key.

30. Raise and safely support the vehicle.

31. Remove the splash shield.

32. Disconnect the exhaust pipe from the exhaust manifold.

33. Lower the vehicle.

34. Remove the exhaust manifold and the exhaust manifold heat insulator.

35. Remove the thermostat housing mounting bolts. Remove the thermostat housing from the intake manifold and the connecting pipe by pulling and twisting the housing. Discard the O-rings.

36. Remove the fuel rail and fuel injectors.

37. Remove the intake manifold bracket bolts.

38. Remove the intake manifold chamber with the throttle body attached.

39. Remove the intake manifold.

40. Remove the cylinder head bolts in the proper crisscross sequence starting at the outer edges and working inward. Then, remove the cylinder head.

➡To prevent warpage, loosen the bolts in reverse of the tightening sequence ⅓ turn at a time. Repeat the sequence until all bolts are loosened.

To install:

41. Be sure all cylinder head and block gasket surfaces are clean. Check the cylinder head for warpage. If warpage is less than 0.002 in. (0.05mm), cylinder head resurfacing is not required. The maximum resurface limit is 0.008 in. (0.2mm) based on a cylinder head total height of 3.94 in. (100mm).

42. Install a new head gasket.

43. Be sure the No. 1 cylinder is at TDC/compression.

44. Clean the oil control orifice and install a new O-ring. Replace the oil control orifice if necessary.

45. Install the dowel pins to the engine block.

46. Install the bolts that secure the intake manifold to its bracket, but do not tighten them.

47. Position the camshaft so that the **UP** mark is facing upward.

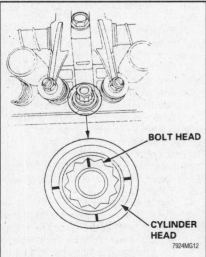

Fig. 40 Cylinder head bolt tightening marks—1998 Odyssey models

BOLT HEAD

CYLINDER HEAD

7924MG12

48. Install the cylinder head and be sure it is properly seated onto its dowel pins.

On 1996–97 engines, apply clean engine oil to the threads of the cylinder head bolts and to the underside of their heads. Install all of the head bolts. Following a crisscross pattern, tighten the bolts sequentially in three steps:
- Step 1: 29 ft. lbs. (39 Nm)
- Step 2: 51 ft. lbs. (69 Nm)
- Step 3: 72.3 ft. lbs. (98.1 Nm)

On 1998 engines, apply clean engine oil to the threads of the cylinder head bolts and to the underside of their heads. Install all of the head bolts. Tighten the cylinder head bolts following this procedure:
- Step 1: 22 ft. lbs. (29 Nm)
- Step 2: Mark the bolt head and cylinder head as illustrated
- Step 3: Tighten the head bolts in sequence 90 degrees
- Step 4: Tighten the head bolts in sequence another 90 degrees
- Step 5: If using new head bolts, tighten the head bolts in sequence a final 90 degrees

49. Install the intake manifold, manifold chamber and throttle body.

50. Install new O-rings, cushion rings, and seal rings onto the fuel injectors, fuel rail, and intake orifice. Install the fuel rail to the intake manifold as an assembly with the fuel injectors.

51. Install the exhaust manifold.

52. Lower the vehicle.

53. Install the timing belt back cover to the cylinder head. Tighten the cover bolts to 106 inch lbs. (12 Nm).

54. Install the key into the camshaft groove, then install the camshaft sprocket. Tighten the sprocket bolt to 27 ft. lbs. (37 Nm).

55. Be sure the camshaft sprocket and the crankshaft pulleys are aligned to TDC for the compression stroke. The camshaft sprocket **UP** mark should face up. The camshaft keyway should also face up.

56. Install the timing belt and the balancer shaft belt.

57. Install the lower timing belt cover and tighten the bolts to 106 inch lbs. (12 Nm).

58. Install a new seal around the adjusting nut. Do not loosen the adjusting nut.

59. Install the crankshaft pulley. Coat the threads and seating face of the pulley bolt with engine oil. Install and tighten the bolt to 181 ft. lbs. (245 Nm).

60. Install the side engine mount. Tighten the bolt and nut attaching the mount to the engine to 40 ft. lbs. (55 Nm). Tighten the through-bolt and nut to 47 ft. lbs. (65 Nm). Remove the jack from under the engine.

61. Adjust the valves, as outlined in Section 1.

62. Install the upper timing belt cover. Tighten the bolt on the intake side of the head to 106 inch lbs. (12 Nm) and tighten the bolt on the exhaust side of the head to 88 inch lbs. (10 Nm).

63. Tighten the crankshaft pulley bolt to 181 ft. lbs. (245 Nm) if it broke loose while adjusting the valves.

64. Install the splash shield.

65. Thoroughly clean the valve cover gasket mating surfaces . Install the valve cover gasket to the groove of the cylinder head cover. Be sure the gasket is seated securely in the corners of the recesses.

66. Apply sealant to the four corners of the recesses of the valve cover gasket. Do not install the parts if 5 minutes or more have elapsed since

applying sealant. After assembly, wait at least 20 minutes before filling the engine with oil.

67. Clean the valve cover contact surface with a shop towel. Install the valve cover. Tighten the valve cover capnuts in a clockwise sequence to 88 inch lbs. (10 Nm).

68. Install a new O-ring to the coolant connecting pipe, and to the thermostat housing. Install the housing to the coolant pipe and the intake manifold. Tighten the mounting bolts to 16 ft. lbs. (22 Nm).

69. Install the coolant bypass hoses.

70. Connect the lower radiator hose to the thermostat housing.

71. Connect the upper radiator hose and the heater inlet hose to the cylinder head.

72. Install the distributor to the cylinder head. Only hand-tighten the mounting bolts at this time.

73. Connect the ignition wires to the spark plugs. Attach the distributor electrical connectors. Install the ignition coil wire to the distributor.

74. Attach the all electrical engine wiring harness connectors, as tagged during removal.

75. Install the engine wiring harness and bypass hose to the lower side of the intake manifold.

76. Install and adjust the alternator drive belt.

77. Install the power steering pump to the power steering pump mounting bracket.

78. Install and adjust the power steering belt.

79. Install the alternator wiring harness to the valve cover. Connect the terminal to the alternator.

80. Connect the ground cable and the wiring harness clamp to the intake manifold.

81. Connect the power steering hose clamp to the engine block.

82. Connect the brake booster vacuum hose to the intake manifold. Connect the other vacuum hoses to the intake manifold.

83. Connect the vacuum hoses located near the fuel feed and return hoses.

84. Connect the fuel return hose and the fuel feed hose to the fuel rail. Install new washers to the fuel feed hose connection. Tighten the fuel feed hose banjo bolt to 16 ft. lbs. (22 Nm). Tighten the service bolt to 106 inch lbs. (12 Nm).

85. Install the breather hose, PCV hose, and the EVAP control canister hose.

86. Install the air intake duct.

87. Connect and adjust the throttle cable. Connect and adjust the throttle control cable and the cruise control cable, if equipped.

88. Drain the engine oil into a sealable container. Install the drain plug with a new crush washer.

89. Refill the engine with clean oil.

90. Fill and bleed the air from the cooling system.

91. Connect the positive and the negative battery cables. Enter the radio security code.

92. Start the engine, checking carefully for any coolant, fuel, oil, or air leaks.

93. Check and adjust the ignition timing if necessary.

V6 ENGINE

⬥ See Figures 41, 42, 43 and 44

✳✳ WARNING

To avoid damaging the cylinder head, allow the coolant temperature to drop below 100°F (38°C) before removing the head bolts.

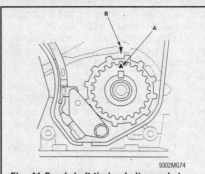

Fig. 41 Crankshaft timing belt sprocket TDC marks. Align sprocket mark (A) with pointer (B)—V6 Odyssey

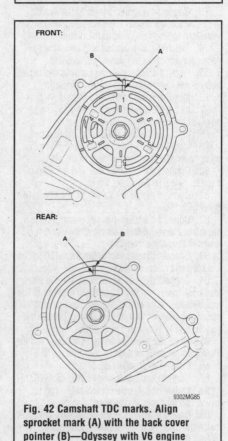

Fig. 42 Camshaft TDC marks. Align sprocket mark (A) with the back cover pointer (B)—Odyssey with V6 engine

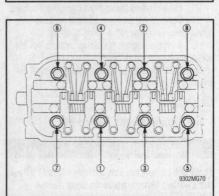

Fig. 43 Cylinder head torque sequence—Odyssey V6 engines

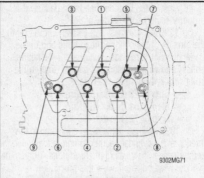

Fig. 44 Intake manifold torque sequence—Odyssey 3.5L V6 engines

1. Note the radio security code and station presets.

2. Disconnect the negative and positive battery cables.

3. Drain the engine coolant into a sealable container.

4. Remove the emissions evaporative hose from the throttle body.

5. Remove the vacuum hose and breather pipe from the air intake duct.

6. Remove the intake air duct.

7. Remove the covers for the ignition coils and intake manifold.

8. Remove the throttle cable and cruise control cable.

✳✳ CAUTION

The fuel injection system remains under pressure after the engine has been turned-OFF. Properly relieve fuel pressure before disconnecting any fuel lines. Failure to do so may result in fire or personal injury.

9. Relieve the residual fuel pressure in the fuel lines before removing. To relieve fuel line pressure remove the fuel filler cap, place a suitable rag or shop towel over the fuel pulsation damper and slowly loosen the fuel pulsation damper one complete turn using a suitable wrench. Always replace the sealing washers whenever the pulsation damper is removed or loosened.

10. Remove the fuel inlet and return hoses.

11. Remove the crankcase ventilation hose.

12. Remove the large and small diameter vacuum hoses from the brake booster.

13. Remove the valve cover breather hose and remove the three water bypass hoses at the throttle body.

14. Move the alternator belt tensioner to relieve tension on the alternator belt and remove the belt.

15. Remove the belt tensioner release arm.

16. Place a wood block on a floor jack and support the engine carefully by lifting on the oil pan.

17. Remove engine side mount bracket.

18. Loosen the power steering adjustment nut, and remove the adjustment locking nut, the pump mounting bolt and the power steering hose guide clamp bolt.

19. Remove the power steering belt and the power steering pump without removing the power steering hoses.

20. Remove the wire harness at the connector from the back of the alternator.

21. Remove the nut securing the large black wire at the back of the alternator and remove the wire.

22. Remove the alternator mounting bolt, the bracket mounting bolt and remove the harness clamp from the alternator bracket.

23. Remove the alternator.

24. Label and detach the wire harness connectors and harness clamps from the following:
   - Intake Air Temperature (IAT) sensor connector
   - Idle Air Control (IAC) valve connector
   - Throttle Position Sensor (TPS) connector
   - Manifold Absolute Pressure (MAP) sensor connector
   - Heated Oxygen Sensor (HO2S) connector
   - Engine Coolant Temperature (ECT) sensor connector
   - ECT switch connector
   - ECT gauge sending unit connector
   - Exhaust Gas Recirculation (EGR) valve lift sensor
   - CKP/TDC/CYP sensor connector
   - Ignition coil connectors
   - VTEC solenoid valve terminal
   - VTEC oil pressure switch terminal
   - Oil pressure switch connector
   - Radiator fan switch A terminal
   - Radiator fan switch B terminal

25. Remove the six ignition coils from the cylinder head covers.

26. Remove the intake manifold.

27. Detach the connectors from the six fuel injectors and remove the fuel rails.

28. Remove the two vacuum hoses from the fuel injection air control valve.

29. Remove the timing belt, as outlined in this section.

30. Remove the upper and lower radiator hoses located near the throttle body.

31. Remove both heater hoses.

32. Detach the Oxygen Sensor (O2S) wire connector.

33. Remove the front exhaust pipe with the O2S attached, and move it to a safe place out of the immediate work area.

34. Remove both exhaust manifolds.

35. Remove the thermostat housing water passage assembly.

36. Remove both camshaft sprockets and rear covers.

37. Remove both valve covers.

38. Loosen the cylinder head bolts ⅓ a turn in reverse order of the tightening sequence.

39. Continue the loosening sequence until all the bolts are loose.

40. Remove the cylinder head(s).

To install:

41. Be sure all cylinder head and block gasket surfaces are clean. Check the cylinder head for warpage. If warpage is less than 0.002 in. (0.05mm), cylinder head resurfacing is not required. The maximum resurface limit is 0.008 in. (0.2mm) based on a cylinder head total height of 4.76 in. (121mm).

42. Install a new head gasket.

43. Clean the oil control orifice and install new O-rings. Replace the oil control orifice if necessary.

44. Install the dowel pins to the engine block.

45. Check the timing belt drive pulley and clean if necessary.

46. Align the timing Top Dead Center (TDC)

mark on the drive belt pulley with the pointer on the oil pump cover.

47. Be sure the No. 1 cylinder is at TDC/compression.

48. Inspect both camshaft cam belt pulleys for cleanliness and clean as necessary.

49. Align the camshaft sprocket TDC marks of both cylinder heads with the pointers located on the back cover.

50. Inspect the cylinder head bolts for cleanliness and clean as necessary.

51. Apply a thin layer of clean engine oil to the bolt threads and flange area of the cylinder head bolts.

52. Carefully place the cylinder heads on the engine block.

53. Following the accompanying torque sequence, **perform each step twice** for each cylinder head. Tighten the head bolts for each cylinder head sequentially in following three steps:
- Step 1: 29 ft. lbs. (39 Nm)
- Step 2: 51 ft. lbs. (69 Nm)
- Step 3: 72.3 ft. lbs. (98.1 Nm)

54. Install a new exhaust manifold gasket on each cylinder head.

55. Install the exhaust manifolds and tighten the manifold nuts in three stages to a final torque of 23 ft. lbs. (31 Nm), using a crisscross pattern, starting with the inner manifold nut and working outward.

56. Install the exhaust pipe using new gaskets and torque the manifold flange self locking nuts to 40 ft. lbs. (54 Nm).

57. Torque the exhaust pipe flange mounting nuts to 25 ft. lbs. (33 Nm)

58. Install the exhaust pipe mounting bracket bolts and torque to 28 ft. lbs. (38 Nm).

59. Connect the O₂S wire harness plug.

60. Install the manifold heat shields and tighten the heat shield bolts to 16 ft. lbs. (22 Nm).

61. Install the timing belt, as outlined in this section.

62. Check and adjust the valve clearances as necessary.

63. Inspect the valve cover gaskets and bolt sealing grommets for damage or deterioration and replace as necessary.

64. Install the valve covers and torque the bolts from the inside out in a crisscross pattern to 104 inch lbs. (12 Nm).

65. Install the thermostat housing water passage assembly using a new O-ring and new gaskets and torque the mounting bolts to 16 ft. lbs. (22 Nm).

66. Install the intake manifold using a new gasket and torque the bolts from the inside out in a crisscross pattern to 16 ft. lbs. (22 Nm).

67. Install the ignition coils and torque the bolts to 104 inch lbs. (12 Nm).

68. Attach the wire harness connectors and harness clamps to the engine electrical components, as tagged during removal.

69. Install the alternator, mounting bolt, the bracket mounting bolt, and install the harness clamp to the alternator bracket.

70. Install the nut securing the large black wire at the back of the alternator and install the wire.

71. Install the wire harness at the connector to the back of the alternator.

72. Install the power steering pump, the hose guide clamp bolt, and the power steering belt.

73. Tension the power steering belt such that a 22 pound pull on the belt halfway between the two

drive pulleys will allow the belt to move 0.51–0.65 in. (13.0–16.5mm).

74. Tighten the power steering pump mounting bolt and adjustment lock nut.

➡️ If a new belt is used, set the tension such that a 22 pound pull on the belt halfway between the two drive pulleys will allow the belt to move 0.33–0.43 in. (8.5–11mm). After the engine has run for five minutes readjust the new belt to the used belt specification.

75. Place a wood block on a floor jack and support the engine carefully by lifting on the oil pan.

76. Install engine side mount bracket.

77. Install the alternator belt tensioner arm.

78. Move the alternator belt tensioner to relieve tension on the alternator belt and install the belt.

79. Attach the valve cover breather hose and the three water bypass hoses to the throttle body.

80. Connect the large and small diameter vacuum hoses to the brake booster.

81. Install the crankcase ventilation hose.

82. Connect the fuel inlet and return hoses.

83. Attach the throttle cable and cruise control cable.

84. Install the covers for the ignition coils and intake manifold.

85. Install the intake air duct.

86. Connect the vacuum hose and breather pipe to the air intake duct.

87. Install the emissions evaporative hoses onto the throttle body.

88. Drain the engine oil into a sealable container and replace the engine oil filter.

89. Fill the engine oil to the specified amount using fresh engine oil that meets the standards of the vehicle manufacturer.

90. Open the heater control valve, fill the cooling system with the recommended coolant mix, and bleed all air from the cooling system.

91. Install the negative and positive battery cables.

92. Start the engine and allow it to reach normal operating temperature.

93. Check for proper adjustment of the cruise control and throttle cables once the engine has been started, reaches normal operating temperature, and is idling at the normal idle speed. The correct cable free play for the cruise control cable should be 0.13–0.17 in. (3.25–4.25mm). The throttle cable should have enough free play that the cable can be moved side to side ⅜–½ inch (10–12mm) at the throttle linkage.

94. Check all fluid levels and top off if necessary. Check for signs of fluid or fuel leaks.

95. Check the operation of the heater and air conditioner and verify proper adjustment of all belts and cables.

96. Enter the radio security code and radio presets.

97. Road test the vehicle and check for proper operation of all accessories.

Oil Pan

REMOVAL & INSTALLATION

CR-V

♦ See Figures 45 and 46

1. Note the radio security code and station presets, then disconnect the negative battery cable.

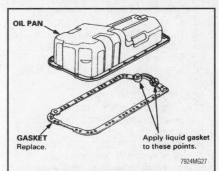

Fig. 45 Oil pan gasket installation—CR-V and 4-cylinder Odyssey

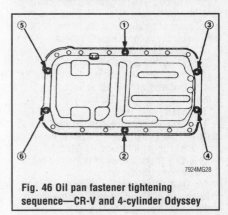

Fig. 46 Oil pan fastener tightening sequence—CR-V and 4-cylinder Odyssey

2. Raise and safely support the vehicle.

3. Drain the engine oil into a sealable container. Install the drain bolt with a new crush washer, tighten the bolt to 33 ft. lbs. (44 Nm).

4. Loosen the oil pan nuts and bolts in a crisscross pattern. Remove the oil pan. If necessary, use a seal cutter, or a mallet to tap the corners of the oil pan. Do not pry on the pan to get it loose.

5. Clean the oil pan mounting surface of old gasket material and engine oil.

6. Inspect the oil screen and pick-up tube for blockage, residue, or build-up. Replace the oil screen and pick-up tube if necessary.

To install:

7. Apply sealant where the oil pump and rear oil seal housing attach to the engine block. Work quickly so that the sealant doesn't set before the oil pan is installed.

8. Install the oil pan gasket and oil pan.

9. Tighten the nuts and bolts at six points as shown.

10. Tighten the nuts and bolts in a three-step, crisscross pattern to 123 inch lbs. (14 Nm). Do not over-tighten the bolts, this can distort the gasket and cause oil leakage.

11. Lower the vehicle. Ensure the sealant has cured and fill the engine with oil.

12. Connect the negative battery cable and enter the radio security code.

13. Start the engine and check for oil leaks.

Odyssey

♦ See Figures 45, 46, 47 and 48

1. Note the radio security code and station presets, then disconnect the negative battery cable.

2. Raise and safely support the vehicle.

3. Drain the engine oil into a sealable container.

4. Install the drain bolt with a new crush washer, tighten the bolt to 33 ft. lbs. (44 Nm).

5. Remove the splash shield.

6. On 4-cylinder engines, perform the following:

   a. Remove the front wheels.

   b. Remove the subframe center beam.

7. Detach the Oxygen Sensor (O2S) electrical wiring harness.

8. Remove the nuts attaching the exhaust pipe to the exhaust manifold(s) and the mid pipe. Remove the exhaust pipe and discard the gaskets.

9. On 4-cylinder engines, remove the torque converter cover.

10. Loosen the oil pan nuts and bolts in a criss-cross pattern. Remove the oil pan. If necessary, use a seal cutter, or a mallet to tap the corners of the oil pan. Do not pry on the pan to get it loose.

11. Clean the oil pan mounting surface of old gasket material and engine oil.

12. Inspect the oil screen and pick-up tube for blockage, residue, or build-up. Replace the oil screen and pick-up tube if necessary.

To install:

13. Apply a suitable liquid gasket where the oil pump and rear oil seal housing attach to the engine block and to the inner threads of the bolt holes. Work quickly so that the sealant doesn't set before the oil pan is installed.

14. On 4-cylinder engines, apply liquid gasket to the corners of the curved section of the oil pan gasket. Install the oil pan and gasket to the engine block.

15. On V6 engines, perform the following:

   a. Apply a thin, even layer of liquid sealant to the oil pan mating surface on the engine block, forming a continuous bead on the inside edges of the threaded bolt holes.

   b. Apply a thin layer of liquid sealant to the inner threads of the bolt holes on the engine block.

16. Install the oil pan and evenly finger-tighten the nuts and bolts.

17. Tighten the nuts and bolts to the final torque specification in a three-step, crisscross pattern.

18. On 4-cylinder engines, then tighten the retainers as follows:

- Tighten to 123 inch lbs. (14 Nm). Do not over-tighten the bolts, this can distort the gasket and cause oil leakage.
- Once the oil pan is installed, install the

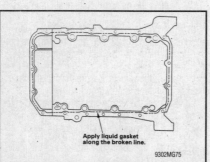

Fig. 47 Apply liquid gasket to the inner threads of the bolt holes and the engine block along the area indicated by the broken line—V6 models

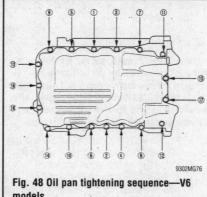

Fig. 48 Oil pan tightening sequence—V6 models

torque converter cover and tighten the bolts to 106 inch lbs. (12 Nm).

19. On V6 engines, tighten the oil pan retainers to 104 inch lbs. (12 Nm).

20. Install the exhaust pipe with new gaskets and new locknuts. Tighten the nuts attaching the exhaust pipe to the exhaust manifold to 40 ft. lbs. (54 Nm), tighten the nuts attaching the exhaust pipe to the middle pipe to 16 ft. lbs. (22 Nm). Install the nuts to the exhaust pipe support bracket and tighten the nuts to 13 ft. lbs. (18 Nm).

21. Connect the O2S electrical wiring harness.

22. On 4-cylinder engines, install the center beam, tighten the mounting bolts to 37 ft. lbs. (50 Nm), and then install the front wheels.

23. Install the splash shield.

24. Lower the vehicle.

25. Ensure the sealant has cured and fill the engine to the correct level with oil.

26. Connect the negative battery cable and enter the radio security code. Start the engine and check for oil leaks.

Oil Pump

REMOVAL & INSTALLATION

CR-V

1. Note the radio security code and station presets.

2. Disconnect the negative battery cable.

3. Drain the engine oil into a sealable container.

4. Raise and safely support the vehicle.

5. Set the engine to No. 1 cylinder Top Deader (TDC).

6. Remove the valve cover and the timing belt middle cover.

7. Remove the accessory drive belts.

8. Remove the crankshaft pulley and the lower timing cover.

9. Remove the timing belt and drive pulley.

10. Remove the oil pan and the oil screen. Discard the screen gasket. Replace the oil screen if it shows signs of blockage.

11. Remove the oil pump mounting bolts and remove the oil pump assembly. Remove the dowel pins from the engine and clean the oil pump mating surfaces of old gasket material, oil, and sludge. Discard the O-rings.

To install:

12. Install a new crankshaft seal into the oil pump housing using an appropriately-sized seal driver.

13. Install the two dowel pins and new O-ring to the cylinder block.

14. Be sure that the mating surfaces are clean and dry. Apply liquid gasket evenly, in a narrow bead centered on the mating surface. Once the sealant is applied, do not wait longer than 20 minutes to install the parts; the sealant will become ineffective. After final assembly, wait at least 30 minutes before adding oil to the engine to give the sealant time to set. To prevent leakage of oil, apply a suitable thread sealer to the inner threads of the bolt holes.

15. Apply engine oil to the lip of the oil pump seal.

16. Install the oil pump and oil screen, tightening the mounting bolts/nuts to 86 inch lbs. (9.8 Nm).

17. Install the oil pan.

18. The completion of installation is the reverse of the removal procedure.

19. Lower the vehicle.

20. Fill the engine with clean engine oil.

21. Connect the negative battery cable, then enter the radio security code.

Odyssey

4-CYLINDER ENGINES

▶ **See Figures 49, 50, 51 and 52**

1. Note the radio security code and disconnect the negative battery cable.

2. Remove the timing belt, balancer belt and tensioners.

3. If equipped with a Top Dead Center (TDC) sensor mounted on the oil pump housing, unbolt the sensor assembly and move it out of the way.

4. Remove the timing belt drive sprocket from the crankshaft.

5. Insert a pin punch or holder tool into the maintenance hole in the front balancer shaft (located behind the balancer sprocket). Hold the shaft steady with the tool and remove the balancer sprocket. Ensure the tool or bolt used is strong enough to resist bending when torque is applied to the sprocket nut.

➡ **Front refers to the side of the engine facing the vehicle's radiator. Rear refers to the side of the engine facing the vehicle's firewall.**

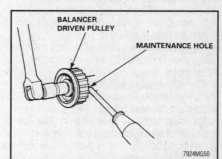

Fig. 49 Use a prytool through the maintenance hole to hold the balancer shaft while removing the pulley retaining bolt—4-cylinder Odyssey

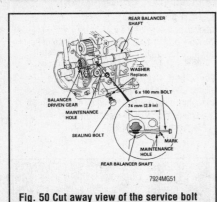

Fig. 50 Cut away view of the service bolt installation—4-cylinder Odyssey

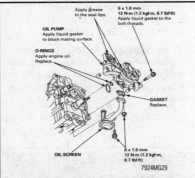

Fig. 51 Exploded view of the oil pump and screen—4-cylinder Odyssey

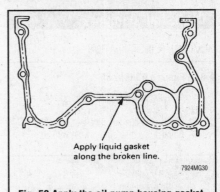

Fig. 52 Apply the oil pump housing gasket sealer as indicated—4-cylinder Odyssey

6. Align the rear timing balancer sprocket using a 6 x 100mm bolt, rod, or pin punch. Mark the bolt or rod at a point 2.9 in. (74mm) from its end.

7. Remove the 12mm sealing bolt from the maintenance hole on the right side of the block below the water pump. Insert the bolt/rod into the hole until the 2.9 in. (74mm) mark you made on it is aligned with the face of the hole. This bolt/rod will act as a pin to hold the shaft in place.

8. Remove the balancer gear case and the dowel pins. Discard the O-ring.

9. Unbolt and remove the balancer driven gear. Leave the holder tool in the maintenance hole.

10. Remove the oil pan and the oil screen. Discard the screen gasket. Replace the oil screen if it shows signs of blockage.

11. Remove the oil pump mounting bolts and remove the oil pump assembly. Remove the dowel pins from the engine and clean the oil pump mating surfaces of old gasket material, oil, and sludge. Discard the O-rings.

To install:

12. Install new crankshaft and balancer shaft seals into the oil pump housing using an appropriately-sized seal driver.

13. Install the two dowel pins and new O-rings to the cylinder block.

14. Be sure that the mating surfaces are clean and dry. Apply liquid gasket evenly in a narrow bead, centered on the mating surface. Once the sealant is applied, do not wait longer than 20 minutes to install the parts; the sealant will become ineffective. After final assembly, wait at least 30 minutes before adding oil to the engine to give the sealant time to set. To prevent leakage of oil, apply a suitable thread sealer to the inner threads of the bolt holes.

15. Install the oil pump to the engine block. Tighten the mounting bolts to 106 inch lbs. (12 Nm).

16. Install the oil screen. Tighten the screen mounting bolts and nuts to 106 inch lbs. (12 Nm).

17. Install the oil pan.

18. Hold the front balancer shaft in place with a suitable tool. Install the balancer driven pulley to the front balancer shaft. Tighten the attaching bolt to 22 ft. lbs. (29 Nm).

19. Install the balancer driven gear to the rear balancer shaft. Tighten the bolt to 18 ft. lbs. (25 Nm).

20. Before installing the balancer driven gear

and the gear case, apply molybdenum disulfide (lithium) grease to the thrust surfaces of the balancer gears.

21. Align the groove on the pulley edge to the pointer on the balancer gear case.

22. Install the balancer gear case to the engine with a new O-ring. Install the mounting bolts and nut. The rear balancer shaft should be held in place with a 6 x 100mm bolt/rod. Tighten the mounting bolts and nut to 18 ft. lbs. (25 Nm).

23. Check the alignment of the pointer on the balancer pulley to the pointer on the oil pump.

24. Remove the 6 x 100mm holder bolt/rod from the maintenance hole. Install the sealing bolt with a new crush washer. Tighten it to 22 ft. lbs. (29 Nm).

25. Install the timing belt and tensioners.

26. Connect the negative battery cable to the battery and enter the radio security code.

V6 ENGINE

1. Note the radio security code and disconnect the negative battery cable from the battery.

2. Drain the engine oil into a sealable container.

3. Turn the crankshaft until the timing marks on the crankshaft pulley and the front cylinder head cam sprocket indicate No. 1 cylinder is at Top Dead Center (TDC).

4. Remove the crankshaft pulley and timing belt, as outlined in this section.

5. Remove the timing belt idler pulley.

6. Remove the Crankshaft Position Sensor (CKP).

7. Remove the crankshaft timing belt sprocket.

8. Disconnect the solenoid wire at the oil filter housing and remove the mounting bolts and oil filter housing assembly.

9. Detach the wire connector from the Oxygen Sensor (O2S).

10. Remove the nuts attaching the exhaust pipe to the exhaust manifolds and the mid pipe. Remove the exhaust pipe hanger bolts, remove the exhaust pipe, and discard the gaskets.

11. Remove the engine oil pan and remove the oil pump pickup screen assembly.

12. Remove the oil pump housing bolts and remove the oil pump assembly.

13. Remove the screws from the oil pump housing and separate the housing and the cover.

To install:

14. Install the oil pump cover on the housing

using a liquid thread locking agent on the pump housing screws.

15. Check that the oil pump spins freely.

16. Clean and dry the oil pump mating surfaces of the engine block and the oil pump.

17. Apply a suitable liquid gasket where the oil pump housing attaches to the engine block and to the inner threads of the bolt holes. Work quickly so that the sealant doesn't set before the oil pump is installed.

18. Apply a thin film of light grease to the lip of the crankshaft oil seal and apply oil to the new O-rings for the oil pump housing.

19. Install the dowel pins in the oil pump cover and align the inner rotor of the oil pump with the crankshaft and install the oil pump assembly. Tighten the oil pump cover bolts to 104 inch pounds (12 Nm).

20. Install the oil pump pickup screen assembly using a new O-ring and tighten the bolts to 104 in. lbs. (12 Nm).

21. Apply a thin, even layer of liquid sealant to the oil pan mating surface on the engine block, forming a continuous bead on the inside edges of the threaded bolt holes.

22. Apply a thin layer of liquid sealant to the inner threads of the bolt holes on the engine block.

23. Install the oil pan and evenly finger-tighten the bolts.

24. Tighten the bolts in a three-step, crisscross pattern to the final torque specification of 104 inch lbs. (12 Nm).

25. Install the oil filter housing assembly, tighten the mounting bolts to 16 ft. lbs. (22 Nm) and connect the solenoid wire at the oil filter housing.

26. Install the exhaust pipe with new gaskets and new locknuts. Tighten the nuts attaching the exhaust pipe to the exhaust manifold to 40 ft. lbs. (54 Nm), tighten the nuts attaching the exhaust pipe to the middle pipe to 16 ft. lbs. (22 Nm). Install the nuts to the exhaust pipe support bracket and tighten the nuts to 13 ft. lbs. (18 Nm).

27. Connect the O2S electrical wiring harness.

28. Install the crankshaft timing belt sprocket.

29. Install the CKP sensor.

30. Install the timing belt idler pulley.

31. Install the timing belt and crankshaft pulley, as outlined in this section

32. Fill the engine oil to the correct level.

33. Connect the negative battery cable to the battery and enter the radio security code.

Crankshaft Damper

REMOVAL & INSTALLATION

♦ **See Figures 53 thru 60**

1. Note the radio security code and station presets.
2. Disconnect the negative battery cable.
3. Raise and safely support the vehicle.

4. Remove the lower engine splash shield.
5. Remove the engine accessory drive belts. For specific details, refer to Section 1.

➡ **Mark the direction of the accessory drive belt's rotation if it is to be reinstalled. If there is any doubt about the condition of a belt, or if it has been contaminated by oil, it should be replaced.**

6. Set the engine at Top Dead Center (TDC) for the No. 1 piston on the compression stroke. The crankshaft pulley **white** mark must be aligned with the mark on the lower timing cover. Once in this position, the engine must not be disturbed.

7. Hold the crankshaft pulley with Honda Tool Nos. 07MAB-PY3010A Holder Attachment and 07JAB-001020A Holder Handle or their equivalents and remove the crankshaft pulley bolt by turning it in a counterclockwise direction.

8. Remove the crankshaft pulley.

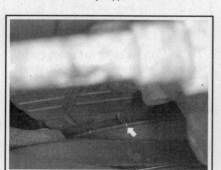

Fig. 53 The engine is at TDC when the white timing mark on the crankshaft pulley is aligned with the raised pointer on the timing belt cover

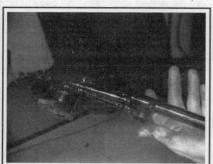

Fig. 54 This crankshaft pulley tool was fabricated by grinding a 2 inch pipe fitting to fit the 50mm hexagon, and welding it onto a used two-stroke connecting rod and a suitable solid steel bar

Fig. 55 The crankshaft pulley is held onto the crankshaft with a special bolt/washer combination, and the bolt should be replaced once removed

Fig. 56 The crankshaft pulley has a 50mm hexagon shape cast into the pulley that allows a tool to be used to hold the pulley in order to remove the bolt

Fig. 57 The crankshaft pulley holding tool is placed into the hexagon cutout of the pulley

Fig. 58 While holding the pulley stationary . . .

Fig. 59 . . . a suitable ½ inch drive 19 mm deep well socket is inserted through the holding tool onto the crankshaft pulley bolt

Fig. 60 While the crankshaft pulley is held, the crankshaft bolt is loosened and removed by turning it counterclockwise

To install:

9. Install the crankshaft pulley. Retighten the crankshaft pulley bolt to:
- CR-V engines: 130 ft. lbs. (177 Nm)
- Odyssey engines: 181 ft. lbs. (245 Nm).

10. Install and adjust the accessory drive belts.

11. Verify that all engine components that may have been removed have been reinstalled correctly.

12. Install the splash shield and lower the vehicle.

13. Connect the negative battery cable, then enter the security code for the radio.

Timing Belt Cover and Seal

REMOVAL & INSTALLATION

Upper Timing Belt Cover/Seal

1. Note the radio security code and disconnect the negative battery cable.

2. Remove the valve cover, then remove the upper timing belt cover.

3. Remove the seal from the groove in the cover.

To install:

4. Secure the seal in the cover. It may be helpful to use a semi drying gasket sealant to hold the seal in place.

5. The remainder of the installation procedure is the reverse of the removal procedure.

6. Enter the radio security code.

Lower Timing Belt Cover/Seal

1. Note the radio security code and disconnect the negative battery cable.

2. Remove the accessory drive belts. For specific details, refer to the drive belt procedures in Section 1.

3. Remove the crankshaft pulley. For specific details, refer to the removal and installation procedure in this section.

4. Remove the lower timing belt cover.

5. Remove the seal from the groove in the cover.

To install:

6. Secure the seal in the cover. It may be helpful to use a semi drying gasket sealant to hold the seal in place.

7. The remainder of the installation procedure is the reverse of the removal procedure.

8. For specific details pertaining to the crankshaft pulley removal, refer to the removal and installation procedure in this section. For specific detail on drive belt installation, refer to the procedures in Section 1.

9. Enter the radio security code.

Timing Belt and Sprockets

The manufacturer recommends replacement of the timing belt (and water pump inspection) under **normal** operating conditions for CR-V and Odyssey models every 84 months (7 years) or 105,000 (168,000 km). If the vehicle is operated in high temperatures (above 110°F or 43°C) or very low temperatures (below -20°F or -29°C) the timing belt should be replaced every 60,000 miles (100,000 km).

If, however, the timing belt is inspected earlier or more frequently than suggested, and shows signs of wear or defects, the belt should be replaced at that time.

✳✳ WARNING

On interference engines, it is very important to replace the timing belt at the recommended intervals, otherwise expensive engine damage will likely result if the belt fails.

REMOVAL & INSTALLATION

✳✳ WARNING

Never allow antifreeze, oil or solvents to come into with a timing belt. If this occurs immediately wash the solution from the timing belt. Also, never excessive bend or twist the timing belt; this can damage the belt so that its lifetime is severely shortened.

CR-V

▶ **See Figures 61 thru 76**

1. Disconnect the negative battery cable.
2. Position crankshaft so that No. 1 piston is at Top Dead Center (TDC).
3. Remove the splash guard.

4. If equipped, remove the cruise control actuator.

5. Loosen and remove the power steering pump drive belt.

6. Remove the two bolts that attach the top power steering hose to the power steering pump. Cover and seal the hose and the open port of the pump.

7. Clamp shut the power steering reservoir return hose, remove it from the return line, and remove the power steering pump and reservoir as an assembly.

8. Remove the remaining accessory drive belts. Refer to Section 1 for specific details.

9. Place a piece of wood between the oil pan and the jack, support the engine with a jack.

10. Remove upper engine bracket.

11. Remove the valve cover.

12. Make sure the engine is at Top Dead Center (TDC) for No. 1 cylinder. The engine is at TDC for No. 1 cylinder when:

a. The white Top Dead Center (TDC) mark on the crankshaft pulley is aligned with the raised pointer.

b. The **UP** marks on both camshaft sprockets are at the topmost (12 O'clock) position.

c. The holes in the No. 1 exhaust and intake cam journals align with the holes in the camshaft. A 4.5 mm or 5⁄32 inch drill bit or Allen key can be placed through the holes to prevent the cams from rotating while removing or installing the cam belt.

13. Remove the crankshaft pulley. For details, see crankshaft pulley removal in this section.

14. Remove the timing belt covers.

15. Loosen the adjusting bolt ½–1 turn. Release the tension from the belt by pushing on the tensioner, then retighten the adjusting bolt.

16. Remove the timing belt.

To install:

17. Be sure the timing marks are properly aligned.

18. Install the timing belt around the crankshaft sprocket and then stuff a clean rag or paper towel between the belt and the sensor guard to hold the belt engaged with the sprocket teeth.

19. Place the flat side of the belt clockwise around the top of the tensioner and then engage the toothed portion of the timing belt counterclockwise around the bottom of the water pump sprocket.

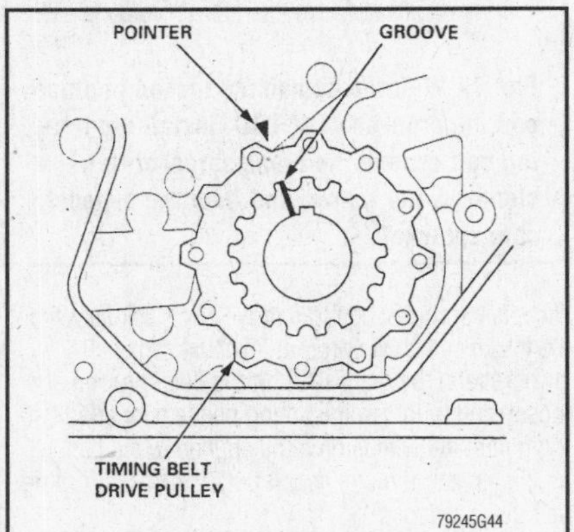

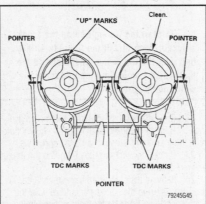

Fig. 61 The Crankshaft timing mark will be easier to verify when clean—Honda CR-V 2.0L engine

Fig. 62 Intake and exhaust camshaft timing marks properly aligned at TDC—Honda CR-V engine

Fig. 63 Removing the cruise control actuator allows for additional work space. The unit is secured to the inner fender with 3 bolts

Fig. 64 Clamp the power steering return line shut before removing it from the metal pipe

Fig. 65 Seal the power steering return line with an absorbent cloth to keep debris from entering the line while it is disconnected

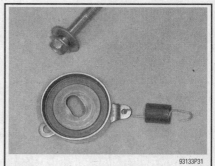

Fig. 66 The timing belt tensioner roller is slotted to allow the tensioner to move when the mounting bolt is loosened

Fig. 67 With the tensioner roller mounting bolt loosened, press on the timing belt to push the tensioner back, then tighten the mounting bolt to hold it in the retracted position

Fig. 68 The "UP" marks should be in the 12 O'clock position when the engine is at Top Dead Center (TDC) for the No. 1 cylinder

Fig. 69 Use two 4.5 mm or ⁵⁄₃₂ inch Allen tools or drill bits to hold the camshafts during belt removal and installation

Fig. 70 The crankshaft timing belt sprocket should line up with the pointer when installing the timing belt

Fig. 71 Start the timing belt on the crank sprocket, then install the flat side of the belt over the top of the tensioner and the toothed portion around the bottom of the water pump sprocket

Fig. 72 With the camshafts locked in place and the crankshaft at TDC, install the timing belt around the crank sprocket, tensioner, water pump, and then the exhaust cam sprocket

20. Carefully pull the timing belt upward but **do not** move the crankshaft. If the crankshaft moved, carefully realign the crankshaft timing belt sprocket with the TDC marks. Carefully engage the teeth of the timing belt onto the exhaust camshaft sprocket, but only install the belt about ⅓ of the way onto the sprocket.

21. Grasp the timing belt on the toothed side and gently lift the belt enough to begin sliding it onto the intake camshaft sprocket.

22. Once the belt has started to slide onto the intake camshaft sprocket, slide the belt equally onto both the intake and exhaust camshaft sprockets.

23. Quickly loosen and then retighten the timing belt tensioner bolt.

24. Remove the tools from the camshaft caps used for securing the camshafts, and remove the cloth used to keep the timing belt engaged in the crankshaft sprocket.

25. Apply a clockwise load on the intake

camshaft sprocket bolt to remove any slack between the intake camshaft sprocket, exhaust camshaft sprocket and the crankshaft timing belt sprocket, then loosen and retighten the timing belt tensioner adjusting bolt to allow tension to be applied to the belt.

26. Install the crankshaft pulley sprocket/timing belt guide washer.

27. Install the lower and upper timing covers.

28. Install the crankshaft pulley and tighten the bolt to 130 ft. lbs. (177 Nm).

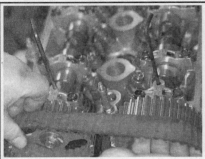

Fig. 73 With both camshafts secured and the timing belt partially installed on the exhaust cam sprocket, pull the belt upward to remove any slack and slide it onto the intake cam sprocket

Fig. 74 Once the timing belt is installed, apply a clockwise load to the intake camshaft sprocket to remove the slack from the belt between the exhaust and crankshaft sprockets

Fig. 75 Continue to apply a clockwise load and loosen the timing belt tensioner mounting bolt to allow it to take up the slack and retighten the bolt

Fig. 76 The rubber plug just above the crankshaft pulley on the lower timing belt cover is removed to access the timing belt tensioner bolt

✷✷ WARNING

If any binding is felt when adjusting the timing belt tension by turning the crankshaft, STOP turning the engine, because the pistons may be hitting the valves.

29. Rotate the crankshaft about 5–6 times counterclockwise to seat the timing belt.
30. Position the No. 1 piston to TDC.
31. Locate and remove the rubber plug for the timing belt tensioner on the lower timing belt cover.
32. Loosen the adjusting bolt ½ turn by
33. Rotate the crankshaft counterclockwise 3 teeth on the camshaft pulley.
34. Tighten the adjusting bolt to 40 ft. lbs. (54 Nm).
35. Retighten the crankshaft pulley bolt to 130 ft. lbs. (177 Nm).
36. Install the valve cover.
37. Install the engine mounting bracket, then remove the jack.
38. If removed, install the cruise control actuator.
39. Install the accessory drive belts.
40. Install the splash guard.
41. Connect the negative battery cable, then check the engine operation and road test.

Odyssey Models

4-CYLINDER ENGINES

♦ **See Figures 77, 78, 79 and 80**

1. Note the radio security code and station presets.
2. Disconnect the negative and positive battery cables.
3. Remove the cylinder head cover.
4. Remove the upper timing belt cover.
5. Turn the crankshaft to align the timing marks and set cylinder No.1 to Top Dead Center (TDC) for the compression stroke. The white mark on the crankshaft pulley should align with the pointer on the timing belt cover. The words **UP** embossed on the camshaft pulley should be aligned in the upward position and the marks on the edge of the pulley should be aligned with the cylinder head or the back cover upper edge. Once in this position, the engine must NOT be turned or disturbed.
6. Remove the splash shield from below the engine.
7. Remove the wheel well splash shield.
8. Loosen and remove the power steering pump belt. Remove the power steering pump.
9. Loosen the adjusting and mounting bolts for the alternator and remove the drive belt.
10. Support the engine with a floor jack cushioned with a piece of wood under the oil pan.
11. Remove the dipstick and the dipstick tube.
12. Remove the through-bolt for the side engine mount and remove the mount.
13. Remove the crankshaft pulley bolt and remove the crankshaft pulley. Use a Crank Pulley Holder tool No. 07MAB-PY3010A and Holder Handle tool No. 07JAB-001020A or their equivalents, to hold the crankshaft pulley while removing the bolt.
14. Remove the lower timing belt cover.

➡ **If only the balance shaft belt is being removed, thread a 6 x 1.0 mm x 25 mm through the timing belt tensioner plate to hold the timing belt tensioner in place.**

15. Loosen the timing belt/timing balancer belt adjuster nut ⅔–1 turn. Move the tension adjuster to release the belt tension and retighten the adjuster nut.
16. Remove the balancer shaft belt, and then the

balance shaft belt crankshaft mounted drive sprocket.

➡ **For servicing the balance shafts, front refers to the side of the engine facing the radiator. Rear refers to the side of the engine facing the firewall.**

17. To remove the rear balance shaft drive sprocket, perform the following:

➡ **The rear balance shaft drive sprocket is part of a gear case and the case is removed as a unit.**

 a. Remove the maintenance bolt located on the back of the engine block. The bolt is inline with the balance shaft about 3 inches behind the balance shaft sprocket.
 b. Make sure the balance shaft sprocket is still in the TDC position. The pointer on the gear

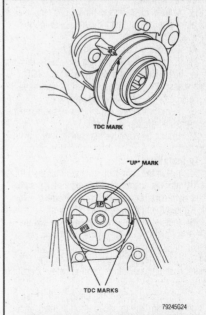

Fig. 77 Align the camshaft, crankshaft and engine marks before removing the timing belt and pulleys—Odyssey with 4-cylinder engines

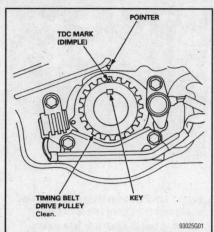

Fig. 78 Align the crankshaft sprocket with the oil pump pointer before installing the timing belt— 4-cylinder Odyssey

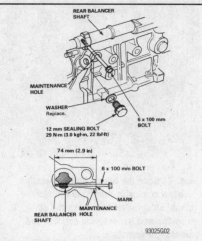

Fig. 79 Holding the rear timing balancer shaft—4-cylinder Odyssey

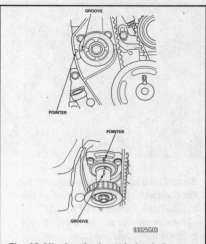

Fig. 80 Aligning the front timing balancer shaft—4-cylinder Odyssey

should align with the pointer on the oil pump housing plate.

  c. Scribe a 3 inch (74mm) line from the end of a 6 x 1.0mm x 100mm bolt.

  d. With the maintenance hole sealing bolt removed, insert the 6 x 1.0mm x 100mm bolt into the maintenance hole to the scribed line to lock the rear balance shaft in the TDC position.

  e. Remove the rear balance shaft gear case mounting bolts and remove the assembly.

18. To remove the front balance shaft drive sprocket:

  a. Install a suitable and sturdy screwdriver or drift through the maintenance hole in the shaft behind the sprocket to hold the front balance shaft.

  b. Remove the front balance shaft mounting nut and sprocket.

19. Loosen the camshaft timing belt tensioner, if not already loose, and lock the tensioner in the released position.

20. Remove the camshaft timing belt.

21. To remove the crankshaft mounted camshaft timing belt drive pulley, if equipped with a TDC sensor assembly, unbolt the assembly and move it to the side before removing the sprocket.

22. Remove the key and the spacers to remove the crankshaft timing sprocket.

23. Unbolt and remove the camshaft timing sprocket.

To install:

24. Install the camshaft timing sprocket so that the **UP** mark is up and the TDC marks are parallel to the cylinder head gasket surface. Install the key and tighten the bolt to 27 ft. lbs. (37 Nm).

25. Install the crankshaft sprocket so that the TDC mark aligns with the pointer on the oil pump. Install the spacers with their concave surfaces facing in. Install the key. If equipped, install the TDC sensor assembly back into position before installing the timing belt.

26. Install and tension the timing belt. Use a 6 x 1.0mm x 25mm bolt threaded through the cam belt tensioner plate to temporarily hold the tensioner.

27. Temporarily install the crankshaft pulley and rotate the crankshaft counterclockwise 5–6 turns to be sure the belt is properly seated.

28. Set the No. 1 piston at TDC for its compression stroke.

✳✳ WARNING

If any binding is felt when adjusting the timing belt tension by turning the crankshaft, STOP turning the engine, because the pistons may be hitting the valves.

29. Rotate the crankshaft counterclockwise so that the camshaft pulley moves only 3 teeth beyond its TDC mark.

30. Loosen, then retighten the temporary cam belt tensioner bolt.

31. If the rear balance shaft sprocket/gear case assembly was removed, perform the following:

  a. If the rear balance shaft was moved, rotate the balance shaft until the 6 x 1.0mm x 100mm bolt can be installed into the maintenance hole to the scribed line.

  b. Align the notch of the balance shaft sprocket edge with the pointer on the gear case. Install the rear balance shaft sprocket/gear case assembly using a new O-ring coated with fresh engine oil. The balance shaft sprocket should be installed in the TDC position. The pointer on the gear should align with the pointer on the oil pump housing plate.

  c. Tighten the mounting bolts to 18 ft. lbs. (25 Nm).

32. If the front balance shaft sprocket was removed, perform the following:

  a. Install a suitable and sturdy screwdriver or drift through the maintenance hole in the shaft behind the sprocket to hold the front balance shaft.

  b. Install the front balance shaft sprocket and mounting nut. Torque the nut to 22 ft. lbs. (29 Nm).

33. Make sure the balance shafts and crankshaft are in the TDC position.

34. Remove the crankshaft pulley, and if removed, install the balance shaft belt drive sprocket.

35. Install the balance shaft belt, making sure the balance shafts and sprockets are still in the TDC position.

36. If removed, install the balance shaft belt tensioner and tension the balance shaft belt.

37. Loosen, then retighten the tensioner adjusting nut to 33 ft. lbs. (45 Nm).

38. Remove the 6 x 1.0mm x 100mm rear balance shaft holding bolt.

39. Temporarily install the crankshaft pulley and rotate the crankshaft 2 revolutions counterclockwise, stopping at TDC.

✳✳ WARNING

If any resistance is felt, stop immediately and determine the cause.

40. Recheck that all of the TDC marks align for both the camshaft and balance shafts.

41. Loosen, then retighten the tensioner adjusting nut to 33 ft. lbs. (45 Nm).

42. Remove the 6 x 1.0mm x 25mm bolt used to secure the camshaft timing belt tensioner.

43. Remove the crankshaft pulley and install the lower cover.

44. Install the crankshaft pulley, lubricate the bolt threads and both sides of the crankshaft pulley bolt with fresh engine oil and tighten the crankshaft pulley bolt to 181 ft. lbs. (245 Nm). **Do Not** use an impact wrench.

45. Install the upper timing cover and the valve cover. Be sure the seals are properly seated.

46. Install the side engine mount. Tighten the through-bolt to 47 ft. lbs. (64 Nm). Tighten the mount nut and bolt to 40 ft. lbs. (55 Nm) each.

47. Remove the floor jack.

48. Install and tension the alternator belt.

49. Install the power steering pump and tension its belt.

50. Install the splash shields.

51. Reconnect the positive and negative battery cables. Enter the radio security code.

52. Check engine operation.

V6 ENGINE

▶ See Figures 81, 82, 83, 84 and 85

1. Note the radio security code and station presets.

2. Disconnect the negative battery terminal.

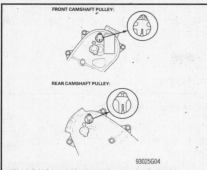

Fig. 81 Crankshaft and camshaft timing marks at Top Dead Center (TDC)—V6 Odyssey

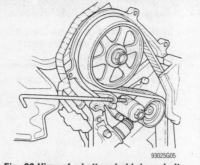

Fig. 82 View of a battery hold-down bolt installed to hold auto-tensioner—V6 Odyssey

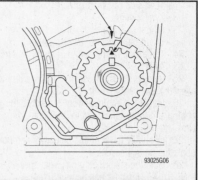

Fig. 83 Crankshaft sprocket Top Dead Center (TDC) mark—V6 Odyssey

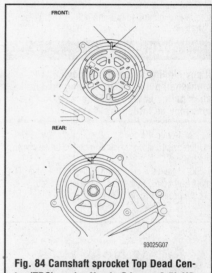

Fig. 84 Camshaft sprocket Top Dead Center (TDC) mark—Honda Odyssey 3.5L V6 engine

Fig. 85 Adjusting the auto-tensioner—V6 Odyssey

3. Turn the crankshaft so the white mark on the crankshaft pulley aligns with the pointer on the oil pump housing cover.

4. Open the inspection plugs on the upper timing belt covers and check that the camshaft sprocket marks align with the upper cover marks.

❋❋ WARNING

Align the camshaft and crankshaft sprockets with their alignment marks before removing the timing belt. Failure to align the timing marks correctly may result in valve damage.

5. Raise and safely support the vehicle and remove both front tires/wheels.

6. Remove the front lower splash shield.

7. Move the alternator tensioner with a suitable belt tensioner release arm tool, to release tension from the belt and remove the alternator drive belt.

8. Remove the alternator belt tensioner release arm.

9. Loosen the power steering pump adjustment nut, adjustment locknut and mounting bolt, then remove the power steering pump with the hoses attached.

10. Support the weight of the engine by placing a wood block on a floor jack and carefully lift on the oil pan.

11. Remove the bolts from the side engine mount bracket and remove the bracket.

12. Remove the dipstick, the dipstick tube and discard the O-ring.

13. Hold the crankshaft pulley with the Handle tool 07JAB-001020A and Crankshaft Holding tool 07MAB-PY3010A, or equivalent. While holding the crankshaft pulley, remove the crankshaft pulley bolt using a heavy duty ¾ in. (19mm) socket and breaker bar.

14. Remove the crankshaft pulley, the upper timing belt covers and the lower timing belt cover.

15. Remove one of the battery clamp fasteners from the battery tray and grind a 45 degree bevel on the threaded end of the battery clamp bolt.

16. Screw in the battery hold-down bolt into the threaded bracket just above the auto-tensioner (automatic timing belt adjuster) and tighten the bolt hand-tight to hold the auto-tensioner adjuster in its current position.

17. Remove the engine mount bracket bolts and the bracket.

18. Loosen the timing belt idler pulley bolt

(located on the right side across from the auto-tensioner pulley) about 5–6 revolutions and remove the timing belt.

To install:

19. Clean the timing belt sprockets and the timing belt covers.

❋❋ WARNING

Align the camshaft and crankshaft sprockets with their alignment marks before installing the timing belt. Failure to align the timing marks correctly may result in valve damage.

20. Align the timing mark on the crankshaft sprocket with the oil pump pointer.

21. Align the camshaft sprocket TDC timing marks with the pointers on the rear cover.

22. If installing a new belt or if the auto-tensioner has extended or if the timing belt cannot be reinstalled easily, the auto-tensioner must be collapsed before installation of the timing belt, perform the following:

a. Remove the battery hold-down bolt from the auto-tensioner bracket.

b. Remove the timing belt auto-tensioner bolts and the auto-tensioner.

c. Secure the auto-tensioner in a soft jawed vise, clamping onto the flat surface of one of the mounting bolt holes with the maintenance bolt facing upward.

d. Remove the maintenance bolt and use caution not to spill oil from the tensioner assembly.

e. Should oil spill from the tensioner, be sure the tensioner is filled with 0.22 ounces (6.5 ml) of fresh engine oil.

f. Using care not to damage the threads or the gasket sealing surface, insert a flat-blade screwdriver through the tensioner maintenance hole and turn the screwdriver clockwise to compress the auto-tensioner bottom while the Tensioner Holder tool 14540-P8A-A01, or equivalent, is installed on the auto-tensioner assembly.

g. Install the auto-tensioner maintenance bolt with a new gasket and tighten to 72 inch lbs. (8 Nm).

h. Install the auto-tensioner on the engine with the tensioner holder tool installed, then tighten the mounting bolts to 104 inch lbs. (12 Nm).

23. Install the timing belt in a counterclockwise pattern starting with the crankshaft drive sprocket. Install the timing belt counterclockwise in the following sequence:

- Crankshaft drive sprocket.
- Idler pulley.

- Left side camshaft sprocket.
- Water pump.
- Right side camshaft sprocket.
- Auto-tensioner adjustment pulley.

24. Torque the timing belt idler pulley bolt to 33 ft. lbs. (44 Nm).

25. Remove the auto-tensioner holding tool to allow the tensioner to extend.

26. Install the engine mount bracket to the engine and torque the bolts to 33 ft. lbs. (44 Nm).

27. Install the lower timing belt cover and both upper timing belt covers.

28. Hold the crankshaft pulley with special tools 07JAB-001020A handle and 07MAB-PY3010A crankshaft holding tool, or equivalent tools. While holding the crankshaft pulley, install the crankshaft pulley bolt using a heavy duty ¾ in. (19mm) socket and a commercially available torque wrench and torque the bolt to 181 ft. lbs. (245 Nm).

✳✳ WARNING

If any binding is felt while moving the crankshaft pulley, STOP turning the crankshaft pulley immediately because the pistons may be hitting the valves.

29. Rotate the crankshaft pulley clockwise 5–6 revolutions to allow the timing belt to be seated in the pulleys.

30. Move the crankshaft pulley to the white TDC mark and inspect the camshaft TDC marks to ensure proper timing of the camshafts.

✳✳ WARNING

If the timing marks do not align, the timing belt removal and installation procedure must be performed again.

31. Install the engine dipstick tube using a new O-ring.

32. Install the power steering pump, and loosely install the mounting bolt, adjustment locknut and adjustment nut.

33. Adjust the power steering belt to a tension such that a 22 lb. (98 N) pull halfway between the 2 drive pulleys will allow the belt to move 0.51–0.65 in. (13.0–16.5mm).

34. Tighten the power steering pump mounting bolt and adjustment locknut.

➡ **If a new belt is used, set the deflection to 0.33–0.43 in. (8.5–11.0mm) and after engine has run for 5 minutes, readjust the new belt to the used belt specification.**

35. Install the alternator belt tensioner arm.

36. Move the alternator tensioner with a Belt Tensioner Release Arm tool YA9317, or equivalent, to release tension from the belt and install the alternator drive belt.

37. Install both engine mount bracket bolts and torque to 33 ft. lbs. (44 Nm).

38. Install the bushing through bolt and tighten to 40 ft. lbs. (54 Nm).

39. Release and carefully remove the floor jack.

40. Install the front lower splash shield.

41. Install both front tires/wheels.

42. Carefully lower the vehicle.

43. Install the battery hold-down bolt in the battery tray.

44. Install the negative battery cable.

45. Enter the radio security code.

INSPECTION

◆ **See Figures 86 thru 95**

Inspect both sides of the timing belt. Replace the belt with a new one if any of the following conditions exist:

- Hardening of the rubber—back side is glossy without resilience and leaves no indentation when pressed with a fingernail
- Cracks on the rubber backing
- Cracks or peeling of the canvas backing
- Cracks on rib root
- Cracks on belt sides
- Missing teeth or chunks of teeth
- Abnormal wear of belt sides—the sides are normal if they are sharp, as if cut by a knife.

If none of these conditions exist, the belt does not need replacement unless it is at the recommended interval. The belt MUST be replaced at the recommended interval.

Camshaft

The camshafts on the CR-V and Odyssey models are installed in the cylinder head and rotates in journals with journal caps that have been machined into the head. No bearings are used between the camshaft and the cylinder head. If a camshaft jour-

Fig. 86 Never bend or twist a timing belt excessively, and do not allow solvents, antifreeze, gasoline, acid or oil to come into contact with the belt

Fig. 87 The timing belt on the left has 60,000 miles of use, the belt on the right has been in service 90,000 miles. The belt on the right is beginning to separate and is ready for replacement

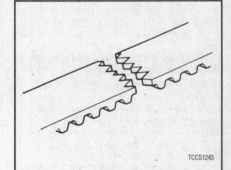

Fig. 88 Check for premature parting of the belt

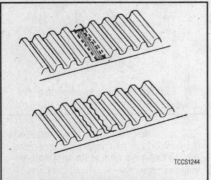

Fig. 89 Check if the teeth are cracked or damaged

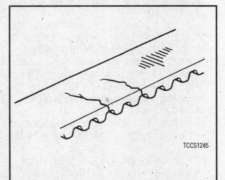

Fig. 90 Look for noticeable cracks or wear on the belt face

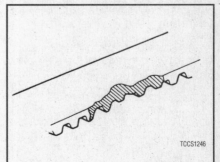

Fig. 91 You may only have damage on one side of the belt; if so, the guide could be the culprit

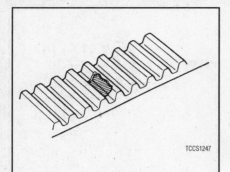

Fig. 92 Foreign materials can get in between the teeth and cause damage

Fig. 93 Inspect the timing belt for cracks, fraying, glazing or damage of any kind

Fig. 94 Damage on only one side of the timing belt may indicate a faulty guide

Fig. 95 ALWAYS replace the timing belt at the interval specified by the manufacturer

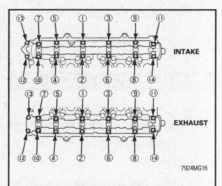

Fig. 96 Camshaft bearing tightening sequence—CR-V models

nal in the cylinder head has been damaged, the head must be replaced, and the cause of the journal failure should be determined before replacing the damaged components.

✳✳ WARNING

Failure to install the camshaft journals in the exact location in which they belong, may cause severe damage to the cylinder head and camshaft.

REMOVAL & INSTALLATION

CR-V

◆ **See Figure 96**

1. Note the radio security code and station presets.
2. Disconnect the negative battery cable.
3. Label and disconnect the spark plug wires.
4. Remove the valve cover and timing belt, as outlined in the procedures in this section.
5. Loosen the rocker arm locknuts and adjusting screws.
6. Remove the camshaft bearing caps, then carefully remove the camshafts.
7. Remove the rocker arms, noting their positions, and inspect for wear.

To install:

➡Use new O-rings, seals, and gaskets when installing the camshaft.

8. Clean and inspect the camshaft bearing caps in the cylinder head.
9. Lubricate the lobes and journals of the camshaft prior to installation. Install the camshaft and the bearing caps.
10. Tighten the camshaft bearing caps to 86 inch lbs. (9.8 Nm), in sequence.
11. Set the camshafts at Top Dead Center (TDC) for No. 1 piston, align the holes in the camshafts with the holes in the No. 1 camshaft holder and insert a 5mm pin punch into the holes.
12. Install the keys into the keyways on the camshafts and install the pulleys, then tighten the retaining bolts to 27 ft. lbs. (37 Nm).
13. Install the timing belt, as outlined in this section.
14. Adjust the valve clearance.
15. Install the valve cover and tighten the nuts to 86 inch lbs. (9.8 Nm).
16. Connect the spark plug wires.
17. Connect the negative battery cable.
18. Enter the security code for the radio.

Odyssey

4-CYLINDER ENGINES

◆ **See Figure 97**

1. Note the security code for the radio.
2. Disconnect the negative battery cable.
3. Remove the timing belt, as outlined in this section.
4. Remove the rocker arm and shaft assembly.

Leave the camshaft bearing cap bolts in the camshaft holders to hold the rocker arm/shaft assembly together.

5. Remove the camshaft and camshaft seal.

To install:

➡Use new O-rings, seals, and gaskets when installing the camshaft.

6. Clean and inspect the camshaft bearing caps in the cylinder head.
7. Lubricate the lobes and journals of the camshaft prior to installation. Install the camshaft with the keyway facing up so that the engine remains at TDC/compression for the No. 1 piston.
8. Lubricate a new camshaft seal with engine oil. Use Camshaft Installer Shaft 07NAF-PT0020A, Installer Cap 07NAF-PT0010A, and Seal Guide 07NAG-PT0010A, or their equivalents to install the camshaft seal.
9. Install the rocker shaft assembly.
10. Install the timing belt, as outlined in this section.
11. Connect the negative battery cable, then enter the security code for the radio.

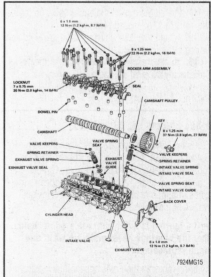

Fig. 97 Exploded view of the camshaft and valve components—4-cylinder Odyssey models

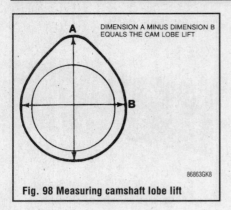

Fig. 98 Measuring camshaft lobe lift

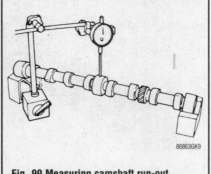

Fig. 99 Measuring camshaft run-out

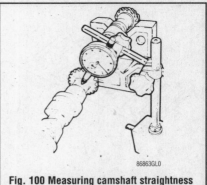

Fig. 100 Measuring camshaft straightness

V6 ENGINE

1. Note the security code for the radio.
2. Disconnect the negative battery cable.
3. Remove the following components, as outlined in this section:
   - Timing belt
   - Intake manifold
   - Valve covers
4. Remove the rocker arm and shaft assembly. Leave the bolts in the rocker shaft to hold the rocker arm/shaft assembly together.
5. Remove the camshaft sprocket bolts and remove the sprockets.
6. Remove the camshaft thrust cover and the camshaft. Replace the oil seal if the oil seal lips are distorted.

To install:

➡**Use new O-rings, seals, and gaskets when installing the camshaft.**

7. Clean and inspect the camshaft bearing caps in the cylinder head.
8. Replace the camshaft oil seals and lubricate the lobes and journals of the camshafts prior to installation.
9. Install the camshafts.
10. Install the camshaft sprockets and torque the bolts to 67 ft. lbs. (90 Nm).
11. Install the rocker shaft assembly and torque the bolts to 17 ft. lbs. (24 Nm).
12. Install the valve covers, intake manifold and timing belt, as outlined in this section.
13. Install the negative battery cable, then enter the security code for the radio.

INSPECTION

▶ **See Figures 98, 99 and 100**

Using solvent, degrease the camshaft and clean out all of the oil holes. Visually inspect the cam lobes and bearing journals for excessive wear. If a lobe is questionable, check all of the lobes as indicated. If a journal or lobe is worn, the camshaft MUST BE or replaced.

➡**If a journal is worn, there is a good chance that the bearings or journals are worn and need replacement.**

If the lobes and journals appear intact, place the front and rear journals in V-blocks and rest a dial indicator on the center journal. Rotate the camshaft to check the straightness. If deviation exceeds 0.001 in. (0.0254mm), replace the camshaft.

Check the camshaft lobes with a micrometer, by

measuring the lobes from the nose to the base and again at 90° (see illustration). The lobe lift is determined by subtracting the second measurement from the first. If all of the exhaust and intake lobes are not identical, the camshaft must be reground or replaced.

Balance Shaft

REMOVAL & INSTALLATION

4-Cylinder Odyssey Models

▶ **See Figure 101**

➡**The CR-V and V6 Odyssey models do not use balance shafts.**

1. Note the radio security code and station presets.
2. Disconnect the negative and positive battery cables.
3. Remove the engine assembly. For details, refer to the engine removal procedures in this section.
4. Remove the cylinder head cover.
5. Remove the upper timing belt cover.
6. Turn the crankshaft to align the timing marks and set cylinder No.1 to Top Dead Center (TDC) for the compression stroke.

7. Remove the crankshaft pulley bolt and remove the crankshaft pulley. Use a Crank Pulley Holder tool No. 07MAB-PY3010A and Holder Handle tool No. 07JAB-001020A or their equivalents, to hold the crankshaft pulley while removing the bolt.
8. Remove the dipstick and the dipstick tube.
9. Remove the through-bolt for the side engine mount and remove the mount.
10. Remove the lower timing belt cover.

➡**If only the balance shaft belt is being removed, thread a 6 x 1.0mm x 25mm through the timing belt tensioner plate to hold the timing belt tensioner in place.**

11. Loosen the timing belt/timing balancer belt adjuster nut ²⁄₃–1 turn. Move the tension adjuster to release the belt tension and retighten the adjuster nut.
12. Remove the balance shaft belt.

➡**For servicing the balance shafts, front refers to the side of the engine facing the radiator. Rear refers to the side of the engine facing the firewall.**

13. Remove the rear balance shaft/gear case assembly.

➡**The rear balance shaft drive sprocket is part of a gear case and the case is removed as a unit.**

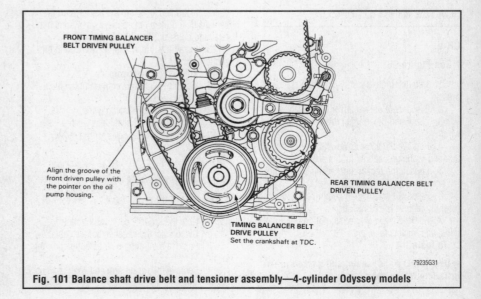

Fig. 101 Balance shaft drive belt and tensioner assembly—4-cylinder Odyssey models

14. Remove the rear balance shaft driven gear as follows:

 a. Remove the maintenance bolt located on the back of the engine block. The bolt is inline with the balance shaft about 3 inches behind the balance shaft sprocket.

 b. Make sure the balance shaft is still in the TDC position.

 c. Scribe a 3 inch (74mm) line from the end of a 6 x 1.0mm x 100mm bolt.

 d. With the maintenance hole sealing bolt removed, insert the 6 x 1.0mm x 100mm bolt into the maintenance hole to the scribed line to lock the rear balance shaft in the TDC position.

 e. Remove the rear balance shaft driven gear bolt and remove the gear.

15. To remove the front balance shaft drive sprocket:

 a. Install a suitable drift through the maintenance hole in the shaft behind the sprocket to hold the front balance shaft.

 b. Remove the front balance shaft mounting nut and sprocket.

16. Remove the front balance shaft outer bearing cap.

17. Remove the oil pan.

18. Remove the oil pump assembly.

19. Remove the front balance shaft retainer plate bolts, then remove the front and rear balance shafts.

20. The installation is the reverse order of disassembly, tighten the front balance shaft retainer plate bolts to 14 ft. lbs. (20 Nm).

Rear Crankshaft Oil Seal

REMOVAL & INSTALLATION

▶ See Figures 102 and 103

1. Before servicing the vehicle, refer to the precautions in the beginning of this section.

2. On CR-V and 4-cylinder Odyssey models remove the transaxle assembly.

3. On V6 Odyssey models, remove the engine and transaxle assembly then separate the transaxle from the engine.

4. On vehicles with an automatic transaxle, remove the driveplate from the crankshaft.

5. On vehicles with a manual transaxle, remove the flywheel from the crankshaft.

6. Carefully pry the crankshaft seal out of the retainer.

Fig. 102 This seal puller made gripping the lip of the rear main seal easy. Simply press the pointed edge into the rubber lip of the seal, pivot the arm, and pull lightly

Fig. 103 Remove the seal by pulling it away from the crankshaft with your fingers

To install:

➡Check the outer edge of the seal housing for burrs or sharp edges. Use a suitable pocket knife of edge reamer to chamfer the edges to prevent seal damage during installation. Do no use any sealant or lubricant on the outer portion of the seal or housing. The outer portion of the seal and the housing should be clean and dry.

7. Apply a light coating clean engine oil to the sealing lip of the new seal. Make sure to keep the outer surface of the oil seal and housing clean and dry.

8. Apply a light coating of lightweight grease such as white grease or petroleum jelly to the crankshaft journal seal surface. **Do not** use wheel bearing, chassis or C/V joint grease.

9. Install the seal onto the crankshaft and into the housing using the appropriate seal driver. Make sure the seal is installed evenly.

10. Install the flywheel or driveplate using new mounting bolts, torque to specification and install the transaxle.

Tighten the mounting bolts in a three step crisscross pattern to the following specifications:

- Manual transaxle flywheel: 75.9 ft. lbs. (103 Nm)
- Automatic transaxle driveplate: 54 ft. lbs. (74 Nm)

Flywheel/Flexplate

REMOVAL & INSTALLATION

▶ See Figures 104, 105 and 106

The flywheel on manual transaxle cars serves as the forward clutch engagement surface. It also serves as the ring gear with which the starter pinion engages to crank the engine. The most common reasons to replace the flywheel are:

- Broken teeth on the flywheel ring gear
- Excessive driveline chatter when engaging the clutch
- Excessive wear, scoring or cracking of the clutch surface

On cars equipped with an automatic transaxle, the torque converter actually forms part of the flywheel. It is bolted to a thin driveplate which, in turn, is bolted to the crankshaft. The driveplate also serves as the ring gear with which the starter

Fig. 104 Installed view of the flywheel and retaining bolts—manual transaxle shown

Fig. 105 Removing the flywheel from a vehicle equipped with a manual transaxle

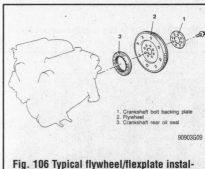

Fig. 106 Typical flywheel/flexplate installation

pinion engages in engine cranking. The driveplate occasionally cracks; the teeth on the ring gear may also break, especially if the starter is often engaged while the pinion is still spinning. The torque converter and driveplate must be separated, and the converter and transaxle are be removed together.

1. Remove the transaxle from the vehicle. For more information, refer to Section 7.

➡On V6 Odyssey models, the engine and transaxle must be removed as a unit.

2. On vehicles equipped with a manual transaxle, remove the clutch assembly from the flywheel, as described in Section 7.

3. Support the flywheel in a secure manner (the flywheel on manual transaxle-equipped vehicles can be heavy).

4. Matchmark the flywheel/flexplate to the rear flange of the crankshaft.

5. Remove the attaching bolts and remove the flywheel/flexplate from the crankshaft.

To install:

6. Clean the flywheel/flexplate attaching bolts, the flywheel/flexplate and the rear crankshaft mounting flange.

7. Position the flywheel/flexplate onto the crankshaft flange so that the matchmarks align.

8. Tighten the mounting bolts, in a three step crisscross pattern, to the following specifications:

- Manual transaxle: 75.9 ft. lbs. (103 Nm)
- Automatic transaxle driveplate: 54 ft. lbs. (74 Nm)

9. On manual transaxle-equipped vehicles, install the clutch assembly. For more information, refer to Section 7.

10. Install the transaxle, as described in Section 7.

EXHAUST SYSTEM

Inspection

▶ See Figures 107 thru 114

➡Safety glasses should be worn at all times when working on or near the exhaust system. Older exhaust systems will almost always be covered with loose rust particles which will shower you when disturbed. These particles are more than a nuisance and could injure your eye.

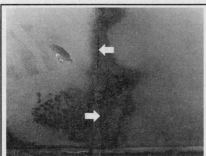

Fig. 107 Cracks in the muffler are a guaranteed leak

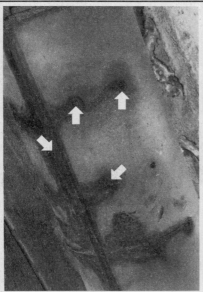

Fig. 108 Check the muffler for rotted spot welds and seams

✳✳ CAUTION

DO NOT perform exhaust repairs or inspection with the engine or exhaust hot. Allow the system to cool completely before attempting any work. Exhaust systems are noted for sharp edges, flaking metal and rusted bolts. Gloves and eye protection are required. A healthy supply of penetrating oil and rags is highly recommended.

Your vehicle must be raised and supported safely to inspect the exhaust system properly. By placing 4 safety stands under the vehicle for support should provide enough room for you to slide under the vehicle and inspect the system completely. Start the inspection at the exhaust manifold or turbocharger pipe where the header pipe is attached and work your way to the back of the vehicle. On dual exhaust systems, remember to inspect both sides of the vehicle. Check the complete exhaust system for open seams, holes loose

Fig. 109 Clean around the edges of the flange gasket with a sharp pick to help with the removal of the sealing ring

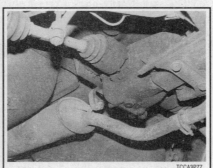

Fig. 110 Make sure the exhaust components are not contacting the body or suspension

connections, or other deterioration which could permit exhaust fumes to seep into the passenger compartment. Inspect all mounting brackets and hangers for deterioration, some models may have

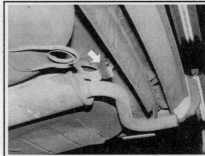

Fig. 111 Check for overstretched or torn exhaust hangers

Fig. 112 Example of a badly deteriorated exhaust pipe

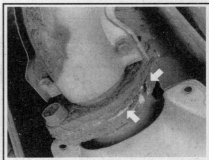

Fig. 113 Inspect flanges for gaskets that have deteriorated and need replacement

Fig. 114 Some systems, like this one, use large O-rings (doughnuts) in between the flanges

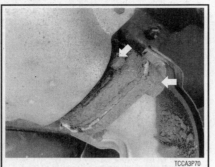

Fig. 115 Nuts and bolts will be extremely difficult to remove when deteriorated with rust

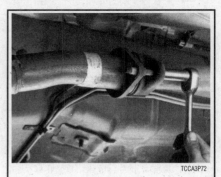

Fig. 116 Example of a flange type exhaust system joint

rubber O-rings that can be overstretched and non-supportive. These components will need to be replaced if found. It has always been a practice to use a pointed tool to poke up into the exhaust system where the deterioration spots are to see whether or not they crumble. Some models may have heat shield covering certain parts of the exhaust system, it will be necessary to remove these shields to have the exhaust visible for inspection also.

REPLACEMENT

♦ See Figure 115

There are basically two types of exhaust systems. One is the flange type where the component ends are attached with bolts and a gasket in-between. The other exhaust system is the slip joint type. These components slip into one another using clamps to retain them together.

✳✳ CAUTION

Allow the exhaust system to cool sufficiently before spraying a solvent exhaust fasteners. Some solvents are highly flammable and could ignite when sprayed on hot exhaust components.

Before removing any component of the exhaust system, ALWAYS squirt a liquid rust dissolving agent onto the fasteners for ease of removal. A lot of knuckle skin will be saved by following this rule. It may even be wise to spray the fasteners and allow them to sit overnight.

Flange Type

♦ See Figure 116

✳✳ CAUTION

Do NOT perform exhaust repairs or inspection with the engine or exhaust hot. Allow the system to cool completely before attempting any work. Exhaust systems are noted for sharp edges, flaking metal and rusted bolts. Gloves and eye protection are required. A healthy supply of penetrating oil and rags is highly recommended. Never spray liquid rust dissolving agent onto a hot exhaust component.

Before removing any component on a flange type system, ALWAYS squirt a liquid rust dissolving agent onto the fasteners for ease of removal. Start by unbolting the exhaust piece at both ends (if required). When unbolting the headpipe from the manifold, make sure that the bolts are free before trying to remove them. if you snap a stud in the exhaust manifold, the stud will have to be removed with a bolt extractor, which often means removal of the manifold itself. Next, disconnect the component from the mounting; slight twisting and turning may be required to remove the component completely from the vehicle. You may need to tap on the component with a rubber mallet to loosen the component. If all else fails, use a hacksaw to separate the parts. An oxy-acetylene cutting torch may be faster but the sparks are DANGEROUS near the fuel tank, and at the very least, accidents could happen, resulting in damage to the under-car parts, not to mention yourself.

Slip Joint Type

♦ See Figure 117

Before removing any component on the slip joint type exhaust system, ALWAYS squirt a liquid rust dissolving agent onto the fasteners for ease of removal. Start by unbolting the exhaust piece at both ends (if required). When unbolting the headpipe from the manifold, make sure that the bolts are free before trying to remove them. if you snap a stud in the exhaust manifold, the stud will have to be removed with a bolt extractor, which often means removal of the manifold itself. Next, remove the mounting U-bolts from around the exhaust pipe you are extracting from the vehicle. Don't be surprised if the U-bolts break while removing the nuts. Loosen the exhaust pipe from any mounting brackets retaining it to the floor pan and separate the components.

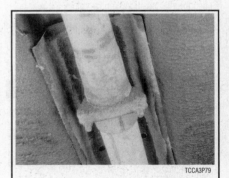

Fig. 117 Example of a common slip joint type system

ENGINE RECONDITIONING

Determining Engine Condition

Anything that generates heat and/or friction will eventually burn or wear out (for example, a light bulb generates heat, therefore its life span is limited). With this in mind, a running engine generates tremendous amounts of both; friction is encountered by the moving and rotating parts inside the engine and heat is created by friction and combustion of the fuel. However, the engine has systems designed to help reduce the effects of heat and friction and provide added longevity. The oiling system reduces the amount of friction encountered by the moving parts inside the engine, while the cooling system reduces heat created by friction and combustion. If either system is not maintained, a break-down will be inevitable. Therefore, you can see how regular maintenance can affect the service life of your vehicle. If you do not drain, flush and refill your cooling system at the proper intervals, deposits will begin to accumulate in the radiator, thereby reducing the amount of heat it can extract from the coolant. The same applies to your oil and filter; if it is not changed often enough it becomes laden with contaminates and is unable to properly lubricate the engine. This increases friction and wear.

There are a number of methods for evaluating the condition of your engine. A compression test can reveal the condition of your pistons, piston rings, cylinder bores, head gasket(s), valves and valve seats. An oil pressure test can warn you of possible engine bearing, or oil pump failures. Excessive oil consumption, evidence of oil in the engine air intake area and/or bluish smoke from the tailpipe may indicate worn piston rings, worn valve guides and/or valve seals. As a general rule, an engine that uses no more than one quart of oil every 1000 miles is in good condition. Engines that use one quart of oil or more in less than 1000 miles should first be checked for oil leaks. If any oil leaks are present, have them fixed before determining how much oil is consumed by the engine, especially if blue smoke is not visible at the tailpipe. In general, the industry standard for acceptable oil consumption is a quart every 600 miles.

COMPRESSION TEST

▶ **See Figure 118**

A noticeable lack of engine power, excessive oil consumption and/or poor fuel mileage measured over an extended period are all indicators of internal engine wear. Worn piston rings, scored or worn cylinder bores, blown head gaskets, sticking or burnt valves, and worn valve seats are all possible culprits. A check of each cylinder's compression will help locate the problem.

➡ **A screw-in type compression gauge is more accurate than the type you simply hold against the spark plug hole. Although it takes slightly longer to use, it's worth the effort to obtain a more accurate reading.**

1. Make sure that the proper amount and viscosity of engine oil is in the crankcase, then ensure the battery is fully charged.

2. Warm-up the engine to normal operating temperature, then shut the engine **OFF**.

3. Disable the ignition system.

4. Label and disconnect all of the spark plug wires from the plugs.

5. Thoroughly clean the cylinder head area around the spark plug ports, then remove the spark plugs.

6. Set the throttle plate to the fully open (wide-open throttle) position. You can block the accelerator linkage open for this, or you can have an assistant fully depress the accelerator pedal.

7. Install a screw-in type compression gauge into the No. 1 spark plug hole until the fitting is snug.

✳✳ WARNING

Be careful not to crossthread the spark plug hole.

8. According to the tool manufacturer's instructions, connect a remote starting switch to the starting circuit.

9. With the ignition switch in the **OFF** position, use the remote starting switch to crank the engine through at least five compression strokes (approximately 5 seconds of cranking) and record the highest reading on the gauge.

10. Repeat the test on each cylinder, cranking the engine approximately the same number of compression strokes and/or time as the first.

11. Compare the highest readings from each cylinder to that of the others. The indicated compression pressures are considered within specifications if the lowest reading cylinder is within 75 percent of the pressure recorded for the highest reading cylinder. For example, if your highest reading cylinder pressure was 150 psi (1034 kPa), then 75 percent of that would be 113 psi (779 kPa). So the lowest reading cylinder should be no less than 113 psi (779 kPa).

12. If a cylinder exhibits an unusually low compression reading, pour a tablespoon of clean engine oil into the cylinder through the spark plug hole and repeat the compression test. If the compression rises after adding oil, it means that the cylinder's piston rings and/or cylinder bore are damaged or worn. If the pressure remains low, the valves may not be seating properly (a valve job is needed), or the head gasket may be blown near that cylinder. If compression in any two adjacent cylinders is low, and if the addition of oil doesn't help raise compression, there is leakage past the head gasket. Oil and coolant in the combustion chamber, combined with blue or constant white smoke from the tailpipe, are symptoms of this problem. However, don't be alarmed by the normal white smoke emitted from the tailpipe during engine warm-up or from cold weather driving. There may be evidence of water droplets on the engine dipstick and/or oil droplets in the cooling system if a head gasket is blown.

OIL PRESSURE TEST

Check for proper oil pressure at the sending unit passage with an externally mounted mechanical oil pressure gauge (as opposed to relying on a factory installed dash-mounted gauge). A tachometer may also be needed, as some specifications may require running the engine at a specific rpm.

1. With the engine cold, locate and remove the oil pressure sending unit.

2. Following the manufacturer's instructions, connect a mechanical oil pressure gauge and, if necessary, a tachometer to the engine.

3. Start the engine and allow it to idle.

4. Check the oil pressure reading when cold and record the number. You may need to run the engine at a specified rpm, so check the specifications.

5. Run the engine until normal operating temperature is reached (upper radiator hose will feel warm).

6. Check the oil pressure reading again with the engine hot and record the number. Turn the engine **OFF**.

7. Compare your hot oil pressure reading to that given in the chart. If the reading is low, check the cold pressure reading against the chart. If the cold pressure is well above the specification, and the hot reading was lower than the specification, you may have the wrong viscosity oil in the engine. Change the oil, making sure to use the proper grade and quantity, then repeat the test.

Low oil pressure readings could be attributed to internal component wear, pump related problems, a low oil level, or oil viscosity that is too low. High oil pressure readings could be caused by an overfilled crankcase, too high of an oil viscosity or a faulty pressure relief valve.

Buy or Rebuild?

Now that you have determined that your engine is worn out, you must make some decisions. The question of whether or not an engine is worth rebuilding is largely a subjective matter and one of personal worth. Is the engine a popular one, or is it an obsolete model? Are parts available? Will it get acceptable gas mileage once it is rebuilt? Is the car it's being put into worth keeping? Would it be less expensive to buy a new engine, have your engine rebuilt by a pro, rebuild it yourself or buy a used engine from a salvage yard? Or would it be simpler and less expensive to buy another car? If you have considered all these matters and more, and have still decided to rebuild the engine, then it is time to decide how you will rebuild it.

➡ **The editors at Chilton feel that most engine machining should be performed by a professional machine shop. Don't think of it as wasting money, rather, as an assurance that the job has been done right the first time. There are many expensive and specialized tools required to perform such tasks as boring and honing an engine block or having a valve job done on a cylinder head. Even inspecting the parts requires expensive micrometers and gauges to properly measure wear and clearances. Also, a machine shop can deliver to you clean, and ready to assemble parts, saving you time and aggravation. Your maximum savings will come from performing the removal, disassembly, assembly and installation of the engine and purchasing or renting only the tools required to perform the above tasks. Depending on the particular circumstances, you may save 40 to 60 percent of the cost doing these yourself.**

A complete rebuild or overhaul of an engine involves replacing all of the moving parts (pistons, rods, crankshaft, camshaft, etc.) with new ones and machining the non-moving wearing surfaces of the block and heads. Unfortunately, this may not be cost effective. For instance, your crankshaft may have been damaged or worn, but it can be machined undersize for a minimal fee.

So, as you can see, you can replace everything inside the engine, but, it is wiser to replace only those parts which are really needed, and, if possible, repair the more expensive ones. Later in this section, we will break the engine down into its two main components: the cylinder head and the engine block. We will discuss each component, and the recommended parts to replace during a rebuild on each.

Engine Overhaul Tips

Most engine overhaul procedures are fairly standard. In addition to specific parts replacement procedures and specifications for your individual engine, this section is also a guide to acceptable rebuilding procedures. Examples of standard rebuilding practice are given and should be used along with specific details concerning your particular engine.

Competent and accurate machine shop services will ensure maximum performance, reliability and

Fig. 118 A screw-in type compression gauge is more accurate and easier to use without an assistant

90943P02

Fig. 119 Use a gasket scraper to remove the old gasket material from the mating surfaces

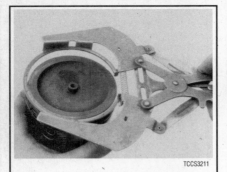

Fig. 120 Use a ring expander tool to remove the piston rings

Fig. 121 Clean the piston ring grooves using a ring groove cleaner tool, or . . .

engine life. In most instances it is more profitable for the do-it-yourself mechanic to remove, clean and inspect the component, buy the necessary parts and deliver these to a shop for actual machine work.

Much of the assembly work (crankshaft, bearings, piston rods, and other components) is well within the scope of the do-it-yourself mechanic's tools and abilities. You will have to decide for yourself the depth of involvement you desire in an engine repair or rebuild.

TOOLS

The tools required for an engine overhaul or parts replacement will depend on the depth of your involvement. With a few exceptions, they will be the tools found in a mechanic's tool kit (see Section 1 of this manual). More in-depth work will require some or all of the following:
- A dial indicator (reading in thousandths) mounted on a universal base
- Micrometers and telescope gauges
- Jaw and screw-type pullers
- Scraper
- Valve spring compressor
- Ring groove cleaner
- Piston ring expander and compressor
- Ridge reamer
- Cylinder hone or glaze breaker
- Plastigage®
- Engine stand

The use of most of these tools is illustrated in this section. Many can be rented for a one-time use from a local parts jobber or tool supply house specializing in automotive work.

Occasionally, the use of special tools is called for. See the information on Special Tools and the Safety Notice in the front of this book before substituting another tool.

OVERHAUL TIPS

Aluminum has become extremely popular for use in engines, due to its low weight. Observe the following precautions when handling aluminum parts:
- Never hot tank aluminum parts (the caustic hot tank solution will eat the aluminum.
- Remove all aluminum parts (identification tag, etc.) from engine parts prior to the tanking.
- Always coat threads lightly with engine oil or anti-seize compounds before installation, to prevent seizure.

- Never overtighten bolts or spark plugs especially in aluminum threads.

When assembling the engine, any parts that will be exposed to frictional contact must be prelubed to provide lubrication at initial start-up. Any product specifically formulated for this purpose can be used, but engine oil is not recommended as a pre-lube in most cases.

When semi-permanent (locked, but removable) installation of bolts or nuts is desired, threads should be cleaned and coated with Loctite• or another similar, commercial non-hardening sealant.

CLEANING

▶ **See Figures 119, 120, 121 and 122**

Before the engine and its components are inspected, they must be thoroughly cleaned. You will need to remove any engine varnish, oil sludge and/or carbon deposits from all of the components to insure an accurate inspection. A crack in the engine block or cylinder head can easily become overlooked if hidden by a layer of sludge or carbon.

Most of the cleaning process can be carried out with common hand tools and readily available solvents or solutions. Carbon deposits can be chipped away using a hammer and a hard wooden chisel. Old gasket material and varnish or sludge can usually be removed using a scraper and/or cleaning solvent. Extremely stubborn deposits may require the use of a power drill with a wire brush. If using a wire brush, use extreme care around any critical machined surfaces (such as the gasket surfaces, bearing saddles, cylinder bores, etc.). USE OF A WIRE BRUSH IS NOT RECOMMENDED ON ANY ALUMINUM COMPONENTS. Always follow any safety recommendations given by the manufacturer of the tool and/or solvent. You should always wear eye protection during any cleaning process involving scraping, chipping or spraying of solvents.

An alternative to the mess and hassle of cleaning the parts yourself is to drop them off at a local garage or machine shop. They will, more than likely, have the necessary equipment to properly clean all of the parts for a nominal fee.

✳✳ CAUTION

Always wear eye protection during any cleaning process involving scraping, chipping or spraying of solvents.

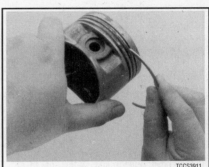

Fig. 122 . . . use a piece of an old ring to clean the grooves. Be careful, the ring can be quite sharp

Remove any oil galley plugs, freeze plugs and/or pressed-in bearings and carefully wash and degrease all of the engine components including the fasteners and bolts. Small parts such as the valves, springs, etc., should be placed in a metal basket and allowed to soak. Use pipe cleaner type brushes, and clean all passageways in the components. Use a ring expander and remove the rings from the pistons. Clean the piston ring grooves with a special tool or a piece of broken ring. Scrape the carbon off of the top of the piston. You should never use a wire brush on the pistons. After preparing all of the piston assemblies in this manner, wash and degrease them again.

✳✳ WARNING

Use extreme care when cleaning around the cylinder head valve seats. A mistake or slip may cost you a new seat.

When cleaning the cylinder head, remove carbon from the combustion chamber with the valves installed. This will avoid damaging the valve seats.

REPAIRING DAMAGED THREADS

▶ **See Figures 123, 124, 125, 126 and 127**

Several methods of repairing damaged threads are available. Heli-Coil® (shown here), Keenserts® and Microdot® are among the most widely used. All involve basically the same principle—drilling out stripped threads, tapping the hole and installing a prewound insert—making welding, plugging and oversize fasteners unnecessary.

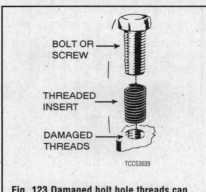

Fig. 123 Damaged bolt hole threads can be replaced with thread repair inserts

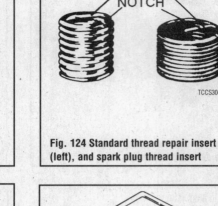

Fig. 124 Standard thread repair insert (left), and spark plug thread insert

Fig. 125 Drill out the damaged threads with the specified size bit. Be sure to drill completely through the hole or to the bottom of a blind hole

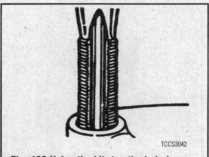

Fig. 126 Using the kit, tap the hole in order to receive the thread insert. Keep the tap well oiled and back it out frequently to avoid clogging the threads

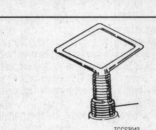

Fig. 127 Screw the insert onto the installer tool until the tang engages the slot. Thread the insert into the hole until it is ¼–½ turn below the top surface, then remove the tool and break off the tang using a punch

Two types of thread repair inserts are usually supplied: a standard type for most inch coarse, inch fine, metric course and metric fine thread sizes and a spark lug type to fit most spark plug port sizes. Consult the individual tool manufacturer's catalog to determine exact applications. Typical thread repair kits will contain a selection of prewound threaded inserts, a tap (corresponding to the outside diameter threads of the insert) and an installation tool. Spark plug inserts usually differ because they require a tap equipped with pilot threads and a combined reamer/tap section. Most manufacturers also supply blister-packed thread repair inserts separately in addition to a master kit containing a variety of taps and inserts plus installation tools.

Before attempting to repair a threaded hole, remove any snapped, broken or damaged bolts or studs. Penetrating oil can be used to free frozen threads. The offending item can usually be removed with locking pliers or using a screw/stud extractor. After the hole is clear, the thread can be repaired, as shown in the series of accompanying illustrations and in the kit manufacturer's instructions.

Engine Preparation

To properly rebuild an engine, you must first remove it from the vehicle, then disassemble and diagnose it. Ideally you should place your engine on an engine stand. This affords you the best access to the engine components. Follow the manufacturer's directions for using the stand with your particular engine. Remove the flywheel or flexplate before installing the engine to the stand.

Now that you have the engine on a stand, and assuming that you have drained the oil and coolant from the engine, it's time to strip it of all but the necessary components. Before you start disassembling the engine, you may want to take a moment to draw some pictures, or fabricate some labels or containers to mark the locations of various components and the bolts and/or studs which fasten them. Modern day engines use a lot of little brackets and clips which hold wiring harnesses and such, and these holders are often mounted on studs and/or bolts that can be easily mixed up. The manufacturer spent a lot of time and money designing your vehicle, and they wouldn't have wasted any of it by haphazardly placing brackets, clips or fasteners on the vehicle. If it's present when you disassemble it, put it back when you assemble, you will regret not remembering that little bracket which holds a wire harness out of the path of a rotating part.

You should begin by unbolting any accessories still attached to the engine, such as the water pump, power steering pump, alternator, etc. Then, unfasten any manifolds (intake or exhaust) which were not removed during the engine removal procedure. Finally, remove any covers remaining on the engine such as the rocker arm, front or timing cover and oil pan. Some front covers may require the vibration damper and/or crank pulley to be removed beforehand. The idea is to reduce the engine to the bare necessities (cylinder head(s), valve train, engine block, crankshaft, pistons and connecting rods), plus any other `in block' components such as oil pumps, balance shafts and auxiliary shafts.

Finally, remove the cylinder head(s) from the engine block and carefully place on a bench. Disassembly instructions for each component follow later in this section.

Cylinder Head

There are two basic types of cylinder heads used on today's automobiles: the Overhead Valve (OHV) and the Overhead Camshaft (OHC). The latter can also be broken down into two subgroups: the Single Overhead Camshaft (SOHC) and the Dual Overhead Camshaft (DOHC). Generally, if there is only a single camshaft on a head, it is just referred to as an OHC head. Also, an engine with an OHV cylinder head is also known as a pushrod engine.

Most cylinder heads these days are made of an aluminum alloy due to its light weight, durability and heat transfer qualities. However, cast iron was the material of choice in the past, and is still used on many vehicles today. Whether made from aluminum or iron, all cylinder heads have valves and seats. Some use two valves per cylinder, while the more hi-tech engines will utilize a multi-valve configuration using 3, 4 and even 5 valves per cylinder. When the valve contacts the seat, it does so on precision machined surfaces, which seals the combustion chamber. All cylinder heads have a valve guide for each valve. The guide centers the valve to the seat and allows it to move up and down within it. The clearance between the valve and guide can be critical. Too much clearance and the engine may consume oil, lose vacuum and/or damage the seat. Too little, and the valve can stick in the guide causing the engine to run poorly if at all, and possibly causing severe damage. The last component all cylinder heads have are valve springs. The spring holds the valve against its seat. It also returns the valve to this position when the valve has been opened by the valve train or camshaft. The spring is fastened to the valve by a retainer and valve locks (sometimes called keepers). Aluminum heads will also have a valve spring shim to keep the spring from wearing away the aluminum.

An ideal method of rebuilding the cylinder head would involve replacing all of the valves, guides, seats, springs, etc. with new ones. However, depending on how the engine was maintained, often this is not necessary. A major cause of valve, guide and seat wear is an improperly tuned engine. An engine that is running too rich, will often wash the lubricating oil out of the guide with gasoline, causing it to wear rapidly. Conversely, an engine which is running too lean will place higher combustion temperatures on the valves and seats allowing them to wear or even burn. Springs fall victim to the driving habits of the individual. A driver who often runs the engine rpm to the redline will wear out or break the springs faster then one that stays well below it. Unfortunately, mileage takes it toll on all of the parts. Generally, the valves, guides, springs and seats in a cylinder head can be machined and re-used, saving you money. However, if a valve is burnt, it may be wise to replace all of the valves, since they were all operating in the same environment. The same goes for any other component on the cylinder head. Think of it as an insurance policy against future problems related to that component.

Unfortunately, the only way to find out which components need replacing, is to disassemble and carefully check each piece. After the cylinder head(s) are disassembled, thoroughly clean all of the components.

DISASSEMBLY

♦ **See Figures 128 thru 138**

Whether it is a single or dual overhead camshaft cylinder head, the disassembly procedure is relatively unchanged. One aspect to pay attention to is careful labeling of the parts on the dual camshaft cylinder head. There will be an intake camshaft and followers as well as an exhaust camshaft and followers and they must be labeled as such. In some cases, the components are identical and could easily be installed incorrectly. DO NOT MIX THEM UP! Determining which is which is very simple; the intake camshaft and components are on the same side of the head as was the intake manifold. Conversely, the exhaust camshaft and components are on the same side of the head as was the exhaust manifold.

Some cylinder heads with rocker arm-type camshaft followers are easily disassembled using a standard valve spring compressor. However, certain models may not have enough open space around the spring for the standard tool and may require you to use a C-clamp style compressor tool with an OHC spring removal tool.

Fig. 128 Exploded view of a valve, seal, spring, retainer and locks from an OHC cylinder head

1. If not already removed, remove the rocker arms and/or shafts and the camshaft. Mark their positions for assembly.
2. Position the cylinder head to allow access to the valve spring.

Fig. 129 Example of a multi-valve cylinder head. Note how it has 2 intake and 2 exhaust valve ports

Fig. 130 C-clamp type spring compressor and an OHC spring removal tool (center) for recessed valve springs

Fig. 131 The cylinder head retains the camshaft using bolt-on bearing cap

3. Use a valve spring compressor tool to relieve the spring tension from the retainer.

➡**Due to engine varnish, the retainer may stick to the valve locks. A gentle tap with a hammer may help to break it loose.**

Fig. 132 Position the OHC spring tool between the jaws of a C-clamp valve spring compressor tool and the spring retainer, then compress the spring

Fig. 133 A sheet of cardboard works well for keeping removed parts in order. The cardboard is easily labeled and holes can be used to help keep the components from moving around

Fig. 134 Compress the valve spring . . .

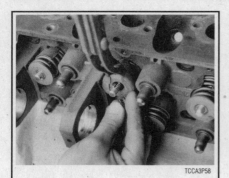

Fig. 135 . . . then remove the valve locks from the valve stem and spring retainer

Fig. 136 Remove the valve spring and retainer from the cylinder head

Fig. 137 Remove the valve seal from the guide. Some gentle prying or pliers may help to remove stubborn ones

Fig. 138 Most aluminum heads will have these valve spring shims. Remove all of them as well

Fig. 139 Valve stems may be rolled on a flat surface to check for bends

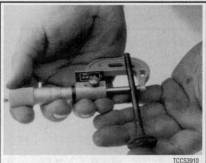

Fig. 140 Use a micrometer to check the valve stem diameter

4. Remove the valve locks from the valve tip and/or retainer. A small magnet may help in removing the small locks.

5. Lift the valve spring, tool and all, off of the valve stem.

6. If equipped, remove the valve seal. If the seal is difficult to remove with the valve in place, try removing the valve first, then the seal. Follow the steps below for valve removal.

7. Position the head to allow access for withdrawing the valve.

➥Cylinder heads that have seen a lot of miles and/or abuse may have mushroomed the valve lock grove and/or tip, causing difficulty in removal of the valve. If this has happened, use a metal file to carefully remove the high spots around the lock grooves and/or tip. Only file it enough to allow removal.

8. Remove the valve from the cylinder head.

9. If equipped, remove the valve spring shim. A small magnetic tool or screwdriver will aid in removal.

10. Repeat Steps 3 though 9 until all of the valves have been removed.

INSPECTION

Now that all of the cylinder head components are clean, it's time to inspect them for wear and/or damage. To accurately inspect them, you will need some specialized tools:

- A 0–1 in. micrometer for the valves
- A dial indicator or inside diameter gauge for the valve guides

- A spring pressure test gauge

If you do not have access to the proper tools, you may want to bring the components to a shop that does.

Valves

▶ See Figures 139 and 140

The first thing to inspect are the valve heads. Look closely at the head, margin and face for any cracks, excessive wear or burning. The margin is the best place to look for burning. It should have a squared edge with an even width all around the diameter. When a valve burns, the margin will look melted and the edges rounded. Also inspect the valve head for any signs of tulipping. This will show as a lifting of the edges or dishing in the center of the head and will usually not occur to all of the valves. All of the heads should look the same, any that seem dished more than others are probably bad. Next, inspect the valve lock grooves and valve tips. Check for any burrs around the lock grooves, especially if you had to file them to remove the valve. Valve tips should appear flat, although slight rounding with high mileage engines is normal. Slightly worn valve tips will need to be machined flat. Last, measure the valve stem diameter with the micrometer. Measure the area that rides within the guide, especially towards the tip where most of the wear occurs. Take several measurements along its length and compare them to each other. Wear should be even along the length with little to no taper. If no minimum diameter is given in the specifications, then the stem should not read more than 0.001 in. (0.025mm) below the unworn area of the

valve stem. Any valves that fail these inspections should be replaced.

Springs, Retainers and Valve Locks

▶ See Figures 141 and 142

The first thing to check is the most obvious, broken springs. Next check the free length and squareness of each spring. If applicable, insure to distinguish between intake and exhaust springs. Use a ruler and/or carpenter's square to measure the length. A carpenter's square should be used to check the springs for squareness. If a spring pressure test gauge is available, check each springs rating and compare to the specifications chart. Check the readings against the specifications given. Any springs that fail these inspections should be replaced.

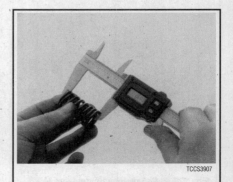

Fig. 141 Use a caliper to check the valve spring free-length

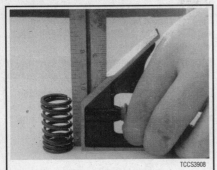

Fig. 142 Check the valve spring for squareness on a flat surface; a carpenter's square can be used

The spring retainers rarely need replacing, however they should still be checked as a precaution. Inspect the spring mating surface and the valve lock retention area for any signs of excessive wear. Also check for any signs of cracking. Replace any retainers that are questionable.

Valve locks should be inspected for excessive wear on the outside contact area as well as on the inner notched surface. Any locks which appear worn or broken and its respective valve should be replaced.

Cylinder Head

There are several things to check on the cylinder head: valve guides, seats, cylinder head surface flatness, cracks and physical damage.

VALVE GUIDES

▶ See Figure 143

Now that you know the valves are good, you can use them to check the guides, although a new valve, if available, is preferred. Before you measure anything, look at the guides carefully and inspect them for any cracks, chips or breakage. Also if the guide is a removable style (as in most aluminum heads), check them for any looseness or evidence of movement. All of the guides should appear to be at the same height from the spring seat. If any seem lower (or higher) from another, the guide has moved. Mount a dial indicator onto the spring side of the cylinder head. Lightly oil the valve stem and insert it into the cylinder head. Position the dial indicator against the valve stem near the tip and zero the

gauge. Grasp the valve stem and wiggle towards and away from the dial indicator and observe the readings. Mount the dial indicator 90 degrees from the initial point and zero the gauge and again take a reading. Compare the two readings for a out of round condition. Check the readings against the specifications given. An Inside Diameter (I.D.) gauge designed for valve guides will give you an accurate valve guide bore measurement. If the I.D. gauge is used, compare the readings with the specifications given. Any guides that fail these inspections should be replaced or machined.

VALVE SEATS

A visual inspection of the valve seats should show a slightly worn and pitted surface where the valve face contacts the seat. Inspect the seat carefully for severe pitting or cracks. Also, a seat that is badly worn will be recessed into the cylinder head. A severely worn or recessed seat may need to be replaced. All cracked seats must be replaced. A seat concentricity gauge, if available, should be used to check the seat run-out. If run-out exceeds specifications the seat must be machined (if no specification is given use 0.002 in. or 0.051mm).

CYLINDER HEAD SURFACE FLATNESS

▶ See Figures 144 and 145

After you have cleaned the gasket surface of the cylinder head of any old gasket material, check the head for flatness.

Place a straightedge across the gasket surface. Using feeler gauges, determine the clearance at the center of the straightedge and across the cylinder head at several points. Check along the centerline and diagonally on the head surface. If the warpage exceeds 0.003 in. (0.076mm) within a 6.0 in. (15.2cm) span, or 0.006 in. (0.152mm) over the total length of the head, the cylinder head must be resurfaced. After resurfacing the heads of a V-type engine, the intake manifold flange surface should be checked, and if necessary, milled proportionally to allow for the change in its mounting position.

CRACKS AND PHYSICAL DAMAGE

Generally, cracks are limited to the combustion chamber, however, it is not uncommon for the head to crack in a spark plug hole, port, outside of the head or in the valve spring/rocker arm area. The first area to inspect is always the hottest: the exhaust seat/port area.

A visual inspection should be performed, b

Fig. 143 A dial gauge may be used to check valve stem-to-guide clearance; read the gauge while moving the valve stem

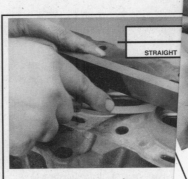

Fig. 144 Check the head for flatness across the center of the head surface using a straightedge and feeler gaug

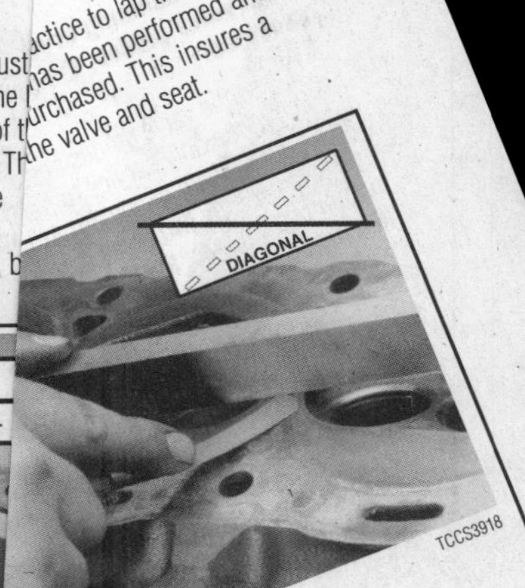

Fig. 145 Checks should also be made along both diagonals of the head surface

izer and precision reaming tools to obtain proper clearances. It would not be cost effective to purchase these tools, unless you plan on rebuilding several of the same cylinder head.

Installing a guide insert involves machining the guide to accept a bronze insert. One style is the coil-type which is installed into a threaded guide. Another is the thin-walled insert where the guide is reamed oversize to accept a split-sleeve insert. After the insert is installed, a special tool is then run through the guide to expand the insert, locking it to the guide. The insert is then reamed to the standard size for proper valve clearance.

Reaming for oversize valves restores normal clearances and provides a true valve seat. Most cast-in type guides can be reamed to accept an valve with an oversize stem. The cost factor for this can become quite high as you will need to purchase the reamer and new, oversize stem valves for all guides which were reamed. Oversizes are generally 0.003 to 0.030 in. (0.076 to 0.762mm), with 0.015 in. (0.381mm) being the most common.

To replace cast-in type valve guides, they must be drilled out, then reamed to accept replacement guides. This must be done on a fixture which will allow centering and leveling off of the original valve seat or guide, otherwise a serious guide-to-seat misalignment may occur making it impossible to properly machine the seat.

Replaceable-type guides are pressed into the cylinder head. A hammer and a stepped drift or punch may be used to install and remove the guides. Before removing the guides, measure the protrusion on the spring side of the head and record it for installation. Use the stepped drift to hammer out the old guide from the combustion chamber side of the head. When installing, determine whether or not the guide also seals a water jacket in the head, and if it does, use the recommended sealing agent. If there is no water jacket, grease the valve guide and its bore. Use the stepped drift, and hammer the new guide into the cylinder head from the spring side of the cylinder head. A stack of washers the same thickness as the measured protrusion may help the installation process.

VALVE SEATS

→Before any valve seat machining can be performed, the guides must be within factory recommended specifications.

→If any machining or replacements were made to the valve guides, the seats must be machined.

If the seats are in good condition, the valves can be lapped to the seats, and the cylinder head assembled. See the valves section for instructions on lapping.

If the valve seats are worn, cracked or damaged, they must be serviced by a machine shop. The valve seat must be perfectly centered to the valve guide, which requires very accurate machining.

CYLINDER HEAD SURFACE

If the cylinder head is warped, it must be machined flat. If the warpage is extremely severe, the head may need to be replaced. In some instances, it may be possible to straighten a warped head enough to allow machining. In either contact a professional machine shop for ser-

→Any OHC cylinder head that shows excessive warpage should have the camshaft bearing journals align bored after the cylinder head has been resurfaced.

Failure to align bore the camshaft bearing journals could result in severe engine damage including but not limited to: valve and piston damage, connecting rod damage, camshaft and/or crankshaft breakage.

CRACKS AND PHYSICAL DAMAGE

Certain cracks can be repaired in both cast iron and aluminum heads. For cast iron, a tapered threaded insert is installed along the length of the crack. Aluminum can also use the tapered inserts, however welding is the preferred method. Some physical damage can be repaired through brazing or welding. Contact a machine shop to get expert advice for your particular dilemma.

ASSEMBLY

▶ See Figure 146

The first step for any assembly job is to have a clean area in which to work. Next, thoroughly clean all of the parts and components that are to be assembled. Finally, place all of the components onto a suitable work space and, if necessary, arrange the parts to their respective positions.

1. Lightly lubricate the valve stems and insert all of the valves into the cylinder head. If possible, maintain their original locations.
2. If equipped, install any valve spring shims which were removed.
3. If equipped, install the new valve seals, keeping the following in mind:
   - If the valve seal presses over the guide, lightly lubricate the outer guide surfaces.
   - If the seal is an O-ring type, it is installed just after compressing the spring but before the valve locks.
4. Place the valve spring and retainer over the stem.
5. Position the spring compressor tool and compress the spring.
6. Assemble the valve locks to the stem.
7. Relieve the spring pressure slowly and

93131P78

Fig. 146 Once assembled, check the valve clearance and correct as needed

insure that neither valve lock becomes dislodged by the retainer.

8. Remove the spring compressor tool.

9. Repeat Steps 2 through 8 until all of the springs have been installed.

10. Install the camshaft(s), rockers, shafts and any other components that were removed for disassembly.

Engine Block

GENERAL INFORMATION

A thorough overhaul or rebuild of an engine block would include replacing the pistons, rings, bearings, timing belt/chain assembly and oil pump. For OHV engines also include a new camshaft and lifters. The block would then have the cylinders bored and honed oversize (or if using removable cylinder sleeves, new sleeves installed) and the crankshaft would be cut undersize to provide new wearing surfaces and perfect clearances. However, your particular engine may not have everything worn out. What if only the piston rings have worn out and the clearances on everything else are still within factory specifications? Well, you could just replace the rings and put it back together, but this would be a very rare example. Chances are, if one component in your engine is worn, other components are sure to follow, and soon. At the very least, you should always replace the rings, bearings and oil pump. This is what is commonly called a "freshen up".

Cylinder Ridge Removal

Because the top piston ring does not travel to the very top of the cylinder, a ridge is built up between the end of the travel and the top of the cylinder bore.

Pushing the piston and connecting rod assembly past the ridge can be difficult, and damage to the piston ring lands could occur. If the ridge is not removed before installing a new piston or not removed at all, piston ring breakage and piston damage may occur.

➡ **It is always recommended that you remove any cylinder ridges before removing the piston and connecting rod assemblies. If you know that new pistons are going to be installed and the engine block will be bored oversize, you may be able to forego this step. However, some ridges may actually prevent the assemblies from being removed, necessitating its removal.**

There are several different types of ridge reamers on the market, none of which are inexpensive. Unless a great deal of engine rebuilding is anticipated, borrow or rent a reamer.

1. Turn the crankshaft until the piston is at the bottom of its travel.

2. Cover the head of the piston with a rag.

3. Follow the tool manufacturers instructions and cut away the ridge, exercising extreme care to avoid cutting too deeply.

4. Remove the ridge reamer, the rag and as many of the cuttings as possible. Continue until all of the cylinder ridges have been removed.

DISASSEMBLY

▶ **See Figures 147 and 148**

The engine disassembly instructions following assume that you have the engine mounted on an engine stand. If not, it is easiest to disassemble the engine on a bench or the floor with it resting on the bell housing or transmission mounting surface. You must be able to access the connecting rod fasteners and turn the crankshaft during disassembly. Also, all engine covers (timing, front, side, oil pan, whatever) should have already been removed. Engines which are seized or locked up may not be able to be completely disassembled, and a core (salvage yard) engine should be purchased.

If not done during the cylinder head removal, remove the timing chain/belt and/or gear/sprocket assembly. Remove the oil pick-up and pump

Fig. 147 Place rubber hose over the connecting rod studs to protect the crankshaft and cylinder bores from damage

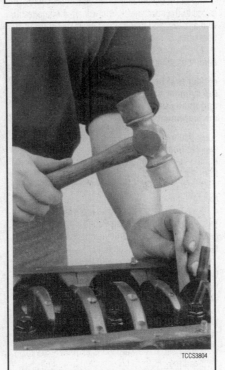

Fig. 148 Carefully tap the piston out of the bore using a wooden dowel

assembly and, if necessary, the pump drive. If equipped, remove any balance or auxiliary shafts. If necessary, remove the cylinder ridge from the top of the bore. See the cylinder ridge removal procedure earlier in this section.

Rotate the engine over so that the crankshaft is exposed. Use a number punch or scribe and mark each connecting rod with its respective cylinder number. The cylinder closest to the front of the engine is always number 1. However, depending on the engine placement, the front of the engine could either be the flywheel or damper/pulley end. Generally the front of the engine faces the front of the vehicle. Use a number punch or scribe and also mark the main bearing caps from front to rear with the front most cap being number 1 (if there are five caps, mark them 1 through 5, front to rear).

✳✳ WARNING

Take special care when pushing the connecting rod up from the crankshaft because the sharp threads of the rod bolts/studs will score the crankshaft journal. Insure that special plastic caps are installed over them, or cut two pieces of rubber hose to do the same.

Again, rotate the engine, this time to position the number one cylinder bore (head surface) up. Turn the crankshaft until the number one piston is at the bottom of its travel, this should allow the maximum access to its connecting rod. Remove the number one connecting rods fasteners and cap and place two lengths of rubber hose over the rod bolts/studs to protect the crankshaft from damage. Using a sturdy wooden dowel and a hammer, push the connecting rod up about 1 in. (25mm) from the crankshaft and remove the upper bearing insert. Continue pushing or tapping the connecting rod up until the piston rings are out of the cylinder bore. Remove the piston and rod by hand, put the upper half of the bearing insert back into the rod, install the cap with its bearing insert installed, and hand-tighten the cap fasteners. If the parts are kept in order in this manner, they will not get lost and you will be able to tell which bearings came form what cylinder if any problems are discovered and diagnosis is necessary. Remove all the other piston assemblies in the same manner. On V-style engines, remove all of the pistons from one bank, then reposition the engine with the other cylinder bank head surface up, and remove that banks piston assemblies.

The only remaining component in the engine block should now be the crankshaft. Loosen the main bearing caps evenly until the fasteners can be turned by hand, then remove them and the caps. Remove the crankshaft from the engine block. Thoroughly clean all of the components.

INSPECTION

Now that the engine block and all of its components are clean, it's time to inspect them for wear and/or damage. To accurately inspect them, you will need some specialized tools:

- Two or three separate micrometers to measure the pistons and crankshaft journals
- A dial indicator
- Telescoping gauges for the cylinder bores

- A rod alignment fixture to check for bent connecting rods

If you do not have access to the proper tools, you may want to bring the components to a shop that does.

Generally, you shouldn't expect cracks in the engine block or its components unless it was known to leak, consume or mix engine fluids, it was severely overheated, or there was evidence of bad bearings and/or crankshaft damage. A visual inspection should be performed on all of the components, but just because you don't see a crack does not mean it is not there. Some more reliable methods for inspecting for cracks include Magnaflux®, a magnetic process or Zyglo®, a dye penetrant. Magnaflux® is used only on ferrous metal (cast iron). Zyglo® uses a spray on fluorescent mixture along with a black light to reveal the cracks. It is strongly recommended to have your engine block checked professionally for cracks, especially if the engine was known to have overheated and/or leaked or consumed coolant. Contact a local shop for availability and pricing of these services.

Engine Block

ENGINE BLOCK BEARING ALIGNMENT

Remove the main bearing caps and, if still installed, the main bearing inserts. Inspect all of the main bearing saddles and caps for damage, burrs or high spots. If damage is found, and it is caused from a spun main bearing, the block will need to be align-bored or, if severe enough, replacement. Any burrs or high spots should be carefully removed with a metal file.

Place a straightedge on the bearing saddles, in the engine block, along the centerline of the crankshaft. If any clearance exists between the straightedge and the saddles, the block must be align-bored.

Align-boring consists of machining the main bearing saddles and caps by means of a flycutter that runs through the bearing saddles.

DECK FLATNESS

The top of the engine block where the cylinder head mounts is called the deck. Insure that the deck surface is clean of dirt, carbon deposits and old gasket material. Place a straightedge across the surface of the deck along its centerline and, using feeler gauges, check the clearance along several points. Repeat the checking procedure with the straightedge placed along both diagonals of the deck surface. If the reading exceeds 0.003 in. (0.076mm) within a 6.0 in. (15.2cm) span, or 0.006 in. (0.152mm) over the total length of the deck, it must be machined.

CYLINDER BORES

▶ See Figure 149

The cylinder bores house the pistons and are slightly larger than the pistons themselves. A common piston-to-bore clearance is 0.0015–0.0025 in. (0.0381–0.0635mm). Inspect and measure the cylinder bores. The bore should be checked for out-of-roundness, taper and size. The results of this inspection will determine whether the cylinder can be used in its existing size and condition, or a rebore to the next oversize is required (or in the case of removable sleeves, have replacements installed).

Fig. 149 Use a telescoping gauge to measure the cylinder bore diameter—take several readings within the same bore

The amount of cylinder wall wear is always greater at the top of the cylinder than at the bottom. This wear is known as taper. Any cylinder that has a taper of 0.0012 in. (0.305mm) or more, must be rebored. Measurements are taken at a number of positions in each cylinder: at the top, middle and bottom and at two points at each position; that is, at a point 90 degrees from the crankshaft centerline, as well as a point parallel to the crankshaft centerline. The measurements are made with either a special dial indicator or a telescopic gauge and micrometer. If the necessary precision tools to check the bore are not available, take the block to a machine shop and have them mike it. Also if you don't have the tools to check the cylinder bores, chances are you will not have the necessary devices to check the pistons, connecting rods and crankshaft. Take these components with you and save yourself an extra trip.

For our procedures, we will use a telescopic gauge and a micrometer. You will need one of each, with a measuring range which covers your cylinder bore size.

1. Position the telescopic gauge in the cylinder bore, loosen the gauges lock and allow it to expand.

➡ Your first two readings will be at the top of the cylinder bore, then proceed to the middle and finally the bottom, making a total of six measurements.

2. Hold the gauge square in the bore, 90 degrees from the crankshaft centerline, and gently tighten the lock. Tilt the gauge back to remove it from the bore.

3. Measure the gauge with the micrometer and record the reading.

4. Again, hold the gauge square in the bore, this time parallel to the crankshaft centerline, and gently tighten the lock. Again, you will tilt the gauge back to remove it from the bore.

5. Measure the gauge with the micrometer and record this reading. The difference between these two readings is the out-of-round measurement of the cylinder.

6. Repeat steps 1 through 5, each time going to the next lower position, until you reach the bottom of the cylinder. Then go to the next cylinder, and continue until all of the cylinders have been measured.

The difference between these measurements will tell you all about the wear in your cylinders. The measurements which were taken 90 degrees from the crankshaft centerline will always reflect the most

wear. That is because at this position is where the engine power presses the piston against the cylinder bore the hardest. This is known as thrust wear. Take your top, 90 degree measurement and compare it to your bottom, 90 degree measurement. The difference between them is the taper. When you measure your pistons, you will compare these readings to your piston sizes and determine piston-to-wall clearance.

Crankshaft

Inspect the crankshaft for visible signs of wear or damage. All of the journals should be perfectly round and smooth. Slight scores are normal for a used crankshaft, but you should hardly feel them with your fingernail. When measuring the crankshaft with a micrometer, you will take readings at the front and rear of each journal, then turn the micrometer 90 degrees and take two more readings, front and rear. The difference between the front-to-rear readings is the journal taper and the first-to-90 degree reading is the out-of-round measurement. Generally, there should be no taper or out-of-roundness found, however, up to 0.0005 in. (0.0127mm) for either can be overlooked. Also, the readings should fall within the factory specifications for journal diameters.

If the crankshaft journals fall within specifications, it is recommended that it be polished before being returned to service. Polishing the crankshaft insures that any minor burrs or high spots are smoothed, thereby reducing the chance of scoring the new bearings.

Pistons and Connecting Rods

PISTONS

▶ See Figure 150

The piston should be visually inspected for any signs of cracking or burning (caused by hot spots or detonation), and scuffing or excessive wear on the skirts. The wrist pin attaches the piston to the connecting rod. The piston should move freely on the wrist pin, both sliding and pivoting. Grasp the connecting rod securely, or mount it in a vise, and try to rock the piston back and forth along the centerline of the wrist pin. There should not be any excessive play evident between the piston and the pin. If there are C-clips retaining the pin in the piston then you have wrist pin bushings in the rods. There should not be any excessive play between the

Fig. 150 Measure the piston's outer diameter, perpendicular to the wrist pin, with a micrometer

wrist pin and the rod bushing. Normal clearance for the wrist pin is approx. 0.001–0.002 in. (0.025–0.051mm).

Use a micrometer and measure the diameter of the piston, perpendicular to the wrist pin, on the skirt. Compare the reading to its original cylinder measurement obtained earlier. The difference between the two readings is the piston-to-wall clearance. If the clearance is within specifications, the piston may be used as is. If the piston is out of specification, but the bore is not, you will need a new piston. If both are out of specification, you will need the cylinder rebored and oversize pistons installed. Generally if two or more pistons/bores are out of specification, it is best to rebore the entire block and purchase a complete set of oversize pistons.

CONNECTING ROD

You should have the connecting rod checked for straightness at a machine shop. If the connecting rod is bent, it will unevenly wear the bearing and piston, as well as place greater stress on these components. Any bent or twisted connecting rods must be replaced. If the rods are straight and the wrist pin clearance is within specifications, then only the bearing end of the rod need be checked. Place the connecting rod into a vice, with the bearing inserts in place, install the cap to the rod and torque the fasteners to specifications. Use a telescoping gauge and carefully measure the inside diameter of the bearings. Compare this reading to the rods original crankshaft journal diameter measurement. The difference is the oil clearance. If the oil clearance is not within specifications, install new bearings in the rod and take another measurement. If the clearance is still out of specifications, and the crankshaft is not, the rod will need to be reconditioned by a machine shop.

➥You can also use Plastigage® to check the bearing clearances. The assembling section has complete instructions on its use.

Camshaft

Inspect the camshaft and rockers as described earlier in this section.

Bearings

All of the engine bearings should be visually inspected for wear and/or damage. The bearing should look evenly worn all around with no deep scores or pits. If the bearing is severely worn,

scored, pitted or heat blued, then the bearing, and the components that use it, should be brought to a machine shop for inspection. Full-circle bearings (used on most camshafts, auxiliary shafts, balance shafts, etc.) require specialized tools for removal and installation, and should be brought to a machine shop for service.

Oil Pump

➥The oil pump is responsible for providing constant lubrication to the whole engine and so it is recommended that a new oil pump be installed when rebuilding the engine.

Completely disassemble the oil pump and thoroughly clean all of the components. Inspect the oil pump gears and housing for wear and/or damage. Insure that the pressure relief valve operates properly and there is no binding or sticking due to varnish or debris. If all of the parts are in proper working condition, lubricate the gears and relief valve, and assemble the pump.

REFINISHING

◆ See Figure 151

Almost all engine block refinishing must be performed by a machine shop. If the cylinders are not to be rebored, then the cylinder glaze can be removed with a ball hone. When removing cylinder glaze with a ball hone, use a light or penetrating type oil to lubricate the hone. Do not allow the hone to run dry as this may cause excessive scoring of the cylinder bores and wear on the hone. If new pistons are required, they will need to be installed to the connecting rods. This should be performed by a machine shop as the pistons must be installed in the correct relationship to the rod or engine damage can occur.

Pistons and Connecting Rods

◆ See Figure 152

Pistons with the wrist pin retained by C-clips on the Odyssey models are an interference fit with the piston and require the use of heat for removal and installation.

Pistons without the wrist pin retained by C-clips on the CR-V and Odyssey models are pressed into the connecting rod small end and require the use of a hydraulic press and special fixtures for removal and installation.

➥The piston and connecting rod assemblies are not serviceable by the average hands-on enthusiast unless specialized training and related equipment are available. Because press fit pistons require special fixtures and/or heaters to remove/install the connecting rod this procedure should only be performed by a machine shop.

All pistons will have a mark indicating the direction to the front of the engine and the must be installed into the engine in that manner. Usually it is a notch or arrow on the top of the piston, or it may be the letter F cast or stamped into the piston.

ASSEMBLY

Before you begin assembling the engine, first give yourself a clean, dirt free work area. Next, clean every engine component again. The key to a good assembly is cleanliness.

Mount the engine block into the engine stand and wash it one last time using water and detergent (dishwashing detergent works well). While washing it, scrub the cylinder bores with a soft bristle brush and thoroughly clean all of the oil passages. Completely dry the engine and spray the entire assembly down with an anti-rust solution such as WD-40® or similar product. Take a clean lint-free rag and wipe up any excess anti-rust solution from the bores, bearing saddles, etc. Repeat the final cleaning process on the crankshaft. Replace any freeze or oil galley plugs which were removed during disassembly.

Crankshaft

◆ See Figures 153, 154, 155 and 156

1. Remove the main bearing inserts from the block and bearing caps.

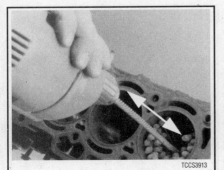
Fig. 151 Use a ball type cylinder hone to remove any glaze and provide a new surface for seating the piston rings

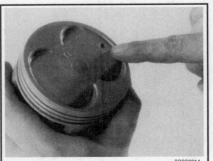
Fig. 152 Most pistons are marked to indicate positioning in the engine (usually a mark means the side facing the front)

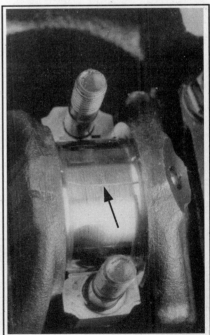
Fig. 153 Apply a strip of gauging material to the bearing journal, then install and torque the cap

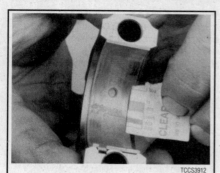

Fig. 154 After the cap is removed again, use the scale supplied with the gauging material to check the clearance

Fig. 155 A dial gauge may be used to check crankshaft end-play

Fig. 156 Carefully pry the crankshaft back and forth while reading the dial gauge for end-play

2. If the crankshaft main bearing journals have been refinished to a definite undersize, install the correct undersize bearing. Be sure that the bearing inserts and bearing bores are clean. Foreign material under inserts will distort bearing and cause failure.

3. Place the upper main bearing inserts in bores with tang in slot.

➡The oil holes in the bearing inserts must be aligned with the oil holes in the cylinder block.

4. Install the lower main bearing inserts in bearing caps.

5. Clean the mating surfaces of block and rear main bearing cap.

6. Carefully lower the crankshaft into place. Be careful not to damage bearing surfaces.

7. Check the clearance of each main bearing by using the following procedure:

a. Place a piece of Plastigage® or its equivalent, on bearing surface across full width of bearing cap and about ¼ in. off center.

b. Install cap and tighten bolts to specifications. Do not turn crankshaft while Plastigage® is in place.

c. Remove the cap. Using the supplied Plastigage® scale, check width of Plastigage® at widest point to get maximum clearance. Difference between readings is taper of journal.

d. If clearance exceeds specified limits, try a 0.001 in. or 0.002 in. undersize bearing in combination with the standard bearing. Bearing clearance must be within specified limits. If standard and 0.002 in. undersize bearing does not bring clearance within desired limits, refinish

crankshaft journal, then install undersize bearings.

8. After the bearings have been fitted, apply a light coat of engine oil to the journals and bearings. Install the rear main bearing cap. Install all bearing caps except the thrust bearing cap. Be sure that main bearing caps are installed in original locations. Tighten the bearing cap bolts to specifications.

9. Install the thrust bearing cap with bolts finger-tight.

10. Pry the crankshaft forward against the thrust surface of upper half of bearing.

11. Hold the crankshaft forward and pry the thrust bearing cap to the rear. This aligns the thrust surfaces of both halves of the bearing.

12. Retain the forward pressure on the crankshaft. Tighten the cap bolts to specifications.

13. Measure the crankshaft end-play as follows:

a. Mount a dial gauge to the engine block and position the tip of the gauge to read from the crankshaft end.

b. Carefully pry the crankshaft toward the rear of the engine and hold it there while you zero the gauge.

c. Carefully pry the crankshaft toward the front of the engine and read the gauge.

d. Confirm that the reading is within specifications. If not, install a new thrust bearing and repeat the procedure. If the reading is still out of specifications with a new bearing, have a machine shop inspect the thrust surfaces of the crankshaft, and if possible, repair it.

14. Rotate the crankshaft so as to position the first rod journal to the bottom of its stroke.

15. Install the rear main seal.

Pistons and Connecting Rods

▶ See Figures 157, 158, 159 and 160

1. Before installing the piston/connecting rod assembly, oil the pistons, piston rings and the cylinder walls with light engine oil. Install connecting rod bolt protectors or rubber hose onto the connecting rod bolts/studs. Also perform the following:

a. Select the proper ring set for the size cylinder bore.

b. Position the ring in the bore in which it is going to be used.

c. Push the ring down into the bore area where normal ring wear is not encountered.

d. Use the head of the piston to position the ring in the bore so that the ring is square with the cylinder wall. Use caution to avoid damage to the ring or cylinder bore.

e. Measure the gap between the ends of the ring with a feeler gauge. Ring gap in a worn cylinder is normally greater than specification. If the ring gap is greater than the specified limits, try an oversize ring set.

f. Check the ring side clearance of the compression rings with a feeler gauge inserted between the ring and its lower land according to specification. The gauge should slide freely around the entire ring circumference without binding. Any wear that occurs will form a step at the inner portion of the lower land. If the lower lands have high steps, the piston should be replaced.

2. Unless new pistons are installed, be sure to install the pistons in the cylinders from which they were removed. The numbers on the connect-

Fig. 157 Checking the piston ring-to-ring groove side clearance using the ring and a feeler gauge

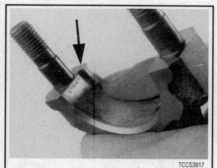

Fig. 158 The notch on the side of the bearing cap matches the tang on the bearing insert

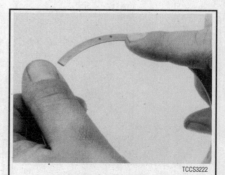

Fig. 159 Most rings are marked to show which side of the ring should face up when installed to the piston

Fig. 160 Install the piston and rod assembly into the block using a ring compressor and the handle of a hammer

ing rod and bearing cap must be on the same side when installed in the cylinder bore. If a connecting rod is ever transposed from one engine or cylinder to another, new bearings should be fitted and the connecting rod should be numbered to correspond with the new cylinder number. The notch on the piston head goes toward the front of the engine.

3. Install all of the rod bearing inserts into the rods and caps.

4. Install the rings to the pistons. Install the oil control ring first, then the second compression ring and finally the top compression ring. Use a piston ring expander tool to aid in installation and to help reduce the chance of breakage.

5. Make sure the ring gaps are properly spaced around the circumference of the piston. Fit a piston ring compressor around the piston and slide the piston and connecting rod assembly down into the cylinder bore, pushing it in with the wooden hammer handle. Push the piston down until it is only slightly below the top of the cylinder bore. Guide the connecting rod onto the crankshaft bearing journal carefully, to avoid damaging the crankshaft.

6. Check the bearing clearance of all the rod bearings, fitting them to the crankshaft bearing journals. Follow the procedure in the crankshaft installation above.

7. After the bearings have been fitted, apply a light coating of assembly oil to the journals and bearings.

8. Turn the crankshaft until the appropriate bearing journal is at the bottom of its stroke, then push the piston assembly all the way down until the connecting rod bearing seats on the crankshaft journal. Be careful not to allow the bearing cap screws to strike the crankshaft bearing journals and damage them.

9. After the piston and connecting rod assemblies have been installed, check the connecting rod side clearance on each crankshaft journal.

10. Prime the oil pump via the oil pump intake tube.

11. On Odyssey 2.2L/2.3L engines, install the balance shaft assemblies.

Cylinder Head(s)

1. Install the cylinder head(s) using new gaskets.

2. Install the timing sprockets/gears and the camshaft belt assembly.

3. On 2.2L/2.3L Odyssey models, install the balance shaft belt assembly.

Engine Covers and Components

Install the timing cover(s) and oil pan. Refer to your notes and drawings made prior to disassembly and install all of the components that were removed. Install the engine into the vehicle.

Engine Start-up and Break-in

STARTING THE ENGINE

Now that the engine is installed and every wire and hose is properly connected, go back and double check that all coolant and vacuum hoses are connected. Check that your oil drain plug is installed and properly tightened. If not already done, install a new oil filter onto the engine. Fill the crankcase with the proper amount and grade of engine oil. Fill the cooling system with a 50/50 mixture of coolant/water.

1. Connect the vehicle battery.

2. Start the engine. Keep your eye on your oil pressure indicator; if it does not indicate oil pressure within 10 seconds of starting, turn the vehicle off.

✳✳ WARNING

Damage to the engine can result if it is allowed to run with no oil pressure. Check the engine oil level to make sure that it is full. Check for any leaks and if found, repair the leaks before continuing. If there is still no indication of oil pressure, you may need to prime the system.

3. Confirm that there are no fluid leaks (oil or other).

4. Allow the engine to reach normal operating temperature (the upper radiator hose will be hot to the touch).

5. At this point you can perform any necessary checks or adjustments, such as checking the ignition timing.

6. Install any remaining components or body panels which were removed.

BREAKING IT IN

Make the first miles on the new engine, easy ones. Vary the speed but do not accelerate hard. Most importantly, do not lug the engine, and avoid sustained high speeds until at least 100 miles. Check the engine oil and coolant levels frequently. Expect the engine to use a little oil until the rings seat. Change the oil and filter at 500 miles, 1500 miles, then every 3000 miles past that.

KEEP IT MAINTAINED

Now that you have just gone through all of that hard work, keep yourself from doing it all over again by thoroughly maintaining it. Not that you may not have maintained it before, heck you could have had one to two hundred thousand miles on it before doing this. However, you may have bought the vehicle used, and the previous owner did not keep up on maintenance. Which is why you just went through all of that hard work. See?

CR-V 2.0L (B20B4 and B20Z2) ENGINE MECHANICAL SPECIFICATIONS

Description	English Specifications	Metric Specifications
General Information		
Engine type	Double Overhead Cam in-line 4 cylinder	
Displacement	120 cubic in.	2.0L (1973cc)
Bore	3.31 in.	84mm
Stroke	3.50 in.	89mm
Compression ratio		
B20B4 Engine	9.2:1	
B20Z2 Engine	9.6:1	
Firing order	1-3-4-2	
Cylinder Head		
Compression		
Minimum	178 psi	1,230 kPa
Maximum deviation	135 psi	930 kPa
	28 psi	200 kPa
Flatness	0.002 in.	0.05mm
Maximum resurface limit	0.008 in.	0.20mm
Cylinder head height (new)	5.195-5.199 in.	131.95-132.05mm
Valve seat width		
Intake	0.049-0.061 in.	1.25-1.55mm
Service limit	0.080 in.	2.0mm
Exhaust	0.049-0.061 in.	1.25-1.55mm
Service limit	0.080 in.	2.0mm
Valve face angle	45°	
Valve seat angle	30°, 45°, 60°	
Cylinder Block		
Bore	3.307-3.308 in.	84.00-84.02mm
Service limit	3.310 in.	84.07mm
Taper (max.)	0.002 in.	0.05mm
Deck surface warpage	0.003 in.	0.07mm
Service limit	0.004 in.	0.10mm
Piston		
Clearance-to-bore	0.0004-0.0016 in.	0.010-0.040mm
Service limit	0.002 in.	0.050mm
*Piston O.D.	3.306-3.307 in.	83.98-83.99mm
Service limit	3.306 in.	83.97mm
*B20B4 engine measured at 0.60 in. (15mm) from bottom of skirt		
*B20Z2 engine measured at 0.80 in. (20mm) from bottom of skirt		
Piston Rings		
End-gap		
Top	0.008-0.012 in.	0.20-0.30mm
Service limit	0.024 in.	0.60mm
Second	0.016-0.022 in.	0.40-0.55mm
Service limit	0.028 in.	0.70mm
Oil	0.008-0.020 in.	0.20-0.50mm
Service limit	0.028 in.	0.70mm
Groove clearance		
Top	0.0022-0.0031 in.	0.055-0.080mm
Service limit	0.005 in.	0.13mm
Second	0.0014-0.0024 in.	0.035-0.060mm
Service limit	0.005 in.	0.13mm
Oil	Not Available	

93133C01

CR-V 2.0L (B20B4 and B20Z2) ENGINE MECHANICAL SPECIFICATIONS

Description	English Specifications	Metric Specifications
Piston Pin		
Diameter	0.8266-0.8268 in.	20.996-21.000mm
Piston-to-pin clearance	0.0004-0.0007 in.	0.010-0.017mm
Connecting rod-to-pin interference	0.0006-0.0013 in.	0.015-0.032mm
Camshaft		
Lobe height		
Intake		
B20B4 Engine	1.3072 in.	33.204mm
B20Z2 Engine	1.3274 in.	33.716mm
Exhaust	1.3200 in.	33.528mm
End play	0.002-0.006 in.	0.05-0.15mm
Service limit	0.020 in.	0.50mm
Journal clearance	0.0012-0.0027 in.	0.030-0.069mm
Service limit	0.006 in.	0.15mm
Crankshaft		
Main bearing journal		
Diameter		
Journal Nos. 1, 2, 4 and 5	2.1644-2.1654 in.	54.976-55.000mm
Journal No. 3	2.1642-2.1651 in.	54.970-55.994mm
Taper	0.0002 in.	0.005mm
Service limit	0.0004 in.	0.10mm
Out-of-round	0.0002 in.	0.005mm
Service limit	0.0004 in.	0.10mm
Main bearing-to-journal clearance		
Journal Nos. 1, 2, 4 and 5	0.0009-0.0017 in.	0.024-0.042mm
Service limit	0.002 in.	0.060mm
Journal No. 3	0.0012-0.0019 in.	0.030-0.048mm
Service limit	0.002 in.	0.060mm
Crankshaft end-play	0.004-0.014 in.	0.10-0.35mm
Service limit	0.018 in.	0.45mm
Crankshaft runout	0.001 in.	0.03mm
Service limit	0.002 in.	0.04mm
Connecting rod journal		
Diameter	1.7707-1.7717 in.	44.976-45.000mm
Taper	0.0002 in.	0.005mm
Service limit	0.0004 in.	0.10mm
Out-of-round	0.0002 in.	0.005mm
Service limit	0.0004 in.	0.10mm
Rod bearing journal clearance	0.0008-0.0015 in.	0.020-0.038mm
Service limit	0.002 in.	0.05mm
Rod side clearance	0.006-0.012 in.	0.10-0.38mm
Service limit	0.016 in.	0.40mm
Connecting rod		
Small end I.D.	0.8255-0.8260 in.	20.968-20.981mm
Big end I.D.	1.890 in.	48.00mm
Valve System		
Type	Pedestal mounted individual rocker mechanically adjusted with adjusting screw and locknut	
Valve face angle	45°	
Cylinder head valve seat angle	30°, 45°, 60°	
Seat width intake and exhaust	0.049-0.061 in.	1.25-1.55mm
Service limit	0.80 in.	2.0mm

93133C02

CR-V 2.0L (B20B4 and B20Z2) ENGINE MECHANICAL SPECIFICATIONS

Description	English Specifications	Metric Specifications
Valve System (cont.)		
Stem-to-guide clearance		
Intake	0.001-0.002 in.	0.02-0.05mm
Service limit	0.003 in.	0.08mm
Exhaust	0.002-0.003 in.	0.05-0.08mm
Service limit	0.004 in.	0.11mm
Stem-to-guide clearance (wobble method)		
Side-to-side valve head movement, valve extended 0.40 in. (10mm) from seat		
Intake	0.002-0.004 in.	0.04-0.10mm
Service limit	0.006 in.	0.16mm
Exhaust	0.004-0.006 in.	0.10-0.16mm
Service limit	0.009 in.	0.22mm
Valve guide installed height		
Intake	0.541-0.561 in.	13.75-14.25mm
Exhaust	0.620-0.640 in.	15.75-16.25mm
Valve guide inside diameter		
Intake	0.260-0.261 in.	6.61-6.63mm
Service limit	0.262 in.	6.65mm
Exhaust	0.260-0.261 in.	6.61-6.63mm
Service limit	0.262 in.	6.65mm
Valve stem installed height		
Intake	1.6049-1.6234 in.	40.765-41.235mm
Service limit	1.6333 in.	41.485mm
Exhaust	1.6837-1.7022 in.	42.765-43.235mm
Service limit	1.7120 in.	43.485mm
Valve clearance (cold)		
Intake	0.003-0.005 in.	0.08-0.12mm
Exhaust	0.006-0.008 in.	0.16-0.20mm
Valve stem outside diameter		
Intake	0.2591-0.2594 in.	6.580-6.590mm
Service limit	0.2580 in.	6.55mm
Exhaust	0.2579-0.2583 in.	6.550-6.560mm
Service limit	0.2570 in.	6.52mm
Valve face margin		
Intake	0.053-0.065 in.	1.35-1.65mm
Service limit	0.045 in.	1.15mm
Exhaust	0.065-0.077 in.	1.65-1.95mm
Service limit	0.057 in.	1.45mm
Valve overall length		
Intake	4.087-4.098 in.	103.80-104.10mm
Exhaust	4.094-4.106 in.	104.00-104.30mm
Valve spring free length		
Intake	1.668 in.	42.36mm
Exhaust	1.745 in.	44.32mm
Oil Pump		
Inner rotor-to-outer rotor radial clearance	0.002-0.006 in.	0.04-0.16mm
Service limit	0.008 in.	0.20mm
Housing-to-rotor axial clearance	0.001-0.003 in.	0.02-0.07mm
Service limit	0.006 in.	0.15mm
Housing-to-outer rotor radial clearance	0.004-0.007 in.	0.10-0.19mm
Service limit	0.008 in.	0.20mm

93133C03

ODYSSEY 2.2L (F22B6) ENGINE MECHANICAL SPECIFICATIONS

Description	English Specifications	Metric Specifications
General Information		
Engine type	Single Overhead Cam in-line 4 cylinder	
Displacement	132 cubic in.	2.2L (2156cc)
Bore	3.35 in.	85mm
Stroke	3.74 in.	95mm
Compression ratio	8.8:1	
Firing order	1-3-4-2	
Cylinder Head		
Compression	178 psi	1,230 kPa
Minimum	135 psi	930 kPa
Maximum deviation	28 psi	200 kPa
Flatness	0.002 in.	0.05mm
Maximum resurface limit	0.008 in.	0.20mm
Cylinder head height (new)	3.935-3.939 in.	99.5-100.05mm
Valve seat width		
Intake	0.049-0.061 in.	1.25-1.55mm
Service limit	0.079 in.	2.0mm
Exhaust	0.049-0.061 in.	1.25-1.55mm
Service limit	0.079 in.	2.0mm
Valve face angle	45°	
Valve seat angle	30°, 45°, 60°	
Cylinder Block		
① Bore		
Diameter		
Cylinder bores marked A or I	3.3468-3.3472 in.	85.010-85.020mm
Cylinder bores marked B or II	3.3465-3.3468 in.	85.000-85.010mm
Service limit	3.3492 in.	85.070mm
Taper (max.)	0.002 in.	0.05mm
Deck surface warpage	0.003 in.	0.07mm
Service limit	0.004 in.	0.10mm
Piston		
Clearance-to-bore	0.0008-0.0016 in.	0.020-0.040mm
Service limit	0.002 in.	0.050mm
Piston O.D. measured at 0.80 in. (21mm) from bottom of skirt		
Piston crowns with no letter or stamped with the letter A	3.3457-3.3461 in.	84.980-84.990mm
Service limit	3.3453 in.	84.970mm
Piston crowns stamped with the letter B	3.3453-3.3457 in.	84.970-84.980mm
Service limit	3.3449 in.	84.960mm
Piston Rings		
End-gap		
Top	0.008-0.014 in.	0.20-0.35mm
Service limit	0.024 in.	0.60mm
Second	0.016-0.022 in.	0.40-0.55mm
Service limit	0.028 in.	0.70mm
Oil	0.008-0.028 in.	0.20-0.70mm
Service limit	0.031 in.	0.80mm
Groove clearance		
Top	0.0014-0.0022 in.	0.035-0.055mm
Service limit	0.005 in.	0.13mm
Second	0.0012-0.0022 in.	0.030-0.055mm
Service limit	0.005 in.	0.13mm
Oil	Not Available	

93133C04

ODYSSEY 2.2L (F22B6) ENGINE MECHANICAL SPECIFICATIONS

Description	English Specifications	Metric Specifications
Piston Pin		
Diameter	0.8659-0.8661 in.	21.994-22.000mm
Piston-to-pin clearance	0.0004-0.0009 in.	0.010-0.022mm
Connecting rod-to-pin interference	0.0005-0.0013 in.	0.013-0.032mm
Camshaft		
Lobe height		
Intake	1.5252 in.	38.741mm
Exhaust	1.5343 in.	38.972mm
End play	0.002-0.006 in.	0.05-0.15mm
Service limit	0.020 in.	0.50mm
Journal clearance	0.0020-0.0035 in.	0.05-0.089mm
Service limit	0.006 in.	0.15mm
Crankshaft		
Main bearing journal		
Diameter		
Journal Nos. 1 and 4	1.9679-1.9688 in.	49.984-50.008mm
Journal No. 2	1.9676-1.9685 in.	49.976-50.000mm
Journal No. 3	1.9674-1.9683 in.	49.972-49.996mm
Journal No. 5	1.9680-1.9690 in.	49.988-50.012mm
Taper	0.0002 in.	0.005mm
Service limit	0.0002 in.	0.006mm
Out-of-round	0.0002 in.	0.005mm
Service limit	0.0002 in.	0.006mm
Main bearing-to-journal clearance		
Journal Nos. 1 and 4	0.0005-0.0015 in.	0.013-0.037mm
Service limit	0.0020 in.	0.050mm
Journal No. 2	0.0008-0.0018 in.	0.021-0.045mm
Service limit	0.0020 in.	0.050mm
Journal No. 3	0.0010-0.0019 in.	0.025-0.049mm
Service limit	0.0022 in.	0.055mm
Journal No. 5	0.0004-0.0013 in.	0.009-0.033mm
Service limit	0.0016 in.	0.040mm
Crankshaft end-play	0.004-0.014 in.	0.10-0.35mm
Service limit	0.018 in.	0.45mm
Crankshaft runout	0.001 in.	0.03mm
Service limit	0.002 in.	0.04mm
Connecting rod journal		
Diameter	1.8888-1.8898 in.	47.976-48.000mm
Taper	0.0002 in.	0.005mm
Service limit	0.0002 in.	0.006mm
Out-of-round	0.0002 in.	0.005mm
Service limit	0.0002 in.	0.005mm
Rod bearing journal clearance	0.0008-0.0019 in.	0.021-0.049mm
Service limit	0.0024 in.	0.06mm
Rod side clearance	0.006-0.012 in.	0.15-0.30mm
Service limit	0.016 in.	0.40mm
Connecting rod		
Small end I.D.	0.8649-0.8654 in.	21.968-21.981mm
Big end I.D.	2.010 in.	51.00mm

93133C05

ODYSSEY 2.2L (F22B6) ENGINE MECHANICAL SPECIFICATIONS

Description	English Specifications	Metric Specifications
Balance shaft		
Journal diameter		
No. 1 front journal	1.6820-1.6824 in.	42.722-42.734mm
Service limit	1.681 in.	42.71mm
No. 1 rear journal	0.8243-0.8248 in.	20.938-20.950mm
Service limit	0.824 in.	20.92mm
No. 2 front and rear journal	1.5241-1.5246 in.	38.712-38.724mm
Service limit	1.524 in.	38.70mm
No. 3 front and rear journals	1.3670-1.3675 in.	34.722-34.734mm
Service limit	1.367 in.	34.71mm
Taper	0.0002 in.	0.005mm
Runout	0.001 in.	0.02mm
End-play, front	0.001 in.	0.03mm
Service limit	0.004-0.016 in.	0.10-0.40mm
End-play, rear	0.002-0.006 in.	0.04-0.15mm
Balance shaft-to-bearing oil clearance		
Nos. 1 and 3 front and no. 3 rear journals	0.0026-0.0039 in.	0.066-0.098mm
Service limit	0.005 in.	0.12mm
No. 1 rear journal	0.0020-0.0030 in.	0.050-0.075mm
Service limit	0.004 in.	0.09mm
No. 2 front and rear journal	0.0030-0.0043 in.	0.076-0.108mm
Service limit	0.005 in.	0.13mm
Balance shaft bearing I.D.		
No. 1 front journal	1.6850-1.6858 in.	42.800-42.820mm
Service limit	1.686 in.	42.83mm
No. 1 rear journal	0.8268-0.8273 in.	21.000-21.013mm
Service limit	0.828 in.	21.02mm
No. 2 front and rear journals	1.5276-1.5283 in.	38.800-38.820mm
Service limit	1.529 in.	38.83mm
No. 3 front and rear journals	1.3701-1.3709 in.	34.800-34.820mm
Service limit	1.371 in.	34.83mm
Valve System		
Type	Shaft mounted rocker arm mechanically adjusted with adjusting screw and locknut	
Valve face angle	45°	
Cylinder head valve seat angle	30°, 45°, 60°	
Seat width intake and exhaust	0.049-0.061 in.	1.25-1.55mm
Service limit	0.79 in.	2.0mm
Stem-to-guide clearance		
Intake	0.0008-0.0018 in.	0.020-0.045mm
Service limit	0.003 in.	0.08mm
Exhaust	0.0022-0.0031 in.	0.055-0.080mm
Service limit	0.005 in.	0.12mm
Stem-to-guide clearance (wobble method)		
Side-to-side valve head movement, valve extended 0.40 in. (10mm) from seat		
Intake		
Service limit	0.002-0.004 in.	0.04-0.09mm
Exhaust	0.006 in.	0.16mm
Service limit	0.004-0.006 in.	0.11-0.16mm
Service limit	0.009 in.	0.24mm

93133C06

ODYSSEY 2.2L (F22B6) ENGINE MECHANICAL SPECIFICATIONS

Description	English Specifications	Metric Specifications
Valve System (cont.)		
Valve guide installed height		
Intake	0.925-0.965 in.	23.50-24.50mm
Exhaust	0.583-0.622 in.	14.80-15.80mm
Valve guide inside diameter		
Intake	0.2171-0.2177 in.	5.515-5.530mm
Service limit	0.219 in.	5.55mm
Exhaust	0.2171-0.2177 in.	5.515-5.530mm
Service limit	0.219 in.	5.55mm
Valve stem installed height		
Intake	1.893-1.924 in.	48.08-48.88mm
Service limit	1.934 in.	49.13mm
Exhaust	1.974-2.006 in.	50.15-50.95mm
Service limit	2.016 in.	51.20mm
Valve clearance (cold)		
Intake	0.009-0.011 in.	0.24-0.28mm
Exhaust	0.011-0.013 in.	0.28-0.32mm
Valve stem outside diameter		
Intake	0.2159-0.2163 in.	5.485-5.495mm
Service limit	0.2148 in.	5.455mm
Exhaust	0.2146-0.2150 in.	5.450-5.460mm
Service limit	0.2134 in.	5.420mm
Valve face margin		
Intake	0.033-0.045 in.	0.85-1.15mm
Service limit	0.026 in.	0.65mm
Exhaust	0.041-0.053 in.	1.05-1.35mm
Service limit	0.037 in.	0.95mm
Valve overall length		
Intake	4.365-4.377 in.	110.88-111.18mm
Exhaust	4.809-4.821 in.	122.15-122.45mm
Valve spring free length		
Intake	2.103 in.	53.42mm
Exhaust	2.152 in.	54.66mm
Oil Pump		
Inner rotor-to-outer rotor radial clearance	0.001-0.006 in.	0.02-0.16mm
Service limit	0.008 in.	0.20mm
Housing-to-rotor axial clearance	0.001-0.003 in.	0.02-0.07mm
Service limit	0.005 in.	0.12mm
Housing-to-outer rotor radial clearance	0.004-0.007 in.	0.10-0.19mm
Service limit	0.008 in.	0.21mm
Oil pressure at warm idle	69 kPa	10 psi minimum
Oil pressure at 3,00 rpm	340 kPa	50 psi minimum

9313C08

ODYSSEY 2.3L (F23A7) ENGINE MECHANICAL SPECIFICATIONS

Description	English Specifications	Metric Specifications
General Information		
Engine type	Single Overhead Cam in-line 4 cylinder	
Displacement	138 cubic in.	2.3L (2254cc)
Bore	3.39 in.	86mm
Stroke	3.82 in.	97mm
Compression ratio	9.3:1	
Firing order	1-3-4-2	
Cylinder Head		
Compression	242 psi	1,670 kPa
Minimum	135 psi	930 kPa
Maximum deviation	28 psi	200 kPa
Flatness	0.002 in.	0.05mm
Maximum resurface limit	0.008 in.	0.20mm
Cylinder head height (new)	3.935-3.939 in.	99.5-100.05mm
Valve seat width		
Intake	0.049-0.061 in.	1.25-1.55mm
Service limit	0.079 in.	2.0mm
Exhaust	0.049-0.061 in.	1.25-1.55mm
Service limit	0.079 in.	2.0mm
Valve face angle	45°	
Valve seat angle	30°, 45°, 60°	
Cylinder Block		
① Bore		
Diameter		
Cylinder bores marked A or I	3.3862-3.3866 in.	86.010-86.020mm
Cylinder bores marked B or II	3.3858-3.3862 in.	86.000-86.010mm
Service limit	3.3070 in.	86.070mm
Taper (max.)	0.002 in.	0.05mm
Deck surface warpage	0.003 in.	0.07mm
Service limit	0.004 in.	0.10mm
Piston		
Clearance-to-bore	0.0008-0.0016 in.	0.020-0.040mm
Service limit	0.002 in.	0.050mm
Piston O.D. measured at 0.60 in. (16mm) from bottom of skirt		
Piston crowns with no letter or stamped with the letter A	3.3850-3.3854 in.	85.980-85.990mm
Service limit	3.3846 in.	85.970mm
Piston crowns stamped with the letter B	3.3846-3.3850 in.	85.970-85.980mm
Service limit	3.3842 in.	85.960mm
Piston Rings		
End-gap		
Top	0.008-0.014 in.	0.20-0.35mm
Service limit	0.024 in.	0.60mm
Second	0.016-0.022 in.	0.40-0.55mm
Service limit	0.028 in.	0.70mm
Oil	0.008-0.028 in.	0.20-0.70mm
Service limit	0.031 in.	0.80mm
Groove clearance		
Top	0.0014-0.0024 in.	0.035-0.060mm
Service limit	0.005 in.	0.13mm
Second	0.0012-0.0022 in.	0.030-0.055mm
Service limit	0.005 in.	0.13mm
Oil	Not Available	

9313C09

① The cylinder bore markings are stamped on the front deck surface of the engine block. Read left-to-right for cylinders 1 through 4

ODYSSEY 2.3L (F23A7) ENGINE MECHANICAL SPECIFICATIONS

Description	English Specifications	Metric Specifications
Piston Pin		
Diameter	0.8646-0.8648 in.	21.961-21.965mm
Service limit	0.8643 in.	21.954mm
Piston-to-pin fit		
Minimum clearance	-0.0002 in.	-0.0050mm
Maximum clearance	+0.00004 in.	+0.0010mm
Service limit	+0.00020 in.	+0.0040mm
Connecting rod-to-pin clearance	0.0002-0.0006 in.	0.005-0.014mm
Service limit	0.0007 in.	0.019mm
Camshaft		
Lobe height		
Intake		
Primary	1.4872 in.	37.775mm
Mid	1.5640 in.	39.725mm
Secondary	1.3575 in.	34.481mm
Exhaust	1.5105 in.	38.366mm
End play	0.002-0.006 in.	0.05-0.15mm
Service limit	0.020 in.	0.50mm
Journal clearance	0.0020-0.0035 in.	0.050-0.089mm
Service limit	0.006 in.	0.15mm
Crankshaft		
Main bearing journal		
Diameter		
Journal Nos. 1, 2, and 4	2.1646-2.1655 in.	54.980-55.004mm
Journal No. 3	2.1644-2.1654 in.	54.976-55.000mm
Journal No. 5	2.1650-2.1660 in.	54.992-55.016mm
Taper	0.0002 in.	0.005mm
Service limit	0.0002 in.	0.006mm
Out-of-round	0.0002 in.	0.005mm
Service limit	0.0002 in.	0.006mm
Main bearing-to-journal clearance		
Journal Nos. 1, 2, and 4	0.0008-0.0018 in.	0.021-0.045mm
Service limit	0.020 in.	0.050mm
Journal No. 3	0.0010-0.0019 in.	0.025-0.049mm
Service limit	0.0022 in.	0.055mm
Journal No. 5	0.0004-0.0013 in.	0.009-0.033mm
Service limit	0.0016 in.	0.040mm
Crankshaft end-play	0.004-0.014 in.	0.10-0.35mm
Service limit	0.018 in.	0.45mm
Crankshaft runout	0.001 in.	0.03mm
Service limit	0.02 in.	0.04mm
Connecting rod journal		
Diameter	1.8888-1.8898 in.	47.976-48.000mm
Taper	0.0002 in.	0.005mm
Service limit	0.0002 in.	0.006mm
Out-of-round	0.0002 in.	0.005mm
Service limit	0.0002 in.	0.005mm
Rod bearing journal clearance	0.0008-0.0019 in.	0.021-0.049mm
Service limit	0.0020 in.	0.06mm
Rod side clearance	0.006-0.012 in.	0.15-0.30mm
Service limit	0.016 in.	0.40mm

93133C10

ODYSSEY 2.3L (F23A7) ENGINE MECHANICAL SPECIFICATIONS

Description	English Specifications	Metric Specifications
Connecting rod		
Small end I.D.	0.8650-0.8652 in.	21.970-21.976mm
Big end I.D.	1.900 in.	48.00mm
Balance shaft		
Journal diameter		
No. 1 front journal	1.6820-1.6824 in.	42.722-42.734mm
Service limit	1.681 in.	42.71mm
No. 1 rear journal	0.8243-0.8248 in.	20.938-20.950mm
Service limit	0.824 in.	20.92mm
No. 2 front and rear journals	1.5241-1.5246 in.	38.712-38.724mm
Service limit	1.524 in.	38.70mm
No. 3 front and rear journals	1.3670-1.3675 in.	34.722-34.734mm
Service limit	1.367 in.	34.71mm
Taper	0.0002 in.	0.005mm
Runout	0.001 in.	0.02mm
Service limit	0.001 in.	0.03mm
End-play, front	0.004-0.016 in.	0.10-0.40mm
End-play, rear	0.002-0.006 in.	0.04-0.15mm
Balance shaft-to-bearing oil clearance		
Nos. 1 and 3 front and no. 3 rear journals	0.0026-0.0039 in.	0.066-0.098mm
Service limit	0.005 in.	0.12mm
No. 1 rear journal	0.0020-0.0030 in.	0.050-0.075mm
Service limit	0.004 in.	0.09mm
No. 2 front and rear journals	0.0030-0.0043 in.	0.076-0.108mm
Service limit	0.005 in.	0.13mm
Balance shaft bearing I.D.		
No. 1 front journal	1.6850-1.6858 in.	42.800-42.820mm
Service limit	1.686 in.	42.83mm
No. 1 rear journal	0.8268-0.8273 in.	21.000-21.013mm
Service limit	0.828 in.	21.02mm
No. 2 front and rear journals	1.5276-1.5283 in.	38.800-38.820mm
Service limit	1.529 in.	38.83mm
No. 3 front and rear journals	1.3701-1.3709 in.	34.800-34.820mm
Service limit	1.371 in.	34.83mm
Valve System		
Type	Shaft mounted rocker arm mechanically adjusted with adjusting screw and locknut	
Valve face angle	45°	
Cylinder head valve seat angle	30°, 45°, 60°	
Seat width intake and exhaust	0.049-0.061 in.	1.25-1.55mm
Service limit	0.79 in.	2.0mm
Stem-to-guide clearance		
Intake	0.0008-0.0018 in.	0.020-0.045mm
Service limit	0.003 in.	0.08mm
Exhaust	0.0022-0.0031 in.	0.055-0.080mm
Service limit	0.005 in.	0.12mm
Stem-to-guide clearance (wobble method)		
Side-to-side valve head movement, valve extended 0.40 in. (10mm) from seat		
Intake	0.002-0.004 in.	0.04-0.09mm
Service limit	0.06 in.	0.16mm
Exhaust	0.004-0.006 in.	0.11-0.16mm
Service limit	0.009 in.	0.24mm

93133C11

ODYSSEY 2.3L (F23A7) ENGINE MECHANICAL SPECIFICATIONS

Description	English Specifications	Metric Specifications
Valve System (cont.)		
Valve guide installed height		
Intake	0.835-0.874 in.	21.20-22.20mm
Exhaust	0.812-0.852 in.	20.63-21.63mm
Valve guide inside diameter		
Intake	0.2171-0.2177 in.	5.515-5.530mm
Service limit	0.219 in.	5.55mm
Exhaust	0.2171-0.2177 in.	5.515-5.530mm
Service limit	0.219 in.	5.55mm
Valve stem installed height		
Intake	1.841-1.872 in.	46.75-47.55mm
Service limit	1.921 in.	47.80mm
Exhaust	1.838-1.869 in.	46.67-47.48mm
Service limit	1.879 in.	47.73mm
Valve clearance (cold)		
Intake	0.009-0.011 in.	0.24-0.28mm
Exhaust	0.011-0.013 in.	0.28-0.32mm
Valve stem outside diameter		
Intake	0.2159-0.2163 in.	5.485-5.495mm
Service limit	0.2148 in.	5.455mm
Exhaust	0.2146-0.2150 in.	5.450-5.460mm
Service limit	0.2134 in.	5.420mm
Valve face margin		
Intake	0.033-0.045 in.	0.85-1.15mm
Service limit	0.026 in.	0.65mm
Exhaust	0.041-0.053 in.	1.05-1.35mm
Service limit	0.037 in.	0.95mm
Valve overall length		
Intake	4.522-4.533 in.	114.85-115.15mm
Exhaust	4.443-4.455 in.	112.85-113.15mm
Valve spring free length		
Intake	2.011 in.	51.08mm
Exhaust	2.188 in.	55.58mm
Oil Pump		
Inner rotor-to-outer rotor radial clearance	0.001-0.006 in.	0.02-0.16mm
Service limit	0.008 in.	0.20mm
Housing-to-rotor axial clearance	0.001-0.003 in.	0.02-0.07mm
Service limit	0.005 in.	0.12mm
Housing-to-rotor radial clearance	0.004-0.007 in.	0.10-0.19mm
Service limit	0.008 in.	0.21mm
Oil pressure at warm idle	69 kPa	10 psi minimum
Oil pressure at 3,00 rpm	340 kPa	50 psi minimum

① The cylinder bore markings are stamped on the front deck surface of the engine block. Read left-to-right for cylinders 1 through 4

93133C12

ODYSSEY 3.5L (J35A1) ENGINE MECHANICAL SPECIFICATIONS

Description	English Specifications	Metric Specifications
General Information		
Engine type	Single Overhead Cam 60° V-6	
Displacement	222 cubic in.	3.5L (3471cc)
Bore	3.50 in.	89mm
Stroke	3.66 in.	93mm
Compression ratio	9.4:1	
Firing order	1-4-2-5-3-6	
Cylinder Head		
Compression	206 psi	1,420 kPa
Minimum	135 psi	930 kPa
Maximum deviation	28 psi	200 kPa
Flatness	0.002 in.	0.05mm
Maximum resurface limit	0.008 in.	0.20mm
Cylinder head height (new)	4.762-4.766 in.	120.95-121.05mm
Valve seat width		
Intake	0.049-0.061 in.	1.25-1.55mm
Service limit	0.079 in.	2.0mm
Exhaust	0.049-0.061 in.	1.25-1.55mm
Service limit	0.079 in.	2.0mm
Valve face angle	45°	
Valve seat angle	30°, 45°, 60°	
Cylinder Block		
Bore		
Diameter	3.5039-3.5045 in.	89.000-89.015mm
Service limit	3.5065 in.	89.065mm
Taper (max.)	0.002 in.	0.05mm
Deck surface warpage	0.003 in.	0.07mm
Service limit	0.004 in.	0.10mm
Piston		
Clearance-to-bore	0.0006-0.0016 in.	0.015-0.040mm
Service limit	0.003 in.	0.080mm
Piston O.D. measured at 0.63 in. (16mm) from bottom of skirt		
Piston O.D.	3.5029-3.5033 in.	88.975-88.985mm
Service limit	3.5026 in.	88.965mm
Piston Rings		
End-gap		
Top	0.008-0.014 in.	0.20-0.35mm
Service limit	0.024 in.	0.60mm
Second	0.016-0.022 in.	0.40-0.55mm
Service limit	0.028 in.	0.70mm
Oil	0.008-0.028 in.	0.20-0.70mm
Service limit	0.031 in.	0.80mm
Groove clearance		
Top	0.0014-0.0024 in.	0.035-0.060mm
Service limit	0.005 in.	0.13mm
Second	0.0012-0.0022 in.	0.030-0.055mm
Service limit	0.005 in.	0.13mm
Oil	Not Available	
Piston Pin		
Diameter	0.8646-0.8648 in.	21.962-21.965mm
Service limit	0.8643 in.	21.954mm

93133C13

ODYSSEY 3.5L (J35A1) ENGINE MECHANICAL SPECIFICATIONS

Description	English Specifications	Metric Specifications
Piston Pin (cont.)		
Piston-to-pin fit		
Minimum clearance	-0.0002 in.	-0.0050mm
Maximum clearance	+0.00004 in.	+0.0010mm
Service limit	+0.00020 in.	+0.0040mm
Connecting rod-to-pin clearance	0.0002-0.0006 in.	0.005-0.014mm
Service limit	0.0007 in.	0.019mm
Camshaft		
Lobe height		
Intake		
Primary	1.4107 in.	35.832mm
Secondary	1.2231 in.	31.066mm
Exhaust	1.4080 in.	35.763mm
End play	0.002-0.008 in.	0.05-0.20mm
Service limit	0.008 in.	0.20mm
Journal clearance	0.0020-0.0035 in.	0.050-0.089mm
Service limit	0.006 in.	0.15mm
Crankshaft		
Main bearing journal		
Diameter	2.8337-2.8346 in.	71.976-72.000mm
Taper	0.0002 in.	0.005mm
Service limit	0.0004 in.	0.010mm
Out-of-round	0.0002 in.	0.005mm
Service limit	0.0004 in.	0.010mm
Main bearing-to-journal clearance	0.0008-0.0017 in.	0.020-0.044mm
Service limit	0.0020 in.	0.050mm
Crankshaft end-play	0.004-0.014 in.	0.10-0.450mm
Service limit	0.0180 in.	0.450mm
Crankshaft runout	0.0008 in.	0.020mm
Service limit	0.0012 in.	0.030mm
Connecting rod journal		
Diameter	2.1644-2.1654 in.	54.976-55.000mm
Taper	0.0002 in.	0.005mm
Service limit	0.0004 in.	0.010mm
Out-of-round	0.0002 in.	0.005mm
Service limit	0.0004 in.	0.010mm
Rod bearing journal clearance	0.0008-0.0017 in.	0.020-0.044mm
Service limit	0.0020 in.	0.050mm
Rod side clearance	0.006-0.014 in.	0.15-0.35mm
Service limit	0.0180 in.	0.450mm
Connecting rod		
Small end I.D.	0.8650-0.8652 in.	21.970-21.976mm
Big end I.D.	2.280 in.	58.00mm
Valve System		
Type	Shaft mounted rocker arm mechanically adjusted with adjusting screw and locknut	
Valve face angle	45°	
Cylinder head valve seat angle	30°, 45°, 60°	
Seat width intake and exhaust	0.049-0.061 in.	1.25-1.55mm
Service limit	0.79 in.	2.0mm

9313C14

ODYSSEY 3.5L (J35A1) ENGINE MECHANICAL SPECIFICATIONS

Description	English Specifications	Metric Specifications
Valve System (cont.)		
Stem-to-guide clearance		
Intake	0.0008-0.0018 in.	0.020-0.045mm
Service limit	0.003 in.	0.08mm
Exhaust	0.0022-0.0031 in.	0.055-0.080mm
Service limit	0.005 in.	0.12mm
Stem-to-guide clearance (wobble method)		
Side-to-side valve head movement, valve extended 0.40 in. (10mm) from seat		
Intake	0.002-0.004 in.	0.04-0.09mm
Service limit	0.006 in.	0.16mm
Exhaust	0.004-0.006 in.	0.11-0.16mm
Service limit	0.009 in.	0.24mm
Valve guide installed height		
Intake	0.835-0.874 in.	21.20-22.20mm
Exhaust	0.812-0.852 in.	20.63-21.63mm
Valve guide inside diameter		
Intake	0.2171-0.2177 in.	5.515-5.530mm
Service limit	0.219 in.	5.55mm
Exhaust	0.2171-0.2177 in.	5.515-5.530mm
Service limit	0.219 in.	5.55mm
Valve stem installed height		
Intake	1.841-1.872 in.	46.75-47.55mm
Service limit	1.921 in.	47.80mm
Exhaust	1.838-1.869 in.	46.68-47.48mm
Service limit	1.879 in.	47.73mm
Valve clearance (cold)		
Intake	0.008-0.009 in.	0.20-0.24mm
Exhaust	0.011-0.013 in.	0.28-0.34mm
Valve stem outside diameter		
Intake	0.2159-0.2163 in.	5.485-5.495mm
Service limit	0.2148 in.	5.455mm
Exhaust	0.2146-0.2150 in.	5.450-5.460mm
Service limit	0.2134 in.	5.420mm
Valve face margin		
Intake	0.033-0.045 in.	0.85-1.15mm
Service limit	0.026 in.	0.65mm
Exhaust	0.041-0.053 in.	1.05-1.35mm
Service limit	0.037 in.	0.95mm
Valve overall length		
Intake	4.522-4.533 in.	114.85-115.15mm
Exhaust	4.443-4.455 in.	112.85-113.15mm
Valve spring free length		
Intake	1.9713 in.	50.07mm
Exhaust	2.106 in.	53.48mm
Oil Pump		
Inner rotor-to-outer rotor radial clearance	0.002-0.006 in.	0.04-0.16mm
Service limit	0.008 in.	0.20mm
Housing-to-rotor axial clearance	0.001-0.003 in.	0.02-0.07mm
Service limit	0.005 in.	0.12mm
Housing-to-outer rotor radial clearance	0.006-0.007 in.	0.14-0.19mm
Service limit	0.008 in.	0.20mm
Oil pressure at warm idle	70 kPa	10 psi minimum
Oil pressure at 3.00 rpm	490 kPa	71 psi minimum

9313C15

CR-V ENGINE TORQUE SPECIFICATIONS

Component	English	Metric
Camshaft		
Camshaft sprocket bolt	27 ft. lbs.	37 Nm
Journal-to-cylinder head bolt (follow tightening sequence)	86 inch lbs.	9.8 Nm
Connecting Rod Bearings		
Rod journal cap bolts (apply engine oil to bolt threads)	23 ft. lbs.	31 Nm
Crankshaft		
Pulley bolt	130 ft. lbs.	177 Nm
Flywheel oil seal housing-to-block bolts	86 inch lbs.	9.8 Nm
Flywheel-to-crankshaft (manual transmission)	75.9 ft. lbs.	103 Nm
Drive plate-to-crankshaft (automatic transmission)	54 ft. lbs.	74 Nm
Cylinder Head		
Valve cover fasteners	86 inch lbs.	9.8 Nm
Cylinder head bolts (Oil bolt threads and follow torque sequence)		
Step 1	22 ft. lbs.	29 Nm
Step 2	63 ft. lbs.	85 Nm
Distributor		
Mounting bolts	17 ft. lbs.	24 Nm
Exhaust Manifold		
Exhaust manifold-to-cylinder head	23 ft. lbs.	31 Nm
Front pipe-to-exhaust manifold nuts	40 ft. lbs.	54 Nm
Intake Manifold		
Intake manifold-to-cylinder head	17 ft. lbs.	23 Nm
Main Bearings		
Cap bolts (apply engine oil to bolt threads)		
Step 1	18 ft. lbs.	25 Nm
Step 2	56 ft. lbs.	76 Nm
Baffle plate fasteners	86 inch lbs.	9.8 Nm
Oil Pan		
Oil pan bolts	104 inch lbs.	12 Nm
Drain plug (always use a new crush washer)	33 ft. lbs.	44 Nm
Oil Pump		
Housing-to-block bolts		
6 x 1.0 mm	86 inch lbs.	9.8 Nm
8 x 1.25 mm	17 ft. lbs.	24 Nm
Relief valve sealing bolt	29 ft. lbs.	39 Nm
Pump cover-to-housing bolts	48 inch lbs.	5 Nm
Rocker Arms		
Valve adjustment locknut	18 ft. lbs.	25 Nm
Pivot bolt-to-cylinder head	46 ft. lbs.	63 Nm
Thermostat		
Thermostat housing-to-cover	104 inch lbs.	12 Nm
Timing Belt and Cover		
Tensioner bolt	40 ft. lbs.	54 Nm
Cover bolts	86 inch lbs.	9.8 Nm
Water Pump		
Water pump-to-block bolts	104 inch lbs.	12 Nm

93133C16

ODYSSEY ENGINE TORQUE SPECIFICATIONS

Component	English	Metric
Balance shaft		
2.2L and 2.3L engine only		
Balance shaft gear case bolt	18 ft. lbs.	25 Nm
Rear balance shaft sealing bolt	22 ft. lbs.	29 Nm
Rear balance shaft driven gear	18 ft. lbs.	25 Nm
Front balance shaft belt driven pulley	22 ft. lbs.	29 Nm
Rear balance shaft retainer plate bolts	14 ft. lbs.	20 Nm
Camshaft		
Camshaft sprocket bolt		
2.2L engine	27 ft. lbs.	37 Nm
2.3L engine	43 ft. lbs.	59 Nm
3.5L engine	67 ft. lbs.	90 Nm
Bearing journal-to-cylinder head (follow tightening sequence)		
6 x 1.0mm bolts	104 inch lbs.	12 Nm
8 x 1.25mm bolts	16 ft. lbs.	22 Nm
Connecting Rod Bearings		
Rod journal cap bolts (apply engine oil to bolt threads)		
2.2L engine	34 ft. lbs.	46 Nm
2.3L and 3.5L engine		
Step 1	14 ft. lbs.	20 Nm
Step 2	90°	90°
Crankshaft		
Pulley bolt	181 ft. lbs.	245 Nm
Flywheel oil seal housing-to-block bolts	86 inch lbs.	9.8 Nm
Flywheel-to-crankshaft (manual transaxle)	76 ft. lbs.	103 Nm
Drive plate-to-crankshaft (automatic transaxle)	54 ft. lbs.	74 Nm
Cylinder Head		
Valve cover fasteners	86 inch lbs.	9.8 Nm
Cylinder head bolts (Oil bolt threads and follow torque sequence)		
2.2L and 3.5L engines		
Step 1	29 ft. lbs.	39 Nm
Step 2	51 ft. lbs.	69 Nm
Step 3	72.3 ft. lbs.	98.1 Nm
2.3L engine		
Step 1	22 ft. lbs.	29 Nm
Step 2	90°	90°
Step 3	90°	90°
Step 4 (Only if using new bolts)	90°	90°
Distributor		
Mounting bolts		
2.2L engine	16 ft. lbs.	22 Nm
2.3L engine	13 ft. lbs.	18 Nm

93133C17

ODYSSEY ENGINE TORQUE SPECIFICATIONS

Component	English	Metric
Exhaust Manifold		
Exhaust manifold-to-cylinder head	23 ft. lbs.	31 Nm
Front pipe-to-exhaust manifold nuts	40 ft. lbs.	54 Nm
Intake Manifold		
Intake manifold-to-cylinder head	16 ft. lbs.	22 Nm
Main Bearings		
Cap bolts (apply engine oil to bolt threads)		
2.2L engine		
Step 1	22 ft. lbs.	29 Nm
Step 2	54 ft. lbs.	74 Nm
2.3L engine		
Step 1 (11 x 1.5 mm bolts)	22 ft. lbs.	29 Nm
Step 2 (11 x 1.5 mm bolts)	58 ft. lbs.	78 Nm
Step 3 (6 x 1.0 mm bolts)	104 inch lbs.	12 Nm
Cap bolts (apply engine oil to bolt threads)		
3.5L engine (follow sequence)		
Step 1 (11 x 1.5 mm bolts)	56 ft. lbs.	76 Nm
Step 2 (10 x 1.25 mm side bolts)	36 ft. lbs.	49 Nm
Oil Pan		
Oil pan fasteners		
2.2L engine	120 inch lbs.	14 Nm
2.3L and 3.5L engine	104 inch lbs.	12 Nm
Drain plug (always use a new crush washer)		
2.2L and 2.3L	33 ft. lbs.	44 Nm
3.5L engine	29 ft. lbs.	39 Nm
Oil Pump		
Relief valve sealing bolt	29 ft. lbs.	39 Nm
Pump cover-to-housing bolts		
2.2L and 2.3L engine	61 inch lbs.	7 Nm
3.5L engine	48 inch lbs.	6 Nm
Housing-to-block 6 x 1.0 mm bolts (apply liquid sealant to threads)	104 inch lbs.	12 Nm
Balancer gear case-to-housing 8 x 1.25 mm bolts (2.2L and 2.3L engine only)	18 ft. lbs.	25 Nm
Rocker Arms		
Valve adjustment locknut	14 ft. lbs.	20 Nm
Thermostat		
Thermostat housing-to-cover	104 inch lbs.	12 Nm
Thermostat housing-to-cylinder head	16 ft. lbs.	22 Nm
Timing Belt and Cover		
Cover bolts	104 inch lbs.	12 Nm
Tensioner nut	33 ft. lbs.	44 Nm
Water Pump		
Water pump-to-block bolts	104 inch lbs.	12 Nm

93133C18

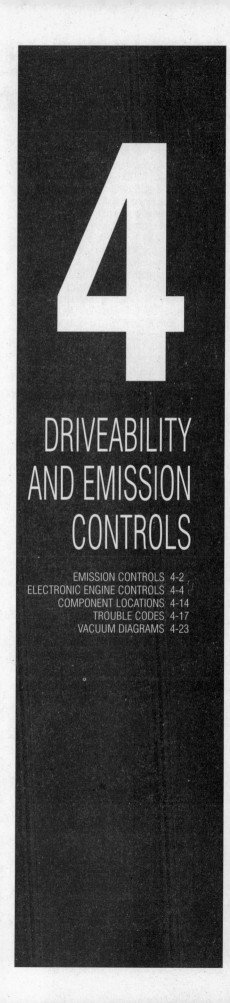

4

DRIVEABILITY AND EMISSION CONTROLS

EMISSION CONTROLS

The following systems can be checked individually, and most of them can be checked using suitable diagnostic equipment. Beginning with model year 1996, Honda passenger vehicles are On Board Diagnostic version II (OBD-II) compliant. Using a suitable OBD-II Data Scan Tool (DST) can save precious diagnostic time and allows the systems to be checked while the engine is running without chance of damaging the component, wire connections or the insulation.

Another advantage of using a suitable OBD-II DST is that the systems can be checked how they interact with one another, and can be checked during initial start-up, monitored during the warm up period and at normal operating temperatures.

A suitable OBD-II DST also allows for any stored Diagnostic Trouble Codes (DTCs) faults to be accessed and cleared.

Crankcase Ventilation System

OPERATION

♦ See Figure 1

The Positive Crankcase Ventilation (PCV) system is used to control and purge the crankcase blow-by vapors. The gases are recycled in the following way:

As the engine is running, clean, filtered air is drawn through the air filter and into the crankcase. As the air passes through the crankcase, it picks up the combustion gases and carries them out of the crankcase, through the PCV valve, and into the induction system. As they enter the intake manifold, they are drawn into the combustion chamber where they are burned.

The most critical component in the system is the PCV valve. This valve controls the amount of gases that are recycled into the combustion chamber. At low engine speeds, the valve is partially closed, limiting the flow of gases into the intake manifold. As engine speed increases, the valve opens to admit greater quantities of gases into the intake manifold. If the PCV valve becomes clogged, the system is designed to allow excessive amounts of blow-by gases to back flow through the crankcase tube into the air cleaner to be consumed by normal combustion.

The Positive Crankcase Ventilation (PCV) system must be operating correctly to provide complete removal of the crankcase vapors. Fresh air is supplied to the crankcase from the air filter, mixed with the internal exhaust gases, passed through the PCV valve and into the intake manifold.

The PCV valve meters the flow at a rate depending upon the manifold vacuum. If the manifold vacuum is high, the PCV restricts the flow to the intake manifold. If abnormal operating conditions occur, excessive amounts of internal exhaust gases back flow through the crankcase vent tube into the air filter to be burned by normal combustion.

Because the PCV valve vents the crankcase, a defective valve allows the build up of harmful blow-by gases that dilute and damage the lubricating properties of the engine oil. Additionally, the crankcase operating pressure increases and may cause a gasket or seal failure, resulting in an engine oil leak. In extreme cases, a seal or gasket could be completely forced away from the sealing surfaces, causing a severe oil leak.

TESTING

➤**Never operate an engine without a PCV valve or a ventilation system, except as directed by testing procedures, for it can become damaged.**

Incorrect operation of the PCV system can cause multiple driveability symptoms.

A plugged valve or hose may cause:
- Rough idle
- Stalling or slow idle speed
- Oil leaks
- Sludge in engine

A leaking valve or hose would cause:
- Rough idle
- Stalling
- High idle speed

PCV Valve
♦ See Figures 2 and 3

1. Check the PCV lines and connections for restrictions and leaks.
2. Start the engine and allow the engine to reach a warm idle.
3. With the engine running at idle, using a suitable pliers or fingers, squeeze the hose between the PCV valve and the intake manifold. The PCV valve should make a clicking noise when the hose is squeezed closed.
4. If the PCV does not make a clicking noise:
   a. Shut off the engine, refer to PCV valve removal as outlined in Section 1 and remove the valve.
   b. Shake the valve and listen for a rattling noise:
   - If the PCV valve doesn't rattle or doesn't move freely when shaken, replace it and recheck the system.
   - If the PCV valve does rattle freely when shaken, check the valve's grommet and hoses for leaks and replace any parts that are cracked or damaged. Recheck the PCV valve operation.

REMOVAL & INSTALLATION

Refer to Section 1 for removal and installation of the PCV valve. The PCV valve should be inspected every 2 years or 60,000 miles (96,000 km) and replaced as necessary.

Evaporative Emission Controls

OPERATION

♦ See Figure 4

Changes in atmospheric temperature cause fuel tanks to breathe, that is, the air within the tank expands and contracts with outside temperature changes. If an unsealed system was used, when the temperature rises, air would escape through the tank vent tube or the vent in the tank cap. The air which escapes contains gasoline vapors.

The Evaporative Emission Control System provides a sealed fuel system with the capability to store and condense fuel vapors. When the fuel evaporates in the fuel tank, the vapor passes through the EVAP emission valve, through vent hoses or tubes to a carbon filled evaporative canister. When the engine is operating the vapors are drawn into the intake manifold and burned during combustion.

A sealed, maintenance free evaporative canister is used. The canister is filled with granules of an

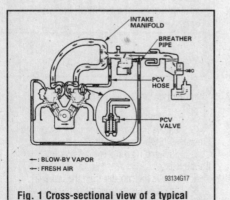

**: BLOW-BY VAPOR
**: FRESH AIR

93134G17

Fig. 1 Cross-sectional view of a typical PCV system

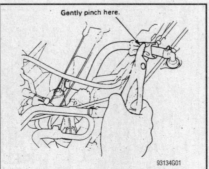

93134G01

Fig. 2 When the engine is at a warm idle, a clicking sound should be heard from the PCV valve when the PCV hose is pinched

93131P56

Fig. 3 The PCV valve is located on the valve cover and sealed with a rubber O-ring. The PCV valve, seal, hose and clamp should be inspected during routine maintenance

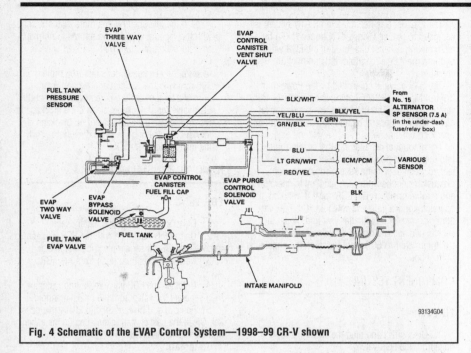

Fig. 4 Schematic of the EVAP Control System—1998–99 CR-V shown

activated carbon mixture. Fuel vapors entering the canister are absorbed by the charcoal granules. A vent cap is located on the top of the canister to provide fresh air to the canister when it is being purged. The vent cap opens to provide fresh air into the canister, which circulates through the charcoal, releasing trapped vapors and carrying them to the engine to be burned.

Fuel tank pressure vents fuel vapors into the canister. They are held in the canister until they can be drawn into the intake manifold. The canister purge valve allows the canister to be purged at a pre-determined time and engine operating conditions.

Vacuum to the canister is controlled by the canister purge valve. The valve is operated by the PCM. The PCM regulates the valve by switching the ground circuit on and off based on engine operating conditions. When energized, the valve prevents vacuum from reaching the canister. When not energized the valve allows vacuum to purge the vapors from the canister.

During warm up and for a specified time during hot starts, the PCM energizes the valve-preventing vacuum from reaching the canister. The EVAP purge control solenoid begins to operate when the engine coolant temperature reaches a predetermined operating temperature.

Once the proper coolant temperature is achieved, the PCM controls the ground circuit to the valve. When the PCM opens the ground, this allows vacuum to flow through the canister and vapors are purged from the canister into the throttle body. During certain idle conditions, the PCM may energize the purge valve to control fuel mixture calibrations.

The fuel tank is sealed with a pressure-vacuum relief filler cap. The relief valve in the cap is a safety feature, preventing excessive pressure or vacuum in the fuel tank. If the cap is malfunctioning, and needs to be replaced, ensure that the replacement is the identical cap to ensure correct system operation.

The following components are part of and affect the operation of the EVAP (Evaporative Emission) Control system:

- Fuel Tank
- Fuel Fill Cap
- Evap Two Way Valve
- Evap Control Canister
- Evap Three Way Valve
- Fuel Tank Pressure Sensor
- Powertrain (PCM) Control Module
- Evap Purge Control Solenoid Valve
- Evap Control Canister Vent Shut Valve

COMPONENT TESTING

The Evaporative Emission (EVAP) Controls are monitored by the Powertrain Control Module (PCM) and if found to be malfunctioning the PCM records the problem in the fault memory as a Diagnostic Trouble Code (DTC). If the problem persists or compromises the vehicle's emissions, the Malfunction Indicator Light (MIL) could be activated.

Evaporative Emissions (EVAP) Control Canister

▶ See Figure 5

This canister is used as a storage facility for fuel vapors that have escaped from components such as

Fig. 5 EVAP control canister—1997 CR-V shown

the fuel tank. This canister prevents these vapors from entering the atmosphere.

Generally, the only testing done to the canister is a visual inspection. Look the canister over and replace it with a new one if there is any evidence of cracks or other damage.

Evaporative Hoses and Tubes

Inspect all system hoses and tubes for signs of damage or cracks. Any damage or leakage must be repaired.

Evaporative Emissions Purge Control Solenoid Valve

▶ See Figure 6

The evaporative emissions control solenoid valve is located at between the canister and the intake manifold.

1. Disconnect the vacuum hose from the valve.
2. Connect a vacuum pump to the vacuum hose.
3. Turn the ignition switch **ON**.
4. Apply vacuum to the hose.
5. If the valve holds vacuum, the valve is OK.
6. If the valve does not hold vacuum:
   a. Turn the ignition switch **OFF**.
   b. Detach the electrical connector from the valve.
   c. Check for continuity between the red/yellow wire and ground. If continuity is present, replace the valve. If no continuity is present, check for an open circuit in the red/yellow wire between the valve and the PCM.
7. When finished testing, attach all disconnected hoses, connectors, and wires.

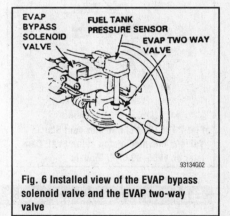

Fig. 6 Installed view of the EVAP bypass solenoid valve and the EVAP two-way valve

REMOVAL & INSTALLATION

Evaporative Emissions Canister

1. Raise and support the vehicle.
2. Remove the bolts retaining the Evaporative Emissions (EVAP) canister and bracket assembly.
3. Label and disconnect the vapor hoses from the canister.
4. Remove the canister from the bracket.
5. Installation is the reverse of the removal procedure.

Evaporative Emissions Control Shut Valve

▶ **See Figure 7**

1. Disconnect the vacuum hose from the EVAP shut valve.
2. Remove the fasteners that hold the EVAP shut valve to the canister.
3. Remove the EVAP control shut valve from the canister.

To install:

4. Install the EVAP control shunt valve and fasteners.
5. Connect all vacuum hoses.

Canister Purge Valve (Two-Way Valve)

▶ **See Figure 8**

1. Raise and support the vehicle.
2. Detach the electrical harness from the valve.
3. Disconnect the fuel vapor hoses and remove the valve.
4. Installation is the reverse of the removal procedure.

Exhaust Gas Recirculation System

OPERATION

▶ **See Figure 9**

➡ **CR-V Models are not equipped with an Exhaust Gas Recirculation (EGR) system.**

The Exhaust Gas Recirculation (EGR) system is designed to reduce Oxides of Nitrogen (NO_x) by recirculating exhaust gas through the EGR valve and into the intake manifold and combustion chambers.

The EGR Valve is controlled by the Powertrain Control Module (PCM) that relies on feedback from various sensors. The PCM contains a memory for ideal EGR Valve operation and lift suited to various operating conditions.

The amount of exhaust gas that is reintroduced into the combustion cycle is determined by several factors, such as: engine speed, engine vacuum, exhaust system backpressure, coolant temperature, and throttle position. The EGR valve is vacuum operated and via an inline solenoid. The EGR vacuum diagram for a particular year and model of vehicle is displayed on the Vehicle Emission Control Information (VECI) label found on the underside of the hood.

COMPONENT TESTING

EGR Valve

1. Disconnect and plug the vacuum supply hose from the EGR valve.
2. Start the engine, then apply the parking brake, block the rear wheels and position the transmission in Neutral. Allow the engine to reach normal operating temperature.
3. Using a hand-held vacuum pump, slowly apply 8 in. Hg (26 kPa) of vacuum to the EGR valve nipple.

a. If the idle speed drops more than 100 rpm with the vacuum applied and returns to normal after the vacuum is removed, the EGR valve is OK.

b. If the idle speed does not drop more than 100 rpm with the vacuum applied and return to normal after the vacuum is removed, inspect the EGR valve for a blockage; clean it if a blockage is found. Replace the EGR valve if no blockage is found, or if cleaning the valve does not remedy the malfunction.

REMOVAL & INSTALLATION

EGR Valve

1. Disconnect the negative battery cable.
2. On models equipped with the EGR lift sensor, remove the EGR lift sensor electrical connector.
3. Detach the vacuum hose from the EGR valve.
4. Unfasten the EGR valve mounting fasteners, then separate the valve from the intake manifold.
5. Remove and discard the old EGR valve gasket. Clean the gasket mating surfaces on the valve and the intake manifold.

To install:

6. Install the EGR valve, along with a new gasket, on the upper intake manifold, then install and tighten the mounting bolts
7. Attach the vacuum hose to the EGR valve.
8. If equipped, install the EGR lift sensor electrical connector.
9. Connect the negative battery cable.

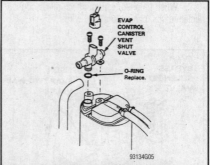

Fig. 7 The Control Canister Vent Shut Valve is mounted on top of the EVAP Canister on 1998–99 CR-V Models

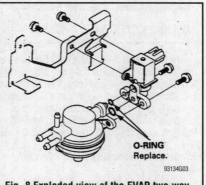

Fig. 8 Exploded view of the EVAP two-way valve

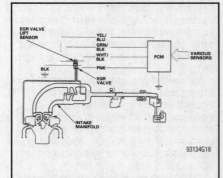

Fig. 9 Cross-sectional view of a typical EGR system

ELECTRONIC ENGINE CONTROLS

The following systems can be checked individually, and most of them can be checked using suitable diagnostic equipment. Beginning with model year 1996 the Honda passenger vehicles are On Board Diagnostic version II (OBD-II) compliant. Using a suitable OBD-II Data Scan Tool (DST) can save precious diagnostic time and allows the systems to be checked while the engine is running without chance of damaging the component, wire connections or the insulation.

Another advantage of using a suitable OBD-II DST is that the systems can be checked how they interact with one another, and can be checked during initial start-up, monitored during the warm up period and at normal operating temperatures.

A suitable OBD-II DST also allows for any stored Diagnostic Trouble Codes (DTCs) faults to be accessed and cleared.

Engine Control Module (ECM)

OPERATION

➡ **The term Powertrain Control Module (PCM) is used in this manual to refer to the engine control computer, whether it is a Powertrain Control Module (PCM) or an Engine Control Module (ECM):**

The heart of the electronic engine management system, which is found on the vehicles covered by this manual, is the Engine or Powertrain control module (ECM/PCM). On vehicles equipped with a manual transaxle, there is no need for a control unit to control shift points as the transaxle is shifted manually. On these models, the engine management system uses an ECM. The 1995 Odyssey models used a separate Transmission Control Module (TCM) that linked with the ECM to control the automatic transaxle shift points.

Beginning with the 1996 Odyssey and 1997 CR-V models equipped with an automatic transaxle, the TCM and ECM have been combined into one unit, called the Powertrain Control Module (PCM). The

PCM processes input information from various sensors, compares the input with pre-programmed information and sends output signals to control the fuel supply, ignition timing, and the engine emission system. The PCM also controls the shift functions of the on vehicles equipped with an automatic transaxle.

Regardless of who the manufacturer may be, all computer control modules are serviced in a similar manner. Care must be taken when handling these expensive electronic components in order to protect them from damage. Carefully follow all instructions included with the replacement part. Avoid touching pins or connectors to prevent damage from static electricity or contaminating the electrical connection. Some input voltages and resistance values are quite small and the readings very sensitive. A poor electrical connection could drastically affect the values recognized by the PCM and cause a poor running condition.

As the PCM is a sensitive electronic component and must be kept away from areas of heat, debris and fluids, the PCM is located in the interior on both the CR-V and Odyssey models. The PCM is located as follows:

- CR-V models: Behind the front passenger's right side kick panel
- 1995–98 Odyssey models: Behind the front passenger's right side footrest
- 1999–00 Odyssey models: In lower portion of the center console

All of the computer control modules contain a Programmable Read Only Memory (PROM) chip that contains calibration information specific to the vehicle application.

✳✳ WARNING

To prevent the possibility of permanent control module damage, the ignition switch MUST always be OFF when disconnecting power from or reconnecting power to the module. This includes unplugging the module connector, disconnecting the negative battery cable, removing the module fuse or even attempting to jump start your dead battery using jumper cables.

In case of an ECM failure, the system will default to a pre-programmed set of values. These are compromise values which allow the engine to operate, although at a reduced efficiency. This is variously known as the default, limp or back-up mode. Driveability is usually affected when the ECM enters this mode and should trigger the Malfunction Indicator Lamp (MIL) indicator.

REMOVAL & INSTALLATION

Sometimes substituting a known good ECM/PCM can be helpful when attempting to diagnose a problem in the engine management system. When substituting a control unit, make sure that both control units are identical. Installing the wrong control unit could damage the substituted unit, and/or possibly damage other related sensors or components in the vehicle being tested.

The control units are very sensitive to changes in the charging system operating voltage and voltage spikes. Make sure the alternator and battery are functioning properly. An alternator that is over charging will not only damages the battery, the volt-

age output may be enough to cause damage to other electrical components and control units.

Operating a vehicle with a discharged or defective battery can cause the vehicle's charging system to be overworked. Never operate a vehicle with a battery cable disconnected. If the vehicle requires a jump start, be careful to connect the battery cables properly, and wait at least one minute after the cables have been installed the start the vehicle.

➥**If the PCM must be replaced on a 1998 2.3L or 1999–00 V6 Odyssey, the immobilizer code must be rewritten using a Honda PGM Tester in order for the engine to start.**

CR-V and 4-Cylinder Odyssey Models

▸ **See Figures 10 and 11**

1. Make sure the ignition switch is turned **OFF**, then disconnect the negative battery cable.

✳✳ WARNING

To prevent the possibility of permanent control module damage, the ignition switch MUST always be OFF when disconnecting power from or reconnecting power to the module. This includes unplugging the module connector, disconnecting the negative battery cable, removing the module fuse or even attempting to jump your dead battery using jumper cables.

2. Locate the computer control module.
3. On CR-V models, remove the front passenger's right side kick panel.

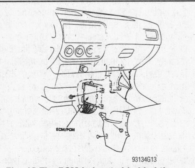

93134G13

Fig. 10 The PCM is located behind the front passenger's right side kick panel on CR-V models

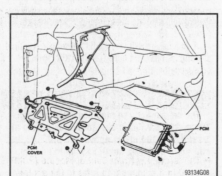

93134G08

Fig. 11 On 4-cylinder Odyssey models, the PCM is located behind the front passenger foot rest

4. On 4-cylinder Odyssey models, if necessary, remove the right side door sill molding, then pull back the front passenger's carpet and remove the control unit cover.
5. Remove the control module mounting hardware.
6. Detach the electrical connectors from the control module.
7. Remove the control module.

To install:

8. Attach the electrical connectors to the computer control module.
9. Position the control module in its mounting location and secure with the mounting hardware.
10. Install the remaining items in the reverse order of disassembly.
11. Check that the ignition switch is **OFF**, then connect the negative battery cable.

➥**On 1998 2.3L Odyssey models, the immobilizer code must be rewritten using a Honda PGM Tester in order for the engine to start.**

V6 Odyssey Models

▸ **See Figures 12 and 13**

➥**If the PCM must be replaced on a V6 Odyssey, the immobilizer code must be rewritten using a Honda PGM Tester in order for the engine to start.**

1. Make sure the ignition switch is turned **OFF**, then disconnect the negative battery cable.

✳✳ WARNING

To prevent the possibility of permanent control module damage, the ignition switch MUST always be OFF when disconnecting power from or reconnecting power to the module. This includes unplugging the module connector, disconnecting the negative battery cable, removing the module fuse or even attempting to jump your dead battery using jumper cables.

2. Locate the computer control module.
3. Pull back both front carpets.
4. Remove the passenger's and driver's side lower center console covers.
5. Remove the PCM cover fasteners and remove the cover through the passenger's side lower center console.
6. Remove the control module mounting hardware.

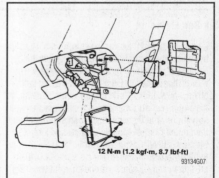

12 N·m (1.2 kgf·m, 8.7 lbf·ft)

93134G07

Fig. 12 The PCM is located in the lower center console on V6 Odyssey models

7. Detach the electrical connectors from the control module.

8. Remove the control module.

To install:

9. Attach the electrical connectors to the computer control module.

10. Position the control module in its mounting location and secure with the mounting hardware.

11. Install the remaining items in the reverse order of disassembly.

12. Check that the ignition switch is **OFF**, then connect the negative battery cable.

When substituting a control unit on V6 Odyssey model, the following steps must be followed.

13. Using a non-immobilizer ignition key blank, cut a temporary ignition key for the vehicle to be tested.

14. Refer to the removal and installation procedures in this section and remove the PCM from both the donor vehicle and the vehicle to be tested. Label each PCM with the vehicle's serial number to avoid confusing the control units.

15. Install the known good PCM into the vehicle to be tested, following the procedures outlined in this section.

16. Tape the ignition key from the donor vehicle to the test vehicle's temporary key head to head so the PCM will recognize the immobilizer code from the donor vehicle, allowing the engine to be started.

17. Once the test is completed reinstall the PCM for each vehicle and destroy the temporary key.

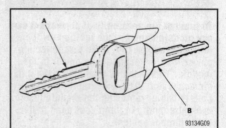

Fig. 13 Tape a temporary ignition key (A) to the donor vehicle's immobilizer ignition key (B) when substituting a PCM on V6 Odyssey models

Oxygen Sensor

OPERATION

▶ **See Figure 14**

An Oxygen (O_2) Sensor is an input device used by the engine control computer to monitor the amount of oxygen in the exhaust gas stream. The information is used by the computer, along with other inputs, to fine-tune the air/fuel mixture so that the engine can run with the greatest efficiency in all conditions. The O_2 sensor sends this information to the Engine Control Module/Powertrain Control Module (ECM/PCM) in the form of a 100–900 millivolt (mV) reference signal. The signal is actually created by the O_2 sensor itself through chemical interactions between the sensor tip material (zirconium dioxide in almost all cases) and the oxygen levels in the exhaust gas stream and ambient atmo-

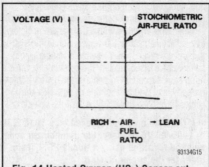

Fig. 14 Heated Oxygen (HO_2) Sensor output voltage vs. mixture ratio

sphere gas. At operating temperatures, approximately 1100°F (600°C), the element becomes a semiconductor. Essentially, through the differing levels of oxygen in the exhaust gas stream and in the surrounding atmosphere, the sensor creates a voltage signal that is directly and consistently related to the concentration of oxygen in the exhaust stream. Typically, a higher than normal amount of oxygen in the exhaust stream indicates that not all of the available oxygen was used in the combustion process, because there was not enough fuel (lean condition) present. Inversely, a lower than normal concentration of oxygen in the exhaust stream indicates that a large amount was used in the combustion process, because a larger than necessary amount of fuel was present (rich condition). Thus, the engine ECM/PCM can correct the amount of fuel introduced into the combustion chambers by controlling the fuel injector opening time.

The ECM/PCM uses the HO_2 sensor output voltage as an indication of the oxygen content of the burnt exhaust gasses. Because the oxygen content directly affects the HO_2 sensor output, the signal voltage from the sensor to the ECM/PCM fluctuates constantly. This fluctuation is caused by interaction between the ECM/PCM and the HO_2 sensor, which follows a general pattern: detect, compare, compensate, detect, compare, compensate, etc. This means that when the ECM/PCM detects a lean signal from the HO_2 sensor, it compares the reading with known parameters stored within its memory. It calculates that there is too much oxygen present in the exhaust gases, so it compensates by adding more fuel to the air/fuel mixture. This, in turn, causes the HO_2 sensor to send a rich signal to the computer, which, then compares this new signal, and adjusts the air/fuel mixture again. This pattern constantly repeats itself: detect rich, compare, compensate lean, detect lean, compare, compensate rich, etc. Since the HO_2 sensor fluctuates between rich and lean, and because the lean limit for sensor output is 100 mV and the rich limit is 900 mV, the proper voltage signal from a normally functioning O_2 sensor consistently fluctuates between 100–300 and 700–900 mV.

➡ **The sensor voltage may never quite reach 100 or 900 mV, but it should fluctuate from at least below 300 mV to above 700 mV, and the mid-point of the fluctuations should be centered around 500 mV.**

To improve O_2 sensor efficiency, newer O_2 sensors were designed with a built-in heating element, and were called Heated Oxygen (HO_2) Sensors. The heating element was incorporated into the sensor so

that the sensor would reach optimal operating temperature quicker, meaning that the O_2 sensor output signal could be used by the engine control computer sooner and also stabilizes the sensor's output. Because the sensor reaches optimal temperature quicker, vehicles can enjoy improved driveability and fuel economy even before the engine reaches normal operating temperature.

Beginning with model year 1996, the On-Board Diagnostics second generation (OBD-II), an updated system based on the former OBD-I became mandatory for passenger vehicles produced for sale in the United States. The OBD-II system used on the CR-V and Odyssey models is also installed on vehicles sold in Canada. This system requires the use of two HO_2 sensors, the Primary Heated Oxygen (PHO_2) Sensor and the Secondary Heated Oxygen (SHO_2) Sensor. The PHO_2 sensor is located before the catalytic converter and performs the same functions as the HO_2 sensor found on vehicles equipped with a single sensor. The Secondary Heated Oxygen (SHO_2) Sensor is located after the catalytic converter and enables the ECM/PCM to monitor the PHO_2 sensor and catalytic converter efficiency. The SHO_2 sensor mounted in the exhaust system after the catalytic converter is not used to affect air/fuel mixture, it is used solely to monitor the catalytic converter and PHO_2 sensor efficiency.

TESTING

The best, and most accurate method to test the operation of an O_2 sensor is with the use of either an oscilloscope or a Diagnostic Scan Tool (DST), following their specific instructions for testing. It is possible, however, to test whether the O_2 sensor is functioning properly within general parameters using a Digital Volt-Ohmmeter (DVOM), also referred to as a Digital Multi-Meter (DMM). Newer DMM's are often designed to perform many advanced diagnostic functions. Some are constructed to be used as an oscilloscope. Two in-vehicle testing procedures, and one bench test procedure, will be provided for the common zirconium dioxide oxygen sensor. The first in-vehicle test makes use of a standard DVOM with a 10 megohms impedance, whereas the second in-vehicle test presented necessitates the usage of an advanced DMM with MIN/MAX/Average functions. Both of these in-vehicle test procedures are likely to set Diagnostic Trouble Codes (DTC's) in the engine control computer. Therefore, after testing, be sure to clear all DTC's before retesting the sensor, if necessary.

✷✷ WARNING

When testing or servicing a Heated Oxygen (O_2) Sensor, the vehicle will need to be started and the engine warmed up to operating temperature in order to perform the necessary testing procedures or to easily remove the sensor from its threaded fitting. This will create a situation that requires working around a HOT exhaust system. The following is a list of precautions to consider during this service:

• Do not pierce any wires when testing a HO_2 sensor, as this can lead to wiring harness damage. Backprobe the connector, when necessary.

• While testing the sensor, be sure to keep out of the way of moving engine components, such as the cooling fan. Refrain from wearing loose clothing that may become tangled in moving engine components.

• Safety glasses must be worn at all times when working on or near the exhaust system. Older exhaust systems may be covered with loose rust particles that can fall off when disturbed. These particles are not only a nuisance, they can cause eye injuries.

• Be cautious when working on and around the hot exhaust system. Painful burns will result if skin is exposed to the exhaust system pipes or manifolds.

• The HO_2 sensor may be difficult to remove when the engine temperature is below 120°F (48°C). Excessive force may damage the threads in the exhaust pipe, therefore always start the engine and allow it to reach normal operating temperature prior to removal.

• Since HO_2 sensors are usually designed with a permanently attached wiring pigtail (this allows the wiring harness and sensor connectors to be positioned away from the hot exhaust system), it may be necessary to use a socket or wrench that is designed specifically for this purpose.

CR-V and Odyssey Model In-Vehicle Testing

▶ See Figure 15

※ WARNING

The four wire Heated Oxygen (HO₂) Sensor have two separate circuits, the signal circuit and the heater circuit which must not be confused. Never apply voltage to the signal wiring of a HO₂ sensor, otherwise it may be damaged. Also, never connect an ohmmeter (or a DVOM set on the ohm function) to both of the signal wires of a HO₂ sensor at the same time, otherwise the sensor may be damaged.

The color of the wires for the HO_2 sensor vary from model to model, however the positioning of the wires is consistent. The signal and heater connector circuit locations are identical on the CR-V and the Odyssey models. With HO_2 sensor disconnected, hold the electrical multi-connector such that the locking tab is at the top, while facing the electrical connectors. The two top electrical connectors are the sensor terminals. The two bottom electrical connectors are the heater terminals. The two electri-

cal connectors on the left side are the (+) positive part of the circuit and the two electrical connectors on the right side are the (-) negative part of the circuit.

Test 1 makes use of a standard DVOM with a 10 megohms impedance, whereas Test 2 necessitates the usage of an advanced Digital Multi-Meter (DMM) with MIN/MAX/Average functions or a sliding bar graph function. Both of these in-vehicle test procedures are likely to set Diagnostic Trouble Codes (DTC's) in the Engine Control Module/Powertrain Control Module (ECM/PCM). Therefore, after testing, be sure to clear all DTC's before retesting the sensor, if necessary. The Test 3 in-vehicle test is designed for the use of a scan tool or oscilloscope. The Test 4 Heating Circuit Test is designed to check the function of the heating circuit of the HO_2 sensor.

The Honda models covered in this book produced prior to 1996 use one Heated Oxygen (HO_2). Beginning with model year 1996, passenger vehicles sold in the United States were mandated to be On Board Diagnostic version II (OBD-II) compliant. The OBD-II equipped vehicles use two HO_2 sensors. The Primary Heated Oxygen (PHO_2)

Sensor is located before the catalytic converter and is also referred to as Sensor 1 (S1). This is the sensor the ECM/PCM uses to monitor the oxygen content of the exhaust. The sensor located down stream from the catalytic converter is the Secondary Heated Oxygen (SHO_2). This sensor is also referred to as Sensor 2 (S2), and is used only to monitor the efficiency of the PHO_2 and the catalytic converter.

The in-vehicle tests may be performed for the SHO_2 sensor, however under normal conditions, the SHO_2 sensor should not fluctuate like the PHO_2). Because the SHO_2 sensor is used only to monitor the efficiency of the PHO_2 sensor and the catalytic converter, if the HO_2 sensor exhibits a fluctuating signal, the catalytic converter is most likely defective.

The following is a list of wire colors and the related circuit for the Heated Oxygen (HO_2) Sensor, Primary Heated Oxygen (PHO_2) Sensors, and Secondary Heated Oxygen (SHO_2)Sensors used on CR-V and Odyssey models.

CR-V Models— PHO_2:
• + Signal Output: white, - Signal Ground: green/black
• + Heater Element Power: black/yellow,
- Heater Element Ground: black/white

CR-V Models— SHO_2:
• + Signal Output: white/red,
- Signal Ground: green/white
• + Heater Element Power: black/white,
- Heater Element Ground: black/white

1995 Odyssey Models— HO_2:
• + Signal Output: white/red,
- Signal Ground: green/blue
• + Heater Element Power: yellow/black,
- Heater Element Ground: orange/black

1996–97 Odyssey Models— PHO_2:
• + Signal Output: white/red,
- Signal Ground: green/blue
• + Heater Element Power: black/yellow,
- Heater Element Ground: orange/black

1996–97 Odyssey Models— SHO_2:
• + Signal Output: white/red, - Signal Ground: red/white
• + Heater Element Power: yellow/black,
- Heater Element Ground: orange/black

1998 Odyssey Models—PHO_2:
• + Signal Output: white, - Signal Ground: green/black
• + Heater Element Power: black/yellow,
- Heater Element Ground: black/white

1998 Odyssey Models—SHO_2:
• + Signal Output: white/red, - Signal Ground: green/black
• + Heater Element Power: yellow/black,
- Heater Element Ground: orange/black

1999–00 Odyssey Models— PHO_2:
• + Signal Output: white, - Signal Ground: green/black
• + Heater Element Power: black/yellow,
- Heater Element Ground: black/white

1999–00 Odyssey Models—SHO_2:
• + Signal Output: white/red, - Signal Ground: green/black
• + Heater Element Power: black/yellow,
- Heater Element Ground: black/white

TEST 1—DIGITAL VOLT-OHMMETER

This test will not only verify proper sensor functioning, but is also designed to ensure the engine control computer and associated wiring is functioning properly as well.

1. Start the engine and allow it to warm up to normal operating temperature.

➡If you are using the opening of the thermostat to gauge normal operating temperature, be forewarned: a defective thermostat can open too early and prevent the engine from reaching normal operating temperature. This can cause a slightly rich condition in the exhaust, which can throw the HO₂ sensor readings off slightly.

2. Turn the ignition switch **OFF**, then locate the two signal wires of the HO_2 sensor pigtail connector.

3. Perform a visual inspection of the connector to ensure it is properly engaged and all terminals are straight, tight and free from corrosion or damage.

4. Disengage the sensor pigtail connector from the vehicle harness connector.

5. Using a DVOM set to read DC voltage, attach the positive lead to the **Signal Output** terminal of the sensor pigtail connector, and the DVOM negative lead to a good engine ground.

※ CAUTION

While the engine is running, keep clear of all moving and hot components. Do not wear loose clothing. Otherwise severe personal injury or death may occur.

6. Have an assistant start the engine and hold it at approximately 2000 rpm. Wait at least 1 minute before commencing with the test to allow the HO_2 sensor to sufficiently warm up.

7. Using a jumper wire, connect the **Signal Output** terminal of the vehicle harness connector to a good engine ground. This will fool the engine control computer into thinking it is receiving a lean signal from the HO_2 sensor, therefore, the computer will richen the air/fuel ratio. With the **Signal Output** terminal so grounded, the DVOM should register at least 800 mV, as the control computer adds additional fuel to the air/fuel ratio.

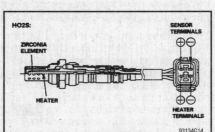

Fig. 15 A Heated Oxygen Sensor has two separate electrical circuits. The sensor circuit, which measures the oxygen content of the exhaust and the heater circuit, used to stabilize the sensor

93134G14

8. While observing the DVOM, disconnect the vehicle harness connector **Signal Output** jumper wire from the engine ground. Use the jumper wire to apply slightly less than 1 volt to the **signal Output** terminal of the vehicle harness connector. One method to do this is by grasping and squeezing the end of the jumper between your forefinger and thumb of one hand while touching the positive terminal of the battery post with your other hand. This allows your body to act as a resistor for the battery positive voltage, and fools the engine control computer into thinking it is receiving a rich signal. Or, use a mostly-drained AA battery by connecting the positive terminal of the AA battery to the jumper wire and the negative terminal of the battery to a good engine ground. (Another jumper wire may be necessary to do this.) The computer should lean the air/fuel mixture out. This lean mixture should register as 150 mV or less on the DVOM while connected to the **Signal Output** terminals of the HO$_2$ sensor.

9. If the DVOM did not register millivoltages as indicated, the problem may be either the sensor, the engine control computer or the associated wiring. Perform the following to determine which is the defective component:

a. Remove the vehicle harness connector **Signal Output** jumper wire.

b. While observing the DVOM, artificially enrich the air/fuel charge using propane. The DVOM reading should register higher than normal millivoltages. (Normal voltage for an ideal air/fuel mixture is approximately 450–550 mV DC). Then, lean the air/fuel intake charger by either disconnecting one of the fuel injector wiring harness connectors (to prevent the injector from delivering fuel) or by detaching 1 or 2 vacuum lines (to add additional non-metered air into the engine). The DVOM should now register lower than normal millivoltages. If the DVOM functioned as indicated, the problem lies elsewhere in the fuel delivery and control system. If the DVOM readings were still unresponsive, the O$_2$ sensor is defective; replace the sensor and retest.

➡**Poor wire connections and/or ground circuits may shift a normal O$_2$ sensor's millivoltage readings up into the rich range or down into the lean range. It is a good idea to check the wire condition and continuity before replacing a component that will not fix the problem.**

10. Turn the engine **OFF**, remove the DVOM and all associated jumper wires. Reattach the vehicle harness connector to the sensor pigtail connector. If applicable, reattach the fuel injector wiring connector and/or the vacuum line(s).

11. Clear any DTCs present in the ECM/PCM memory, as necessary.

TEST 2—DIGITAL MULTI-METER

This test method is a more straightforward Heated Oxygen (HO$_2$) Sensor test, and does not test the engine control computer's response to the HO$_2$ sensor signal. The use of a DMM with the MIN/MAX/Average function or sliding bar graph/wave function is necessary for this test. Don't forget that the Secondary Heated Oxygen (SHO$_2$) Sensor mounted after the catalytic converter (if equipped) will not fluctuate like the other Primary Heated Oxygen (PHO$_2$) Sensor will.

1. Start the engine and allow it to warm up to normal operating temperature.

➡**If using the opening of the thermostat to gauge normal operating temperature, be forewarned: a defective thermostat can open too early and prevent the engine from reaching normal operating temperature. This can cause a slightly rich condition in the exhaust, which can throw the HO$_2$ sensor readings off slightly.**

2. Turn the ignition switch **OFF**, then locate the HO$_2$ sensor pigtail connector.

3. Perform a visual inspection of the connector to ensure it is properly engaged and all terminals are straight, tight and free from corrosion or damage.

4. Backprobe the HO$_2$ sensor connector terminals. Attach the DMM positive test lead to the **Signal Output** terminal of the sensor pigtail connector. Attach the negative lead to either the **Signal Ground** terminal of the sensor pigtail or to a good, clean engine ground.

5. Activate the MIN/MAX/Average or sliding bar graph/wave function on the DMM.

✳✳ CAUTION

While the engine is running, keep clear of all moving and hot components. Do not wear loose clothing. Otherwise severe personal injury or death may occur.

6. Have an assistant start the engine and wait a few minutes before commencing with the test to allow the HO$_2$ sensor to sufficiently warm up.

7. Read the minimum, maximum and average readings exhibited by the HO$_2$ sensor or observe the bar graph/wave form. The average reading for a properly functioning HO$_2$ sensor is be approximately 450–550 mV DC. The minimum and maximum readings should vary more than 300–600 mV. A typical HO$_2$ sensor can fluctuate from as low as 100 mV to as high as 900 mV; if the sensor range of fluctuation is not large enough, the sensor is defective. Also, if the fluctuation range is biased up or down in the scale. For example, if the fluctuation range is 400 mV to 900 mV the sensor is defective, because the readings are pushed up into the rich range (as long as the fuel delivery system is functioning properly). The same goes for a fluctuation range pushed down into the lean range. The midpoint of the fluctuation range should be around 400–500 mV. Finally, if the HO$_2$ sensor voltage fluctuates too slowly (usually the voltage wave should oscillate past the mid-way point of 500 mV several times per second) the sensor is defective. (When an O$_2$ sensor fluctuates too slowly, it is referred to as being "lazy.")

➡**Poor wire connections and/or ground circuits may shift a normal HO$_2$ sensor's millivoltage readings up into the rich range or down into the lean range. It is a good idea to check the wire condition and continuity before replacing a component that will not fix the problem.**

8. Using the propane method, richen the air/fuel mixture and observe the DMM readings. The average HO$_2$ sensor output signal voltage should rise into the rich range.

9. Lean the air/fuel mixture by either disconnecting a fuel injector wiring harness connector or

by disconnecting a vacuum line. The HO$_2$ sensor average output signal voltage should drop into the lean range.

10. If the HO$_2$ sensor did not react as indicated, the sensor is defective and should be replaced.

11. Turn the engine **OFF**, remove the DMM and all associated jumper wires. Reattach the vehicle harness connector to the sensor pigtail connector. If applicable, reattach the fuel injector wiring connector and/or the vacuum line(s).

12. Clear any DTC's present in the ECM/PCM memory, as necessary.

TEST 3—OSCILLOSCOPE

▶ **See Figure 16**

This test is designed for the use of an oscilloscope to test the functioning of an Heated Oxygen (HO$_2$ Sensor.

➡**This test is only applicable for HO$_2$ and Primary Heated Oxygen (PHO$_2$) Sensors mounted in the exhaust system before the catalytic converter.**

1. Start the engine and allow it to reach normal operating temperature.

2. Turn the engine **OFF**, and locate the HO$_2$ sensor connector. Backprobe the scope lead to the O$_2$ sensor connector **Signal Output** terminal. Refer to the scope manufacturer's instructions for more information on attaching the scope to the vehicle.

3. Turn the scope ON.

4. Set the oscilloscope amplitude to 200 mV per division, and the time to 1 second per division. Use the 1:1 setting of the probe, and be sure to connect the scope's ground lead to a good, clean engine ground. Set the signal function to automatic or internal triggering.

5. Start the engine and run it at 2000 rpm.

6. The oscilloscope should display a waveform, representative of the HO$_2$ sensor switching between lean (100–300 mV) and rich (700–900 mV). The sensor should switch between rich and lean, or lean and rich (crossing the mid-point of 500 mV) several times per second. In addition, the range of each wave should reach at least above 700 mV and below 300 mV. However, an occasional low peak is acceptable.

7. Force the air/fuel mixture rich by introducing propane into the engine, then observe the oscil-

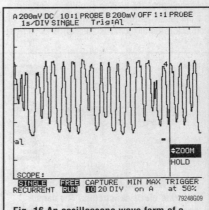

Fig. 16 An oscilloscope wave form of a typical good HO$_2$ sensor as it fluctuates from rich to lean

loscope readings. The fluctuating range of the HO$_2$ sensor should climb into the rich range.

8. Lean the air/fuel mixture out by either detaching a vacuum line or by disengaging one of the fuel injector's wiring connectors. Watch the scope readings; the HO$_2$ sensor waveform should drop toward the lean range.

9. If the HO$_2$ sensor's wave form does not fluctuate adequately, is not centered around 500 mV during normal engine operation, does not climb toward the rich range when propane is added to the engine, or does not drop toward the lean range when a vacuum hose or fuel injector connector is detached, the sensor is defective.

10. Reattach the fuel injector connector or vacuum hose.

11. Disconnect the oscilloscope from the vehicle.

TEST 4—HEATING CIRCUIT TEST

◆ See Figure 17

The heating circuit in a Heated Oxygen (HO$_2$) Sensor is designed heat and stabilize the sensor quicker than a non-heated sensor. This provides an advantage of increased engine driveability and fuel economy while the engine temperature is still below normal operating temperature, because the fuel management system can enter closed loop operation (more efficient than open loop operation) sooner.

Therefore, if the heating element goes bad, the HO$_2$ sensor may still function properly once the sensor warms up to its normal temperature. This will take longer than normal and may cause mild driveability-related problems while the engine has not reached normal operating temperature.

If the heating element is found to be defective, replace the HO$_2$ sensor.

1. Locate the O$_2$ sensor pigtail connector.

2. Perform a visual inspection of the connector to ensure it is properly engaged and all terminals are straight, tight and free from corrosion or damage.

3. Disengage the sensor pigtail connector from the vehicle harness connector.

4. Using a DVOM set to read resistance (ohms), attach 1 DVOM test lead to the **Heater Element Power** terminal, and the other lead to the **Heater Element Ground** terminal, of the sensor pigtail connector, then observe the resistance readings.

a. If there is no continuity between the **Heater Element Power** and **Heater Element Ground** terminals, the sensor is defective. Replace it with a new one and retest.

b. If there is continuity between the 2 terminals, but the resistance is less than 10 ohms or greater than 40 ohms, the sensor is defective. Replace it with a new one and retest.

5. Turn the engine **OFF**, remove the DVOM and all associated jumper wires. Reattach the vehicle harness connector to the sensor pigtail connector.

6. Clear any DTC's present in the ECM/PCM memory, as necessary.

REMOVAL & INSTALLATION

◆ See Figures 18, 19 and 20

✴✴ WARNING

The sensors use a pigtail and connector. This pigtail should not be removed from the sensor. Damage or removal of the pigtail or connector could affect proper operation of the oxygen sensor. Keep the electrical connector and louvered end of the sensor clean and free of grease. NEVER use cleaning solvents of any type on the sensor! The sensor may be difficult to remove when the engine temperature is below 120°F (48°C). Excessive removal force may damage the threads in the exhaust manifold or pipe; follow the removal procedure carefully.

1. Make sure the ignition is **OFF**, then disconnect the negative battery cable.

2. Raise and safely support the vehicle.

3. Locate the oxygen sensor. It protrudes from the exhaust pipe (it looks somewhat like a spark plug).

4. Unplug the sensor electrical connector.

➡**There are special wrenches, either socket or open-end available from reputable retail outlets for removing the oxygen sensor. These tools make the job much easier and often prevent unnecessary damage.**

5. Carefully unscrew the sensor counterclockwise, then remove the oxygen sensor from the manifold or pipe.

To install:

6. During and after the removal, be very careful to protect the tip of the sensor if it is to be reused. Do not let it to come in contact with fluids or dirt. Do not clean it or wash it.

7. Apply a light coat of anti-seize compound to the sensor threads but DO NOT allow any to get on the tip of the sensor.

8. Install the sensor into the exhaust pipe.

9. Attach the electrical connector and ensure a clean, tight connection.

10. Carefully lower the vehicle.

11. Connect the negative battery cable and enter the radio security code.

Idle Air Control Valve

OPERATION

◆ See Figure 21

The engine idle speed is monitored and controlled by the Engine Control Module/Powertrain Control Module (ECM/PCM) which uses the Idle Air Control (IAC) Valve to regulate the idle speed. The valve controls the amount of air that is allowed to bypass the intake throttle plate, which enables the engine idle speed to remain constant even though the engine loads change during idle. This is especially true when electrical consumers such as the air conditioner are used.

The minimum idle air speed is set at the factory with a stop screw. This setting allows a certain amount of air to bypass the throttle valves regardless of IAC valve positioning. A combination of this airflow and IAC positioning allows the ECM/PCM to control engine idle speed. During normal engine idle operation, the IAC valve is controlled by the ECM/PCM and properly positioned. No adjustment

Fig. 17 The heating circuit of the O$_2$ sensor can be tested with a DMM set to measure resistance

89714P27

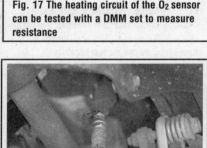

Fig. 18 The Heated Oxygen (HO$_2$) Sensor threads into the exhaust system. Always disconnect the sensor pigtail before attempting removal

93134P02

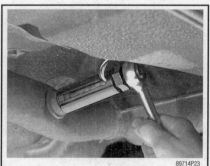

Fig. 19 A deep well socket with a slot for the pig tail wire is one type of tool used for removal of a Heated Oxygen (HO$_2$) Sensor

89714P23

Fig. 20 Coat only the threads of the Heated Oxygen (HO$_2$) Sensor with an anti-seize compound

89714P24

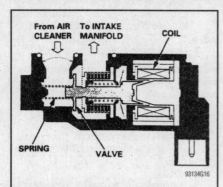

Fig. 21 Cutaway of the IAC Valve. The valve regulates the air bypassed by the intake throttle plate into the intake manifold to control idle speed

should be required during routine maintenance. Tampering with the minimum idle speed adjustment may result in premature failure of the IAC valve or improperly controlled engine idle operation.

TESTING

Prior to testing the Idle Air Control (IAC) Valve, inspect the IAC valve mounting, hoses, connections and O-rings for damage, looseness or leakage.
1. Start the vehicle's engine.
2. Allow to run until it reaches normal operating temperature that is indicated by one complete fan cycle.
3. Detach the electrical connector for the IAC valve.
4. With the IAC valve disconnected, there should be a noticeable drop in engine speed. If a drop in idle speed was noted but an intermittent idle still persists, check the wiring harness for high resistance connections or exposed wires.

REMOVAL & INSTALLATION

1. Disconnect the negative battery cable.
2. Disconnect the wiring harness from the IAC valve.
3. Remove the two retaining bolts.
4. Remove the IAC valve and discard the old seals or gaskets.
   To install:
5. Clean the gasket mating surfaces thoroughly.
6. Using new seals or gaskets, position the IAC valve on the throttle body.
7. Install and tighten the retaining bolts.
8. Connect the wiring harness to the IAC valve.
9. If raised, lower the vehicle.
10. Connect the negative battery cable.

Engine Coolant Temperature Sensor

OPERATION

▶ See Figure 22

The Engine Coolant Temperature (ECT) Sensor is a "thermistor", a sensor whose resistance changes in response to engine coolant temperature. The sen-

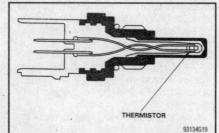

Fig. 22 The ECT sensor is a "thermistor", a sensor whose resistance changes in response to coolant temperature

sor resistance decreases as the coolant temperature increases, and increases as the coolant temperature decreases. This input signal is used by the PCM help determine the correct air-to-fuel ratio for the engine's operating temperature. The PCM controls the fuel mixture by controlling how long the electrically triggered fuel injectors stay open. If the ECT sensor is unplugged, the PCM senses a very high resistance, and the engine may start when cold, however as the engine's temperature increases, a rich running condition will cause the engine to loose power and stall.

TESTING

1. Disconnect the engine wiring harness from the ECT sensor.
2. Connect an ohmmeter between the two ECT sensor terminals.
3. With the engine cold and the ignition switch in the **OFF** position, measure and note the ECT sensor resistance.
4. Connect the engine wiring harness to the sensor.
5. Start the engine and allow the engine to reach normal operating temperature.
6. Once the engine has reached normal operating temperature, turn the engine **OFF**.
7. Again, disconnect the engine wiring harness from the ECT sensor.
8. Measure and note the ECT sensor resistance with the engine hot.
9. The ECT sensor should have 5,000 ohms resistance when the engine coolant temperature is cold. The ECT sensor resistance should decrease as the engine temperature increases. At operating temperature the ECT sensor resistance should be 100–400 ohms.
10. If readings are not close, the sensor may be faulty.

REMOVAL & INSTALLATION

1. Disconnect the negative battery cable.
2. Drain and recycle the engine coolant.

✳✳ CAUTION

Never open, service or drain the radiator or cooling system when hot; serious burns can occur from the steam and hot coolant. In addition, when draining engine coolant, keep in mind that cats and dogs are attracted to ethylene glycol antifreeze and could drink any that is left in an uncovered

container or in puddles on the ground. This will prove fatal in sufficient quantities. Always drain coolant into a sealable container. Coolant should be reused unless it is contaminated or is several years old.

3. Detach the ECT sensor connector.
4. Remove the ECT sensor from the thermostat housing
   To install:
5. Installation is the reverse of the removal procedure. Make sure to coat the sensor threads with Teflon® sealant.
6. Refill the engine cooling system.
7. Start the engine and check for coolant leaks.
8. Bleed the cooling system as necessary.

Intake Air Temperature Sensor

OPERATION

▶ See Figure 23

The Intake Air Temperature (IAT) Sensor is used by the PCM to monitor the air temperature inside the intake manifold. The resistance decreases as the air temperature increases. This provides a signal to the PCM indicating the temperature of the incoming air charge. This sensor helps the PCM to determine spark timing and the air-to-fuel ratio. Information from this sensor is added to the pressure sensor information to calculate the density of the air mass being sent to the cylinders.

Fig. 23 The tip of the IAT sensor has an exposed thermistor that changes the resistance of the sensor. The resistance decreases as the air temperature increases

TESTING

▶ See Figures 24 and 25

1. Turn the ignition switch **OFF**.
2. Disconnect the wiring harness from the IAT sensor.
3. Measure the resistance between the sensor terminals.
4. Compare the resistance reading with the accompanying chart.
5. If the resistance is not within specification, the IAT may be faulty.
6. Connect the wiring harness to the sensor.

Fig. 24 The IAT sensor can be monitored with an appropriate Data-stream capable scan tool

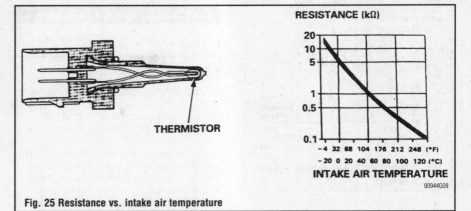

Fig. 25 Resistance vs. intake air temperature

REMOVAL & INSTALLATION

1. Disconnect the negative battery cable.
2. Detach the IAT sensor electrical connector.
3. Remove the retaining screws from the sensor (some models may unscrew from the manifold).
4. Remove the IAT sensor from the intake manifold.

To install:

5. Coat the sensor threads with Teflon® sealant.
6. Install the sensor into the intake manifold.
7. Attach the connectors on the IAT.
8. Connect the negative battery cable.

Manifold Absolute Pressure Sensor

OPERATION

▶ **See Figure 26**

The Manifold Absolute Pressure (MAP) Sensor measures and converts intake manifold vacuum into a voltage signal. The higher the vacuum, the lower the voltage signal that is sent to the PCM. The range of operation of the MAP sensor varies from approximately 0.5–3.0 volts. The PCM compares the Throttle Position (TP) sensor with the MAP sensor readings to verify proper operation. Any discrepancy between the MAP sensor and the TP sensor is likely to trigger the Malfunction Indicator Lamp (MIL). The MAP sensor provides the PCM information on engine load.

TESTING

1. Check the connection at the Manifold Absolute Pressure (MAP) Sensor connector.
2. Check the terminals within the connector for corrosion or poor contacts causing high resistance.
3. Repair or replace electrical connections as necessary.
4. If code 3 is detected, an electrical problem in the system may be present.
5. Remove the electrical connector from the MAP sensor.
6. Turn the ignition key to the **ON** position.
7. Connect the positive lead of a voltmeter to the terminal No. 1, the leftmost electrical terminal.
8. Connect the negative probe to the (terminal No. 2) green/white wire in the harness. Do not probe the MAP sensor side.
9. With the voltmeter connected properly there should be a voltage of 5 volts.

REMOVAL & INSTALLATION

1. Disconnect the negative battery cable.
2. Detach the MAP sensor vacuum lines.
3. Remove the mounting screws from the MAP sensor.
4. Remove the MAP sensor.
5. Installation is the reverse of the removal procedure.

Throttle Position Sensor

OPERATION

▶ **See Figures 27 and 28**

The Throttle Position (TP) sensor is a potentiometer that provides a signal to the PCM that is directly proportional to the throttle plate position. The TP sensor is mounted on the side of the throttle body and is connected to the throttle plate shaft. The TP sensor monitors throttle plate movement and position, and transmits an appropriate electrical signal to the PCM. These signals are used by the PCM to adjust the air/fuel mixture, spark timing and if installed, EGR operation according to engine load at idle, part throttle, or full throttle. The TP sensor is not adjustable.

The TP sensor receives a 5 volt reference signal and a ground circuit from the PCM. A return signal circuit is connected to wiper that runs on a resistor internally on the sensor. The further the throttle is opened, the further the wiper moves along the resistor. At full throttle, the wiper essentially creates a loop between the reference signal and the signal return returning the full or nearly full 5 volt signal back to the PCM. At idle the signal return should be approximately 0.9 volts.

The PCM compares the TP sensor with the MAP sensor to determine if the system is functioning properly.

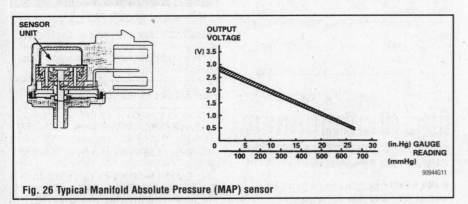

Fig. 26 Typical Manifold Absolute Pressure (MAP) sensor

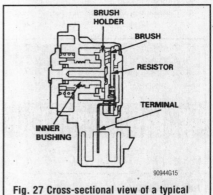

Fig. 27 Cross-sectional view of a typical Honda Throttle Position (TP) sensor

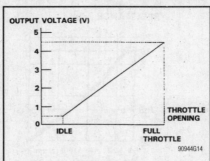

Fig. 28 Output voltage vs. throttle opening of a TP sensor

TESTING

♦ See Figure 29

1. With the engine **OFF** and the ignition **ON**, check the voltage at the signal return circuit of the TP sensor by carefully backprobing the connector using a DVOM.
2. Voltage should be between 0.2 and 1.4 volts at idle.
3. Slowly move the throttle pulley to the Wide Open Throttle (WOT) position and watch the voltage on the DVOM. The voltage should slowly rise to slightly less than 4.8v at Wide Open Throttle (WOT).
4. If no voltage is present, check the wiring harness for supply voltage (5.0v) and ground (0.3v or less), by referring to your corresponding wiring guide. If supply voltage and ground are present, but no output voltage from TP, replace the TP sensor. If supply voltage and ground do not meet specifications, make necessary repairs to the harness or PCM.

REMOVAL & INSTALLATION

1. Disconnect the negative battery cable.
2. Disconnect the wiring harness from the TP sensor.
3. Remove the two sensor mounting screws.
4. Pull the TP sensor off the throttle shaft.
To install:
5. Install the TP sensor onto the shaft.
6. Install and tighten the sensor mounting screws.
7. Connect the wiring harness to the sensor.
8. Connect the negative battery cable.

Fig. 29 The TP sensor can be monitored with an appropriate and Data-stream capable scan tool

Crankshaft Position Sensor

OPERATION

♦ See Figure 30

The Crankshaft Position (CKP) Sensor is used to monitor engine speed and determines the timing for the for the fuel injectors for each cylinder. On Odyssey models, the CKP sensor is also used to detect an engine misfire.

The CKP sensor is located in the lower distributor housing on CR-V and 1995 Odyssey models. If the CKP sensor in the distributor housing fails, the distributor ignition housing must be replaced.

On 1996–00 Odyssey models, the CKP sensor is located underneath the lower timing belt cover behind the crankshaft pulley.

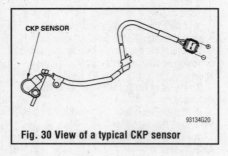

Fig. 30 View of a typical CKP sensor

TESTING

CR-V and 1995 Odyssey Models

1. With the ignition switch **OFF**, detach the electrical connector on the side of the distributor housing.
2. Measure the resistance between the following two CKP wires:
   - CR-V models: The blue and white wires. The resistance should be 300–700 ohms.
   - 1995 Odyssey models: The blue/green and blue/yellow wires. The resistance should be 700–1,300 ohms.
3. If the resistance is not in the specified range, replace the distributor ignition housing.

1996–00 Odyssey models

1. With the ignition switch **OFF**, detach the electrical connector for the CKP sensor along the lower timing belt cover.
2. Measure the resistance between the two CKP sensor wires:
   - 1996–97 Odyssey models: 500–1,000 ohms.
   - 1998–00 Odyssey models: 1,850–2,450 ohms.
3. If the resistance is not within the specified range, replace CKP sensor.

REMOVAL & INSTALLATION

CR-V and 1995 Odyssey Models

♦ See Figure 31

1. Remove the negative battery cable.
2. Remove the distributor cap leaving the wires attached and place aside.

Fig. 31 The Crankshaft Position (CKP) Sensor rotor looks like a small gear in the lower distributor housing—CR-V and 1995 Odyssey models

3. Disconnect the electrical connectors at the side of the distributor housing.
4. Make a matchmark reference mark between the distributor housing and the cylinder head and remove the distributor housing assembly.
To install:
5. Transfer the components not supplied with the replacement distributor housing assembly.
6. Install the distributor housing assembly in the reverse order of removal.
7. Check and reset the ignition timing as outlined in Section 1.

1996–00 Odyssey Models

1. Remove the negative battery cable.
2. Detach the CKP sensor electrical connector at the front of the lower timing belt cover.
3. Remove the accessory drive belts. Refer to Section 1 for specific details on belt removal.
4. Remove the crankshaft pulley. Refer to Section 3 timing belt replacement for specific details.
5. Remove the lower timing belt cover.
6. Remove the CKP sensor.

➡The CKP sensor is part of the Top Dead Center (TDC) Sensor on 1996–98 Odyssey models and must be replaced as an unit.

7. Install the CKP sensor in the reverse order of removal.

Crankshaft Speed Fluctuation Sensor

➡The Odyssey models do not use a Crankshaft Speed Fluctuation (CKF) sensor. The Odyssey models use a Crankshaft Position (CKP) Sensor to monitor crankshaft engine speed fluctuation.

OPERATION

The Crankshaft Speed Fluctuation (CKF) Sensor is used by the PCM to monitor crankshaft speed fluctuation. The diagnostic system is composed of a pulser rotor mounted on the crankshaft, and a pulse pick-up sensor on the engine block. The PCM monitors the crankshaft speed fluctuations based on the CKF signal and determines if an engine misfire has occurred if the crankshaft speed fluctuates beyond a predetermined limit.

TESTING

1. With the ignition switch **OFF**, disconnect the Crankshaft Fluctuation (CKF) sensor connector.
2. Measure the resistance between the two terminals.
3. The resistance should measure 1.6–3.2 k ohms.
4. If the resistance is not within the specified range, replace the sensor.

REMOVAL & INSTALLATION

▶ **See Figure 32**

The sensor is located underneath the lower timing belt cover behind the crankshaft pulley.
1. Remove the negative battery cable.
2. Raise and safely support the vehicle.
3. Remove the engine splash shield.
4. Remove the power steering, alternator and air conditioner belts. For details, refer to Section 1.
5. Remove the crankshaft pulley and lower timing belt cover. For details, refer to the timing belt removal procedures in Section 3.
6. Disconnect the CKF sensor electrical connector near the alternator. Remove the sensor mounting bolts and remove the sensor.
7. Install in the reverse order of removal.

Fig. 32 The CKF Sensor is located under the timing belt cover, behind the crankshaft pulley and uses the large cogged wheel to monitor crankshaft speed

Knock Sensor

OPERATION

▶ **See Figure 33**

The Knock Sensor (KS) is used to monitor detonation in the combustion chamber. Detonation occurs when the fuel does not burn evenly and completely in the combustion chamber. Detonation is also referred to as pre-ignition, "engine knocks" or "engine pinging." Detonation can be caused by a variety of conditions including excessive ignition timing advance, excessive carbon build up in the combustion chamber, incorrect spark plug heat

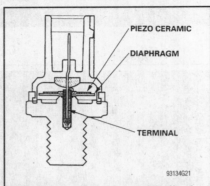

Fig. 33 Cross-sectional view of the Knock Sensor (KS) used on the 1999 Odyssey

range and/or gap or using gasoline with too low of an octane rating.

To maximize the efficiency of the engine, a knock sensor is used to send a signal to the PCM. If a knock is detected, the PCM responds by adjusting the ignition timing until the "knock" stops. The sensor works by generating a signal produced by the frequency of the knock as recorded by the piezo-electric ceramic disc inside the KS. The disc absorbs the shock waves from the knocks and exerts a pressure on the metal diaphragm inside the KS. This compresses the crystals inside the disc and the disc generates a voltage signal proportional to the frequency of the knocks ranging from zero to 1 volt.

TESTING

Although the sensor is designed to detect internal engine knocks, a loose bracket or fastener near the sensor location could cause the sensor to mistake a loose bracket or fastener for an internal knock. A sensor that has come loose or has been replaced but over-tightened during installation, could also cause an incorrect signal to be sent to the ECM/PCM.

There is real no test for this sensor, the sensor produces it's own signal based on information gathered while the engine is running. The sensors also are mounted on the side of the engine block near the cylinder head. The sensors can be monitored with an appropriate scan tool using a data display or other data stream information. Follow the instructions included with the scan tool for information on accessing the data. The only test available is to test the continuity of the harness from the PCM to the sensor and make sure all of the electrical connectors are clean and secure.

REMOVAL & INSTALLATION

1. Disconnect the negative battery cable.
2. Locate the sensor installed in the side of the engine block. If the vehicle needs to be raised, raise and securely support the vehicle in a safe manner.
3. Unplug the sensor connector.
4. Using the proper size socket, loosen and remove the knock sensor.

To install:
5. Carefully thread the sensor into the engine block.
6. Tighten the sensor to 23 ft. lbs. (31 Nm).
7. Attach the sensor connector.
8. Lower the vehicle if raised for accessibility.
9. Connect the negative battery cable.

Vehicle Speed Sensor

OPERATION

▶ **See Figure 34**

The Vehicle Speed (VSS) Sensor is a magnetic pick-up sensor that sends a signal to the Powertrain Control Module (PCM) and the speedometer. The sensor measures the rotation of the output shaft on the transaxle and sends an AC voltage signal to the PCM that determines the corresponding vehicle speed.

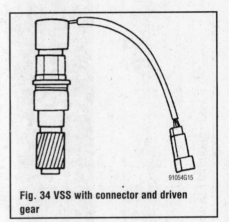

Fig. 34 VSS with connector and driven gear

TESTING

1. Disconnect the negative battery cable.
2. Disengage the wiring harness connector from the VSS.
3. Using a Digital Volt-Ohmmeter (DVOM), measure the resistance (ohmmeter function) between the sensor terminals. If the resistance is 190–250 ohms, the sensor is okay.

REMOVAL & INSTALLATION

1. Disconnect the negative battery cable.
2. Disconnect the three terminal connector from the vehicle speed sensor (VSS).
3. Remove the fasteners that secure the VSS to the transaxle housing assembly.
4. Remove the VSS.
To install:
5. Install the VSS.
6. Install the mounting bolts.
7. Connect the three terminal connector to the sensor.
8. Connect the negative battery cable.

COMPONENT LOCATIONS

♦ See Figures 35, 36, 37 and 38

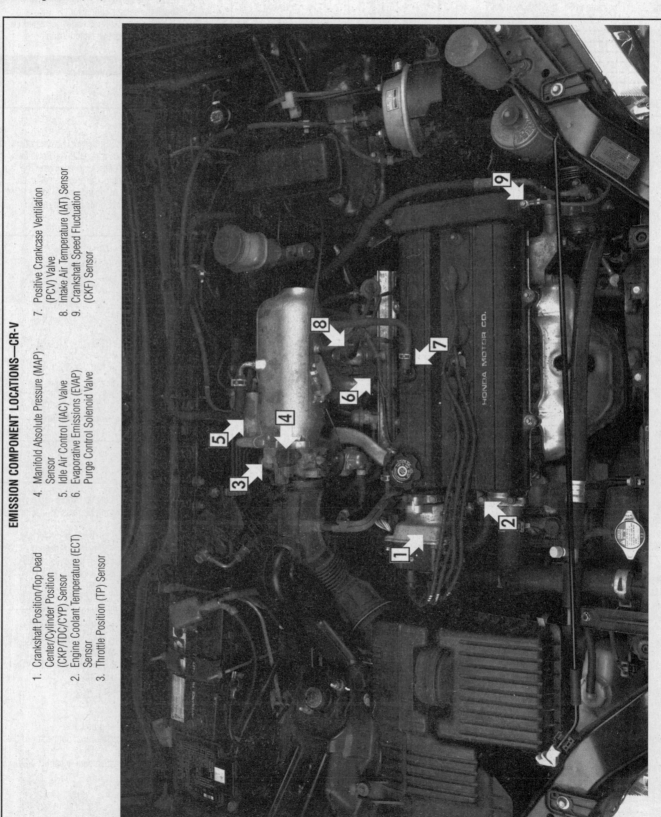

EMISSION COMPONENT LOCATIONS—CR-V

1. Crankshaft Position/Top Dead Center/Cylinder Position (CKP/TDC/CYP) Sensor
2. Engine Coolant Temperature (ECT) Sensor
3. Throttle Position (TP) Sensor
4. Manifold Absolute Pressure (MAP) Sensor
5. Idle Air Control (IAC) Valve
6. Evaporative Emissions (EVAP) Purge Control Solenoid Valve
7. Positive Crankcase Ventilation (PCV) Valve
8. Intake Air Temperature (IAT) Sensor
9. Crankshaft Speed Fluctuation (CKF) Sensor

93134PU2

EMISSION COMPONENT LOCATIONS—V6 ODYSSEY

1. Top Dead Center 1/2 (TDC1), (TDC2) Sensor
2. Crankshaft Position (CKP) Sensor
3. Knock Sensor (KS)
4. Engine Coolant Temperature (ECT) Sensor
5. Positive Crankcase Ventilation (PCV) Valve
6. Intake Air Temperature (IAT) Sensor
7. Manifold Absolute Pressure (MAP) Sensor
8. Idle Air Control (IAC) Valve
9. Throttle Position (TP) Sensor
10. Evaporative Emissions (EVAP) Purge Control Solenoid Valve

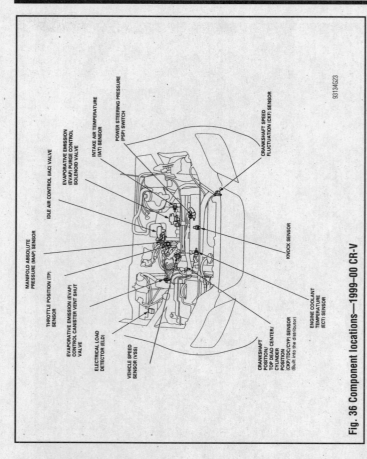

Fig. 36 Component locations—1999–00 CR-V

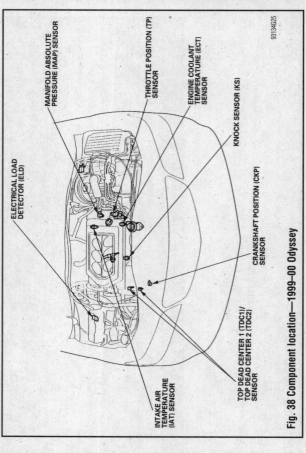

Fig. 38 Component location—1999–00 Odyssey

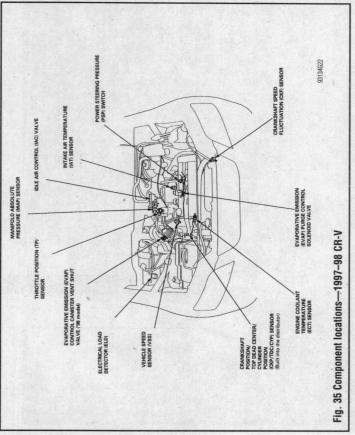

Fig. 35 Component locations—1997–98 CR-V

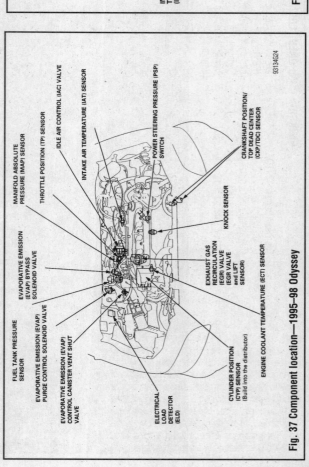

Fig. 37 Component location—1995–98 Odyssey

TROUBLE CODES

General Information

The CR-V and Odyssey models both use an Engine Control Module/Powertrain Control Module (ECM/PCM) to control the fuel, ignition and emission systems of the engine. The ECM/PCM relies on a variety of sensors to evaluate the engine's operating condition. The ECM/PCM also has the ability to recognize when a sensor's value or input is beyond the normal operating range for that component.

If a sensor's wire is damaged, disconnected, or the sensor fails, the ECM/PCM receives an invalid signal for that sensor. The ECM/PCM has no idea what the cause of the problem is, however it does recognize that the signal is not within the acceptable operating range for that particular component. In order for the engine to run, the ECM/PCM will substitute a default value for the sensor that allows the engine to continue running, however the engine's performance and efficiency may be compromised. When this condition occurs, the ECM/PCM stores Diagnostic Trouble Codes (DTCs) into its fault memory.

If the condition is severe enough to cause potential damage to another component, the MALFUNCTION INDICATOR LAMP (USA Models and 1996 and later Canadian Models) or the CHECK ENGINE LIGHT (1995 Canadian Models) is turned on and the warning light remains on after the vehicle is started.

Diagnostic testing is done by checking the inputs and the outputs for the ECM/PCM control unit, and by accessing the fault memory of the ECM/PCM. The ECM used in the 1995 Odyssey models has on board diagnostic capabilities that are decoded by using the blink code method. The CR-V and 1996–00 Odyssey models are OBD-II compliant and the PCM fault memory is accessed by using a suitable OBD-II capable Data Scan Tool (DST), and the fault codes are displayed on the DST screen.

SCAN TOOLS

On all 1996–00 models, an OBD-II compliant scan tool must be used. To retrieve the ECM/PCM Diagnostic Trouble Codes (DTCs). There are many manufacturers of these tools; a purchaser must be certain that the tool is proper for the intended use. A suitable good quality Data Scan Tool (DST) should come with comprehensive instructions on its proper use. Be sure to follow the instructions that came with the unit if they differ from what is provided in this manual.

The scan tool allows any stored codes to be read from the ECM/PCM memory. The tool also allows the operator to view the data being sent to the computer control module while the engine is running. This ability has obvious diagnostic advantages; as the use of the scan tool is frequently required for component testing. The scan tool makes collecting information easier; however, an operator familiar with the system must correctly interpret the data.

An example of the usefulness of the scan tool may be seen in the case of a temperature sensor, which has changed its electrical characteristics. The ECM/PCM is reacting to an apparently warmer engine (causing a driveability problem), but the sensor's voltage has not changed enough to set a fault code. Connecting the scan tool, the voltage signal being sent to the ECM/PCM may be viewed; and comparison to normal values or a known good vehicle reveals the problem quickly.

ELECTRICAL TOOLS

The most commonly required electrical diagnostic tool is the digital multimeter, allowing voltage, ohms (resistance) and amperage to be read by one instrument. The multimeter must be a high-impedance unit, with 10 megohms of impedance in the voltmeter. This type of meter will not place an additional load on the circuit it is testing; which is extremely important in low voltage circuits. The multimeter must be of high quality in all respects. It should be handled carefully and protected from impact or damage. Replace batteries frequently in the unit.

Other necessary tools include an unpowered test light, and electrical leads capable of back-probing electrical terminals without damaging them. A vacuum pump/gauge is also needed for checking some sensors, solenoids and valves.

Diagnosis and Testing

Diagnosis of a driveability and/or emissions problems requires attention to detail and following the diagnostic procedures in the correct order. Resist the temptation to perform any repairs before performing the preliminary diagnostic steps. In many cases this will shorten diagnostic time and often cure the problem without electronic testing.

The proper troubleshooting procedure for these vehicles is as follows:

VISUAL/PHYSICAL INSPECTION

This is possibly the most critical step of diagnosis and should be performed immediately after retrieving any codes. A detailed examination of connectors, wiring and vacuum hoses can often lead to a repair without further diagnosis. Performance of this step relies on the skill of the technician performing it; a careful inspector will check the undersides of hoses as well as the integrity of hard-to-reach hoses blocked by the air cleaner or other component. Wiring should be checked carefully for any sign of strain, burning, crimping, or terminal pullout from a connector. Checking connectors at components or in harnesses is required; usually, pushing them together will reveal a loose fit.

INTERMITTENTS

If a fault occurs intermittently, such as a loose connector pin breaking contact as the vehicle hits a bump, the PCM will note the fault as it occurs and may energize the dash-warning lamp. If the problem self-corrects, as with the terminal pin again making contact, the dash lamp will extinguish after 10 seconds but a code will remain stored in the computer control module's memory.

When an unexpected code appears during diagnostics, it may have been set during an intermittent failure that self-corrected itself. These codes are still useful in diagnosis and should not be discounted.

CIRCUIT/COMPONENT REPAIR

The fault codes and the scan tool data will lead to diagnosis and checking of a particular circuit. It is important to note that the fault code indicates a fault or loss of signal in an ECM/PCM-controlled system, not necessarily in the specific component. A sensor's wire may be shorted, corroded or disconnected, and though the actual sensor is operating properly, the signal received by the ECM/PCM is beyond specification.

Refer to the appropriate Diagnostic Code chart to determine the code's meaning. The component may then be tested following the appropriate component test procedures found in this section. If the component is OK, check the wiring for shorts or an open circuit. Sometimes a second opinion is valuable from an experienced driveability technician.

If a code indicates the ECM/PCM to be faulty and the ECM/PCM is replaced, but does not correct the problem, one of the following may be the reason:

- There is a problem with the ECM/PCM terminal connections: The terminals may have to be removed from the connector in order to check them properly.
- The ECM/PCM or PROM is not correct for the application: The incorrect ECM/PCM or PROM may cause a malfunction and may or may not set a code.
- The problem is intermittent: This means that the problem is not present at the time the system is being checked. In this case, make a careful physical inspection of all portions of the system involved.
- Shorted solenoid, relay coils or harness: Solenoids and relays are turned on and off by the ECM/PCM using internal electronic switches called drivers. Each driver is part of a group of four called Quad-Drivers. A shorted solenoid, relay coil or harness could cause an PCM to fail, and a replacement PCM to fail when it is installed.
- The Programmable Read Only Memory (PROM) may be faulty: Although the PROM rarely fails, it operates as part of the ECM/PCM. Therefore, it could be the cause of the problem. Substitute a known good PROM.
- The replacement ECM/PCM may be faulty: After the ECM/PCM is replaced, the system should be rechecked for proper operation. If the diagnostic code again indicates the ECM/PCM is the problem, substitute a known good PCM. Although this is a very rare condition, it could happen.

Diagnostic Connector

OBD-I SYSTEMS

1995 Odyssey Models
▶ See Figure 39

The Service Check Connector (SCS) is a two wire electrical connector with a blue housing located under the dash near the center console, on the passenger side of the vehicle.

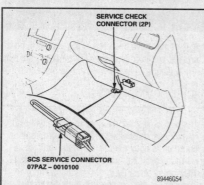

Fig. 39 The SCS Service Connector is used to access the blink codes on 1995 Odyssey models. A paper clip can be substituted by carefully back-probing the connector

➡The Diagnostic Trouble Codes (DTCs) on this model are displayed as blink codes.

OBD-II SYSTEMS

♦ See Figure 40

The 16-pin On Board Diagnostic version II (OBD-II) compliant Data Link Connector (DLC) is used to access the Diagnostic Trouble Codes (DTCs) using an OBD-II compliant Data Scan Tool (DST).

CR-V Models

The 16-pin OBD-II compliant DLC is an electrical connector with a gray housing located under the dash near the center console, on the passenger side of the vehicle.

The two wire electrical connector with a blue housing next to the DLC is the Service Check Connector (SCS).

1996–98 Odyssey Models

The 16-pin OBD-II compliant DLC is an electrical connector with a gray housing located under the dash near the center console, on the passenger side of the vehicle.

The Service Check Connector (SCS) is a two wire electrical connector with a blue housing located on the passenger side of the vehicle under the dash.

1999–00 Odyssey Models

The 16-pin OBD-II compliant DLC is an electrical connector with a gray housing located under the dash behind the center console one the driver's side of the vehicle.

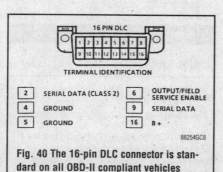

Fig. 40 The 16-pin DLC connector is standard on all OBD-II compliant vehicles

➡The two wire Service Check Connector (SCS) is not used on these models.

Reading Codes

OBD-I SYSTEMS

1995 Odyssey Models

♦ See Figures 41 and 42

Listings of the trouble codes for the various engine control systems covered in this manual are located in this section. Remember that a code only points to the faulty circuit NOT necessarily to a faulty component. Loose, damaged or corroded connections may contribute to a fault code on a circuit when the sensor or component is operating properly. Be sure that the components are faulty before replacing them, especially the expensive ones.

To activate the blink code system proceed as follows:

1. Turn the ignition switch **OFF**.
2. Locate the two wire Service Check Connector (SCS) located behind the passenger's side center console.
3. Install the SCS Service Connector tool no. 07PAZ-0010100 or equivalent into the connector, or carefully back probe the connector using a suitable small paper clip.
4. Turn the ignition switch to the **ON** position and observe the Malfunction Indicator Lamp (MIL) or Check Engine Light. If the warning light stays on, there are no stored faults. If the warning light begins to blink, for each fault that is stored, a blink code will be present.

➡After making repairs, clear the trouble codes and operate the vehicle to see if it will reset, indicating further problems.

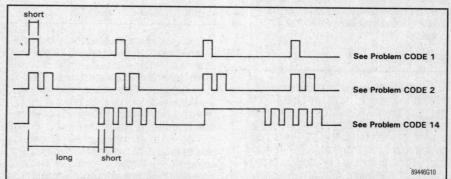

Fig. 41 It's a good idea to have a pencil and paper handy when reading a blink code to note the long and short flashes of the warning light

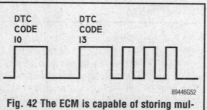

Fig. 42 The ECM is capable of storing multiple blink codes. Using the codes can be useful for diagnosis purposes

OBD-II SYSTEMS

♦ See Figure 43

On all 1996–00 models, an On Board Diagnostic version II (OBD-II) compliant Data Scan Tool (DST) must be used to retrieve the Diagnostic Trouble Codes (DTCs). Follow the DST manufacturer's instructions on how to connect the scan tool to the vehicle and how to retrieve the DTCs.

Clearing Codes

OBD-I SYSTEMS

1995 Odyssey Models

✳✳ WARNING

The ignition switch must be OFF any time power is disconnected or restored to the ECM/PCM. Severe damage may result if this precaution is not observed.

1. Locate the 7.5 amp **BACK UP** (Radio) fuse in the under-hood fuse panel.
2. Turn the ignition switch to the **OFF** position
3. Remove the fuse for 10 seconds, then reinstall the fuse.

OBD-II SYSTEMS

CR-V and 1996–00 Odyssey Models

The Diagnostic Trouble Codes (DTCs) can be cleared using one of two methods. A suitable On Board Diagnostic version II (OBD-II) Data Scan Tool (DST) can be used to clear the DTCs or the Back-Up Radio fuse can be removed to clear the codes.

The advantage of using a DST is that all of the stored fault codes can be read before clearing them. This may be handy for future diagnostic purposes.

When clearing the stored DTCs by removing the fuse, all of the codes are cleared at one time. Once the codes are cleared, the stored information is lost.

✳✳ WARNING

The ignition switch must be OFF any time power is disconnected or restored to the

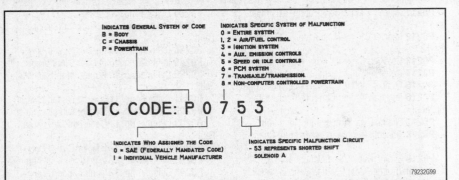

INDICATES GENERAL SYSTEM OF CODE
B = BODY
C = CHASSIS
P = POWERTRAIN

INDICATES SPECIFIC SYSTEM OF MALFUNCTION
0 = ENTIRE SYSTEM
1, 2 = AIR/FUEL CONTROL
3 = IGNITION SYSTEM
4 = AUX. EMISSION CONTROLS
5 = SPEED OR IDLE CONTROLS
6 = PCM SYSTEM
7 = TRANSAXLE/TRANSMISSION
8 = NON-COMPUTER CONTROLLED POWERTRAIN

DTC CODE: P 0 7 5 3

INDICATES WHO ASSIGNED THE CODE
0 = SAE (FEDERALLY MANDATED CODE)
1 = INDIVIDUAL VEHICLE MANUFACTURER

INDICATES SPECIFIC MALFUNCTION CIRCUIT
- 53 REPRESENTS SHORTED SHIFT
SOLENOID A

79232G99

Fig. 43 The Diagnostic Trouble Codes (DTCs) are easily interpreted when using an OBD-II compliant scan tool

ECM/PCM. Severe damage may result if this precaution is not observed.

To clear the stored DTCs locate the 7.5 amp **BACK-UP** (Radio) fuse and proceed as follows:
- CR-V and 2.2L/2.3L Odyssey models: Located in the under-hood fuse panel.
- V6 Odyssey models: Fuse No. 13 in the passenger's side under-dash fuse box.
1. Turn the ignition switch to the off position
2. Remove the fuse for 10 seconds, then reinstall the fuse.

Diagnostic Trouble Codes

OBD-I DIAGNOSTIC TROUBLE CODES

The following is a list of On Board Diagnostic version I (OBD-I) Diagnostic Trouble Codes (DTCs). These codes are also known as flash codes or blink codes because the warning light pulses are counted to determine the code.

Code 0 Engine Control Module (ECM)
Code 1 Heated Oxygen (HO2) Sensor
Code 3 Manifold Absolute Pressure
Code 4 Crankshaft Position (CKP) Sensor
Code 5 Manifold Absolute Pressure (MAP) Sensor
Code 6 Engine Coolant Temperature (ECT) Sensor
Code 7 Throttle Position (TP) Sensor
Code 8 Top Dead Center Position (TDC) Sensor
Code 9 No. 1 Cylinder Position (CYP) Sensor
Code 10 Intake Air Temperature (IAT) Sensor
Code 12 Exhaust Gas Recirculation (EGR) Valve Lift Sensor
Code 13 Barometric Pressure (BARO) Sensor
Code 14 Idle Air Control (IAC) Valve
Code 15 Ignition Output Signal
Code 16 Fuel Injector
Code 17 Vehicle Speed Sensor (VSS)
Code 20 Electric Load Detector (ELD)
Code 30 Automatic Transaxle FI Signal A
Code 31 Automatic Transaxle FI Signal B
Code 41 Heated Oxygen (HO2) Sensor Heater
Code 43 Fuel Supply System

OBD-II DIAGNOSTIC TROUBLE CODES

The following is a list of On Board Diagnostic version II (OBD-II) Diagnostic Trouble Codes (DTCs).

P0000 No Failures
P0100 Mass or Volume Air Flow Circuit Malfunction
P0101 Mass or Volume Air Flow Circuit Range/Performance Problem
P0102 Mass or Volume Air Flow Circuit Low Input
P0103 Mass or Volume Air Flow Circuit High Input
P0104 Mass or Volume Air Flow Circuit Intermittent
P0105 Manifold Absolute Pressure/Barometric Pressure Circuit Malfunction
P0106 Manifold Absolute Pressure/Barometric Pressure Circuit Range/Performance Problem
P0107 Manifold Absolute Pressure/Barometric Pressure Circuit Low Input
P0108 Manifold Absolute Pressure/Barometric Pressure Circuit High Input
P0109 Manifold Absolute Pressure/Barometric Pressure Circuit Intermittent
P0110 Intake Air Temperature Circuit Malfunction
P0111 Intake Air Temperature Circuit Range/Performance Problem
P0112 Intake Air Temperature Circuit Low Input
P0113 Intake Air Temperature Circuit High Input
P0114 Intake Air Temperature Circuit Intermittent
P0115 Engine Coolant Temperature Circuit Malfunction
P0116 Engine Coolant Temperature Circuit Range/Performance Problem
P0117 Engine Coolant Temperature Circuit Low Input
P0118 Engine Coolant Temperature Circuit High Input
P0119 Engine Coolant Temperature Circuit Intermittent
P0120 Throttle/Pedal Position Sensor/Switch "A" Circuit Malfunction
P0121 Throttle/Pedal Position Sensor/Switch "A" Circuit Range/Performance Problem
P0122 Throttle/Pedal Position Sensor/Switch "A" Circuit Low Input
P0123 Throttle/Pedal Position Sensor/Switch "A" Circuit High Input
P0124 Throttle/Pedal Position Sensor/Switch "A" Circuit Intermittent
P0125 Insufficient Coolant Temperature For Closed Loop Fuel Control
P0126 Insufficient Coolant Temperature For Stable Operation
P0130 O2 Circuit Malfunction (Bank no. 1 Sensor no. 1)

P0131 O2 Sensor Circuit Low Voltage (Bank no. 1 Sensor no. 1)
P0132 O2 Sensor Circuit High Voltage (Bank no. 1 Sensor no. 1)
P0133 O2 Sensor Circuit Slow Response (Bank no. 1 Sensor no. 1)
P0134 O2 Sensor Circuit No Activity Detected (Bank no. 1 Sensor no. 1)
P0135 O2 Sensor Heater Circuit Malfunction (Bank no. 1 Sensor no. 1)
P0136 O2 Sensor Circuit Malfunction (Bank no. 1 Sensor no. 2)
P0137 O2 Sensor Circuit Low Voltage (Bank no. 1 Sensor no. 2)
P0138 O2 Sensor Circuit High Voltage (Bank no. 1 Sensor no. 2)
P0139 O2 Sensor Circuit Slow Response (Bank no. 1 Sensor no. 2)
P0140 O2 Sensor Circuit No Activity Detected (Bank no. 1 Sensor no. 2)
P0141 O2 Sensor Heater Circuit Malfunction (Bank no. 1 Sensor no. 2)
P0142 O2 Sensor Circuit Malfunction (Bank no. 1 Sensor no. 3)
P0143 O2 Sensor Circuit Low Voltage (Bank no. 1 Sensor no. 3)
P0144 O2 Sensor Circuit High Voltage (Bank no. 1 Sensor no. 3)
P0145 O2 Sensor Circuit Slow Response (Bank no. 1 Sensor no. 3)
P0146 O2 Sensor Circuit No Activity Detected (Bank no. 1 Sensor no. 3)
P0147 O2 Sensor Heater Circuit Malfunction (Bank no. 1 Sensor no. 3)
P0150 O2 Sensor Circuit Malfunction (Bank no. 2 Sensor no. 1)
P0151 O2 Sensor Circuit Low Voltage (Bank no. 2 Sensor no. 1)
P0152 O2 Sensor Circuit High Voltage (Bank no. 2 Sensor no. 1)
P0153 O2 Sensor Circuit Slow Response (Bank no. 2 Sensor no. 1)
P0154 O2 Sensor Circuit No Activity Detected (Bank no. 2 Sensor no. 1)
P0155 O2 Sensor Heater Circuit Malfunction (Bank no. 2 Sensor no. 1)
P0156 O2 Sensor Circuit Malfunction (Bank no. 2 Sensor no. 2)
P0157 O2 Sensor Circuit Low Voltage (Bank no. 2 Sensor no. 2)
P0158 O2 Sensor Circuit High Voltage (Bank no. 2 Sensor no. 2)
P0159 O2 Sensor Circuit Slow Response (Bank no. 2 Sensor no. 2)
P0160 O2 Sensor Circuit No Activity Detected (Bank no. 2 Sensor no. 2)
P0161 O2 Sensor Heater Circuit Malfunction (Bank no. 2 Sensor no. 2)
P0162 O2 Sensor Circuit Malfunction (Bank no. 2 Sensor no. 3)
P0163 O2 Sensor Circuit Low Voltage (Bank no. 2 Sensor no. 3)
P0164 O2 Sensor Circuit High Voltage (Bank no. 2 Sensor no. 3)
P0165 O2 Sensor Circuit Slow Response (Bank no. 2 Sensor no. 3)
P0166 O2 Sensor Circuit No Activity Detected (Bank no. 2 Sensor no. 3)
P0167 O2 Sensor Heater Circuit Malfunction (Bank no. 2 Sensor no. 3)
P0170 Fuel Trim Malfunction (Bank no. 1)

P0171 System Too Lean (Bank no. 1)
P0172 System Too Rich (Bank no. 1)
P0173 Fuel Trim Malfunction (Bank no. 2)
P0174 System Too Lean (Bank no. 2)
P0175 System Too Rich (Bank no. 2)
P0176 Fuel Composition Sensor Circuit Malfunction
P0177 Fuel Composition Sensor Circuit Range/Performance
P0178 Fuel Composition Sensor Circuit Low Input
P0179 Fuel Composition Sensor Circuit High Input
P0180 Fuel Temperature Sensor "A" Circuit Malfunction
P0181 Fuel Temperature Sensor "A" Circuit Range/Performance
P0182 Fuel Temperature Sensor "A" Circuit Low Input
P0183 Fuel Temperature Sensor "A" Circuit High Input
P0184 Fuel Temperature Sensor "A" Circuit Intermittent
P0185 Fuel Temperature Sensor "B" Circuit Malfunction
P0186 Fuel Temperature Sensor "B" Circuit Range/Performance
P0187 Fuel Temperature Sensor "B" Circuit Low Input
P0188 Fuel Temperature Sensor "B" Circuit High Input
P0189 Fuel Temperature Sensor "B" Circuit Intermittent
P0190 Fuel Rail Pressure Sensor Circuit Malfunction
P0191 Fuel Rail Pressure Sensor Circuit Range/Performance
P0192 Fuel Rail Pressure Sensor Circuit Low Input
P0193 Fuel Rail Pressure Sensor Circuit High Input
P0194 Fuel Rail Pressure Sensor Circuit Intermittent
P0195 Engine Oil Temperature Sensor Malfunction
P0196 Engine Oil Temperature Sensor Range/Performance
P0197 Engine Oil Temperature Sensor Low
P0198 Engine Oil Temperature Sensor High
P0199 Engine Oil Temperature Sensor Intermittent
P0200 Injector Circuit Malfunction
P0201 Injector Circuit Malfunction—Cylinder no. 1
P0202 Injector Circuit Malfunction—Cylinder no. 2
P0203 Injector Circuit Malfunction—Cylinder no. 3
P0204 Injector Circuit Malfunction—Cylinder no. 4
P0205 Injector Circuit Malfunction—Cylinder no. 5
P0206 Injector Circuit Malfunction—Cylinder no. 6
P0207 Injector Circuit Malfunction—Cylinder no. 7
P0208 Injector Circuit Malfunction—Cylinder no. 8
P0209 Injector Circuit Malfunction—Cylinder no. 9
P0210 Injector Circuit Malfunction—Cylinder no. 10

P0211 Injector Circuit Malfunction—Cylinder no. 11
P0212 Injector Circuit Malfunction—Cylinder no. 12
P0213 Cold Start Injector no. 1 Malfunction
P0214 Cold Start Injector no. 2 Malfunction
P0215 Engine Shutoff Solenoid Malfunction
P0216 Injection Timing Control Circuit Malfunction
P0217 Engine Over Temperature Condition
P0218 Transmission Over Temperature Condition
P0219 Engine Over Speed Condition
P0220 Throttle/Pedal Position Sensor/Switch "B" Circuit Malfunction
P0221 Throttle/Pedal Position Sensor/Switch "B" Circuit Range/Performance Problem
P0222 Throttle/Pedal Position Sensor/Switch "B" Circuit Low Input
P0223 Throttle/Pedal Position Sensor/Switch "B" Circuit High Input
P0224 Throttle/Pedal Position Sensor/Switch "B" Circuit Intermittent
P0225 Throttle/Pedal Position Sensor/Switch "C" Circuit Malfunction
P0226 Throttle/Pedal Position Sensor/Switch "C" Circuit Range/Performance Problem
P0227 Throttle/Pedal Position Sensor/Switch "C" Circuit Low Input
P0228 Throttle/Pedal Position Sensor/Switch "C" Circuit High Input
P0229 Throttle/Pedal Position Sensor/Switch "C" Circuit Intermittent
P0230 Fuel Pump Primary Circuit Malfunction
P0231 Fuel Pump Secondary Circuit Low
P0232 Fuel Pump Secondary Circuit High
P0233 Fuel Pump Secondary Circuit Intermittent
P0234 Engine Over Boost Condition
P0261 Cylinder no. 1 Injector Circuit Low
P0262 Cylinder no. 1 Injector Circuit High
P0263 Cylinder no. 1 Contribution/Balance Fault
P0264 Cylinder no. 2 Injector Circuit Low
P0265 Cylinder no. 2 Injector Circuit High
P0266 Cylinder no. 2 Contribution/Balance Fault
P0267 Cylinder no. 3 Injector Circuit Low
P0268 Cylinder no. 3 Injector Circuit High
P0269 Cylinder no. 3 Contribution/Balance Fault
P0270 Cylinder no. 4 Injector Circuit Low
P0271 Cylinder no. 4 Injector Circuit High
P0272 Cylinder no. 4 Contribution/Balance Fault
P0273 Cylinder no. 5 Injector Circuit Low
P0274 Cylinder no. 5 Injector Circuit High
P0275 Cylinder no. 5 Contribution/Balance Fault
P0276 Cylinder no. 6 Injector Circuit Low
P0277 Cylinder no. 6 Injector Circuit High
P0278 Cylinder no. 6 Contribution/Balance Fault
P0279 Cylinder no. 7 Injector Circuit Low
P0280 Cylinder no. 7 Injector Circuit High
P0281 Cylinder no. 7 Contribution/Balance Fault
P0282 Cylinder no. 8 Injector Circuit Low
P0283 Cylinder no. 8 Injector Circuit High
P0284 Cylinder no. 8 Contribution/Balance Fault
P0285 Cylinder no. 9 Injector Circuit Low

P0286 Cylinder no. 9 Injector Circuit High
P0287 Cylinder no. 9 Contribution/Balance Fault
P0288 Cylinder no. 10 Injector Circuit Low
P0289 Cylinder no. 10 Injector Circuit High
P0290 Cylinder no. 10 Contribution/Balance Fault
P0291 Cylinder no. 11 Injector Circuit Low
P0292 Cylinder no. 11 Injector Circuit High
P0293 Cylinder no. 11 Contribution/Balance Fault
P0294 Cylinder no. 12 Injector Circuit Low
P0295 Cylinder no. 12 Injector Circuit High
P0296 Cylinder no. 12 Contribution/Balance Fault
P0300 Random/Multiple Cylinder Misfire Detected
P0301 Cylinder no. 1—Misfire Detected
P0302 Cylinder no. 2—Misfire Detected
P0303 Cylinder no. 3—Misfire Detected
P0304 Cylinder no. 4—Misfire Detected
P0305 Cylinder no. 5—Misfire Detected
P0306 Cylinder no. 6—Misfire Detected
P0307 Cylinder no. 7—Misfire Detected
P0308 Cylinder no. 8—Misfire Detected
P0309 Cylinder no. 9—Misfire Detected
P0310 Cylinder no. 10—Misfire Detected
P0311 Cylinder no. 11—Misfire Detected
P0312 Cylinder no. 12—Misfire Detected
P0320 Ignition/Distributor Engine Speed Input Circuit Malfunction
P0321 Ignition/Distributor Engine Speed Input Circuit Range/Performance
P0322 Ignition/Distributor Engine Speed Input Circuit No Signal
P0323 Ignition/Distributor Engine Speed Input Circuit Intermittent
P0325 Knock Sensor no. 1—Circuit Malfunction (Bank no. 1 or Single Sensor)
P0326 Knock Sensor no. 1—Circuit Range/Performance (Bank no. 1 or Single Sensor)
P0327 Knock Sensor no. 1—Circuit Low Input (Bank no. 1 or Single Sensor)
P0328 Knock Sensor no. 1—Circuit High Input (Bank no. 1 or Single Sensor)
P0329 Knock Sensor no. 1—Circuit Input Intermittent (Bank No. 1 or Single Sensor)
P0330 Knock Sensor no. 2—Circuit Malfunction (Bank no. 2)
P0331 Knock Sensor no. 2—Circuit Range/Performance (Bank no. 2)
P0332 Knock Sensor no. 2—Circuit Low Input (Bank no. 2)
P0333 Knock Sensor no. 2—Circuit High Input (Bank no. 2)
P0334 Knock Sensor no. 2—Circuit Input Intermittent (Bank no. 2)
P0335 Crankshaft Position Sensor "A" Circuit Malfunction
P0336 Crankshaft Position Sensor "A" Circuit Range/Performance
P0337 Crankshaft Position Sensor "A" Circuit Low Input
P0338 Crankshaft Position Sensor "A" Circuit High Input
P0339 Crankshaft Position Sensor "A" Circuit Intermittent
P0340 Camshaft Position Sensor Circuit Malfunction
P0341 Camshaft Position Sensor Circuit Range/Performance

P0342 Camshaft Position Sensor Circuit Low Input

P0343 Camshaft Position Sensor Circuit High Input

P0344 Camshaft Position Sensor Circuit Intermittent

P0350 Ignition Coil Primary/Secondary Circuit Malfunction

P0351 Ignition Coil "A" Primary/Secondary Circuit Malfunction

P0352 Ignition Coil "B" Primary/Secondary Circuit Malfunction

P0353 Ignition Coil "C" Primary/Secondary Circuit Malfunction

P0354 Ignition Coil "D" Primary/Secondary Circuit Malfunction

P0355 Ignition Coil "E" Primary/Secondary Circuit Malfunction

P0356 Ignition Coil "F" Primary/Secondary Circuit Malfunction

P0357 Ignition Coil "G" Primary/Secondary Circuit Malfunction

P0358 Ignition Coil "H" Primary/Secondary Circuit Malfunction

P0359 Ignition Coil "I" Primary/Secondary Circuit Malfunction

P0360 Ignition Coil "J" Primary/Secondary Circuit Malfunction

P0361 Ignition Coil "K" Primary/Secondary Circuit Malfunction

P0362 Ignition Coil "L" Primary/Secondary Circuit Malfunction

P0370 Timing Reference High Resolution Signal "A" Malfunction

P0371 Timing Reference High Resolution Signal "A" Too Many Pulses

P0372 Timing Reference High Resolution Signal "A" Too Few Pulses

P0373 Timing Reference High Resolution Signal "A" Intermittent/Erratic Pulses

P0374 Timing Reference High Resolution Signal "A" No Pulses

P0375 Timing Reference High Resolution Signal "B" Malfunction

P0376 Timing Reference High Resolution Signal "B" Too Many Pulses

P0377 Timing Reference High Resolution Signal "B" Too Few Pulses

P0378 Timing Reference High Resolution Signal "B" Intermittent/Erratic Pulses

P0379 Timing Reference High Resolution Signal "B" No Pulses

P0380 Glow Plug/Heater Circuit "A" Malfunction

P0381 Glow Plug/Heater Indicator Circuit Malfunction

P0382 Glow Plug/Heater Circuit "B" Malfunction

P0385 Crankshaft Position Sensor "B" Circuit Malfunction

P0386 Crankshaft Position Sensor "B" Circuit Range/Performance

P0387 Crankshaft Position Sensor "B" Circuit Low Input

P0388 Crankshaft Position Sensor "B" Circuit High Input

P0389 Crankshaft Position Sensor "B" Circuit Intermittent

P0400 Exhaust Gas Recirculation Flow Malfunction

P0401 Exhaust Gas Recirculation Flow Insufficient Detected

P0402 Exhaust Gas Recirculation Flow Excessive Detected

P0403 Exhaust Gas Recirculation Circuit Malfunction

P0404 Exhaust Gas Recirculation Circuit Range/Performance

P0405 Exhaust Gas Recirculation Sensor "A" Circuit Low

P0406 Exhaust Gas Recirculation Sensor "A" Circuit High

P0407 Exhaust Gas Recirculation Sensor "B" Circuit Low

P0408 Exhaust Gas Recirculation Sensor "B" Circuit High

P0410 Secondary Air Injection System Malfunction

P0411 Secondary Air Injection System Incorrect Flow Detected

P0412 Secondary Air Injection System Switching Valve "A" Circuit Malfunction

P0413 Secondary Air Injection System Switching Valve "A" Circuit Open

P0414 Secondary Air Injection System Switching Valve "A" Circuit Shorted

P0415 Secondary Air Injection System Switching Valve "B" Circuit Malfunction

P0416 Secondary Air Injection System Switching Valve "B" Circuit Open

P0417 Secondary Air Injection System Switching Valve "B" Circuit Shorted

P0418 Secondary Air Injection System Relay "A" Circuit Malfunction

P0419 Secondary Air Injection System Relay "B" Circuit Malfunction

P0420 Catalyst System Efficiency Below Threshold (Bank no. 1)

P0421 Warm Up Catalyst Efficiency Below Threshold (Bank no. 1)

P0422 Main Catalyst Efficiency Below Threshold (Bank no. 1)

P0423 Heated Catalyst Efficiency Below Threshold (Bank no. 1)

P0424 Heated Catalyst Temperature Below Threshold (Bank no. 1)

P0430 Catalyst System Efficiency Below Threshold (Bank no. 2)

P0431 Warm Up Catalyst Efficiency Below Threshold (Bank no. 2)

P0432 Main Catalyst Efficiency Below Threshold (Bank no. 2)

P0433 Heated Catalyst Efficiency Below Threshold (Bank no. 2)

P0434 Heated Catalyst Temperature Below Threshold (Bank no. 2)

P0440 Evaporative Emission Control System Malfunction

P0441 Evaporative Emission Control System Incorrect Purge Flow

P0442 Evaporative Emission Control System Leak Detected (Small Leak)

P0443 Evaporative Emission Control System Purge Control Valve Circuit Malfunction

P0444 Evaporative Emission Control System Purge Control Valve Circuit Open

P0445 Evaporative Emission Control System Purge Control Valve Circuit Shorted

P0446 Evaporative Emission Control System Vent Control Circuit Malfunction

P0447 Evaporative Emission Control System Vent Control Circuit Open

P0448 Evaporative Emission Control System Vent Control Circuit Shorted

P0449 Evaporative Emission Control System Vent Valve/Solenoid Circuit Malfunction

P0450 Evaporative Emission Control System Pressure Sensor Malfunction

P0451 Evaporative Emission Control System Fuel Tank Pressure Sensor Range/Performance

P0452 Evaporative Emission Control System Fuel Tank Pressure Sensor Low Input

P0453 Evaporative Emission Control System Fuel Tank Pressure Sensor High Input

P0454 Evaporative Emission Control System Pressure Sensor Intermittent

P0455 Evaporative Emission Control System Leak Detected (Gross Leak)

P0460 Fuel Level Sensor Circuit Malfunction

P0461 Fuel Level Sensor Circuit Range/Performance

P0462 Fuel Level Sensor Circuit Low Input

P0463 Fuel Level Sensor Circuit High Input

P0464 Fuel Level Sensor Circuit Intermittent

P0465 Purge Flow Sensor Circuit Malfunction

P0466 Purge Flow Sensor Circuit Range/Performance

P0467 Purge Flow Sensor Circuit Low Input

P0468 Purge Flow Sensor Circuit High Input

P0469 Purge Flow Sensor Circuit Intermittent

P0470 Exhaust Pressure Sensor Malfunction

P0471 Exhaust Pressure Sensor Range/Performance

P0472 Exhaust Pressure Sensor Low

P0473 Exhaust Pressure Sensor High

P0474 Exhaust Pressure Sensor Intermittent

P0475 Exhaust Pressure Control Valve Malfunction

P0476 Exhaust Pressure Control Valve Range/Performance

P0477 Exhaust Pressure Control Valve Low

P0478 Exhaust Pressure Control Valve High

P0479 Exhaust Pressure Control Valve Intermittent

P0480 Cooling Fan no. 1 Control Circuit Malfunction

P0481 Cooling Fan no. 2 Control Circuit Malfunction

P0482 Cooling Fan no. 3 Control Circuit Malfunction

P0483 Cooling Fan Rationality Check Malfunction

P0484 Cooling Fan Circuit Over Current

P0485 Cooling Fan Power/Ground Circuit Malfunction

P0500 Vehicle Speed Sensor Malfunction

P0501 Vehicle Speed Sensor Range/Performance

P0502 Vehicle Speed Sensor Circuit Low Input

P0503 Vehicle Speed Sensor Intermittent/Erratic/High

P0505 Idle Control System Malfunction

P0506 Idle Control System RPM Lower Than Expected

P0507 Idle Control System RPM Higher Than Expected

P0510 Closed Throttle Position Switch Malfunction

P0520 Engine Oil Pressure Sensor/Switch Circuit Malfunction

P0521 Engine Oil Pressure Sensor/Switch Range/Performance

P0522 Engine Oil Pressure Sensor/Switch Low Voltage

P0523 Engine Oil Pressure Sensor/Switch High Voltage

P0530 A/C Refrigerant Pressure Sensor Circuit Malfunction

P0531 A/C Refrigerant Pressure Sensor Circuit Range/Performance

P0532 A/C Refrigerant Pressure Sensor Circuit Low Input

P0533 A/C Refrigerant Pressure Sensor Circuit High Input

P0534 A/C Refrigerant Charge Loss

P0550 Power Steering Pressure Sensor Circuit Malfunction

P0551 Power Steering Pressure Sensor Circuit Range/Performance

P0552 Power Steering Pressure Sensor Circuit Low Input

P0553 Power Steering Pressure Sensor Circuit High Input

P0554 Power Steering Pressure Sensor Circuit Intermittent

P0560 System Voltage Malfunction

P0561 System Voltage Unstable

P0562 System Voltage Low

P0563 System Voltage High

P0565 Cruise Control On Signal Malfunction

P0566 Cruise Control Off Signal Malfunction

P0567 Cruise Control Resume Signal Malfunction

P0568 Cruise Control Set Signal Malfunction

P0569 Cruise Control Coast Signal Malfunction

P0570 Cruise Control Accel Signal Malfunction

P0571 Cruise Control/Brake Switch "A" Circuit Malfunction

P0572 Cruise Control/Brake Switch "A" Circuit Low

P0573 Cruise Control/Brake Switch "A" Circuit High

P0574 **Through P0580** Reserved for Cruise Codes

P0600 Serial Communication Link Malfunction

P0601 Internal Control Module Memory Check Sum Error

P0602 Control Module Programming Error

P0603 Internal Control Module Keep Alive Memory (KAM) Error

P0604 Internal Control Module Random Access Memory (RAM) Error

P0605 Internal Control Module Read Only Memory (ROM) Error

P0606 PCM Processor Fault

P0608 Control Module VSS Output "A" Malfunction

P0609 Control Module VSS Output "B" Malfunction

P0620 Generator Control Circuit Malfunction

P0621 Generator Lamp "L" Control Circuit Malfunction

P0622 Generator Field "F" Control Circuit Malfunction

P0650 Malfunction Indicator Lamp (MIL) Control Circuit Malfunction

P0654 Engine RPM Output Circuit Malfunction

P0655 Engine Hot Lamp Output Control Circuit Malfunction

P0656 Fuel Level Output Circuit Malfunction

P0700 Transmission Control System Malfunction

P0701 Transmission Control System Range/Performance

P0702 Transmission Control System Electrical

P0703 Torque Converter/Brake Switch "B" Circuit Malfunction

P0704 Clutch Switch Input Circuit Malfunction

P0705 Transmission Range Sensor Circuit Malfunction (PRNDL Input)

P0706 Transmission Range Sensor Circuit Range/Performance

P0707 Transmission Range Sensor Circuit Low Input

P0708 Transmission Range Sensor Circuit High Input

P0709 Transmission Range Sensor Circuit Intermittent

P0710 Transmission Fluid Temperature Sensor Circuit Malfunction

P0711 Transmission Fluid Temperature Sensor Circuit Range/Performance

P0712 Transmission Fluid Temperature Sensor Circuit Low Input

P0713 Transmission Fluid Temperature Sensor Circuit High Input

P0714 Transmission Fluid Temperature Sensor Circuit Intermittent

P0715 Input/Turbine Speed Sensor Circuit Malfunction

P0716 Input/Turbine Speed Sensor Circuit Range/Performance

P0717 Input/Turbine Speed Sensor Circuit No Signal

P0718 Input/Turbine Speed Sensor Circuit Intermittent

P0719 Torque Converter/Brake Switch "B" Circuit Low

P0720 Output Speed Sensor Circuit Malfunction

P0721 Output Speed Sensor Circuit Range/Performance

P0722 Output Speed Sensor Circuit No Signal

P0723 Output Speed Sensor Circuit Intermittent

P0724 Torque Converter/Brake Switch "B" Circuit High

P0725 Engine Speed Input Circuit Malfunction

P0726 Engine Speed Input Circuit Range/Performance

P0727 Engine Speed Input Circuit No Signal

P0728 Engine Speed Input Circuit Intermittent

P0730 Incorrect Gear Ratio

P0731 Gear no. 1 Incorrect Ratio

P0732 Gear no. 2 Incorrect Ratio

P0733 Gear no. 3 Incorrect Ratio

P0734 Gear no. 4 Incorrect Ratio

P0735 Gear no. 5 Incorrect Ratio

P0736 Reverse Incorrect Ratio

P0740 Torque Converter Clutch Circuit Malfunction

P0741 Torque Converter Clutch Circuit Performance or Stuck Off

P0742 Torque Converter Clutch Circuit Stuck On

P0743 Torque Converter Clutch Circuit Electrical

P0744 Torque Converter Clutch Circuit Intermittent

P0745 Pressure Control Solenoid Malfunction

P0746 Pressure Control Solenoid Performance or Stuck Off

P0747 Pressure Control Solenoid Stuck On

P0748 Pressure Control Solenoid Electrical

P0749 Pressure Control Solenoid Intermittent

P0750 Shift Solenoid "A" Malfunction

P0751 Shift Solenoid "A" Performance or Stuck Off

P0752 Shift Solenoid "A" Stuck On

P0753 Shift Solenoid "A" Electrical

P0754 Shift Solenoid "A" Intermittent

P0755 Shift Solenoid "B" Malfunction

P0756 Shift Solenoid "B" Performance or Stuck Off

P0757 Shift Solenoid "B" Stuck On

P0758 Shift Solenoid "B" Electrical

P0759 Shift Solenoid "B" Intermittent

P0760 Shift Solenoid "C" Malfunction

P0761 Shift Solenoid "C" Performance Or Stuck Off

P0762 Shift Solenoid "C" Stuck On

P0763 Shift Solenoid "C" Electrical

P0764 Shift Solenoid "C" Intermittent

P0765 Shift Solenoid "D" Malfunction

P0766 Shift Solenoid "D" Performance Or Stuck Off

P0767 Shift Solenoid "D" Stuck On

P0768 Shift Solenoid "D" Electrical

P0769 Shift Solenoid "D" Intermittent

P0770 Shift Solenoid "E" Malfunction

P0771 Shift Solenoid "E" Performance Or Stuck Off

P0772 Shift Solenoid "E" Stuck On

P0773 Shift Solenoid "E" Electrical

P0774 Shift Solenoid "E" Intermittent

P0780 Shift Malfunction

P0781 1–2 Shift Malfunction

P0782 2–3 Shift Malfunction

P0783 3–4 Shift Malfunction

P0784 4–5 Shift Malfunction

P0785 Shift/Timing Solenoid Malfunction

P0786 Shift/Timing Solenoid Range/Performance

P0787 Shift/Timing Solenoid Low

P0788 Shift/Timing Solenoid High

P0789 Shift/Timing Solenoid Intermittent

P0790 Normal/Performance Switch Circuit Malfunction

P0801 Reverse Inhibit Control Circuit Malfunction

P0803 1–4 Upshift (Skip Shift) Solenoid Control Circuit Malfunction

P0804 1–4 Upshift (Skip Shift) Lamp Control Circuit Malfunction

P1106 Barometric Pressure Circuit Range Performance Problem

P1107 Barometric Pressure Circuit Low Input

P1108 Barometric Pressure Circuit High Input

P1111 IAT Sensor Circuit Intermittent High Voltage

P1112 IAT Sensor Circuit Intermittent Low Voltage

P1114 ECT Sensor Circuit Intermittent Low Voltage

P1115 ECT Sensor Circuit Intermittent High Voltage

P1121 Throttle Position Lower Than Expected

P1122 Throttle Position Higher Than Expected

P1128 Manifold Absolute Pressure Lower Than Expected

P1129 Manifold Absolute Pressure Higher Than Expected

P1133 HO2S-11 Insufficient Switching (Bank 1 Sensor 1)

P1134 HO2S-11 Transition Time Ratio (Bank 1 Sensor 1)

P1153 HO2S-21 Insufficient Switching (Bank 2 Sensor I)

P1154 HO2S-21 Transition Time Ratio (Bank 2 Sensor 1)

P1171 Fuel System Lean During Acceleration
P1259 VTEC System Malfunction
P1297 Electrical Load Detector Circuit Low Input
P1298 Electrical Load Detector Circuit High Input
P1300 Random Misfire
P1336 Crankshaft Speed Fluctuation Sensor Intermittent Interruption
P1337 Crankshaft Speed Fluctuation Sensor No Signal
P1359 Crankshaft Position/Top Dead Center Sensor/Cylinder Position Connector Disconnected
P1361 Top Dead Center Sensor Intermittent Interruption
P1362 Top Dead Center Sensor No Signal
P1366 Top Dead Center Sensor2 Intermittent Interruption
P1367 Top Dead Center Sensor2 No Signal
P1381 Cylinder Position Sensor Intermittent Interruption
P1382 Cylinder Position Sensor No Signal

P1391 G-Acceleration Sensor Intermittent Low Voltage
P1390 G-Acceleration (Low G) Sensor Performance
P1392 Rough Road G-Sensor Circuit Low Voltage
P1393 Rough Road G-Sensor Circuit High Voltage
P1394 G-Acceleration Sensor Intermittent High Voltage
P1406 EGR Valve Pintle Position Sensor Circuit Fault
P1441 EVAP System Flow During Non-Purge
P1442 EVAP System Flow During Non-Purge
P1456 EVAP System Leak Detected (Fuel Tank)
P1457 EVAP System Leak Detected (Control Canister)
P1491 EGR Valve Lift Insufficient Detected
P1498 EGR Valve Lift Sensor High Voltage
P1508 Idle Speed Control System-Low
P1509 Idle Speed Control System-High
P1607 Powertrain Control Module Internal Circuit Failure A

P1618 Serial Peripheral Interface Communication Error
P1640 Output Driver Module 'A' Fault
P1676 FPTDR Signal Line Failure
P1678 FPTDR Signal Line Failure
P1705 Automatic Transaxle
P1706 Automatic Transaxle
P1709 Automatic Transaxle
P1738 Automatic Transaxle
P1739 Automatic Transaxle
P1753 Automatic Transaxle
P1768 Automatic Transaxle
P1773 Automatic Transaxle
P1790 PCM ROM (Transmission Side) Check Sum Error
P1792 PCM EPROM (Transmission Side) Check Sum Error
P1835 Kick Down Switch Always On
P1850 Brake Band Apply Solenoid Electrical Fault
P1860 TCC PWM Solenoid Electrical Fault
P1870 Transmission Component Slipping

VACUUM DIAGRAMS

▶ **See Figures 44, 45, 46, 47 and 48**

Following are vacuum diagrams for most of the engine and emissions package combinations covered by this manual. Because vacuum circuits will vary based on various engine and vehicle options, always refer first to the vehicle emission control information label, if present. Should the label be missing, or should vehicle be equipped with a different engine from the vehicle's original equipment, refer to the diagrams below for the same or similar configuration. If you wish to obtain a replacement emissions label, most manufacturers make the labels available for purchase. The labels can usually be ordered from a local dealer.

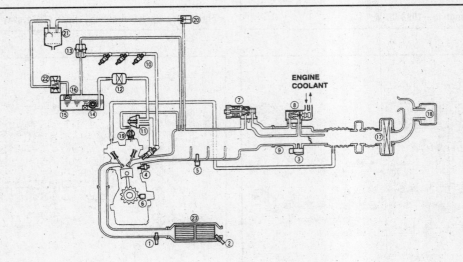

① PRIMARY HEATED OXYGEN SENSOR (PRIMARY HO2S, SENSOR 1)
② SECONDARY HEATED OXYGEN SENSOR (SECONDARY HO2S, SENSOR 2)
③ MANIFOLD ABSOLUTE PRESSURE (MAP) SENSOR
④ ENGINE COOLANT TEMPERATURE (ECT) SENSOR
⑤ INTAKE AIR TEMPERATURE (IAT) SENSOR
⑥ CRANKSHAFT SPEED FLUCTUATION (CKF) SENSOR
⑦ IDLE AIR CONTROL (IAC) VALVE
⑧ FAST IDLE THERMO VALVE
⑨ THROTTLE BODY (TB)
⑩ FUEL INJECTOR
⑪ FUEL PULSATION DAMPER
⑫ FUEL FILTER
⑬ FUEL PRESSURE REGULATOR
⑭ FUEL PUMP
⑮ FUEL TANK
⑯ FUEL TANK EVAPORATIVE EMISSION (EVAP) VALVE
⑰ AIR CLEANER
⑱ RESONATOR
⑲ POSITIVE CRANKCASE VENTILATION (PCV) VALVE
⑳ EVAPORATIVE EMISSION (EVAP) PURGE CONTROL SOLENOID VALVE
㉑ EVAPORATIVE EMISSION (EVAP) CONTROL CANISTER
㉒ EVAPORATIVE EMISSION (EVAP) TWO WAY VALVE
㉓ THREE WAY CATALYTIC CONVERTER (TWC)

93134G26

Fig. 44 Vacuum hose routing—1997 CR-V

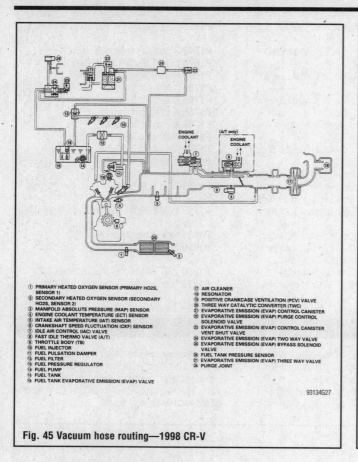

① PRIMARY HEATED OXYGEN SENSOR (PRIMARY HO2S, SENSOR 1)
② SECONDARY HEATED OXYGEN SENSOR (SECONDARY HO2S, SENSOR 2)
③ MANIFOLD ABSOLUTE PRESSURE (MAP) SENSOR
④ ENGINE COOLANT TEMPERATURE (ECT) SENSOR
⑤ INTAKE AIR TEMPERATURE (IAT) SENSOR
⑥ CRANKSHAFT SPEED FLUCTUATION (CKF) SENSOR
⑦ IDLE AIR CONTROL (IAC) VALVE
⑧ FAST IDLE THERMO VALVE (A/T)
⑨ THROTTLE BODY (TB)
⑩ FUEL INJECTOR
⑪ FUEL PULSATION DAMPER
⑫ FUEL FILTER
⑬ FUEL PRESSURE REGULATOR
⑭ FUEL PUMP
⑮ FUEL TANK
⑯ FUEL TANK EVAPORATIVE EMISSION (EVAP) VALVE

⑰ AIR CLEANER
⑱ RESONATOR
⑲ POSITIVE CRANKCASE VENTILATION (PCV) VALVE
⑳ THREE WAY CATALYTIC CONVERTER (TWC)
㉑ EVAPORATIVE EMISSION (EVAP) CONTROL CANISTER
㉒ EVAPORATIVE EMISSION (EVAP) PURGE CONTROL SOLENOID VALVE
㉓ EVAPORATIVE EMISSION (EVAP) CONTROL CANISTER VENT SHUT VALVE
㉔ EVAPORATIVE EMISSION (EVAP) TWO WAY VALVE
㉕ EVAPORATIVE EMISSION (EVAP) BYPASS SOLENOID VALVE
㉖ FUEL TANK PRESSURE SENSOR
㉗ EVAPORATIVE EMISSION (EVAP) THREE WAY VALVE
㉘ PURGE JOINT

93134G27

Fig. 45 Vacuum hose routing—1998 CR-V

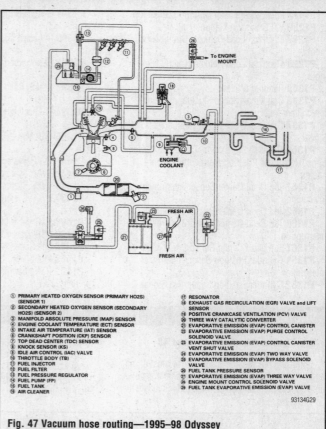

① PRIMARY HEATED OXYGEN SENSOR (PRIMARY HO2S) (SENSOR 1)
② SECONDARY HEATED OXYGEN SENSOR (SECONDARY HO2S) (SENSOR 2)
③ MANIFOLD ABSOLUTE PRESSURE (MAP) SENSOR
④ ENGINE COOLANT TEMPERATURE (ECT) SENSOR
⑤ INTAKE AIR TEMPERATURE (IAT) SENSOR
⑥ CRANKSHAFT POSITION (CKP) SENSOR
⑦ TOP DEAD CENTER (TDC) SENSOR
⑧ KNOCK SENSOR (KS)
⑨ IDLE AIR CONTROL (IAC) VALVE
⑩ THROTTLE BODY (TB)
⑪ FUEL INJECTOR
⑫ FUEL FILTER
⑬ FUEL PRESSURE REGULATOR
⑭ FUEL PUMP (FP)
⑮ FUEL TANK
⑯ AIR CLEANER

⑰ RESONATOR
⑱ EXHAUST GAS RECIRCULATION (EGR) VALVE and LIFT SENSOR
⑲ POSITIVE CRANKCASE VENTILATION (PCV) VALVE
⑳ THREE WAY CATALYTIC CONVERTER
㉑ EVAPORATIVE EMISSION (EVAP) CONTROL CANISTER
㉒ EVAPORATIVE EMISSION (EVAP) PURGE CONTROL SOLENOID VALVE
㉓ EVAPORATIVE EMISSION (EVAP) CONTROL CANISTER VENT SHUT VALVE
㉔ EVAPORATIVE EMISSION (EVAP) TWO WAY VALVE
㉕ EVAPORATIVE EMISSION (EVAP) BYPASS SOLENOID VALVE
㉖ FUEL TANK PRESSURE SENSOR
㉗ EVAPORATIVE EMISSION (EVAP) THREE WAY VALVE
㉘ ENGINE MOUNT CONTROL SOLENOID VALVE
㉙ FUEL TANK EVAPORATIVE EMISSION (EVAP) VALVE

93134G29

Fig. 47 Vacuum hose routing—1995–98 Odyssey

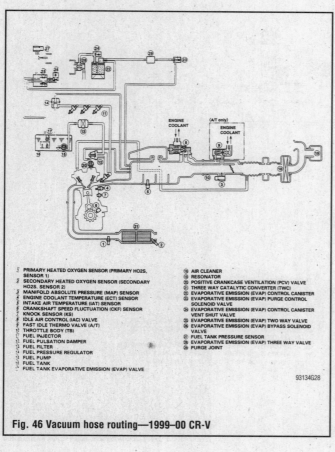

① PRIMARY HEATED OXYGEN SENSOR (PRIMARY HO2S, SENSOR 1)
② SECONDARY HEATED OXYGEN SENSOR (SECONDARY HO2S, SENSOR 2)
③ MANIFOLD ABSOLUTE PRESSURE (MAP) SENSOR
④ ENGINE COOLANT TEMPERATURE (ECT) SENSOR
⑤ INTAKE AIR TEMPERATURE (IAT) SENSOR
⑥ CRANKSHAFT SPEED FLUCTUATION (CKF) SENSOR
⑦ KNOCK SENSOR (KS)
⑧ IDLE AIR CONTROL (IAC) VALVE
⑨ FAST IDLE THERMO VALVE (A/T)
⑩ THROTTLE BODY (TB)
⑪ FUEL INJECTOR
⑫ FUEL PULSATION DAMPER
⑬ FUEL FILTER
⑭ FUEL PRESSURE REGULATOR
⑮ FUEL PUMP
⑯ FUEL TANK
⑰ FUEL TANK EVAPORATIVE EMISSION (EVAP) VALVE

⑱ AIR CLEANER
⑲ RESONATOR
⑳ POSITIVE CRANKCASE VENTILATION (PCV) VALVE
㉑ THREE WAY CATALYTIC CONVERTER (TWC)
㉒ EVAPORATIVE EMISSION (EVAP) CONTROL CANISTER
㉓ EVAPORATIVE EMISSION (EVAP) PURGE CONTROL SOLENOID VALVE
㉔ EVAPORATIVE EMISSION (EVAP) CONTROL CANISTER VENT SHUT VALVE
㉕ EVAPORATIVE EMISSION (EVAP) TWO WAY VALVE
㉖ EVAPORATIVE EMISSION (EVAP) BYPASS SOLENOID VALVE
㉗ FUEL TANK PRESSURE SENSOR
㉘ EVAPORATIVE EMISSION (EVAP) THREE WAY VALVE
㉙ PURGE JOINT

93134G28

Fig. 46 Vacuum hose routing—1999–00 CR-V

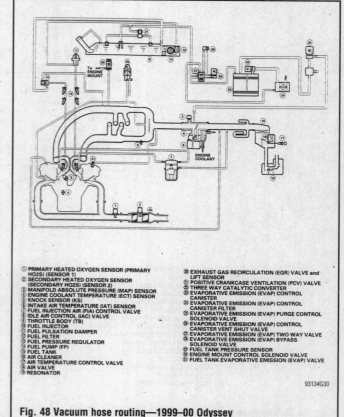

① PRIMARY HEATED OXYGEN SENSOR (PRIMARY HO2S) (SENSOR 1)
② SECONDARY HEATED OXYGEN SENSOR (SECONDARY HO2S) (SENSOR 2)
③ MANIFOLD ABSOLUTE PRESSURE (MAP) SENSOR
④ ENGINE COOLANT TEMPERATURE (ECT) SENSOR
⑤ KNOCK SENSOR (KS)
⑥ INTAKE AIR TEMPERATURE (IAT) SENSOR
⑦ FUEL INJECTION AIR (FIA) CONTROL VALVE
⑧ IDLE AIR CONTROL (IAC) VALVE
⑨ THROTTLE BODY (TB)
⑩ FUEL INJECTOR
⑪ FUEL PULSATION DAMPER
⑫ FUEL FILTER
⑬ FUEL PRESSURE REGULATOR
⑭ FUEL PUMP (FP)
⑮ FUEL TANK
⑯ AIR CLEANER
⑰ AIR TEMPERATURE CONTROL VALVE
⑱ AIR VALVE
⑲ RESONATOR

⑳ EXHAUST GAS RECIRCULATION (EGR) VALVE and LIFT SENSOR
㉑ POSITIVE CRANKCASE VENTILATION (PCV) VALVE
㉒ THREE WAY CATALYTIC CONVERTER
㉓ EVAPORATIVE EMISSION (EVAP) CONTROL CANISTER
㉔ EVAPORATIVE EMISSION (EVAP) CONTROL CANISTER FILTER
㉕ EVAPORATIVE EMISSION (EVAP) PURGE CONTROL SOLENOID VALVE
㉖ EVAPORATIVE EMISSION (EVAP) CONTROL CANISTER VENT SHUT VALVE
㉗ EVAPORATIVE EMISSION (EVAP) TWO WAY VALVE
㉘ EVAPORATIVE EMISSION (EVAP) BYPASS SOLENOID VALVE
㉙ FUEL TANK PRESSURE SENSOR
㉚ ENGINE MOUNT CONTROL SOLENOID VALVE
㉛ FUEL TANK EVAPORATIVE EMISSION (EVAP) VALVE

93134G30

Fig. 48 Vacuum hose routing—1999–00 Odyssey

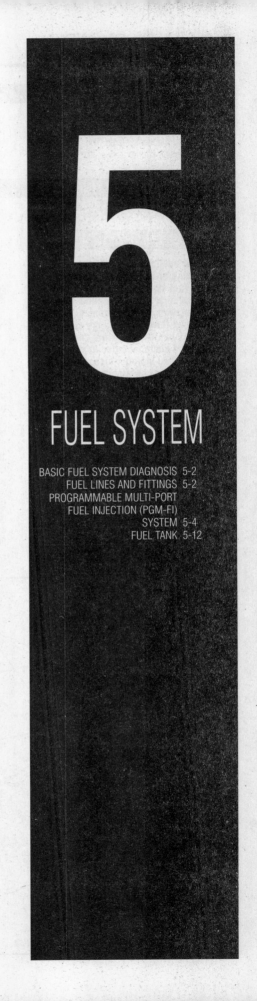

5

FUEL SYSTEM

BASIC FUEL SYSTEM DIAGNOSIS

When there is a problem starting or driving a vehicle, two of the most important checks involve the ignition and the fuel systems. The questions most mechanics attempt to answer first, "is there spark?" and "is there fuel?" will often lead to solving most basic problems. For ignition system diagnosis and testing, please refer to the information on engine electrical components and ignition systems found earlier in this manual. If the ignition system checks out (there is spark), then you must determine if the fuel system is operating properly (is there fuel?).

FUEL LINES AND FITTINGS

♦ See Figure 1

✳✳ CAUTION

Observe all applicable safety precautions when working around fuel. Whenever servicing the fuel system, always work in a well ventilated area. Do not allow fuel spray or vapors to come in contact with a spark or open flame. Keep a dry chemical fire extinguisher near the work area. Always keep fuel in a container specifically designed for fuel storage; also, always properly seal fuel containers to avoid the possibility of fire or explosion.

The fuel system is inter-connected using a network of lines and connectors. At times these connectors must be disconnected in order to properly repair the system. Pay careful attention to the following.

The fuel lines and fittings found on the Honda CR-V and Odyssey models are one of four basic types:
• Clamped fitting
• Compression fitting
• Banjo bolt fitting
• Quick-connect fitting

Due to the construction of the fuel lines, acid may damage the integrity of the line. Replace the fuel tubing if there is any suspect of an acid or electrolyte contamination. When disconnecting the lines, be cautious not to twist the connectors. As always, replace any component if damaged.

Clamped Fittings

REMOVAL & INSTALLATION

♦ See Figures 2 and 3

The conventional clamped fitting is used when a flexible hose is installed over a fitting and clamped in place. This type of fuel fitting is found in a variety of locations and sizes throughout the vehicle, such as the fuel filler neck and Evaporative Canister hoses. The flexible fuel hose is installed over a fitting with a clamp to secure the hose to the fitting. The clamp is either spring loaded and released using a pliers, or mechanically tightened, requiring a screwdriver or related tool to loosen or tighten.

To remove a clamped type fitting, perform the following:

1. Release the clamp's tension and slide the clamp off the section of hose that is attached to the fitting.
2. Carefully slide the hose off the fitting.

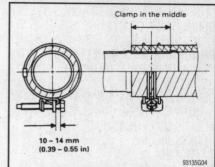

Fig. 2 The mechanically tightened clamp should be centered on the fitting and properly secured. Use care to not overtighten

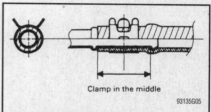

Fig. 3 The spring-loaded clamp is released by using flat-nosed pliers to squeeze the tabs together and slide the clamp off the clamped portion of the fitting

To install:
3. Carefully slide the hose over the fitting.
4. Center the clamp over the middle of the section of hose covering the fitting.
5. Release the clamp or tighten as necessary.

Compression Fittings

REMOVAL & INSTALLATION

♦ See Figures 4, 5, 6 and 7

The compression fitting has a flared metal tube or a compression fitting that is surrounded by a threaded flare nut. Because the tube is flared or has a compression fitting installed, the threaded flare nut cannot be removed from the line and is considered part of the assembly.

Compression fittings are most often used when a pressure line attaches to an assembly, much like the inlet fuel line for the firewall mounted fuel filter found on CR-V and 4-cylinder Odyssey models.

The compression fitting does not have a gasket or seal, rather it uses the threaded flare nut to seal the flared end of the line or a compression fitting on the line to the assembly. The flared end of the fuel

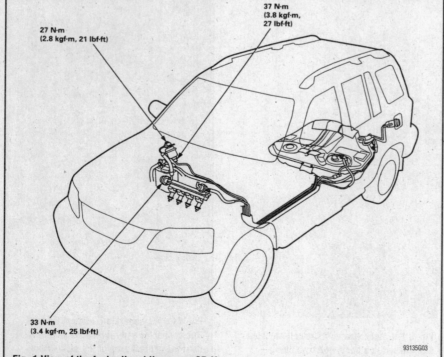

Fig. 1 View of the fuel rail and lines on a CR-V

line or the compression fitting is sealed between the component and the flare nut.

A compression fitting is most often found where the fluid in the line is under considerable pressure.

The flare nut is one of two types:

• The externally threaded flare nut: An example of this type of fitting is most easily seen on the CR-V and Odyssey models where the flare nut is threaded into the brake master cylinder.

Fig. 4 An example of an internally threaded flare nut on this fuel line. Note the use of a flare nut wrench; loosen the nut while the component is held with another wrench

Fig. 5 The open-end wrench on the left compared to a flare nut wrench on the right. The slot allows the flare nut wrench to clear the line, yet will grip the flare nut on all 6 sides

Fig. 6 The fuel inlet line on a Honda fire-wall mounted fuel filter is a compression fitting. The flare nut has external threads and is threaded into the bottom of the fuel filter

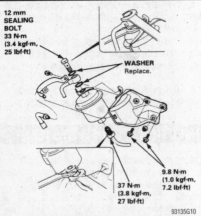

Fig. 7 An exploded view of a Honda fire-wall-mounted fuel filter and mounting bracket. The filter outlet (top) uses a banjo bolt fitting, the inlet (bottom) is a compression fitting

• An internally threaded flare nut: This type of fitting uses a compression fitting on the line and the nut threads onto a threaded fitting.

1. To disconnect a fuel line using a compression fitting, hold the component that the flare nut is threaded onto securely, and using a flare nut type wrench, loosen the flare nut.

2. Installation is the reverse of the removal procedure.

Banjo Bolt Fittings

REMOVAL & INSTALLATION

▶ **See Figures 8 and 9**

The banjo bolt fitting has a hollow bolt that is installed through a round hollowed out chamber with a hose fitting incorporated onto the chamber. The hollowed out chamber and hose fitting resemble the shape of a banjo, hence the name banjo bolt. The banjo bolt uses a sealing washer on each side of the hollowed chamber that should be replaced during reassembly.

Banjo bolt fittings are used where the fluid in the fluid lines is under pressure.

To remove a banjo bolt type of fitting:

Fig. 8 The outlet line on a firewall-mounted fuel filter uses a banjo bolt type fitting—CR-V and 4-cylinder Odyssey models

Fig. 9 When reinstalling the banjo bolt, always use new sealing washers

1. Secure the component the banjo bolt is threaded into and loosen the banjo bolt using a boxed end wrench if room permits.

To install:

2. Using new sealing washer on either side of the banjo fitting, install the banjo bolt and carefully tighten to specification. The sealing washers should be slightly "crushed" between the banjo bolt the banjo fitting and the component.

Quick-Connect Fittings

REMOVAL & INSTALLATION

▶ **See Figures 10 and 11**

A disconnected quick-connect fitting can be re-attached. The retainer on the mating pipe should not be reused once disconnected. It should be replaced when:

• Replacing the fuel pump.

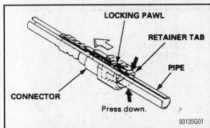

Fig. 10 Press both retainer tabs in to release the fuel line from the connector on quick-connect fittings

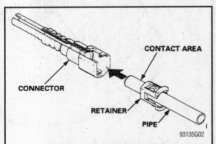

Fig. 11 Once separated, inspect the fuel line connector and replace the retainer. Coat the contact area of the pipe with a light coating of fresh engine oil

- Replacing the fuel feed pipe.
- It has been removed from the pipe.
- It is damaged.

To disconnect a quick-connect fitting, perform the following:

1. Properly relieve the fuel system pressure, as outlined later in this section.

2. Clean all dirt off the fuel system connectors before removal of the fitting.

3. Hold the connector with one hand, then pull the connector off with your other hand by pressing down on the retainer tabs.

4. Inspect the contact area of the connector for dirt and grime. If the surface is dirty, clean it. If the surface area is rusty or damaged, replace it.

5. To keep foreign material out of the fitting, cover the end of the line/fitting assembly with a plastic bag such as a sandwich style or locking freezer bag.

To install:

6. Insert a new retainer into the connector.

7. Apply a light coating of fresh engine oil to the fuel pipe.

8. Carefully press the fuel pipe into the connector making sure the retainer snaps in place completely.

9. Inspect for leakage and repair as necessary.

PROGRAMMABLE MULTI-PORT FUEL INJECTION (PGM-FI) SYSTEM

General Information

▶ See Figure 12

The fuel system includes components such as the fuel tank, fuel filler cap, fuel lines, a high-pressure fuel pump, PGM-FI main relay, filter, pressure regulator, injectors, and fuel pulsation damper. The fuel injection system delivers pressurized fuel to the injectors with the engine **ON** and cuts that fuel delivery when the engine is turned **OFF**.

The fuel is circulated in a pressurized loop from the fuel tank to the injectors and back to the fuel tank. That is why some of the components are labeled in and out, or feed and return, as the component must be installed properly. This is also useful when doing system diagnosis, because the fuel pressure characteristics could differ depending on where it is being checked.

The fuel is circulated in a loop so each fuel injector has a continuous supply of fuel. The fuel injectors are electrically operated and their operation is controlled by the Powertrain Control Module (PCM). Each injector has a small electromagnet, that when triggered by electricity, causes the injector to open and spray fuel. Sometimes an audible clicking noise can be heard from an electrically operated injector when the engine is running.

The fuel requirements for an engine differ depending on the temperature of the engine and the surrounding atmospheric conditions. A cold engine being started in freezing temperatures requires significantly more fuel to be delivered to the cylinders than a warm engine idling in a hot climate.

Any atmospheric condition that affects the amount of available oxygen molecules in the air also affects the needed fuel mixture for a gasoline engine. The amount of available oxygen molecules in the air is affected by both temperature and altitude, and the fuel injection system must be able to adapt to ensure the correct fuel delivery for the engine to run properly.

During a cold engine startup more fuel is needed to get the engine started. The fuel does not atomize efficiently on a cold engine, as the fuel tends to enter the combustion chamber in the form of small droplets, which are more difficult to ignite than an atomized vapor. Once the engine has reached operating temperature, the fuel is atomized into a highly combustible vapor by the engine's increased operating temperature. This fuel vapor is much more combustible than raw fuel droplets, therefore the engine needs less fuel to operate.

To accommodate the ever-changing fuel requirements for an engine to run and perform properly, the PCM must be capable of monitoring the atmospheric conditions and the engine's operating parameters.

Engine related conditions that affect fuel requirements are engine operating temperature, engine speed (RPM), throttle position and engine load. Atmospheric conditions that affect an engine's fuel requirements are altitude and outside air (ambient air) temperature

Based on the information provided to the PCM via the input sensors, the PCM manages the fuel delivery by controlling the amount of time that it allows each injector to stay open. Because the fuel injectors are in a fuel loop where the pressure is relatively constant, the fuel mixture can be controlled by the amount of time a fuel injector stays open.

The added benefits of a precisely controlled fuel delivery system include reduced emissions, improved driveability, increased performance and improved fuel economy

The fuel injection system rarely requires maintenance and there are no routine adjustments to the fuel metering system that can be performed. Preventative maintenance tips that will help prolong the life of a fuel injection system include:

- Frequently inspect the air filter, and replace as needed
- Never operate the vehicle with a missing fuel filler cap
- Keeping the fuel system free of contaminants and debris
- Follow the recommended fuel filter replacement intervals
- Keep the fuel injector and engine management sensor wiring and connectors clean and dry

SERVICE PRECAUTIONS

Safety is an important factor when servicing the fuel system. Failure to conduct maintenance and repairs in a safe manner may result in serious personal injury. Maintenance and testing of the vehicle's fuel system components can be accomplished safely and effectively by adhering to the following rules and guidelines.

- To avoid the possibility of fire and personal injury, always disconnect the negative battery cable unless the repair or test procedure requires that battery voltage be applied.
- Always relieve the fuel system pressure prior to disconnecting any fuel system component (injector, fuel rail, pressure regulator, etc.), fitting or fuel line connection. Exercise extreme caution whenever relieving fuel system pressure to avoid exposing skin, face and eyes to fuel spray. Please be advised

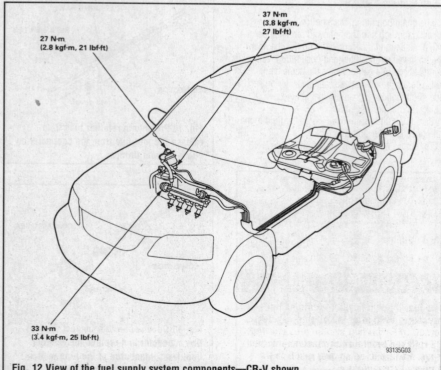

27 N·m
(2.8 kgf·m, 21 lbf·ft)

37 N·m
(3.8 kgf·m,
27 lbf·ft)

33 N·m
(3.4 kgf·m, 25 lbf·ft)

93135G03

Fig. 12 View of the fuel supply system components—CR-V shown

that fuel under pressure may penetrate the skin or any part of the body that it contacts.

• Always place a shop towel or cloth around the fitting or connection prior to loosening to absorb any excess fuel due to spillage. Ensure that all fuel spillage is quickly removed from engine surfaces. Ensure that all fuel soaked cloths or towels are deposited into a suitable waste container.

• Always keep a dry chemical (Class B) fire extinguisher near the work area.

• Do not allow fuel spray or fuel vapors to come into contact with a spark or open flame.

• Always use a backup wrench when loosening and tightening fuel line connection fittings. This will prevent unnecessary stress and torsion to fuel line piping. Always follow the proper torque specifications.

• Always replace worn fuel fitting O-rings. Do not substitute fuel hose where fuel pipe is installed.

Relieving Fuel System Pressure

PROCEDURE

CR-V and 4-Cylinder Odyssey Models

▶ See Figure 13

❊❊ CAUTION

Be sure that the ignition switch is OFF before relieving the fuel system. Never work near an open flame, a source of sparks or smoke while working on the fuel system!

1. Disconnect the negative battery cable.
2. Remove the fuel filler cap.
3. Place a shop towel over the banjo bolt to absorb any fuel that may spray out as the bolt is loosened.
4. Using a 12mm box-end wrench, loosen the banjo bolt from the top of the fuel filter. Be sure to hold the fuel filter with another wrench.
5. Slowly unscrew the banjo bolt one turn.
6. Always replace the banjo bolt sealing washers whenever the bolt is loosened.
7. After the fuel system pressure is relieved, tighten the bolt, install the fuel filler cap, then connect the negative battery cable.

Fig. 13 To relieve fuel system pressure, place a rag over the banjo bolt and slowly turn the banjo bolt on the fuel filter

V6 Odyssey Models

▶ See Figure 14

1. Disconnect the negative battery cable.
2. Remove the fuel filler cap.
3. Use a wrench to loosen the fuel pulsation damper on the fuel rail near the throttle linkage.
4. Place a shop towel over the fuel pulsation damper to absorb any fuel that may leak out as the damper is loosened.
5. Slowly unscrew the fuel pulsation damper one turn.
6. Always replace the sealing washer whenever the fuel pulsation damper loosened.
7. After the fuel system pressure is relieved, tighten the fuel pulsation damper, install the fuel filler cap, then connect the negative battery cable.

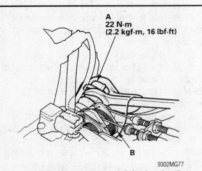

Fig. 14 Place a rag over the fuel pulsation damper (A), protect the throttle linkage (B), then use a wrench to loosen the damper to relieve the residual fuel pressure—V6 Odyssey

Fuel Pump

REMOVAL & INSTALLATION

❊❊ CAUTION

Observe all applicable safety precautions when working around fuel. Whenever servicing the fuel system, always work in a well-ventilated area. Do not allow fuel spray or vapors to come in contact with a spark or open flame. Keep a dry chemical fire extinguisher near the work area. Always keep fuel in a container specifically designed for fuel storage; also, always properly seal fuel containers to avoid the possibility of fire or explosion.

CR-V Models

▶ See Figures 15, 16, 17, 18 and 19

❊❊ CAUTION

The fuel injection system remains under pressure, even after the engine has been turned OFF. The fuel system pressure MUST BE relieved before disconnecting any fuel lines. Failure to do so may result in fire and/or personal injury.

1. Disconnect the negative battery cable.
2. Open the fuel tank filler cap to vent off pressure in the tank.
3. Relieve the fuel pressure, as outlined earlier in this section.
4. Tilt the left rear seat bottom forward.
5. Remove the Phillips screws securing the seat frame cover, then remove the cover.
6. Remove the Phillips screws in the floor fuel pump floor pan cover and lift the cover up to access the fuel pump wiring electrical connector.
7. Detach the fuel pump electrical connector and place the floor pan cover aside.
8. Using a pair of square-nosed pliers, squeeze the spring loaded fuel clamp tabs together

Fig. 15 With the left rear seat tilted forward, remove the seat frame cover fasteners—CR-V shown

Fig. 16 Once the fasteners are removed, remove the seat frame cover upward and out of the vehicle—CR-V shown

Fig. 17 With the floor pan access panel removed, detach the electrical connector from the fuel pump—CR-V shown

Fig. 18 After the electrical connector is detached and the access panel aside, remove the clamped and quick-connect fuel lines, then the 8mm mounting nuts—CR-V shown

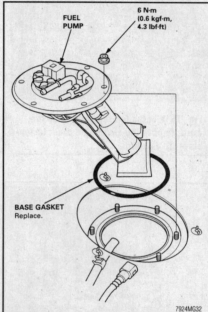

Fig. 19 Always replace the fuel pump base gasket when reinstalling the fuel pump—4-cylinder Odyssey

to release the clamp's tension and slide the clamp down the fuel line.

9. Press the two tabs on the quick-connect fuel line in and slide the fuel hose away from the fuel line.

10. Remove the 8mm nuts securing the fuel pump mounting plate to the fuel tank, and carefully extract the fuel pump assembly from the fuel tank.

✳✳ WARNING

Ensure that the battery is disconnected before any wires are removed.

11. Installation is the reverse of the removal procedure, making sure to replace the fuel pump mounting plate seal.

Odyssey Models

✳✳ CAUTION

The fuel injection system remains under pressure, even after the engine has been turned OFF. The fuel system pressure MUST BE relieved before disconnecting any fuel lines. Failure to do so may result in fire and/or personal injury.

4-CYLINDER ENGINES

▶ See Figure 19

1. Disconnect the negative battery cable.
2. Open the fuel tank filler cap to vent off pressure in the tank.
3. Relieve the fuel pressure, as outlined earlier in this section.
4. Remove the fuel tank assembly. For details, refer to the fuel tank removal procedures later in this section.
5. Detach the fuel pump electrical connector.
6. Using a pair of square-nosed pliers, squeeze the spring loaded fuel clamp tabs together to release the clamp's tension and slide the clamp down the fuel line.
7. Press the two tabs on the quick-connect fuel line in and slide the fuel hose away from the fuel line.
8. Remove the 8mm nuts securing the fuel pump mounting plate to the fuel tank, and carefully extract the fuel pump assembly from the fuel tank.

✳✳ WARNING

Ensure that the battery is disconnected before any wires are removed.

9. Installation is the reverse of the removal procedure, making sure to replace the fuel pump mounting plate seal.

V6 ENGINE

➡ **The radio may contain a coded theft protection circuit. Always make note of the code number before disconnecting the battery.**

➡ **The fuel pump on the V6 Odyssey is located in the fuel tank.**

1. Disconnect the negative battery cable.
2. Remove the fuel filler cap, then relieve the fuel system pressure as outlined earlier in this section.
3. Remove the rear seats and carpet.
4. Remove the access panel from the floor.
5. Make sure the ignition switch is in the **OFF** position, then detach the electrical connector at the fuel pump wire harness.
6. Disconnect the quick-connect fuel fittings from the fuel pump.
7. Remove the fuel pump locknut ring.
8. Remove fuel pump/filter assembly from the fuel tank.
9. Remove fuel filter, then the fuel pump.
To install:
10. Install the fuel pump, then the fuel filter.
11. Install and tighten the locknut ring.
12. Reconnect the fuel lines and electrical connections.

13. Reconnect the negative battery cable and enter the radio security code.
14. Turn the ignition **ON**, but don't start the engine. Then, turn the ignition **OFF**. Repeat this step two or three times to pressurize the fuel system.
15. Check the fuel lines and fuel fittings for leakage.

TESTING

Fuel Pump Circuit

▶ See Figures 20 thru 25

If you suspect a problem with the fuel pump, listen for the pump to operate by removing the fuel fill cap and checking to see if the pump can be heard running during the first two seconds after the ignition key is turned to the **ON** position. You should hear the fuel pump motor run.

➡ **If the fuel pump can be heard running, the fuel pump's electrical circuit is likely to be OK and the fuel pump operating pressure should be checked as outlined later in this section.**

Once the engine has started, the fuel pump operation is controlled by the Powertrain Control Module (PCM) via the PGM-FI Main Relay. The fuel pump receives its electrical power from the PGM-FI Main Relay, which is triggered for two seconds when the ignition switch is initially turned to the **ON** position.

After the initial two-second startup signal is received, the PGM-FI Main Relay is controlled by the PCM. Because the fuel pump receives its power from the PGM-FI Main Relay, a problem with the ignition switch, PCM, or electrical wiring may not allow battery voltage to reach the pump.

To check the fuel pump wiring proceed as follows:

1. Make sure the ignition switch is in the **OFF** position.
2. Locate and detach the fuel pump electrical connector at the fuel tank.
3. On CR-V and V6 Odyssey models, remove the floor access panel. For specific details, see the fuel pump removal procedure in this section.
4. On 4-cylinder Odyssey models, perform the following:
    a. Raise the vehicle and safely support it on suitable jackstands.
    b. Remove the protective cover for the fuel tank fuel hoses.
5. Detach the fuel pump electrical connector.
6. Connect a suitable voltmeter between the fuel pump positive terminal of the electrical connector and a known good chassis ground. See the accompanying figures for details.
   - CR-V models: Terminal position No. 4
   - 2.2L Odyssey models: Terminal Position No. 3
   - 2.3L Odyssey models: Terminal Position No. 2
   - V6 Odyssey models: Terminal Position 5
7. Hold the electrical connector of the PGM-FI Main Relay so the wire side of the female terminals is visible and install a jumper wire between terminal Nos. 4 and 5.

8. When the ignition switch is turned to the **ON** position, battery voltage should be present at the fuel pump electrical connector.

9. If the battery voltage is present, check the fuel pump's ground.

10. If the ground is OK, check the fuel pump.

11. If battery voltage is not present, trace the wiring harness and check the cause for an open or shorted circuit.

12. If all wiring checks out, test the fuel pressure, as outlined later in this section.

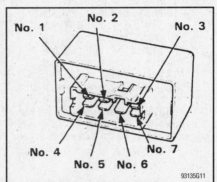

Fig. 20 PGM-FI Main Relay Terminals: (1) PCM (2) Starter Solenoid (3) Ground (4) Fuel Pump (5) Ignition Switch (6) PCM (7) Battery (+)

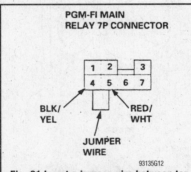

Fig. 21 Insert a jumper wire between terminal Nos. 4 and 5 of the PGM-FI Main Relay. With the ignition switch ON, battery voltage should be present at the fuel pump connector

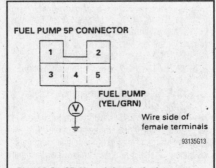

Fig. 22 On CR-V models, the fuel pump receives its electrical power from the PGM-FI Main Relay at terminal position No. 4

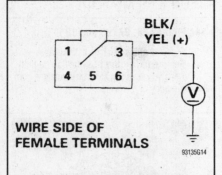

Fig. 23 On 2.2L Odyssey models, the fuel pump receives its electrical power from the PGM-FI Main Relay at terminal position No. 3

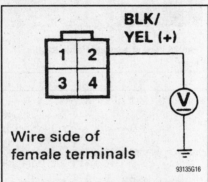

Fig. 24 On 2.3L Odyssey models, the fuel pump receives its electrical power from the PGM-FI Main Relay at terminal position No. 2

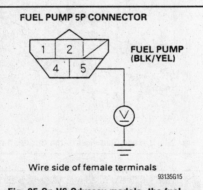

Fig. 25 On V6 Odyssey models, the fuel pump receives its electrical power from the PGM-FI Main Relay at terminal position No. 5

Fuel Pump Pressure

The fuel pressure should be checked at the fuel rail or at the fuel feed line for the fuel rail. The fuel pressure is checked with the engine started, thus the fuel pressure gauge must not interrupt the flow of fuel to the fuel rail and the fuel injectors.

To attach a fuel pressure gauge to the pressurized fuel loop you will need an adapter that is capable of safely withstanding the fuel system fuel pressure.

✴✴ WARNING

Checking the fuel system fuel pressure requires the use of an inline fuel pressure gauge with the engine running. Do not perform this check if suitable test equipment and fuel fittings are not available. The fuel system operates under pressure, if any fuel leakage is noticed while performing this check STOP immediately and do not continue until the source of the leak is resolved. Do not perform this test near sources of heat, spark, or flames. This test must be performed in a well-ventilated area.

✴✴ CAUTION

The fuel injection system remains under pressure, even after the engine has been turned OFF. The fuel system pressure MUST BE relieved before disconnecting any fuel lines. Failure to do so may result in fire and/or personal injury.

To check the fuel system pressure proceed as follows:

1. Remove the fuel filler cap and relieve the fuel pressure, as outlined in this section.

2. Attach a suitable fuel pressure gauge to the fuel injection fuel loop as follows:

- CR-V models: Remove the banjo bolt from the fuel filter outlet and install the pressure gauge using a suitable fitting to temporarily substitute for the banjo bolt and supply fuel to the gauge and the fuel rail.
- 2.2L Odyssey models: Remove the service/banjo bolt from the end of the fuel rail. Install the fuel pressure gauge using a suitable fitting to temporarily substitute for the banjo bolt or in place of the service bolt that will allow fuel to be supplied to the gauge and the fuel rail.
- 2.3L Odyssey models: Remove the banjo bolt from the fuel filter outlet and install the pressure gauge using a suitable fitting to temporarily substitute for the banjo bolt and supply fuel to the gauge and the fuel rail.
- V6 Odyssey models: Remove the fuel pulsation damper from the end of the fuel rail and install a suitable fuel pressure gauge in its place.

3. Remove and plug the vacuum line for the fuel pressure regulator located near the end of the fuel rail.

4. Start the engine and note the fuel pressure. With the pressure regulator vacuum hose disconnected and plugged, the fuel pressure should register as follows:

➡The engine number on the CR-V models is located on the side of the engine facing the radiator, near the transmission bell housing. Refer to Section 1 for specific details.

- CR-V models with the B20B4 Engine: 38–46 psi (260–310 kPa)
- CR-V models with the B20Z2 Engine: 40–47 psi (270–320 kPa)

- 2.2L Odyssey models: 38–46 psi (260–310 kPa)
- 2.3L Odyssey models: 47–54 psi (320–370 kPa)
- V6 Odyssey models: 41–48 psi (280–330 kPa)

➡ **If the engine won't start, turn the ignition switch ON, wait two seconds, then turn the ignition switch OFF. Turn the ignition switch back ON again and read the fuel pressure.**

5. If the fuel pressure is higher than specification, check for a pinched or restricted fuel return hose or line.

6. If the fuel pressure is lower than the specification, check for a damaged fuel pressure regulator, clogged fuel filter, fuel feed line or a leak in the fuel feed line. If the fuel pressure regulator, fuel feed lines, and fuel pump are OK, replace the fuel pump and fuel filter.

➡ **The fuel pressure regulator testing procedures are located later in this section.**

Once the test is complete, perform the following:

7. Carefully remove the fuel pressure gauge and test fittings.

8. Install the removed fasteners using new sealing washers.

9. Install the fuel filler cap.

10. Start the engine and check for any fuel leaks, and repair as necessary.

Throttle Body

The throttle body used on Honda CR-V and Odyssey models is a single-barrel side draft design. The lower portion of the throttle body has a coolant passage that is heated by the coolant flowing from the cylinder head. The throttle body is heated to prevent throttle icing and to help stabilize the fuel mixture.

The Throttle Position (TP) Switch and the Manifold Absolute Pressure (MAP) Sensor are attached to the throttle body. The TP switch and the MAP sensor are important input sensors used by the PCM, and based on the information received will affect the ignition timing and fuel mixture.

The idle speed adjusting screw is located toward the top of the throttle body, in a vertical position facing the air inlet of the throttle body. The idle speed screw is used to increase/decrease the bypass air required to achieve the recommended idle speed.

The throttle cable is attached to the throttle body, and should have enough free play such that the cable has 0.39–0.47 inches (10–12mm) of deflection.

The throttle stop screw is located on the side of the throttle body, near the throttle linkage. The throttle stop screw is non-adjustable and **MUST NOT** be disturbed. The throttle stop screw is set at the factory and usually has a light coat of paint on it to permanently lock it in place. With the throttle in the closed or idle position, if there is clearance between the throttle stop screw and the throttle stop, the throttle body must be replaced.

➡ **Replace the throttle body if there is excessive play in the throttle shaft, if the shaft is sticking or binding, or if clearance exists between the throttle stop screw and the throttle stop.**

REMOVAL & INSTALLATION

▶ **See Figures 26, 27, 28 and 29**

1. Disconnect the negative battery cable.
2. Remove the air duct from the throttle body.
3. Remove the wiring harness connector from the throttle body.

Fig. 26 View of a typical Honda throttle body

4. Label and detach all vacuum hoses from the throttle body.
5. Detach the accelerator cable.
6. Detach and plug the coolant hoses from the throttle body.
7. Remove the throttle body mounting fasteners.
8. Remove the throttle body.
9. Using a suitable plastic scraper, remove any gasket material from the throttle body and air intake plenum.
10. Installation is the reverse of the removal procedure making sure of the following:
- The throttle cable is properly routed, installed, and has 0.39–0.47 inches (10–12mm) of deflection.
- If equipped, make sure the transmission and cruise control cables are properly routed and installed correctly. With the engine at a warm idle the cruise control cable should have 0.18–0.22 inches (4.5–5.5mm) of free play.
- The cooling system is topped off and bled as necessary.

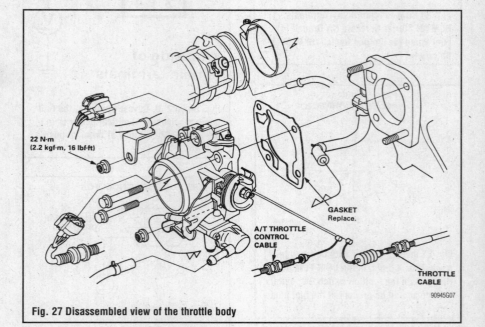

Fig. 27 Disassembled view of the throttle body

Fig. 28 View of throttle body and fast idle thermo valve

Fig. 29 Periodic cleaning of the throttle body is recommended

Fuel Injector(s)

REMOVAL & INSTALLATION

♦ See Figures 30 thru 37

✳✳ CAUTION

Observe all applicable safety precautions when working around fuel. Whenever servicing the fuel system, always work in a well-ventilated area. Do not allow fuel spray or vapors to come in contact with a spark or open flame. Keep a dry chemical fire extinguisher near the work area. Always keep fuel in a container specifically designed for fuel storage; also, always properly seal fuel containers to avoid the possibility of fire or explosion.

1. Disconnect the negative battery cable.
2. Relieve the fuel system pressure.

✳✳ CAUTION

Fuel injection systems remain under pressure, even after the engine has been turned OFF. The fuel system pressure must be relieved before disconnecting any fuel lines. Failure to do so may result in fire and/or personal injury.

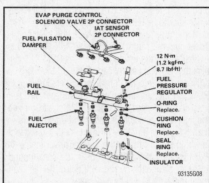

Fig. 30 Exploded view of the fuel rail and injectors—1997–98 CR-V shown

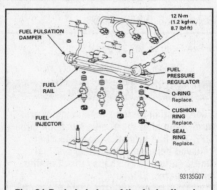

Fig. 31 Exploded view of the fuel rail and injectors—1999 CR-V shown

Fig. 32 Remove the fuel rail and injectors from the intake manifold

Fig. 33 Always replace the injector O-rings when ever the injectors are removed and reinstalled. Coat the O-rings with a light film of fresh engine oil during reassembly

Fig. 34 Remove the injector from the fuel rail

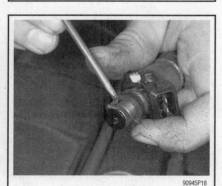

Fig. 35 Use a pick tool to carefully remove the injector O-ring

Fig. 36 Check needle and seat of the injector for carbon deposits that may inhibit the injector from closing all of the way

Fig. 37 The fuel injectors have a spacer and an O-ring gasket. Both must be replaced whenever the injectors have been removed

3. Detach the electrical connectors from the fuel rail.

4. Disconnect the vacuum hose and fuel return from the fuel pressure regulator.

5. Loosen and remove the fasteners on the fuel rail, then remove the fuel rail.

6. Grasp the fuel injector body and pull up while gently rocking the fuel injector from side to side.

7. Once removed, inspect the fuel injector cap and body for signs of deterioration. Replace as required.

8. Remove and discard the injector O-rings. If an O-ring or end cap is missing, look in the intake manifold for the missing part.

To install:

9. Replace the O-rings and apply a small amount of clean engine oil to them. Install the lubricated O-rings onto each injector.

10. Install the injectors using a slight twisting downward motion.

11. Install the injector retaining clips.

12. Install the fuel injection supply manifold (fuel rail).

13. Connect the negative battery cable.

14. Turn the ignition switch **ON** for 5 seconds, then turn it **OFF** and check for fuel leaks.

15. If no fuel leaks are noticed, run the engine at idle for 2 minutes, then turn the engine **OFF** and recheck for fuel leaks and proper operation.

TESTING

The easiest way to test the operation of the fuel injectors is to listen for a clicking sound coming from the injectors while the engine is running. This is accomplished using a mechanic's stethoscope, or a long screwdriver.

Place the end of the stethoscope or the screwdriver (tip end, not handle) onto the body of the injector. Place the two earpieces of the stethoscope in your ears, or if using a screwdriver, place your ear on top of the handle. An audible clicking noise should be heard; as the solenoid in the injector is operating. If the injector makes this noise, the injector driver circuit and computer are operating as designed. Continue testing all the injectors this way.

※※ CAUTION

Be extremely careful while working on an operating engine, make sure you have no dangling jewelry, extremely loose clothes, power tool cords or other items that might get caught in a moving part of the engine.

The Honda fuel injectors are triggered by electrical pulses. The injector is either on (open) or off (closed). The amount of fuel the injector provides is determined by the fuel pressure and how long the injector is opened.

When diagnosing a fuel related running problem, it's a good idea to remove the spark plugs and check their color. A rich mixture (too much fuel) is characterized by a black sooty appearing spark plug electrode. A lean mixture (too little fuel) is characterized by a dry, very whitish colored spark plug.

A fuel injector could cause a rich mixture if:
• The pressure regulator is defective
• The system fuel pressure is too high
• The injector leaks when not being triggered
• The pressure regulator vacuum line is restricted
A fuel injector could cause a lean mixture if:
• The pressure regulator is defective
• The system fuel pressure is too low
• The injector has fuel flow related blockage
• The injector sticks or binds when being triggered
• The internal electrical windings of the injector have failed
• The injector does not receive an electrical pulse or has a bad ground

All Injectors Clicking

If all the injectors are clicking, but you have determined that the fuel system is the cause of your driveability problem, continue diagnostics. Make sure that you have checked fuel pump pressure as outlined earlier in this section. An easy way to determine a weak or unproductive cylinder is a cylinder drop test. This is accomplished by grounding one spark plug wire at a time, or interrupting the voltage signal to an individual ignition coil pack, one unit at a time and seeing which cylinder causes the least difference in the idle. The one that causes the least change is the weak cylinder.

If the injectors were all clicking and the ignition system is functioning properly, remove the injector of the suspect cylinder and bench test it. This is accomplished by checking for a spray pattern from the injector itself. Install a fuel supply line to the injector (or rail if the injector is left attached to the rail) and momentarily apply 12 volts DC and a ground to the injector itself; a visible fuel spray should appear. If no spray is achieved, replace the injector and check the running condition of the

engine. If the injector leaks fuel without being triggered, replace the leaking injector.

One or More Injectors Are Not Clicking

▶ See Figures 38, 39, 40 and 41

If one or more injectors are found to be not operating, testing the injector driver circuit and computer can be accomplished using a "noid" light. First, with the engine not running and the ignition key in the **OFF** position, remove the connector from the injector to be tested, then plug the "noid" light tool into the injector connector. Start the engine and the "noid" light should flash, signaling that the injector driver circuit is working. If the "noid" light flashes, but the injector does not click when

Fig. 38 Unplug the fuel injector connector

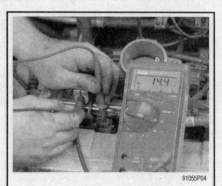
Fig. 39 Probe the two terminals of a fuel injector to check its resistance

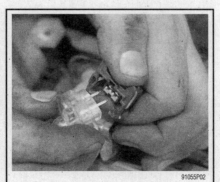
Fig. 40 Plug the correct "noid" light directly into the injector harness connector

Fig. 41 If the correct "noid" light flashes while the engine is running, the injector driver circuit of the PCM is working

plugged in, test the injector's resistance. The resistance should be between 1.5–2.5 ohms.

If the "noid" light does not flash, the injector driver circuit is faulty. Check the PGM-FI Main Relay operation and the wiring between the PCM. Disconnect the negative battery cable. Unplug the "noid" light from the injector connector and also unplug the PCM. Check the harness between the appropriate pins on the harness side of the PCM connector and the injector connector. Resistance should be less than 5.0 ohms; if not, repair the circuit. If resistance is within specifications, the injector driver inside the PCM is faulty. If available, substitute a known good PCM for diagnostic purposes. If defective, replacement of the PCM will be necessary.

Fuel Rail Assembly

REMOVAL & INSTALLATION

▶ See Figures 30, 31 and 42

1. Disconnect the negative battery cable.

※※ CAUTION

Fuel injection systems remain under pressure, even after the engine has been turned OFF. The fuel system pressure must be relieved before disconnecting any fuel lines. Failure to do so may result in fire and/or personal injury.

2. Relieve the fuel system pressure, as outlined earlier in this section.
3. Detach the electrical harness connectors.
4. Remove the vacuum hose and fuel return hose from the fuel pressure regulator.
5. Remove the fuel line from the fuel rail.
6. Unfasten the fuel rail retaining nuts, then remove the fuel rail.

To install:

➡**When installing the fuel rail, be sure to lubricate all rubber O-rings with fresh engine oil and to replace any sealing washer that was removed.**

7. Coat the fuel injector O-rings with a light coating of fresh engine oil and install the fuel rail and secure with the retaining fasteners.
8. Connect the fuel line to the fuel rail.
9. Install the vacuum hose and fuel return hose to the fuel pressure regulator.

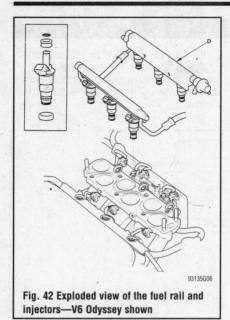

Fig. 42 Exploded view of the fuel rail and injectors—V6 Odyssey shown

10. Attach the electrical harness connectors.
11. Connect the negative battery cable.
12. Pressurize the fuel system by turning the ignition switch to the **ON** position.
13. Check for leaks, if none are found, start the engine and recheck for any leaks. If any leakage is found, repair as necessary.

Fuel Pressure Regulator

REMOVAL & INSTALLATION

▶ See Figure 43

✳✳ CAUTION

Observe all applicable safety precautions when working around fuel. Whenever servicing the fuel system, always work in a well ventilated area. Do not allow fuel spray or vapors to come in contact with a spark or open flame. Keep a dry chemical fire extinguisher near the work area. Always keep fuel in a container specifically designed for fuel storage; also, always properly seal fuel containers to avoid the possibility of fire or explosion.

1. Properly relieve the fuel system pressure, as outlined earlier in this section.
2. Disconnect the negative battery cable.
3. Detach the vacuum hose from the fuel pressure regulator.
4. Unfasten the two fuel pressure regulator retaining bolts.
5. Remove the fuel pressure regulator and the O-rings. Discard the O-rings.
To install:
6. Lubricate the new O-rings with light engine oil.
7. Position a new O-ring onto the fuel pressure regulator.
8. Place the fuel pressure regulator into position and install the retainers.
9. Attach the vacuum line to the fuel pressure regulator.

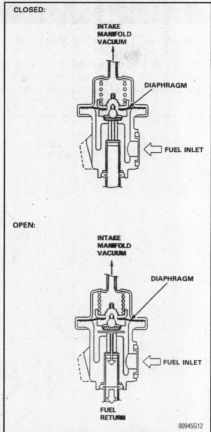

Fig. 43 Cross-sectional views of the fuel pressure regulator in both the open and closed positions

10. Connect the negative battery cable.
11. Run the engine at idle for 2 minutes, then turn the engine **OFF** and check for fuel leaks and proper operation.

PGM-FI Main Relay

▶ See Figure 44

The PGM-FI Main Relay is actually comprised of two individual internal relays. When the ignition switch is initially turned **ON**, the Powertrain Control Module (PCM) supplies ground to the PGM-FI Main Relay. This ground triggers one of the PGM-FI internal relays that sends battery voltage to the fuel pump for two seconds to pressurize the fuel system.

When the engine is running the PCM supplies a continuous ground to the PGM-FI Main Relay. The supplied ground keeps the relay in the "closed" position providing electrical current to the fuel pump, keeping the fuel loop pressurized while the engine runs.

If the engine is not running with the ignition on, the PCM cuts the ground to the PGM-FI Main Relay, causing the relay to "open" and stop the electric current flow to the fuel pump. As mentioned previously, if the engine is not running, the PCM will only supply ground to the PGM-FI Main Relay for two seconds when the ignition switch is initially switched to the ON position.

The PGM-FI Main Relay also supplies electrical power to the Idle Air Control (IAC) Valve and to the fuel injectors.

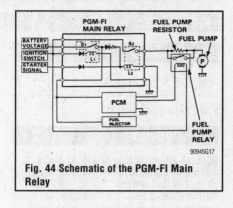

Fig. 44 Schematic of the PGM-FI Main Relay

TESTING

▶ See Figure 45

➡**If the engine starts and continues to run, the PGM-FI Main Relay is working and does not need to be replaced.**

The PGM-FI Main Relay is located as follows:
• CR-V models: Near the passenger right side kick panel under the dash
• 2.2L/2.3L Odyssey models: Near the driver left side kick panel under the dash
• V6 Odyssey models: To the left of the steering column under the dash

1. Locate and remove the relay.
2. Apply battery voltage to the number three terminal.
3. Ground the No. 2 terminal.
4. Check for continuity between terminals five and two.
5. If continuity is detected, proceed to the step 7.
6. If there is no continuity, replace the relay.
7. Connect the No. 4 terminal to the positive side of the battery.
8. Ground the No. 2 terminal of the relay.
9. Check for continuity between the No. 5 terminal and the No. 2 terminal of the relay.
10. If there is continuity, the relay checks out OK. If the fuel pump still does not function, check the wiring harness and electrical connectors.
11. If there is no continuity, replace the relay and retest.

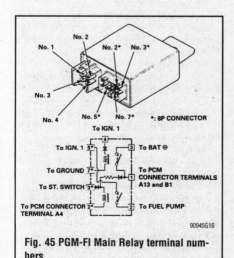

Fig. 45 PGM-FI Main Relay terminal numbers

FUEL TANK

Tank Assembly

REMOVAL & INSTALLATION

▶ See Figures 46 and 47

✳✳ CAUTION

Observe all applicable safety precautions when working around fuel. Whenever servicing the fuel system, always work in a well ventilated area. Do not allow fuel spray or vapors to come in contact with a spark or open flame. Keep a dry chemical fire extinguisher near the work area. Always keep fuel in a container specifically designed for fuel storage; also, always properly seal fuel containers to avoid the possibility of fire or explosion.

The vehicle must be raised and safely supported to allow the fuel tank to be removed from underneath the vehicle.

1. Note the radio security code and disconnect the negative battery cable.

2. Relieve the residual fuel system pressure as outlined in this section.

3. On CR-V models, fold the left rear seat cushion forward and remove the plastic seat base, then remove the floor pan access panel.

    a. Detach the fuel pump electrical connector, then disconnect the fuel feed and return lines.

4. On V6 Odyssey models, perform the following:

    a. Disconnect the fuel feed and return lines, and detach the fuel pump electrical connector.

    b. Remove the fuel pump. For specific details, see the fuel pump removal procedures in this section.

    c. Using an approved hand pump and storage container, remove the fuel from the fuel tank through the fuel pump access hole.

5. Carefully jack up and safely support the vehicle.

6. On CR-V models, perform the following:

    a. Remove the middle floor beam.

    b. Remove the fuel tank drain bolt and drain the fuel into an approved container.

    c. Install the fuel tank drain bolt using a new sealing washer, tighten the bolt to 36 ft. lbs. (49 Nm) and apply a coating of a rust preventative to the bolt.

7. On 4-cylinder Odyssey models:

    a. Remove the fuel tank drain bolt and drain the fuel into an approved container.

    b. Remove the fuel hose joint protection cover.

    c. Install the fuel tank drain bolt using a new sealing washer, tighten the bolt to 36 ft. lbs. (49 Nm) and apply a coating of a rust preventative to the bolt.

    d. Disconnect the fuel return hose, vapor hose and quick-connect fittings.

    e. Detach the fuel pump electrical connector.

8. On clamped fuel lines, release the clamp tension and slide the hose clamps away from the fitting. Carefully twist the hoses while pulling to remove them. Make sure all fuel hoses and electrical connectors have been properly disconnected.

9. Support the fuel tank with a jack.

10. Remove the fuel tank strap fasteners and allow the straps to fall freely.

11. Carefully remove the fuel tank. The tank may stick in place due to being undercoated. Carefully using a suitable pry tool, remove it from its mount.

12. The installation is in the reverse order of disassembly. If the tank is to be replaced, transfer the needed components as necessary using new seals, O-rings, and quick-connect connectors.

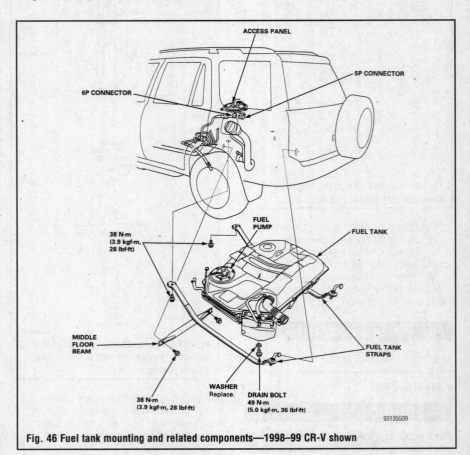

Fig. 46 Fuel tank mounting and related components—1998–99 CR-V shown

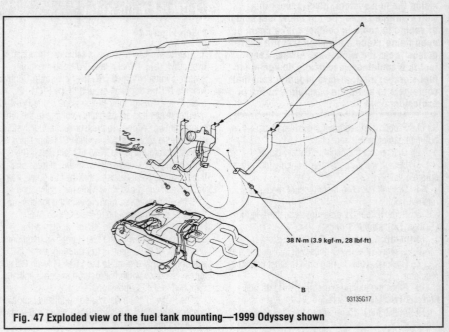

Fig. 47 Exploded view of the fuel tank mounting—1999 Odyssey shown

6

CHASSIS ELECTRICAL

UNDERSTANDING AND TROUBLESHOOTING ELECTRICAL SYSTEMS

Basic Electrical Theory

▶ See Figure 1

For any 12 volt, negative ground, electrical system to operate, the electricity must travel in a complete circuit. This simply means that current (power) from the positive (+) terminal of the battery must eventually return to the negative (-) terminal of the battery. Along the way, this current will travel through wires, fuses, switches and components. If, for any reason, the flow of current through the circuit is interrupted, the component fed by that circuit will cease to function properly.

Perhaps the easiest way to visualize a circuit is to think of connecting a light bulb (with two wires attached to it) to the battery—one wire attached to the negative (-) terminal of the battery and the other wire to the positive (+) terminal. With the two wires touching the battery terminals, the circuit would be complete and the light bulb would illuminate. Electricity would follow a path from the battery to the bulb and back to the battery. It's easy to see that with longer wires on our light bulb, it could be mounted anywhere. Further, one wire could be fitted with a switch so that the light could be turned on and off.

The normal automotive circuit differs from this simple example in two ways. First, instead of having a return wire from the bulb to the battery, the current travels through the frame of the vehicle. Since the negative (-) battery cable is attached to the frame (made of electrically conductive metal), the frame of the vehicle can serve as a ground wire to complete the circuit. Secondly, most automotive circuits contain multiple components which receive power from a single circuit. This lessens the amount of wire needed to power components on the vehicle.

HOW DOES ELECTRICITY WORK: THE WATER ANALOGY

Electricity is the flow of electrons—the subatomic particles that constitute the outer shell of an

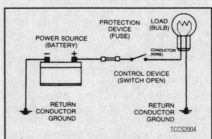

Fig. 1 This example illustrates a simple circuit. When the switch is closed, power from the positive (+) battery terminal flows through the fuse and the switch, and then to the light bulb. The light illuminates and the circuit is completed through the ground wire back to the negative (-) battery terminal. In reality, the two ground points shown in the illustration are attached to the metal frame of the vehicle, which completes the circuit back to the battery

atom. Electrons spin in an orbit around the center core of an atom. The center core is comprised of protons (positive charge) and neutrons (neutral charge). Electrons have a negative charge and balance out the positive charge of the protons. When an outside force causes the number of electrons to unbalance the charge of the protons, the electrons will split off the atom and look for another atom to balance out. If this imbalance is kept up, electrons will continue to move and an electrical flow will exist.

Many people have been taught electrical theory using an analogy with water. In a comparison with water flowing through a pipe, the electrons would be the water and the wire is the pipe.

The flow of electricity can be measured much like the flow of water through a pipe. The unit of measurement used is amperes, frequently abbreviated as amps (a). You can compare amperage to the volume of water flowing through a pipe. When connected to a circuit, an ammeter will measure the actual amount of current flowing through the circuit. When relatively few electrons flow through a circuit, the amperage is low. When many electrons flow, the amperage is high.

Water pressure is measured in units such as pounds per square inch (psi); the electrical pressure is measured in units called volts (v). When a voltmeter is connected to a circuit, it is measuring the electrical pressure.

The actual flow of electricity depends not only on voltage and amperage, but also on the resistance of the circuit. The higher the resistance, the higher the force necessary to push the current through the circuit. The standard unit for measuring resistance is an ohm. Resistance in a circuit varies depending on the amount and type of components used in the circuit. The main factors which determine resistance are:

• Material—some materials have more resistance than others. Those with high resistance are said to be insulators. Rubber materials (or rubber-like plastics) are some of the most common insulators used in vehicles as they have a very high resistance to electricity. Very low resistance materials are said to be conductors. Copper wire is among the best conductors. Silver is actually a superior conductor to copper and is used in some relay contacts, but its high cost prohibits its use as common wiring. Most automotive wiring is made of copper.

• Size—the larger the wire size being used, the less resistance the wire will have. This is why components which use large amounts of electricity usually have large wires supplying current to them.

• Length—for a given thickness of wire, the longer the wire, the greater the resistance. The shorter the wire, the less the resistance. When determining the proper wire for a circuit, both size and length must be considered to design a circuit that can handle the current needs of the component.

• Temperature—with many materials, the higher the temperature, the greater the resistance (positive temperature coefficient). Some materials exhibit the opposite trait of lower resistance with higher temperatures (negative temperature coefficient). These principles are used in many of the sensors on the engine.

OHM'S LAW

There is a direct relationship between current, voltage and resistance. The relationship between current, voltage and resistance can be summed up by a statement known as Ohm's law.

Voltage (E) is equal to amperage (I) times resistance ®: $E = I \times R$

Other forms of the formula are $R = E/I$ and $I = E/R$

In each of these formulas, E is the voltage in volts, I is the current in amps and R is the resistance in ohms. The basic point to remember is that as the resistance of a circuit goes up, the amount of current that flows in the circuit will go down, if voltage remains the same.

The amount of work that the electricity can perform is expressed as power. The unit of power is the watt (w). The relationship between power, voltage and current is expressed as:

Power (w) is equal to amperage (I) times voltage (E): $W = I \times E$

This is only true for direct current (DC) circuits; The alternating current formula is a tad different, but since the electrical circuits in most vehicles are DC type, we need not get into AC circuit theory.

Electrical Components

POWER SOURCE

Power is supplied to the vehicle by two devices: The battery and the alternator. The battery supplies electrical power during starting or during periods when the current demand of the vehicle's electrical system exceeds the output capacity of the alternator. The alternator supplies electrical current when the engine is running. Just not does the alternator supply the current needs of the vehicle, but it recharges the battery.

The Battery

In most modern vehicles, the battery is a lead/acid electrochemical device consisting of six 2 volt subsections (cells) connected in series, so that the unit is capable of producing approximately 12 volts of electrical pressure. Each subsection consists of a series of positive and negative plates held a short distance apart in a solution of sulfuric acid and water.

The two types of plates are of dissimilar metals. This sets up a chemical reaction, and it is this reaction which produces current flow from the battery when its positive and negative terminals are connected to an electrical load. The power removed from the battery is replaced by the alternator, restoring the battery to its original chemical state.

The Alternator

On some vehicles there isn't an alternator, but a generator. The difference is that an alternator supplies alternating current which is then changed to direct current for use on the vehicle, while a generator produces direct current. Alternators tend to be more efficient and that is why they are used.

Alternators and generators are devices that consist of coils of wires wound together making big electromagnets. One group of coils spins within another set and the interaction of the magnetic fields causes a current to flow. This current is then drawn off the coils and fed into the vehicles electrical system.

GROUND

Two types of grounds are used in automotive electric circuits. Direct ground components are grounded to the frame through their mounting points. All other components use some sort of ground wire which is attached to the frame or chassis of the vehicle. The electrical current runs through the chassis of the vehicle and returns to the battery through the ground (-) cable; if you look, you'll see that the battery ground cable connects between the battery and the frame or chassis of the vehicle.

➡**It should be noted that a good percentage of electrical problems can be traced to bad grounds.**

PROTECTIVE DEVICES

It is possible for large surges of current to pass through the electrical system of your vehicle. If this surge of current were to reach the load in the circuit, the surge could burn it out or severely damage it. It can also overload the wiring, causing the harness to get hot and melt the insulation. To prevent this, fuses, circuit breakers and/or fusible links are connected into the supply wires of the electrical system. These items are nothing more than a built-in weak spot in the system. When an abnormal amount of current flows through the system, these protective devices work as follows to protect the circuit:

• Fuse—when an excessive electrical current passes through a fuse, the fuse "blows" (the conductor melts) and opens the circuit, preventing the passage of current.

• Circuit Breaker—a circuit breaker is basically a self-repairing fuse. It will open the circuit in the same fashion as a fuse, but when the surge subsides, the circuit breaker can be reset and does not need replacement.

• Fusible Link—a fusible link (fuse link or main link) is a short length of special, high temperature insulated wire that acts as a fuse. When an excessive electrical current passes through a fusible link, the thin gauge wire inside the link melts, creating an intentional open to protect the circuit. To repair the circuit, the link must be replaced. Some newer type fusible links are housed in plug-in modules, which are simply replaced like a fuse, while older type fusible links must be cut and spliced if they melt. Since this link is very early in the electrical path, it's the first place to look if nothing on the vehicle works, yet the battery seems to be charged and is properly connected.

⁙ WARNING

Always replace fuses, circuit breakers and fusible links with identically rated components. Under no circumstances should a component of higher or lower amperage rating be substituted.

SWITCHES & RELAYS

◗ **See Figure 2**

Switches are used in electrical circuits to control the passage of current. The most common use is to open and close circuits between the battery and the various electric devices in the system. Switches are rated according to the amount of amperage they can handle. If a sufficient amperage rated switch is not used in a circuit, the switch could overload and cause damage.

Some electrical components which require a large amount of current to operate use a special switch called a relay. Since these circuits carry a large amount of current, the thickness of the wire in the circuit is also greater. If this large wire were connected from the load to the control switch, the switch would have to carry the high amperage load and the fairing or dash would be twice as large to accommodate the increased size of the wiring harness. To prevent these problems, a relay is used.

Relays are composed of a coil and a set of contacts. When the coil has a current passed though it, a magnetic field is formed and this field causes the contacts to move together, completing the circuit. Most relays are normally open, preventing current from passing through the circuit, but they can take any electrical form depending on the job they are intended to do. Relays can be considered "remote control switches." They allow a smaller current to operate devices that require higher amperages. When a small current operates the coil, a larger current is allowed to pass by the contacts. Some common circuits which may use relays are the horn, headlights, starter, electric fuel pump and other high draw circuits.

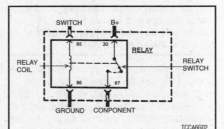

TCCA6G02

Fig. 2 Relays are composed of a coil and a switch. These two components are linked together so that when one operates, the other operates at the same time. The large wires in the circuit are connected from the battery to one side of the relay switch (B+) and from the opposite side of the relay switch to the load (component). Smaller wires are connected from the relay coil to the control switch for the circuit and from the opposite side of the relay coil to ground

LOAD

Every electrical circuit must include a "load" (something to use the electricity coming from the source). Without this load, the battery would attempt to deliver its entire power supply from one pole to another. This is called a "short circuit." All

this electricity would take a short cut to ground and cause a great amount of damage to other components in the circuit by developing a tremendous amount of heat. This condition could develop sufficient heat to melt the insulation on all the surrounding wires and reduce a multiple wire cable to a lump of plastic and copper.

WIRING & HARNESSES

The average vehicle contains meters and meters of wiring, with hundreds of individual connections. To protect the many wires from damage and to keep them from becoming a confusing tangle, they are organized into bundles, enclosed in plastic or taped together and called wiring harnesses. Different harnesses serve different parts of the vehicle. Individual wires are color coded to help trace them through a harness where sections are hidden from view.

Automotive wiring or circuit conductors can be either single strand wire, multi-strand wire or printed circuitry. Single strand wire has a solid metal core and is usually used inside such components as alternators, motors, relays and other devices. Multi-strand wire has a core made of many small strands of wire twisted together into a single conductor. Most of the wiring in an automotive electrical system is made up of multi-strand wire, either as a single conductor or grouped together in a harness. All wiring is color coded on the insulator, either as a solid color or as a colored wire with an identification stripe. A printed circuit is a thin film of copper or other conductor that is printed on an insulator backing. Occasionally, a printed circuit is sandwiched between two sheets of plastic for more protection and flexibility. A complete printed circuit, consisting of conductors, insulating material and connectors for lamps or other components is called a printed circuit board. Printed circuitry is used in place of individual wires or harnesses in places where space is limited, such as behind instrument panels.

Since automotive electrical systems are very sensitive to changes in resistance, the selection of properly sized wires is critical when systems are repaired. A loose or corroded connection or a replacement wire that is too small for the circuit will add extra resistance and an additional voltage drop to the circuit.

The wire gauge number is an expression of the cross-section area of the conductor. Vehicles from countries that use the metric system will typically describe the wire size as its cross-sectional area in square millimeters. In this method, the larger the wire, the greater the number. Another common system for expressing wire size is the American Wire Gauge (AWG) system. As gauge number increases, area decreases and the wire becomes smaller. An 18 gauge wire is smaller than a 4 gauge wire. A wire with a higher gauge number will carry less current than a wire with a lower gauge number. Gauge wire size refers to the size of the strands of the conductor, not the size of the complete wire with insulator. It is possible, therefore, to have two wires of the same gauge with different diameters because one may have thicker insulation than the other.

It is essential to understand how a circuit works before trying to figure out why it doesn't. An electrical schematic shows the electrical current paths when a circuit is operating properly. Schematics break the entire electrical system down into individual circuits. In a schematic, usually no attempt is made to represent wiring and components as they physically appear on the vehicle; switches and other components are shown as simply as possible. Face views of harness connectors show the cavity or terminal locations in all multi-pin connectors to help locate test points.

CONNECTORS

▶ **See Figures 3 and 4**

Three types of connectors are commonly used in automotive applications—weatherproof, molded and hard shell.

• Weatherproof—these connectors are most commonly used where the connector is exposed to the elements. Terminals are protected against moisture and dirt by sealing rings which provide a weather-tight seal. All repairs require the use of a special terminal and the tool required to service it. Unlike standard blade type terminals, these weatherproof terminals cannot be straightened once they are bent. Make certain that the connectors are properly seated and all of the sealing rings are in place when connecting leads.

• Molded—these connectors require complete replacement of the connector if found to be defective. This means splicing a new connector assembly into the harness. All splices should be soldered to insure proper contact. Use care when probing the connections or replacing terminals in them, as it is possible to create a short circuit between opposite terminals. If this happens to the wrong terminal pair,

Fig. 3 Hard shell (left) and weatherproof (right) connectors have replaceable terminals

Fig. 4 Weatherproof connectors are most commonly used in the engine compartment or where the connector is exposed to the elements

it is possible to damage certain components. Always use jumper wires between connectors for circuit checking and NEVER probe through weatherproof seals.

• Hard Shell—unlike molded connectors, the terminal contacts in hard-shell connectors can be replaced. Replacement usually involves the use of a special terminal removal tool that depresses the locking tangs (barbs) on the connector terminal and allows the connector to be removed from the rear of the shell. The connector shell should be replaced if it shows any evidence of burning, melting, cracks, or breaks. Replace individual terminals that are burnt, corroded, distorted or loose.

Test Equipment

Pinpointing the exact cause of trouble in an electrical circuit is most times accomplished by the use of special test equipment. The following describes different types of commonly used test equipment and briefly explains how to use them in diagnosis. In addition to the information covered below, the tool manufacturer's instructions booklet (provided with the tester) should be read and clearly understood before attempting any test procedures.

JUMPER WIRES

✳✳ CAUTION

Never use jumper wires made from a thinner gauge wire than the circuit being tested. If the jumper wire is of too small a gauge, it may overheat and possibly melt. Never use jumpers to bypass high resistance loads in a circuit. Bypassing resistances, in effect, creates a short circuit. This may, in turn, cause damage and fire. Jumper wires should only be used to bypass lengths of wire or to simulate switches.

Jumper wires are simple, yet extremely valuable, pieces of test equipment. They are basically test wires which are used to bypass sections of a circuit. Although jumper wires can be purchased, they are usually fabricated from lengths of standard automotive wire and whatever type of connector (alligator clip, spade connector or pin connector) that is required for the particular application being tested. In cramped, hard-to-reach areas, it is advisable to have insulated boots over the jumper wire terminals in order to prevent accidental grounding. It is also advisable to include a standard automotive fuse in any jumper wire. This is commonly referred to as a "fused jumper". By inserting an in-line fuse holder between a set of test leads, a fused jumper wire can be used for bypassing open circuits. Use a 5 amp fuse to provide protection against voltage spikes.

Jumper wires are used primarily to locate open electrical circuits, on either the ground (-) side of the circuit or on the power (+) side. If an electrical component fails to operate, connect the jumper wire between the component and a good ground. If the component operates only with the jumper installed, the ground circuit is open. If the ground circuit is good, but the component does not operate, the circuit between the power feed and component may be open. By moving the jumper wire successively back from the component toward the power source, you

can isolate the area of the circuit where the open is located. When the component stops functioning, or the power is cut off, the open is in the segment of wire between the jumper and the point previously tested.

You can sometimes connect the jumper wire directly from the battery to the "hot" terminal of the component, but first make sure the component uses 12 volts in operation. Some electrical components, such as fuel injectors or sensors, are designed to operate on about 4 to 5 volts, and running 12 volts directly to these components will cause damage.

TEST LIGHTS

▶ **See Figure 5**

The test light is used to check circuits and components while electrical current is flowing through them. It is used for voltage and ground tests. To use a 12 volt test light, connect the ground clip to a good ground and probe wherever necessary with the pick. The test light will illuminate when voltage is detected. This does not necessarily mean that 12 volts (or any particular amount of voltage) is present; it only means that some voltage is present. It is advisable before using the test light to touch its ground clip and probe across the battery posts or terminals to make sure the light is operating properly.

✳✳ WARNING

Do not use a test light to probe electronic ignition, spark plug or coil wires. Never use a pick-type test light to probe wiring on computer controlled systems unless specifically instructed to do so. Any wire insulation that is pierced by the test light probe should be taped and sealed with silicone after testing.

Like the jumper wire, the 12 volt test light is used to isolate opens in circuits. But, whereas the jumper wire is used to bypass the open to operate the load, the 12 volt test light is used to locate the presence of voltage in a circuit. If the test light illuminates, there is power up to that point in the circuit; if the test light does not illuminate, there is an open circuit (no power). Move the test light in successive steps back toward the power source until the light in the handle illuminates. The open is between the probe and a point which was previously probed.

Fig. 5 A 12 volt test light is used to detect the presence of voltage in a circuit

The self-powered test light is similar in design to the 12 volt test light, but contains a 1.5 volt penlight battery in the handle. It is most often used in place of a multimeter to check for open or short circuits when power is isolated from the circuit (continuity test).

The battery in a self-powered test light does not provide much current. A weak battery may not provide enough power to illuminate the test light even when a complete circuit is made (especially if there is high resistance in the circuit). Always make sure that the test battery is strong. To check the battery, briefly touch the ground clip to the probe; if the light glows brightly, the battery is strong enough for testing.

➡**A self-powered test light should not be used on any computer controlled system or component. The small amount of electricity transmitted by the test light is enough to damage many electronic automotive components.**

MULTIMETERS

Multimeters are an extremely useful tool for troubleshooting electrical problems. They can be purchased in either analog or digital form and have a price range to suit any budget. A multimeter is a voltmeter, ammeter and ohmmeter (along with other features) combined into one instrument. It is often used when testing solid state circuits because of its high input impedance (usually 10 megaohms or more). A brief description of the multimeter main test functions follows:

• Voltmeter—the voltmeter is used to measure voltage at any point in a circuit, or to measure the voltage drop across any part of a circuit. Voltmeters usually have various scales and a selector switch to allow the reading of different voltage ranges. The voltmeter has a positive and a negative lead. To avoid damage to the meter, always connect the negative lead to the negative (-) side of the circuit (to ground or nearest the ground side of the circuit) and connect the positive lead to the positive (+) side of the circuit (to the power source or the nearest power source). Note that the negative voltmeter lead will always be black and that the positive voltmeter will always be some color other than black (usually red).

• Ohmmeter—the ohmmeter is designed to read resistance (measured in ohms) in a circuit or component. Most ohmmeters will have a selector switch which permits the measurement of different ranges of resistance (usually the selector switch allows the multiplication of the meter reading by 10, 100, 1,000 and 10,000). Some ohmmeters are "auto-ranging" which means the meter itself will determine which scale to use. Since the meters are powered by an internal battery, the ohmmeter can be used like a self-powered test light. When the ohmmeter is connected, current from the ohmmeter flows through the circuit or component being tested. Since the ohmmeter's internal resistance and voltage are known values, the amount of current flow through the meter depends on the resistance of the circuit or component being tested. The ohmmeter can also be used to perform a continuity test for suspected open circuits. In using the meter for making continuity checks, do not be concerned with the actual resistance readings. Zero resistance, or any ohm reading, indicates continuity in the circuit.

Infinite resistance indicates an opening in the circuit. A high resistance reading where there should be none indicates a problem in the circuit. Checks for short circuits are made in the same manner as checks for open circuits, except that the circuit must be isolated from both power and normal ground. Infinite resistance indicates no continuity, while zero resistance indicates a dead short.

✳✳ WARNING

Never use an ohmmeter to check the resistance of a component or wire while there is voltage applied to the circuit.

• Ammeter—an ammeter measures the amount of current flowing through a circuit in units called amperes or amps. At normal operating voltage, most circuits have a characteristic amount of amperes, called "current draw" which can be measured using an ammeter. By referring to a specified current draw rating, then measuring the amperes and comparing the two values, one can determine what is happening within the circuit to aid in diagnosis. An open circuit, for example, will not allow any current to flow, so the ammeter reading will be zero. A damaged component or circuit will have an increased current draw, so the reading will be high. The ammeter is always connected in series with the circuit being tested. All of the current that normally flows through the circuit must also flow through the ammeter; if there is any other path for the current to follow, the ammeter reading will not be accurate. The ammeter itself has very little resistance to current flow and, therefore, will not affect the circuit, but it will measure current draw only when the circuit is closed and electricity is flowing. Excessive current draw can blow fuses and drain the battery, while a reduced current draw can cause motors to run slowly, lights to dim and other components to not operate properly.

Troubleshooting Electrical Systems

When diagnosing a specific problem, organized troubleshooting is a must. The complexity of a modern automotive vehicle demands that you approach any problem in a logical, organized manner. There are certain troubleshooting techniques, however, which are standard:

• Establish when the problem occurs. Does the problem appear only under certain conditions? Were there any noises, odors or other unusual symptoms? Isolate the problem area. To do this, make some simple tests and observations, then eliminate the systems that are working properly. Check for obvious problems, such as broken wires and loose or dirty connections. Always check the obvious before assuming something complicated is the cause.

• Test for problems systematically to determine the cause once the problem area is isolated. Are all the components functioning properly? Is there power going to electrical switches and motors. Performing careful, systematic checks will often turn up most causes on the first inspection, without wasting time checking components that have little or no relationship to the problem.

• Test all repairs after the work is done to make sure that the problem is fixed. Some causes can be

traced to more than one component, so a careful verification of repair work is important in order to pick up additional malfunctions that may cause a problem to reappear or a different problem to arise. A blown fuse, for example, is a simple problem that may require more than another fuse to repair. If you don't look for a problem that caused a fuse to blow, a shorted wire (for example) may go undetected.

Experience has shown that most problems tend to be the result of a fairly simple and obvious cause, such as loose or corroded connectors, bad grounds or damaged wire insulation which causes a short. This makes careful visual inspection of components during testing essential to quick and accurate troubleshooting.

Testing

OPEN CIRCUITS

▶ **See Figure 6**

This test already assumes the existence of an open in the circuit and it is used to help locate the open portion.

1. Isolate the circuit from power and ground.
2. Connect the self-powered test light or ohmmeter ground clip to the ground side of the circuit and probe sections of the circuit sequentially.
3. If the light is out or there is infinite resistance, the open is between the probe and the circuit ground.
4. If the light is on or the meter shows continuity, the open is between the probe and the end of the circuit toward the power source.

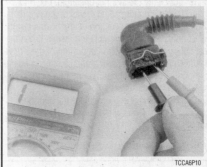

TCCA6P10

Fig. 6 The infinite reading on this multimeter indicates that the circuit is open

SHORT CIRCUITS

➡**Never use a self-powered test light to perform checks for opens or shorts when power is applied to the circuit under test. The test light can be damaged by outside power.**

1. Isolate the circuit from power and ground.
2. Connect the self-powered test light or ohmmeter ground clip to a good ground and probe any easy-to-reach point in the circuit.
3. If the light comes on or there is continuity, there is a short somewhere in the circuit.
4. To isolate the short, probe a test point at either end of the isolated circuit (the light should be on or the meter should indicate continuity).

5. Leave the test light probe engaged and sequentially open connectors or switches, remove parts, etc. until the light goes out or continuity is broken.

6. When the light goes out, the short is between the last two circuit components which were opened.

If a short circuit has caused a blown fuse, a suitable automotive test light can be used to help locate the cause. A test light is connected in series to the fuse terminals to diagnose the source of the short circuit. Using a suitable automotive test light proceed as follows:

7. Carefully remove the blown fuse.

✳✳ WARNING

Make sure the test light leads and jumper wires, if used, are properly insulated and DO NOT contact any other electrical terminals, wiring or chassis grounds. Failure to properly attach or insulate the test light and/or jumper wires could cause physical injury or component damage.

8. Attach one lead of the automotive test light to one of the fuse terminals, and the second lead of the test light to the other fuse terminal.

➡**It may be necessary to use a suitable jumper wire to properly connect the test light leads to the fuse terminals.**

9. If the circuit is a switched circuit, turn on the ignition switch and/or the switch for the component that is causing the fuse to blow. When the appropriate switch is turned on, the test light should begin working.

10. Once the test light is operating, begin to inspect the wiring and components of the circuit. Systematically disconnect and reconnect the electrical connectors in the circuit being tested. When the test light goes out, the shorted portion of the circuit has been located. The short could be either a failed component or a shorted portion of the electrical circuit for the component.

11. Repair the short, or replace the shorted component and reinstall the correct amperage fuse and retest.

VOLTAGE

This test determines voltage available from the battery and should be the first step in any electrical troubleshooting procedure after visual inspection. Many electrical problems, especially on computer controlled systems, can be caused by a low state of charge in the battery. Excessive corrosion at the battery cable terminals can cause poor contact that will prevent proper charging and full battery current flow.

1. Set the voltmeter selector switch to the 20V position.

2. Connect the multimeter negative lead to the battery's negative (-) post or terminal and the positive lead to the battery's positive (+) post or terminal.

3. Turn the ignition switch **ON** to provide a load.

4. A well charged battery should register over 12 volts. If the meter reads below 11.5 volts, the battery power may be insufficient to operate the electrical system properly.

VOLTAGE DROP

▶ **See Figure 7**

When current flows through a load, the voltage beyond the load drops. This voltage drop is due to the resistance created by the load and also by small resistances created by corrosion at the connectors and damaged insulation on the wires. The maximum allowable voltage drop under load is critical, especially if there is more than one load in the circuit, since all voltage drops are cumulative.

1. Set the voltmeter selector switch to the 20 volt position.

2. Connect the multimeter negative lead to a good ground.

3. Operate the circuit and check the voltage prior to the first component (load).

4. There should be little or no voltage drop in the circuit prior to the first component. If a voltage drop exists, the wire or connectors in the circuit are suspect.

5. While operating the first component in the circuit, probe the ground side of the component with the positive meter lead and observe the voltage readings. A small voltage drop should be noticed. This voltage drop is caused by the resistance of the component.

6. Repeat the test for each component (load) down the circuit.

7. If a large voltage drop is noticed, the preceding component, wire or connector is suspect.

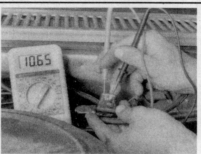

Fig. 7 This voltage drop test revealed high resistance (low voltage) in the circuit

RESISTANCE

▶ **See Figures 8 and 9**

✳✳ WARNING

Never use an ohmmeter with power applied to the circuit. The ohmmeter is designed to operate on its own power supply. The normal 12 volt electrical system voltage could damage the meter!

1. Isolate the circuit from the vehicle's power source.

2. Ensure that the ignition key is **OFF** when disconnecting any components or the battery.

3. Where necessary, also isolate at least one side of the circuit to be checked, in order to avoid reading parallel resistances. Parallel circuit resis-

Fig. 8 Checking the resistance of a coolant temperature sensor with an ohmmeter. Reading is 1.04 kilohms

tances will always give a lower reading than the actual resistance of either of the branches.

4. Connect the meter leads to both sides of the circuit (wire or component) and read the actual measured ohms on the meter scale. Make sure the selector switch is set to the proper ohm scale for the circuit being tested, to avoid misreading the ohmmeter test value.

Wire and Connector Repair

Almost anyone can replace damaged wires, as long as the proper tools and parts are available. Wire and terminals are available to fit almost any need. Even the specialized weatherproof, molded and hard shell connectors are now available from aftermarket suppliers.

Be sure the ends of all the wires are fitted with the proper terminal hardware and connectors. Wrapping a wire around a stud is never a permanent solution and will only cause trouble later. Replace wires one at a time to avoid confusion. Always route wires exactly the same as the factory.

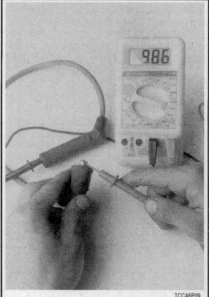

Fig. 9 Spark plug wires can be checked for excessive resistance using an ohmmeter

➡If connector repair is necessary, only attempt it if you have the proper tools. Weatherproof and hard shell connectors require special tools to release the pins inside the connector. Attempting to repair these connectors with conventional hand tools will damage them.

If reliability is a concern, solder wires with rosin core solder whenever possible and insulate them using shrink wrap, or a good quality electrical tape. Exercise care when soldering wires, as proper heat sinks may be needed to prevent component damage from excessive heat. Do not solder a wire or component if there is a potential for heat related damage to occur.

BATTERY CABLES

Disconnecting the Battery Cables

When working on any electrical component on the vehicle, it is always a good idea to disconnect the negative (-) battery cable. This will prevent potential damage to many sensitive electrical components such as the Powertrain Control Module (PCM), radio, alternator, etc.

✳✳ WARNING

Never disconnect a battery cable when the engine is running. Disconnecting a battery cable with the engine running is likely to cause expensive and permanent damage to the alternator, voltage regulator, and control modules, such as the PCM.

➡**Any time you disconnect or remove the battery cables, it is recommended that you disconnect the negative (-) battery cable first. This will prevent your accidentally grounding the positive (+) terminal to the body of the vehicle when disconnecting it, thereby preventing damage to the above mentioned components.**

Before you disconnect the cable(s), first turn the ignition to the **OFF** position. This will prevent a draw on the battery which could cause arcing (electricity trying to ground itself to the body of a vehicle, just like a spark plug jumping the gap) and, of course, damaging some components such as the alternator diodes.

When reconnecting or installing a battery, always attach the negative cable last. This is done as a safety measure, should a tool or component slip while installing the positive battery cable. If the tool touches the battery positive terminal and a chassis ground simultaneously, as long as the negative battery cable is not connected, no damage will occur. Make sure when installing a battery that the positive battery cable is fully installed and tightened before installing the negative battery cable.

When the battery cable(s) are reconnected (negative cable last), be sure to check that your lights, windshield wipers and other electrically operated safety components are all working correctly. If your vehicle contains an Electronically Tuned Radio (ETR), don't forget to reset your radio security code, the radio station presets, and reset the clock.

AIR BAG (SUPPLEMENTAL RESTRAINT SYSTEM)

General Information

The Air Bag is referred to as a Supplemental Restraint System (SRS) component because it is designed to work with, or as a supplement to, the seat belts supplied with the vehicle.

✳✳ CAUTION

Air bags should never be assumed to take the place of seat belts. The air bag is designed to work in conjunction with the seat belts. Most states have instituted laws requiring the use of seat belts. Consult your local and state laws regarding seat belt usage.

✳✳ WARNING

If the air bags have deployed, the air bags, SRS control unit, and if installed, the seat belt tensioner assemblies must be replaced.

A basic SRS is comprised of the following components:
- SRS Airbag
- SRS Sensors
- SRS Control Unit
- SRS Indicator Light (SRS Warning Light)

The SRS Sensors are used by the SRS Control Unit to detect a moderate to severe frontal collision. If such is the case, the SRS Sensors send a signal to the SRS Control Unit, which in turn activates the SRS Airbag. The SRS Control Unit also has it's own emergency backup power in case the vehicle's electrical system is disconnected in a crash.

The SRS Control Unit also monitors the integrity of the SRS System once the ignition key is switched **ON**. Under normal operating conditions, when the ignition key is initially turned to the **ON** position, the SRS Indicator Light should come on for 6 seconds, and then go out. This serves as a bulb check for the SRS Indicator Light. If the SRS Control Unit detects a problem in the SRS system, the SRS Indicator Light will remain ON until the problem is resolved and the SRS Diagnostic Trouble Codes (DTCs) erased.

✳✳ CAUTION

If the SRS Indicator Light fails to light, or is on continuously, the cause should be determined immediately. The system may have a problem that could compromise the safe operation and/or deployment of the SRS system.

SERVICE PRECAUTIONS

▸ **See Figures 10 and 11**

✳✳ CAUTION

The Supplemental Restraint System (SRS) must be disabled before performing service on or around system components, steering column, instrument panel components, wiring and sensors. Failure to follow safety and disabling procedures could result in accidental air bag deployment, possible personal injury and unnecessary system repairs.

Please take note of the following precautions whenever working on or near SRS air bag system components:

• When carrying a live air bag module, point the bag and trim cushion away from your body. When placing a live air bag on a bench or other surface, always face the bag and trim cushion up, away from the surface. Following these precautions will reduce the chance of injury if the air bag is accidentally deployed.

• Use only a digital multimeter when checking any part of the air bag system. The multimeter's output must be 0.01Amps (10mA) or less when it is switched to its smallest ohmmeter range value.

• Do not bump, strike, or drop any SRS component. Store SRS components away from any source of electricity, including static electricity, moisture, oil, grease, and extreme heat and humidity.

• Do not cut, damage, or attempt to alter the SRS wiring harness or its yellow insulation.

• Do not install SRS components that have been recovered from wrecked or dismantled vehicles.

• Always disconnect both battery cables when working around SRS components or wiring.

• Always disable the air bag when working under the dashboard.

• Always check the alignment of the air bag cable reel during steering-related service procedures.

93138P10

Fig. 10 If removed, always place the inflator module facing up to avoid injury should accidental deployment occur

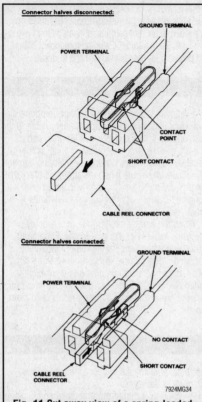

Connector halves disconnected:

GROUND TERMINAL
POWER TERMINAL
CONTACT POINT
SHORT CONTACT
CABLE REEL CONNECTOR

Connector halves connected:

GROUND TERMINAL
POWER TERMINAL
NO CONTACT
CABLE REEL CONNECTOR
SHORT CONTACT

7924MG34

Fig. 11 Cut away view of a spring-loaded SRS electrical connector. Never modify an SRS electrical connector

- Take extra care when working in the area of the dashboard. Avoid direct exposure of the SRS unit or wiring to heat guns, welding, or spraying equipment.
- Disconnect the driver's/front passenger's air bag and if equipped, the seat belt tensioner connections before working below the dashboard close to the SRS control unit.
- If the vehicle is involved in a frontal impact or after a collision without airbag deployment, inspect the SRS unit for physical damage. If the SRS control unit is dented, cracked, or deformed, replace it.
- If removed or replaced, make sure the SRS control unit is installed securely.
- Never disassemble the SRS control unit.
- When installing or replacing the SRS control unit, be careful not to bump or strike the area around the SRS control unit. Avoid using impact wrenches, hammers, etc. in the area surrounding the SRS control unit
- Never reach through the steering wheel to start an air bag equipped vehicle.
- If the air bag has deployed, the air bags, control unit, and if equipped, the seat belt tensioners must be replaced.

DISARMING THE SRS

✳✳ CAUTION

The Supplemental Restraint System (SRS) must be disarmed before any of its components are disconnected or the air bag is removed. Failing to disarm the SRS before

servicing its components may cause accidental deployment of the air bag, resulting in unnecessary SRS repairs and possible personal injury.

➡To fully disarm the SRS system requires that both the driver's and passenger's air bag be disconnected and shunted. Also, on 1998 and later CR-V models, and V6 Odyssey models, the driver's and passenger's front seat belt tensioner must also be disconnected.

The battery must be disconnected at least 3 minutes prior to proceeding with disarming the SRS components, otherwise DTCs will be stored and the SRS Indicator Light will remain on once the system is activated.

Driver's Side Air Bag

1. Write down the sound system security code before disconnecting the battery.
2. Disconnect the negative battery cable first and then the positive battery cable.
3. Wait at least three minutes after disconnecting the battery before working on or around the air bag.
4. On CR-V, 2.3L and V6 Odyssey models, remove the steering wheel lower access cover and disconnect the driver's side 2-pin air bag electrical connector.
5. On 2.2L Odyssey models, remove the steering wheel lower access panel and locate the red shorting connector. Disconnect the driver's side air bag 3-pin electrical connector and install the red shorting connector onto the 3-pin air bag connector.

Passenger's Side Air Bag

1. If not previously disconnected, disconnect the negative battery cable first and then the positive battery cable.
2. Wait at least three minutes after disconnecting the battery before working on or around the air bag.
3. Remove the glove box or dashboard compartment. The air bag electrical connector is located in the dash just above the glove or storage box.
4. On 2.2L Odyssey models, locate the front passenger's air bag connector and proceed as follows:
   a. If the air bag connector is a 2-pin electrical connector, detach the connector.
   b. If the air bag connector is a 3-pin electrical connector, locate the red shorting connector. Disconnect the 3-pin passenger's side air bag connector, and then install the air bag 3-pin electrical connector onto the red shorting connector.
5. On CR-V models and 2.3L and 3.5L Odyssey models, disconnect the 2-pin passenger's side air bag connector.

Seat Belt Tensioner

The seat belt tensioner system is part of the Supplemental Restraint System (SRS) on 1998 and later CR-V models and V6 Odyssey models. The seat belt tensioner system is activated when the air bag is deployed. If the air bag has deployed, the SRS control unit, air bags, and seat belt tensioners must be replaced.

1. Remove the left and right center pillar trim.
2. Detach the 2-pin electrical connector for the driver's and passenger's side seat belt tensioner.

ARMING THE SRS

➡To properly arm the Supplemental Restraint (SRS) System, all SRS components must be completely and properly installed. This includes the driver's and passenger's air bag, and on 1998 and later CR-V models, and V6 Odyssey models, the driver's and passenger's front seat belt tensioners.

Driver's Side Air Bag

1. On CR-V, 2.3L and V6 Odyssey models, attach the driver's side 2-pin air bag electrical connector.
2. On 2.2L Odyssey models, perform the following:
   a. Detach the shorting connector from the air bag module connector.
   b. Immediately couple the air bag and cable reel connectors.
   c. Place the red shorting connector back into its holder.
3. Install the steering wheel lower access panel.
4. Make sure the passenger's air bag and, if equipped, the driver's and passenger's seat belt tensioners are properly installed before connecting the battery.
5. Connect the positive battery cable first and then the negative battery cable.
6. Enter the sound system security code.
7. Turn the ignition switch to the **ON** position, but don't start the engine. The SRS indicator light should turn ON for 6 seconds and then turn OFF. If the SRS indicator light doesn't come ON, or stays ON longer than six seconds, the system fault must be diagnosed, repaired and the SRS DTC fault memory cleared.

Passenger's Side Air Bag

1. On CR-V models, and 2.3L and 3.5L Odyssey models, attach the 2-pin passenger's side air bag connector.
2. On 2.2L Odyssey models locate the front passenger's air bag connector and proceed as follows:
   a. If the air bag connector is a 2-pin electrical connector, attach the electrical connector.
   b. If the air bag connector is a 3-pin electrical connector, remove the red shorting connector and immediately connect the 3-pin passenger's side air bag electrical connector. Then place the red shorting connector back into its holder.
3. Install the glove box or dashboard compartment.
4. Make sure the driver's air bag and, if equipped, the driver's and passenger's seat belt tensioners are properly installed before connecting the battery.
5. Connect the positive battery cable first and then the negative battery cable.
6. Enter the sound system security code.
7. Turn the ignition switch to the **ON** position, but don't start the engine. The SRS indicator light should turn ON for 6 seconds and then turn OFF. If the SRS indicator light doesn't come ON, or stays ON longer than six seconds, the system fault must

be diagnosed, repaired and the SRS DTC fault memory cleared.

Seat Belt Tensioner

1. Attach the 2-pin electrical connector for the driver's and passenger's side seat belt tensioner.

2. Install the left and right center pillar trim.

3. Make sure the driver's and passenger's air bags are properly installed before connecting the battery.

4. Connect the positive battery cable first and then the negative battery cable.

5. Enter the sound system security code.

6. Turn the ignition switch to the **ON** position, but don't start the engine. The SRS indicator light should turn ON for 6 seconds and then turn OFF. If the SRS indicator light doesn't come ON, or stays ON longer than six seconds, the system fault must be diagnosed, repaired and the SRS DTC fault memory cleared.

HEATING AND AIR CONDITIONING

❊❊ WARNING

When working on components located near or under the dash be aware of the location of the Supplemental Restraint (SRS) System components and wiring and take care not to damage them.

❊❊ CAUTION

The SRS system should always be disarmed before performing dash related repairs, otherwise physical injury or component damage could occur.

Front Blower Motor

REMOVAL & INSTALLATION

The front blower motor is located in the front passenger's right side foot well area.

1. If additional access is needed, remove the front passenger's right side lower kick panel.

2. Detach the electrical connectors from the blower motor.

3. Remove the fasteners on the blower motor mounting flange.

4. Remove the blower motor downward from the blower unit.

5. Installation is the reverse of the removal procedure.

Rear Blower Motor

REMOVAL & INSTALLATION

Odyssey Models

4-CYLINDER ENGINES

1. Carefully remove the left and right side lids located on the side of the blower unit at the upper door pillar, by unsnapping them from their 3 mounting points.

2. Carefully unsnap the rear A/C switch, detach the electrical connector and remove the switch.

3. Carefully unsnap the left and right lids at the ends of both the intake and outlet grilles.

4. Remove two self tapping screws from each grille, and remove the intake and outlet grilles.

5. Disconnect the left and right drain hoses from the lower trim panel.

6. Remove the 9 fasteners securing the lower panel and remove the panel.

7. Detach the electrical connector from the blower motor assembly.

8. Remove the 4 self tapping screws from the

blower motor assembly and remove the blower assembly.

9. Remove the blower motor bracket and blower motor housing screws, then remove the blower from the housing just enough to expose the set screw attaching the fan assembly to the blower.

10. Remove the fan assembly set screw, then remove the blower motor.

11. Installation is the reverse of the removal procedure.

V6 ENGINE

1. Carefully remove the right side rear trim panel.

2. Detach the electrical connectors from the blower motor and resistor pack.

3. Remove the fasteners securing the blower motor unit to the vehicle.

4. Remove the fasteners securing the blower motor flange to the blower motor housing.

5. Installation is the reverse of the removal procedure.

Heater Core

REMOVAL & INSTALLATION

➡**Removing the heater core requires removal of the dashboard and the air conditioner evaporator. Removal of the air conditioner evaporator requires the A/C system to be discharged. The legal ramifications of discharging A/C systems without the proper EPA certification, experience, and equipment dictate that the A/C components on your vehicle should be serviced only by a Motor Vehicle Air Conditioning (MVAC) trained, and EPA certified automotive technician using approved equipment.**

If you insist upon servicing the heater core and you are not a Motor Vehicle Air Conditioning (MVAC) trained, and EPA certified automotive technician and/or you do have the approved equipment for discharging and recovery of the A/C refrigerant, before disabling your vehicle, take your vehicle to an approved repair facility and have the A/C system discharged prior to beginning the heater core repair procedure.

1. Take your vehicle to an approved repair facility and have the A/C system discharged.

2. Turn the ignition to the **ON** position and set the heater temperature knob to the full heat position, then turn the ignition switch to the **OFF** position.

3. Disconnect the negative battery cable.

4. From under the hood, locate the heater control valve on the lower passenger's side firewall area just below the fuel filter. Disconnect the clamp securing the heater valve cable to the heater valve and remove the cable.

5. Make sure the heater valve is in the full hot position by pressing the arm toward the firewall.

6. Allow the engine to cool if the coolant temperature is above 100°F (37°C).

7. Drain the engine coolant from the radiator into a suitable and sealable container.

8. On 4-cylinder Odyssey models, remove the upper intake manifold.

9. Place a drain pan below the two heater hoses at the firewall, release the tension on both heater hose clamps and slide the clamps up the heater hose away from the firewall and remove the two hoses.

10. Drain the coolant from the hoses into the drain pan and then into a suitable and sealable container.

11. Remove the nut attached to the stud protruding through the firewall, just above and to the right of the heater hoses.

12. Remove the dashboard assembly. Refer to Section 10 for specific details.

13. On 4-cylinder Odyssey models, remove the steering hanger beam, center dash supports and the upper cover plate.

14. Remove the evaporator as follows:

a. Note the entertainment system security code, then disconnect the negative battery cable, then the positive cable and remove the battery.

b. From under the hood, unbolt and remove the suction and receiver lines from the evaporator. Plug of cap the lines and the receiver immediately to avoid moisture and debris contamination.

c. Remove the glove box assembly.

d. Remove the passenger dashboard lower cover, then remove the glove box frame and knee bolster bracket.

e. Disconnect the evaporator temperature sensor and wire harness.

f. Remove the evaporator mounting screws, mounting bolt and mounting nut, disconnect the drain hose and remove the evaporator assembly.

15. Detach the electrical connectors from the heater mode control motor and air mix control motor, then remove the wire harness clips and wire harness from the heater unit.

16. Remove the clip from the heater duct, and remove the heater unit mounting nuts and remove the heater unit.

➡**Take care not to tip the heater unit as residual coolant may spill.**

17. Remove the heater core cover.

18. Remove the heater core pipe grommet.

19. Remove the heater core pipe clamp.

20. Carefully remove the heater core assembly.

To install:

21. The installation procedure is in reverse order of disassembly making note of the following points.

22. For the air conditioning system:

- Replace any removed A/C O-rings and coat them with a light coating of refrigerant oil before installing them.
- Make sure any replaced O-rings are compatible with R-134a refrigerant.
- Once the repair procedure is completed, have a certified repair facility add the proper type and amount of refrigerant oil if necessary, charge the A/C system, and test for normal operation and refrigerant leaks.

23. For the heater system:
- Apply a suitable sealant to the grommets.
- Make sure the heater inlet and outlet hoses are installed in the correct location.
- Refill the engine coolant with a 50/50 mixture of approved coolant and water, and bleed as necessary.
- Once the heater core repair is completed, make sure the heater control valve is properly adjusted by placing the temperature setting to the max cool position. Unclamp the heater valve cable sheathing and move the heater valve arm away from the firewall. The apply a light pull to the cable and cable sheathing to make sure all slack is removed from the cable, and reinstall the cable.

Heater Water Control Valve

REMOVAL & INSTALLATION

▶ See Figure 12

❊❊ WARNING

Before working on a cooling system component, the engine coolant temperature must be below 100°F (37°C).

Fig. 12 A pair of hose crimping pliers is useful when doing cooling system related repairs

39133P09

1. Turn the ignition switch to the **ON** position, then turn the heater temperature control to full hot, then turn the ignition switch **OFF**.
2. Drain the coolant from the radiator into a suitable sealable container, or using two pair of suitable hose crimping pliers, carefully clamp shut the two heater hoses attached to the heater control valve.
3. Squeeze the hose clamp ends together using a flat-nosed pliers to release the tension of the hose clamps, and slide the clamps off of the heater valve spigots.
4. Place a suitable coolant drain pan below the heater control valve, then remove the control valve cable clamp and control valve cable.
5. Carefully remove the heater hoses from the control valve and remove the control valve from the vehicle.

To install:
6. The installation is the reverse of the removal procedure making sure of the following points:

- Make sure the cooling system is topped off with the proper mixture of coolant and bled if necessary.
- Once the repair is completed, check the operation of the heater control valve.

Air Conditioning Components

REMOVAL & INSTALLATION

Repair or service of air conditioning components is not covered by this manual, because of the risk of personal injury or death, and because of the legal ramifications of servicing these components without the proper EPA certification and experience. Cost, personal injury or death, environmental damage, and legal considerations (such as the fact that it is a federal crime to vent refrigerant into the atmosphere), dictate that the A/C components on your vehicle should be serviced only by a Motor Vehicle Air Conditioning (MVAC) trained, and EPA certified automotive technician.

Control Panel

REMOVAL & INSTALLATION

1. On 4-cylinder Odyssey models, disconnect the air mix control cable from the heater assembly.
2. Remove the center console, as outlined in Section 10.
3. Remove the self tapping screws that mount the control unit to the center console trim panel.
4. Installation is the reverse of the removal procedure.

CRUISE CONTROL

The cruise control system a vacuum-based system and is designed to work at speeds above 25 mph. To activate the system, the cruise control dash mounted main switch must be in the on position. The main switch toggles between on and off by simply pressing it. When in the on position, an indicator light in the switch will light.

The cruise control system works a mechanical linkage to the throttle by way of a vacuum motor which is inside a server. This is a diaphragm moved by vacuum applied to one side. A solenoid driven valve connects the vacuum motor to a vacuum tank. Another solenoid vents the vacuum. The cruise control module controls the servo and the throttle by pulsing these solenoid valves on and off.

One input to the cruise control module is the vehicle speed, which is sent to the Powertrain Control Module (PCM) by the Vehicle Speed Sensor (VSS)

To diagnose the system, first note the symptom. If the system does not engage at all:
- Check the main switch, make sure it is in the on position.
- Check the brake and clutch (if installed) pedal adjustments.
- Check the wiring for the cruise vacuum unit and control unit.

- Check the vacuum hose connections for the vacuum unit.
- Check the vacuum unit throttle cable and verify that it is connected.
- Check the speedometer operation. If the speedometer does not work, the VSS may be faulty.
If the system loses speed:
- Check the vacuum hoses for the vacuum unit for leaks.
- Check the vacuum storage tank for leaks.
If the vehicle loses speed before the system engages:
- Check the cable adjustment from the vacuum unit to the throttle for excessive free play.

ENTERTAINMENT SYSTEMS

Radio Receiver/Tape Player

REMOVAL & INSTALLATION

CR-V Models

▶ See Figures 13, 14, 15, 16 and 17

Radio removal requires removal of the driver's dashboard lower cover, glove box, center pocket or console and center dashboard lower cover.

➡**Before disconnecting the battery cable(s) or the radio electrical connectors, make sure to note the radio security code. Once disconnected, the radio will not function until the code is entered.**

1. Note the radio security code.
2. Remove the glove box, and the driver's side lower dash trim from below the steering wheel, as outlined in Section 10.
3. Remove the lower, center console trim, as outlined in Section 10.
4. Remove the center console change box and the cup holder assembly from the center console, as follows:

    a. Open the change box and remove the 6 Phillips screws that mount the change box onto the console.

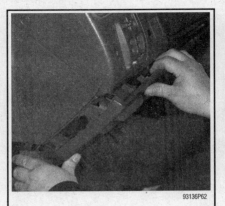

Fig. 13 Carefully release the driver's side lower dash panel by pulling it away from the dash

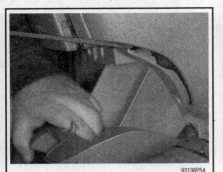

Fig. 14 Use a small flat-bladed tool or suitable curved pick, pull outward on the hook on the upper right hand side of the change box, while pulling on the box to remove it

Fig. 15 To access the radio and heater control assembly, remove the left and right side fasteners from the dash brackets with an 8mm wrench or Phillips screwdriver

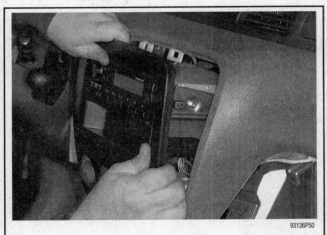

Fig. 16 With the two fasteners removed, carefully pull the assembly from the center dash. The assembly is secured with 6 clips and may require a little patience and finesse to remove it

Fig. 17 The radio is held in place by four 8mm/Phillips fasteners. Disconnect the radio wires, antenna, and the mounting fasteners to remove the radio

b. Using a small flat-bladed prytool or a small curved pick, pull outward on the hook located on the upper right hand side of the change box, while pulling on the box to remove it from the console.

5. Remove the center console center cover.

a. Remove the 2 lower and 2 right side Phillips screws from the cover.

b. Carefully pull the left side of the console away from the dash to release the left side clips.

6. Remove the combination radio and heater control assembly from the center dash.

a. Use an 8mm wrench or Phillips screwdriver to remove the left and right side bolts that mount the assembly to the dash brackets.

b. Once both bolts are removed, carefully pull the combination radio and heater control assembly from the center dash. The assembly is secured with 6 clips and may require a little patience and finesse to release it from the console.

c. Once the assembly has been loosened, reach behind it to release the two wire terminals from the heater controls, and the wire terminal and antenna lead from the radio.

7. To remove the radio, remove the two bolts on the left and right sides using an 8mm wrench or Phillips screwdriver.

8. Installation is the reverse of the removal.

9. Enter the radio security code and radio station presets.

Odyssey Models

4-CYLINDER ENGINES

1. Note the radio security code.

2. Remove the center console. For specific details, refer to Section 10.

3. Remove the cup holder. For specific details, refer to Section 10.

4. Remove the two mounting bolts from the underneath back portion of the radio, and remove the radio.

5. Detach the electrical connectors and antenna lead and remove the radio.

6. Installation is the reverse of the removal procedure. Once installed, enter the security code.

V6 ENGINE

1. Note the radio security code.

2. Disconnect the negative battery cable.

3. Remove the center console panel. For specific details, refer to Section 10.

4. Remove the bolts securing the radio bracket to the center panel, detach the electrical connector and the antenna, then remove the audio unit.

5. Remove the mounting hardware from the mounting brackets and separate the audio unit and the case.

6. Installation is the reverse of the removal procedure. Once installed, enter the security code.

Speakers

REMOVAL & INSTALLATION

▶ **See Figures 18 and 19**

1. Locate the small rectangular opening at the bottom of the speaker grills.

2. Using a suitable, small flat blade prytool, carefully pry the speaker grill from the door panel.

3. Remove the 3 Phillips screws that mount the speaker to the door panel.

4. Carefully remove the speaker from the door panel to gain access the electrical connector.

5. Remove the wire connector from the speaker.

6. Installation is the reverse of the removal procedure.

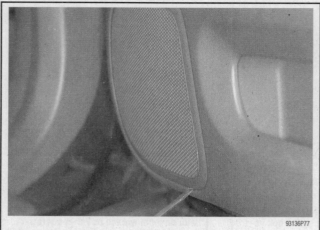

Fig. 18 Carefully pry the speaker cover away from the door panel using a suitable prytool in the small rectangular access hole at the bottom of the speaker

Fig. 19 Remove the Phillips screws holding the speaker in place, and then remove the speaker

WINDSHIELD WIPERS AND WASHERS

Windshield Wiper Blade and Arm

REMOVAL & INSTALLATION

Wiper Arm Removal

▶ See Figures 20, 21 and 22

FRONT

1. Remove the mounting nut from the wiper pivot using a 14mm wrench.
2. Mark the wiper arm and pivot bolt alignment using touch up paint or a suitable maker.
3. Carefully press down on the wiper arm about 4 inches (100mm) from the wiper pivot bolt. Press down and release several times until the wiper arm releases from the pivot.
4. While holding the wiper arm on the pivot, fold the arm upward until it locks in position.
5. Lift the wiper arm off of the pivot.

6. Installation is the reverse of removal, noting the following:
- Be sure to properly align the wiper arm with the pivot bolt.
- Once the arms are installed, operate the

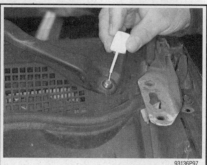

Fig. 21 Matchmark the wiper arm and the wiper pivot to ensure proper alignment during reassembly

wipers in the fast position with the windshield wet. Use the washers to wet the windshield. If the wipers strike the windshield trim, reposition the arms to so they do not touch the surrounding trim.

REAR

The rear wiper arm removal is the same as the front wiper arm procedure, with exception of the wrench size needed. Most of the rear wiper assemblies typically require a 12mm wrench for removal.

Wiper Blade Removal

▶ See Figures 23 and 24

1. Lift the wiper arm up and press the small tab at the wiper pivot inward while pressing downward on the blade to release it.

To install:

2. Lift the blade assembly upward into the arm until the pivoting clip snaps in place.

Fig. 20 Remove the wiper arm mounting nut

Fig. 22 Temporarily reinstall the wiper mounting nut about 3 turns, then press downward on the wiper arm until it frees itself from the tapered pivot

Fig. 23 To remove a wiper blade, press and hold the wiper pivot tab inward . . .

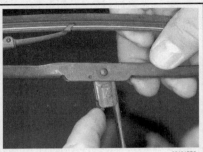

Fig. 24 . . . then, press downward on the blade assembly to release it from the wiper arm

Windshield Wiper Motor

REMOVAL & INSTALLATION

Front

▶ **See Figures 25 thru 32**

1. Make sure the wipers are in the park position. If not, turn the ignition key to the **ON** position and operate the wipers one time. Turn the wiper switch to the off position and then turn the ignition switch **OFF**.

2. Remove the wiper arms from the wiper pivots.

3. Using a suitable trim panel removal tool,

remove the upper clips from the plastic windshield wiper linkage cover.

4. Using two small suitable prytools, carefully remove the lower panel clips from the wiper linkage cover.

5. Remove the 2 wiper pivot trim covers, and then remove the plastic wiper linkage cover.

6. Using a 10mm socket, extension and ratchet, remove the four wiper assembly mounting bolts.

7. Remove the wiper motor electrical connector from the wiper motor.

8. Carefully remove the wiper motor and linkage assembly from the center cowling.

9. Make a reference mark with touch up paint or a suitable marker between the motor pivot shaft and the pivot arm.

10. Using a 12mm wrench, remove the pivot arm mounting nut, and then tap the arm with a suitable plastic handle of a screwdriver. It may take several taps to loosen the link arm. Once the arm is loose, lift it off of the pivot shaft.

11. Using a 10mm socket, extension and ratchet, remove the three bolts that mount the motor to the bracket assembly.

To install:

12. Installation is the reverse of the removal. If the wiper motor is being replaced, cycle the motor one time to make sure it is in the park position. To do this proceed as follows:

a. Before installing the wiper motor onto the linkage assembly, plug the wiper electrical connector onto the wiper motor.

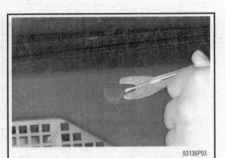

Fig. 25 Use a trim panel removal tool and a small flat-blade screwdriver to carefully lift the front wiper cowling pressed in fasteners . . .

Fig. 26 . . . then use the trim panel tool to remove the fastener from the front wiper cowling

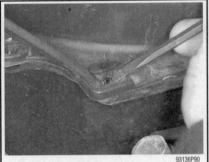

Fig. 27 Use two small flat-blade screwdrivers to remove the lower fasteners of the front wiper cowling

Fig. 28 Once the cowling is removed, the wiper motor/pivot assembly mounting bolts can be removed

Fig. 29 Matchmark the wiper motor shaft to the arm before removing the arm

Fig. 30 Unfasten the wiper pivot arm mounting nut from the wiper motor shaft . . .

Fig. 31 . . . then tap lightly on the wiper pivot arm to release it from the tapered shaft

Fig. 32 Unfasten the three mounting bolts from the wiper motor to remove the motor

b. Secure and place the wiper motor such that it can be operated safely and will not contact a painted surface.

c. Turn the ignition switch to the **ON** position, but do not start the engine.

d. While the ignition switch is in the **ON** position, turn the wiper switch to the low speed on position. Make sure the wiper motor spins, then turn the wiper switch **OFF**. The wiper motor should stop moving once it reaches the park position.

e. Turn the ignition switch to the **OFF** position, and install the wiper motor in the reverse order as removal.

Rear

♦ See Figure 33

1. Make sure the wipers are in the park position. If not, turn the ignition key to the **ON** position and operate the wipers one time. Turn the wiper switch to the off position and then turn the ignition switch **OFF**.

2. Lift up the rear wiper pivot cover, and using a 10mm wrench, remove the rear wiper mounting nut.

3. Matchmark the wiper arm and the wiper pivot, then remove the wiper arm from the wiper pivot.

4. Remove the outer wiper pivot trim from the wiper pivot.

5. Using a suitable 23mm wrench, loosen and remove the wiper pivot mounting nut.

6. Open the rear hatch glass and press in on the two wiper motor cover tabs, and remove the cover.

7. Detach the electrical connector from the wiper motor.

93136PB3

Fig. 33 Once the wiper arm is removed, the trim cover can be taken off to access the mounting nut

8. Using a 10mm socket, extension and ratchet, remove the fastener that secures the motor assembly to the window lift handle and carefully remove the wiper motor and bracket assembly from the rear hatch glass.

9. Using a 10mm socket, extension and ratchet, remove the fasteners that secure the motor to the wiper motor bracket assembly.

To install:

10. Installation is the reverse of the removal procedure. If the wiper motor is being replaced, cycle the motor one time to make sure it is in the park position. To do this proceed as follows:

a. Before installing the wiper motor onto the linkage assembly, plug the wiper electrical connector onto the wiper motor.

b. Carefully hold the wiper motor such that it can be operated safely and will not contact a painted surface or the rear hatch glass.

c. Turn the ignition switch to the **ON** position, but do not start the engine.

d. While the ignition switch is in the **ON** position, turn the wiper switch to the low speed on position. Make sure the wiper motor spins, then turn the wiper switch off. The wiper motor should stop moving once it reaches the park position.

e. Turn the ignition switch to the **OFF** position and install the wiper motor in the reverse order as removal.

➡**Use extreme care to not overtighten the fasteners.**

Windshield Washer Pump

REMOVAL & INSTALLATION

The front and rear windshield washer pumps are attached to the washer bottle which is located on the lower left or right side of the vehicle, behind the front bumper. On CR-V models, the front bumper must be removed to access the washer motor.

1. On CR-V models, remove the front bumper. See Section 10 for details.

2. On 4-cylinder Odyssey models, remove the left front inner fender well.

3. On V6 Odyssey models, remove the right front inner fender well.

4. Detach the washer motor electrical connector and fluid hose.

5. Release the washer pump from the washer bottle and grommet.

6. Installation is the reverse of the removal procedure.

INSTRUMENTS AND SWITCHES

Instrument Cluster

REMOVAL & INSTALLATION

CR-V Models

♦ See Figures 34, 35, 36 and 37

1. Remove the 2 Phillips screws from the top of the instrument cluster assembly trim.

2. Carefully remove the trim by pulling on the lower portion of the trim to release the lower the lower clips.

3. Remove the 2 upper and 2 lower Phillips screws from the cluster assembly.

4. Carefully remove the instrument cluster assembly enough to access the electrical connectors on the back of the assembly.

5. Once the electrical connectors are removed, the assembly can be removed.

6. Installation is the reverse of the removal procedure.

Odyssey Models

4-CYLINDER ENGINES

1. Carefully pry off the left side outlet.

2. Remove the 2 upper and 1 left side Phillips screws, then remove the instrument cluster trim.

3. Place a soft protective cloth on the upper steering column trim and remove the 4 cluster assembly mounting screws.

4. Carefully pry the cluster assembly partially out and unplug the electrical connectors.

93136P33

Fig. 34 To remove the instrument cluster trim, locate and remove the Phillips screws securing the trim to the dash

93136P31

Fig. 35 Once the trim is removed, the gauge assembly fasteners can be removed

93136P30

Fig. 36 Pull the instrument cluster partially out, detach the electrical connector(s), then remove the cluster

5. Once the electrical connectors are removed, the assembly can be removed.

6. Installation is the reverse of the removal procedure.

V6 ENGINE

1. Remove the four steering column cover fasteners from the lower cover and remove the upper and lower covers.

2. Remove the center panel by carefully prying the panel away from the dash. Wrap the end of the prytool in protective tape to avoid damaging the components.

3. Remove the driver's center switch panel by carefully prying the panel away from the dash. Detach the electrical connectors and remove the panel.

4. Tilt the steering wheel to the full down position.

5. Remove the 6 screws located along the bottom, and the 2 screws by the instruments in the top of the instrument cover panel.

6. Carefully pull along the top of the panel to release the pressed in clips, and once loose, detach the electrical connectors and remove the panel.

7. Place a soft protective cloth on the upper steering column trim and remove the 4 gauge assembly mounting screws.

8. Carefully pull the gauge assembly outward and detach the electrical connectors.

9. Once the electrical connectors are removed, the assembly can be removed.

10. Installation is the reverse of the removal procedure.

Gauges

REMOVAL & INSTALLATION

The individual gauges are not replaceable on V6 Odyssey models. If a problem occurs with any of the components in the instrument cluster, the entire instrument cluster assembly must be replaced.

CR-V And 4-Cylinder Odyssey Models

♦ See Figure 38

The tachometer, speedometer, and the combination fuel level/engine coolant temperature gauges can be replaced individually without replacing the entire instrument cluster.

1. Remove the instrument cluster assembly as outlined earlier in this section.

2. Carefully remove the clear gauge assembly meter lens.

3. From the back side of the instrument cluster, remove the self tapping fasteners to remove the desired gauge.

4. Installation is the reverse of the removal procedure.

Back-up Light Switch

REMOVAL & INSTALLATION

Manual Transaxle

On vehicles equipped with manual transaxles, the back-up light switch is located on the top of the transaxle gear case. The switch looks similar to a large nut with two wires protruding from it. The switch is not adjustable.

1. Detach the electrical connector at the switch.

2. Loosen and remove the switch by turning it counterclockwise.

➡ **When replacing the switch always use a new sealing washer.**

3. Installation is the reverse of the removal procedure.

Automatic Transaxle

On vehicles with automatic transaxles, the back-up light switch is located on the right side of the transaxle, under a protective cover. The switch is actually a combination switch for the neutral safety circuit, gear shift indicator and back-up lights. The switch is adjustable.

1. Set the parking brake and place the transaxle in Neutral.

2. Remove the protective cover for the switch.

3. Detach the electrical connector for the switch.

4. Loosen the switch mounting bolts, and remove the switch by lifting it away from the transaxle.

To install:

5. Make sure the transmission is in Neutral.

6. Set the switch such that it is in the neutral position. The switch will click when it is in the neutral position.

7. The remainder of the installation is the reverse of removal, making sure of the following:

   a. Turn the ignition switch **ON** and move the gear selector from position to position making sure all the gear indicator lights work properly.

   b. Then place the gear selector in the Reverse position and verify that the reverse lights are functioning.

   c. Next test to make sure the engine will start in the Neutral and Park positions, but will NOT start in any other position. If, necessary, adjust the switch as needed.

Fig. 37 Once the instrument cluster is removed, you can replace any burned-out bulbs as necessary

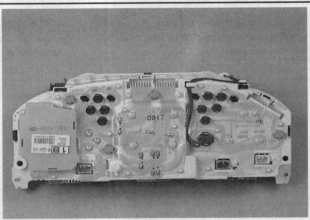

Fig. 38 Once the instrument cluster is removed, the individual gauges can be removed by removing the fasteners on the back of the assembly

LIGHTING

Headlights

REMOVAL & INSTALLATION

▶ **See Figures 39, 40, 41 and 42**

To replace the headlight bulb, proceed as follows:
1. Open the hood.
2. On 4-cylinder Odyssey models, to replace the passenger's side headlight bulb, remove the upper air filter housing.
3. On V6 Odyssey models, to replace the driver's side headlight bulb, remove the upper air filter housing.
4. Squeeze both ends of the headlight electrical connector to unlock the tab and carefully pull the electrical connector off.
5. Carefully pull on the rubber tab to remove the weather seal.
6. Unclip the wire bracket securing the bulb and pivot it away and remove the bulb.
7. Installation is the reverse of removal, making sure to **never** touch the glass portion of the bulb. If the bulb glass has been touched, clean the glass with rubbing alcohol and a clean oil free cloth.

AIMING THE HEADLIGHTS

▶ **See Figures 43, 44 and 45**

The headlights must be properly aimed to provide the best, safest road illumination. The lights should be checked for proper aim and adjusted as necessary. Certain state and local authorities have requirements for headlight aiming; these should be checked before adjustment is made.

❊❊ CAUTION

About once a year, if the headlight assembly is replaced, or any time front end work is performed on your vehicle, the headlight should be accurately aimed by a reputable repair shop using the proper equipment. Headlights not properly aimed can make it virtually impossible to see and may blind other drivers on the road, possibly causing an accident. Note that the following procedure is a temporary fix, until you can take your vehicle to a repair shop for a proper adjustment.

Headlight adjustment may be temporarily made

using a wall, as described below, or on the rear of another vehicle. When adjusted, the lights should not glare in oncoming car or truck windshields, nor should they illuminate the passenger compartment of vehicles driving in front of you. These adjustments are rough and should always be fine-tuned by a repair shop which is equipped with headlight aiming tools. Improper adjustments may be both dangerous and illegal.

The headlamps for the vehicles covered by this manual, horizontal and vertical aiming of each headlamp is provided by two adjusting wheels which move the lens assembly. The adjustment wheels are turned by using a long No. 2 Phillips screw driver. There is no adjustment for focus; this is done during headlight manufacturing.

Before removing the headlight bulb or disturbing the headlamp in any way, note the current settings in order to ease headlight adjustment upon reassembly. The high or low beam adjustment setting can be done using the wall of a garage or a building:
1. Park the vehicle on a level surface, with the fuel tank about ½ full and with the vehicle empty of all extra cargo (unless normally carried). The vehicle should be facing a wall which is no less than 6 feet (1.8m) high and 12 feet (3.7m) wide.

Fig. 39 After unplugging the electrical connector, carefully pull the weather seal off—CR-V shown

Fig. 40 With the electrical connector and weather seal removed, the headlight bulb wire bracket is easily seen—CR-V shown

Fig. 41 With the electrical connector and weather seal removed, release the headlight wire bracket—CR-V shown

Fig. 42 Pivot the wire bracket out of the way, and then carefully remove the bulb. Be careful to not touch the glass—CR-V shown

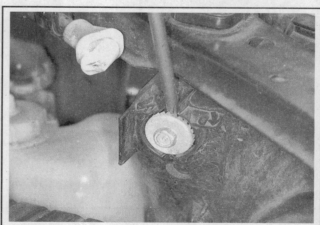

Fig. 43 Example of headlight adjustment wheel being turned with a No. 2 Phillips screwdriver—CR-V shown

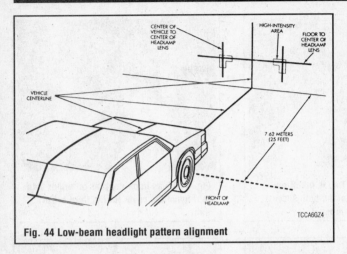

Fig. 44 Low-beam headlight pattern alignment

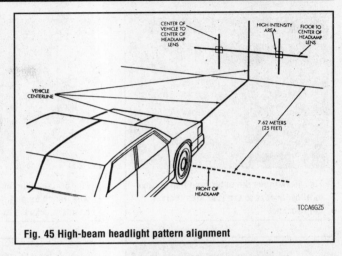

Fig. 45 High-beam headlight pattern alignment

The front of the vehicle should be about 25 feet (7.6 m) from the wall.

2. If aiming is to be performed outdoors, it is advisable to wait until dusk in order to properly see the headlight beams on the wall. If done in a garage, darken the area around the wall as much as possible by closing shades or hanging cloth over the windows.

3. Using a tape measure, measure from the ground to the center of the headlamp assembly and write down the measurement.

4. Then measure the distance between the center of the grill to the center of one of the headlights and write down the measurement.

5. Stand behind the center of the vehicle. If possible, use the third brake light and rear view mirror to sight the center of the vehicle. Look through the windshield, or over the vehicle toward the flat surface that is to be used to aim the headlights, and place a piece of tape on the flat surface to mark the center.

6. Using the measurement taken from the center of the grill to the center of the headlamp, measure on both sides of the center mark on the flat surface and place a piece of tape on the flat surface.

7. Then using the ground to headlamp center measurement, subtract 1 inch (25 mm) from the measurement, and move the two outer tape marks on the flat surface to that height.

8. Turn the headlights ON low beam and note where the center of each light's beam is aimed, then switch on the high beams and note the center of each light's high beam.

9. Adjust the headlights on low beam such that the light is on the center of the tape marks on the flat surface.

10. Have the headlight adjustment checked as soon as possible by a reputable repair shop.

Signal and Marker Lights

REMOVAL & INSTALLATION

Front Turn Signal and Parking Lights

CR-V MODELS AND V6 ODYSSEY MODELS

▶ See Figures 46 and 47

1. Turn the steering wheel in the opposite direction from which the bulb is to be removed.

2. Using a flat blade screwdriver, remove the fasteners securing the inner fender behind the headlight and pull back on the inner fender liner.

3. Remove the bulb socket from the light assembly by turning it counterclockwise ¼ of a turn.

4. To remove the turn signal/side marker bulb, press in slightly and turn it counterclockwise to release the bulb.

5. On CR-V models, to remove the marker bulb, pull the bulb straight out of the socket.

6. Installation is the reverse of the removal procedure.

4-CYLINDER ODYSSEY MODELS

1. Remove the Phillips screw at the top of the light assembly.

2. Remove the lens assembly forward away from the body.

3. Remove the bulb socket from the light assembly by turning it counterclockwise ¼ of a turn.

4. To remove the turn signal/side marker bulb, press in slightly and turn it counterclockwise to release the bulb.

5. Installation is the reverse of the removal procedure.

Rear Turn Signal and Parking Lights

▶ See Figure 48

1. Open the rear tailgate.

2. On CR-V models, remove the fasteners securing the taillight assembly, and lift the assembly from the vehicle.

3. On 4-cylinder Odyssey models, swing the taillight cover open and remove it.

4. On V6 Odyssey models, perform the following:

   a. Carefully pry off the taillight trim covers.

   b. Remove the two Phillips screws securing the taillight and slide the taillight assembly backwards away from the vehicle.

5. Remove the bulb socket from the light assembly by turning it counterclockwise ¼ of a turn.

Fig. 46 Press down on the inner fender to access the front marker bulb sockets—CR-V model shown

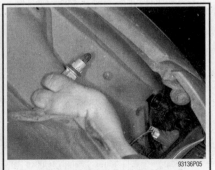

Fig. 47 Remove the bulb socket from the headlamp assembly to replace the bulb—CR-V model shown

Fig. 48 The bulbs for the rear lights are removed from the socket by pulling them straight out—CR-V shown

Fig. 49 Remove the outer mud flap screws to allow access to the rear side marker bulb socket

Fig. 50 Once the mud flap is out of the way, reach up and twist the bulb socket counterclockwise to remove it

Fig. 51 Press in on the tabs on either side to release the cover for the third brake light

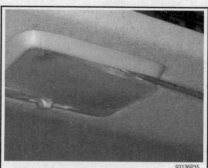

Fig. 52 Using a thin flat-bladed prytool, carefully pry the lens away from the light assembly

Fig. 53 Disengage the spring clip which retains one tapered end of this dome light bulb, then withdraw the bulb

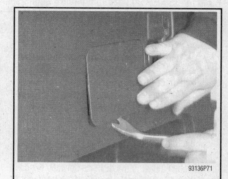

Fig. 54 Carefully pry the license plate light access panel open

6. To remove the bulb, carefully pull it straight out of the socket.

7. Installation is the reverse of the removal procedure.

Side Marker Light

▶ See Figures 49 and 50

The CR-V is the only model covered in this book that uses a separate side marker bulb for the rear. To replace the bulb, proceed as follows.

1. Remove the rear mud flap to access the bulb socket.

2. Remove the bulb socket from the light assembly by turning it counterclockwise ¼ of a turn.

3. To remove the bulb, carefully pull it straight out of the socket.

4. Installation is the reverse of the removal procedure.

High-mount Brake Light

CR-V MODELS

▶ See Figure 51

1. Open the tailgate.

2. Press in on the tabs on either side to release the cover for the third brake light.

3. Remove the bulb socket from the light assembly by turning it counterclockwise ¼ of a turn.

4. To remove the bulb, carefully pull it straight out of the socket.

5. Installation is the reverse of the removal procedure.

4-CYLINDER ODYSSEY MODELS

1. Remove the small rectangular covers on the left and right side of the LED brake light.

2. Remove the two screws securing the light in place.

3. Carefully pry the LED light assembly out of the spoiler.

4. Detach the electrical connector and remove the wire harness fastener.

5. Installation is the reverse of the removal procedure.

V6 ODYSSEY MODELS

1. Remove the small end covers on the left and right side of the brake light lens.

2. Remove the two screws securing the light in place.

3. Carefully pull the light assembly out of the tailgate.

4. Remove the bulb socket from the light assembly by turning it counterclockwise ¼ of a turn.

5. To remove the bulb, carefully pull it straight out of the socket.

6. Installation is the reverse of the removal procedure.

Dome Light

▶ See Figures 52 and 53

1. Using a small prytool, carefully remove the cover lens from the lamp assembly.

2. Remove the bulb from its retaining clip contacts. If the bulb has tapered ends, gently depress

the spring clip/metal contact and disengage the light bulb, then pull it free of the two metal contacts.

To install:

3. Before installing the light bulb into the metal contacts, ensure that all electrical conducting surfaces are free of corrosion or dirt.

4. Position the bulb between the two metal contacts.

5. To ensure that the replacement bulb functions properly, activate the applicable switch to illuminate the bulb which was just replaced. If the replacement light bulb does not illuminate, either it is faulty or there is a problem in the bulb circuit or switch. Correct as necessary.

6. Install the cover lens until its retaining tabs are properly engaged.

Cargo or Passenger Area Lamps

1. Carefully pry the lens cover off of the light assembly

2. Remove the light from the light socket.

3. Installation is the reverse of the removal procedure.

License Plate Lights

CR-V MODELS

▶ See Figures 54 and 55

1. Carefully pry open the bottom of the access panel in the rear tailgate near the luggage hook.

2. Remove the bulb socket from the light assembly by turning it counterclockwise ¼ of a turn.

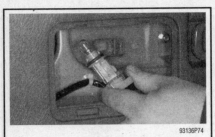

Fig. 55 Remove the bulb and socket in order to access the bulb

3. To remove the bulb, carefully pull it straight out of the socket.

4. Installation is the reverse of the removal procedure.

4-CYLINDER ODYSSEY MODELS

1. Remove the 2 Phillips screws securing the lens assembly and remove the lens.

2. To remove the bulb, pull it carefully straight out of the socket.

3. Installation is the reverse of the removal procedure.

V6 ODYSSEY MODELS

1. Carefully pry open the left side of the license plate light.

2. Remove the bulb sockets from the light assembly by pressing the tabs and pulling it away.

3. To remove the bulb, pull it carefully straight out of the socket.

4. Installation is the reverse of the removal procedure.

TRAILER WIRING

▶ **See Figures 56, 57 and 58**

The CR-V and Odyssey models have a trailer lighting connector in the left side of the cargo area. Wiring the vehicle for towing is fairly easy. There are a number of good wiring kits available and these should be used, rather than trying to design your own.

All trailers will need brake lights and turn signals as well as tail lights and side marker lights. Most areas require extra marker lights for overwide trailers. Also, most areas have recently required back-up lights for trailers, and most trailer manufacturers have been building trailers with back-up lights for several years.

Additionally, some Class I, most Class II and just about all Class III and IV trailers will have electric brakes. Add to this number an accessories wire, to operate trailer internal equipment or to charge the trailer's battery, and you can have as many as seven wires in the harness.

Determine the equipment on your trailer and buy the wiring kit necessary. The kit will contain all the wires needed, plus a plug adapter set which includes the female plug, mounted on the bumper or hitch, and the male plug, wired into, or plugged into the trailer harness.

When installing the kit, follow the manufacturer's instructions. The color coding of the wires is usually standard throughout the industry. One point to note: some domestic vehicles, and most imported vehicles, have separate turn signals. On most domestic vehicles, the brake lights and rear turn signals operate with the same bulb. For those vehicles without separate turn signals, you can purchase an isolation unit so that the brake lights won't blink whenever the turn signals are operated. Companies such as Draw-Tite® have ready to install wiring kits available to fit the CR-V and Odyssey models.

One, final point, the best kits are those with a spring loaded cover on the vehicle mounted socket. This cover prevents dirt and moisture from corroding the terminals. Never let the vehicle socket hang loosely; always mount it securely to the bumper or hitch.

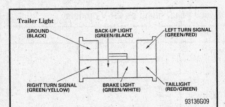

Fig. 56 The CR-V and Odyssey model trailer lighting connector in the cargo area is pre-wired for an accessory electrical connector

Fig. 57 Easy to install Draw-Tite® trailer hitch and wiring kits are available for many Honda models, including the CR-V and Odyssey—CR-V kit shown

Fig. 58 The Draw-Tite® trailer wiring kit makes easy work of trailer wiring. Simply remove the left cargo area speaker to access the vehicle's trailer wiring connector, and plug in the kit's electrical connector

CIRCUIT PROTECTION

Fuses

REPLACEMENT

▶ **See Figure 57**

Fuses are located either in the engine compartment or passenger compartment fuse and relay panels. If a fuse blows, a single component or single circuit will not function properly. Excessive current draw is what causes a fuse to blow. Observing the condition of the fuse will provide insight as to what caused this to occur.

A fuse with signs of burns, melting of the plastic shell, or little to no trace of the wire that once served as the conductor indicates that a direct short to ground exists.

1. Remove the fuse or relay box cover.
2. Inspect the fuses to determine which is faulty.
3. Unplug and discard the fuse.

Fig. 57 Remove the cover, usually located near the steering column, for access to the fuses

4. Inspect the box terminals and clean if corroded. If any terminals are damaged, replace the terminals.
5. Plug in a new fuse of the same amperage rating.

✳✳ WARNING

Never exceed the amperage rating of a blown fuse. If the replacement fuse also blows, check for a problem in the circuit.

6. Check for proper operation of the affected component or circuit.

Maxi-Fuses (Fusible Links)

Maxi-fuses are located in the engine compartment relay box. If a maxi-fuse blows, an entire circuit or several circuits will not function properly.

REPLACEMENT

▶ **See Figure 58**

1. Remove the fuse and relay box cover.
2. Inspect the fusible links to determine which is faulty.
3. Unplug and discard the fusible link.
4. Inspect the box terminals and clean if corroded. If any terminals are damaged, replace the terminals.
5. Plug in a new fusible link of the same amperage rating.

❊❊ WARNING

Never exceed the amperage rating of a blown maxi-fuse. If the replacement fuse also blows, check for a problem in the circuit(s).

6. Check for proper operation of the affected circuit(s).

93136P69

Fig. 58 The engine compartment relay box contains the maxi-fuses

Circuit Breakers

RESETTING AND/OR REPLACEMENT

Circuit breakers are located inside the fuse panel. They are automatically reset when the problem corrects itself, is repaired, or the circuit cools down to allow operation again.

Flashers

REPLACEMENT

Turn Signal Flasher/Hazard Warning Relay

▶ **See Figures 59 thru 64**

1. Grasp and pull the flasher from the connector located near the top of the fuse panel.
2. Inspect the socket for corrosion or any other signs of a bad contact.
3. Installation is the reverse of the removal procedure.

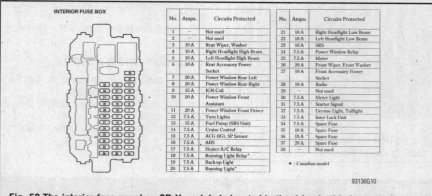

INTERIOR FUSE BOX

No.	Amps.	Circuits Protected	No.	Amps.	Circuits Protected
1	–	Not used	21	10 A	Right Headlight Low Beam
2	–	Not used	22	10 A	Left Headlight Low Beam
3	10 A	Rear Wiper, Washer	23	10 A	SRS
4	10 A	Right Headlight High Beam	24	7.5 A	Power Window Relay
5	10 A	Left Headlight High Beam	25	7.5 A	Meter
6	10 A	Rear Accessory Power Socket	26	20 A	Front Wiper, Front Washer
7	20 A	Power Window Rear Left	27	10 A	Front Accessory Power Socket
8	20 A	Power Window Rear Right	28	10 A	Radio
9	15 A	IGN Coil	29	–	Not used
10	20 A	Power Window Front Assistant	30	7.5 A	Meter Light
			31	7.5 A	Starter Signal
11	20 A	Power Window Front Driver	32	7.5 A	License Light, Taillight
12	7.5 A	Turn Lights	33	7.5 A	Inter Lock Unit
13	15 A	Fuel Pump (SRS Unit)	34	7.5 A	Spare Fuse
14	7.5 A	Cruise Control	35	10 A	Spare Fuse
15	7.5 A	ACG (IG), SP Sensor	36	15 A	Spare Fuse
16	7.5 A	ABS	37	20 A	Spare Fuse
17	7.5 A	Heater A/C Relay	38	–	Not used
18	7.5 A	Running Light Relay*			
19	7.5 A	Back-up Light			
20	7.5 A	Running Light*			

* : Canadian model

93136G10

Fig. 59 The interior fuse panel on CR-V models is located in the driver's side lower dash area

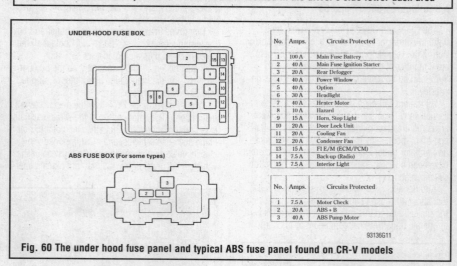

UNDER-HOOD FUSE BOX

No.	Amps.	Circuits Protected
1	100 A	Main Fuse Battery
2	40 A	Main Fuse Ignition Starter
3	20 A	Rear Defogger
4	40 A	Power Window
5	40 A	Option
6	30 A	Headlight
7	40 A	Heater Motor
8	10 A	Hazard
9	15 A	Horn, Stop Light
10	20 A	Door Lock Unit
11	20 A	Cooling Fan
12	20 A	Condenser Fan
13	15 A	FI E/M (ECM/PCM)
14	7.5 A	Back-up (Radio)
15	7.5 A	Interior Light

ABS FUSE BOX (For some types)

No.	Amps.	Circuits Protected
1	7.5 A	Motor Check
2	20 A	ABS + B
3	40 A	ABS Pump Motor

93136G11

Fig. 60 The under hood fuse panel and typical ABS fuse panel found on CR-V models

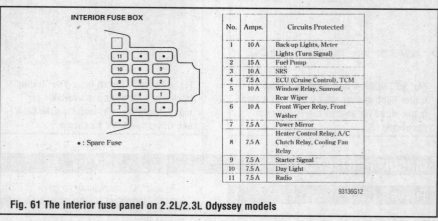

INTERIOR FUSE BOX

No.	Amps.	Circuits Protected
1	10 A	Back-up Lights, Meter Lights (Turn Signal)
2	15 A	Fuel Pump
3	10 A	SRS
4	7.5 A	ECU (Cruise Control), TCM
5	10 A	Window Relay, Sunroof, Rear Wiper
6	10 A	Front Wiper Relay, Front Washer
7	7.5 A	Power Mirror
8	7.5 A	Heater Control Relay, A/C Clutch Relay, Cooling Fan Relay
9	7.5 A	Starter Signal
10	7.5 A	Day Light
11	7.5 A	Radio

• : Spare Fuse

93136G12

Fig. 61 The interior fuse panel on 2.2L/2.3L Odyssey models

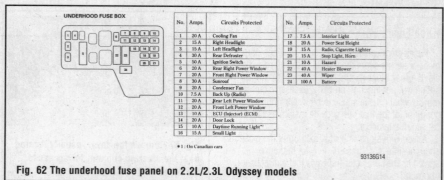

UNDERHOOD FUSE BOX

No.	Amps.	Circuits Protected	No.	Amps.	Circuits Protected
1	20 A	Cooling Fan	17	7.5 A	Interior Light
2	15 A	Right Headlight	18	20 A	Power Seat Height
3	15 A	Left Headlight	19	15 A	Radio, Cigarette Lighter
4	20 A	Rear Defroster	20	15 A	Stop Light, Horn
5	50 A	Ignition Switch	21	10 A	Hazard
6	20 A	Rear Right Power Window	22	40 A	Heater Blower
7	20 A	Front Right Power Window	23	40 A	Wiper
8	30 A	Sunroof	24	100 A	Battery
9	20 A	Condenser Fan			
10	7.5 A	Back Up (Radio)			
11	20 A	Rear Left Power Window			
12	20 A	Front Left Power Window			
13	10 A	ECU (Injector) (ECM)			
14	20 A	Door Lock			
15	10 A	Daytime Running Light*¹			
16	15 A	Small Light			

*1 : On Canadian cars

93136G14

Fig. 62 The underhood fuse panel on 2.2L/2.3L Odyssey models

INTERIOR FUSE BOX
Driver's Side

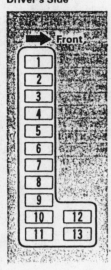

No.	Amps.	Circuits Protected
1	15 A	Fuel Pump
2	10 A	SRS
3	7.5 A	Heater Control, A/C Clutch Relay, Cooling Fan Relay
4	7.5 A	Power Mirror
5	7.5 A	Daytime Running Light*
6	15 A	ECU (PCM), Cruise Control
7	10 A	Rear Wiper
8	7.5 A	ACC Relay
9	10 A	Back-up Lights, Instrument Lights
10	7.5 A	Turn Signals
11	15 A	IG Coil
12	30 A	Front Wiper
13	7.5 A	Starter Signal

* : On Canadian models

Passenger's Side

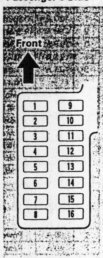

No.	Amps.	Circuits Protected
1	20 A	Driver's Side Automatic Sliding Door
2	20 A	Power Seat Reclining*1
3	10 A	BSC*1
4	20 A	Power Seat Sliding*1
5	20 A	Passenger's Side Automatic Sliding Door
6	10 A	Daytime Running Light*2
7	7.5 A	Left Power Vent
8	20 A	Front Passenger's Power Window
9	15 A	ACC Socket
10	15 A	Small Light, License Light
11	15 A	Interior Light, Radio
12	20 A	Power Door Locks
13	7.5 A	Clock, Back Up
14	7.5 A	ABS Motor Check
15	20 A	Driver's Power Window
16	7.5 A	Right Power Vent

*1 : EX
*2 : Canadian models

93136G15

Fig. 63 The interior fuse panel on V6 Odyssey models

PRIMARY UNDER-HOOD FUSE BOX

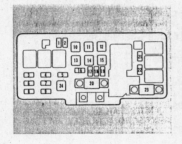

No.	Amps.	Circuits Protected	No.	Amps.	Circuits Protected
1	20 A	Spare Fuse	14	40 A	Power Seat*
2	30 A	Spare Fuse	15	40 A	Heater Motor
3	15 A	Right Headlight	16	30 A	Cooling Fan
4	15 A	ACG S	17	7.5 A	Spare Fuse
5	15 A	Hazard	18	10 A	Spare Fuse
6	—	Not Used	19	15 A	Spare Fuse
7	20 A	Stop	20	120 A	Battery
8	15 A	Left Headlight	21	30 A	Condenser Fan
9	20 A	ABS F/S	22	7.5 A	MG Clutch
10	40 A	Power Window Motor	23	50 A	Ignition Switch (IG 1 Main)
11	30 A	Power Sliding Door*	24	30 A	ABS Motor
12	30 A	Rear Defroster			
13	40 A	Back Up, ACC			

* : EX model

SECONDARY UNDER-HOOD FUSE BOX

No.	Amps.	Circuits Protected
1	30 A	Power Sliding Door*
2	40 A	Rear A/C

* : EX model

93136G16

Fig. 64 The underhood fuse panel on V6 Odyssey models

WIRING DIAGRAMS

INDEX OF WIRING DIAGRAMS

93136W01

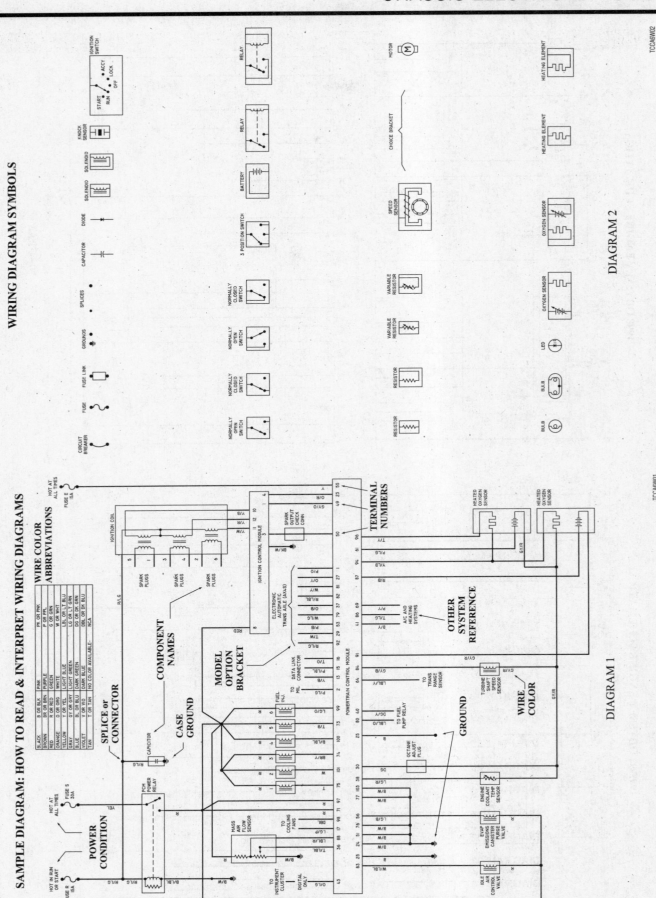

1998 ODYSSEY ENGINE SCHEMATIC

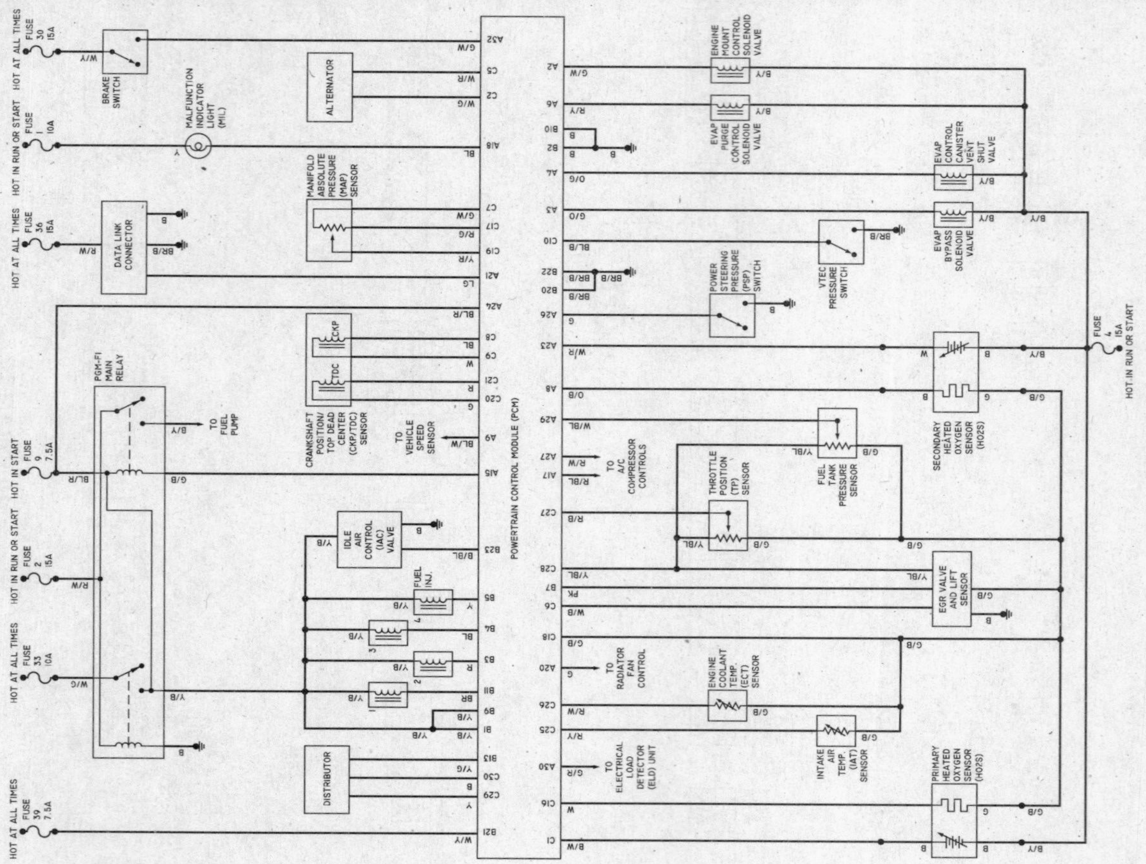

DIAGRAM 4

1995-97 ODYSSEY ENGINE SCHEMATIC

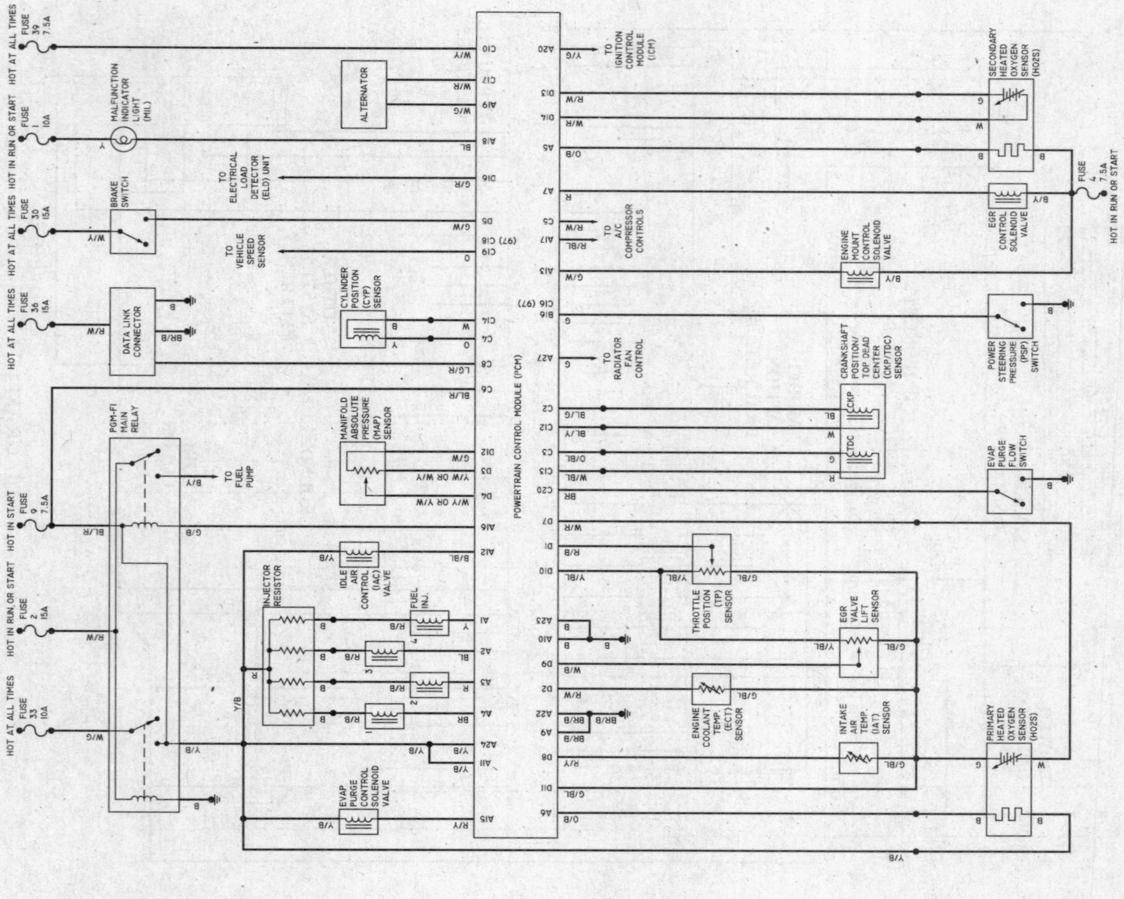

DIAGRAM 3

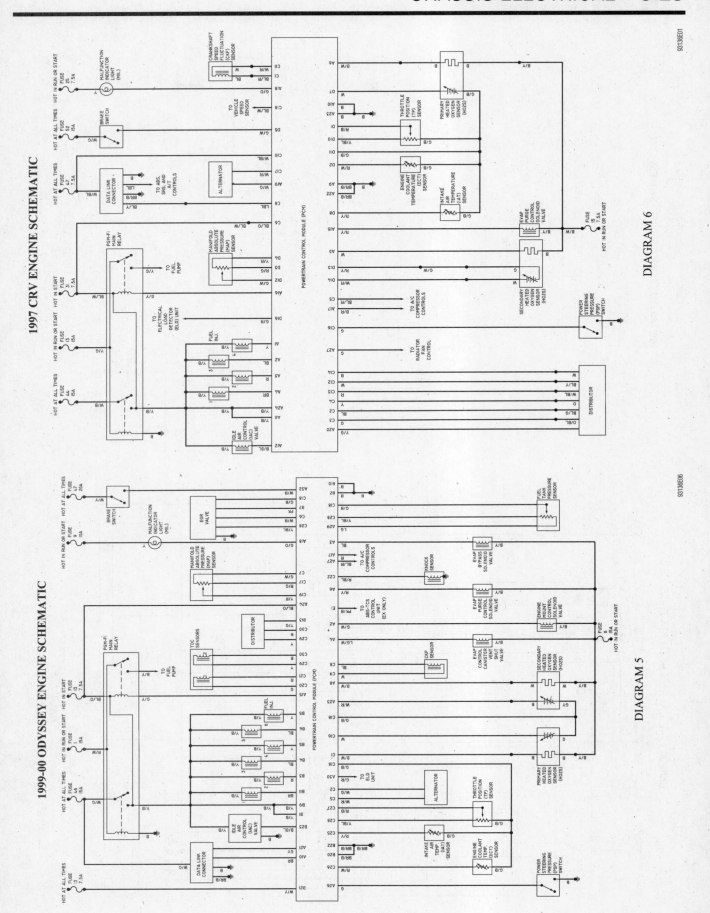

1997 CRV ENGINE SCHEMATIC

1999-00 ODYSSEY ENGINE SCHEMATIC

DIAGRAM 6

DIAGRAM 5

1995-00 ODYSSEY CHASSIS SCHEMATIC

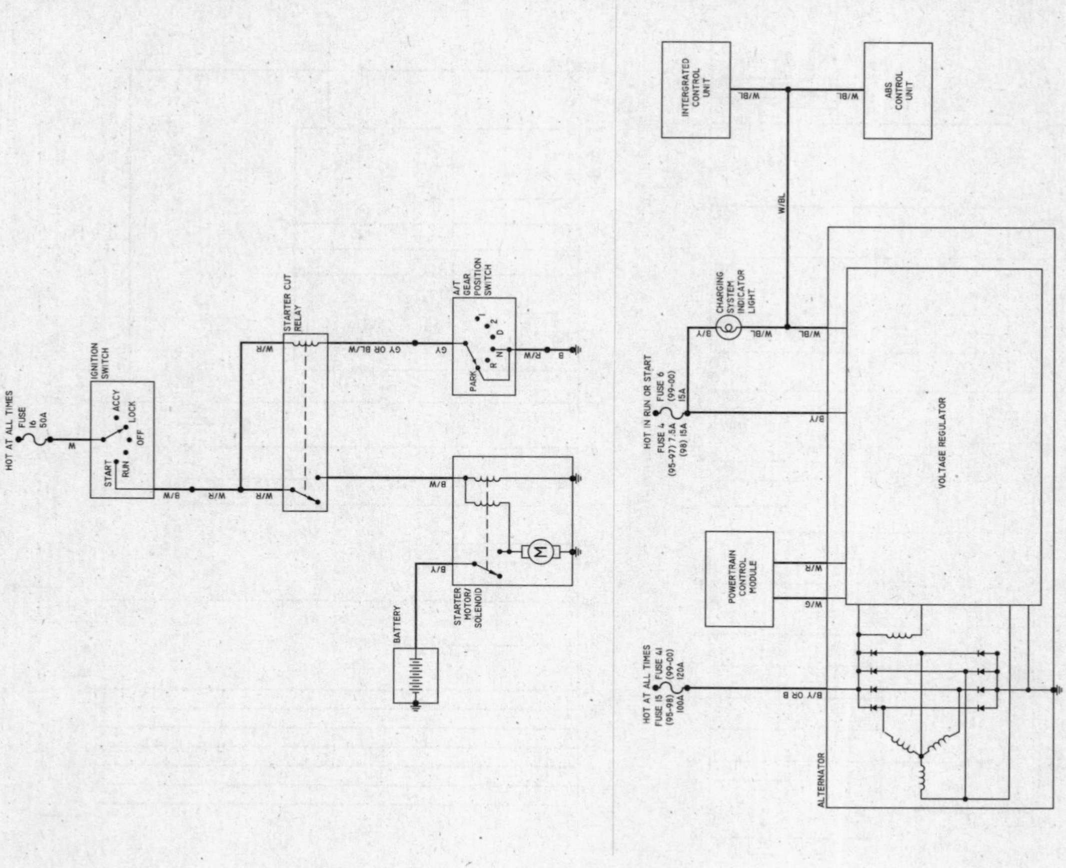

DIAGRAM 8

1998-00 CRV ENGINE SCHEMATIC

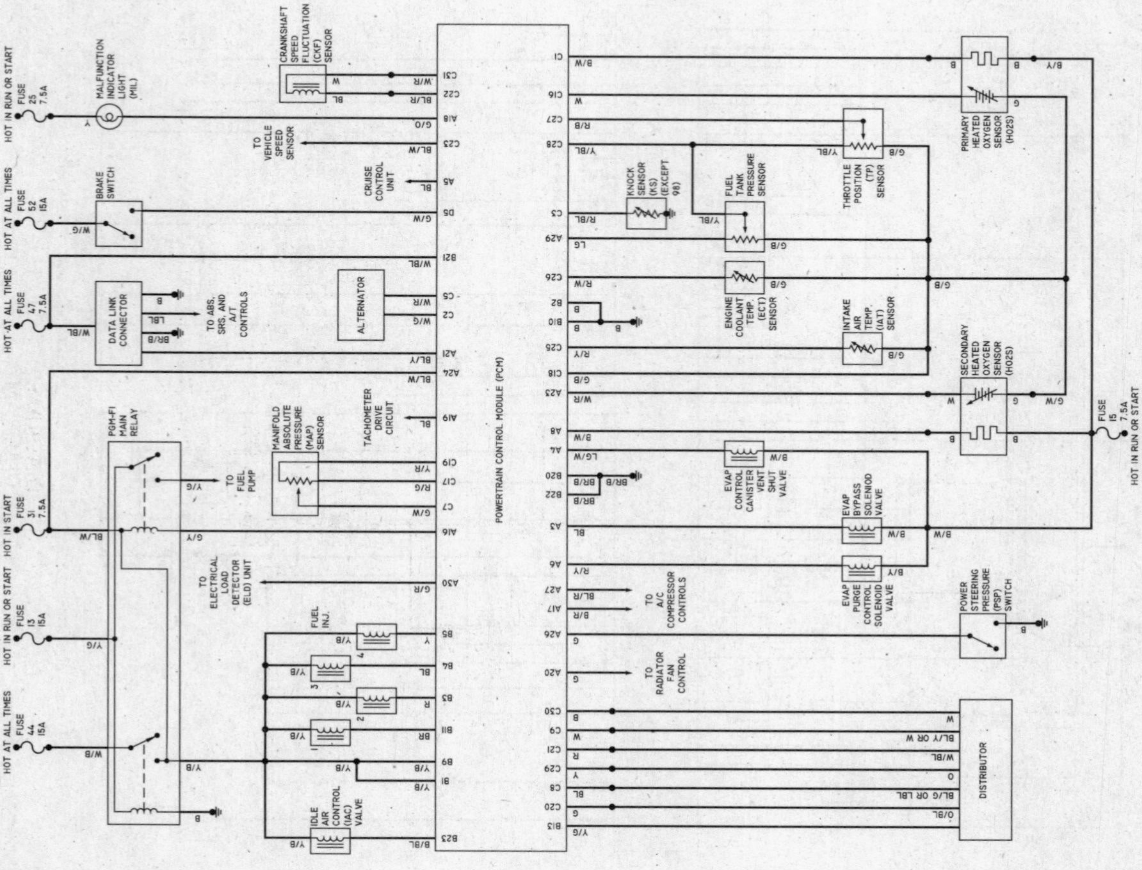

DIAGRAM 7

1995-00 ODYSSEY CHASSIS SCHEMATIC

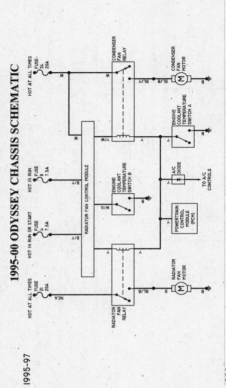

1995-97

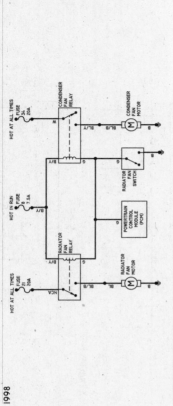

1998

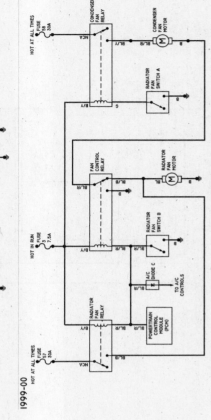

DIAGRAM 10

1999-00

1995-00 ODESSEY CHASSIS SCHEMATIC

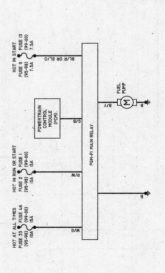

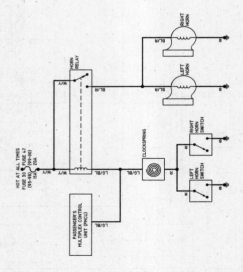

DIAGRAM 9

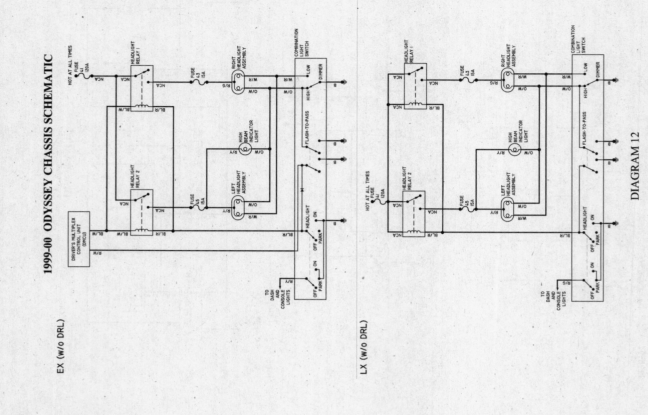

1999-00 ODYSSEY CHASSIS SCHEMATIC

EX (w/o DRL)

LX (w/o DRL)

DIAGRAM 12

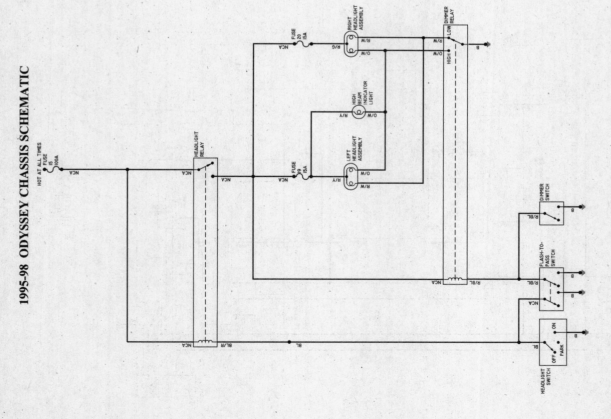

1995-98 ODYSSEY CHASSIS SCHEMATIC

DIAGRAM 11

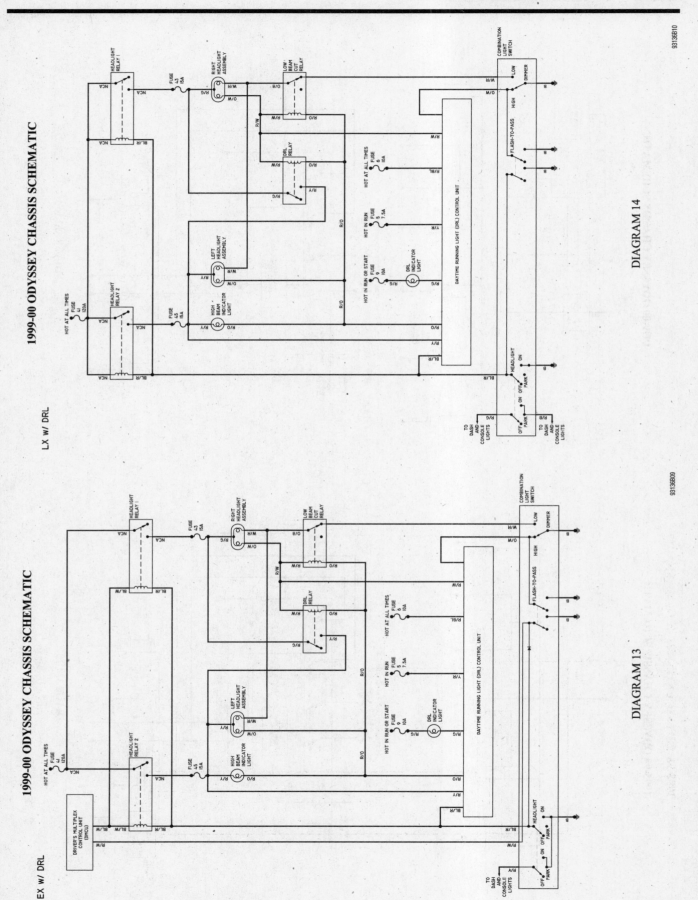

1999-00 ODYSSEY CHASSIS SCHEMATIC

LX w/ DRL

DIAGRAM 14

1999-00 ODYSSEY CHASSIS SCHEMATIC

EX w/ DRL

DIAGRAM 13

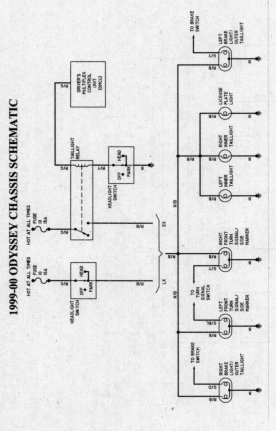

1999-00 ODYSSEY CHASSIS SCHEMATIC

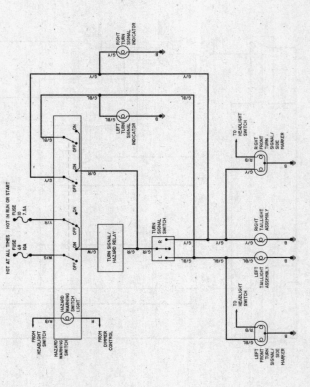

DIAGRAM 16

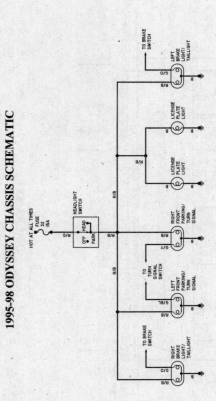

1995-98 ODYSSEY CHASSIS SCHEMATIC

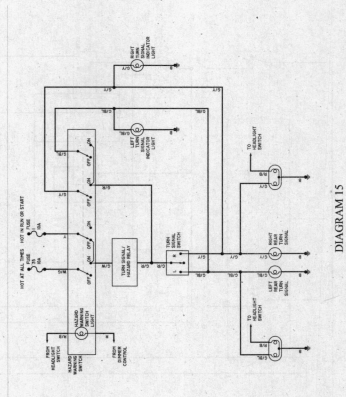

DIAGRAM 15

1999-00 ODYSSEY CHASSIS SCHEMATIC

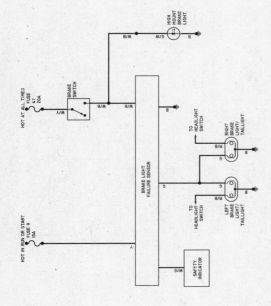

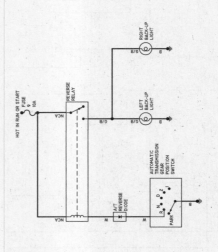

DIAGRAM 18

1995-98 ODYSSEY CHASSIS SCHEMATIC

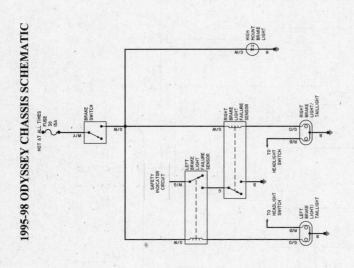

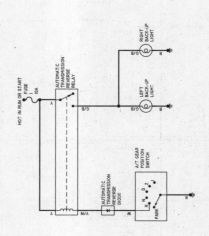

DIAGRAM 17

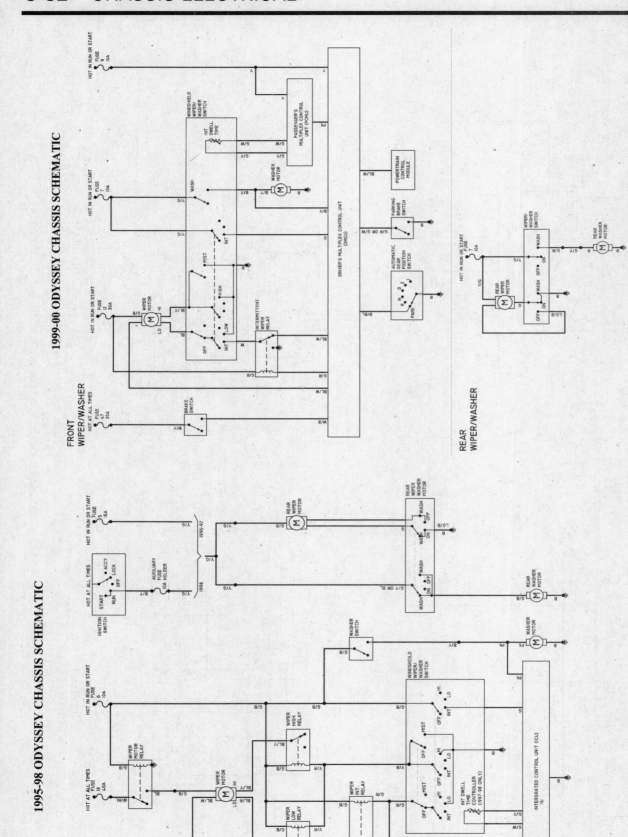

1999-00 ODYSSEY CHASSIS SCHEMATIC

FRONT
WIPER/WASHER

REAR
WIPER/WASHER

DIAGRAM 20

1995-98 ODYSSEY CHASSIS SCHEMATIC

DIAGRAM 19

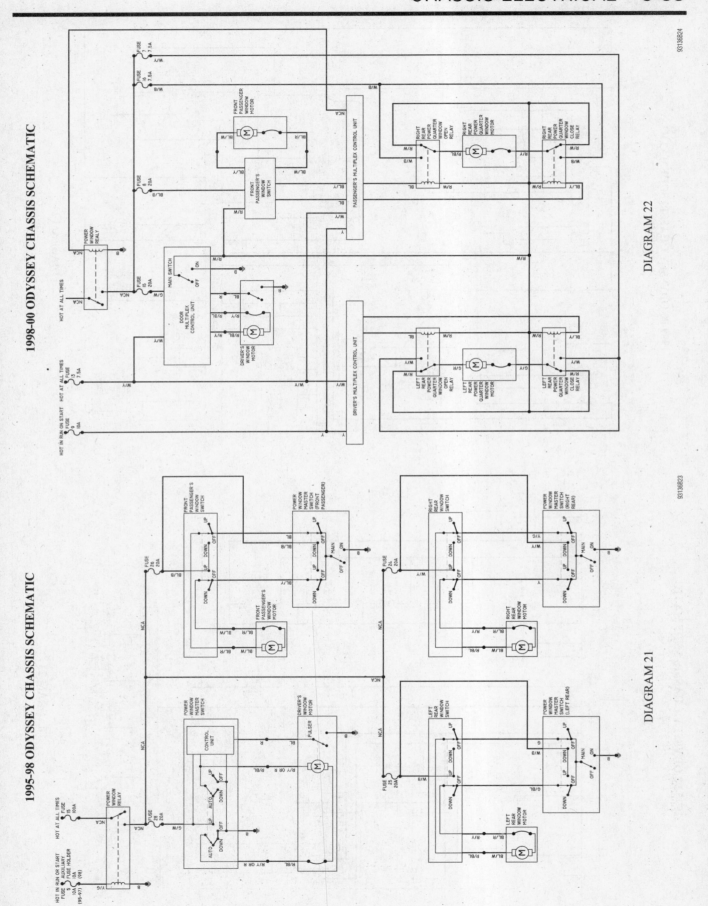

1998-00 ODYSSEY CHASSIS SCHEMATIC

DIAGRAM 22

1995-98 ODYSSEY CHASSIS SCHEMATIC

DIAGRAM 21

1999-00 ODYSSEY CHASSIS SCHEMATIC

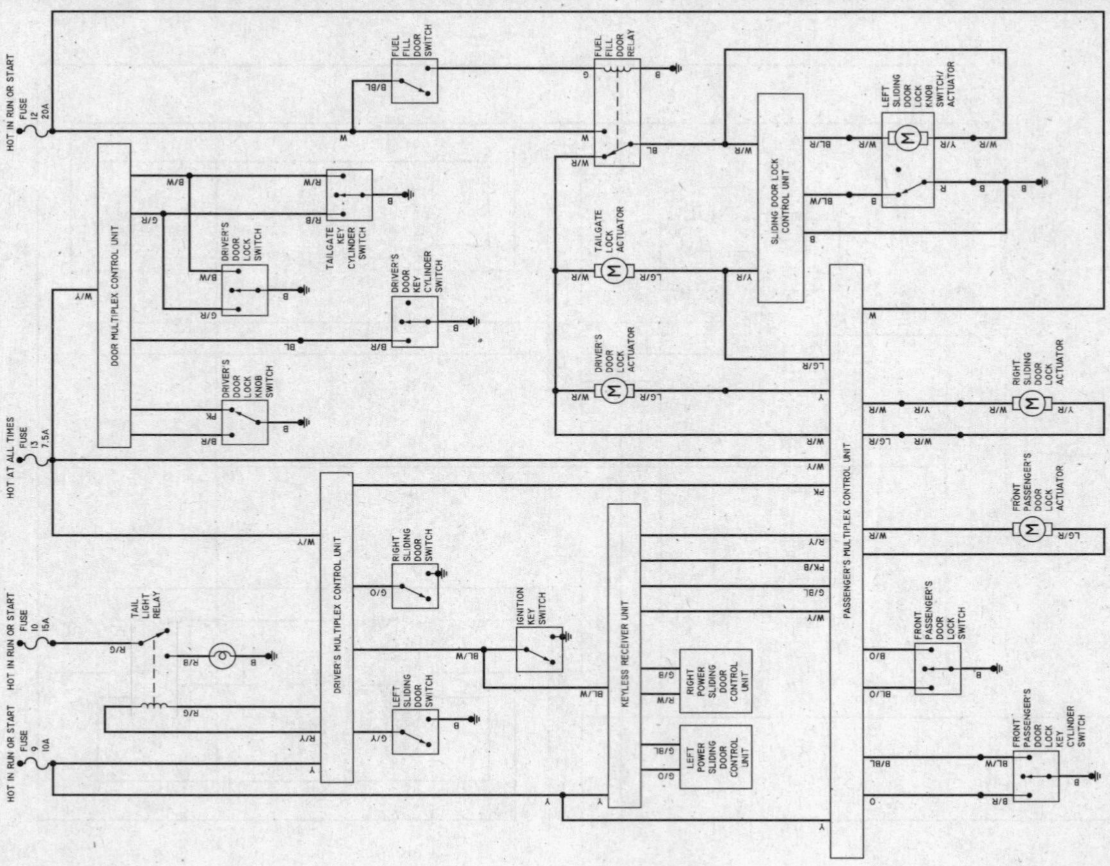

DIAGRAM 24

93136830

EX

1995-98 ODYSSEY CHASSIS SCHEMATIC

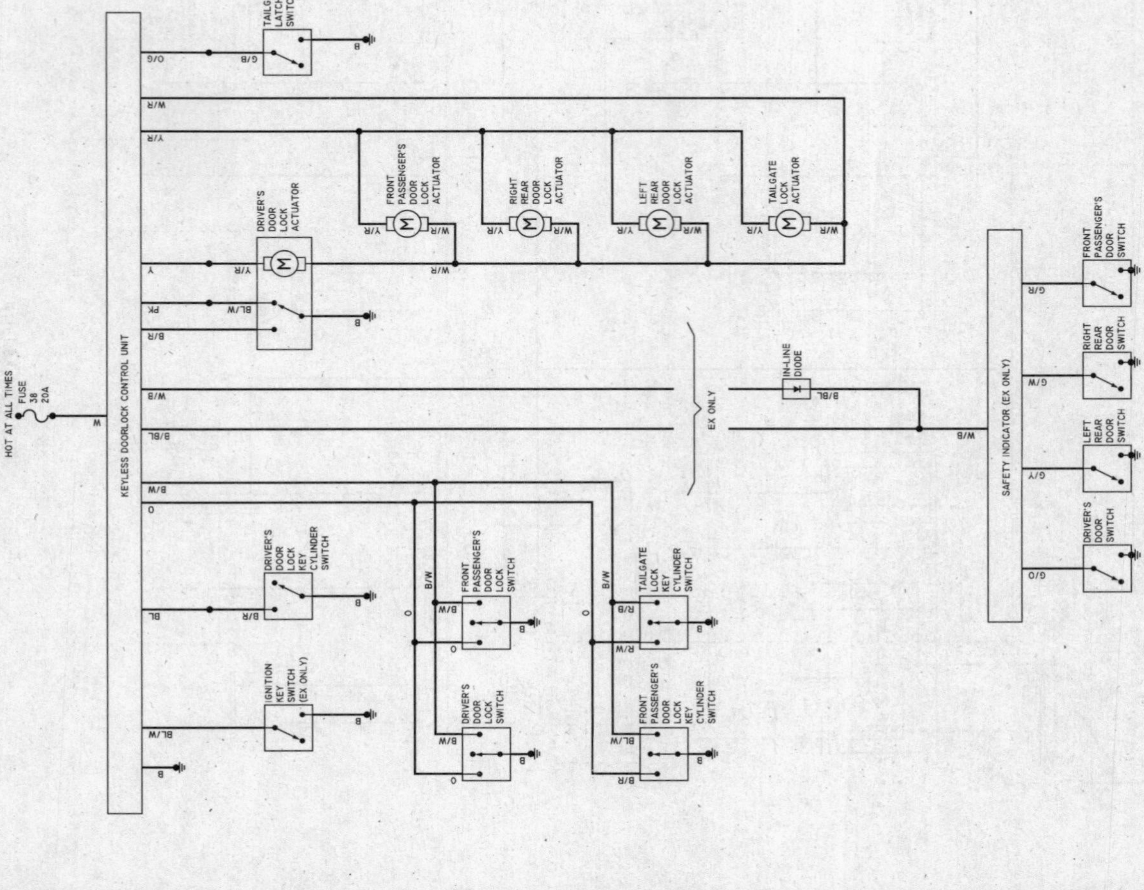

DIAGRAM 23

93136827

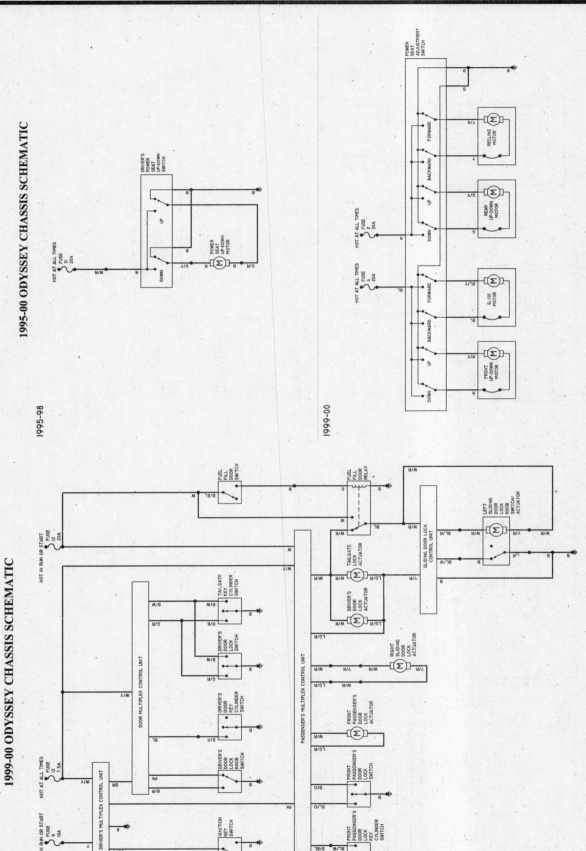

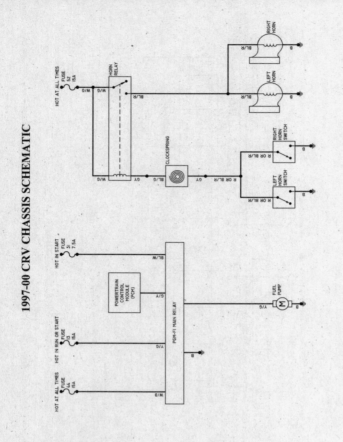

1997-00 CRV CHASSIS SCHEMATIC

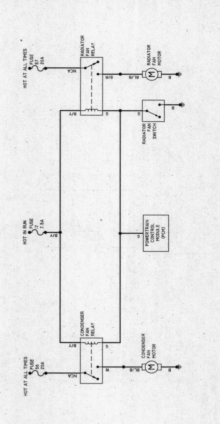

DIAGRAM 28

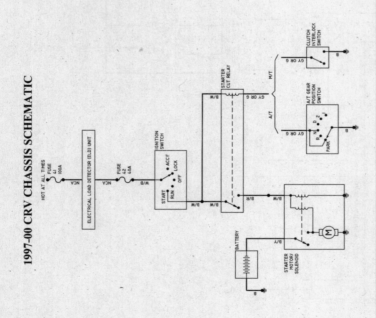

1997-00 CRV CHASSIS SCHEMATIC

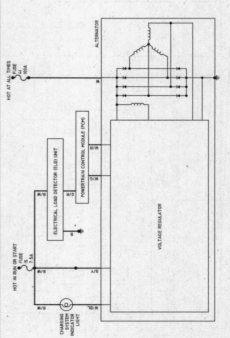

DIAGRAM 27

1997-00 CRV CHASSIS SCHEMATIC

w/o DRL

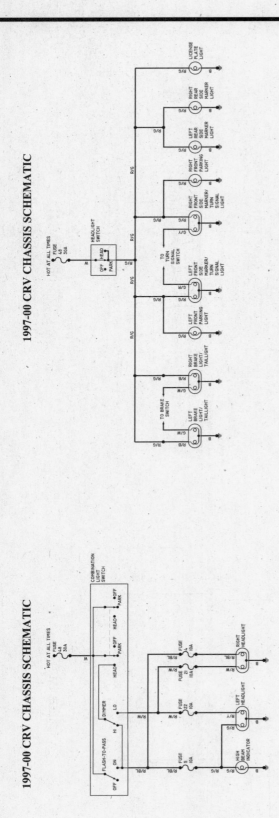

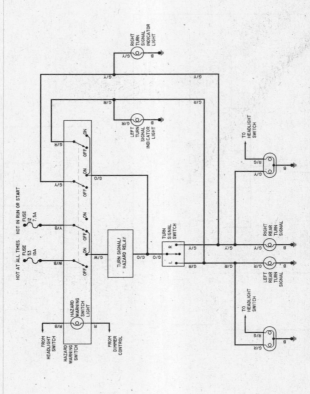

DIAGRAM 30

DIAGRAM 29

w/ DRL

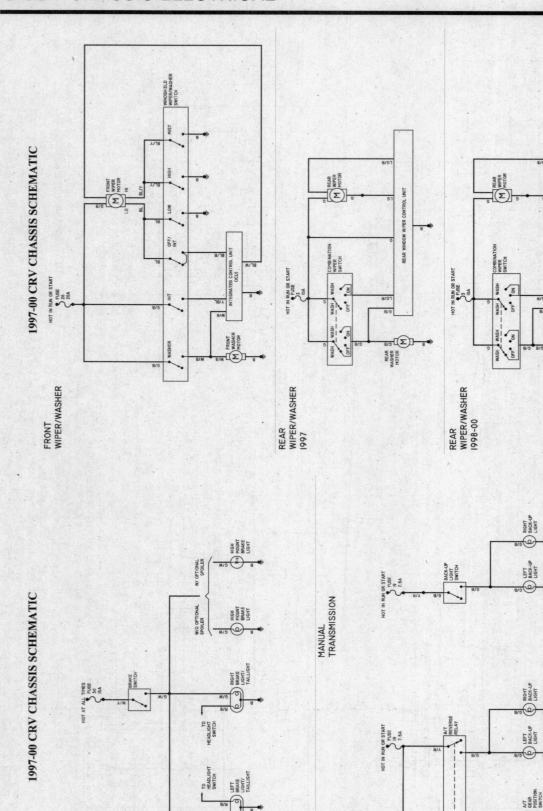

1997-00 CRV CHASSIS SCHEMATIC

FRONT WIPER/WASHER

REAR WIPER/WASHER 1997

REAR WIPER/WASHER 1998-00

DIAGRAM 32

1997-00 CRV CHASSIS SCHEMATIC

MANUAL TRANSMISSION

AUTOMATIC TRANSMISSION

DIAGRAM 31

1997-00 CRV CHASSIS SCHEMATIC

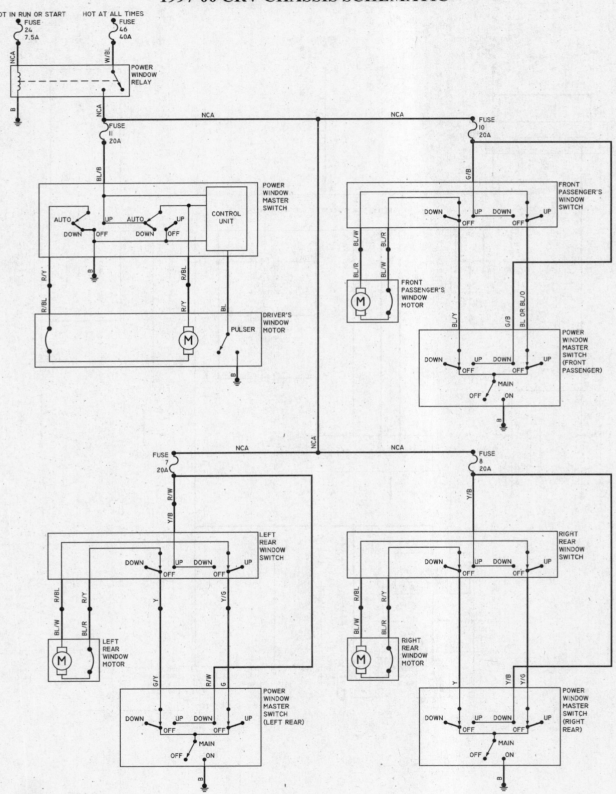

DIAGRAM 33

1996-00 CRV CHASSIS SCHEMATIC

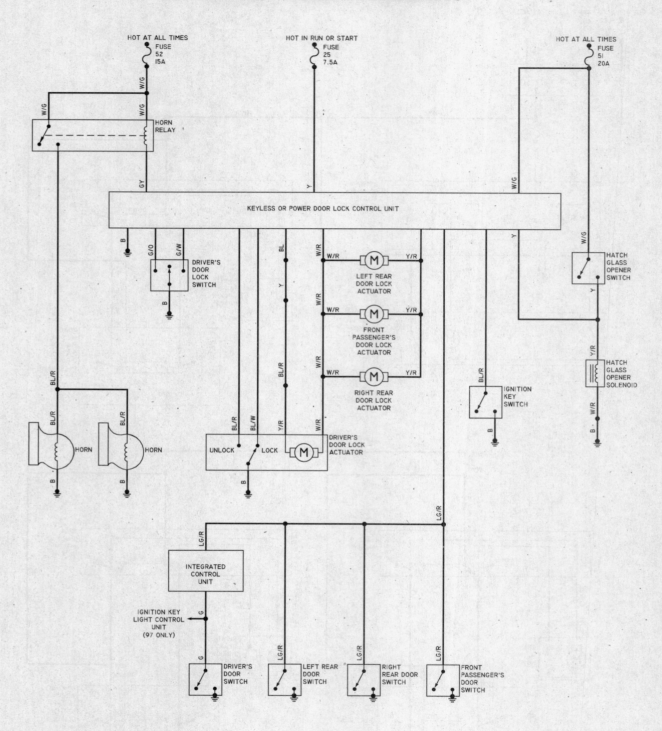

DIAGRAM 34

93136B25

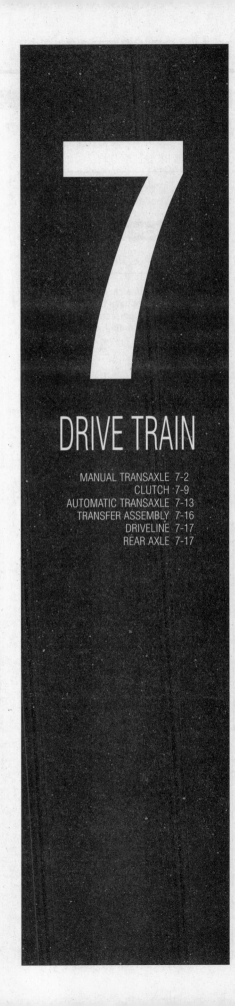

7

DRIVE TRAIN

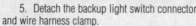

MANUAL TRANSAXLE

Back-up Light Switch

REMOVAL & INSTALLATION

For back-up light switch replacement, please refer to the procedure located in Section 6 of this manual.

Transaxle Assembly

REMOVAL & INSTALLATION

➡**The radio may have a coded theft protection circuit. Make sure you have the code before disconnecting the battery, removing the radio fuse, or removing the radio.**

CR-V Models

♦ **See Figures 1 thru 8**

1. Disconnect the negative battery cable, then the positive battery cable.
2. Remove the air cleaner case and the air intake tube.
3. Remove the clutch pipe bracket and slave cylinder. Do not operate the clutch pedal once the slave cylinder has been removed.
4. Disconnect the starter motor cables, transmission ground cable and the Vehicle Speed Sensor (VSS) connector.

5. Detach the backup light switch connector and wire harness clamp.
6. Remove the cotter keys and bolts securing the shift cable assembly to the shift linkage. Be sure to note that the location of the plastic washer should between the cable end and the steel washer.

➡**Be careful not to bend or kink the cable when removing it.**

7. Remove the cable bracket from the clutch housing.
8. Remove the four upper transaxle-to-engine mounting bolts and the lower starter mounting bolt.
9. Safely raise and support the vehicle.
10. Remove the front wheels.
11. Drain the transaxle oil into a suitable container. Install the drain plug with a new washer.
12. Remove the front lower splash shield and guard bar. There are three types of fasteners securing these in place:
   a. The inner fender fasteners are two pieces. The inner button looking piece must be carefully pried out of the holder, then the holder can be removed.
   b. The guard bar and front center fasteners are attached with a 6mm bolt and are removed with a 10mm socket, on a 6 inch extension and a ratchet.
   c. The outer forward fasteners are Phillips head screws.
13. Disconnect the heated Oxygen (O_2S) sensor connector.

14. Remove and discard the two nuts attaching exhaust pipe "A" to the hanger bracket.
15. Remove and discard the nuts attaching exhaust pipe "A" to the exhaust manifold, then discard the exhaust gaskets.
16. Remove and discard the nuts attaching the exhaust system to the catalytic converter, then discard the exhaust gasket. Remove exhaust pipe "A" from the vehicle.
17. On 4-Wheel Drive (4WD) models do the following:
   a. Make matchmarks on the output shaft flange and the driveshaft flange prior to removal for proper alignment when reinstalling.
   b. Remove the four bolts that attach the driveshaft to the transfer assembly and separate them.
18. Remove the cotter pins and castle nuts from the front lower ball joints. Separate the ball joints from the lower control arms. Discard the cotter pins.
19. Remove the right strut fork pinch bolt and lower through bolt and nut, then remove the strut fork from the lower control arm.
20. Pry the right halfshaft out of the differential, then discard the set ring on the inner joint.
21. Pry the left halfshaft out of the intermediate shaft, discard the set ring on the inner joint.
22. Tie plastic bags over the halfshaft joints to keep the splines of the joints clean.
23. Remove the intermediate shaft mounting bolts, and remove the intermediate shaft.

Fig. 1 Remove the air cleaner housing assembly

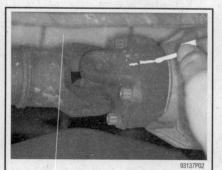

Fig. 2 Matchmark the driveshaft to output flange to make sure both are properly aligned during assembly

Fig. 3 Unfasten the retaining bolts, then remove the clutch slave cylinder

Fig. 4 Carefully pull the transaxle away from the engine assembly

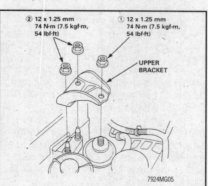

Fig. 5 Upper bracket tightening sequence—CR-V models

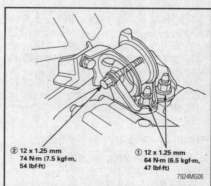

Fig. 6 Transition mount fastener tightening sequence and values—CR-V models

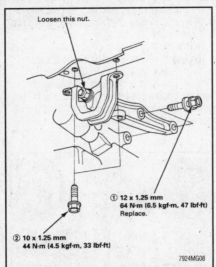

① 12 x 1.25 mm
64 N·m (6.5 kgf·m, 47 lbf·ft)
Replace.

② 10 x 1.25 mm
44 N·m (4.5 kgf·m, 33 lbf·ft)

7924MG08

Fig. 7 Right front mount/bracket tightening sequence—CR-V models

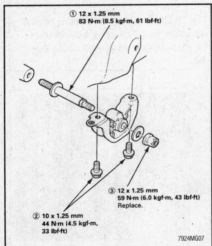

① 12 x 1.25 mm
83 N·m (8.5 kgf·m, 61 lbf·ft)

③ 12 x 1.25 mm
59 N·m (6.0 kgf·m, 43 lbf·ft)
Replace.

② 10 x 1.25 mm
44 N·m (4.5 kgf·m, 33 lbf·ft)

7924MG07

Fig. 8 Left front mount/bracket tightening sequence—CR-V models

24. Remove the set ring from the intermediate shaft and install a new set ring.

25. Remove the rear engine stiffener.

26. Remove the lower clutch housing cover.

27. Remove the right front mount/bracket.

28. Place a transaxle jack under the transaxle and raise it just enough to take tension off the mount, then remove the transaxle mount bracket and mount.

29. Remove the rear engine mount bolts and the transaxle mounting bolts.

30. While supporting the transaxle on a suitable transaxle jack, pull the transaxle away from the engine until the mainshaft is clear, and then lower the transmission.

➥**Be careful not to bend the clutch line.**

31. Remove the starter motor, clutch release bearing, fork and boot.

To install:

32. Install the dowel pins to the clutch housing.

33. Apply a suitable super high temperature grease to the following components:
    a. The release fork bolt.
    b. The spline of the transaxle input shaft.
    c. The inside of the release bearing and the sleeve on the transaxle input shaft where the release bearing rides.
    d. The tips of the release fork and where the slave cylinder pin rides on the release fork.

34. Install the release fork boot.

35. Place the transaxle assembly on the transaxle jack and raise it to engine level.

36. Install the transaxle mounting bolts and new rear mount bracket bolts. Tighten the transaxle mounting bolts to 47 ft. lbs. (64 Nm) and the rear mount bolts to 61 ft. lbs. (83 Nm).

37. Raise the transaxle and install the transaxle mount. First tighten the mounting nuts and bolt to the transaxle to 47 ft. lbs. (64 Nm), then tighten the mounting through bolt to 54 ft. lbs. (74 Nm).

38. Install the four upper transaxle mounting bolts and the lower starter bolt. Tighten the upper transaxle mounting bolts to 47 ft. lbs. (54 Nm), then tighten the lower starter bolt to 33 ft. lbs. (44 Nm).

39. Install the right front mount/bracket. Tighten the three engine bolts to 47 ft. lbs. (64 Nm), and tighten the two frame mounting bolts to 33 ft. lbs. (44 Nm).

40. Install the clutch cover. Tighten the 6x1mm bolts to 104 inch lbs. (12 Nm), tighten the 8x1.25mm bolts to 17 ft. lbs. (24 Nm). Tighten the 12x1.25mm bolt to 22 ft. lbs. (29 Nm).

41. Install the rear engine stiffener. Tighten the bolt attaching the stiffener to the transaxle to 33 ft. lbs. (44 Nm). Tighten the bolts attaching the stiffener(s) to the engine to 18 ft. lbs. (24 Nm).

42. Pour 1 quart (1 liter) of transmission fluid into the transaxle through the opening where the intermediate shaft is installed.

43. Install the intermediate shaft with a new snap ring and tighten the bolts to 29 ft. lbs. (39 Nm).

44. Remove the transaxle jack and the jackstand from the engine.

45. Install new set ring to the halfshafts.

46. Turn the right steering knuckle fully outward and slide the halfshaft into the differential unit until you feel the spring clip engage. Turn the left steering knuckle fully outward and slide the halfshaft onto the intermediate shaft until you feel the spring clip engage.

47. Install the right strut fork. Tighten the pinch bolt to 32 ft. lbs. (43 Nm) and tighten the fork lower through bolt and nut to 47 ft. lbs. (64 Nm).

48. Connect the lower ball joints to the lower control arms, tighten the castle nuts to 36–43 ft. lbs. (49–59 Nm). Install new cotter pins.

49. Install exhaust pipe "A" using new gaskets and locknuts. Tighten the nuts attaching the exhaust pipe to the exhaust manifold to 40 ft. lbs. (54 Nm). Tighten the nuts attaching the exhaust system to the catalytic converter to 16 ft. lbs. (22 Nm). Tighten the exhaust pipe hanger nuts to 12 ft. lbs. (16 Nm).

50. Install the engine splash shield.

51. Apply a suitable super high temperature grease to the tip of the slave cylinder and install the slave cylinder to the transaxle. Tighten the mounting bolts to 16 ft. lbs. (22 Nm). Install the clutch bracket pipe and tighten the mounting bolts to 56 inch lbs. (9.8 Nm).

52. Install the front wheels and lower the vehicle.

53. Attach the VSS sensor and the starter motor connectors.

54. Connect the transaxle ground cable and the backup light switch connector.

55. Install the shift cable bracket and cable.

56. Install the air cleaner housing assembly with the air intake tube.

57. Refill the transaxle with the proper type and amount of lubricant.

58. Connect the positive, then the negative battery cables.

59. Check the operation of the clutch and smooth operation of the shifter.

60. Check the front wheel alignment and road test the vehicle.

61. Enter the radio security code.

Halfshafts

♦ **See Figure 9**

The Honda CR-V and Odyssey models use the front halfshafts to couple the transaxle to the road wheels. This allows power to be delivered as the suspension moves up and down and while the wheels are turned side to side to negotiate turns. In order to accomplish the ability to simultaneously supply rotational power and the ability to change direction, an axle must have a component that can pivot and rotate at the same time.

On the Honda CR-V and Odyssey models, this is accomplished by using a halfshaft with an inner and outer Constant Velocity (CV) joint. In order to lubricate the CV-joint, the joint is assembled using an approved high temperature molybdenum disulfide grease capable of withstanding extreme pressure and heat. The grease is retained in the CV-joint by a tapered accordion boot, which is installed over the axle and the CV-joint.

The CV-boot allows the CV-joint to rotate and pivot, while retaining the lubricant and protecting the CV-joint from water and debris.

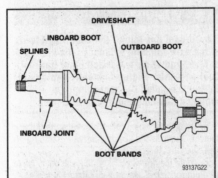

93137G22

Fig. 9 A typical halfshaft used on the CR-V and Odyssey models. Note the small doughnut shaped dynamic damper in the center of the driveshaft of this halfshaft

HALFSHAFT INSPECTION

When inspecting a halfshaft, it is more likely to have an outer CV-joint or CV-boot failure because the outer CV-joint pivots more when the vehicle is turning than the inner CV-joint. The outer CV-boot is more vulnerable to physical damage because of its location, unlike the inner CV-joint/boot, which is surrounded by the transaxle, engine, and the vehicle's body.

A rear halfshaft failure on the 4WD CR-V model is much less likely than a front halfshaft failure because the CV-joints do not have to pivot like the front halfshafts must and because the power delivery is only present at the rear wheels when the front wheels loose traction.

Although the CV-joint lubricant is sealed in place via the CV-boot, grease does lose its ability to lubricate with time and use. If a vehicle is used in extreme conditions under severe loads, it's likely the CV-joint lubricant could loose its ability to lubricate within 5 years or 100,000 miles (160,000 km) or less.

In these extreme cases, the CV-boots should be removed, and the CV-joints cleaned and repacked with the recommended lubricant.

To diagnose a CV-joint failure, proceed as follows:

1. Road test the vehicle and listen for a "clicking" noise from the left front or right front wheel area, especially during moderate acceleration from a stop while turning. Use a large, safe parking lot and accelerate from a stop, alternately turning left and right. A clicking noise from the front of the vehicle is an indication of a worn CV-joint.

2. Apply the parking brake and put the transmission in neutral with the ignition in the **OFF** position.

3. Carefully raise and safely support the vehicle.

4. Rotate the tire/wheel assembly slowly by hand. Turn the front wheels side to side to simulate a turn to inspect the halfshaft Constant Velocity (CV) joint boots for leakage, wear, cracks, punctures or tears.

➡ **If an outer CV-boot is leaking, the inside portion of the road wheel and surrounding suspension components will be covered with grease. The cost of a typical CV joint is many times more expensive than a CV-boot.**

❊❊ WARNING

If a CV-boot has failed, the centrifugal force of the axle spinning will cause the lubricant to leak, and allow water and other harmful debris to enter and permanently damage the CV-joint. A failed CV-boot should be replaced immediately.

5. Wrap a suitable protective cloth around the center of the axle and securely fasten a clamping-type pliers to the axle.

6. Hold the tire/wheel assembly stationary while trying to rotate the axle back and forth while checking for excessive looseness from the outer CV-joint. Then hold the inner CV-joint and move the axle back and forth to check for excessive looseness. A slight amount of free movement is acceptable, however, if the axle can be moved ³⁄₁₆ inches (5mm) or more, the CV-joint should be replaced.

Symptoms of a failed CV-joint could include:
• A clicking noise during moderate acceleration, especially when turning.
• A shuddering vibration or rumbling noise when driving, especially when accelerating.
• A clunking noise when shifting from, or moving from, forward to reverse to forward.

➡ **A shuddering vibration or rumbling noise can also be caused by a failed wheel bearing, severe tire imbalance, or a tire with internal belt damage. Should this symptom occur, the problem should be diagnosed immediately.**

REMOVAL & INSTALLATION

▶ **See Figures 10 thru 19**

The outer CV-joint cannot be removed from the halfshaft with the halfshaft installed in the vehicle. Replacement of the CV-joint(s) or CV-boot(s) requires removal of the halfshaft. If the outer CV-joint has failed on vehicles produced before 1998, the shaft and CV-joint must be replaced as an assembly.

➡ **If the halfshaft assembly or outer CV-joint is to be replaced, make sure to note whether or not the vehicle is equipped with ABS brakes to ensure the correct replacement parts.**

The following procedure covers vehicles equipped with manual or automatic transaxles.

1. Disconnect the negative battery cable.

2. With the vehicle on the ground, raise the locking tab on the axle nut and loosen it using a sturdy ½ inch drive breaker bar and a 32mm (1¼) inch socket, then loosen the wheels.

3. Raise and safely support the vehicle and remove the axle spindle nut(s) and front wheel(s).

4. Drain the differential or transaxle lubricant as needed. On CR-V and 4-cylinder Odyssey models, the differential does not have to be drained if the left driveshaft is to be removed. On V6 Odyssey models, the differential does not have to be drained if the right driveshaft is to be removed.

5. Remove the sway bar stabilizer link from the shock or control arm assembly.

6. On CR-V and 4-cylinder Odyssey models, remove the strut fork through bolt and nut and the strut pinch bolt, then remove the strut fork. Discard and replace the through bolt nut.

7. Remove and discard the cotter key for the lower ball joint nut, remove the nut, then separate the lower ball joint from the lower control arm using a suitable ball joint removal tool.

8. Pull downward on the lower control arm to allow the steering knuckle to be removed from the ball joint.

9. Pull the knuckle outward and remove the halfshaft outboard CV-joint from the knuckle using a plastic mallet or a hammer and a suitable punch.

10. To remove the inner CV-joint from the transaxle assembly, perform the following:

a. Using a suitable prytool, carefully pry out the inboard CV-joint approximately ½inch (13mm) in order to force the spring clip out of the groove in the differential side gears or intermediate shaft.

❊❊ WARNING

Be careful not to damage the oil seal. Do not pull on the axle to release the retainer as the inboard CV-joint may come apart.

11. To remove the inner CV-joint from the intermediate shaft assembly, perform the following:

a. Tap on the inboard CV-joint with a plastic hammer or a suitable blunt drift to release the CV-joint from the intermediate shaft.

12. Pull the halfshaft straight out of the differential or the intermediate shaft. Replace the spring clip on the end of the inboard joint.

To install:

13. Install new retainer clips on the splined shafts of the axle.

14. If the axle is being installed into the transaxle, apply a thin film of light grease to the lips of the transaxle seal and the portion of the CV-joint that contacts the seal.

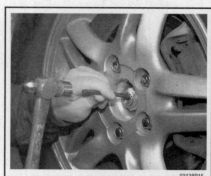

93138P15

Fig. 10 Before raising the vehicle, remove the center cap, then using a chisel, carefully tap the lock tab upward on the axle nut

93138P16

Fig. 11 Choose chisel that will fit in the notch of the threaded portion of the axle to relieve the lock tab

93138P17

Fig. 12 Once the axle nut lock tab is relieved, use a heavy duty ½ inch drive breaker bar and a 32mm socket to loosen the nut

15. If the axle is being installed onto the intermediate shaft, apply a high temperature grease to the splines of the shaft, then wipe the grease away from the snap ring groove and intervals of 2–3 splines on the shaft to allow air to bleed.

16. Install the inner CV-joints making sure they "snap" into place allowing the retainer clips to be fully seated.

The balance of the installation is the reverse of removal, noting the following points:

17. On CR-V and 4-cylinder Odyssey models:
   a. Tighten the lower ball joint to 36–43 ft. lbs. (49–59 Nm) and install a new cotter key.

Fig. 13 Use a tie rod end/ball joint removal tool to remove the ball joint from the lower control arm

Fig. 14 Use a 14mm box end wrench and a 5mm hex wrench to remove the stabilizer link—CR-V model shown

Fig. 15 Once the axle nut has been removed and the knuckle released from the ball joint, drive the axle out of the hub assembly with a hammer and a punch, or a plastic mallet

   b. Tighten the damper fork pinch bolt to 32 ft. lbs. (43 Nm), and the though bolt with a new self locking nut to 47 ft. lbs. (64 Nm).

18. On V6 Odyssey models:
   a. Tighten the lower ball joint to 43–51 ft. lbs. (59–69 Nm) and install a new locking key.
   b. Tighten the stabilizer link to 58 ft. lbs. (78 Nm).

19. Use a new axle nut, tighten the axle nut to 181 ft. lbs. (245 Nm), and then stake the nut into the slot in the axle using a hammer and a suitable punch.

Fig. 16 Pull the steering knuckle assembly outward and away from the outer CV-joint—CR-V model shown

Fig. 17 Using a suitable prytool, carefully release the inner CV-joint from the transaxle. When reinstalling make sure to use a new retainer snap-ring

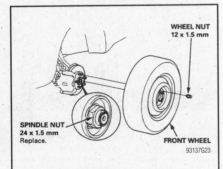

Fig. 18 When installing the halfshaft, always use a new spindle nut, tighten the spindle nut and wheel nuts to specification, and then stake the spindle nut into the slot of the spindle

Fig. 19 A click-type torque wrench works well when having to tighten a nut to 181 ft. lbs. (245 Nm). The audible click can be heard even as the technician strains to tighten the nut

20. Tighten the wheel nuts to 80 ft. lbs. (108 Nm).
21. Refill the transaxle assembly with the approved and appropriate lubricant.
22. Connect the negative battery cable.
23. Enter the radio security code.
24. Check the wheel alignment and adjust as necessary.

CV-JOINT OVERHAUL

▶ See Figures 20 thru 38

The replacement CV-boot clamps can be one of three types, a folding double clamped band, a double loop band, or an ear clamp band. Do not substitute ordinary radiator hose clamps or plastic ties in place of a CV-boot clamp.

> **✳✳ CAUTION**
>
> When replacing a CV-joint or CV-boot, do NOT reuse the CV-boot clamps.

➥The Canadian and USA versions of the CR-V and Odyssey models produced before 1999 use different outer CV-boots and clamps. The Canadian models use outer CV-boots made of Thermoplastic Polyester Elastomer (TPE), while the USA models use rubber.

> **✳✳ WARNING**
>
> When removing a CV-joint, make sure to matchmark all the components before disassembly to ensure the components are installed exactly in the same location from which they were removed. If a component is to be replaced, make sure to install the replacement part in the exact location as the component being replaced. Failure to reinstall the components correctly could result in premature failure or excessive driveline vibration.

If a CV-boot has failed and is to be replaced, the CV-joint from where the failed boot was located **must** be cleaned and repacked with the appropriate lubricant.

When the outer CV-boot is to be replaced and/or the outer CV-joint serviced, if special tools are not available to remove the outer CV-joint, simply dis-

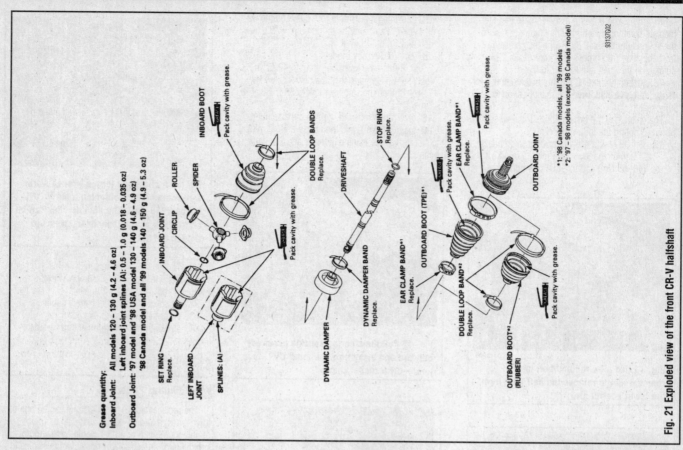

Grease quantity:
Inboard Joint: All models 120 – 130 g (4.2 – 4.6 oz)
   Left inboard joint splines (A): 0.5 – 1.0 g (0.018 – 0.035 oz)
Outboard Joint: '97 model and '98 USA model 130 – 140 g (4.6 – 4.9 oz)
   '98 Canada model and all '99 models 140 – 150 g (4.9 – 5.3 oz)

INBOARD BOOT
Pack cavity with grease.

ROLLER
SPIDER
CIRCLIP
INBOARD JOINT
SET RING
Replace.
LEFT INBOARD JOINT
SPLINES (IA)
Pack cavity with grease.

DOUBLE LOOP BANDS
Replace.

DRIVESHAFT
STOP RING
Replace.

DYNAMIC DAMPER
DYNAMIC DAMPER BAND
Replace.

EAR CLAMP BAND*¹
Replace.

OUTBOARD BOOT (TPE)*¹
Pack cavity with grease.

EAR CLAMP BAND*²
Replace.
Pack cavity with grease.

OUTBOARD JOINT

DOUBLE LOOP BAND*²
Replace.

OUTBOARD BOOT*²
(RUBBER)
Pack cavity with grease.

*1: '98 Canada models, all '99 models
*2: '97 – 98 models (except '98 Canada model)

Fig. 21 Exploded view of the front CR-V halfshaft

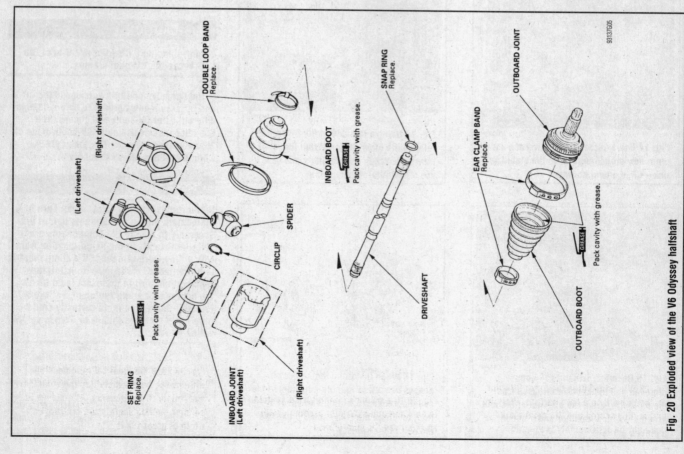

(Right driveshaft)
(Left driveshaft)

DOUBLE LOOP BAND
Replace.

INBOARD BOOT
Pack cavity with grease.

SNAP RING
Replace.

OUTBOARD JOINT

EAR CLAMP BAND
Replace.
Pack cavity with grease.

SPIDER
CIRCLIP

Pack cavity with grease.

SET RING
Replace.

INBOARD JOINT
(Left driveshaft)
(Right driveshaft)

DRIVESHAFT

OUTBOARD BOOT

Fig. 20 Exploded view of the V6 Odyssey halfshaft

assemble and remove the inner CV-joint and boot, then slide the outer boot off of the axle.

If the outer CV-joint has failed, on vehicles produced before 1998, the shaft and CV-joint must be replaced as an assembly.

☀☀ WARNING

If the outer CV-joint is to be replaced, make sure to note whether or not the vehicle is equipped with ABS brakes to ensure the correct replacement parts.

Due to the popularity of halfshafts on front wheel drive and four wheel drive vehicles, axle and halfshaft rebuilding facilities have become increasingly popular. Before removing and disassembling a halfshaft, check locally to see if there is a facility available that will sell a rebuilt halfshaft, or rebuild your halfshaft. You may discover that this is more cost effective and convenient, especially if you remove the halfshaft yourself.

1. Remove the halfshaft assembly.
2. Mark the location of the dynamic damper (if installed) and the CV-boots on the drive axle.
3. Be sure to mark the inner CV-joint roller grooves during disassembly to ensure proper positioning during reassembly.
4. Remove the CV-boot clamps, then remove the boot from the inner CV-joint housing and remove

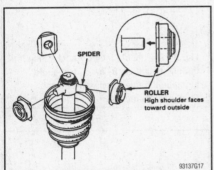

Fig. 22 Matchmark the location of the rollers when removing them from the spider, and matchmark the location of the spider to the splined axle to ensure proper reassembly

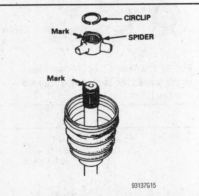

Fig. 23 The spider is held onto the splined drive axle with a circlip. Use a new circlip during reassembly

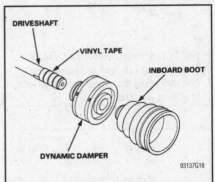

Fig. 24 When removing the components from the drive axle, wrap vinyl tape around the spines to prevent damaging the boot or damper

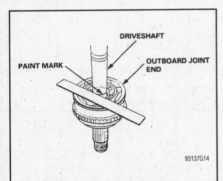

Fig. 25 If removing the outer CV-joint on a 1998 or later vehicle, lay a straight edge across the joint and make a paint mark to ensure proper reassembly

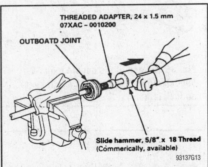

Fig. 26 Removal an outer CV-joint on 1998 or later vehicles requires using a suitable slide hammer and an adapter. If not available, remove the inner components to replace the boot

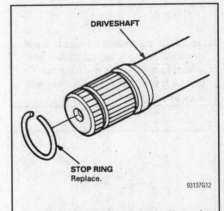

Fig. 27 If the outer CV-joint was removed, replace the stop ring

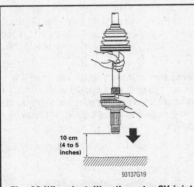

Fig. 28 When installing the outer CV-joint, tap the spindle on a hard surface, until the joint is fully seated and the paint mark made during disassembly is aligned

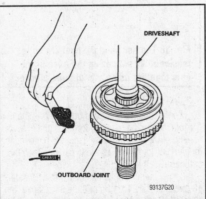

Fig. 29 Use a 2 inch (50mm) wide spatula to pack the outer CV-joint assembly with an approved CV-joint grease

Fig. 30 Pack the inner CV-joint housing with grease before installing the spider and rollers. If the housing (A) attaches to an intermediate shaft, put a tablespoon's worth of grease in it

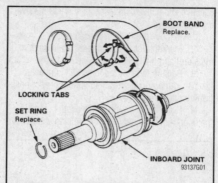

Fig. 31 The folding double clamped CV-boot clamp is removed by opening the tabs and lifting the curved section upward to release the tension

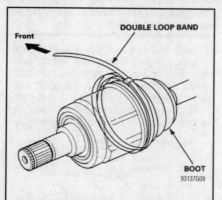

Fig. 32 The double loop CV-boot clamp wraps around the boot and through the clip two times

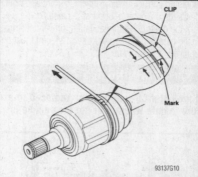

Fig. 33 The double loop CV-boot clamp is initially tensioned by hand, and while being held a line is scribed ½ inch (12mm) from the clip

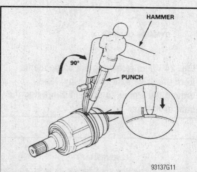

Fig. 34 The double loop CV-boot clamp is then tensioned such that the scribed line is lined up with the clip and folded up. The clip is then crimped using a hammer and a pointed punch

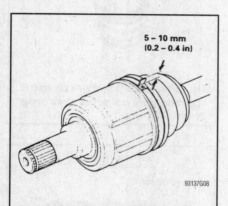

Fig. 35 The end of the double loop CV-boot clamp is then trimmed about ³⁄₁₆ of an inch (10mm) . . .

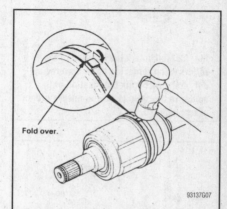

Fig. 36 . . . then fold the clamp over and tap it flush with a small hammer

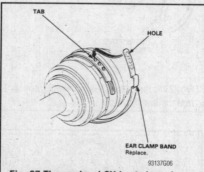

Fig. 37 The ear band CV-boot clamp is assembled by placing the tabs through the holes in the clamp

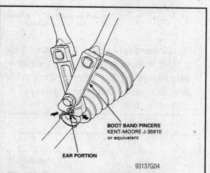

Fig. 38 The ear band CV-boot clamp is tensioned by squeezing the base of the ears together using a boot band pincher

the housing from the inboard spider gear rollers. If the CV-boot clamps are welded, the clamps must be cut using a pair of suitable side cutters.

5. Mark the rollers to the spider gear yoke, and the yoke to the driveshaft so they can be installed in their original positions.

6. Remove the rollers, snapring, and spider gear yoke, then remove the stopper ring.

➡ It may be necessary to use a small universal gear puller to remove the spider gear yoke from the axle.

7. On vehicles produced before 1998, the outer CV-joint cannot be removed from the shaft. Wrap the end of the axle with vinyl tape, the remove the inboard CV-joint boot, dynamic damper, then the outboard CV-joint boot.

8. If a suitable slide hammer with a ⅝ inch x 18 thread and a 24 x 1.5mm threaded adapter Tool No. 07XAC-0010200 or its equivalent are available, the outer CV-joint can be removed on 1998 and later vehicles as follows:

a. Matchmark the CV-joint to the axle for reassembly.

b. Wrap a shop towel around the axle and install the axle securely in a suitable vise.

c. Install the adapter onto the threaded portion of the outer CV-joint and the slide hammer, and remove the CV-joint using the slide hammer.

d. Remove the stop ring.

e. Wrap the end of the axle with vinyl tape and remove the CV-boot.

To install:

9. Wrap the end of the axle splines with vinyl tape to prevent damage to the boots. Install the outboard boot, dynamic strut, and inboard boot, along with their small CV-joint clamps, then remove the vinyl tape.

➡ Make sure to loosely install the small CV-boot and dynamic strut clamps at this time. In some cases it may be impossible to install the small clamps once the CV-joints are reinstalled.

10. If the outer CV-joint was removed from the axle:

a. Install a new stop ring.

b. Align the matchmarks on the axle and CV-joint and lightly seat the axle into the CV-joint until the stop ring end gap is closed.

c. Seat the axle into the CV-joint by holding the axle and CV-joint and tapping the CV-joint using 5 inch (10 cm) strokes onto a hard surface while holding the axle until the stop ring is fully seated into the CV-joint.

d. Place a straight edge across the CV-joint to see if it aligns with the paint mark on the axle, to ensure the CV-joint is fully seated.

11. Using a 2 inch (50mm) paint or gasket scraper, or its equivalent, thoroughly pack the CV-joint with an approved CV-joint grease.

12. Install the CV-boot onto the outer CV-joint.

13. Install the large CV-boot clamp to secure the boot to the outer CV-joint. Do not tighten the small clamp at this time.

The CV-boot clamps can be one of three types, a folding double clamped band, a double loop band, or an ear clamp band. The folding double clamped band has thick curved portion of band that seats into a small bracket and applies tension as the curved portion is pressed downward, and held in place by two folding tabs. The double loop band wraps around the CV-boot twice and through a small clip. The ear clamp band has a series of holes and locking tabs that are locked into the holes.

14. To install a folding double clamped band:

a. Seat the end of the thick curved section into the small bracket.

b. Press the thick curved section down, flush with the band.

c. While holding the curved section down, fold over the locking tabs and seat them by tapping them lightly with a small hammer.

15. To install a double loop band CV-boot clamp proceed as follows:

a. Install the clamp in the direction such that if the axle were installed on the vehicle the clip of the clamp is at the top, with the end of the clamp is facing forward.

b. Wrap the clamp around the boot 2 times, and seat the clamp into the groove of the boot.

c. Pull the end of the clamp by hand to remove any slack in the band, and scribe a mark in the band ½ inch (12mm) from the clip.

d. Using a boot band tool or an equivalent device, pull the end of the clamp until the line is flush with the rear edge of the clip, and then fold the end of the clamp upward so it is at a 90° angle with the clip.

e. While holding the end of the clamp in this position, center punch the clip using a pointed center punch and a hammer.

f. Trim the end of the clamp ⅜ of an inch (10mm) from the end of the clip, fold the clamp end over the clip and seat the folded clamp end by tapping it with a hammer.

16. To install an ear clamp style band clamp proceed as follows:

a. Feed the tab of the band into the holes of the band. Sometimes a small flat blade jewelers screwdriver can be placed through the clamp's hole and the tab levered into place.

b. Squeeze the small raised ear portion at the base of the clamp using a pair of boot band pinchers, or carefully alternate side to side with a thin pair of needle nose pliers, until the gap at the base of the clamp's ear is ⅛ of an inch (3mm) apart.

17. Install the spider gear in its original position by aligning the matchmarks.

18. Fit the snapring onto the halfshaft groove.

19. Fit the rollers to the spider gear with their high shoulders facing outward. Reinstall the rollers in their original positions on the spider gear.

20. Pack the inboard joint housing with an approved CV-joint grease. Do not use a substitute, or mix types of grease.

21. Fit the inboard joint onto the halfshaft while holding the axle with the rollers facing downward to prevent them from falling off, and place the rollers into the inboard joint housing.

22. Install the CV-boot onto the inner CV-joint.

23. Install the large CV-boot clamp to secure the boot to the inner CV-joint. Do not install the small clamp at this time.

24. With the boots installed onto the CV-joints, adjust the CV-boots on the axle in or out to place the boot ends in their original positions.

25. Tighten the new clamps on the small end of the boots and secure as necessary to ensure a good fit.

26. Always use a new set ring whenever the driveshaft is being installed. When reinstalling, be sure the driveshaft ends lock securely in place into the differential or intermediate shaft.

27. Reinstall the halfshaft into the vehicle.

28. Install a new axle nut onto the axle, tighten the axle nut to 181 ft. lbs. (245 Nm).

29. Stake the axle nut into the slot in the axle.

CLUTCH

⁂⁂ CAUTION

The clutch driven disc may contain asbestos, which has been determined to be a cancer causing agent. Never clean clutch surfaces with compressed air! Avoid inhaling any dust from any clutch surface! When cleaning clutch surfaces, use a commercially available brake cleaning fluid.

Driven Disc and Pressure Plate

REMOVAL & INSTALLATION

CR-V Models

▶ See Figures 39 thru 54

➡The radio may have a coded theft protection circuit. Make sure you have the code before disconnecting the battery, removing the radio fuse, or removing the radio.

When removing the transaxle to replace the clutch disk, always replace the clutch disk, release bearing, pilot bearing and pressure plate. Often times these components are sold more economically as a clutch kit.

If the flywheel is damaged or excessively worn, check to see if the flywheel is sold with the clutch replacement parts as a kit. Usually it is more cost effective to buy a complete kit than to purchase the parts individually.

➡If a flywheel with surface irregularities is reused, it is very likely that when driving, the clutch will chatter as it is engaged.

Try to avoid the use of rebuilt parts, as at times, the expense saved on parts may be far less justified than the labor cost (or time) to do the job a second time.

1. Before servicing the vehicle, refer to the precautions in the beginning of this section.

2. Disconnect the negative battery cable.

3. Remove the manual transaxle assembly from the vehicle.

4. Install a suitable flywheel holder tool to aid in the removal of the pressure plate and flywheel (if being removed).

5. Install a suitable clutch alignment tool through the clutch disk splines and into the pilot bearing.

6. Matchmark the pressure plate and flywheel for easy reassembly. Remove the pressure plate bolts in a criss-cross pattern, 2 turns at a time to prevent warpage.

7. Remove the pressure plate, then the clutch disc with the alignment shaft.

8. Inspect the flywheel for surface irregularities or the presence of oil which may be leaking from the rear main oil seal or transmission input shaft seal. If the flywheel has surface irregularities, cracks, hot spots, or shows signs of bluing (over-

Fig. 39 View of the transaxle, once it is separated from the engine

Fig. 40 Loosen the pressure plate bolts in a criss-cross pattern. This will prevent the plate from bending during the removal procedure

heated), replace the flywheel. If the rear main oil seal is leaking, remove the flywheel and replace the oil seal. If removing the flywheel, loosen the bolts in a crisscross pattern.

To install:

9. If the rear crankshaft oil seal was removed, install the seal as follows:

    a. Carefully chamfer the edges of the seal housing with a suitable sharp pocket knife or chamfering tool.

    b. Thoroughly clean the housing-to-seal mating surface with rubbing alcohol or a suitable brake cleaner and allow to dry.

    c. Make sure the seal is dry and clean. **DO NOT** use sealant on the seal. Install the seal using a suitable seal driver until it is flush with the seal housing.

    d. Once installed, lubricate the seal lips with a thin coating of light petroleum grease.

10. If the flywheel was removed, perform the following:

    a. Inspect the mounting bolts. Replace them if they show signs of stretching, distortion or if the flywheel showed signs of severe overheating.

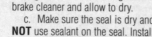

✳✳ WARNING

If the flywheel bolts are to be replaced, use new, original equipment bolts designed specifically for the application. Substituting bolts other than original equipment may break due to insufficient hardness, or cause an engine imbalance due to weight variations.

Fig. 41 Remove the pressure plate and clutch disc from the flywheel

Fig. 42 Clutch disc and alignment tool removal. The tip of the tool can be changed for different sized pilot bearings

Fig. 43 Inspect the clutch disc for signs of uneven wear

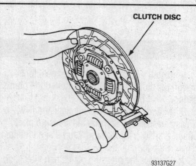

Fig. 44 To check wear, measure the clutch lining thickness. A new clutch is 0.33–0.36 inches (8.4–9.1mm). Replace the disk if it is 0.24 inches (6.0mm) or less

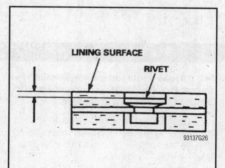

Fig. 45 You must also replace the clutch if the distance between the lining surface and the rivet is 0.008 inches (0.2mm) or less

Fig. 46 Always check the rear main seal for oil leaks that may contaminate the friction surface of the clutch disc. Replace the seal if a leak is detected

Fig. 47 The irregularities on the surface of this flywheel were caused by constant overheating of its surface. While machining may be possible, it should be replaced

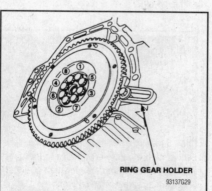

Fig. 48 Tighten the flywheel bolts to 76 ft. lbs. (103 Nm) following the illustrated tightening sequence. Replace the bolts if they are distorted or stretched

Fig. 49 The pilot bearing is installed into the center of the flywheel

b. Make sure the flywheel is clean. If necessary, clean the flywheel using rubbing alcohol or a suitable brake cleaner. Allow the flywheel to dry, then apply a thin coating of light petroleum

Fig. 50 This is how the clutch alignment tool should appear after it has been inserted into the pilot bearing

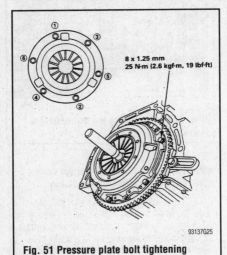

Fig. 51 Pressure plate bolt tightening sequence

8 x 1.25 mm
25 N·m (2.6 kgf·m, 19 lbf·ft)

Fig. 52 The clutch fork pivots on a steel ball. Inspect the fork for cracks. Lubricate the splined transmission shaft, ball and fork with high temperature grease during reassembly

grease to the portion of the flywheel that contacts the engine oil seal.

c. Align the hole in the flywheel with the crankshaft dowel pin and install the mounting bolts finger-tight.

d. Install a suitable flywheel holder, and tighten the flywheel mounting bolts in several steps using a criss-cross pattern as illustrated. The mounting bolt final torque should be 76 ft. lbs. (103 Nm).

11. If the clutch pilot bearing was removed or the flywheel replaced, install the clutch pilot bearing.

12. Install a clutch pilot tool through the clutch disk splines and into the clutch pilot bearing to hold the clutch disk in place.

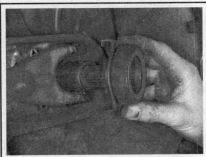

Fig. 53 On reassembly, apply a high temperature grease to the ears of the release fork where it contacts the release bearing, and to the inner surface of the release bearing and its guide tube

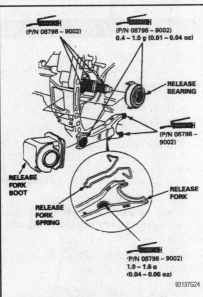

Fig. 54 Make sure to apply a suitable super high temperature grease to these components for smooth operation of the of the clutch release mechanisms

13. Inspect the clutch pressure plate bolts for damage. Replace the bolts as necessary. Install the pressure plate, tightening the mounting bolts to 19 ft. lbs. (25 Nm), in the proper sequence as illustrated.

14. Remove the flywheel holding tool and the clutch alignment tool.

15. Apply a suitable super high temperature grease to the following components:
- Transaxle input shaft
- Release bearing guide tube
- Release bearing inner sleeve
- Release fork pivot cavity and pivot
- Release fork-to-release bearing ears
- Release fork-to-slave cylinder rod cavity

16. Install the transaxle assembly.

17. Connect the negative battery cable and enter the radio security code.

ADJUSTMENTS

Clutch Pedal Free-Play

▶ See Figure 55

➡The hydraulic clutch is self-adjusting to compensate for wear.

1. Loosen the locknut at the base of the clutch switch (for the cruise control, if equipped), or for the adjusting bolt that contacts the clutch pedal when the pedal is fully released. Back off the switch or adjustment bolt until it no longer contacts the clutch pedal.

2. Loosen the locknut at the rear of the push rod for the clutch master cylinder.

3. Turn the clutch master cylinder push rod in or out until:
- The clutch pedal height from the floor is 7 3/16 inches (183mm).
- The clutch pedal stroke is 5 5/16–5 11/16 inches (135–145mm).

4. Tighten the push rod locknut.

5. Thread in the clutch switch or adjusting bolt until it contacts the clutch pedal, then thread the component an additional 3/4–1 turn, and tighten the locknut.

6. Loosen the locknut on the clutch interlock switch.

7. Measure the clearance between the clutch pedal and the floor board with the clutch pedal fully depressed.

8. Allow the clutch pedal to rise from the floor until it is 9/16–3/4 inches (15–20mm) above the full bottom measurement.

9. Adjust the interlock switch so that the engine will start from this position.

10. Turn the interlock switch in an additional 3/4–1 turn, and tighten the locknut.

11. Tighten the locknut to secure the clutch interlock switch in this position.

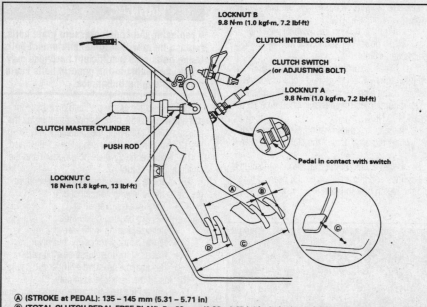

LOCKNUT B
9.8 N·m (1.0 kgf·m, 7.2 lbf·ft)

CLUTCH INTERLOCK SWITCH

CLUTCH SWITCH
(or ADJUSTING BOLT)

LOCKNUT A
9.8 N·m (1.0 kgf·m, 7.2 lbf·ft)

CLUTCH MASTER CYLINDER

PUSH ROD

Pedal in contact with switch

LOCKNUT C
18 N·m (1.8 kgf·m, 13 lbf·ft)

Ⓐ (STROKE at PEDAL): 135 – 145 mm (5.31 – 5.71 in)
Ⓑ (TOTAL CLUTCH PEDAL FREE PLAY): 7 – 22 mm (0.28 – 0.87 in) include the pedal play 1 – 9 mm (0.04 – 0.35 in)
Ⓒ (CLUTCH PEDAL HEIGHT): 183 mm (7.20 in) to the floor
Ⓓ (CLUTCH PEDAL DISENGAGEMENT HEIGHT): 72 mm (2.83 in) minimum to the floor

93137G28

Fig. 55 Clutch pedal components, lubrication points, and adjustment specifications

93137P01

Fig. 56 The clutch slave cylinder is mounted onto the transaxle housing, just behind the radiator

90947P15

Fig. 57 Disconnecting the hydraulic line from the slave cylinder

Master Cylinder

REMOVAL & INSTALLATION

✳✳ WARNING

Do not spill brake fluid on any of the vehicles painted surfaces. It will damage the paint!

1. Use a suitable siphon or a clean turkey baster to remove the old fluid, or remove the clutch master cylinder reservoir bracket mounting bolts and pour the old fluid into a suitable container.
2. Clean the reservoir thoroughly using a clean shop cloth or paper towel.
3. Disconnect the clutch pipe from the master cylinder.
4. Remove the reservoir hose from the master cylinder reservoir.
5. If additional room is needed, remove the driver's side lower dash panel and the following items from under the dash:
   a. Remove the cotter pin on the clutch pedal rod.
   b. Remove the clutch pedal pin out of the yoke.
   c. Remove the master cylinder retaining nuts.
6. Remove the clutch master cylinder from under the hood.

✳✳ WARNING

Do not spill brake fluid on the clutch master cylinder damper.

7. Installation is the reverse of removal.

➡ **Use only fresh DOT 3 or 4 brake fluid from a sealed container to refill the clutch hydraulic system.**

8. Fill and bleed the clutch system, using a suitable DOT 3 or 4 brake fluid.

Slave Cylinder

REMOVAL & INSTALLATION

♦ See Figures 56 and 57

1. Locate the slave cylinder mounted on the transaxle assembly, near the radiator.
2. Remove the flare fitting and steel line from the slave cylinder assembly.
3. Remove the slave cylinder from the clutch housing by removing the attaching bolts.
4. Installation is the reverse of the removal procedure

➡ **Use only fresh DOT 3 or 4 brake fluid from a sealed container to refill the clutch hydraulic system.**

5. Fill, then bleed the clutch system, using a suitable DOT 3 or 4 brake fluid.

HYDRAULIC SYSTEM BLEEDING

➡ **Use only DOT 3 or 4 brake fluid from a clean, sealed container, for the clutch master reser-** voir. As brake fluid will damage the vehicle's paint, clean up any spills immediately.

1. Use a suitable siphon or a clean turkey baster to remove the old brake fluid, or remove the clutch master cylinder reservoir bracket mounting bolts and pour the old fluid into a suitable container.
2. Clean the reservoir thoroughly using a clean shop cloth or paper towel.
3. Fit a flare or box end wrench onto the slave cylinder bleeder screw.
4. Attach a (clear if available) rubber tube to the slave cylinder bleed screw and suspend it into a suitable clear drain container partially filled with brake fluid.
5. Fill the clutch master cylinder with brake fluid.
6. Open the bleeder screw and have an assistant press the clutch pedal to the floor.
7. While holding the clutch pedal to the floor, close the bleed screw.
8. Slowly release the clutch pedal to its fullest extension and recheck the reservoir fluid level. Top off as necessary.
9. Repeat the above steps until the fluid exiting the bleed screw is clean and free of all air bubbles.
10. Top off the clutch master cylinder reservoir as necessary.

AUTOMATIC TRANSAXLE

Neutral Safety Switch

◆ **See Figure 58**

The neutral safety switch is a combination switch that also controls the backup lights and gear position indicators. The switch is located on the transaxle assembly.

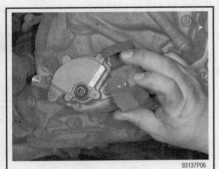

Fig. 58 The combination neutral safety, backup light and gear position switch is located on the transaxle—CR-V shown

REMOVAL & INSTALLATION

See backup light switch procedures in section 6, for removal and installation procedures.

ADJUSTMENT

See backup light switch procedures in section 6, for adjustment procedures.

Automatic Transaxle Assembly

REMOVAL & INSTALLATION

CR-V and 4-Cylinder Odyssey Models

◆ **See Figure 59**

➡ **The radio may contain a code anti-theft circuit. Always obtain the security code number before disconnecting the battery cables.**

1. Shift the transaxle into **N** (neutral).
2. Disconnect the negative and positive battery cables and remove the battery.
3. Remove the air intake hose, air cleaner case, and battery tray. Disconnect the ground cable and the cable bracket from the battery tray.
4. Disconnect the throttle cable from the throttle control lever.
5. Detach the transaxle ground cable and the mainshaft speed sensor connectors. Detach the shift and lock-up solenoid valve connectors.
6. Disconnect the starter cables from the starter motor and unbolt the cable bracket from the transaxle case.
7. Disconnect the Vehicle Speed Sensor (VSS) wiring harness. The VSS is located on the rear of the transaxle case near the cooler line inlet.

8. Detach the gear position switch and counter shaft speed sensor connectors.
9. Loosen the four upper transaxle case bolts, but leave them threaded into the engine block. Move the lower radiator hose slightly upward and toward the engine block if more clearance is needed for a socket and extension.
10. Loosen, but do not remove, the three front engine mount bracket bolts.
11. Raise and safely support the vehicle. Remove the front wheels.
12. Remove the splash shield.
13. Drain the transaxle fluid and reinstall the drain plug with a new crush washer.
14. Disconnect the transaxle cooler hoses from the joint pipes. Plug the hoses to keep out dirt and moisture.
15. Remove the subframe center beam.
16. Remove the cotter pins and lower arm ball joint nuts, then separate the ball joints from the lower arms using a suitable ball joint tool.
17. Remove the right damper pinch bolt. Separate the damper fork from the strut.
18. Unbolt the right radius rod from the right lower control arm and remove it from the front subframe beam.
19. Using a suitable tool, carefully pry the right and left halfshafts out of the differential. Pull on the inboard CV-joints and remove the right and left halfshafts. Tie plastic bags over the halfshaft ends to prevent damage to the CV boots and splines. Don't let the left halfshaft hang by its own weight; use a piece of wire to suspend it out of the way.
20. Turn the right driveshaft toward the front of the vehicle so that it is resting on the lower control arm. Use a piece of wire to support the halfshaft.
21. Remove the intermediate shaft by unbolting its mounting bracket from the engine block.
22. Remove the torque converter cover and shift cable holder.
23. Remove the shift control cable by removing the lockbolt. Remove the shift cable lever from the control shaft. Don't disconnect the control lever from the shift cable. Wire the shift cable out of the work area and be careful not to kink it.

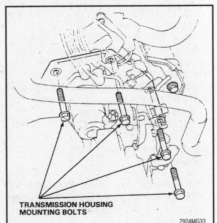

TRANSMISSION HOUSING MOUNTING BOLTS

7924MG33

Fig. 59 Upper transaxle case bolt locations—CR-V and 4-cylinder Odyssey models

24. On CR-V models, remove the driveshaft bolts from the transfer unit.
25. Remove the eight drive plate bolts one at a time while rotating the crankshaft pulley.
26. Place a suitable jack under the transaxle and raise the jack just enough to take weight off of the mounts.
27. Remove the transaxle mount from the transaxle case. Don't remove the bracket.
28. Remove the upper and lower transaxle case bolts. Unbolt the rear engine mount bracket from the transaxle case. The rear engine mount bracket through-bolt may have to be loosened first.
29. Pull the transaxle away from the engine until it clears the dowel pins. Lower the transaxle from the vehicle.

To install:

➡ **Use new self-locking nuts when assembling the front suspension components. Install new set rings onto the halfshaft inboard joint splines. Replace any color-coded self-locking bolts.**

30. Flush the transaxle cooler lines:
    a. Use a suitable pressurized flusher (Honda or Kent-Moore part No. J38405-A or equivalent). Use only Honda flushing fluid; other fluids will damage the system.
    b. Fill the flusher with 21 ounces (600 grams) of fluid. Pressurize the flusher to 80–120 psi (551–827 kPa), following the procedure on the fluid container and flusher.
    c. Clamp the discharge hose of the flusher to the cooler return line. Clamp the drain hose to the cooler inlet line and route it into a bucket or drain tank. Ensure the drain hose is securely clamped to the drain container.
    d. Connect the flusher to air and water lines. Use hot water if it's available.
    e. Open the flusher water valve and flush the cooler for ten seconds.
    f. Depress the flusher trigger to mix flushing fluid with the water. Flush for two minutes, turning the air valve on and off for five seconds every 15–20 seconds. The maximum air pressure for the flushing procedure is 120 psi (827 kPa).
    g. After finishing one flushing cycle, reverse the hoses and flush in the opposite direction.
    h. Dry the cooler lines with compressed air so that no moisture is left in the cooler system.
31. Ensure the two 14mm dowel pins are installed into the torque converter housing.
32. Install the torque converter onto the transaxle mainshaft with a new hub O-ring. Install the starter motor onto the transaxle case and tighten its mounting bolts to 33 ft. lbs. (44 Nm).
33. Raise the transaxle into position and install the transaxle housing mounting bolts. Evenly tighten the bolts to 47 ft. lbs. (65 Nm).
34. Connect the rear engine mount bracket to the transaxle case and evenly tighten the three new self-locking bolts to 40 ft. lbs. (54 Nm). Tighten the rear mount through-bolt to 47 ft. lbs. (64 Nm) if it was loosened.
35. Install the intake manifold bracket and tighten the bolts to 16 ft. lbs. (22 Nm).
36. Install the transaxle mount and hand-tighten the through-bolt. Tighten the three nuts to 28 ft. lbs.

(38 Nm). Tighten the through-bolt to 47 ft. lbs. (65 Nm).

37. Tighten the three front engine mount bracket bolts to 28 ft. lbs. (38 Nm).

38. Remove the transmission jack.

39. Attach the torque converter to the drive plate and hand-tighten the bolts. Tighten the eight bolts in two steps in a crisscross pattern: first to 53 inch lbs. (6 Nm), and finally to 106 inch lbs. (12 Nm). Check for free rotation after tightening the last bolt.

40. Install the shift control cable and control cable holder. Tighten the shift cable lockbolt to 123 inch lbs. (14 Nm). Tighten the control cable holder bolts to 13 ft. lbs. (18 Nm).

41. Install the torque converter cover and tighten the bolts to 106 inch lbs. (12 Nm).

42. Install the intermediate shaft and tighten the mounting bolts to 28 ft. lbs. (38 Nm).

43. On CR-V models, install the driveshaft to the transfer unit.

44. Install the radius rod and damper fork.

45. Install a new set ring on the end of each halfshaft.

46. Turn the right steering knuckle fully outward and slide the axle into the differential until the set ring snaps into the differential side gear. Repeat the procedure on the left side. Ensure the halfshafts are fully seated in the differential and intermediate shaft.

47. Install the damper fork bolts and ball joint nuts to the lower arms. Tighten the ball joint nut to 40 ft. lbs. (55 Nm) and install a new cotter pin.

48. Install the subframe center beam and tighten its bolts to 37 ft. lbs. (50 Nm). Install the splash shield.

49. Install the front wheels and lower the vehicle.

50. Use a pulley holder tool, in conjunction with a torque wrench, to tighten the crankshaft pulley bolt to:
  • CR-V models: 130 ft. lbs. (177 Nm).
  • 4-cylinder Odyssey models: 181 ft. lbs. (245 Nm).

51. Reconnect the speed sensor.

52. Raise the right front knuckle with a floor jack until the weight of the vehicle is supported by the jack. Tighten the damper fork pinch bolt to 32 ft. lbs. (44 Nm). Tighten the radius rod bolts to 76 ft. lbs. (103 Nm), and the radius rod nut to 32 ft. lbs. (44 Nm). Hold the damper fork bolt with a wrench and tighten the nut to 40 ft. lbs. (55 Nm).

53. Connect the cables to the starter. Place the radiator hose back into its bracket.

54. Reconnect the throttle control cable.

55. Attach the lock-up control solenoid valve and shift control solenoid valve connectors.

56. Attach the mainshaft and countershaft speed sensor connectors and the transaxle ground cable.

57. Connect the transaxle cooler hoses to the joint pipes.

58. Install the battery base, air cleaner case and air intake hose. Reconnect the ground cable and the cable bracket to the battery base.

59. Install the battery. Connect the positive and negative battery cables.

60. Refill the transaxle with ATF. Use only Honda Premium ATF or an equivalent DEXRON®II or III ATF. Connect the battery cables.

61. Leave the flusher drain hose attached to the cooler return line.

62. With the transaxle in **P** (park), run the engine for 30 seconds, or until approximately 1 qt.

(0.9 L) of fluid is discharged. This completes the cooler flushing process.

63. Remove the drain hose and reconnect the cooler return line.

64. Refill the transaxle fluid to the proper level.

65. Start the engine, set the parking brake and shift the transaxle through all gears three times. Check for proper shift cable and throttle cable adjustment.

66. Let the engine reach operating temperature with the transaxle in **P** (park) or **N** (neutral). Then, shut the engine **OFF** and check the fluid level.

67. Road test the vehicle. Check for proper shifting.

68. After road testing the vehicle, loosen the front engine mount bracket bolts, then retighten them to 28 ft. lbs. (39 Nm).

69. Check and adjust the vehicle's front wheel alignment. Tighten the front wheel nuts to 80 ft. lbs. (110 Nm).

70. Enter the radio security code.

V6 Odyssey Models

♦ **See Figures 60 thru 65**

1. Note the radio security code.

2. Disconnect the negative terminal of the battery.

3. Remove the bolt for the lower portion of the windshield washer reservoir.

4. Fix the hood in a vertical position using the support rod.

5. Remove the air intake duct assembly, the resonator cover and the air filter housing assembly.

6. Remove the battery hold down bracket, the battery and the battery tray.

7. Remove the battery connector, cable clamps, and the relay bracket from the battery base.

8. Remove the battery base.

9. Raise and support the vehicle and drain the transaxle into a sealable container. Reinstall the drain plug using a new sealing washer.

10. Remove the trans cooler hose clamps on the starter and remove both hoses from the cooler lines. Turn the hoses upward to prevent leakage and seal the ends of the hoses and lines to prevent contamination.

11. Remove the starter cable clamps, cables and starter.

12. Remove the transmission grounding cable.

13. Disconnect the shift control solenoid valve connectors and remove the harness clamp.

14. Detach the connectors for the mainshaft speed sensor, 3rd clutch pressure switch, clutch pressure control solenoid, and remove the harness clamps from the clamp brackets.

15. Unplug the connector for the lock-up control/ shift control solenoid valve, and remove the connector from the harness cover.

16. Remove the bolt for the connector bracket.

17. Remove the bolt for the harness cover and push the cover rearward to remove it from the transmission hanger.

18. Detach the connectors from the clutch pressure switch and the countershaft speed sensor.

19. Remove the gear position switch connector from the bracket and disconnect it.

20. Remove the nut for the front engine mount and disconnect the vacuum tube near the joint.

21. Remove the transmission housing retaining bolts.

22. Remove the engine trim covers.

23. Attach a lifting bracket to the engine that will allow the engine to be supported safely and securely in three places, then slightly lift the engine.

24. Remove the lower engine splash shield.

25. Disconnect the Oxygen (O_2S) sensor and remove the front pipe and catalytic converter as an assembly.

26. Disconnect the lower ball joints and the lower stabilizer link.

27. Remove the shift cable holder bolts and the shift cable cover.

28. Remove the shift control cable lock bolt and shift cable.

✳✳ WARNING

Use care to not severely bend or kink the cable. If the cable is damaged in any manner, replace the cable.

29. Install a 6mm x 1.0mm x 14mm bolt and nut on the shift cable cover and reinstall the cover to the torque converter housing to enable removal of the torque converter during the transmission removal.

30. Remove the torque converter cover.

31. Remove the eight torque converter drive

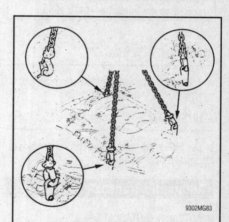

9302MG83

Fig. 60 During transmission removal, attach the engine lifting hoist in three places to secure the engine before the subframe is removed—V6 Odyssey engine

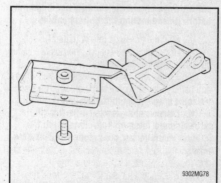

9302MG78

Fig. 61 Reinstall the shift cable cover with a 6mm nut and 6 x 1 x 14mm bolt installed to allow the torque converter to be removed during transaxle removal

plate bolts one at a time while rotating the crankshaft pulley.

32. Remove the engine stiffener bolts.

33. Remove the clip for the power steering fluid return hose from the bracket.

34. Remove the power steering fluid pipe bracket bolts, bracket and steering gearbox mounting bolt.

35. Remove the stiffener bracket from the steering gearbox.

36. Remove the steering gear box mounting bolts and stiffener nut and bolt.

37. Remove the rear drivetrain mounting bolts.

38. Remove the power steering bracket bolts and unclamp the power steering pipe clamps.

39. Remove the lower transmission mount nuts.

40. Make side-to-side and front-to-rear reference marks between the lower subframe and the vehicle to ensure proper alignment during installation.

41. Carefully support the subframe with a piece of wood 4 in. x 4 in. x 58 in. long and a jack.

42. Remove the subframe mounting bolts and stiffeners.

43. Carefully lower the subframe.

44. Support the end of the steering gearbox with a suitable rope wrapped around the passenger end of the steering gearbox and attached to the vehicle body.

45. Remove the lower transmission mounts.

46. Using a suitable prytool, pry the driveshafts out of the differential and the intermediate shaft.

47. Cover the exposed machined surfaces of the driveshaft with a plastic bag to protect them.

48. Remove the bolts from the intermediate shaft bracket and remove the shaft.

49. Cover the machined surfaces of the shaft to protect it with plastic bags.

50. Remove the front drivetrain mount bracket assembly.

51. Remove the transmission housing mounting fasteners.

52. Lower the transmission and tilt the engine carefully to allow the transmission to clear the end cover from the side frame.

53. Put a jack under the transmission to support it.

54. Move the transmission away from the engine until it clears the dowel pins and then lower it onto the transmission jack.

➡ **If the torque converter is stuck on the drive plate, move it toward the transmission housing through the opening for the starter motor.**

55. Remove the shift cable cover and the torque converter assembly from the torque converter housing.

56. Inspect the drive plate carefully and replace it if there is damage.

To install:

➡ **Use new self-locking nuts when assembling the front suspension components. Install new set rings onto the halfshaft inboard joint splines. Replace any color-coded self-locking bolts.**

57. Flush the transaxle cooler lines:

　a. Use a pressurized flusher (Honda or Kent-Moore part No. J38405-A or equivalent). Use only Honda flushing fluid (Honda part No. J35944–20); other fluids will damage the system.

　b. Fill the flusher with 21 ounces (600 grams) of fluid. Pressurize the flusher to 80–120 psi (551–827 kPa), following the procedure on the fluid container and flusher.

　c. Clamp the discharge hose of the flusher to the cooler return line. Clamp the drain hose to the cooler inlet line and route it into a bucket or drain tank. Ensure the drain hose is securely clamped to the drain container.

　d. Connect the flusher to air and water lines. Use hot water if it's available.

　e. Open the flusher water valve and flush the cooler for ten seconds.

　f. Depress the flusher trigger to mix flushing fluid with the water. Flush for two minutes, turning the air valve on and off for five seconds every 15–20 seconds. The maximum air pressure for the flushing procedure is 120 psi (827 kPa).

　g. After finishing one flushing cycle, reverse the hoses and flush in the opposite direction.

58. Install the transmission lower mount and tighten the bolts to 28 ft. lbs. (38 Nm).

59. Install the torque converter onto the transaxle mainshaft with a new O-ring.

60. Install the 14mm and 10mm dowel pins in the torque converter housing.

61. Carefully place the transmission on a jack and raise the transmission level with the engine.

62. Attach the transmission to the engine and install the transmission housing mounting bolts and tighten to a torque of 47 ft. lbs. (64 Nm).

63. Install the front engine mount bracket and tighten the bolts to 28 ft. lbs. (38 Nm).

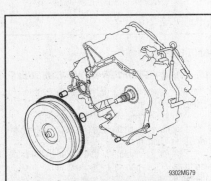

Fig. 62 Install the torque converter on the transmission mainshaft with a new O-ring—V6 Odyssey models

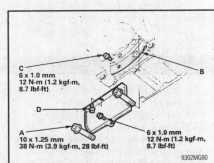

Fig. 63 Torque converter bolts are accessed with the trans housing lower cover plate removed. (A) Engine stiffener bolts (C) Torque converter bolts (D) Access cover bolts—V6 Odyssey models

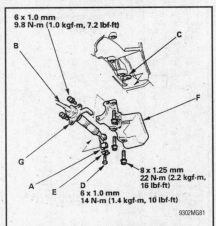

Fig. 64 Shift cable control lever, cover plate, and cover bracket tightening torque and components. (A) Control lever (B) Shift cable (C) Control shaft (D) Lock bolt (E) Lock bolt locking tab (F) Shift cable cover (G) Shift cable holder—V6 Odyssey models

64. Install the engine stiffener bolts and tighten to 28 ft. lbs. (38 Nm).

65. Install the torque converter drive plate bolts in two steps using a crisscross pattern as follows:

- First step: 52 inch lbs. (6 Nm).
- Second step: 104 inch lbs. (12 Nm)

66. Rotate the crankshaft and check that it moves freely.

67. Install the torque converter access cover.

68. Check the crankshaft pulley bolt for the proper torque, and if necessary, tighten the crankshaft pulley bolt to 181 ft. lbs. (245 Nm).

69. Install the shift cable control lever bolt to 120 inch lbs. (14 Nm), and the cable cover bolts to 16 ft. lbs. (22 Nm).

70. Install the shift cable holder bolts and tighten to 86 inch lbs. (9.8 Nm).

71. Install the intermediate shaft using a new set ring, and tighten the mounting bolts to 29 ft. lbs. (39 Nm).

72. Install new set rings on the left and right driveshafts and install the driveshafts.

73. Carefully support the subframe with a piece of wood 4 in. x 4 in. x 58 in. long and a jack and lift up to the body.

74. Align the side-to-side and front-to-rear reference marks between the lower subframe and the vehicle to ensure proper alignment during installation.

75. Install the sub-frame mounting bolts and stiffeners and tighten the bolts to the specifications shown in the accompanying illustration.

76. Install the lower transmission mount nuts.

77. Install the power steering bracket bolt and fluid pipe bracket.

78. Install the rear drivetrain mounting bolts and tighten the bolts to the torque shown in the rear drivetrain mount illustration.

79. Install the stiffener bracket to the steering gearbox and tighten the nuts and bolts to 43 ft. lbs. (58 Nm).

80. Install the steering gear box mounting bolt and torque to 29 ft. lbs.

81. Install the power steering fluid return pipe clip on the bracket.

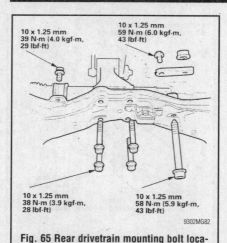

10 x 1.25 mm
39 N·m (4.0 kgf·m, 29 lbf·ft)

10 x 1.25 mm
59 N·m (6.0 kgf·m, 43 lbf·ft)

10 x 1.25 mm
38 N·m (3.9 kgf·m, 28 lbf·ft)

10 x 1.25 mm
58 N·m (5.9 kgf·m, 43 lbf·ft)

9302MG82

Fig. 65 Rear drivetrain mounting bolt location and torque specifications

82. Connect the lower ball joints and tighten the nuts to 43–51 ft. lbs. (59–69 Nm) and install the lower stabilizer link nuts to a torque of 51 ft. lbs. (69 Nm).

83. Install the front pipe using new gaskets and the catalytic converter as an assembly and connect the O2S connector. Tighten the manifold-to-exhaust pipe nuts to 40 ft. lbs. (54 Nm), and the converter to exhaust pipe nuts to 25 ft. lbs. (33 Nm).

84. Install the lower engine splash shield.

85. Install the transmission housing retaining bolts and torque to 47 ft. lbs. (64 Nm).

86. Install and tighten the front engine mount nut to 40 ft. lbs. (54 Nm).

87. Install the gear position switch connector and install on it on the bracket.

88. Attach the connectors for the mainshaft speed sensor, 3rd clutch pressure switch, clutch pressure control solenoid, and install the harness clamps on the clamp brackets.

89. Install the harness cover and install it on the transmission hanger.

90. Engage the connector for the lock-up control/shift control solenoid valve, and install the connector.

91. Attach the connectors from the clutch pressure switch and the countershaft speed sensor.

92. Connect the shift control solenoid valve connectors and install the harness clamp.

93. Install the transmission grounding cable.

94. Install the starter cable clamps, cables and starter. Tighten the short starter motor mounting bolt to 33 ft. lbs. (44 Nm), and the longer bolt to 47 ft. lbs. (64 Nm).

95. Install the ATF cooler hose clamps on the starter and install both ATF hoses onto the cooler lines.

96. Install the battery base.

97. Install the battery connector, cable clamps, and the relay bracket for the battery base.

98. Install the battery tray, the battery, and the battery hold down bracket.

99. Install the air intake duct assembly, the resonator cover and the air filter housing assembly.

100. Install the engine trim covers.

101. Refill the transmission to the correct level with ATF.

102. Connect the negative terminal of the battery.

103. Set the parking brake, start the engine and shift through the all of the transmission gears three times.

104. Check for proper shift lever operation, gear position indicator operation and shift cable adjustment.

105. Check for proper front wheel alignment and correct as necessary.

106. Allow the engine to reach normal operation temperature in the **P** or **N** position, and then turn the engine off and recheck the ATF fluid level.

107. Install the hood support rod in its normal position.

108. Install the bolt for the lower portion of the windshield washer reservoir.

109. Road test the vehicle and check for normal operation of transmission and the shift points.

110. Enter the security code for the radio.

111. Loosen the front engine mount nut after the road test and tighten the nut to 40 ft. lbs. (54 Nm).

ADJUSTMENTS

Shift Linkage

CR-V AND 4-CYLINDER ODYSSEY MODELS

1. Remove the lower right steering column access hole cover.

2. Shift the transmission to the **N** position.

3. Remove the shift cable end lock pin from the adjustable cable end.

4. Check the alignment of the hole in the cable end to see if it is perfectly aligned with the linkage adjusting rod.

5. If the holes are not aligned, loosen the cable end locknut and adjust the cable end until the hole in the cable end and the adjusting rod are perfectly aligned.

6. Reinstall the lock pin. If any resistance is felt when inserting the lock pin, readjust the cable end.

7. Make sure the lock pin snaps firmly into

place. If the lock pin is not secure, it must be replaced.

8. Move the gear selector through each gear position and verify the operation of the gear position indicators.

9. Insert the ignition key into the key cylinder on the upper steering column cover and check to see that the shift lock lever releases.

V6 ODYSSEY MODELS

1. Remove the steering column covers. Refer to Section 10 for details if necessary.

2. Shift the transmission to the **N** position.

3. Remove the shift cable end attachment nut and remove the shift cable end from the shift linkage.

4. Pull the shift cable until it stops and release it. Then pull the cable back until two steps are felt.

5. Turn the ignition switch **ON** and verify that the **N** position indicator light is lit.

6. Insert a 0.24 inch (6mm) pin into the hole of the detent plate and through the positioning hole on the control bracket.

7. Reinstall the shift cable end onto the mounting stud and make sure it is fully seated.

8. Install the shift cable locking nut and tighten to 16 ft. lbs. (22 Nm).

9. Remove the lock pin from the shift detent alignment hole.

10. Move the gear selector through each gear position and verify the operation of the gear position indicators.

11. Push the shift lock release and verify that the shift lock lever releases.

Throttle Linkage

1. Start the engine and allow the engine to run in **P** at 3,000 RPM until the radiator fan comes on, then allow the engine to idle.

2. Check the throttle cable side-to-side deflection. The total deflection should be ⅜–½ inches (10–12mm).

3. If the deflection is not within specification, loosen the locknut and adjust the throttle cable as necessary.

Halfshafts

REMOVAL & INSTALLATION

Please refer to the halfshaft removal procedures under Manual Transaxle in this section for specific details.

TRANSFER ASSEMBLY

Output Shaft Seal

REMOVAL & INSTALLATION

❋❋ WARNING

Do not remove the output flange nut with an impact wrench, otherwise the transfer assembly could be damaged.

1. Matchmark the driveshaft and output flange and remove the driveshaft.

2. Cut the lock tabs of the output flange mounting nut with a chisel.

3. Hold the output flange and remove the following components in this order:
   - Output flange mounting nut (Replace when reassembling)
   - Conical spring washer (Replace when reassembling)
   - Back-up ring

   - O-ring (Replace when reassembling)
   - Output flange

4. Carefully remove the output flange seal.

To install:

5. Install a new seal. Once installed coat the lip of the seal with a light petroleum grease.

6. Coat the output flange seal surface with a light petroleum grease and install the flange.

7. Install a new O-ring, then the back-up ring and a new conical washer. Make sure the conical washer is installed such that the raised portion is facing out.

8. Coat the shaft and mounting nut with ATF before installing the nut.

9. Hold the output flange and tighten the mounting nut to 98 ft. lbs. (132 Nm), then stake the nut into the groove.

10. Align the matchmark between the driveshaft and the output flange and reinstall the driveshaft. Tighten the bolts to 24 ft. lbs. (32 Nm).

11. Check the transmission fluid level and top off as necessary.

Transfer Assembly

REMOVAL & INSTALLATION

▶ **See Figure 66**

1. Raise and safely support the front of the vehicle.

2. Drain the transaxle lubricant and remove the guard bar/splash shield.

3. Disconnect the header pipe from the vehicle.

4. Remove the shift cable. Do not bend the shift cable excessively.

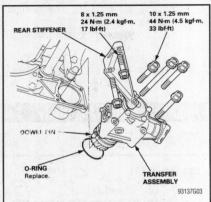

Fig. 66 Exploded view of the transfer assembly

5. Matchmark the driveshaft and transfer assembly flanges, then separate.

6. Clean the area around the transfer assembly to keep dirt and debris form entering the transaxle.

7. Remove the mounting bolts for the rear stiffener and the transfer assembly.

➡ **Do not allow dust or other foreign material to enter the transmission while servicing the transfer unit.**

To install:

8. Install a new O-ring on the transfer assembly.

9. Install the transfer assembly and tighten the mounting bolts to 33 ft. lbs. (44 Nm).

10. Install and tighten the rear stiffener mounting bolts to 17 ft. lbs. (24 Nm).

11. Line up the marks on the driveshaft and tighten the bolts to 24 ft. lbs. (32 Nm).

12. Install the shift cable and cover.

13. Attach the exhaust header pipe and install the splash shield/guard bar.

14. Fill the transmission with Honda Automatic transmission fluid or ATF, then start the engine and allow it to reach operation temperature. Turn the engine **OFF** and recheck the fluid level.

DRIVELINE

Rear Driveshaft and U-Joints

REMOVAL & INSTALLATION

▶ **See Figures 67 and 68**

1. Matchmark the driveshaft flange to the front transfer and rear differential flanges.

2. Remove the driveshaft protective hoop.

3. Temporarily support the driveshaft with technician's wire or have an assistant hold it.

4. Remove the 12-point bolts from the rear differential flange.

5. Remove the 2 center support bearing mounting bolts.

6. Remove the 12-point bolts from the front transfer flange.

7. Remove the driveshaft.

8. Installation is the reverse of the removal procedure, observing the following torque specifications:

- 12-point flange bolts: 24 ft. lbs. (32 Nm)
- Center support bearing bolts: 29 ft. lbs. (39 Nm)
- Driveshaft protective hoop bolts: 16 ft. lbs. (22 Nm)

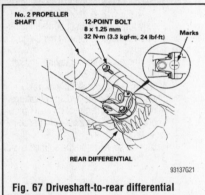

Fig. 67 Driveshaft-to-rear differential mounting

U-JOINT REPLACEMENT

The manufacturer states that should a failure occur with any component of the driveshaft assembly, the assembly must be replaced as a unit.

DRIVESHAFT BALANCING

The manufacturer states that should a failure occur with any component of the driveshaft assem-

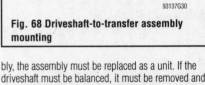

Fig. 68 Driveshaft-to-transfer assembly mounting

bly, the assembly must be replaced as a unit. If the driveshaft must be balanced, it must be removed and taken to a vendor specializing in driveshaft balancing.

Center Bearing

REMOVAL & INSTALLATION

Refer to the driveshaft removal procedure for center bearing removal and installation.

REAR AXLE

Axle Shaft

REMOVAL & INSTALLATION

1. Loosen the wheel nuts.

2. Carefully raise the locking tab of the axle spindle nut using a hammer and chisel.

3. Loosen and remove the axle nut.

4. Raise and safely support the vehicle.

5. Remove the rear wheel.

6. Remove the halfshafts from the differential. Refer to the differential removal procedure in this section for specific details.

7. Carefully remove the halfshaft from the trailing arm assembly by tapping on it with a plastic hammer, or using a suitable drift and hammer.

To install:

8. Installation is the reverse of removal taking note of the following points:

- Install new set rings in the groove of the splined inner CV-joint shafts.
- Top off the differential fluid as necessary.
- Install a new spindle nut and torque to 134 ft. lbs. (181 Nm), and once tightened, stake the nut.
- Tighten the wheel nuts to 80 ft. lbs. (108 Nm).

Inner Axle Oil Seals

REMOVAL & INSTALLATION

1. Remove the differential. For specific information refer to procedures in this section.
2. Remove the axle seal.

To install:

3. Install a new axle seal squarely into the differential housing, then apply a thin coat of light petroleum grease to the lip of the seal.
4. The balance of the installation is the reverse of the removal.

Pinion Seal

REMOVAL & INSTALLATION

1. Remove the driveshaft.
2. Carefully raise the lock tab of the pinion flange mounting nut with a hammer and chisel.
3. Hold the pinion flange and remove the pinion flange mounting nut.

❊❊ WARNING

Do not use an impact wrench to remove the nut.

4. Remove the spring washer, back-up ring and O-ring.
5. Remove the pinion flange.
6. Remove the oil seal.

To install:

7. Install the pinion flange seal squarely into the differential housing, then coat the lip of the seal with a thin coating of light petroleum grease.
8. Install the pinion flange.
9. Install a new O-ring coated with ATF.
10. Install the back-up ring.

11. Install the disc spring washer with the raise portion facing out.
12. Install a new locknut and tighten to 87 ft. lbs. (118 Nm).
13. Top off the differential with Honda CVT Fluid. ATF Dexron II can be substituted temporarily.

Rear Differential Assembly

REMOVAL & INSTALLATION

▶ **See Figure 69**

1. Drain the differential fluid.
2. Matchmark the driveshaft flange and differential flange and remove the driveshaft from the differential.
3. Remove the rear differential damper.
4. Support the differential assembly with a suitable jack and remove the left and right support brackets.
5. Remove the breather tube from the fitting near the crossmember mount.
6. Using a suitable prytool, carefully pry out the inner CV-joint assemblies enough to release the locking rings from the differential.
7. Remove the upper support bracket bolts and washers.
8. Carefully lower the jack supporting the differential assembly enough to remove the CV-joints from the differential.
9. Remove the differential mounting bracket.

To install:

10. Installation is the reverse of removal, observing the following points and specifications:
   - Thinly coat the differential oil seal lips with a light petroleum grease before installing the axles.
   - Install new set rings on the splined shafts of the inner CV-joints.

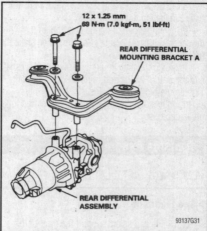

Fig. 69 Exploded view of the rear differential and mounting bracket

   - Make sure the inner CV-joints are fully seated into the differential.
   - Align the matchmarks of the driveshaft flange and differential flange.
   - Refill the differential with Honda CVT Fluid. ATF Dexron II can be substituted temporarily.

11. Tighten the fasteners to the following specifications:
   - Differential damper bolts: 40 ft. lbs. (54 Nm)
   - Driveshaft mounting bolts: 24 ft. lbs. (32 Nm)
   - Differential mounting bracket-to-body bolts: 36 ft. lbs. (49 Nm)
   - Differential side bracket-to-differential bolts: 40 ft. lbs. (54 Nm)
   - Differential mounting bracket-to-differential bolts: 51 ft. lbs. (69 Nm)

TORQUE SPECIFICATIONS

Components	Ft. Lbs.	Nm
Automatic Transaxle		
CR-V - 2.2L/2.3L Odyssey		
Starter motor-to-transaxle case bolts	33 ft. lbs.	44 Nm
Transaxle housing mounting bolts	47 ft. lbs.	65 Nm
Rear engine mount bracket-to-transaxle case self-locking bolts	40 ft. lbs.	54 Nm
Rear mount through-bolt	47 ft. lbs.	64 Nm
Intake manifold bracket	16 ft. lbs.	22 Nm
Transaxle mount nuts	28 ft. lbs.	38 Nm
Subframe center beam bolts	37 ft. lbs.	50 Nm
Transaxle mount through-bolt	47 ft. lbs.	65 Nm
Front engine mount bracket bolts	28 ft. lbs.	38 Nm
Torque converter to the drive plate		
First step	53 inch lbs.	6 Nm
Second step	106 inch lbs.	12 Nm
Shift cable lockbolt	123 inch lbs.	14 Nm
Control cable holder bolts	13 ft. lbs.	18 Nm
Torque converter cover bolts	106 inch lbs.	12 Nm
3.5L V6 Odyssey		
Transmission lower mount bolts	28 ft. lbs.	38 Nm
Transmission to engine housing mounting bolts	47 ft. lbs.	64 Nm
Front engine mount bracket bolts	28 ft. lbs.	38 Nm
Engine stiffener bolts	28 ft. lbs.	38 Nm
Torque converter drive plate bolts two steps		
First step	52 inch lbs.	6 Nm
Second step	104 inch lbs.	12 Nm
Shift cable locking nut	16 ft. lbs.	22 Nm
Manual Transaxle		
CR-V		
Transaxle mounting bolts	47 ft. lbs.	64 Nm
Rear mount bolts	61 ft. lbs.	83 Nm
Transaxle mount	47 ft. lbs.	64 Nm
Through bolt	54 ft. lbs.	74 Nm
Upper transaxle mounting bolts	47 ft. lbs.	54 Nm
Lower starter bolt	33 ft. lbs.	44 Nm
Front mount-to-bracket engine bolts	47 ft. lbs.	64 Nm
Frame mounting bolts	33 ft. lbs.	44 Nm
Subframe center beam bolts	37 ft. lbs.	50 Nm
Rear engine stiffener-to-transaxle	33 ft. lbs.	44 Nm
Stiffener(s)-to-engine	18 ft. lbs.	24 Nm
Intermediate shaft (Axle) bolts	29 ft. lbs.	39 Nm
Strut fork pinch bolt	32 ft. lbs.	43 Nm

93137C01

TORQUE SPECIFICATIONS

Components	Ft. Lbs.	Nm
Clutch		
CR-V		
Flywheel mounting bolts	76 ft. lbs.	103 Nm
Pressure plate mounting bolts	19 ft. lbs.	25 Nm
Clutch cover		
6x1mm bolts	104 inch lbs.	12 Nm
8x1.25mm bolts	17 ft. lbs.	24 Nm
12x1.25mm bolt	22 ft. lbs.	29 Nm
Slave cylinder to the transaxle mounting bolts	16 ft. lbs.	22 Nm
Clutch bracket pipe bolts	56 inch lbs.	9.8 Nm
Transfer Assembly		
CR-V		
Output flange mounting nut	98 ft. lbs.	132 Nm
Output flange-to-driveshaft bolts	24 ft. lbs.	32 Nm
Transfer assembly mounting bolts	33 ft. lbs.	44 Nm
Rear stiffener mounting bolts	17 ft. lbs.	24 Nm
Driveshaft		
CR-V		
12 point flange bolts	24 ft. lbs.	32 Nm
Center support bearing bolts	29 ft. lbs.	39 Nm
Driveshaft protective hoop bolts	16 ft. lbs.	22 Nm
Rear Differential Assembly		
CR-V		
Pinion flange nut	87 ft. lbs.	118 Nm
Differential damper bolts	40 ft. lbs.	54 Nm
Driveshaft mounting bolts	24 ft. lbs.	32 Nm
Differential mounting bracket-to-body bolts	36 ft. lbs.	49 Nm
Differential side bracket-to-differential bolts	40 ft. lbs.	54 Nm
Differential mounting bracket-to-differential bolts	51 ft. lbs.	69 Nm
Axles		
Intermediate shaft mounting bolts	28 ft. lbs.	38 Nm
Front spindle nut	181 ft. lbs.	245 Nm
Rear spindle nut		
CR-V	134 ft. lbs.	181 Nm
Odyssey	181 ft. lbs.	245 Nm
Wheel lug nuts	80 ft. lbs.	108 Nm

93137C02

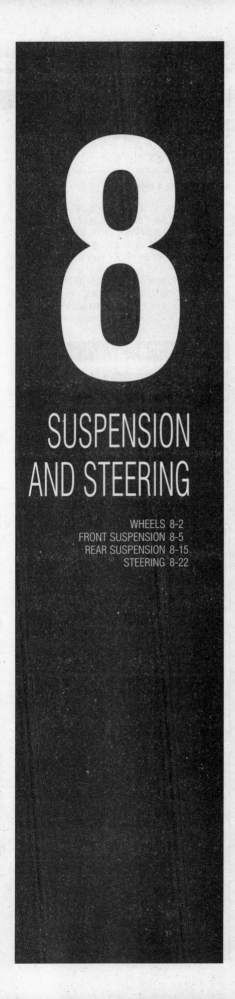

8

SUSPENSION AND STEERING

WHEELS

Front And Rear Wheels

REMOVAL & INSTALLATION

▶ **See Figures 1 thru 11**

There are four reinforced jacking points located along the lower seam of the vehicle's rocker panel. The two jack points per side are located behind the front wheel opening, for accessing a front wheel and forward of the rear wheel opening to access a rear wheel.

These jack points can be used to lift the vehicle with the supplied scissors-style jack, or a suitable hydraulic floor jack. If lifting the vehicle using a suitable lift, the lift arms can be placed under the four jack points.

✳ CAUTION

Never compromise safety when lifting and supporting a vehicle. Make sure the equipment being used is rated for the vehicle's weight. Never work underneath a vehicle supported by a jack. Always use a suitable jackstand to support the vehicle's weight. As an added measure of safety, if tire/wheel assembly is being removed from the vehicle to allow a repair procedure to be performed, place the tire/wheel assembly under the vehicle. If the vehicle were acci-dentally knocked off it's support by an external force, the tire/wheel assembly could protect the vehicle from coming into contact with the ground. When placing a jack or jackstand under a vehicle, never place a finger, hand or other body part between the vehicle and the support or lifting tool. When lifting only one side (left, right, front, or rear) of a vehicle, always set the parking brake and block the wheels remaining in contact with the ground.

1. Park the vehicle on a hard level surface.
2. Remove the jack, tire iron and, if necessary, the spare tire from their storage compartments.
3. Locate the reinforced jack point located along the lower seam of the vehicle's rocker panel for the part of the vehicle that is to be lifted.

➡**This procedure is also covered in the vehicle's owner's manual.**

4. Place the jack in the proper position.
5. Apply the parking brake and block the diagonally opposite wheel with a wheel chock or two.

➡**Wheel chocks may be purchased at your local auto parts store, or a block of wood cut into wedges may be used. If possible, keep one or two of the chocks in your tire storage compartment, in case any of the tires has to be removed on the side of the road.**

6. If equipped with an automatic transaxle, place the selector lever in **P** or Park; with a manual transaxle, place the shifter in first gear.
7. With the tires still on the ground, use the wheel nut tool to loosen the wheel nuts ½ turn.

➡**If a nut is stuck, never use heat to loosen it. Damage to the wheel and/or bearings may occur. If the nuts are seized, spray the seized nut with a penetrating lubricant and give it one or two heavy hammer blows directly on the end of the bolt to loosen the corrosion. Be careful, as continued pounding will likely damage the nut, wheel stud, brake drum or rotor. Use a large ½ inch breaker bar and a six sided 19mm (¾ inch) deep well socket if available to increase the mechanical advantage.**

8. Using the jack, raise the vehicle until the tire is clear of the ground. Support the vehicle safely using suitable jackstands.
9. Remove the lug nuts, then remove the tire and wheel assembly.

To install:

10. Make sure the wheel, hub mating surfaces, and wheel lug studs, are clean and free of all foreign material. Always remove corrosion from the wheel mounting surface and the brake rotor or drum. Failure to do so may cause the wheel to corrode onto the mounting surface or the lug nuts to either seize in place or loosen in service.
11. Apply an anti-seize compound the wheel studs.

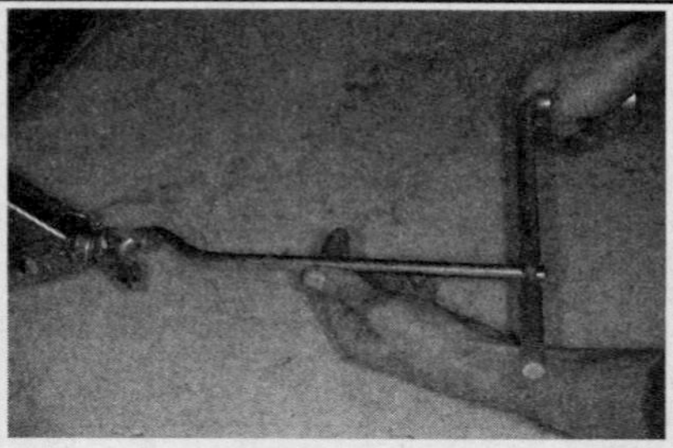

Fig. 1 Connect the vehicle's jack handle as shown. Rotate the jack handle clockwise to raise or counterclockwise to lower the vehicle

Fig. 2 Place the jack at one of the four reinforced lifting points along the seam of the lower rocker panel

Fig. 3 Before jacking the vehicle, block the diagonally opposite wheel with one or, preferably, two chocks

Fig. 4 With the vehicle still on the ground, loosen the lug nuts ½ turn

Fig. 5 For seized wheel nuts, spray them with a penetrating lubricant and use a sturdy ½ inch drive breaker bar and a six sided 19mm (¾ inch) deep well socket

Fig. 6 After the lug nuts have been loosened, raise the vehicle using the jack until the tire is clear of the ground

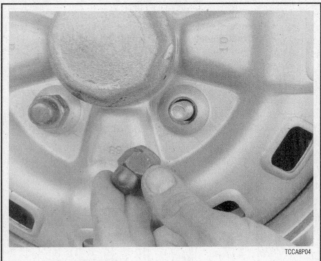

Fig. 7 Remove the lug nuts from the studs

Fig. 8 Remove the wheel and tire assembly from the vehicle

Fig. 9 Apply an anti-seize compound to the threads before reinstalling the wheel and lug nuts.

Fig. 10 Always torque the lug nuts to avoid causing a brake pulsation. A click type torque wrench makes quick work of this procedure

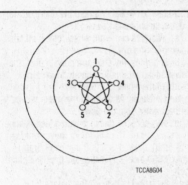

Fig. 11 On wheels with 5 lug nuts, tighten the nuts in star shaped pattern skipping every other nut until all of them are torqued to 80 ft. lbs. (108 Nm)

12. Install the tire/wheel assembly, and if equipped install the wheel covers making sure the valve stem protrudes through the proper opening in the cover. Install then hand-tighten the lug nuts.

13. Using the lug nut tool, tighten all the lug nuts, in a star shaped crisscross pattern, until they are snug.

14. Raise the vehicle and withdraw the jack-stand, then lower the vehicle until the tire contacts the ground.

15. Using a torque wrench, tighten the lug nuts in a star shaped crisscross pattern to 80 ft. lbs. (108 Nm).

❊❊ WARNING

Do not overtighten the lug nuts, as this may cause the wheel studs to stretch, break or crossthread and/or cause a brake pulsation due to component warpage.

16. Remove the jack from under the vehicle, and place the jack and tire tool in their storage compartments. Remove the wheel chock(s).

17. If you have removed a flat or damaged tire, place it in the storage compartment of the vehicle

and take it to your local repair station to have it fixed or replaced as soon as possible.

INSPECTION

◆ **See Figures 12 and 13**

Inspect the tires for proper inflation, lacerations, puncture marks, nails and other sharp objects. Repair or replace as necessary. Remove any debris that is wedged into the tire's tread, as this could cause an annoying clicking noise when driving. Periodically check the tire treadwear. Uneven wear could be a sign of an alignment related condition. As the treadwear approaches the wear bars on the tire, the tire loses its ability to disperse water when driven in wet weather conditions and could compromise the vehicle's handling and safety.

Check the wheel assemblies for dents, cracks, rust and metal fatigue. Repair or replace as necessary. If a wheel vibration is felt, check the wheel axial and radial runout and tire balance. A tire which has aged, or has had a severe impact such as from a pot hole, may have an internal belt damage and must be replaced immediately.

To inspect the wheel axial runout proceed as follows:

1. Raise and safely support the vehicle.

2. To measure the axial runout, place a sturdy object near the wheel that will allow a dial indicator to be attached to it and zero the dial indicator to the side of the rim. To check the axial runout without a dial indicator use a strong wooden dowel and attach it to a sturdy object and adjust it so that it is almost touching the side of the wheel rim.

3. Rotate the wheel and read the dial indicator, or if using the wooden dowel:

   a. Watch to see if the wheel moves in and out from the dowel.

   b. If it does move in and out, adjust the dowel such that it is just barely touching the side of the wheel.

   c. Rotate the wheel until the wheel moves furthest away from the dowel.

   d. Measure the distance with a feeler gauge or a small ruler. The maximum movement (service limit) allowed is 0.080 inches (2.0mm). Note 0.080 inches is just a little over 1/16 of an inch.

4. Next measure the radial runout. Zero the dial indicator downward on the rim, or adjust the dowel such that it is just above the inside of the rim.

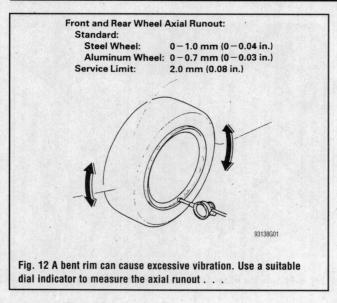

Front and Rear Wheel Axial Runout:
Standard:
  Steel Wheel: 0 − 1.0 mm (0 − 0.04 in.)
  Aluminum Wheel: 0 − 0.7 mm (0 − 0.03 in.)
Service Limit: 2.0 mm (0.08 in.)

93138G01

Fig. 12 A bent rim can cause excessive vibration. Use a suitable dial indicator to measure the axial runout . . .

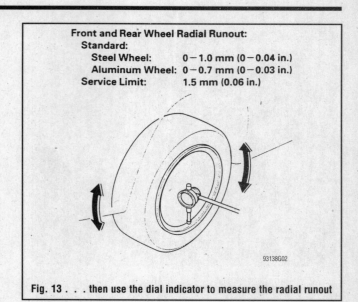

Front and Rear Wheel Radial Runout:
Standard:
  Steel Wheel: 0 − 1.0 mm (0 − 0.04 in.)
  Aluminum Wheel: 0 − 0.7 mm (0 − 0.03 in.)
Service Limit: 1.5 mm (0.06 in.)

93138G02

Fig. 13 . . . then use the dial indicator to measure the radial runout

5. Rotate the wheel and read the dial indicator, or if using the wooden dowel:

  a. Watch to see if the wheel moves up and down from the dowel.

  b. If it does move up and down, adjust the dowel such that it is just barely touching the inside of the wheel.

  c. Rotate the wheel until the wheel moves furthest away from the dowel.

  d. Measure the distance with a feeler gauge or a small ruler. The maximum movement (service limit) allowed is 0.060 inches (1.5mm). Note 0.060 inches is just a less than 1⁄16 of an inch.

6. If the wheel is beyond the service limit, replace the wheel, or have it straightened.

Wheel Lug Studs

REPLACEMENT

Front

Replacing a front wheel lug stud will require removal of the front steering knuckle from the vehicle and replacement of the axle nut. In addition to replacing the axle nut, on CR-V and V6 Odyssey models, the front wheel bearing must be replaced, as the front hub is pressed into the bearing. On these models, the hub must be pressed out of the bearing to allow enough room for the wheel lug stud to be removed from and installed into the hub.

To replace a front wheel lug stud proceed as follows:

1. Remove the front knuckle assembly. For specific details, refer to the procedure in this section.

2. On CR-V and V6 Odyssey models, press the front hub out of the wheel bearing assembly.

3. On 4-cylinder Odyssey models, unbolt the hub sub-assembly from the knuckle.

4. Place the back side of the hub squarely over a suitable deep well impact socket just large enough to clear the button head of the stud.

5. Using a hydraulic press, or a suitable ball peen hammer, drive the stud out of the hub into the socket.

To install:

6. Place the front side of the hub flush with the deep well socket used for removal. Make sure the socket is deep enough to ensure that the threaded portion of the stud will not contact the bottom of the socket when it is fully installed.

7. Drive the threaded portion of the stud though the back of the hub until the button head portion of the stud bottoms on the hub.

8. On CR-V and V6 Odyssey models:

  a. Replace the wheel bearing. For specific details follow the bearing removal and installation procedures in this section.

  b. Press the hub into the wheel bearing assembly.

9. On 4-cylinder Odyssey models, install the hub sub-assembly onto the knuckle.

10. The balance of the installation procedure is the reverse of removal, noting the following points:

- For every stud replaced, use a new wheel lug nut. Torque the lug nuts to 80 ft. lbs. (108 Nm).
- Install a new axle nut and torque the nut to 181 ft. lbs. (245 Nm), then stake the nut.

Rear

1. Remove the rear hub assembly. For specific details follow the hub removal and installation procedures in this section.

2. Place the back side of the hub squarely over a suitable deep well impact socket just large enough to clear the button head of the stud.

3. Using a hydraulic press, or a suitable ball peen hammer, drive the stud out of the hub into the socket.

To install:

4. Place the front side of the hub flush with the deep well socket used for removal. Make sure the socket is deep enough to ensure that the threaded portion of the stud will not contact the bottom of the socket when it is fully installed.

5. Drive the threaded portion of the stud though the back of the hub until the button head portion of the stud bottoms on the hub.

6. The balance of installation is the reverse of the removal procedure, noting the following points:

- For every stud replaced, use a new wheel lug nut. Torque the lug nuts to 80 ft. lbs. (108 Nm).
- On CR-V models, install a new axle nut and torque the nut to 134 ft. lbs. (181 Nm), then stake the nut.
- On Odyssey models, install a new axle nut and torque the nut to 181 ft. lbs. (245 Nm), then stake the nut.
- On V6 Odyssey models, install a new spindle nut hub cap.
- On Odyssey models, install a new axle nut and torque the nut to 181 ft. lbs. (245 Nm), then stake the nut.

FRONT SUSPENSION

FRONT SUSPENSION COMPONENTS—CR-V

1. Steering knuckle
2. Tie rod end
3. Lower control arm
4. Upper control arm
5. Lower control arm bushing
6. Lower control arm bushing
7. Sway bar
8. Upper ball joint
9. Shock fork
10. Lower ball joint

93138PU2

FRONT SUSPENSION COMPONENTS—V-6 Odyssey

1. Tie rod end
2. Inner steering rod
3. Lower ball joint
4. Lower control arm
5. Coil spring
6. Lower control arm bushing
7. Sway bar
8. Sway bar link
9. Steering knuckle

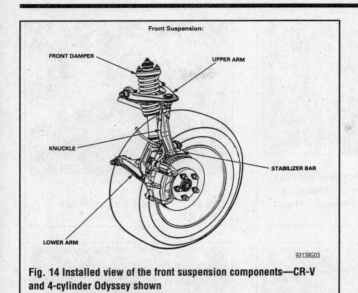

Fig. 14 Installed view of the front suspension components—CR-V and 4-cylinder Odyssey shown

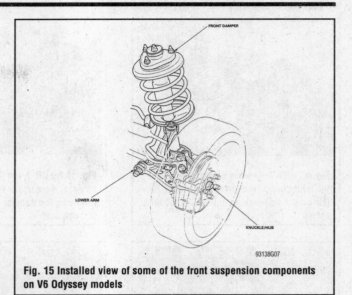

Fig. 15 Installed view of some of the front suspension components on V6 Odyssey models

Coil Springs

REMOVAL & INSTALLATION

▶ **See Figures 16 and 17**

1. Remove the strut assembly from the vehicle.
2. Place the strut in a vice and install a suit-able spring compressor onto the coil spring. Follow the spring compressor manufacturer's instructions.

3. Compress the spring, then using a 14mm boxed end wrench, remove the self-locking nut from the top of the strut using a 5mm hex key to hold the strut dampening rod. Remove the upper strut mount, then remove the coil spring.

To install:

➡**Use new self-locking nuts when assembling and installing the struts.**

4. Install the spring compressor onto the coil spring. Set the spring onto the strut cartridge. The flat part of the coil spring is its top.

5. Assemble the strut mount and its washer

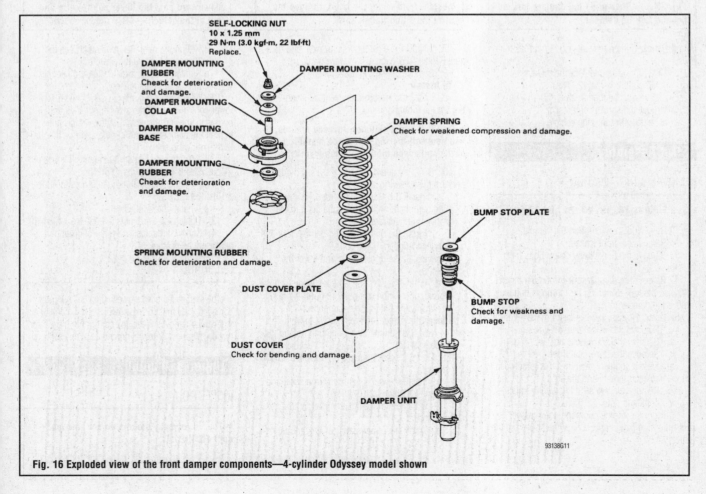

Fig. 16 Exploded view of the front damper components—4-cylinder Odyssey model shown

Fig. 17 With the spring compressed, hold the strut shaft with a 5mm hex wrench to loosen the self-locking nut—CR-V model shown

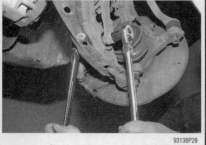

Fig. 18 On CR-V and 4-cylinder Odyssey models, the damper fork is removed by removing the damper fork-to-control arm through bolt . . .

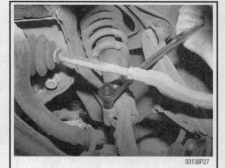

Fig. 19 . . . remove the damper fork pinch bolt . . .

Fig. 20 . . . then slide the damper fork down off of the damper

Fig. 21 Once the fork damper is disconnected, from under the hood, remove the strut mounting flange nuts . . .

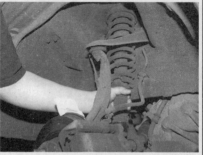

Fig. 22 . . . then lower the strut assembly downward past the lower control arm and out of the vehicle—CR-V model shown

onto the strut. Tighten the self-locking nut, as follows:

- CR-V models and 4-cylinder Odyssey models: 22 ft. lbs. (29 Nm).
- V6 Odyssey models: 33 ft. lbs. (44 Nm)

6. Remove the spring compressor.
7. Install the strut into the vehicle.

Strut Assembly

REMOVAL & INSTALLATION

◆ See Figures 18, 19, 20, 21 and 22

1. Raise and safely support the vehicle.
2. Remove the front wheels.
3. Remove the brake hose clamp bolts from the strut.
4. Remove the damper fork-to-damper pinch bolt, then the fork-to-control arm through bolt and remove the damper fork.
5. On V6 Odyssey models, perform the followng:
   a. Remove the wheel sensor wire bracket.
   b. Remove the brake hose bracket.
   c. Remove the upper stabilizer link.
   d. Make alignment reference marks between the knuckle assembly and the strut.
   e. Remove the two strut to steering knuckle pinch bolts and nuts.
6. From the engine compartment, remove the strut mounting flange nuts. Lower the strut from the vehicle.

7. Inspect the strut mounts for wear and damage. Replace any damaged or worn parts.
8. Remove the spring assembly.

To install:

9. Install the strut into the vehicle. Hand-tighten the mounting nuts.

➡ **On CR-V and 4-cylinder Odyssey models, use new self-locking nuts when installing the struts and assembling the damper forks.**

10. On CR-V and 4-cylinder Odyssey models, perform the following steps:
    a. Install the strut into the damper fork. The alignment mark on the strut tube fits into the groove on the damper fork.
    b. Install the pinch bolt and damper fork bolt. Only hand-tighten these bolts.
    c. Install the front wheels and lower the vehicle.
    d. With all four of the vehicle's wheels on the ground, tighten the damper fork nut to 47 ft. lbs. (65 Nm) while holding the damper fork bolt. Tighten the damper fork pinch bolt to 32 ft. lbs. (44 Nm). Tighten the strut mounting nuts to 28 ft. lbs. (39 Nm).
11. On V6 Odyssey models, perform the following steps:
    a. Install the wheel sensor wire bracket and tighten to 83 inch lbs. (9.3 Nm).
    b. Install the brake hose bracket, and tighten to 16 ft. lbs. (22 Nm).
    c. Install the upper stabilizer link and tighten to 58 ft. lbs. (78 Nm).

d. Align the reference marks between the knuckle assembly and the strut.
e. Install the two strut-to-steering knuckle pinch bolts and nuts loosely.
12. With a floor jack placed safely under the lower control arm, lift the steering knuckle until it begins to support the weight of the vehicle and tighten the damper mounting nuts and pinch bolts to the following specifications:
    a. Tighten the two strut to steering knuckle pinch bolts to 116 ft. lbs. (157 Nm).
    b. Tighten the strut mounting nuts to 28 ft. lbs. (39 Nm).
    c. Install the front wheels.
13. Tighten the wheel nuts to 80 ft. lbs. (108 Nm).
14. Check and adjust the vehicle's front end alignment as needed.

OVERHAUL

The strut assemblies are sealed units. If worn or damaged, they must be replaced. The only component that can be removed is the coil spring. For more information, please refer to that procedure in this section.

Upper Ball Joint

INSPECTION

➡ **The V6 Odyssey models do not have an upper ball joint.**

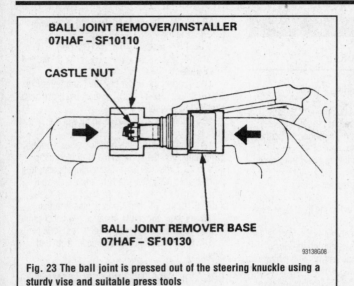

Fig. 23 The ball joint is pressed out of the steering knuckle using a sturdy vise and suitable press tools

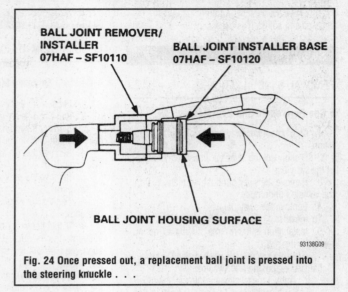

Fig. 24 Once pressed out, a replacement ball joint is pressed into the steering knuckle . . .

The ball joint is part of the upper control arm. If the ball joint has failed the control arm assembly must be replaced.

1. Raise and safely support the vehicle.
2. Place a suitable jack under the lower control arm and lift the arm upward 2 inches (50mm).
3. Carefully grasp the upper and lower portion of the front tires and attempt to rock back and forth.
4. If looseness is felt at the upper portion of the tire:

   a. Remove the tire/wheel assembly and inspect the upper control arm bushings using a suitable prytool to check for looseness. If looseness is felt, replace the upper control arm.

   b. Using a suitable prytool pry between the steering knuckle and the upper control arm. If looseness is present, replace the control arm assembly.

REMOVAL & INSTALLATION

The upper ball joints cannot be replaced separately. If the ball joints become worn or damaged, the upper control arm must be replaced.

Lower Ball Joint

INSPECTION

1. Raise and safely support the vehicle.
2. Place a suitable jack under the lower control arm and lift the arm upward 2 inches (50mm).
3. Carefully grasp the upper and lower portion of the front tires and attempt to rock back and forth.
4. If looseness is felt at the lower portion of the tire proceed as follows:

   a. Using a suitable prytool pry between steering knuckle and the lower control arm.

   b. If looseness is present, on CR-V and 4-cylinder Odyssey models, replace the lower joint. On V6 Odyssey models, replace the lower control arm assembly.

REMOVAL & INSTALLATION

➡On V6 Odyssey models, the lower ball joints cannot be replaced separately. If the ball joints become worn or damaged, the lower control arm assembly must be replaced.

CR-V and 4-Cylinder Odyssey models

▶ See Figures 23, 24 and 25

➡This procedure is performed after the removal of the steering knuckle and requires the use of special press tools. In addition a large sturdy vise is needed. After replacement of the ball joint, the ball joint retaining clip is installed onto the boot using Clip Guide Tool No. 07974-SA50700 or 07GAG-SD40700 or their equivalents.

1. Remove the brake caliper, and brake rotor from the steering knuckle assembly. For more information, refer to Section 9 of this manual.
2. Remove the steering knuckle assembly from the vehicle, as outlined later in this section.
3. Pry off the ball joint boot snapring and remove the boot.
4. Check the boot condition and replace if damaged or deteriorated.
5. Install the ball joint removal/installer Tool No. 07HAF-SF101110 around the ball joint spindle with the large end facing out. Install and tighten the ball joint castle nut to hold the tool in position.
6. Position the knuckle with the installed tool into a suitable vise, with the ball joint removal base Tool No. 07HAF-SF10130 installed over the ball joint base. Tighten the vise to press the ball joint out of the steering knuckle.
7. Tighten the vise to press the ball joint out of the steering knuckle.

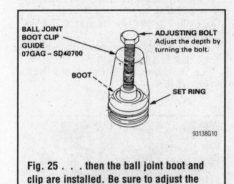

Fig. 25 . . . then the ball joint boot and clip are installed. Be sure to adjust the ball joint boot clip before reinstalling the steering knuckle

To install:

8. Position the new ball joint into the hole of the steering knuckle.
9. Install the ball joint removal/installer Tool No. 07HAF-SF101110 on the ball joint spindle side of the steering knuckle the small end facing out.
10. Position the installation base Tool No. 07HAF-SF10120 on the ball joint base and set the assembly in a large vise. Tighten the vise to press the ball joint into the steering knuckle.
11. Pack the interior of the ball joint boot with grease.
12. Adjust the boot clip guide tool with its adjusting bolt until the end of the tool aligns with the groove on the boot. Slide the clip over the installed onto the boot using the clip guide Tool No. 07974-SA50700 or 07GAG-SD40700 or their equivalent and into position on the ball joint boot and seat the ball joint boot snapring in the groove of the ball joint.
13. Install the hub assembly and brake disc onto the knuckle.
14. Install the steering knuckle assembly into the vehicle.

15. Have the vehicle's front end alignment checked and adjusted as necessary.

Sway Bar

REMOVAL & INSTALLATION

♦ **See Figures 26 and 27**

1. Matchmark the sway bar for proper reinstallation.
2. Disconnect the sway bar links from the end of the sway bar.
3. Remove the sway bar bushing brackets from the vehicle's underbody.
4. Remove the sway bar.
To install:
5. Installation is the reverse of removal, noting the following steps:
　a. Apply silicone grease between the sway bar bracket busing and sway bar.
　b. Tighten the sway bar retainers, as follows:
- Sway bar bracket-to-body bolts: 16 ft. lbs. (22 Nm)
- CR-V models: Link nut and bolt 22 ft. lbs. (29 Nm)
- 4-cylinder Odyssey models: Link nut and bolt 14 ft. lbs. (19 Nm)
- V6 Odyssey models: Link nut 58 ft. lbs. (78 Nm)

93138P36

Fig. 26 To remove the sway bar links, use a 14mm wrench to loosen the flange bolt and a 5mm hex key to hold the threaded spindle—CR-V shown

93138P40

Fig. 27 Unfasten the retaining bolts from the sway bar bushing bracket—CR-V shown

Radius Rod

REMOVAL & INSTALLATION

4-Cylinder Odyssey Models

1. Loosen the front wheel lug nuts ½ turn.
2. Raise and safely support the vehicle.
3. Remove the radius rod self-locking nut from the front subframe.
4. Remove the two radius rod-to-control arm fasteners.
5. Remove the radius rod assembly.
To install:
6. Apply silicone grease to the front radius rod bushings.
7. Install the larger bushing on the front of the subframe and the smaller bushing on the rear of the subframe both with the small end of the bushing facing out.
8. Install the washer onto the radius rod then the sleeve, and install the radius rod through the bushings in the lower subframe.
9. Install the front radius rod washer, then install and hand tighten a new self-locking radius rod nut.
10. Install the radius rod-to-control arm flange bolts and tighten to 76 ft. lbs. (103 Nm).
11. Tighten the radius rod bushing bolt to 40 ft. lbs. (54 Nm).
12. The balance of assembly is the reverse of the removal procedure. Make sure to tighten the lug nuts to 80 ft. lbs. (108 Nm).

Upper Control Arm

REMOVAL & INSTALLATION

➡ **The V6 Odyssey models do not have an upper control arm.**

1. Raise and safely support the vehicle.
2. Remove the front wheels. Support the lower control arm assembly with a floor jack.
3. Remove the damper fork bolt and damper fork pinch bolt. Remove the damper fork.
4. Separate the upper ball joint from the steering knuckle using a ball joint separator tool.
5. Unbolt the brake hose clips from the strut tube.
6. Remove the three strut mounting nuts. Remove the strut from the vehicle.
7. Remove the self-locking nuts from the upper control arm anchor bolts. Remove the upper arm from the vehicle.

➡ **Do not disassemble the upper arm. If the ball joint or bushings are faulty, or the upper arm is damaged, the entire upper arm must be replaced.**

To install:

➡ **Use new self-locking nuts when installing the upper arm and strut.**

8. Install the upper control arm assembly into the strut tower.
9. Install the strut into the vehicle. Connect the damper fork bolt and pinch bolt.

10. Tighten the upper control arm bushing fasteners, as follows:
- CR-V models: 40 ft. lbs. (54 Nm).
- 4-cylinder Odyssey models: 47 ft. lbs. (64 Nm).
11. Connect the upper ball joint and tighten to 29–35 ft. lbs. (39–47 Nm). Connect the brake hose clips to the strut tube.
12. Install the front wheels and lower the vehicle.
13. With all four of the vehicle's wheels on the ground, loosen, then tighten the strut mounting nuts to 28 ft. lbs. (39 Nm). Tighten the damper fork pinch bolt to 32 ft. lbs. (44 Nm) and the damper fork bolt to 47 ft. lbs. (65 Nm). Tighten the castle nut to 32 ft. lbs. (44 Nm), then tighten it further, if necessary, only enough to install a new cotter pin.
14. Tighten the lug nuts to 80 ft. lbs. (108 Nm).
15. Check and adjust the vehicle's front end alignment.

CONTROL ARM BUSHING REPLACEMENT

The upper control arm bushings are part of the control arm. If the bushings are worn or damaged, the control arm must be replaced as an assembly

Lower Control Arm

REMOVAL & INSTALLATION

♦ **See Figures 28, 29 and 30**

1. Loosen the front wheel nuts ½ turn.
2. Raise and safely support the vehicle.
3. Remove the front tire/wheel assembly
4. On CR-V and 4-cylinder Odyssey models, perform the following:
　a. Disconnect the lower sway bar link.
　b. Remove the strut fork through bolt.
5. On 4-cylinder Odyssey models, remove the radius rod-to-control arm fasteners.
6. Loosen the lower ball joint flange nut, then using a suitable ball joint removal tool, disconnect the ball joint from the control arm.
7. Remove the lower control arm bushing fasteners, then remove the control arm.
To install:
8. Installation is the reverse of the removal procedure, noting the following steps and tightening specifications:

93138P29

Fig. 28 Loosen the fork through bolt flange nut, then tap on the nut using a plastic hammer to loosen and remove the through bolt—CR-V shown

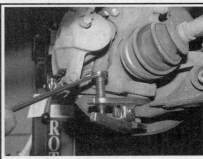

Fig. 29 Use a ball joint/tie rod end removal tool to remove the lower ball joint assembly—CR-V shown

Fig. 30 If the ball joint spindle spins when trying to install a new flange nut, temporarily install a C-clamp to hold the tapered portion of the spindle seated into the control arm. Then, tighten the flange nut

a. On CR-V and 4-cylinder Odyssey models, perform the following:
- Lubricate the lower control arm bushings with silicone grease
- Replace the strut fork-to-control arm flange nut and torque the nut and through bolt to: 47 ft. lbs. (64 Nm)
- Install the lower ball joint castle nut using a new cotter pin and torque to: 36–43 ft. lbs. (49–59 Nm)

b. On CR-V models, tighten the control arm retainers, as follows:

- Front flange bolt: 76 ft. lbs. (103 Nm)
- Rear bushing bracket bolts: 66 ft. lbs. (89 Nm)
- Rear busing self-locking nut (replace): 61 ft. lbs. (83 Nm)

c. On 4-cylinder Odyssey models, tighten the control arm front flange bolt to 40 ft. lbs. (54 Nm).

d. On V6 Odyssey models, tighten the control arm retainers, as follows:

- Front and rear flange bolts: 69 ft. lbs. (93 Nm)
- Rear bushing bracket bolts: 66 ft. lbs. (89 Nm)
- Install the lower ball joint castle nut using a new lock pin and torque to: 43–51 ft. lbs. (59–69 Nm)

e. Torque the lug nuts to 80 ft. lbs. (108 Nm)

CONTROL ARM BUSHING REPLACEMENT

With exception of the rear control arm bushing on the CR-V models, if a control arm bushing is worn or damaged the control arm assembly must be replaced. To replace the rear control arm bushing, proceed as follows:

1. Remove the front lower control arm bushing flange bolt.
2. Remove the rear lower control arm bushing self-locking nut.
3. Remove the rear lower control arm bushing bracket.
4. Remove the rear lower control arm bushing from the control arm spindle.
5. Installation is the reverse of the removal procedure. Refer to the control arm installation procedures for tightening specifications.

Knuckle

REMOVAL & INSTALLATION

▶ **See Figures 31 thru 41**

1. Using a suitable sized chisel, lift the lock tab of the front axle spindle nut from the groove in the spindle.
2. Loosen and remove the front axle spindle nut.
3. Loosen the wheel lug nuts ½ turn.
4. Raise and safely support the vehicle.

5. Remove the tire/wheel assembly.
6. Remove the brake hose and caliper mounting bolts and place the caliper assembly aside supported by mechanic's wire to prevent the hydraulic hose from being damaged.
7. Remove the ABS wheel sensor bolts and remove the wheel sensor.
8. Remove the cotter key from the tie rod end spindle, and remove the castle nut, then using a tie rod end removal tool, remove the tie rod end from the knuckle.
9. Remove the cotter key from the lower ball joint spindle, then loosen and remove the castle nut and release the ball joint from the lower control arm.
10. On CR-V and 4-cylinder Odyssey models, remove the cotter key from the upper ball joint spindle, then loosen and remove the castle nut and release the ball joint from the upper control arm.
11. On V6 Odyssey models, remove the strut-to-knuckle mounting nuts and bolts.
12. Pull the knuckle away from the vehicle. If necessary, use a plastic hammer to tap on the spindle to help release it from the hub splines.
13. On CR-V and V6 Odyssey models, using a hydraulic press and suitable press tools, remove the front hub/bearing assembly. For specific details, refer to the hub/bearing removal and installation procedures in this section.
14. On 4-cylinder Odyssey models, remove the flange bolts securing the hub unit to the knuckle.
15. Remove the splash guard.

➡**Carefully inspect the lug bolt studs. If they have been damaged, replace them while the hub is removed from the knuckle.**

To install:
16. Install the splash guard.
17. On CR-V and V6 Odyssey models, install the wheel bearing, snapring and hub.
18. On 4-cylinder Odyssey models, install the wheel bearing/hub assembly and tighten the flange bolts to 33 ft. lbs. (44 Nm)
19. The balance of installation is the reverse of the removal procedure, making note of the following points and specifications:

a. CR-V and 4-cylinder Odyssey model torque specifications:
- Upper ball joint torque: 29–35 ft. lbs. (39–47 Nm), install using a new cotter pin
- Lower ball joint torque: 36–43 ft. lbs. (49–59 Nm), install using a new cotter pin

Fig. 31 Drive the lock tab upward out of the groove in the spindle before removing the nut

Fig. 32 With the center cap removed, removed, loosen and remove the spindle flange nut

Fig. 33 Loosen the spindle from the hub splines by driving it inward using a plastic hammer, or a suitable tapered punch and hammer

Fig. 34 After removing the cotter key, loosen and remove the tie rod end castle nut. When reinstalling, use a new cotter key

Fig. 35 Use a tie rod end removal tool to release the tie rod from the steering knuckle

Fig. 36 Remove the ABS wheel sensor fasteners, then lift the sensor away from the knuckle

Fig. 37 Use a hand impact driver to remove the Phillips screws that hold the brake rotor to the wheel hub

Fig. 38 Thread two 8 x 1.25mm bolts into the brake rotor two turns at a time to push it off the hub

Fig. 39 When reinstalling the tie rod end into the knuckle, use a pair of locking pliers to keep the tapered spindle seated and from spinning freely

Fig. 40 Install a new axle spindle nut, tighten it to 181 ft. lbs. (245 Nm), then stake the nut into the spindle groove

- Tie rod end: 32 ft. lbs. (43 Nm), install using a new cotter pin
- ABS sensor fasteners: 16 ft. lbs. (22 Nm)
  b. 4-cylinder Odyssey model torque specifications:
- Hub unit flange bolts: 33 ft. lbs. (44 Nm)
  c. V6 Odyssey model torque specifications:
- Lower ball joint castle nut: 43–51 ft. lbs. (59–69 Nm), install using a new lock pin
- Damper pinch bolts flange nuts: 116 ft. lbs. (157 Nm)
- ABS wheel sensor: 82 inch lbs. (9.3 Nm)
  d. Tighten as follows for all models:
- Brake rotor mounting screws: 82 inch lbs. (9.3 Nm)

- Brake caliper bolt: 80 ft. lbs. (108 Nm)
- Lug nuts: 80 ft. lbs. (108 Nm)
- Axle spindle nut: 181 ft. lbs. (245 Nm), stake nut afterwards

Front Hub and Bearing

INSPECTION

1. Raise and support the vehicle safely.
2. Remove the front and/or rear wheels.
3. Install the lug nuts and tighten them to 80 ft. lbs. (108 Nm).
4. Use a dial gauge to measure front bearing end-play at the hub flange, or to measure rear bearing end-play at the center of the hub's grease cap.
5. Pull the rotor assembly in and out to measure the bearing play. Compare the dial gauge readings.
6. The standard bearing end-play for both front and rear wheels is 0.000–0.002 in. (0.00–0.05mm). If the end-play measurement exceeds the standard, the wheel bearings must be replaced. The wheel bearings cannot be adjusted.

REMOVAL & INSTALLATION

▶ See Figures 42, 43, 44 and 45

➡Once the wheel bearing is removed, it must be replaced. A hydraulic press and bearing

drivers are required to remove and install the wheel bearing. The following Honda tools or their equivalents are needed: Hub Assembly tool 07GAF-SE0100, Hub Bases 07965-SD90100, Bearing Driver 07749–0010000, 52 x 55mm Driving Attachment 07746–0010400.

1. Remove the steering knuckle assembly. For specific details, refer to the repair procedures in this section.
2. On 4-cylinder Odyssey models, remove the flange bolts securing the hub unit to the knuckle and remove the hub unit.
3. On CR-V and V6 Odyssey models, support the knuckle in a suitable press plate.
4. On 4-cylinder Odyssey models, support the hub unit in a suitable press plate.
5. Using a suitable press tool that is slightly smaller than the inner race of the wheel bearing, press the hub out of the inner wheel bearing race.
6. Remove the inner race remaining on the hub from the hub assembly using a bearing separator.
7. On CR-V and V6 Odyssey models, remove the large circlip.
8. Support the knuckle or hub unit in a suitable press plate, and using a press tool slightly smaller than the outer race of the wheel bearing, press the wheel bearing out.
9. If the knuckle is being replaced, transfer the splash guard shield.
10. Carefully inspect the lug nut studs, and replace them at this time, if necessary.

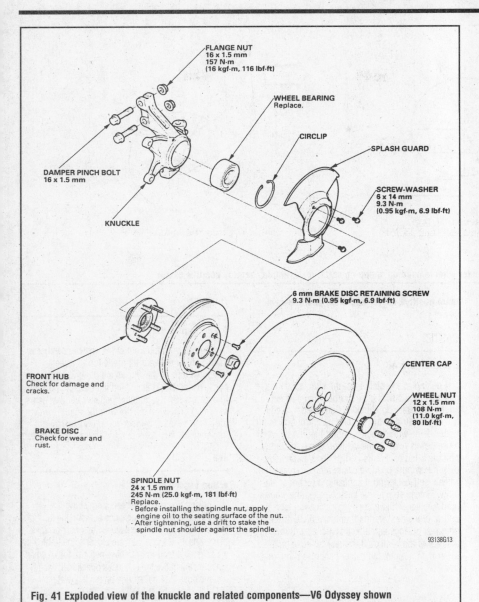

Fig. 41 Exploded view of the knuckle and related components—V6 Odyssey shown

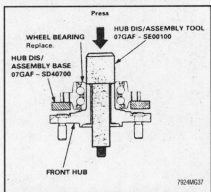

Fig. 42 Removing the hub from the wheel bearing using the disassembly tools

To install:

11. Using a press tool slightly smaller than the outer race of the wheel bearing, support the knuckle or hub unit, and press the wheel bearing into the knuckle or hub unit. If used, install the large circlip.

12. Support the inner wheel bearing race, and press the hub into the wheel bearing.

13. On 4-cylinder Odyssey models, install the hub unit onto the knuckle and torque the flange bolts to 33 ft. lbs. (44 Nm).

14. The balance of installation is in reverse order of removal, noting the following:

- Tighten the axle spindle nut to 181 ft. lbs. (245 Nm)
- Tighten the wheel nuts to 80 ft. lbs. (108 Nm)

Wheel Alignment

If the tires are worn unevenly, if the vehicle is not stable on the highway or if the handling seems uneven in spirited driving, the wheel alignment should be checked. If an alignment problem is suspected, first check for improper tire inflation and other possible causes. These can be worn suspension or steering components, accident damage or even unmatched tires. If any worn or damaged components are found, they must be replaced before the wheels can be properly aligned. Wheel

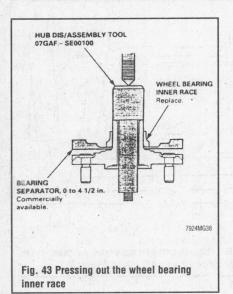

Fig. 43 Pressing out the wheel bearing inner race

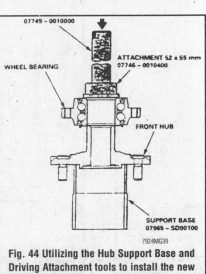

Fig. 44 Utilizing the Hub Support Base and Driving Attachment tools to install the new wheel bearing

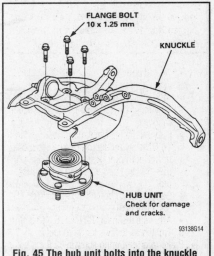

Fig. 45 The hub unit bolts into the knuckle on 4-cylinder Odyssey models

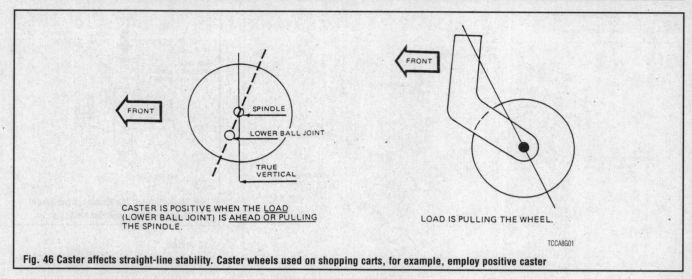

Fig. 46 Caster affects straight-line stability. Caster wheels used on shopping carts, for example, employ positive caster

alignment requires very expensive equipment and involves minute adjustments which must be accurate. This should only be performed by a trained technician. Take your vehicle to a properly equipped shop.

The following is a description of the alignment angles which are adjustable on most vehicles and how they affect vehicle handling. The caster angle only applies the vehicle's front wheel however both camber and toe apply to both the front and rear wheels. The toe is adjustable on both the front and rear wheels on the CR-V and Odyssey models. The caster can be adjusted by substituting shims on the 4-cylinder Odyssey models. The front camber can be adjusted by substitution of a special different shank size bolt on the V6 Odyssey model. Neither camber nor caster is adjustable on the CR-V models. Only the toe can be adjusted on the rear of the CR-V and Odyssey models.

➡**When diagnosing a vehicle for pulling, be aware most road surfaces are crowned. Typically, a vehicle will pull to the side with the least positive caster and most positive camber.**

CASTER

▶ **See Figure 46**

Looking at a vehicle from the side, caster angle describes the steering axis rather than a wheel angle. The steering knuckle is attached to a control arm or strut at the top and a control arm at the bottom. The wheel pivots around the line between these points to steer the vehicle. When the upper point is tilted back, this is described as positive caster. Having a positive caster tends to make the wheels self-centering, increasing directional stability. Excessive positive caster makes the wheels hard to steer, while an uneven caster will cause a pull to one side. Overloading the vehicle or sagging rear springs will affect caster, as will raising the rear of the vehicle. If the rear of the vehicle is lower than normal, the caster becomes more positive.

CAMBER

▶ **See Figure 47**

Looking from the front of the vehicle, camber is the inward or outward tilt of the top of wheels. When the tops of the wheels are tilted in, this is negative camber; if they are tilted out, it is positive. In a turn, a slight amount of negative camber helps maximize contact of the tire with the road. However, too much negative camber compromises straight-line stability, increases bump steer and torque steer.

TOE

▶ **See Figure 48**

Looking down at the wheels from above the vehicle, toe angle is the distance between the front of the wheels, relative to the distance between the back of the wheels. If the wheels are closer at the front, they are said to be toed-in or to have negative toe. A small amount of negative toe enhances directional stability and provides a smoother ride on the highway.

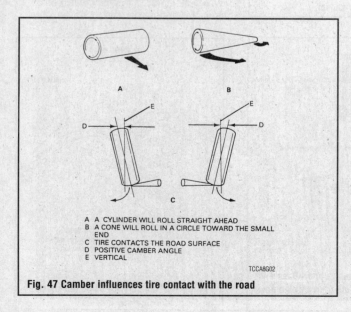

A A CYLINDER WILL ROLL STRAIGHT AHEAD
B A CONE WILL ROLL IN A CIRCLE TOWARD THE SMALL END
C TIRE CONTACTS THE ROAD SURFACE
D POSITIVE CAMBER ANGLE
E VERTICAL

Fig. 47 Camber influences tire contact with the road

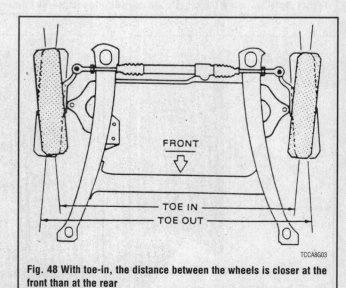

Fig. 48 With toe-in, the distance between the wheels is closer at the front than at the rear

REEAR SUSPENSION

REAR SUSPENSION COMPONENTS—CR-V

1. Shock absorber
2. Upper arm
3. Sway bar link
4. Axle
5. Lower arm bushing
6. Coil spring
7. Lower arm
8. Trailing arm

REAR SUSPENSION COMPONENTS—V-6 Odyssey

1. Trailing arm
2. Lower arm A
3. Lower arm B
4. Lower arm A bushing
5. Coil spring
6. Shock absorber
7. Rear knuckle

93138PU3

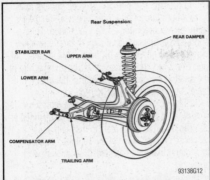

Fig. 49 Rear suspension components used on CR-V models

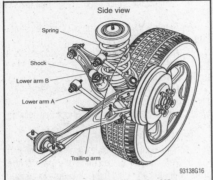

Fig. 51 Cutaway side view of the V6 Odyssey double wishbone rear suspension

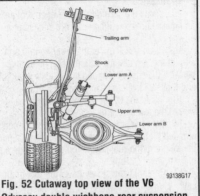

Fig. 52 Cutaway top view of the V6 Odyssey double wishbone rear suspension

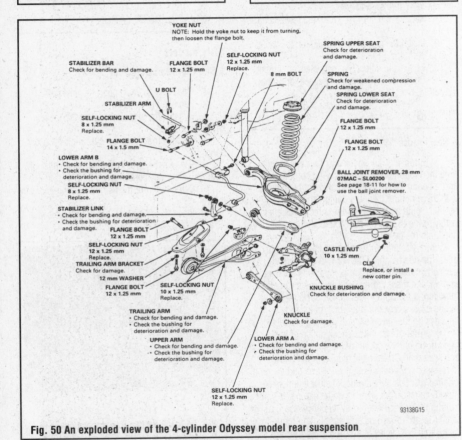

Fig. 50 An exploded view of the 4-cylinder Odyssey model rear suspension

➡On 4-cylinder Odyssey models, after removing and installing any rear suspension component, the Load Sensing Proportioning Valve (LSPV) spring length must be checked and adjusted. This step is important; the LSPV determines the fluid pressure for the rear brakes. Please refer to the Load Sensing Proportioning Valve procedures in Section 9.

Coil Springs

REMOVAL & INSTALLATION

CR-V Models

1. Raise and safely support the vehicle.
2. Remove rear wheels.

3. Remove the strut assembly. For details, see strut assembly removal in this section.
4. Place the strut assembly in a vise and using a suitable spring compressor, compress the spring.
5. Use a 5mm hex key to hold the strut dampening rod and remove the self-locking nut.
6. Remove the washer, rubber busing collar, mounting base, mounting bushing, and spring mounting rubber.
7. Remove the spring.
8. Installation is the reverse of disassembly, noting the following:
   • Install a new self-locking nut and tighten to 22 ft. lbs. (29 Nm).
   • Tighten the strut flange mounting nuts to 36 ft. lbs. (49 Nm).
   • Tighten the strut-to-control arm through bolt to 40 ft. lbs. (54 Nm).

4-Cylinder Odyssey Models

1. Raise and safely support the vehicle.
2. Remove the rear wheels.
3. Place a floor jack under the lower control arm spring perch and raise it slightly.
4. Remove the shock absorber flange through bolt and the knuckle flange through bolt from the lower control arm.
5. Collapse and remove and the shock assembly. For specific details, see the shock removal procedures in this section.
6. Slowly lower the floor jack to release the tension on the coil spring.
7. Remove the coil spring and the upper and lower spring seats.

To install:

8. Replace the upper and lower spring seats if they are distorted or have disintegrated.
9. Install the spring seats into position.
10. Install the coil spring. Align the ends of the coil with the notches on the spring seats.
11. Raise the floor jack under the lower control arm to compress the spring.
12. Install the shock absorber and knuckle flange bolts and hand tighten them only at this point.
13. Lower the jack and move it under the knuckle. Raise the jack under the knuckle until it is supporting the weight of the vehicle. Tighten each of the two flange bolts to 76 ft. lbs. (103 Nm) and the shock flange nuts to 28 ft lbs. (38 Nm).
14. Lower the floor jack. Install the rear wheels. Lower the vehicle.
15. Tighten the wheel nuts to 80 ft. lbs. (108 Nm).
16. Check and adjust the rear wheel alignment as necessary.

V6 Odyssey Models

1. Carefully raise and support the vehicle.
2. Remove the rear wheel and tire assembly.
3. Place a jack under the lower control arm and lift the arm slightly.
4. Remove the wheel sensor clamp bolts and wire from the lower control arm, but do not disconnect the wire.
5. Remove the flange bolt that attaches the lower control arm to the knuckle assembly.
6. Carefully and slowly lower the jack gradually.
7. Remove the spring from the vehicle.

To install:

8. Install the spring to the lower control arm and make sure the spring seats are aligned properly.

9. Place a jack under the lower control arm and lift the arm slightly until the bolt holes align between the control arm and the knuckle assembly and loosely install the flange bolt.

10. Install the wheel sensor clamp bolts and wire to the lower control arm.

11. With the jack placed under the lower control arm and lift the arm until the jack begins to support the weight of the vehicle and torque the flange bolt to 54 ft. lbs. (74 Nm).

12. Carefully and slowly lower the jack gradually.

13. Install the rear wheel and tighten the wheel nuts to 80 ft. lbs. (108 Nm).

14. Check and adjust the rear wheel alignment.

15. Test drive the vehicle and check for proper operation.

Shock Absorbers

REMOVAL & INSTALLATION

4-Cylinder Odyssey Models

1. Remove the cup holder from the top of the right rear interior trim. Remove the cup holder, storage tray, and jack from the left rear interior trim.

2. Raise and support the vehicle safely.

3. Remove the rear wheels.

4. Place a floor jack under the lower control arm and raise it slightly to compress the spring.

5. Remove the lower shock mount flange bolt and the knuckle flange bolt.

6. Unbolt the shock mount from inside the vehicle. Remove the shock from the vehicle.

To install:

7. Check the shock mount and bushings and replace any that are damaged. Assemble the mount, bushing, and stopper on the shock.

8. Install the shock into the vehicle. Install new self-locking upper mounting nuts.

9. Raise the lower control arm with a floor jack. Be sure the coil spring is properly seated.

10. Install the shock absorber and knuckle flange bolts.

11. Raise the jack enough to take up the weight of the vehicle. Tighten both of the flange bolts to 76 ft. lbs. (103 Nm).

12. Lower the floor jack. Install the rear wheels. Lower the vehicle.

13. Tighten the shock mount nuts to 28 ft. lbs. (39 Nm), and the shock piston nut to 22 ft. lbs. (29 Nm). Install the jack, tool tray, and cup holders.

14. Tighten the wheel nuts to 80 ft. lbs. (108 Nm).

15. Check and adjust the rear wheel alignment as necessary.

V6 Odyssey Models

1. Carefully raise and support the vehicle.

2. Remove the rear wheel.

3. Place a jack under the lower control arm and lift the arm slightly.

4. Remove the shock upper flange bolt from the body.

5. Remove the self-locking nut from the stud on the knuckle.

6. Compress the shock by hand and remove it from the vehicle.

To install:

7. Compress the shock by hand and install it on knuckle mounting stud.

8. Loosely install the lower shock self-locking nut.

9. Extend the shock upward into the upper flange on the body and loosely install the flange bolt.

10. With the jack placed under the lower control arm and lift the arm until the jack begins to support the weight of the vehicle and torque the upper flange bolt to 47 ft. lbs. (64 Nm), and the self-locking nut to 47 ft. lbs. (64 Nm).

11. Remove the floor jack from the lower control arm.

12. Install the rear wheel and tighten the wheel nuts to 80 ft. lbs. (108 Nm).

13. Check and adjust the rear wheel alignment.

14. Test drive the vehicle and check for proper operation.

TESTING

▶ **See Figure 53**

The purpose of the shock absorber is simply to limit the motion of the spring during compression and rebound cycles. If the vehicle is not equipped with these motion dampers, the up and down motion would multiply until the vehicle was alternately trying to leap off the ground and to pound itself into the pavement.

Contrary to popular rumor, the shocks do not affect the ride height of the vehicle. This is controlled by other suspension components such as springs and tires. Worn shock absorbers can affect handling; if the front of the vehicle is rising or falling excessively, the "footprint" of the tires changes on the pavement and steering is affected.

The simplest test of the shock absorber is simply push down on one corner of the unladen vehicle and release it. Observe the motion of the body as it is released. In most cases, it will come up beyond it original rest position, dip back below it and settle quickly to rest. This shows that the damper is controlling the spring action. Any tendency to excessive pitch (up-and-down) motion or failure to return to rest within 2-3 cycles is a sign of poor function

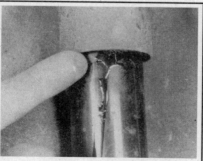

Fig. 53 When fluid is seeping out of the shock absorber, it's time to replace it

within the shock absorber. Oil-filled shocks may have a light film of oil around the seal, resulting from normal breathing and air exchange. This should NOT be taken as a sign of failure, but any sign of thick or running oil definitely indicates failure. Gas filled shocks may also show some film at the shaft; if the gas has leaked out, the shock will have almost no resistance to motion.

While each shock absorber can be replaced individually, it is recommended that they be changed as a pair (both front or both rear) to maintain equal response on both sides of the vehicle. Chances are quite good that if one has failed, its mate is weak also.

Strut Assembly

REMOVAL & INSTALLATION

CR-V models

▶ **See Figures 54 thru 59**

1. Raise and safely support the vehicle.

2. Remove rear wheels.

3. Remove the side access panel in the rear cargo area.

4. Remove the flange bolts through the access panel.

5. Remove the strut assembly flange through bolt from the lower control arm.

6. Carefully lower the rear strut assembly from the vehicle.

7. Place the strut assembly in a suitable vise

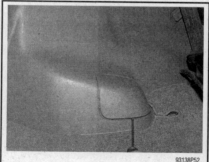

Fig. 54 Remove the side access cover in the cargo area

Fig. 55 Remove the strut mount flange nuts from the top of the strut assembly

Fig. 56 Remove the strut-to-control arm through bolt

Fig. 59 Using the drift, center the shock sleeve with the control arm, then install the through bolt by lightly tapping it to displace the drift

Fig. 57 Carefully lower the strut assembly away from the vehicle

Fig. 58 Once the strut assembly is reinstalled, use a tapered drift to help align the strut with the lower control arm

and using a suitable spring compressor, compress the spring.

8. Use a 5mm hex key to hold the strut dampening rod and remove the self-locking nut.

9. Remove the washer, rubber busing collar, mounting base, mounting bushing, and spring mounting rubber.

10. Remove the spring.

11. Installation is the reverse of the removal procedure, noting the following:
- Install a new strut damper rod self-locking nut and tighten to 22 ft. lbs. (29 Nm).
- Tighten the strut flange mounting nuts to 36 ft. lbs. (49 Nm).
- Tighten the strut-to-control arm through bolt to 40 ft. lbs. (54 Nm).

OVERHAUL

The strut assembly cannot be overhauled. If worn or damaged, it must be replaced. The only component that can be removed is the coil spring, which is covered earlier in this section.

Control Arms/Links

REMOVAL & INSTALLATION

CR-V Models

UPPER ARM

1. Raise and safely support the vehicle.
2. Remove the rear tire/wheel assembly.

3. Remove the upper arm-to-body through bolts.
4. Remove the upper arm through bolt.
5. Remove the upper arm.
To install:
6. Installation is the reverse of removal, noting the following steps:
- Lubricate the body side bushing with silicone grease.
- Tighten the arm-to-body flange bolts to 29 ft lbs. (39 Nm)
- Tighten the upper arm through bolt to 40 ft. lbs. (54 Nm)
- Tighten the lug nuts to 80 ft. lbs. (108 Nm)

LOWER ARM

1. Raise and safely support the vehicle.
2. Remove the rear tire/wheel assembly.
3. Remove the inner and outer bushing flanged through bolts.
4. Remove the stabilizer bar link flange nut.
5. Remove the lower arm.
To install:
6. Installation is the reverse of removal, noting the following steps:
- Lubricate the outer arm bushing with silicone grease.
- Tighten the stabilizer bar link flange nut to 22 ft lbs. (29 Nm)
- Tighten the bushing through bolts to 40 ft. lbs. (54 Nm)
- Tighten the lug nuts to 80 ft. lbs. (108 Nm)

4-Cylinder Odyssey Models

UPPER ARM

1. Raise and safely support the vehicle.
2. Remove the rear tire/wheel assembly.
3. Remove the upper arm-to-body through bolt.
4. Remove the upper arm ball joint bolt.
5. Using a suitable ball joint/tie end removal tool, remove the ball joint.
6. Remove the upper arm.
To install:
7. Installation is the reverse of removal, noting the following steps:
- Lubricate the body side bushing with silicone grease.
- Tighten the ball joint nut to 29–35 ft lbs. (39–47 Nm), install using a new cotter pin
- Tighten the upper arm through bolt to 76 ft. lbs. (103 Nm)
- Tighten the lug nuts to 80 ft. lbs. (108 Nm)

LOWER ARM A

1. Raise and safely support the vehicle.
2. Remove the rear tire/wheel assembly.
3. Remove the inner bushing flanged through bolt.
4. Remove the flange nut, then remove the lower arm.
To install:
5. Installation is the reverse of removal, noting the following steps:
- Lubricate the inner arm bushing with silicone grease.
- Tighten the flange nut to 47 ft lbs. (64 Nm)
- Tighten the bushing through bolts to 69 ft. lbs. (93 Nm)
- Tighten the lug nuts to 80 ft. lbs. (108 Nm)

LOWER ARM B

1. Raise and safely support the vehicle.
2. Remove the rear wheels.
3. Place a floor jack under the lower control arm spring perch and raise it slightly.
4. Remove the shock absorber flange through bolt and the knuckle flange through bolt from the lower control arm.
5. Collapse and remove and the shock assembly. For specific details, see the shock removal procedures in this section.
6. Slowly lower the floor jack to release the tension on the coil spring.
7. Remove the coil spring and the upper and lower spring seats.
8. Matchmark the inner bushing concentric washer location for reassembly.
9. Remove the inner arm bushing through bolt.
10. Remove the lower arm.
To install:
11. Lubricate the inner busing with silicone grease.
12. Install the lower arm and it's through bolt using a new flange nut. Do not tighten it at this time.
13. Replace the upper and lower spring seats if they are distorted or have disintegrated.
14. Install the spring seats into position.
15. Install the coil spring. Align the ends of the coil with the notches on the spring seats.
16. Raise the floor jack under the lower control arm to compress the spring.
17. Install the shock absorber and knuckle flange bolts and hand tighten them only at this point.

18. Lower the jack and move it under the knuckle. Raise the jack under the knuckle until it is supporting the weight of the vehicle. Tighten each of the inner bushing flange nut to 40 ft. lbs. (54 Nm), the two flange bolts to 76 ft. lbs. (103 Nm) and the shock flange nuts to 28 ft lbs. (38 Nm).

19. Lower the floor jack. Install the rear wheels. Lower the vehicle.

20. Tighten the wheel nuts to 80 ft. lbs. (108 Nm).

21. Check and adjust the rear wheel alignment as necessary.

V6 Odyssey Models

UPPER ARM

1. Raise and safely support the vehicle.
2. Remove the rear tire/wheel assembly.
3. Remove the upper arm-to-body through bolt.
4. Remove the upper arm ball joint bolt.
5. Using a suitable ball joint/tie end removal tool, remove the ball joint.
6. Remove the upper arm.

To install:

7. Installation is the reverse of removal, noting the following steps:
   - Tighten the ball joint nut to 36–43 ft lbs. (49–58 Nm), install using a new cotter pin
   - Tighten the upper arm through bolt to: 47 ft. lbs. (64 Nm)
   - Tighten the lug nuts to: 80 ft. lbs. (108 Nm)

LOWER ARM A

1. Raise and safely support the vehicle.
2. Remove the rear tire/wheel assembly.
3. Remove the flanged through bolt.
4. Remove the flange nut.
5. Remove the lower arm.

To install:

6. Installation is the reverse of removal, noting the following steps:
   - Tighten the flange nut to 47 ft lbs. (64 Nm)
   - Tighten the bushing through bolts to: 69 ft. lbs. (93 Nm)
   - Tighten the lug nuts to: 80 ft. lbs. (108 Nm)

LOWER ARM B

1. Raise and safely support the vehicle.
2. Remove the rear wheels.
3. Remove the rear coil spring assembly. For details, please refer to the removal and installation procedures in this section.
4. Matchmark the inner bushing eccentric washer location for reassembly.
5. Remove the inner arm bushing through bolt.
6. Remove the lower arm.

To install:

7. Install the lower arm and it's through bolt using a new flange nut. Align the eccentric washer matchmarks. Do not tighten it at this time.
8. Install the spring assembly, following the procedures in this section.
9. Raise the floor jack under the lower control arm to compress the spring. Tighten the new inner bushing flange nut to 61 ft. lbs. (83 Nm)
10. Lower the floor jack. Install the rear wheels. Lower the vehicle.
11. Tighten the wheel nuts to 80 ft. lbs. (108 Nm).
12. Check and adjust the rear wheel alignment as necessary.

Sway Bar

REMOVAL & INSTALLATION

1. Matchmark the sway bar for proper reinstallation.
2. Disconnect the sway bar links from the end of the sway bar.
3. Remove the sway bar bushing brackets from the vehicle's under body.
4. Remove the sway bar.

To install:

5. Installation is the reverse of removal noting the following steps:
   - Apply silicone grease between the sway bar bracket bushing and sway bar.
   - Tighten the sway bar bracket-to-body bolts: 16 ft. lbs. (22 Nm)
   - On CR-V models, tighten the link nut and bolt 22 ft. lbs. (29 Nm)
   - On 4-cylinder Odyssey models, tighten the link nut and bolt 14 ft. lbs. (19 Nm)
   - On V6 Odyssey models, tighten the link nut 58 ft. lbs. (78 Nm)

Rear Hub & Bearings

REMOVAL & INSTALLATION

CR-V

▶ **See Figures 60 thru 66**

➡**The rear wheel bearing is part of the rear hub bearing unit. The bearing cannot be replaced separately from the hub.**

1. Raise and safely support the rear of the vehicle.
2. Remove the rear wheels.
3. Raise the lock tab on the spindle nut, then remove the nut.
4. Remove the brake drum from the hub assembly. If the drum is difficult to remove, thread two 8 x 1.25mm bolts into the threaded holes of the brake drum. Turn each bolt two turns at a time to remove the drum evenly.
5. Remove the brake shoes and disconnect the parking brake cable from the actuating arm. For details, refer to Section 9.
6. Slide a 12mm box end wrench up the parking brake cable to compress the lock clip, then slide the cable through the backing plate.
7. Disconnect the brake line from the wheel cylinder. If the brake line flare nut is seized onto the brake line, remove the wheel cylinder mounting bolts, hold the flare nut and spin the wheel cylinder.
8. Remove the three flange bolts that mount the backing plate onto the trailing arms.
9. On 4-Wheel Drive (4WD) models, remove the backing plate/hub bearing assembly from the trailing arm using a suitable two jaw puller.
10. Using a suitable press tool that is slightly smaller than the inner race of the wheel bearing, support the backing plate and press the hub out of the inner wheel bearing race.

✷✷ WARNING

Do not distort the backing plate.

11. Remove the inner race remaining on the hub from the hub assembly using s bearing separator.

➡**Carefully inspect the lug nut studs, and replace them at this time, if necessary.**

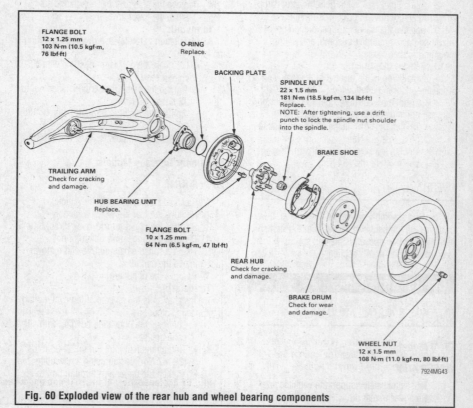

Fig. 60 Exploded view of the rear hub and wheel bearing components

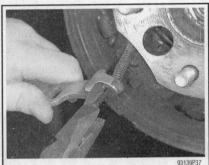

Fig. 61 Remove the parking brake cable from the actuating arm using a pair of flat-nosed pliers

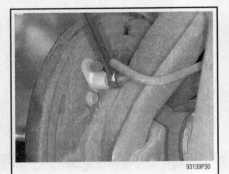

Fig. 62 Loosen the wheel cylinder hydraulic flare nut using a line wrench

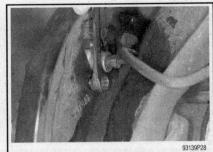

Fig. 63 If the brake line is seized onto the flare nut, loosen the flare nut slightly, remove the wheel cylinder mounting bolts . . .

Fig. 64 . . . then hold the flare nut and spin the wheel cylinder off the flare nut. This sure beats breaking the hydraulic line

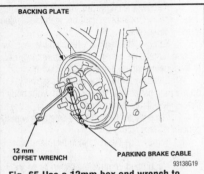

Fig. 65 Use a 12mm box end wrench to compress the parking brake cable retainer clip

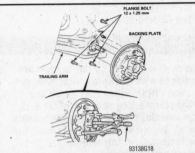

Fig. 66 On 4WD models, once the brake hydraulic line and flange bolts are removed, use a two-jaw puller to remove the hub from the splined axle shaft

12. Remove the flange bolts mounting the hub bearing unit to the backing plate and remove the hub bearing unit.

To install:

13. Install a new O-ring on the hub bearing unit.

14. Attach the hub to the backing plate and tighten the bolts to 47 ft. lbs. (64 Nm). Support the rear hub on a suitable press plate and using a suitable press tool press the inner bearing race/bearing assembly onto the hub.

15. Bolt the backing plate to the trailing arm and tighten to 76 ft. lbs. (103 Nm).

16. Connect the brake line to the wheel cylinder.

17. The completion of installation is the reverse order of the removal procedure, noting the following steps:

- Apply some motor oil to the seating surface of the nut and tighten to 134 ft. lbs. (181 Nm).
- Using a drift, stake the spindle nut.
- Bleed the brakes as necessary. Please refer to Section 9 for details
- Adjust the parking brake. Please refer to Section 9 for details.
- Have the rear wheel alignment checked and adjusted, as necessary.

Odyssey Models

♦ See Figure 67

➡The rear wheel bearing is part of the rear hub bearing unit. The bearing cannot be replaced separately from the hub.

1. Raise and safely support the vehicle and remove the rear wheels.

2. Engage the parking brake.

3. On V6 Odyssey models, perform the following:
   a. Release the parking brake.
   b. Remove the metal dust cap from the center of the brake drum.
   c. Remove the brake drum from the hub

assembly. If the drum is difficult to remove, thread two 8 x 1.25mm bolts into the threaded holes of the brake drum. Turn each bolt two turns at a time to remove the drum evenly.

4. On 4-cylinder Odyssey models, perform the following:

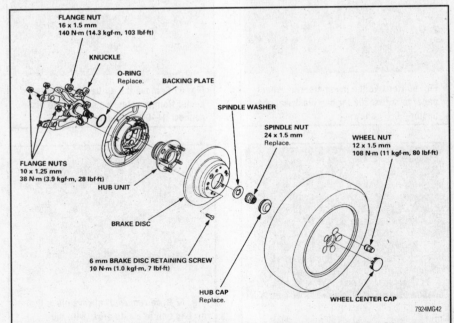

Fig. 67 Exploded view of the rear hub and wheel bearing components—4-cylinder Odyssey shown

a. Remove the caliper bracket mounting bolts. Use a piece of wire to hang the caliper out of the way.

b. Remove the two 6mm brake rotor retaining screws. If the rotor has seized onto the hub, thread two 8 x 1.25mm bolts into the threaded holes to pop the rotor loose.

c. Release the parking brake. Remove the brake rotor.

5. Raise the lock tab on the rear spindle nut and remove the nut.

6. Remove the spindle nut and remove the rear hub and bearing assembly as a unit.

To install:

7. Clean the hub unit in solvent. Inspect the hub unit and wheel bearing for damage.

➡ **If the wheel bearing is faulty, the entire hub unit must be replaced.**

8. Clean excess brake dust and grease from the backing plate and brake drum.

9. Install the hub unit, and spindle nut.

10. Using a new nut, tighten the spindle nut to 181 ft. lbs. (245 Nm), then stake the nut.

11. The balance of the installation is in reverse order of removal noting the following steps:

a. On 4-cylinder Odyssey models, tighten the brake caliper retainers to 28 ft. lbs. (38 Nm)

b. On V6 Odyssey models, install a new metal dust cap on the center of the brake drum.

c. Tighten the wheel nuts to 80 ft. lbs. (108 Nm) and road test the vehicle to check the operation of the brakes.

STEERING

Steering Wheel

REMOVAL & INSTALLATION

◆ **See Figures 68 thru 74**

✳✳ CAUTION

The models covered by this manual are equipped with a Supplemental Restraint System (SRS), which uses an air bag. Whenever working near any of the SRS components, such as the impact sensors, the air bag module, steering column and instrument panel, disable the SRS, as described in Section 6.

1. Disconnect the negative, then the positive battery cables.

2. Disable the air bag system, as outlined in Section 6 of this manual.

3. Remove the access panel from the steering wheel bottom to access the electrical connector.

4. Remove the connector from its holder and detach the electrical connector between the air bag and the cable reel.

5. Remove the steering wheel side access panels and remove the fasteners that mount the air bag to the steering wheel using a T-30 Torx® bit.

6. Carefully remove the air bag assembly, holding the padded surface away from your body in case of accidental deployment.

7. Place the air bag unit in a safe area with the padded surface facing UP.

8. Remove the electrical connectors for the horn.

9. If equipped, remove the electrical connector for the cruise control.

10. Remove the steering wheel mounting fastener.

11. Turn the steering wheel to the straight ahead position, so the steering wheel is properly centered.

12. Matchmark the steering wheel to the splined steering shaft for proper alignment during reassembly.

13. Remove the steering wheel by rocking it slowly from side to side while pulling steadily with both hands, or if necessary, use a commercially available steering wheel puller.

✳✳ WARNING

If using a steering wheel puller, use care to not thread the puller-to-steering wheel attachment bolts in more than 5 turns, otherwise the air bag cable reel could be damaged.

To install:

14. Before installing the steering wheel, center the cable reel by pointing the arrow up. This can be done by rotating the cable reel clockwise until it

Fig. 68 Remove the lower steering wheel panel to access the air bag electrical connector—CR-V shown

Fig. 69 Remove the air bag electrical connector from the steering wheel, and disconnect it—CR-V model shown

Fig. 70 Remove the side access panels to expose the air bag mounting fasteners—CR-V model shown

Fig. 71 Carefully pull the air bag unit from the steering wheel

Fig. 72 Once removed, always place the air bag unit in a safe area, with the padded surface facing up—CR-V model shown

Fig. 73 Once the air bag unit has been removed and the appropriate electrical connectors unplugged, remove the steering wheel mounting fastener

Fig. 74 Once the steering wheel is removed, the air bag cable reel is exposed. Avoid moving the cable reel if possible. If it has been moved, make sure to properly position it during installation

stops. Then rotate the cable reel about two turns counterclockwise, and the arrow should face up.

15. Install the steering wheel and make sure the wheel shaft engages the cable reel and the turn signal canceling sleeve.

16. Tighten the steering wheel fastener, as follows:
- CR-V and 4-cylinder Odyssey models: 29 ft. lbs. (39 Nm).
- V6 Odyssey models: 36 ft. lbs. (49 Nm).

17. Attach all wires and harnesses.

18. Install the air bag assembly using new air bag mounting fasteners, then torque the fasteners to 86 inch lbs. (9.8 Nm).

19. Install all covers.

20. Connect the positive battery cable first and then the negative.

21. After installation, confirm normal system operation of all related equipment, and that all controls are working properly.

Combination Headlight & Turn Signal Switch

REMOVAL & INSTALLATION

✳✳ CAUTION

The models covered by this manual are equipped with a Supplemental Restraint System (SRS), which uses an air bag. Whenever working near any of the SRS components, such as the impact sensors, the air bag module, steering column and instrument panel, disable the SRS, as described in Section 6.

1. Disable the air bag system, as outlined in Section 6 of this manual.

2. Remove the driver's side lower dashboard cover and knee bolster.

3. Remove the steering column covers.

4. Disconnect the harness by gently depressing the tab on the connector and pulling.

5. Remove the combination switch mounting screws, then remove the switch.

6. Installation is the reverse of the removal procedure.

Fig. 75 Once the steering column covers are removed, the column mounted combination switches are relatively easy to remove. First, use a long Phillips screwdriver to remove the mounting screws . . .

Windshield Wiper Switch

REMOVAL & INSTALLATION

▶ See Figures 75, 76 and 77

✳✳ CAUTION

The models covered by this manual are equipped with a Supplemental Restraint System (SRS), which uses an air bag. Whenever working near any of the SRS components, such as the impact sensors, the air bag module, steering column and instrument panel, disable the SRS, as described in Section 6.

1. Disable the air bag system, as outlined in Section 6 of this manual.

2. Remove the driver's side lower dashboard cover and knee bolster.

3. Remove the steering column covers.

4. Disconnect the harness by gently depressing the tab on the connector and pulling.

5. Remove the combination switch mounting screws.

6. Remove the switch.

7. Installation is the reverse of the removal procedure.

Ignition Switch

REMOVAL & INSTALLATION

✳✳ CAUTION

The models covered by this manual are equipped with a Supplemental Restraint System (SRS), which uses an air bag. Whenever working near any of the SRS components, such as the impact sensors, the air bag module, steering column and instrument panel, disable the SRS, as described in Section 6.

1. Disable the air bag system, as outlined in Section 6 of this manual.

2. Remove the lower panel of the dashboard.

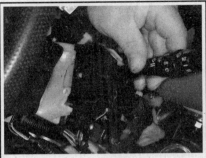

Fig. 76 . . . then release the switch assembly and pull outward, away from the steering column

Fig. 77 Finally, locate the lock tabs on the electrical connectors, and release and remove the connectors from the switch assembly

3. Remove the knee bolster.

4. Remove the steering column covers.

5. Unplug the connectors from the under dash fuse block.

6. Remove the steering column upper and lower covers.

7. Position the ignition switch to the "0" position.

8. Remove the two screws that secure the switch to the mount.

9. Pull the ignition switch away from the mount.

10. Installation is the reverse of the removal procedure.

Ignition Lock Cylinder

REMOVAL & INSTALLATION

✳✳ CAUTION

The models covered by this manual are equipped with a Supplemental Restraint System (SRS), which uses an air bag. Whenever working near any of the SRS components, such as the impact sensors, the air bag module, steering column and instrument panel, disable the SRS, as described in Section 6.

1. Disable the air bag system, as outlined in Section 6 of this manual.

2. On CR-V and V6 Odyssey models, remove the steering column as follows:

   a. Remove the steering wheel.

   b. Remove the driver's side dash lower covers and knee bolster.

   c. Remove the steering column covers.

   d. If equipped with an automatic transaxle, place the gear selector to **N** and disconnect the selector cable.

   e. Remove the combination switches from the steering column.

   f. Matchmark and disconnect the steering joint in the engine compartment.

   g. Remove the steering column mounting fasteners.

3. On 4-cylinder Odyssey models, perform the following:

   a. Remove the lower dash cover.

   b. Remove the steering column covers.

   c. Detach the 7-pin and 8-pin electrical connectors.

   d. Remove the steering column mounting nuts and bolts.

   e. Lower the steering column assembly.

4. Center punch the shear bolt(s).

5. Use a 3/16 inch (5mm) drill bit to drill out the head(s) of the bolt(s).

6. Remove the shear bolt(s).

7. Insert the ignition key and turn the ignition switch to the **"I"** position.

8. Press down the lock pin at the service hole in the top of the clamp and remove the lock assembly from the column.

To install:

9. On CR-V and 4-cylinder Odyssey models:

   a. Insert the ignition key and turn the ignition switch to the **"I"** position.

   b. Press down the lock key and install the lock assembly onto the column until it clicks in place.

10. On V6 Odyssey models, install the lock body without the key installed.

11. Finger-tighten the new shear bolts.

12. Insert the key into the new lock cylinder and check for proper switch operation.

13. Tighten the shear bolt(s) until the head(s) can be snapped off.

14. Align the steering column and tighten the bolts.

15. Plug the harness into the ignition switch.

16. Install the steering column covers.

17. Install the dashboard panel and knee bolster.

18. Enable the air bag system., as outlined in Section 6.

Steering Linkage

REMOVAL & INSTALLATION

Inner Steering Rods

1. Raise and safely support the vehicle.

2. Remove the front wheel/tire assembly.

3. Clean the steering rod between the steering boot and outer tie rod end lock nut with a suitable penetrating lubricant and a clean cloth or shop towel.

4. Loosen the outer tie rod end locking nut ⅛ turn.

5. Loosen the steering boot clamp(s), and slide the small clamp off the boot.

6. Carefully loosen the boot and slide outward off the steering rack and onto the shaft to expose the inner steering rod mounting fastener.

7. If necessary, position the inner steering rack shaft in or out to allow for additional access.

8. Relieve the steering rod nut locking tab from the inner steering rack shaft, then loosen the steering rod ball socket nut 1 turn.

9. Matchmark the tie rod end to the threaded shaft.

10. Remove the cotter key and castle nut from the outer tie rod end threaded spindle, and using a tie rod end removal tool, remove the tie rod from the steering knuckle.

11. Hold the tie rod with a wrench, and remove the outer tie rod end from the threaded rod, counting the number of complete turns it takes to remove the tie rod end from the shaft. Write the number of turns on a piece of note paper.

12. Remove the tie rod end lock nut from the threaded steering shaft.

13. Slide the steering rack boot off the shaft.

14. Remove the inner steering rod ball socket nut from the inner steering rack shaft.

To install:

15. Inspect the tie rod end for looseness, and the steering rack boot and tie rod end boot for cracks deterioration or damage and replace as necessary.

16. Clean steering rack shaft and apply a light coating of Genuine Honda Power steering fluid as necessary.

17. Apply a medium strength locking agent to the threads where the inner steering rod ball socket mounts. Use a new locking washer, and on Odyssey models, an new stop washer, and install the inner tie rod onto the steering rack shaft.

18. Tighten the inner tie rod end fastener as follows:

- CR-V models: 40 ft. lbs. (54 Nm)
- 4-cylinder Odyssey models: 58 ft. lbs. (78 Nm)
- V6 Odyssey models: 61 ft. lbs. (83 Nm)

19. Peen the lock washer over the nut or onto the flat surface of the steering rack shaft.

20. Apply silicone grease to the outer circumference of the inner tie rod end ball socket, and onto the groove just outside of the socket.

21. Apply silicone grease to the inside of the small end of the steering rack boot, and slide the boot over the steering shaft and onto the rack and install the boot clamps. If the boot has air hose fittings make sure they are installed as removed.

22. Apply a light film of an anti-seize compound onto the threaded tie rod end, and install the tie rod end lock nut.

23. Install the tie rod end onto the tie rod, turning it in exactly the number of turns it took to remove it.

24. Install the tie rod end following the tie rod end installation procedures in this section

25. The balance of installation is the reverse of the removal procedure.

26. Check the front end alignment and adjust as necessary.

Outer Tie Rod Ends

▶ See Figures 78, 79, 80, 81 and 82

1. Raise and safely support the vehicle.

2. Remove the front wheel/tire assembly.

3. Loosen the outer tie rod end locking nut ⅛ turn.

4. Matchmark the tie rod end to the threaded shaft.

5. Remove the cotter key and castle nut from the outer tie rod end threaded spindle, and using a tie rod end removal tool, remove the tie rod from the steering knuckle.

6. Hold the tie rod with a wrench, and remove the outer tie rod end from the threaded rod, counting the number of complete turns it takes to remove the tie rod end from the shaft. Write the number of turns on a piece of note paper.

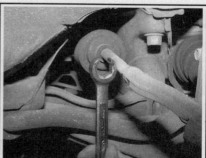

Fig. 78 A line wrench works well when loosening a tie rod end lock nut

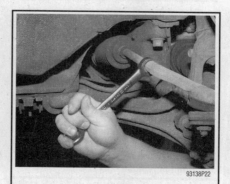

Fig. 79 Loosen the tie rod end lock nut ⅛ turn to allow for removal of the tie rod end

Fig. 80 After removing the cotter key from the threaded tie rod end spindle, remove the mounting nut

Fig. 81 Use a tie rod end removal tool to separate the tie rod end from the knuckle

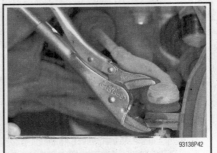

Fig. 82 When installing the tie rod end, the tapered spindle can be held and seated into the knuckle using locking pliers while the nut is tightened

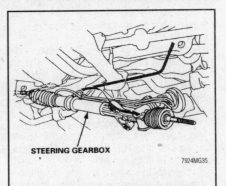

Fig. 83 Remove and install the rack and pinion gear by moving it as shown

To install:

7. Apply a light film of an anti-seize compound onto the threaded tie rod end, and install the tie rod end lock nut.

8. Install the tie rod end onto the tie rod, turning it exactly the number of turns it took to remove it.

9. Install the tapered spindle of the tie rod end into the knuckle and tighten the castle head nut to:

- CR-V models using a castle nut: 29–35 ft. lbs. (39–47 Nm)
- CR-V models using a non-castle nut: 32 ft. lbs. (43 Nm)
- 4-cylinder Odyssey models: 32 ft. lbs. (43 Nm)
- V6 Odyssey models: 40 ft. lbs. (54 Nm)

10. Install a new cotter pin in the tie rod end threaded spindle.

11. Tighten the tie rod end lock nut.

12. The balance of installation is the reverse of the removal procedure.

13. Have the front end alignment checked and adjusted as necessary.

Power Rack and Pinion Steering Gear

REMOVAL & INSTALLATION

▶ See Figure 83

✳✳ CAUTION

The models covered by this manual are equipped with a Supplemental Restraint System (SRS), which uses an air bag. Whenever working near any of the SRS components, such as the impact sensors, the air bag module, steering column and instrument panel, disable the SRS, as described in Section 6.

➡**The original radio may contain a coded anti-theft circuit. Obtain the security code number before disconnecting the battery cable.**

1. Drain the fluid from the power steering system, as follows:

a. Lift the power steering reservoir off of its mount and disconnect the inlet hose.

b. Insert a length of tubing into the inlet hose and route the tubing into a drain container.

c. With the engine running at idle, turn the steering wheel lock-to-lock several times until fluid stops running out of the hose. Then, immediately shut the engine **OFF**.

2. Position the front wheels straight ahead. Lock the steering column with the ignition key. Reconnect the reservoir inlet hose.

3. Disconnect the negative and positive battery cables. Wait at least three minutes before working around the airbags.

4. Raise and safely support the vehicle.

5. Remove the steering joint cover on the driver's side floor and remove the lower steering joint bolts.

6. Disconnect the steering joint by sliding it up toward the steering column.

7. Remove the front wheels.

8. Remove the tie-rod ends, cotter pins and castle nuts. Install a 10mm nut onto the end of the ball joint stud so the threads won't be damaged by the ball joint remover. Using a ball joint removal tool, disconnect the tie rod ends from the steering knuckles.

9. Remove the self-locking nuts and separate the catalytic converter and the joint pipe from exhaust pipe and the front muffler. Remove the catalytic converter. Be careful not to damage the Oxygen Sensor (O_2S); disconnect their electrical leads if necessary.

10. On the CR-V and 4-cylinder Odyssey models perform the following:

a. Unbolt the fluid return line clamp from the top of the rear subframe beam.

b. Use a flare nut wrench to disconnect the two hydraulic lines from the rack valve body. Plug the lines to keep dirt and moisture out. Carefully move the disconnected lines to the rear of the rack assembly so that they are not damaged when the rack is removed.

c. Push on the left side inner tie rod to position the rack all the way to the right.

d. Remove the rack stiffener plate, then remove the right steering rack mounting bolts.

e. Pull the steering rack down to release it from the pinion shaft.

f. Drop the steering rack far enough to permit the end of the pinion shaft to come out of the hole in the frame channel.

g. Slide the steering rack to the right until the left tie rod clears the subframe, then drop it down and out of the vehicle to the left.

11. On V6 Odyssey models, perform the following:

a. Remove the front lower splash shield.

b. Disconnect the feed line mounting brackets from the front sub frame.

c. Loosen the 14mm flare nut on the steering housing and disconnect the feed line.

d. Loosen the hose clamp for the return hose, and remove the return hose.

e. Attach a chain hoist to the engine, and carefully lift the engine up slightly.

f. Remove the bolts that attach the rear engine mount to the sub-frame.

g. Remove the through bolt that attaches the rear engine mount busing to the bracket.

h. Lift the engine mount bushing assembly upward and install the bracket through bolt such that the bushing assembly rests on the through bolt, to allow clearance between the bushing assembly and the sub-frame.

i. Attach a sturdy wood block between both sides of the lower center of the sub-frame.

j. Secure a jack to the center of the wood block and support the sub-frame by lifting with the jack.

k. Tighten the slack on the engine chain hoist caused by lifting the sub-frame with the jack.

l. Loosen the four sub-frame bushing through bolts 1 3/16 inch (30mm) from the mounting surface, using care not to loosen the bolts more than necessary.

m. Remove the front and rear sub-frame stiffener bolts and plates.

n. Slowly and carefully lower the jack that is supporting the sub-frame, and allow the sub-frame to rest on the mounting bolts that were previously loosened.

o. Remove the right feed line clamp and bracket.

p. Remove the two left side steering gearbox mounting nuts and bolts.

q. Move the steering gearbox to the left between the sub-frame and the body to remove.

To install:

➡**Use new gaskets and self-locking nuts when installing the catalytic converter.**

12. Before installing the rack and pinion, slide the rack's ends all the way to the right. Install the pinion shaft grommet. Align the lug and the slot of the grommet and the valve body.

✳✳ WARNING

Use only genuine Honda Type-V power steering fluid. Any other type or brand of fluid will damage the power steering pump.

13. Move the steering rack into position. Install the pinion shaft grommet and insert the pinion through the hole in the firewall.

14. On the CR-V and 4-cylinder Odyssey models, perform the following:

a. Install the rack mounting bolts. Tighten the bracket bolts to 28 ft. lbs. (39 Nm). Tighten the stiffener plate mounting bolts to 32 ft. lbs. (43 Nm).

b. Reconnect the two hydraulic lines to the rack valve body. Carefully tighten the 14mm inlet fitting to 27 ft. lbs. (37 Nm) and the 16mm outlet fitting to 21 ft. lbs. (28 Nm).

c. Install the catalytic converter using new gaskets and self-locking nuts. Tighten the self-locking nuts to 16 ft. lbs. (22 Nm). Reconnect the O_2S if it was disconnected.

d. Center the rack ends within their steering strokes.

e. Install the tie rod ends onto the rack ends. Connect the tie rod ends to the steering knuckles and install the castle nuts. Install the front wheels.

f. Verify that the rack is centered within its strokes.

15. Center the SRS cable reel, as follows:
- Turn the steering wheel clockwise until it stops.
- Turn the steering wheel counterclockwise until the yellow gear tooth lines up with the alignment mark on the lower column cover.

16. On V6 Odyssey models, perform the following:

a. Install the two left side steering gearbox mounting nuts and bolts loosely.

b. Install the right side mounting bracket and feed line clamp.

c. Carefully raise the sub-frame with the jack.

d. Install the front and rear sub-frame stiffener plate bolts and torque to 54 ft. lbs. (74 Nm).

e. Tighten the four sub-frame bushing bolts to 75.9 ft. lbs. (103 Nm), and lower the jack and remove the wooden support block.

f. Install the rear engine mount and torque the sub-frame to engine mount bolts to 29 ft. lbs. (39 Nm), and the engine mount bushing through bolt to 61 ft. lbs. (83 Nm).

g. Remove the engine chain hoist from the engine.

h. Connect and secure the return hose and clamp, and the feed line flare nut.

i. Install the feed line mounting brackets onto the front of the sub-frame.

j. Using new gaskets, install the front exhaust pipe and catalytic converter and connect the O_2S wires.

k. Install the front lower splash shield.

l. Install the tie rod ends and torque the nuts to 40 ft. lbs. (54 Nm). Install a new cotter pin through the hole at the end of the tie rod end and spread the ends of the cotter pin flush with the assembly.

m. Install the steering joint onto the pinion shaft of the steering gearbox taking care to align the hole of the steering shaft joint with the flat portion of the pinion.

17. Line up the bolt hole in the steering joint with the groove in the pinion shaft. Slip the joint onto the pinion shaft. Pull the joint up and down to be sure the splines are fully seated. Tighten the joint bolts to 22 ft. lbs. (30 Nm).

➡Connect the steering joint and pinion shaft with the cable reel and steering rack centered. Verify that the lower joint bolt is securely seated in the pinion shaft groove. If the steering wheel and rack are not centered, reposition the serrations at the lower end of the steering joint.

18. Install the steering joint cover.

19. On CR-V and 4-cylinder Odyssey models, tighten the tie rod end castle nuts to 29–35 ft. lbs. (40–48 Nm). Then, tighten them only enough to install new cotter pins.

20. Lower the vehicle. Reconnect the negative battery cable.

21. Be sure the reservoir inlet line has been reconnected. Fill the reservoir to the upper line with Honda power steering fluid. Run the engine at idle and turn the steering wheel lock-to-lock several times to bleed any air from the system and fill the rack valve body with fluid. Recheck the fluid level and add more if necessary.

22. Check the power steering system for leaks.

23. Check the front wheel alignment and steering wheel spoke angle. Make adjustments by turning the left and right tie rod ends equally.

24. Road test the vehicle, then enter the radio security code.

Power Steering Pump

REMOVAL & INSTALLATION

◆ See Figures 84, 85 and 86

1. Note the radio security code and disconnect the negative battery cable.

2. Place a suitable drain pan under the vehicle.

3. Drain the power steering fluid from the reservoir.

4. Remove the belt by loosening the pivot and lock bolts.

5. Cover the air conditioner compressor and drive belts with several shop towels to absorb any spilled fluid.

✳✳ WARNING

If any power steering fluid is spilled on a painted surface, wipe it off immediately.

6. Squeeze the power steering hose clamp at the pump, slide it up the hose and remove the hose from the pump.

7. Loosen the power steering pump outlet hose retaining bolts, and remove the hose fitting along with its O-ring from the pump.

✳✳ WARNING

Protect all open power steering lines and fittings from debris and contaminants, otherwise internal damage may occur.

8. Wrap a clean cloth around the outlet hose fitting, and the port on the pump and hold in place with duct electrical tape.

9. Plug and cap the reservoir hose and metal hose fitting on the pump.

✳✳ WARNING

Do not turn the steering wheel with the pump removed.

10. Remove the pivot and lock bolts, then remove the pump.

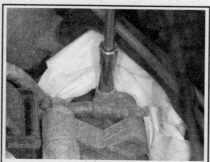

Fig. 84 The power steering outlet hose bolts onto the power steering pump—CR-V model shown

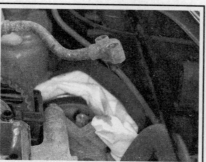

Fig. 85 When the bolts are removed, place shop towels to absorb any leakage, replace the O-ring on the fitting and coat with Genuine Honda Power Steering Fluid during reinstallation

Fig. 86 Wrap a clean cloth around the fitting and secure in place with tape to absorb any seepage, and to prevent debris from contaminating the power steering system

To install:

11. Install the pump and loosely install the lock and pivot bolts.

12. Install a new O-ring on the power steering hose outlet fitting, lubricate the O-ring with a light coating of Honda power steering fluid and install the fitting.

13. The balance of the installation is the reverse of the removal procedure. Please refer to Section 1 for belt adjustment procedures.

14. Make note of the following points:

- Make sure all fasteners, hose clamps and fittings are properly installed and tightened.
- When topping off the system use only Genuine Honda Power Steering Fluid-V or S. Substituting another brand may damage internal components.
- Clean any spilled fluid before starting the vehicle.
- Bleed the system and top off as necessary.

BLEEDING

1. Fill the reservoir to the upper line with Genuine Honda Power Steering Fluid-V or S.

2. Run the engine at idle and turn the steering wheel lock-to-lock several times to bleed air from the system and fill the rack valve body.

3. Recheck the fluid level and add more if necessary. Don't overfill the reservoir.

4. Check the power steering system for leaks.

TORQUE SPECIFICATIONS

Components	Ft. Lbs.	Nm
Front Suspension		
Axle nut	181 ft. lbs.	245 Nm
Lug nuts (front and rear)	80 ft. lbs.	109 Nm.
Strut dampening rod self-locking nut		
CR-V-2.2L/2.3L Odyssey	22 ft. lbs.	29 Nm.
3.5L Odyssey	33 ft. lbs.	44 Nm
Strut mounting nuts	28 ft. lbs.	39 Nm
Damper fork through bolt/nut		
CR-V-2.2L/2.3L Odyssey	47 ft. lbs.	65 Nm
Damper fork pinch bolt		
CR-V-2.2L/2.3L Odyssey	32 ft. lbs.	44 Nm
Strut-to-steering knuckle pinch bolts		
3.5L V-6 Odyssey	116 ft. lbs.	157 Nm.
Sway Bar		
Sway bar bracket-to-body bolts	16 ft. lbs.	22 Nm
Link nut/bolt		
CR-V	22 ft. lbs.	29 Nm
2.2L/2.3L Odyssey	14 ft. lbs.	19 Nm
3.5L V-6 Odyssey	58 ft. lbs.	78 Nm
Radius Rod		
2.2L/2.3L Odyssey		
Radius rod-to-control arm flange bolts	76 ft. lbs.	103 Nm.
Radius rod bushing bolt	40 ft. lbs.	54 Nm.
Upper Control Arm bushings		
CR-V	40 ft. lbs.	54 Nm.
Odyssey 2.2L/2.3L	47 ft. lbs.	64 Nm.
Lower Control Arm		
CR-V		
Front flange bolt	76 ft. lbs.	103 Nm
Rear bushing bracket bolts	66 ft. lbs.	89 Nm
Rear busing self locking nut	61 ft. lbs.	83 Nm
2.2L/2.3L Odyssey		
Front flange bolt	40 ft. lbs.	54 Nm
3.5L V-6 Odyssey		
Front and rear flange bolts	69 ft. lbs.	93 Nm
Rear bushing bracket bolts	66 ft. lbs.	89 Nm
Knuckle		
Upper ball joint		
CR-V/2.2L/2.3L Odyssey	29-35 ft. lbs.	39-47 Nm
Lower ball joint		
CR-V/2.2L/2.3L Odyssey	36-43 ft. lbs.	49-59 Nm
3.5L V-6 Odyssey	43-51 ft. lbs.	59-69 Nm
Wheel bearing hub flange bolts		
2.2L/2.3L Odyssey	33 ft. lbs.	44 Nm
Brake caliper bracket bolt	80 ft. lbs.	108 Nm

93138C01

TORQUE SPECIFICATIONS

Components	Ft. Lbs.	Nm
Rear Suspension		
Axle spindle nut		
CR-V	134 ft. lbs.	181 Nm
Odyssey	181 ft. lbs.	245 Nm
Struts		
CR-V		
Strut damper rod self locking nut	22 ft. lbs.	29 Nm.
Strut flange mounting nuts	36 ft. lbs.	49 Nm.
Strut-to-control arm through bolt	40 ft. lbs.	54 Nm.
Control Arms/Links		
Upper arm		
Arm-to-body flange bolts		
CR-V	29 ft lbs.	39 Nm
Upper arm through bolt		
CR-V	40 ft. lbs.	54 Nm
2.2L/2.3L Odyssey	76 ft. lbs.	103 Nm
3.5L V-6 Odyssey	47 ft. lbs.	64 Nm
Upper arm ball joint		
2.2L/2.3L Odyssey	29-35 ft lbs.	39-47 Nm
3.5L V-6 Odyssey	36-43 ft lbs.	49-58 Nm
Lower arm A		
Odyssey		
Flange nut	47 ft lbs.	64 Nm
Bushing through bolts	69 ft. lbs.	93 Nm
Lower arm B		
Inner bushing flange nut		
2.2L/2.3L Odyssey	40 ft. lbs.	54 Nm
3.5L V-6 Odyssey	61 ft. lbs.	83 Nm
Rear Hub & Bearings		
CR-V		
Hub to the backing plate bolts	47 ft. lbs.	64 Nm.
Backing plate to the trailing arm	76 ft. lbs.	103 Nm.
Brake caliper bracket torque		
2.2L/2.3L Odyssey	28 ft. lbs.	38 Nm
Steering		
Steering Wheel		
CR-V/2.2L/2.3L Odyssey	29 ft. lbs.	39 Nm.
3.5L V-6 Odyssey	36 ft. lbs.	49 Nm.
Air bag mounting fasteners	86 inch lbs.	9.8 Nm.
Inner Steering Rods		
CR-V	40 ft. lbs.	54 Nm
2.2L/2.3L Odyssey	58 ft. lbs.	78 Nm
3.5L V-6 Odyssey	61 ft. lbs.	83 Nm
Outer Tie Rod Ends		
CR-V		
Castle nut	29-35 ft. lbs.	39-47 Nm
Non-castle nut	32 ft. lbs.	43 Nm
2.2L/2.3L Odyssey	32 ft. lbs.	43 Nm
3.5L V-6 Odyssey	40 ft. lbs.	54 Nm
Steering joint-to-pinion shaft	22 ft. lbs.	30 Nm

93138C02

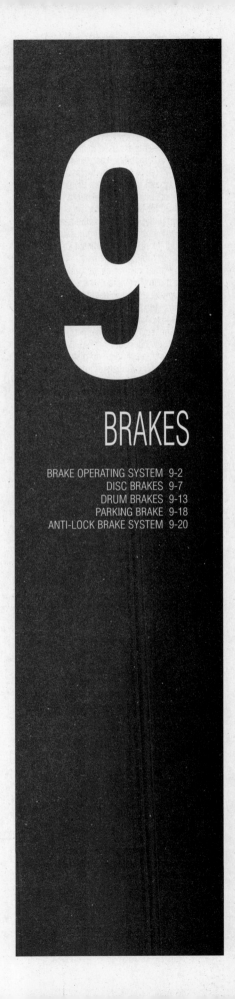

9

BRAKES

BRAKE OPERATING SYSTEM

Basic Operating Principles

Hydraulic systems are used to actuate the brakes of all modern automobiles. The system transports the power required to force the frictional surfaces of the braking system together from the pedal to the individual brake units at each wheel. A hydraulic system is used for two reasons.

First, fluid under pressure can be carried to all parts of an automobile by small pipes and flexible hoses without taking up a significant amount of room or posing routing problems.

Second, a great mechanical advantage can be given to the brake pedal end of the system, and the foot pressure required to actuate the brakes can be reduced by making the surface area of the master cylinder pistons smaller than that of any of the pistons in the wheel cylinders or calipers.

The master cylinder consists of a fluid reservoir along with a double cylinder and piston assembly. Double type master cylinders are designed to separate the front and rear braking systems hydraulically in case of a leak. The master cylinder coverts mechanical motion from the pedal into hydraulic pressure within the lines. This pressure is translated back into mechanical motion at the wheels by either the wheel cylinder (drum brakes) or the caliper (disc brakes).

Steel lines carry the brake fluid to a point on the vehicle's frame near each of the vehicle's wheels. The fluid is then carried to the calipers and wheel cylinders by flexible tubes in order to allow for suspension and steering movements.

In drum brake systems, each wheel cylinder contains two pistons, one at either end, which push outward in opposite directions and force the brake shoe into contact with the drum.

In disc brake systems, the cylinders are part of the calipers. At least one cylinder in each caliper is used to force the brake pads against the disc.

All pistons employ some type of seal, usually made of rubber, to minimize fluid leakage. A rubber dust boot seals the outer end of the cylinder against dust and dirt. The boot fits around the outer end of the piston on disc brake calipers, and around the brake actuating rod on wheel cylinders.

The hydraulic system operates as follows: When at rest, the entire system, from the piston(s) in the master cylinder to those in the wheel cylinders or calipers, is full of brake fluid. Upon application of the brake pedal, fluid trapped in front of the master cylinder piston(s) is forced through the lines to the wheel cylinders. Here, it forces the pistons outward, in the case of drum brakes, and inward toward the disc, in the case of disc brakes. The motion of the pistons is opposed by return springs mounted outside the cylinders in drum brakes, and by spring seals, in disc brakes.

Upon release of the brake pedal, a spring located inside the master cylinder immediately returns the master cylinder pistons to the normal position. The pistons contain check valves and the master cylinder has compensating ports drilled in it. These are uncovered as the pistons reach their normal position. The piston check valves allow fluid to remain in the fluid lines for the wheel cylinders or calipers as the master cylinder piston withdraws. Then, as the return springs force the brake pads or shoes

into the released position, the excess fluid enters the reservoir through the compensating ports. It is during the time the pedal is in the released position that any fluid that has leaked out of the system will be replaced through the compensating ports.

Dual circuit master cylinders employ two pistons, located one behind the other, in the same cylinder. The primary piston is actuated directly by mechanical linkage from the brake pedal through the power booster. The secondary piston is actuated by fluid trapped between the two pistons. If a leak develops in front of the secondary piston, it moves forward until it bottoms against the front of the master cylinder, and the fluid trapped between the pistons will operate the rear brakes. If the rear brakes develop a leak, the primary piston will move forward until direct contact with the secondary piston takes place, and it will force the secondary piston to actuate the front brakes. In either case, the brake pedal moves farther when the brakes are applied, and less braking power is available.

All dual circuit systems use a switch to warn the driver when only half of the brake system is operational. This switch is usually located in a valve body which is mounted on the firewall or the frame below the master cylinder. A hydraulic piston receives pressure from both circuits, each circuit's pressure being applied to one end of the piston. When the pressures are in balance, the piston remains stationary. When one circuit has a leak, however, the greater pressure in that circuit during application of the brakes will push the piston to one side, closing the switch and activating the brake warning light.

In disc brake systems, this valve body also contains a metering valve and, in some cases, a proportioning valve. The metering valve keeps pressure from traveling to the disc brakes on the front wheels until the brake shoes on the rear wheels have contacted the drums, ensuring that the front brakes will never be used alone. The proportioning valve controls the pressure to the rear brakes to lessen the chance of rear wheel lock-up during very hard braking.

Warning lights may be tested by depressing the brake pedal and holding it while opening one of the wheel cylinder bleeder screws. If this does not cause the light to go on, substitute a new lamp, make continuity checks, and, finally, replace the switch as necessary.

The hydraulic system may be checked for leaks by applying pressure to the pedal gradually and steadily. If the pedal sinks very slowly to the floor, the system has a leak. This is not to be confused with a springy or spongy feel due to worn flexible brake lines or the compression of air within the lines. If the system leaks, there will be a gradual change in the position of the pedal with a constant pressure.

Check for leaks along all lines and at the master and wheel cylinders. If no external leaks are apparent, the problem is inside the master cylinder. Either the check valve is contaminated with debris and/or the seals are worn.

The typical cause of a brake pulsation is an irregular surface or a worn mechanical component. Possible causes include:

- Bent suspension hub
- Improper wheel lug nut torque
- Worn or damaged wheel bearing

- Improper machined surfaces of a brake drum or rotor
- Thickness variations and/or warpage of a brake drum or rotor

DISC BRAKES

Instead of the traditional expanding brakes that press outward against a circular drum, disc brake systems utilize a disc (rotor) with brake pads positioned on either side of it. An easily-seen analogy is the hand brake arrangement on a bicycle. The pads squeeze onto the rim of the bike wheel, slowing its motion. Automobile disc brakes use the identical principle but apply the braking effort to a separate disc instead of the wheel.

The disc (rotor) is a casting, usually equipped with cooling fins between the two braking surfaces. This enables air to circulate between the braking surfaces making them less sensitive to heat buildup and more resistant to fade. Dirt and water do not drastically affect braking action since contaminants are thrown off by the centrifugal action of the rotor or scraped off the by the pads. Also, the equal clamping action of the two brake pads tends to ensure uniform, straight line stops. Disc brakes are inherently self-adjusting. There are three general types of disc brake:

1. A fixed caliper.
2. A floating caliper.
3. A sliding caliper.

The fixed caliper design uses two hydraulic pistons mounted on either side of the rotor (on each side of the caliper). The caliper is mounted rigidly and does not move.

The sliding and floating designs are quite similar. In fact, these two types are often lumped together. In both designs, the pad on the inside of the rotor is moved into contact with the rotor by hydraulic force. The caliper, which is not held in a fixed position, moves slightly, bringing the outside pad into contact with the rotor. There are various methods of attaching floating calipers. Some pivot at the bottom or top, and some slide on mounting bolts. In any event, the end result is the same.

DRUM BRAKES

Drum brakes employ two brake shoes mounted on a stationary backing plate. These shoes are positioned inside a circular drum which rotates with the wheel assembly. The shoes are held in place by springs. This allows them to slide toward the drums (when they are applied) while keeping the linings and drums in alignment. The shoes are actuated by a wheel cylinder which is mounted at the top of the backing plate. When the brakes are applied, hydraulic pressure forces the wheel cylinder's actuating links outward. Since these links bear directly against the top of the brake shoes, the tops of the shoes are then forced against the inner side of the drum. This action forces the bottoms of the two shoes to contact the brake drum by rotating the entire assembly slightly (known as servo action). When pressure within the wheel cylinder is relaxed, return springs pull the shoes back away from the drum.

Most modern drum brakes are designed to self-adjust themselves during application when the vehicle is moving in reverse. This motion causes both shoes to rotate very slightly with the drum, rocking an adjusting lever, thereby causing rotation of the adjusting screw. Some drum brake systems are designed to self-adjust during application whenever the brakes are applied. This on-board adjustment system reduces the need for maintenance adjustments and keeps both the brake function and pedal feel satisfactory.

PARKING BRAKES

Parking brakes are most often actuated by a mechanical linkage. Typically a cable moves a linkage to actuate the brake lining as the cable is pulled via a foot pedal or hand lever. The parking brake can be either a disc or a drum design. A drum parking brake is engaged by mechanically forcing the brake shoes outward into the brake drum. The parking brake may use the same brake shoes as the hydraulic brake system, or it could be a completely separate system.

Such is the case where a disc brake rotor also incorporates a drum brake on the inside area of the brake rotor. In this instance, the hydraulic brake is a disc brake, while the parking brake is a mechanically operated drum brake. On a combination system of this type, the parking brake functions separately from the hydraulic brake and shares no common parts with exception of the combination brake disc/drum.

Some manufactures use a disc brake caliper with an internal mechanical linkage. On this system, the parking brake and the hydraulic brake share the same brake linings.

POWER BRAKE BOOSTER

Virtually all modern vehicles use a vacuum assisted power brake system to multiply the braking force and reduce pedal effort. Since vacuum is always available when the engine is operating, the system is simple and efficient. A vacuum diaphragm is located on the front of the master cylinder and assists the driver in applying the brakes, reducing both the effort and travel he must put into moving the brake pedal.

The vacuum diaphragm housing is normally connected to the intake manifold by a vacuum hose. A check valve is placed at the point where the hose enters the diaphragm housing, so that during periods of low manifold vacuum brakes assist will not be lost.

Depressing the brake pedal closes off the vacuum source and allows atmospheric pressure to enter on one side of the diaphragm. This causes the master cylinder pistons to move and apply the brakes. When the brake pedal is released, vacuum is applied to both sides of the diaphragm and springs return the diaphragm and master cylinder pistons to the released position.

If the vacuum supply fails, the brake pedal rod will contact the end of the master cylinder actuator rod and the system will apply the brakes without any power assistance. The driver will notice that much higher pedal effort is needed to stop the car and that the pedal feels harder than usual.

Vacuum Leak Test

1. Operate the engine at idle without touching the brake pedal for at least one minute.

2. Turn off the engine and wait one minute.
3. Test for the presence of assist vacuum by depressing the brake pedal and releasing it several times. If vacuum is present in the system, light application will produce less and less pedal travel. If there is no vacuum, air is leaking into the system.

System Operation Test

1. With the engine **OFF**, pump the brake pedal until the supply vacuum is entirely gone.
2. Put light, steady pressure on the brake pedal.
3. Start the engine and let it idle. If the system is operating correctly, the brake pedal should fall toward the floor if the constant pressure is maintained.

Power brake systems may be tested for hydraulic leaks just as ordinary systems are tested.

✳✳ WARNING

Clean, high quality brake fluid is essential to the safe and proper operation of the brake system. You should always buy the highest quality brake fluid that is available. If the brake fluid becomes contaminated, drain and flush the system, then refill the master cylinder with new fluid. Never reuse any brake fluid. Any brake fluid that is removed from the system should be discarded.

Brake Light Switch

REMOVAL & INSTALLATION

▶ **See Figures 1, 2 and 3**

1. Detach the brake light switch electrical connector.
2. Loosen the locknut.
3. Remove the brake light switch by unthreading it in a counter-clockwise direction.

To install:

4. Thread the brake light switch into its mounting bracket until the threaded end of the switch contacts the pad on the brake pedal. The switch plunger should be fully depressed and not visible at this time.

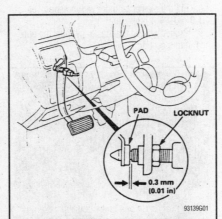

Fig. 1 The brake light switch is threaded into a bracket, and is adjusted or replaced by loosening the locknut and threading the switch in or out as necessary

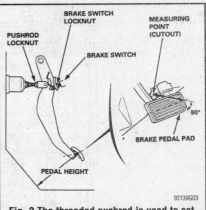

Fig. 2 The threaded pushrod is used to set the brake pedal height—CR-V model shown

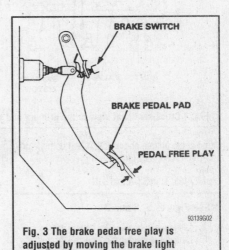

Fig. 3 The brake pedal free play is adjusted by moving the brake light switch—CR-V model shown

5. Back off the switch one quarter turn to allow 0.01 in (0.30mm) of clearance between the threaded portion of the switch and the pedal pad.
6. Attach the brake light switch electrical connector.
7. Connect the negative battery cable.

Master Cylinder

▶ **See Figure 4**

✳✳ CAUTION

The Honda anti-lock brake system contains brake fluid under extremely high pressure within the pump, accumulator and modulator assembly. Do not disconnect or loosen any lines, hoses, fittings or components without properly relieving the system pressure. Use only a bleeder T-wrench 07HAA-SG00100, or equivalent, to relieve pressure. Improper procedures or failure to discharge the system pressure may result in severe personal injury and/or property damage.

Honda vehicles have a tandem master cylinder that is used to improve the safety of the vehicle. The master cylinder has one reservoir tank with two feed

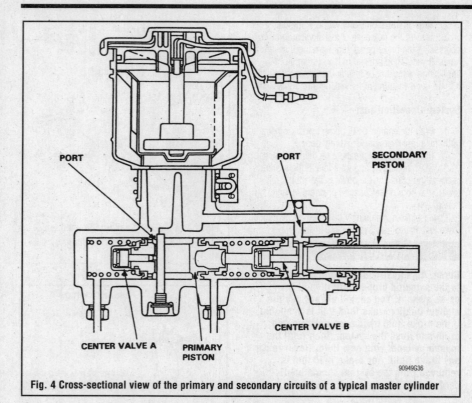

Fig. 4 Cross-sectional view of the primary and secondary circuits of a typical master cylinder

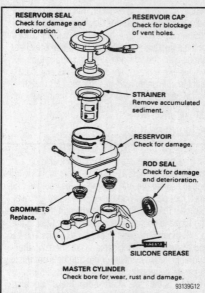

Fig. 7 Exploded view of a typical brake master cylinder and related components— CR-V shown

holes at the bottom of the tank to feed both the primary and secondary circuit.

REMOVAL & INSTALLATION

▶ See Figures 5, 6 and 7

1. Disconnect the negative battery cable.
2. Detach the electrical connectors from the master cylinder.
3. Remove the master cylinder reservoir cap.
4. Remove the brake fluid from the master cylinder using a siphon or clean turkey baster.

✲✲ CAUTION

Brake fluid contains polyglycol ethers and polyglycols. Avoid contact with the eyes and wash your hands thoroughly after handling brake fluid. If you do get brake fluid in your eyes, flush your eyes with clean, running water for 15 minutes. If eye irritation persists, or if you have taken brake fluid internally, IMMEDIATELY seek medical assistance.

5. Use a flare nut wrench to disconnect the fluid lines from the master cylinder.

✲✲ WARNING

Be cautious not to bend the brake fluid lines upon removal of the master cylinder.

6. Unfasten the mounting nuts that attach the master cylinder to the booster, then remove the master cylinder from the brake booster.
To install:
7. Install the master cylinder in the reverse order of removal.
8. Fill the master cylinder with an approved DOT 3 or DOT 4 brake fluid.
9. Properly bleed the master cylinder, as outlined in this section.

BENCH BLEEDING

✲✲ WARNING

Avoid spilling brake fluid on paint. It will damage most finishes. If a spill does occur, wash it immediately with water and absorbent cloth.

If the master cylinder is off the vehicle, it can be bench bled.
1. Secure the master cylinder in a bench vise.
2. Place a suitable catch pan so as to collect any fluid seepage.
3. Connect 2 short sections of brake line to the outlet fittings. Carefully bend them until the open end is below the fluid level in the master cylinder reservoirs.
4. Fill the reservoir with fresh DOT 3 or DOT 4 type brake fluid.
5. Using a wooden dowel, or equivalent, pump the piston slowly several times until no more air bubbles appear in the reservoirs.
6. Disconnect the 2 short lines, refill the master cylinder and securely install the cylinder cap.
7. If the master cylinder is on the vehicle, it can still be bled as follows:
   a. Using a flare nut wrench to avoid twisting or warping the lines, open one brake line at a time ¼ turn.
   b. Have an assistant press the brake pedal to the floor and hold it there, tighten the brake line, then have the assistant slowly release the brake pedal.
   c. Check the reservoir fluid level and top off as necessary.
   d. Repeat the above procedures on all of the lines until the dispersed fluid is free of all air bubbles.

➡ **Always tighten the line before the brake pedal is released.**

Fig. 5 Use a line wrench to remove the brake line flare nuts from the master cylinder

Fig. 6 Fill the reservoir with fresh DOT 3 or DOT 4 brake fluid from a sealed container

8. Once the master cylinder is bled, flush the surrounding area with water to neutralize the brake fluid.

9. Bleed the complete brake system, if necessary.

➡ **If the master cylinder has been thoroughly bled and filled to the proper level upon installation into the vehicle, it should not be necessary to bleed the entire hydraulic system.**

Power Brake Booster

REMOVAL & INSTALLATION

♦ **See Figure 8**

1. Disconnect the negative battery cable.
2. Detach all electrical connectors from the master cylinder.
3. Remove the brake fluid from the master cylinder, then use a flare nut wrench to disconnect the metal fluid lines.

❋❋ WARNING

Be careful not to bend the lines upon removal of the master cylinder.

4. Remove the master cylinder from the brake booster.
5. Disconnect the vacuum hoses from the brake booster.
6. From under the dash, remove the clevis and its pin from the brake pedal.
7. Remove the booster mounting bolts.
8. Remove the brake booster from the engine compartment.

To install:

9. Install the power brake booster in the reverse order of removal.
10. Fill the master cylinder with Honda approved or equivalent DOT 3 or DOT 4 brake fluid.
11. Properly bleed the master cylinder.

Fig. 8 The power brake booster is the large circular canister that the master cylinder is bolted to

Load Sensing Proportioning Valve

➡ **After removal or installation of a rear suspension component, the Load Sensing Proportioning Valve (LSPV) spring length must be**

checked and adjusted. This step is important; the LSPV affects the fluid pressure for the rear brakes.

REMOVAL & INSTALLATION

4-Cylinder Odyssey Models

♦ **See Figure 9**

1. Raise and safely support the vehicle.
2. Disconnect the hydraulic brake lines from the LSPV.
3. Remove the U-bolt from the stabilizer arm and remove the arm.
4. Remove the LSPV from the frame.

To install:

5. Installation is the reverse of removal, noting the following points:

- Make sure the align the stabilizer arm with the flat portion of the stabilizer.
- Bleed the air from the brake hydraulic system as outlined in this section.
- Lower the vehicle to the ground, settle the suspension, check and if necessary adjust the LSPV.

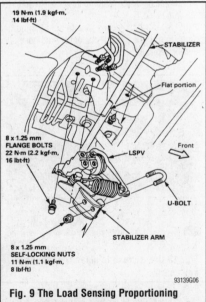

Fig. 9 The Load Sensing Proportioning Valve (LSPV) and related components—4-cylinder Odyssey models

ADJUSTMENT

4-Cylinder Odyssey Models

♦ **See Figures 10, 11 and 12**

Check the adjustment of the load sensing proportioning valve spring as follows:

1. Be sure the vehicle is not loaded with cargo. Release the parking brake.
2. Note the level of fuel in the tank and compare it with the chart to determine the degree of adjustment needed.
3. Insert a ³⁄₁₆ or ¹³⁄₆₄ drill bit or metal pin 5.0–5.3mm in diameter into the 5mm diameter hole in the LSPV arm.
4. Use a precision caliper to measure the distance between the installed pin and the 8mm adjusting bolt thread. This is the length of the LSPV spring.
5. If the measurement is out of specification, loosen the 8mm adjusting bolt and adjust the spring length to specification, according to the values on the accompanying chart. Tighten the adjusting nut to 106 inch lbs. (12 Nm).
6. Check and adjust the rear wheel alignment.
7. Test drive the vehicle and check for proper brake system operation.

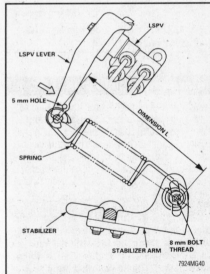

Fig. 10 Load sensing proportioning valve spring length and adjusting bolt

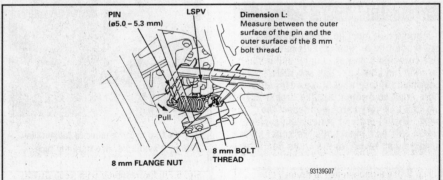

Fig. 11 Use a vernier caliper to measure the distance from the installed pin and the 8mm bolt thread

The table shows that dimension L of fully-fueled 7-passenger LX 7 is 132 mm (5.197 in). However, because the fuel level is 1/2, dimension L should be compensated by – 2 mm.
Therefore, it should be adjusted at 130 mm (5.118 in).

U.S.A. MODEL:

mm (in)

Type	Dimension L	Fuel Level			
		3/4	1/2	1/4	0
LX 6-pass.	131 (5.157)	– 1 (– 0.039)	– 2 (– 0.079)	– 3 (– 0.012)	– 4 (– 0.157)
LX 7-pass.	132 (5.197)	↑	↑	↑	↑
EX	131 (5.157)	↑	↑	↑	↑

CANADA MODEL:

mm (in)

Passenger	Dimension L	Fuel Level			
		3/4	1/2	1/4	0
6-pass.	131 (5.157)	– 1 (– 0.039)	– 2 (– 0.079)	– 3 (– 0.012)	– 4 (– 0.157)
7-pass.	132 (5.197)	↑	↑	↑	↑

NOTE: If the vehicle is equipped with a trailer hitch, add 3 mm to dimension L before compensating for the fuel level.

7924MG41

Fig. 12 Load sensing proportioning valve specifications chart

Brake Hoses and Lines

Metal lines and rubber brake hoses should be checked frequently for leaks and external damage. Metal lines are particularly prone to crushing and kinking under the vehicle. Any such deformation can restrict the proper flow of fluid and therefore impair braking at the wheels. Rubber hoses should be checked for cracking or scraping; such damage can create a weak spot in the hose and it could fail under pressure.

Any time the lines are removed or disconnected, extreme cleanliness must be observed. Clean all joints and connections before disassembly (use a stiff bristle brush and clean brake fluid); be sure to plug the lines and ports as soon as they are opened. New lines and hoses should be flushed clean with brake fluid before installation to remove any contamination.

✳✳ CAUTION

If a brake line must be replaced, use a pre-made line or factory replacement part. Use care and a proper tubing bender when forming the new line. Use only DOT approved replacement brake hoses. If a flare must be formed, use the proper flaring tool and very carefully inspect the work. The integrity of the braking system relies on safe connections. Personal injury or death can result from a brake line failure.

REMOVAL & INSTALLATION

▶ See Figures 13, 14, 15 and 16

✳✳ CAUTION

The Honda anti-lock brake system contains brake fluid under extremely high pressure within the pump, accumulator and modulator assembly. Do not disconnect or loosen any lines, hoses, fittings or components without properly relieving the system pressure. Use only a bleeder T-wrench 07HAA-SG00100 or equivalent to relieve pressure. Improper procedures or failure to discharge the system pressure may result in severe personal injury and/or property damage.

1. Disconnect the negative battery cable.
2. Raise and safely support the vehicle on jackstands.
3. Remove any wheel and tire assemblies necessary for access to the particular line you are removing.
4. Thoroughly clean the surrounding area at the joints to be disconnected.
5. Place a suitable catch pan under the joint to be disconnected.
6. Using two wrenches (one to hold the joint and one to turn the fitting), disconnect the hose or line to be replaced.

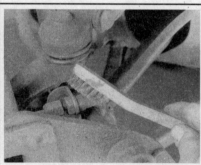

TCCA9P09

Fig. 13 Use a brush to clean the fittings of any debris

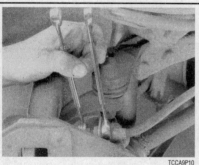

TCCA9P10

Fig. 14 Use two wrenches to loosen the fitting. If available, use flare nut type wrenches

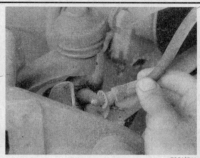

TCCA9P11

Fig. 15 Gaskets, seals and crush washers should always be replaced during installation

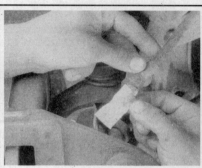

TCCA9P12

Fig. 16 Tape or plug the line to prevent contamination

7. Disconnect the other end of the line or hose, moving the drain pan if necessary. Always use a back-up wrench to avoid damaging the fitting.
8. Disconnect any retaining clips or brackets holding the line and remove the line from the vehicle.

➡If the brake system is to remain open for more time than it takes to swap lines, tape or plug each remaining clip and port to keep contaminants out and fluid in.

To install:
9. Install the new line or hose, starting with the end farthest from the master cylinder. Connect the other end, then confirm that both fittings are correctly threaded and turn smoothly using finger pressure. Make sure the new line will not rub against any other part. Brake lines must be at least ½ in. (13mm) from the steering column and other moving parts. Any protective shielding or insulators must be reinstalled in the original location.

✳✳ WARNING

Make sure the hose is NOT kinked or touching any part of the exhaust, frame or suspension after installation. These conditions may cause the hose to fail prematurely.

10. Using two wrenches as before, tighten each fitting.
11. Install any retaining clips or brackets on the lines.

12. If removed, install the wheel and tire assemblies, then carefully lower the vehicle to the ground.

13. Refill the brake master cylinder reservoir with clean, fresh brake fluid, meeting DOT 3 specifications. Properly bleed the brake system.

14. Connect the negative battery cable.

Bleeding the Brake System

➡ The brake fluid should be replaced at least every 3 years or 45,000 miles (72,000 km).

❊❊ WARNING

Avoid spilling brake fluid on the vehicle's paint. It will damage the finish. If a spill does occur, wash it immediately with water.

The purpose of bleeding the brakes is to expel air trapped in the hydraulic system. The system should be checked for fluid condition, brake hose condition and air whenever the pedal feels spongy. The system must be bled whenever it has been opened, repaired, or a hydraulic component replaced. If you are not using a pressure bleeder, you will need an assistant for this job.

❊❊ WARNING

Never reuse brake fluid which has been bled from the brake system. Brake fluid absorbs moisture which can lower its boiling point, therefore re-using old, used, or contaminated fluid can decrease the effectiveness of the braking system.

BLEEDING

▶ See Figures 17, 18 and 19

➡ If the ABS modulator has been opened or replaced it may be necessary to bleed each line at the modulator unit.

When bleeding the brakes, air may be trapped in the brake lines or valves far upstream, as much as 10 feet from the bleeder screw. Therefore, it is very important to have a fast flow of a large volume of brake fluid when bleeding the brakes, to make sure all of the air is expelled from the system.

➡ Proper manual bleeding of the hydraulic brake system will require the use of an assistant unless a suitable self-bleeding tool is available. If using a self-bleeding tool, refer to the manufacturer's directions for tool use and follow the proper bleeding sequence listed in this section.

❊❊ WARNING

Avoid spilling brake fluid on the vehicle's paint. It will damage the finish. If a spill does occur, wash it with water immediately.

1. To bleed the brakes, if the ABS modulator has not been opened or replaced, proceed as follows.

➡ If the master cylinder reservoir runs dry during the bleeding process, restart from the first fitting.

2. Remove the old brake fluid and clean the brake master cylinder reservoir with a clean lint-free cloth.

3. Bleed the brake system at each fitting. Do not proceed to the next fitting until all air bubbles are removed from the previous fitting. Bleed the brakes, making sure to following this sequence:
   - Left Front
   - Right Right
   - Right Rear
   - Left Rear

4. Attach a clear plastic hose to the bleeder screw, then place the hose into a clean jar that has enough fresh brake fluid to submerge the end of the hose.

5. Have an assistant pump the brake pedal 3–4 times, and hold pressure on it, then open the bleeder screw at least ¼ turn. When the bleeder screw opens, the brake pedal will drop. Have the assistant hold it there until the bleed valve is closed.

6. Close the bleeder screw and have the assistant slowly release the brake pedal only AFTER the bleeder screw is closed, then check the master cylinder fluid level and top off as necessary.

7. Repeat the bleeding procedure until all there are no air bubbles, or a minimum of 4 or 5 times at each bleeder screw, then check the pedal for travel and feel. If the pedal travel is excessive, or feels spongy, it's possible enough fluid has not passed through the system to expel all of the trapped air.

➡ Constantly check and top off the master cylinder. Do not allow the master cylinder to run dry, otherwise air will re-enter the brake system.

8. Once completed, test drive the vehicle to be sure the brakes are operating correctly and that the pedal feel is firm.

93139P24

Fig. 17 A one man bleeder unit such as this one, can be purchased at you local aftermarket parts supplier

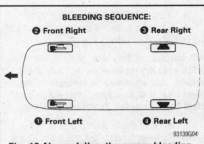

93139G04

Fig. 18 Always follow the proper bleeding sequence when bleeding the brake hydraulic system

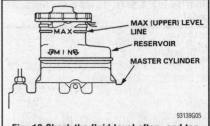

93139G05

Fig. 19 Check the fluid level often, and top off the master cylinder reservoir as necessary as the system is being bled

DISC BRAKES

❊❊ CAUTION

Older brake pads or shoes may contain asbestos, which has been determined to be cancer causing agent. Never clean the brake surface with compressed air! Avoid physical contact or inhaling any dust from any brake surface! When cleaning brake surfaces, use a commercially available brake cleaning fluid.

Brake Pads

The brake pads should be inspected during every oil change. Brake wear varies with vehicle use and driving habits. Constant stop and go driving is likely to wear the linings much more quickly than highway driving. Vehicles equipped with an automatic transaxle are more likely to wear the linings more quickly than those equipped with a manual transmission.

Driving habits also affect brake wear. Aggressive braking from high speeds is likely to wear the linings more quickly than slow gradual stops. Aggressive braking also generates much more heat which could result in premature brake rotor wear, potential rotor warpage and wheel bearing damage, as the heat generated can decrease the ability of the grease to adequately lubricate the sealed wheel bearing.

Some brake pads are equipped with audible wear sensors. When the brake linings reach their wear limit, a small metal tab begins to contact the brake rotor, making an audible, but light scraping noise which initially occurs when the brakes are used. Eventually it will make a high pitched scraping noise any time the vehicle is moving, being most noticeable at slow speeds.

❊❊ WARNING

If a scraping noise is heard when applying the brakes, inspect the brake linings immediately.

Sometimes brakes do squeal even though the brake linings are not worn. In this instance, the brake squeal usually diminishes when the brakes are used hard.

Causes of brake squeal include the following:
• Rust or debris built up between the brake pad backing and caliper bracket
• Insufficient lubricant on the sliding pins
• Loose brake pad shims
• Brake rotor surface wear and/or a ridge on the outer circumference of the brake rotor
• Glazed, contaminated or improper brake linings

REMOVAL & INSTALLATION

Front

▶ See Figures 20 thru 26

1. Use a siphon or clean turkey baster to remove about half of the brake fluid from the master cylinder. Or remove all of the fluid, clean the reservoir with an approved brake cleaner and a clean lint-free cloth and fill ½ full with fresh brake fluid.

2. Raise and safely support the vehicle with jackstands.

3. Remove the front tire/wheel assemblies.

4. If necessary, remove the brake hose mounting bolts from the steering knuckle.

➡Regardless of their wear pattern, when brake pads are replaced on one side of the vehicle, they must also be replaced on the other side. It is advisable, however, to complete one side before beginning the other.

5. Working on one brake caliper at a time, remove the lower brake caliper bolt and pivot the caliper up and out of the way.

✳✳ WARNING

Once a brake caliper has been lifted away from the brake pads, do not press the brake pedal.

6. Remove the brake pads and shims.
To install:
7. If the pad thickness is less than the service requirement, replace the pads.
8. Clean and check the brake rotor for cracks and uneven wear, or an excessive ridge on the outer circumference. Measure the brake rotor thickness with a micrometer and replace the rotor if the measured thickness is less than the minimum thickness specification stamped into the rotor.
9. Clean the caliper brackets, and lubricate the

Fig. 20 To remove the front brake pads, remove the lower caliper mounting bolt . . .

Fig. 21 . . . then pivot the brake caliper up, off of the brake pads

Fig. 22 Once the caliper is pivoted up, you can remove the brake pads from the caliper bracket

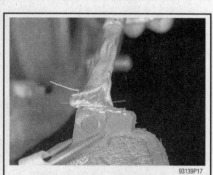

Fig. 23 Before installation, put a light coating of an anti-seizing compound onto the tabs of the brake pad backing . . .

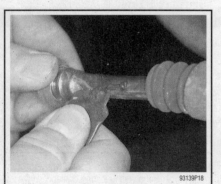

Fig. 24 . . . also lubricate the caliper sliders with a high temperature brake grease

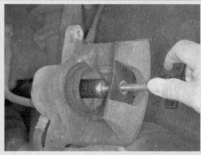

Fig. 25 You must press the brake caliper piston back into the piston bore, smoothly and gradually using a brake caliper piston tool. If necessary, use a suitable socket as a spacer . . .

Fig. 26 . . . you can also use a large C-clamp, centered in the piston cavity to carefully press the piston into the caliper bore

bracket sliding pins with a high temperature brake grease.

10. Apply a light coat of an anti-seizing compound to the brake pad backing tabs and the slots the tabs are installed into on the brake caliper bracket.

11. Make sure all the brake pad shims are properly and securely installed. If equipped with wear indicators, install the brake pad such that the wear indicator is at the top of the inside brake pad.

12. If the brake pads are being replaced, the brake caliper piston must be pressed back into the caliper body as follows:

a. Clean the exposed portion of the brake caliper piston with an approved brake cleaner, and wipe off any residual debris using a clean lint-less cloth.

b. Using a tool designed for retracting brake caliper pistons or a suitable C-clamp, press on the center of the brake piston using a slow, light, even pressure to press the piston into the caliper. If necessary, place a suitable sized socket in the center cavity of the piston to act as a spacer, or, use an old brake pad to lay across the piston.

✳✳ WARNING

Do not force the brake caliper piston back into the caliper. If the piston begins to bind, stop immediately until the cause can be determined.

Possible causes for a brake caliper piston to bind include:
- An out of round brake caliper piston
- An excessively worn brake caliper bore and/or brake piston
- Excessive corrosion or debris built up on the brake piston surface or caliper bore

✳✳ WARNING

When reusing the old brake pads, be sure to install them in the same positions to prevent an increase in stopping distance.

13. Using an old pad as a cushion, push the piston into the caliper to allow enough space for the new pads. Or, you can use a large C-clamp, or other suitable tool, to completely retract the piston into the caliper.

14. Install all the mounting bolts.

15. Check the master cylinder brake reservoir fluid level and top off as necessary.

16. Once the brake calipers are completely installed, press the brake pedal in short 2 inch (50mm) strokes until the brake pedal is firm. Avoid pressing the brake pedal more than 2 inches because the wear in the master cylinder bore could damage the internal seals. Depress and hold the brake several times to ensure they work.

17. Carefully road test the vehicle. Allow approximately 200 miles (320km) of driving for new brake pads to fully seat.

Rear

4-CYLINDER ODYSSEY MODELS

▶ See Figures 27 and 28

The 4-cylinder Odyssey models are equipped with hydraulic disc brakes on the rear wheels. The disc brake rotor also has an internal brake drum machined into the center of the rotor assembly. The drum portion of the rotor assembly is used for the mechanical parking brake.

1. Use a siphon or clean turkey baster to remove about half of the brake fluid from the master cylinder.

2. Raise and properly support the vehicle. Remove the rear tire/wheel assemblies.

3. Unfasten the lower caliper mounting bolt, then pivot the caliper upward from the bracket.

4. Remove the pad shims, retainers and brake pads. If the brake pads are worn below specification, replace the pads.

To install:

5. If the brake pads are being replaced, the brake caliper piston must be pressed back into the caliper body. Refer to the procedure in front disc brake pad replacement in this section for details.

6. Clean and remove any rust from the mounting bracket and caliper assembly.

7. Clean the brake disc and check for cracks.

8. Apply Molykote M77® or equivalent grease to the back of the brake pads and shims.

✳✳ WARNING

Do not apply any grease to the friction material.

9. Install the brake pads and shims into the caliper bracket.

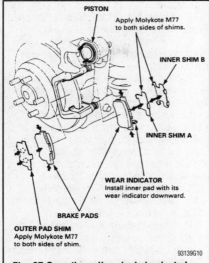

Fig. 27 Once the caliper body is pivoted upward, the brake pads can be removed from the bracket assembly

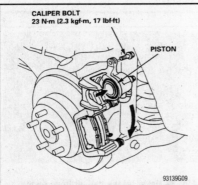

Fig. 28 When lowering the brake caliper assembly in place, make sure the piston is pressed back into the bore, and be careful not to damage the piston dust seal and the lower pin boot

10. Carefully rotate the brake caliper into place, making sure to not damage the piston dust boot and the mounting pin boot, then install and tighten the caliper mounting bolt to 17 ft. lbs. (23 Nm).

11. Check the master cylinder brake reservoir fluid level and top off as necessary.

12. Once the brake calipers are completely installed, press the brake pedal in short 2 inch (50mm) strokes until the brake pedal is firm. Avoid pressing the brake pedal more than 2 inches because the wear in the master cylinder bore could damage the internal seals. Depress and hold the brake several times to ensure they work.

13. Carefully road test the vehicle. Allow approximately 200 miles of driving for new brake pads to fully seat.

INSPECTION

▶ See Figure 29

You should check the brake pads every 6,000 miles (9,600km), any time the oil is changed or wheels are removed. Inspect both ends of the outer

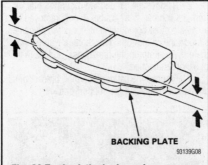

Fig. 29 To check the brake pad wear, measure the thickness of the lining. If the thickness is below the service limit, replace the pads

brake pad by looking in at each end of the caliper. These are the points at which the highest rate of wear normally occurs. Also, check the thickness on the inner brake pad to make sure it is not wearing prematurely. Some inboard pads have a thermal layer against the steel backing surface which is integrally molded with the pad. Do not confuse this extra layer with uneven inboard/outboard brake pad wear.

Look down through inspection hole in the top of the caliper to view the inner brake pad. Replace the pads whenever the thickness of any pad is worn within 0.030 in. (0.76mm) of the steel backing surface. For riveted brake pads, they must be replaced if the pad is worn to 0.030 (0.76mm) of any rivet head. The disc brake pads MUST be replaced in axle sets, for example, if you replace the driver's side front brake pads, you must also replace the passenger's side front brake pads. This will prevent uneven wear and other brake system problems.

1. Remove the brake pads and observe their condition.

2. Measure the thickness of the brake pad's lining material at the thinnest portion of the assembly. Do not include the pad's metal backing plate in the measurement.

3. If you can't accurately determine the condition of the brake pads by visual inspection, you must remove the caliper, then remove the brake pads.

Brake Caliper

REMOVAL & INSTALLATION

▶ See Figures 30, 31, 32, 33 and 34

➡**Do not allow the master cylinder reservoir to empty. An empty reservoir will allow air to enter the brake system and complete system bleeding will be required.**

1. Use a siphon or clean turkey baster to remove about half of the brake fluid from the master cylinder.

2. Raise and safely support the vehicle, then remove the tire and wheel assembly.

3. Unfasten the caliper mounting bolts, then remove the caliper assembly from the rotor.

4. Remove the brake pads and shims.

5. If the caliper is to be completely removed from the vehicle for replacement or overhaul, remove the brake hose attaching bolt, then disconnect the brake hose from the caliper and plug the hose to prevent fluid contamination or loss.

6. Remove the caliper and mounting bracket from the vehicle. If the caliper is only removed for access to other components or for pad replacement, support the caliper using mechanic's wire so that there is no strain on the brake hose, and leave the brake hose attached.

7. Remove the caliper mounting bracket bolts and lift the caliper off the support bracket.

Fig. 30 Use a wrench to loosen the caliper mounting bracket bolts

Fig. 31 Once the bolts have been removed, lift the caliper mounting away from the brake rotor

To install:

8. Completely retract the piston into the caliper using a large C-clamp or other suitable tool.

9. Clean and lubricate both steering knuckle abutments or support brackets with a coating of multi-purpose grease.

10. Position the caliper and brake pad assembly over the brake rotor. Be sure to properly install the caliper assembly into the abutments of the steering knuckle or support bracket. Be sure the caliper guide pin bolts, rubber bushings and sleeves are clear of the steering knuckle bosses.

11. Fill the master cylinder with fresh brake fluid and, if the brake hose was removed, bleed the brake system as outlined in this section.

12. Install the wheel and tire assembly.

13. Carefully lower the vehicle, then tighten the lug nuts to the proper specifications.

14. Depress the brake pedal using short 2 inch (50mm) strokes, in repetitions of 3–4 times until the brake linings are seated and to restore pressure in the system.

> ❋❋ **CAUTION**
>
> Do not move the vehicle until a firm pedal is obtained.

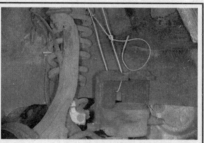

Fig. 32 Never let the caliper hang by the brake hose. Always suspend if with a piece of wire so there is no tension on the hose

Fig. 34 Pull the rear brake caliper away from the mount—4-cylinder Odyssey models

15. Road test the vehicle and check for proper brake operation.

OVERHAUL

▶ **See Figures 35 thru 42**

➥ Some vehicles may be equipped dual piston calipers. The procedure to overhaul the caliper is essentially the same with the exception of multiple pistons, O-rings and dust boots.

1. Remove the caliper from the vehicle and place on a clean workbench.

> ❋❋ **CAUTION**
>
> NEVER place your fingers in front of the pistons in an attempt to catch or protect the pistons when applying compressed air. This could result in personal injury!

➥ Depending upon the vehicle, there are two different ways to remove the piston from the caliper. Refer to the brake pad replacement procedure to make sure you have the correct procedure for your vehicle.

2. The first method is as follows:
   a. Stuff a shop towel or a block of wood into the caliper to catch the piston.
   b. Remove the caliper piston using compressed air applied into the caliper inlet hole. Inspect the piston for scoring, nicks, corrosion and/or worn or damaged chrome plating. The piston must be replaced if any of these conditions are found.

3. For the second method, you must rotate the piston to retract it from the caliper.

4. If equipped, remove the anti-rattle clip.

5. Use a prytool to remove the caliper boot, being careful not to scratch the housing bore.

6. Remove the piston seals from the groove in the caliper bore.

7. Carefully loosen the brake bleeder valve cap and valve from the caliper housing.

8. Inspect the caliper bores, pistons and mounting threads for scoring or excessive wear.

9. Use crocus cloth to polish out light corrosion from the piston and bore.

10. Clean all parts with denatured alcohol and dry with compressed air.

To install:

11. Lubricate and install the bleeder valve and cap.

12. Install the new seals into the caliper bore grooves, making sure they are not twisted.

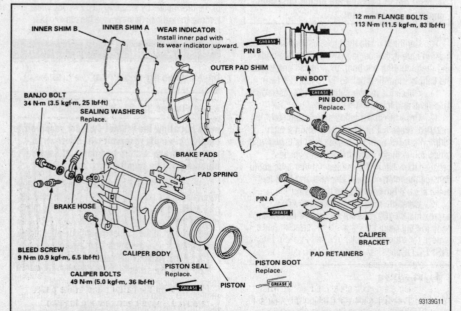

Fig. 33 Exploded view of the front brake caliper and related components—CR-V model shown

INNER SHIM B
INNER SHIM A
WEAR INDICATOR
Install inner pad with its wear indicator upward.
OUTER PAD SHIM
12 mm FLANGE BOLTS
113 N·m (11.5 kgf·m, 83 lbf·ft)
PIN B
PIN BOOT
GREASE
PIN BOOTS
Replace.
BANJO BOLT
34 N·m (3.5 kgf·m, 25 lbf·ft)
SEALING WASHERS
Replace.
BRAKE PADS
PAD SPRING
PIN A
GREASE
BRAKE HOSE
CALIPER BRACKET
PAD RETAINERS
BLEED SCREW
9 N·m (0.9 kgf·m, 6.5 lbf·ft)
CALIPER BODY
CALIPER BOLTS
49 N·m (5.0 kgf·m, 36 lbf·ft)
PISTON SEAL
Replace.
PISTON BOOT
Replace.
PISTON
GREASE
GREASE

Fig. 35 For some types of calipers, use compressed air to drive the piston out of the caliper, but make sure to keep your fingers clear

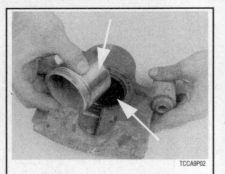

Fig. 36 Withdraw the piston from the caliper bore

Fig. 37 On some vehicles, you must remove the anti-rattle clip

Fig. 38 Use a prytool to carefully pry around the edge of the boot . . .

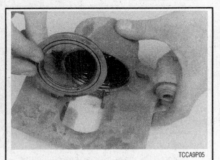

Fig. 39 . . . then remove the boot from the caliper housing, taking care not to score or damage the bore

Fig. 40 Use extreme caution when removing the piston seal; DO NOT scratch the caliper bore

Fig. 41 Use the proper size driving tool and a mallet to properly seal the boots in the caliper housing

Fig. 42 There are tools, such as this Mighty-Vac, available to assist in proper brake system bleeding

13. Lubricate the piston bore.

14. Install the pistons and boots into the bores of the calipers and push to the bottom of the bores.

15. Use a suitable driving tool to seat the boots in the housing.

16. Install the caliper in the vehicle.

17. Install the wheel and tire assembly, then carefully lower the vehicle.

18. Properly bleed the brake system.

Brake Disc (Rotor)

REMOVAL & INSTALLATION

▶ **See Figures 43, 44, 45, 46 and 47**

1. Use a siphon or clean turkey baster to remove about half of the brake fluid from the master cylinder.

2. Raise and safely support the vehicle and remove the tire/wheel assembly.

3. Remove the caliper mounting bolts, then lift the caliper assembly away from the brake rotor.

4. Use a suitable piece of wire to suspend the caliper assembly. This will prevent the weight of the caliper from being supported by the brake flex hose which will damage the hose.

5. Once the caliper body and brake pads are removed, unfasten the caliper bracket mounting bolts, then remove the bracket from the rotor.

6. Remove the rotor retaining screws.

7. Remove the brake rotor by pulling it straight off the wheel mounting studs or if seized in place, remove the stubborn brake rotor by threading in two 8 x 1.25mm bolts, two turns at a time until the brake rotor is released.

To install:

8. If necessary, completely retract the piston into the caliper using a large C-clamp or other suitable tool as provided in the front disc brake pad replacement procedures in this section.

9. Install the brake rotor onto the wheel hub and tighten the mounting screws.

10. Install the caliper mounting bracket and secure with the retaining bolts.

11. Install the caliper and pad assembly over the brake rotor and mounting bracket and install the mounting bolts.

12. Fill the master cylinder to the proper level with fresh brake fluid.

13. Install the tire/wheel assembly and lower the vehicle.

14. Pump the brake pedal until the brake pads are seated and a firm pedal is achieved before attempting to move the vehicle.

❊❊ CAUTION

Do not move the vehicle until a firm pedal is obtained.

Fig. 43 With the caliper and brake pads removed, loosen and remove the two bracket mounting bolts, then . . .

Fig. 44 . . . remove the bracket from the knuckle—CR-V model shown

Fig. 47 Remove a stubborn brake rotor by threading in two 8 x 1.25mm bolts, two turns at a time until the brake rotor is released—CR-V model shown

15. Road test the vehicle to check for proper brake operation.

INSPECTION

▶ **See Figures 48, 49 and 50**

Whenever the brake calipers or pads are removed, inspect the rotors for defects. The brake rotor is an extremely important component of the brake system. Cracks, large scratches or warpage can adversely affect the braking system, at times to the point of becoming very dangerous.

Light scoring is acceptable. Heavy scoring or warping will necessitate refinishing or replacement of the disc. The brake disc must be replaced if cracks or burned marks are evident.

If the rotor needs to be replaced with a new part, the protective coating on the braking surface of the rotor must be removed with an appropriate solvent before installing the rotor to the vehicle.

Check the run-out of the hub (disc removed). It should not be more than 0.002 inch (0.050mm). If so, the hub should be replaced.

All brake discs or rotors have markings for MIN-IMUM allowable thickness cast on an unmachined surface or an alternate surface. Always use this specification as the **minimum** allowable thickness or refinishing limit. Refer to a local auto parts store or machine shop, if necessary, where rotors are resurfaced.

If the rotor needs to be replaced with a new part,

Fig. 45 The use of a hand impact driver may be necessary to remove the brake rotor retaining screws

the protective coating on the braking surface of the rotor must be removed with an appropriate solvent before installing the rotor to the vehicle.

To properly check a brake rotor, the disc runout, thickness and parallelism should be measured. To perform these measurements proceed as follows:

1. Raise and safely support the vehicle.
2. Remove the tire/wheel assembly for the brake rotor to be inspected.
3. Reinstall the lug nuts and torque to 80 ft. lbs. (108 Nm).
4. Remove the brake pads as outlined in this section.
5. Inspect the brake surface for cracks and damage, then thoroughly clean the brake surface.
6. To measure runout:
   a. Attach a dial indicator to a solid portion of the suspension.
   b. Set and zero the dial indicator plunger 0.40 inches (10mm) inside the outer circumference of the brake rotor.
   c. Rotate the brake rotor and note the amount of runout by reading the dial indicator. If the runout exceeds 0.004 inches (0.10mm), measure the minimum thickness. If rotor thickness is within specification, use an approved on-car brake lathe and machine the brake rotor.
7. To measure the brake rotor thickness and parallelism proceed as follows:
   a. Use a micrometer and measure the brake rotor thickness 0.40 inches (10mm) inside the outer circumference of the brake rotor every 45° (⅛ of a rotation).

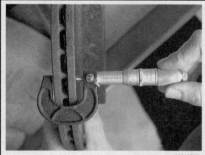

Fig. 48 Using a micrometer to measure the thickness of the brake rotor. Discard the rotor if it is not within the specification stamped on the rotor

Fig. 46 Close up view of the brake rotor retaining screws

   b. Compare the smallest value measured to the minimum thickness specifications stamped on the brake rotor. If the rotor is below the minimum thickness, the rotor must be replaced. If within specification, measure the parallelism.
   c. To measure parallelism, subtract the smallest value measured from the largest value measured. If the parallelism is greater than 0.0006 inches (0.015mm), use an approved on car brake lathe and machine the brake rotor.

➡ **If after machining the brake rotor is below minimum thickness, it must be replaced.**

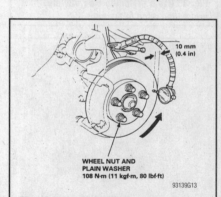

Fig. 49 Use a dial indicator to measure the brake rotor runout

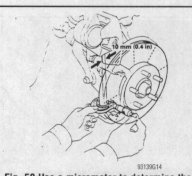

Fig. 50 Use a micrometer to determine the rotor parallelism and to measure rotor thickness. If the rotor thickness is below the minimum thickness, it must be replaced

DRUM BRAKES

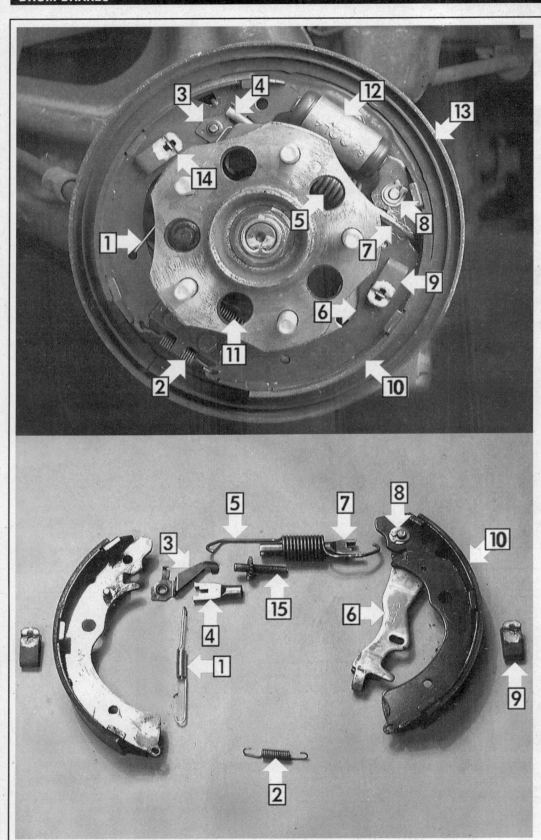

DRUM BRAKE COMPONENTS

1. Self-adjuster spring
2. Lower return spring
3. Self-adjusting lever
4. Free spinning clevis B
5. Upper return spring
6. Parking brake arm
7. Threaded clevis A
8. U-clip
9. Retainer spring
10. Brake shoe
11. Parking brake arm return spring
12. Wheel cylinder
13. Backing plate
14. Retaining spring lock pin
15. Adjuster assembly

93139PU3

The CR-V and V6 Odyssey models use hydraulic drum brakes on the rear wheels. The parking brake is incorporated with the rear hydraulic drum brake on these models. Odyssey models equipped with the 4-cylinder engine, do not use hydraulic drum brakes on the rear wheels, with the exception of the parking brakes. For drum parking brake service information on these models, refer to the parking brake procedures later in this section.

Brake Drums

REMOVAL AND INSTALLATION

▶ **See Figures 51 and 52**

1. Raise and safely support the rear of the vehicle.
2. Remove the rear tire/wheel assemblies.
3. Thread two 8 x 1.25mm bolts into the threaded holes two turns at a time to lift the drum off the hub.

❋❋ WARNING

Do not press the brake pedal with the brake drum removed.

4. Installation is in reverse order of removal.

Fig. 51 Thread two 8 x 1.25mm bolts into the brake drum, two turns at a time, to press it away from the hub

Fig. 52 Pull the brake drum away from the hub to access the rear brake components

INSPECTION

Inspect the drum for cracks, uneven surface wear, scoring, grooves, excessive ridge wear and out of round conditions. If necessary and within wear limits, resurface the brake drum. Otherwise replace it.

Inspect the rear bearing condition with the drum removed. Rotate the rear hub bearings and check for smooth operation.

The maximum allowable inside diameter should be stamped into the brake drum. Measure the inside diameter of the drum to determine if it is within the service limit. If resurfaced, recheck the inside diameter. If the drum exceeds the specification, replace the drum. Compare the measured brake drum inside diameter to the following specifications:

CR-V models:
- Standard: 8.657–8.661 inches (219.9–220.0mm)
- Service Limit: 8.700 inches (221.0mm)

V6 Odyssey models:
- Standard: 9.996–10.000 inches (253.9–254.0mm)
- Service Limit: 10.04 inches (255.0mm)

Brake Shoes

INSPECTION

Inspect the brake linings for cracking, glazing, contamination and wear. If any one shoe is damaged or beyond specification, replace the shoes as a set. Brake shoe lining thickness specifications:

CR-V models:
- Standard: 0.15–0.18 inches (3.9–4.5mm)
- Service Limit: 0.08 inches (2.0mm)

V6 Odyssey models:
- Standard: 0.18 inches (4.5mm)
- Service Limit: 0.08 inches (2.0mm)

REMOVAL AND INSTALLATION

▶ **See Figures 53 thru 63**

1. Raise and safely support the rear of the vehicle.
2. Remove the rear tire/wheel assemblies.
3. Remove the brake drums.

❋❋ WARNING

Do not press the brake pedal when the brake drum is removed.

4. Place a small paint stick or ruler between the wheel cylinder and rear brake shoe.
5. Clamp a pair of locking pliers securely onto the backing plate at the center of the rear brake shoe.
6. Using locking needle-nose pliers, clamp onto the upper brake spring where the brake adjuster meets the rear shoe. Pull back on the spring and remove it.
7. Remove the lower return spring.
8. Support the back of the brake shoe retainer pin with a finger, and using clamping needle-nose pliers, grasp the top of the retainer spring, press inward and turn 90° to release it from the pin.
9. Place a suitable elastic band around the wheel cylinder to keep the pistons in place.

❋❋ WARNING

If the wheel cylinder pistons are not held in place when the brake shoes are removed, they may fall out causing fluid loss and component damage. Brake bleeding is necessary if this occurs.

10. Remove the front brake shoe, brake adjuster and related components, then use a pair of suitable pliers to pull the parking brake cable out of the bracket for the rear brake shoe.
11. Place the brake shoe in a vise so that the jaws do not contact the brake lining, and the pivot pin head and the lever arm are supported.
12. Use a hammer and chisel to drive the U-clip off the pin, then remove the lever arm.
13. Inspect the wheel cylinder for seepage, leaks or damage and replace as necessary.
   To install:
14. Clean the lever arm and lubricate the pivot point and transfer to the replacement brake shoe.

Fig. 53 Place a paint stick between the rear shoe and the wheel cylinder, and clamp locking pliers onto the backing plate to hold the shoe when the upper spring is removed and installed

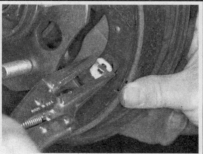

Fig. 54 Hold the locking pin in place with your fingers, press inward on the retaining spring . . .

Fig. 55 . . . then turn the retaining spring 90° to release it

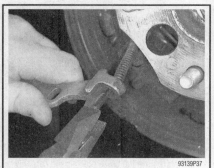

Fig. 56 Use a pair of flat-nosed pliers to remove the parking brake cable from the brake shoe lever arm —CR-V shown

Fig. 57 Place the brake shoe in a suitable vise as shown, to support and remove the lever arm. Do not clamp on the brake linings

Fig. 58 Lubricate the pivot surfaces before reassembling. Use a new U-clamp and washer during assembly

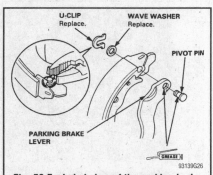

Fig. 59 Exploded view of the parking brake lever and related components—CR-V model shown

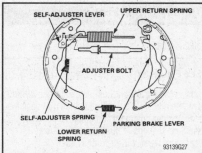

Fig. 60 Detailed view of the rear drum brake components. The adjuster bolt assembly is installed inside the upper return spring

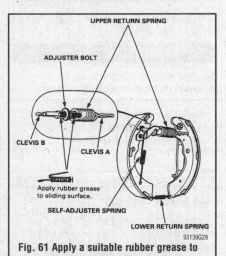

Fig. 61 Apply a suitable rubber grease to the spindle and threaded portion of the adjuster bolt—CR-V shown

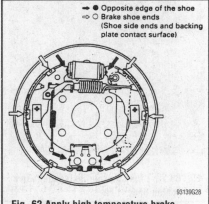

Fig. 62 Apply high temperature brake grease to the areas referenced by the arrows—CR-V model shown

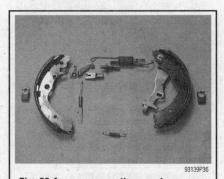

Fig. 63 As you remove the rear drum brake components, make sure to keep them in order to ease reassembly

15. Install the lever arm and brake shoe into the vise, install an new washer, and U-clip, bending the open end of the U-clip closed with flat-nosed pliers.

16. Clean and lubricate the following with an approved high temperature brake grease:
- Brake adjuster threads and clevis pivot
- All raised areas on the brake shoe backing plate that contact the metal portion of the brake shoe.
- The grooves in the wheel cylinder and lower brake shoe resting blocks.

17. Install the brake cable into the rear shoe lever arm, then install the rear shoe onto the backing plate with new retaining pins and springs.

18. Install the paint stick, or suitable ruler, between the rear shoe and the wheel cylinder.

19. Clamp locking pliers securely onto the backing plate at the center of the rear brake shoe.

20. Install the brake adjuster along with the upper and lower springs onto the front shoe, then hook the lower spring into the rear shoe as the front shoe is installed onto the backing plate. Secure the front shoe to the backing plate using a new retaining pin and spring.

21. Remove the elastic band used around the wheel cylinder to keep the pistons in place.

22. Using locking needle-nose pliers, clamp onto the upper brake spring where the brake adjuster meets the rear shoe. Pull back on the spring and install it onto the rear shoe.

23. Remove the locking pliers, and paint stick or ruler. Clean and install the brake drum, and hold in place with two lug nuts.

24. Rotate the brake drum and using a flat blade screwdriver, adjust the brake adjuster until a very light scuffing noise is heard when rotating the drum. If necessary, remove the drum to rotate the adjustment star wheel.

25. Install the wheel/tire assemblies, carefully lower the vehicle and torque the lug nuts to specification.

26. Pump the brake pedal repeatedly several times to set the brake adjusters. If brake pedal pressure is acceptable, test drive the vehicle slowly for approximately 5 minutes and press the brake pedal several times while backing up and pulling forward to set the adjusters and seat the brake shoes.

☀ WARNING

Overtightening or over-adjusting the parking brake cable may cause the brakes to drag causing excessive heat build up and brake failure.

27. Check and top off the brake fluid reservoir as necessary.
28. Check the parking brake adjustment and adjust as necessary.

Wheel Cylinders

INSPECTION

▶ See Figure 64

Inspect the brake backing plate for signs of fluid stains. Remove the brake drums, then pull back the wheel cylinder dust boot and check for signs of brake fluid seepage. If fluid leakage is found in these areas, replace the wheel cylinder.

Fig. 64 Carefully peel the dust boot back and check for signs of fluid seepage. If fluid leaked out or the outside of the wheel cylinder is wet, replace it

REMOVAL AND INSTALLATION

▶ See Figures 65, 66, 67, 68 and 69

1. Raise and safely support the rear of the vehicle.
2. Remove the rear tire/wheel assemblies.
3. Remove the brake drums.
4. Remove the brake shoes.
5. Install a suitable brake line clamp on the flexible brake line to seal the brake fluid in the system. If the proper tool is not available, do NOT use a pair of locking pliers to clamp the brake line shut. Instead, drain the fluid from the disconnected brake line into a suitable container, then plug the fitting to avoid contaminating the system.
6. Place a suitable drain pan directly underneath the wheel cylinder. If necessary wash the residual brake fluid away with cold water.

7. Using a brake line wrench, loosen the flare nut ⅛–¼ turn while watching the metal brake line. If the flare nut moves freely, remove the flare nut and brake line.

☀ WARNING

Do not bend or kink the metal hydraulic brake lines

If the metal line moves as the flare nut turns, the line is seized to the flare nut. To overcome this condition, remove the two wheel cylinder mounting bolts, then remove the brake bleeder and carefully pull the wheel cylinder outward until the wheel cylinder can be rotated while holding the flare nut. Install the wheel cylinder in reverse order if necessary.

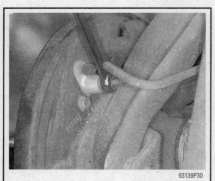

Fig. 65 If a brake line seizes to the flare nut, loosen the flare nut ⅛ of a turn . . .

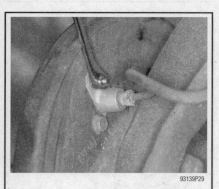

Fig. 66 . . . then loosen the bleeder valve and tighten finger-tight

Fig. 67 Remove the wheel cylinder mounting bolts . . .

Fig. 68 . . . then remove the bleeder valve, pull the wheel cylinder outward and, while holding the flare nut, rotate the wheel cylinder to remove it

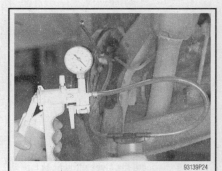

Fig. 69 Bleeding a wheel cylinder is quick work when using a self-bleeder

8. Remove the wheel cylinder mounting bolt(s), and remove the wheel cylinder.

☀ WARNING

Use only original grade wheel cylinder mounting bolts when replacing the bolt.

9. Installation is in reverse order of removal, making sure to remove the brake line clamp, properly torque all fasteners and bleed the brake hydraulic system.

OVERHAUL

▶ See Figures 70 thru 79

Wheel cylinder overhaul kits may be available, but often at little or no savings over a reconditioned wheel cylinder. It often makes sense with these components to substitute a new or reconditioned part instead of attempting an overhaul.

If no replacement is available, or you would prefer to overhaul your wheel cylinders, the following procedure may be used. When rebuilding and installing wheel cylinders, avoid getting any contaminants into the system. Always use clean, new, high quality brake fluid. If dirty or improper fluid has been used, it will be necessary to drain the entire system, flush the system with proper brake fluid, replace all rubber components, then refill and bleed the system.

1. Remove the wheel cylinder from the vehicle and place on a clean workbench.
2. First remove and discard the old rubber boots, then withdraw the pistons. Piston cylinders

Fig. 70 Remove the outer boots from the wheel cylinder

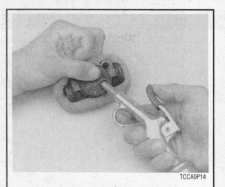

Fig. 71 Compressed air can be used to remove the pistons and seals

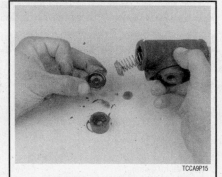

Fig. 72 Remove the pistons, cup seals and spring from the cylinder

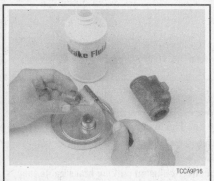

Fig. 73 Use brake fluid and a soft brush to clean the pistons . . .

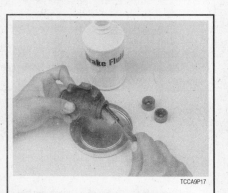

Fig. 74 . . . and the bore of the wheel cylinder

Fig. 75 Once cleaned and inspected, the wheel cylinder is ready for assembly

Fig. 76 Lubricate the cup seals with brake fluid

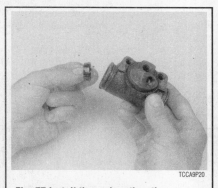

Fig. 77 Install the spring, then the cup seals in the bore

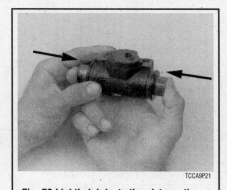

Fig. 78 Lightly lubricate the pistons, then install them

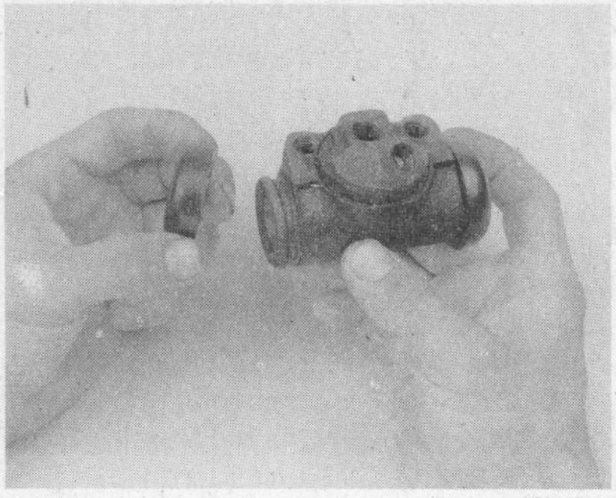

Fig. 79 The boots can now be installed over the wheel cylinder ends

are equipped with seals and a spring assembly, all located behind the pistons in the cylinder bore.

3. Remove the remaining inner components, seals and spring assembly. Compressed air may be useful in removing these components. If no compressed air is available, be VERY careful not to score the wheel cylinder bore when removing parts from it. Discard all components for which replacements were supplied in the rebuild kit.

4. Wash the cylinder and metal parts in denatured alcohol or clean brake fluid.

✳✳ WARNING

Never use a mineral-based solvent such as gasoline, kerosene or paint thinner for cleaning purposes. These solvents will swell rubber components and quickly deteriorate them.

5. Allow the parts to air dry or use compressed air. Do not use rags for cleaning, since lint will remain in the cylinder bore.

6. Inspect the piston and replace it if it shows scratches.

7. Lubricate the cylinder bore and seals using clean brake fluid.

8. Position the spring assembly.

9. Install the inner seals, then the pistons.

10. Insert the new boots into the counterbores by hand. Do not lubricate the boots.

11. Install the wheel cylinder.

PARKING BRAKE

Cable

REMOVAL & INSTALLATION

◆ **See Figures 80, 81 and 82**

1. Disconnect the negative battery cable.
2. Loosen the lug nuts, then raise and safely support the vehicle.
3. On CR-V and 4-cylinder Odyssey models, perform the following:
   a. Remove the Phillips screw(s), then slide the trim cover up and out.
   b. Detach the parking brake switch electrical connector.
   c. Release the parking brake lever, then disconnect the parking brake cable.
   d. Remove the parking brake lever assembly.
4. On V6 Odyssey models, release the parking brake lever, then disconnect the parking brake cable

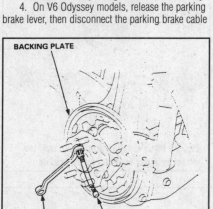

Fig. 80 Use a 12mm offset wrench to remove the parking brake cable from the backing plate

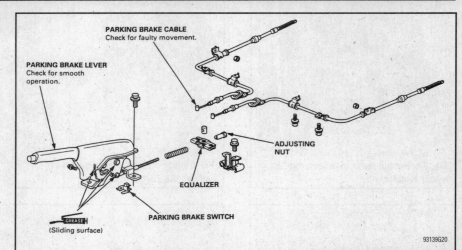

Fig. 82 Exploded view of the parking brake cable and related components—4-cylinder Odyssey models

by removing the adjustment nut at the foot pedal assembly.

5. On CR-V and V6 Odyssey models remove the rear brake drum.
6. On 4-cylinder Odyssey models, remove the disc brake caliper, mounting bracket, brake pads and brake rotor.
7. Remove the brake shoes as necessary to access the cable attached to the brake shoe bracket, and disconnect the cable.
8. Slide a 12mm offset boxed end wrench onto the brake cable to compress the cable-to-backing plate retainer, then slide the cable through the backing plate.
9. Remove the parking brake cable guide brackets attached to the vehicle's underbody and remove the cable.
10. Installation is the reverse of the removal procedure, making sure upon completion, that the parking brake is properly adjusted.

ADJUSTMENT

◆ **See Figures 83, 84 and 85**

❋❋ WARNING

An over-adjusted parking brake cable may not allow the rear brake self-adjusters to function properly.

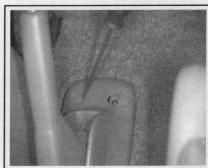

Fig. 83 To access the parking brake adjuster, first remove the trim covers

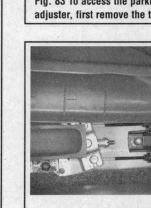

Fig. 84 Remove the Phillips screws, slide the cover back to unhook it, and lift it away—CR-V model shown

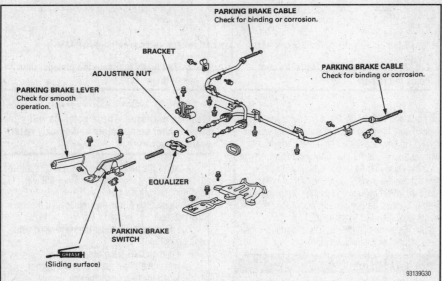

Fig. 81 Exploded view of a typical Honda parking brake cable and related components—CR-V model shown

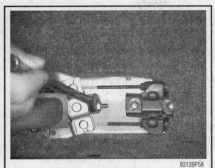

Fig. 85 Turn the adjustment nut in to tighten or out to loosen the parking brake cable, as necessary

On CR-V and V6 Odyssey models, the parking brake shares the brake shoes with the hydraulic brake. If the shoes are worn and the hydraulic brake shoe adjustment is not functioning properly, they should be checked and adjusted before proceeding with the parking brake adjustment. A typical symptom of a brake system that may need adjustment, is when the parking brake is released, the hydraulic brake pedal is pumped repetitively 3 times and the pedal height and/or pedal pressure increases.

On 4-cylinder Odyssey models, the parking brake does not interact with the hydraulic brake system. The parking brake drum is cast into the center of the brake rotor.

✳✳ WARNING

Overtightening the parking brake cable may cause the brakes to drag causing excessive heat build up and brake failure.

1. The rear brakes should be engaged a certain number of notches when a force is applied:
   - CR-V models: 44 lbs. (196 N) pull, 2–6 notches
   - 4-cylinder Odyssey models: 44 lbs. (196 N) pull, 4–8 notches
   - V6 Odyssey models: 66 lbs. (294 N) press 3–5 notches
2. To adjust the parking brake cable, release the parking brake, raise and safely support the rear of vehicle.
3. On CR-V and 4-cylinder Odyssey models, perform the following:
   a. Remove the screw covers, screws and parking brake trim cover.
   b. Turn the adjustment nut as needed to attain the proper adjustment.

➡️**Make sure the brakes do not drag when the parking brake lever is released.**

   c. Reinstall the trim cover.
4. On V6 Odyssey models, perform the following:
   a. Depress the pedal 2 notches.
   b. Tighten the adjusting nut at the pedal assembly until the rear brakes just begin to drag when rotated.
   c. Release the parking brake lever and check that the wheels do not drag when turned. The parking brake should engage in 3–5 notches when a force of 66 lbs. (294 N) is applied to the parking brake pedal.
5. Carefully lower the vehicle.

Parking Brake Shoes

REMOVAL & INSTALLATION

CR-V and V6 Odyssey Models

Please refer to the rear drum brake shoe replacement procedures in this section.

4-Cylinder Odyssey Models

▸ **See Figures 86, 87, 88, 89 and 90**

These models use a parking drum brake located in the center of the rear brake rotor. The shoes are attached to a backing plate inside the rear brake rotor. To service follow the steps below.

1. Loosen the rear parking brake by lowering it to the rest position.
2. Raise the vehicle and support it with the proper jackstands.
3. Remove the rear tires.
4. Remove the two 6mm bolts.
5. Remove the rear brake disc rotor.

➡️**If necessary, install two 8mm bolts into the threaded holes in the rotor and tighten them 2 turns at a time. This will push the rotor from the hub and stud assembly.**

6. Inspect the brake shoe linings for contamination, cracking, glazing, or excessive wear.
7. Measure the linings of the shoes if there is any question as to the amount of life left. The lining thickness is 0.10 in (2.5mm) on a new shoe. The

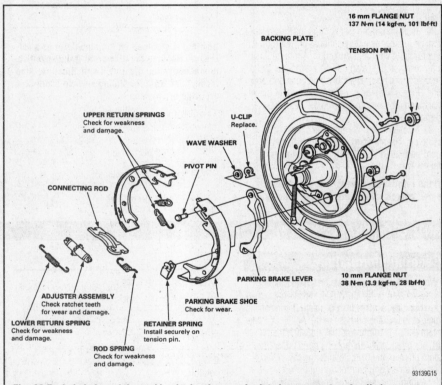

Fig. 86 Exploded view of the parking brake shoes and related components—4-cylinder Odyssey shown

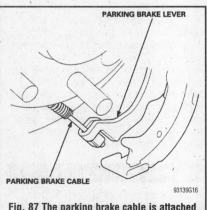

Fig. 87 The parking brake cable is attached to a lever that pivots on the brake shoe

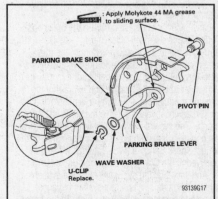

Fig. 88 The lever is attached to the brake shoe by a pivot pin and a U-clip

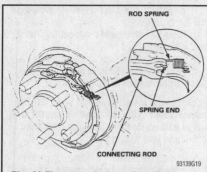

Fig. 89 The top springs are installed so that the curved spring end is facing downward

service limit is a minimum thickness of 0.04 in (1.0mm).

The inner part of the rear rotor is machined in the same manner as a conventional brake drum. It too is prone to wear and distortion. Although it is not as common to see an out-of-round inner drum on a disc/drum rotor assembly it still can and does occur. Driving with the parking brake on can quickly generate enough heat to damage the inner drum assembly.

8. Measure the inner drum as shown in the illustration. The standard inside drum diameter should be 6.69 in (170.0mm). The maximum inside diameter is 6.73 in (171.0mm).

➡ **If the refinishing standard does not match the one on your disc/drum use the specifica-**

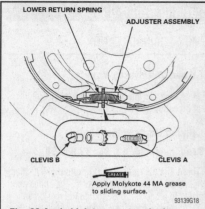

Fig. 90 Apply high temperature brake grease the parking brake adjustment sliding surfaces

tion that is stamped on the disc/drum as a reference. Replace the disc/drum if the specification is above the maximum specification. Also inspect the drum for sliding surface scoring, grooving or cracking.**

9. Push and turn the retainer springs to remove the retaining pins.
10. Remove the adjuster, springs and shoes.
11. Separate the parking brake cable and the brake lever.
12. Remove the following components:
   - Wave washer.
   - Parking brake lever.
   - Pivot pin.
   - U—clip.

To install:

13. Apply a suitable brake cylinder grease to the sliding surface of the pivot pin.
14. Insert the pivot pin into the brake shoe.
15. Attach the parking brake lever and wave washer on the pivot pin.
16. Secure these components with the U-clip.

➡ **Squeeze the U-clip securely to prevent it from coming out of the brake shoe.**

17. Apply a suitable high temperature grease to all of the shoe sliding surfaces on the backing plate.
18. The balance of the assembly is the reverse of removal, making sure to properly adjust the parking brake.

ADJUSTMENT

4-Cylinder Odyssey Models

1. Release the parking brake.
2. Raise and safely support the rear of the vehicle.
3. Remove the rear tire/wheel assemblies.
4. Remove the inspection hole cover from the rear brake rotor.
5. Rotate the brake rotor such that the inspection hole is at the bottom.
6. Adjust the parking brake star nut using a flat-blade screwdriver until the shoes lock, then back the adjuster off 8 notches and reinstall the tire/wheel assemblies.

ANTI-LOCK BRAKE SYSTEM

General Information

When conventional brakes are applied in an emergency stop or on ice, one or more wheels may lock. This may result in loss of steering control and vehicle stability. The purpose of the Anti-lock Brake System (ABS) is to prevent lock up when traction is marginal or under heavy braking conditions. This system offers many benefits allowing the driver increased safety and control during braking. Anti-lock braking operates only at speeds above 3 mph (5 km/h).

Under normal braking conditions, the ABS functions the same as a standard brake system with a diagonally split master cylinder and conventional vacuum assist.

If wheel lock is detected during the brake application, the system will enter anti-lock mode. During anti-lock mode, hydraulic pressure in the four wheel circuits is modulated to prevent any one wheel from locking. Each wheel circuit is designed with a set of electrical valves and hydraulic line to provide modulation, although for vehicle stability, both rear wheel valves receive the same electrical signal. The system can build or reduce pressure at each wheel, depending on signals generated by the Wheel Speed Sensors (WSS) at each wheel and received at the Controller Anti-lock Brake (CAB).

Anti-lock braking systems (ABS) are available on all Honda models. When this system engages, some audible noise as well as pulses in the brake pedal may occur. Do not be alarmed; this is normal system operation.

PRECAUTIONS

Failure to observe the following precautions may result in system damage:

- Before performing electric arc welding on the vehicle, disconnect the control module and the hydraulic unit connectors.
- When performing painting work on the vehicle, do not expose the control module to temperatures in excess of 185°F (85°C) for longer than 2 hours. The system may be exposed to temperatures up to 200°F (95°C) for less than 15 minutes.
- Never disconnect or connect the control module or hydraulic modulator connectors with the ignition switch **ON**.
- Never disassemble any component of the Anti-Lock Brake System (ABS) which is designated unserviceable; the component must be replaced as an assembly.
- When filling the master cylinder, always use brake fluid which meets DOT-3 specifications; petroleum-based fluid will destroy the rubber parts.
- Working on ABS system requires extreme amount of mechanical ability, training and special tools. If you are not familiar, have your vehicle repaired by a certified mechanic.

Diagnosis and Testing

Much like the Powertrain Control Module (PCM), the ABS system is capable of storing Diagnostic Trouble Codes (DTCs) which can be accessed using a suitable 16-pin Data Scan Tool (DST) or by activating the ABS blink codes using the Service Check Connector (SCS). Because of the complexity of the ABS system and the importance of correct system operation, it is a good idea to have a qualified automotive technician inspect the system if any problems have been detected.

If the Anti-lock Braking System (ABS) is OK, the ABS indicator lamp will light and then go out two seconds after turning the ignition switch to the **ON** position. The ABS lamp may illuminate a second time and then go off again. This is also normal.

The ABS lamp may illuminate under the below conditions.

- When only the drive wheels spin.
- If one drive wheel is stuck.
- During vehicle spin.
- If the ABS continues to operate for a long time.
- If there is signal disturbance is detected.

The ABS lamp may or may not stay illuminated continuously if a fault is detected. It depends on which DTC was detected and if the system corrected the problem or not. The ABS lamp may go off only after the problem is corrected and the vehicle has been restarted and driven a few miles. Remember it depends on which code was thrown and the duration or number of times that the code was detected.

This system can perform an initial diagnosis and a regular diagnosis. The initial diagnosis is performed immediately after the engine is started and continues until the ABS lamp goes out. The regular diagnosis is performed after the initial system check and monitors the system constantly until the ignition switch is turned **OFF**.

Diagnostic Trouble Codes (DTCs)

READING DIAGNOSTIC TROUBLE CODES

▶ **See Figure 91**

Reading the control module memory is one of the first steps in system diagnostics. This step should be initially performed to determine the general nature of the fault. Subsequent readings will determine if the fault has been cleared.

Reading codes can be performed using a suitable 16-pin Data Scan Tool (DST) or by activating the ABS system blink codes using the SCS service check connector.

To read the fault codes, connect the 16-pin DST scan tool according to the manufacturer's instructions. Follow the manufacturer's specified procedure for accessing and reading the codes.

To activate the self check ABS blink code, the vehicle must be turned **OFF**, not moving, SCS service connector installed, and the brake pedal released. Then proceed as follows:

1. Block the wheels as necessary to prevent moving.
2. With the ignition in the **OFF** position, locate the SCS service check cable connection under the vehicle's dash as illustrated in Section 4, and install the shunting tool, SCS Service Connector Tool No. 07PAZ-0010100 or its equivalent.
3. Once the SCS tool is installed, make sure the brake pedal is released, turn the ignition **ON** and record the ABS indicator light blinking frequency.
4. The ABS indicator should light for 2 seconds, then shut off for 3.6 seconds and begin to flash the stored DTCs. The ABS indicator light shuts off for 3.6 seconds between flashing each stored DTC. The DTC is a two digit code. The first digit is displayed by the ABS indicator light staying on in 1.3 second increments, then a 0.5 second pause, and the second digit flashed in 0.3 of a second increments. Hence code 32 would be displayed

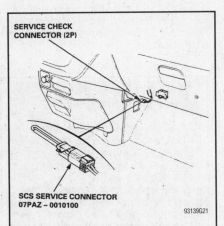

SERVICE CHECK
CONNECTOR (2P)

SCS SERVICE CONNECTOR
07PAZ – 0010100

93139G21

Fig. 91 An SCS Service Connector tool must be used to shunt the 2-pin Service Check Connector—4-cylinder Odyssey model shown

as three long flashes followed by two short flashes of the ABS indicator light.

5. Turn the ignition switch **OFF**, clear the stored DTCs and remove the SCS connector.

ABS trouble codes for CR-V and Odyssey models.

• Code 11: Front right wheel sensor has an open or short to the body ground or a short to power.
• Code 12: Front left wheel sensor electrical noise or an intermittent interruption.
• Code 13: Rear right wheel sensor has an open or short to the body ground or a short to power.
• Code 14: Rear left wheel sensor electrical noise or an intermittent interruption.
• Code 15: Front right wheel sensor has an open or short to the body ground or a short to power.
• Code 16: Front left wheel sensor electrical noise or an intermittent interruption.
• Code 17: Rear right wheel sensor has an open or short to the body ground or a short to power.
• Code 18: Rear left wheel sensor electrical noise or an intermittent interruption.
• Code 21: Pulser
• Code 22: Pulser
• Code 23: Pulser
• Code 24: Pulser
• Code 31: Front right input solenoid has a short to ground or a short to wire.
• Code 32: Front right output solenoid has a short to ground or a short to wire.
• Code 33: Front left input solenoid has a short to ground or a short to wire.
• Code 34: Front left output solenoid has a short to ground or a short to wire.
• Code 35: Rear right input solenoid has a short to ground or a short to wire.
• Code 36: Rear right output solenoid has a short to ground or a short to wire.
• Code 37: Rear left input solenoid has a short to ground or a short to wire.
• Code 38: Rear left output solenoid has a short to ground or a short to wire.
• Code 41: Front right wheel lock.
• Code 42: Front left wheel lock.
• Code 43: Right rear wheel lock.
• Code 44: Left rear wheel lock.
• Code 51: Motor lock.
• Code 52: Motor stuck off.
• Code 53: Motor stuck on.
• Code 54: Fail safe relay.
• Code 61: Ignition voltage.
• Code 62: Ignition voltage.
• Code 71: Different diameter tire.
• Code 81: Central Processing Unit (CPU)

CLEARING DIAGNOSTIC TROUBLE CODES

The Diagnostic Trouble Codes (DTCs) are cleared using a 16-pin Diagnostic Scan Tool (DST), a vehicle manufacturer's specific tester, or by using the shunting tool, SCS Service Connector Tool No. 07PAZ-0010100 or its equivalent.

Follow the tool manufacturer's instructions when using a 16-pin DST to erase the DTCs. To use the SCS shunting tool proceed as follows:

1. Block the wheels as necessary to prevent moving.

2. With the ignition in the **OFF** position, locate the SCS service check cable connection under the vehicle's dash as illustrated in Section 4, and install the SCS shunting tool or its equivalent.
3. Once the SCS tool is installed, press and hold the brake pedal, then turn the ignition **ON** while holding the brake pedal pressed.
4. The ABS indicator should light for 2 seconds, then shut off, then the brake pedal is released.
5. The ABS indicator lights again within 4 seconds, when the indicator light comes on, press and hold the brake pedal until the light goes out, then release the brake pedal.
6. If the ABS indicator shuts off for 4 seconds, then quickly blinks 2 times, the DTCs are erased.
7. Turn the ignition switch **OFF**, remove the SCS connector.
8. Start the engine and check that the ABS indicator lamp goes out. Test drive the vehicle to allow the ABS system to perform a dynamic check.
9. If the ABS indicator light comes on while operating the vehicle, recheck the DTCs, diagnose and repair as necessary.

ABS Modulator

▶ **See Figure 92**

The ABS Modulator Unit (MU) contains solenoid valves for each wheel. These valves are independent of each other and are positioned vertically for improved maintainability. The modulators for the rear wheels act as proportioning control valves to prevent the rear wheels from locking up in the event the anti-lock braking system is malfunctioning or not activated.

The ABS Modulator Unit consists of the inlet solenoid valve, reservoir, pump, pump motor and the damping chamber. The modulator controls pressure reduction, pressure retaining, and pressure intensifying for each wheel.

REMOVAL & INSTALLATION

▶ **See Figure 93**

1. Disconnect the negative battery cable.
2. Remove the modular unit mounting bolts.
3. Detach the pump motors connectors.

✳✳ WARNING

Always use a flare nut wrench on the fittings, to prevent stripping of the flare nuts.

4. Disconnect the brake lines using a flare nut wrench.
5. Remove the modular unit from the bracket assembly.
   To install:
6. Install the modular unit.
7. Connect the brake lines, using a flare nut wrench. Tighten the fittings to 11 ft. lbs. (15Nm).
8. Connect the modulator unit.
9. Attach the pump motor connectors.
10. Bleed the brake system beginning with the left front brake caliper. Bleed each fitting until all air is removed. Proceed in the following order:
    • Left Front
    • Right Front
    • Right Rear
    • Left Rear

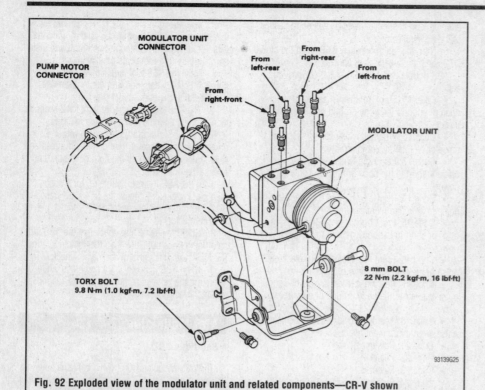

Fig. 92 Exploded view of the modulator unit and related components—CR-V shown

TORX BOLT
9.8 N·m (1.0 kgf·m, 7.2 lbf·ft)

8 mm BOLT
22 N·m (2.2 kgf·m, 16 lbf·ft)

PUMP MOTOR CONNECTOR

MODULATOR UNIT CONNECTOR

From left-rear

From right-rear

From left-front

From right-front

MODULATOR UNIT

93139G25

Fig. 93 View of the ABS modulator unit and mounting bracket—CR-V model shown

93139P12

11. Connect the negative battery cable.

12. After starting the engine, check to make sure the ABS lamp is not illuminated.

13. Drive the vehicle and check that the ABS light does not come on.

14. Check and clear codes as necessary.

ABS Control Unit

The ABS control unit and Powertrain Control Module (PCM) manage the entire system via inputs from various sensors and programmed decisions which are stored within the unit. This management system includes the Vehicle Speed Sensor (VSS), pump motor, various electronic solenoids, ABS wheel sensors and an internal self-diagnostic mode. The main function of the ABS control unit is to perform calculations on the signals received from each one of the sensors at the wheels. This will enable it to control the system by actuating solenoid valves

that regulate the flow and pressure of the brake fluid to each wheel. The system was designed with a sub-function that gives driving signals to the pump motor as well as signals the self diagnostic mode which is a necessity for backing up the anti-lock braking system.

REMOVAL & INSTALLATION

▶ See Figure 94

1. Disconnect the negative battery cable.

2. On CR-V and V6 Odyssey models, remove the passenger's right kick panel.

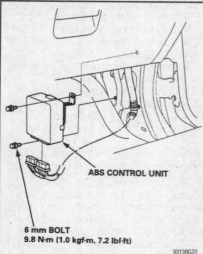

6 mm BOLT
9.8 N·m (1.0 kgf·m, 7.2 lbf·ft)

ABS CONTROL UNIT

93139G22

Fig. 94 The ABS control unit is located under the passenger's side kick panel—CR-V model shown

3. On 4-cylinder Odyssey models, locate the control unit which is found in the driver's side underdash area.

4. Detach the ABS control unit electrical connectors.

5. Remove the ABS control unit by removing the mounting fasteners.

To install:

6. Install the unit in the reverse order of removal.

7. Check that the ABS light comes on briefly and then goes off once the engine has been started.

8. Drive the vehicle to ensure that the ABS light does not come on.

9. Check and clear codes as necessary.

Wheel Speed Sensor

▶ See Figure 95

Each wheel has its own wheel speed sensor which sends a small AC electrical signal to the control module. Correct ABS operation depends on accurate wheel speed signals. The vehicle's wheels and tires must all be the same size and type in order to generate accurate signals. If there is a variation between wheel and tire sizes, inaccurate wheel speed signals will be produced.

✳✳ WARNING

It is very critical that the wheel speed sensor(s) be installed correctly to ensure continued system operation. The sensor cables must be installed, routed and clipped properly. Failure to install the sensor(s) properly could result in contact with moving parts or over extension of sensor cables. This will cause ABS component failure and an open circuit.

Honda uses a contactless type of sensor that detects the rotating speed of the wheel. It is constructed of a permanent magnet and a coil. Attached to the rotating parts are gear pulsers (a.k.a. Tone Rings). When these pulsers turn, the magnetic flux around the coil in the wheel sensor alternates its current. This generates voltages in a frequency or wave pattern. These wave pulses are sent to the ABS control unit which identifies the speed of each of the four wheels.

93139P13

Fig. 95 The ABS rear wheel sensor and tone ring mounting and location—CR-V model shown

REMOVAL & INSTALLATION

▸ See Figures 96 and 97

※※ CAUTION

Vehicles equipped with air bag systems (SRS) have components and wiring in the same area as the front speed sensor wiring harnesses. The air bag system connectors are yellow. Do not use electrical test equipment on these circuits. Do not damage the SRS wiring while working on other wiring or components. Failure to observe correct procedures may cause the air bag system to inflate unexpectedly or render the system totally inoperative.

1. Raise and safely support the vehicle as necessary for access.
2. Make certain the ignition switch is **OFF**.
3. Detach the sensor harness connector.
4. Beginning at the connector end, remove grommets, clips or retainers as necessary to free the harness. Take careful note of the placement and routing of the harness; it must be reinstalled in the exact original position.
5. Remove the bolt holding the speed sensor to its mounting, then remove the sensor. If it is stuck in place, gently tap on the side of the mounting flange with a hammer and small punch; do not tap on the sensor.

To install:

6. Place the sensor in position; install the retaining bolts loosely. Route the harness correctly. Avoid twisting or crimping the harness; use the white line on the wires as a guide.

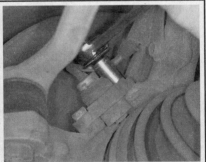

Fig. 96 Typical front wheel speed sensor mounting—CR-V model shown

Fig. 97 The ABS rear wheel speed sensor is held in place by two mounting bolts— CR-V model shown

7. Once the harness and sensor are correctly but loosely placed, tighten the sensor mounting bolts. Tighten bolts to 16 ft. lbs. (22 Nm).
8. Working from the sensor end to the connector, install each clip, retainer, bracket or grommet holding the sensor harness. The harness must not be twisted. Tighten any bolt holding brackets to 84 inch lbs. (10 Nm).
9. Attach the wiring connector.
10. Use the ABS checker to check for proper signal from the wheel speed sensor.
11. Carefully lower the vehicle to the ground.

INSPECTION

▸ See Figures 98 and 99

1. Use a non-metallic feeler gauge to measure the gap between the sensor and the pulser.
2. Rotate the hub or axle slowly by hand, taking measurements at several locations.
3. Compare with the following specifications:
CR-V and 4-cylinder Odyssey models:
   - Front and Rear: 0.020–0.040 in. (0.5–1.0mm)
V6 Odyssey models:
   - Front: 0.020–0.040 in. (0.5–1.0mm)
   - Rear: 0.010–0.040 in. (0.2–1.1mm)

Tone Ring (Pulser)

Inspect the tone ring for any built up debris and clean as necessary. If any one tooth is damaged, it must be replaced.

The ABS tone ring on the front of all vehicles, and on the rear of 4WD CR-Vs, is an integral component of the halfshaft assemblies and therefore,

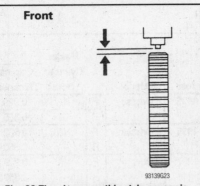

Fig. 98 The air gap on this style sensor is measured from the tip of the ABS sensor core and the tone ring. This is a typical ABS sensor found on disc brakes

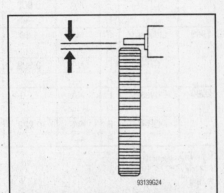

Fig. 99 The air gap on this style sensor is measured between the inside edge of the ABS sensor core and the tone ring. This is a typical ABS sensor used on drum brakes

cannot be serviced separately, therefor if the tone ring requires service, the halfshaft assembly must be replaced.

Bleeding the ABS System

The ABS brake system is bled in the usual fashion with no special procedures required. Refer to the bleeding procedure located earlier in this section. Make certain the master cylinder reservoir is filled before the bleeding is begun and check the level frequently.

BRAKE SPECIFICATIONS
All measurements in inches unless noted

Year	Model		Master Cylinder Bore	Brake Disc Original Thickness	Brake Disc Minimum Thickness	Maximum Runout	Brake Drum Diameter Original Inside Diameter	Brake Drum Diameter Max. Wear Limit	Brake Drum Diameter Maximum Machine Diameter	Minimum Lining Thickness Front	Minimum Lining Thickness Rear	Brake Caliper Bracket Bolts (ft. lbs.)	Brake Caliper Mounting Bolts (ft. lbs.)
1995	Odyssey	F	NA	0.929	0.830	0.004	—	—	—	0.060	—	80	36
		R	—	0.350	0.300	0.004	6.69 ①	6.73 ①	6.73 ①	—	0.060 ②	28	17
1996	Odyssey	F	NA	0.929	0.830	0.004	—	—	—	0.060	—	80	36
		R	—	0.350	0.300	0.004	6.69 ①	6.73 ①	6.73 ①	—	0.060 ②	28	17
1997	Odyssey	F	NA	0.929	0.830	0.004	—	—	—	0.060	—	80	36
		R	—	0.350	0.300	0.004	6.69 ①	6.73 ①	6.73 ①	—	0.060 ②	28	17
	CR-V	F	NA	0.902	0.830	0.004	—	—	—	0.060	—	80	36
		R	—	—	—	—	8.66	8.70	8.70	—	0.080	—	—
1998	Odyssey	F	NA	0.929	0.830	0.004	—	—	—	0.060	—	80	36
		R	—	0.350	0.300	0.004	6.69 ①	6.73 ①	6.73 ①	—	0.060 ②	28	17
	CR-V	F	NA	0.902	0.830	0.004	—	—	—	0.060	—	80	36
		R	—	—	—	—	8.66	8.70	8.70	—	0.080	—	—
1999	Odyssey	F	NA	1.10	1.02	0.004	—	—	—	0.060	—	80	20
		R	—	—	—	—	9.996	10.04	—	—	0.080	—	—
	CR-V	F	NA	0.929	0.830	0.004	—	—	—	0.060	—	80	36
		R	—	—	—	—	8.66	8.70	8.70	—	0.080	—	—
2000	Odyssey	F	NA	1.10	1.02	0.004	—	—	—	0.060	—	80	20
		R	—	—	—	—	9.996	10.04	—	—	0.080	—	—
	CR-V	F	NA	0.929	0.830	0.004	—	—	—	0.060	—	80	36
		R	—	—	—	—	8.66	8.70	8.70	—	0.080	—	—

NA - Not Available

F - Front

R - Rear

① Specifications for rear parking brake drum

② Specifications for rear parking brake shoe lining thickness:
New 0.10 in.
Wear Limit 0.04 in.

93139C01

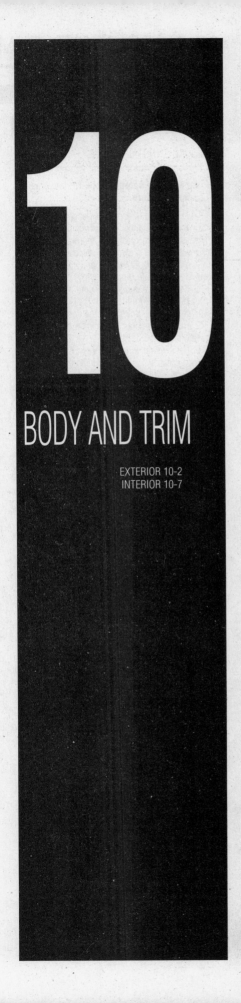

10

BODY AND TRIM

EXTERIOR

Doors

REMOVAL & INSTALLATION

➡ **Front and rear doors may be removed using the same procedure.**

1. Disconnect the negative battery cable.
2. Protect the door and surrounding trim and painted areas using cardboard and masking tape. A thick masking tape is available at local body and paint supply stores. Cover and protect any corners, sharp edges or protruding objects.
3. Support the door, by placing a floor jack and a piece of wood underneath the door.
4. Remove the bolts from the door stop arm.
5. Remove the door panel, detach the wiring connectors, and guide clips.
6. Remove the wiring harness from the door frame. If necessary, use tape to keep the wiring pulled aside.
7. Inspect and make sure all applicable wiring connectors are disconnected and removed.
8. Matchmark the location of the hinges on the door and/or vehicle frame.
9. Unfasten the hinge bolts, then remove the door assembly.

To install:

➡ **If necessary, make shims out of scrap sheet metal, paint stirring sticks or cardboard and tape in place with masking tape to the area to be aligned or shimmed.**

10. Position the door into place and finger tighten the hinge bolts.
11. Align the door with the hinge marks made earlier and tighten the bolts.
12. Attach the wiring connectors.
13. Attach the door stop arm and tighten the bolts to 89 inch lbs. (10 Nm).
14. Remove the supporting jack.
15. Install the door panel.
16. Connect the negative battery cable.

ADJUSTMENT

♦ **See Figures 1, 2, 3 and 4**

When checking door alignment, look carefully at each seam between the door and body. The gap should be constant and even all the way around the door. Pay particular attention to the door seams at the corners farthest from the hinges; this is the area where errors will be most evident. Additionally, the door should pull in against the weatherstrip when latched to seal out wind and water. The contact should be even all the way around and the stripping should be about half compressed.

The position of the door can be adjusted in three dimensions: fore and aft, up and down, in and out. The primary adjusting points are the hinge-to-body bolts. Apply tape to the fender and door edges to protect the paint. Two layers of common masking tape works well. Loosen the bolts just enough to allow the hinge to move in place. With the help of an assistant, position the door and retighten the bolts. Inspect the door seams carefully and repeat the adjustment until correctly aligned.

The in-out adjustment (how far the door "sticks out" from the body) is adjusted by loosening the hinge-to-door bolts. Again, move the door into place, then retighten the bolts. This dimension affects both the amount of crush on the weatherstrips and the amount of "bite" on the striker.

The door should be adjusted such that the leading edge of the door is just below or no more than level with the adjoining body panel. The trailing edge of the door should be adjusted so the edge of the panel is slightly above the adjoining body panel. If not properly adjusted, the doors are likely to cause a wind noise.

Further adjustment for closed position and smoothness of latching is made at the latch plate or striker. This piece is located at the rear edge of the door and is attached to the bodywork; it is the piece the latch engages when the door is closed. Although the striker size and style may vary between models or from front to rear, the method of adjusting it is the same:

1. Loosen the large cross-point screw(s) holding the striker. Know in advance that these bolts will be very tight; an impact screwdriver is a handy tool to have for this job. Make sure you are using the proper size bit.
2. With the bolts just loose enough to allow the striker to move if necessary, hold the outer door handle in the released position and close the door. The striker will move into the correct location to match the door latch. Open the door and tighten the mounting bolts. The striker may be adjusted towards or away from the center of the car, thereby tightening or loosening the door fit.
3. The striker can be moved up and down to compensate for door position, but if the door is correctly mounted at the hinges this should not be necessary.

➡ **Do not attempt to correct height variations (sag) by adjusting the striker.**

Additionally, some models may use one or more spacers or shims behind the striker or at the hinges. These shims may be removed or added in combination to adjust the reach of the striker or hinge.

4. After the striker bolts have been tightened, open and close the door several times. Observe the motion of the door as it engages the striker; it should continue its straight-in motion and not deflect up or down as it hits the striker.

Fig. 1 Matchmark the striker for both up and down and in and out reference marks

Fig. 2 Use a hand impact driver to loosen and tighten the No. 3 Phillips screws

Fig. 3 Use a plastic mallet or hammer to move the striker in a small amount

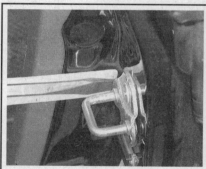

Fig. 4 To move a striker out a small amount, protect the door jamb with a soft object such as a paint stirring stick, and carefully pry with a suitable prytool

5. Check the feel of the latch during opening and closing. It must be smooth and linear, without any trace of grinding or binding during engagement and release.

It may be necessary to repeat the striker adjustment several times (and possibly re-adjust the hinges) before the correct door to body match is produced. This can be a maddening process of loosen and tighten, check and readjust; have patience.

If a door makes a knocking noise over bumps,

it's likely the striker is not centered in the door latch. Inspect, loosen and lightly tap the striker up or down as necessary.

Hood

REMOVAL & INSTALLATION

♦ **See Figures 5 and 6**

➡ **The help of an assistant is recommended when removing or installing the hood.**

1. Open and support the hood.
2. Disconnect the negative battery cable.
3. Protect the body with covers to prevent damage to the paint.
4. Use a suitable marker, or scribe marks around the hinge locations for reference during installation.
5. Unplug any electrical connections and windshield washer hoses that would interfere with hood removal.
6. While an assistant helps secure the hood, unfasten the attaching bolts, then remove the hood from the vehicle.

To install:

7. Place the hood into position. Install and partially tighten attaching bolts.
8. Adjust the hood with the reference marks and tighten the attaching bolts.
9. Check the hood for an even fit between the fenders and for flush fit with the front of the fenders. Also, check for a flush fit with the top of the cowl and fenders. If necessary, adjust the hood latch.
10. Attach any electrical connections or windshield washer hoses that were disconnected during hood removal.

ALIGNMENT

Once the hood is installed, tighten the hood-to-hinge bolts just snug. Close the hood and check for perfect seam alignment. The hood seams are one of the most visible on the car; the slightest error will be plainly obvious to an observer.

Loosen the bolts and position the hood as necessary, then snug the nuts and recheck. Continue the process until the hood latches smoothly and aligns evenly at all the seams.

➡ **Do not adjust hood position by moving the latch.**

The hood bolts and the hinge mount bolts may be loosened to adjust their positions. Shims may be used behind the hinge mounts if necessary. When everything aligns correctly, tighten the bolts securely.

The elevation of the hood at the latch end may be adjusted by turning the rubber stops or cushions. These bumpers have threaded bottoms and move up or down when turned. An annoying hood rattle on bumps may be caused by missing cushions, or misalignment of the hood.

Tailgate

REMOVAL & INSTALLATION

CR-V Models

1. Disconnect the negative battery cable.
2. Protect the tailgate and surrounding trim and painted areas using cardboard and masking tape. A thick masking tape is available at local body and paint supply stores. Cover and protect any corners, sharp edges or protruding objects.
3. Support the tailgate, by placing a floor jack and a piece of wood underneath the tailgate.
4. Remove the bolts from the tailgate stop arm.
5. Remove the tailgate interior trim panel, disconnect the wiring connectors, and guide clips.
6. Remove the wiring harness from the tailgate frame. If necessary, use tape to keep the wiring pulled aside.
7. Inspect and make sure all applicable wiring connectors are disconnected and removed.
8. Matchmark the location of the hinges on the tailgate and/or vehicle frame.
9. Remove the hinge bolts and remove the tailgate assembly.

To install:

➡ **If necessary, make shims out of scrap sheet metal, paint stirring sticks or cardboard and tape in place with masking tape to the area to be aligned or shimmed.**

10. Position the tailgate into place and finger tighten the hinge bolts.
11. Align the tailgate with the hinge marks made earlier and tighten the bolts.
12. Attach the wiring connectors.

13. Attach the tailgate stop arm.
14. Remove the supporting jack.
15. Install the tailgate interior trim panel.
16. Connect the negative battery cable.

Rear Hatch

REMOVAL & INSTALLATION

Odyssey Models

4-CYLINDER ENGINES

➡ **The help of an assistant is recommended when removing or installing the hatch.**

1. Disconnect the negative battery cable.
2. Open and support the hatch.
3. Unsnap the inside side window trim, and remove it.
4. Open the grab handle caps and remove the handle screws and handle.
5. Remove the pins and clips from the lower hatch trim panel, and unsnap the panel from the hatch.
6. Pop off the tailgate light lens, then remove the light retaining screws and detach the electrical connector.
7. Remove the third brake light end caps and mounting screws.
8. Open the tailgate and remove the spoiler mounting bolts.
9. Close the tailgate and pull the spoiler back, just enough to unsnap the end clips, then raise the spoiler upward and disconnect the washer tube and electrical connector.
10. Remove the hatch spoiler.

➡ **Before removing the wiring harness, attach a string to the end of it. This will enable you to pull the harness back through upon installation.**

11. Detach the electrical connectors, remove the attachment bolt, harness clips and remove the wiring harness.
12. Have an assistant hold the hatch and remove the support strut.
13. Remove the hinge bolts at the hatch and remove the hatch.
14. Installation is the reverse of the removal procedure.

V6 ENGINE

➡ **The help of an assistant is recommended when removing or installing the hatch.**

1. Disconnect the negative battery cable.
2. Open and support the hatch.
3. Open the grab handle caps and remove the handle screws and handle.
4. Remove the pins and clips from the lower hatch trim panel, and unsnap the panel from the hatch.
5. Carefully unsnap the upper, left and right side window trim.
6. Remove the rear spoiler mounting nuts, disconnect the rear window washer line, remove the rear access cap and release the clip.
7. Carefully close the tailgate, then lift up on the spoiler. Remove the wire harness grommet, then disconnect the electrical connector and remove the spoiler.

Fig. 5 Use a suitable paint marker to matchmark the installed position of the hood brackets

93130P13

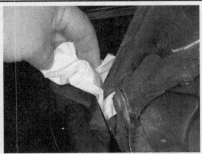

Fig. 6 Stuff a soft clean cloth between the body and the rear edge of the hood. This protects the paint on both components, and allows some support when removing the hood

93130P11

➡️**Before removing the wiring harness, attach a string to the end of it. This will enable you to pull the harness back through upon installation.**

8. Detach the electrical connectors, remove the attachment bolt, harness clips and remove the wiring harness.

9. Have an assistant hold the hatch and lift the metal band from around the support strut pivot and remove the strut. Do not remove the metal band.

10. Remove the hinge bolts at the hatch and remove the hatch.

11. Installation is the reverse of the removal procedure.

Bumpers

REMOVAL & INSTALLATION

CR-V Models

FRONT

▶ **See Figures 7, 8, 9 and 10**

1. Note the radio security code and disconnect the negative battery cable.

2. Remove the front grille as outlined in this section.

3. Carefully pry out the inner clip pin from the clips along the top of the bumper and remove the clips.

4. Remove the self-tapping Phillips screws from the lower part of the bumper just in front of the

Fig. 7 Remove the locking pin from the retaining clip using a suitable prytool

Fig. 8 Remove the lock pin from the retaining clip . . .

Fig. 9 . . . then remove the retaining clip

Fig. 10 Once all the fasteners are removed, the front bumper can be pulled away from the vehicle—CR-V model shown

wheel opening, and rear most portion of the bumper in the forward portion of the front wheel well.

5. Remove the 3 special shouldered bolts from the left and right front lower center portion of the bumper, and from the center of the lower air intake.

6. Have an assistant help guide the bumper away from the vehicle.

7. Installation is the reverse of the removal procedure.

REAR

▶ **See Figures 11, 12 and 13**

1. Note the radio security code and disconnect the negative battery cable.

2. Open the tailgate.

Fig. 11 Remove the bumper mounting bolts with a 10mm socket, extension and ratchet

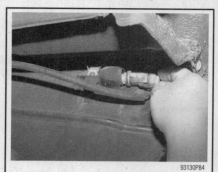

Fig. 12 If a bumper has marker lights mounted to it, the light bulb socket can be disconnected to ease removal

Fig. 13 Once the fasteners are removed, the rear bumper is carefully pulled away from the vehicle —CR-V model shown

3. Carefully pry out the inner clip pin from the clips along the top of the bumper and the rear lower edge, then remove the clips.

4. Remove the self-tapping Phillips screws from the rear mud guards and front most portion of the bumper in the upper rear portion of the wheel well.

5. Remove the 2 special shouldered bolts from the left and right corners, near the tailgate seal.

6. Remove the bulb sockets from the side marker lights.

7. Have an assistant help guide the bumper away from the vehicle.

8. Installation is the reverse of the removal procedure.

Odyssey Models

FRONT

1. Note the radio security code, then disconnect the negative battery cable.

2. Remove the bolt from the lower part of the bumper just in front of the wheel opening, and remove the self-tapping screw from the rear most portion of the bumper at the forward portion of the front wheel well.

3. On V6 Odyssey models, perform the following:

   a. Remove the grille.

   b. Remove the pins and clips from the lower front of the bumper.

4. On 4-cylinder Odyssey models, remove the bolts from the left and right side lower brackets for the bumper at the ends of the lower air intake.

5. Pull the ends of the bumper outward.

6. Have an assistant help guide the bumper up and away from the vehicle.

7. Installation is the reverse of the removal procedure.

REAR

1. Note the radio security code and disconnect the negative battery cable.

2. Open the tailgate.

3. Carefully pry out the inner clip pin from the clips along the top of the bumper and the rear lower edge, then remove the clips.

4. Remove the self-tapping Phillips screws from the front most portion of the bumper in the upper rear portion of the wheel well.

5. On V6 Odyssey models, perform the following:

   a. Remove the clip at the edge of the wheel opening area.

   b. Remove the self-tapping screws at the top outside corners of the bumper.

   c. Remove the 4 trim caps and remove the mounting bolts.

6. Have an assistant help pull the sides of the bumper outward and guide the bumper away from the vehicle.

7. Installation is the reverse of the removal procedure.

Grille

REMOVAL & INSTALLATION

CR-V Models

▶ See Figures 14, 15, 16 and 17

1. Open and support the hood.
2. Disconnect the negative battery cable.
3. Using a suitable flat-bladed prytool, carefully remove the plastic cover from the top of the grille emblem.
4. Remove the combination washer and self-tapping screws from the upper grille mounting tabs.
5. Using a long No. 2 Phillips screwdriver remove the combination washer and self-tapping screw from the center lower grille retaining tab, then loosen and remove the lower left and right side self-tapping screws.
6. Carefully slide the grille away from the vehicle.

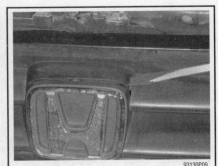

Fig. 14 Carefully pry the cover from the top of the grille emblem to access the lower grille fastener—CR-V model shown

Fig. 15 Once the cover is removed, the lower grille screws can be loosened with a long No. 2 Phillips screwdriver—CR-V model shown

Fig. 16 The small holes at either end of the grille allow removal of the remaining grille fasteners—CR-V model shown

Fig. 17 Carefully lift the grille assembly away from the vehicle once all the fasteners are removed—CR-V model shown

To install:

7. Position the grille, making sure the tabs are lined up with the clips, then install and tighten the retaining screws.

8. Install the plastic cover to the top of the grille emblem.

9. Connect the negative battery cable.

10. Lower the hood.

Odyssey Models

4-CYLINDER ENGINES

1. Open and support the hood.
2. Disconnect the negative battery cable.

3. Remove the grille retaining nuts, unsnap the retaining clips, and remove the grille.

To install:

4. Position the grille, making sure the retaining clips are secured, then tighten the retaining nuts.

5. Connect the negative battery cable.

6. Lower the hood.

V6 ENGINE

1. Open and support the hood.
2. Disconnect the negative battery cable.
3. Remove the front trim panel lock pins and clips, then remove the trim panel.
4. Remove the grille mounting lock pins and clips, and remove the grille.

To install:

5. Replace any damaged clips, then position the grille, making sure the retaining clips are secured, then install the locking pins.

6. Connect the negative battery cable.

7. Lower the hood.

Outside Mirrors

REMOVAL & INSTALLATION

CR-V Models

MIRROR ASSEMBLY

1. Disconnect the negative battery cable.
2. Lower the door glass and unsnap the inside triangular mirror trim by hand.
3. Detach the electrical connector.
4. Remove the mirror mounting bolts, and remove the mirror assembly.
5. Installation is the reverse of the removal procedure.

MIRROR GLASS

▶ See Figures 18, 19 and 20

✵✵ CAUTION

Wear gloves and eye protection when removing the mirror glass.

1. Carefully pull out the bottom edge of the mirror holder by hand.
2. Carefully and evenly, pull the lower edge of the mirror holder slowly, until it unsnaps from the actuator.

Fig. 18 To remove the mirror glass on CR-V and 4-cylinder Odyssey models, slowly tilt the bottom of the mirror outward . . .

93130P75

Fig. 19 . . . then, gently and evenly, pull on the lower portion of the mirror to unsnap it from the mounting clips

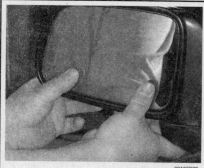

93130P73

Fig. 20 To install the mirror glass on CR-V and 4-cylinder Odyssey models, press evenly to snap the mirror onto the adjustment base

To install:

3. If the hooks stuck to the mirror holder, remove them and reinstall them onto the actuator base.

4. Carefully align the clips and hooks, and using even pressure, snap the mirror holder onto the actuator base.

5. Check the mirror operation.

4-Cylinder Odyssey Models

MIRROR ASSEMBLY

1. Disconnect the negative battery cable.

2. Remove the door panel, as outlined in this section.

3. Apply masking tape to the base of the mirror, then use a clean shop towel to protect the finish, and carefully pry the lower portion of the mirror base cover off the mirror and remove the bolt.

4. Detach the electrical connector and harness clips, then peel away the hole seal and remove the bolts.

5. While holding the mirror, detach the cast in hook from the door skin and remove the mirror.

6. Installation is the reverse of the removal procedure.

MIRROR GLASS

✴✴ CAUTION

Wear gloves and eye protection when removing the mirror glass.

---

1. Remove the hole seal at the bottom of the mirror and remove the screw.

2. Pull out the mirror glass holder along with the actuator, then label and disconnect the actuator wires.

3. Carefully and evenly, pull the lower edge of the mirror holder slowly, until it unsnaps from the actuator.

To install:

4. If the hooks stuck to the mirror holder, remove them and reinstall them onto the actuator base.

5. Carefully align the clips and hooks, and using even pressure, snap the mirror holder onto the actuator base.

6. Check the mirror operation.

V6 Odyssey Models

MIRROR ASSEMBLY

1. Disconnect the negative battery cable.

2. Completely lower the door glass.

3. Carefully unsnap the upper portion of the inside mirror trim by hand, then lift upward and remove the trim.

4. On models equipped with power mirrors, remove the door panel and detach the electrical connector as outlined in this section.

5. Remove the mirror mounting bolts while supporting the mirror.

6. While holding the mirror, release the clip and remove the mirror.

7. Installation is the reverse of the removal procedure.

MIRROR GLASS

✴✴ CAUTION

Wear gloves and eye protection when removing the mirror glass.

---

1. Carefully and evenly, pull up on the lower edge of the mirror holder slowly, until it unsnaps from the actuator. If necessary, disconnect the heated mirror leads.

To install:

2. Carefully align the clips and hooks, and using even pressure, snap the mirror holder downward onto the actuator base.

3. Check the mirror operation.

Antenna

REPLACEMENT

CR-V Models

1. Remove the dash panels as necessary to access and disconnect the antenna lead. Refer to the radio removal procedures in Section 6.

2. Using a T-20 Torx® bit, remove the antenna mounting screws, then remove the mast antenna.

3. Installation is the reverse of the removal procedure.

Odyssey Models

1. Unthread the antenna mast.

2. Using the antenna removal tool No. 07JAA-

0010000C or its equivalent, remove the antenna nut.

3. Remove the right front inner fender well self-tapping screws and pin clips, and remove the inner fender.

4. Remove the antenna housing bracket bolt and remove the antenna housing from the wheel well.

5. Installation is the reverse of the removal procedure. Make sure to tighten the antenna nut before tightening the antenna bracket.

Fenders

REMOVAL & INSTALLATION

1. Disconnect the negative battery cable.

2. Open the hood and support the hood with the prop rod.

3. Remove the grille and front bumper, as outlined .

4. Remove the two piece pin and clips from the inner fender liner, then remove the self-tapping screws and remove the inner fender liner.

5. Detach the electrical connectors for the head lights, remove the headlight mounting bolts and the headlights.

6. Protect the edges of the fender and door with masking tape as necessary.

7. Matchmark the fender to the inner fender for reassembly. Trace the outline of the fender to inner fender with a sharpened No. 2 pencil.

8. Open the front doors as necessary to access and remove the rear fender mounting bolts.

9. Remove the fender mounting bolts at the front cowl, headlight opening and along the top of the fender in the engine compartment.

10. Have an assistant help remove the fender from the vehicle.

11. Installation is the reverse of the removal procedure.

Lower Rocker Side Sill Panel

REMOVAL & INSTALLATION

▶ **See Figure 21**

The side sill panel is mounted along the lower rocker panel.

9094LP49

Fig. 21 View of side sill panel and retaining clips

1. Remove the self-tapping screws from the rear lower portion of the front wheel well.

2. Remove the inner pins from the clips along the bottom of the sill panel, then remove the clips.

3. Slide the sill panel forward and remove.

4. Remove the L-shaped side sill panel clips by turning them 45° and pulling them out of the body.

To install:

5. Slide the L-shaped clips onto the side sill panel.

6. Install the panel on the car by aligning the clips with the holes in the cars body.

7. Press lightly to ensure the clips have fully seated in the body.

8. Install the wheel well screws and lower mounting clips and pins that were previously removed.

Power Sunroof

REMOVAL & INSTALLATION

4-Cylinder Odyssey Models

PANEL REPLACEMENT

1. Open the sunroof halfway.

2. Carefully unsnap the front of the liner by pulling it downward.

3. Slide the liner toward the back to release the pins from the holder and remove the liner.

4. Remove the 6 panel mounting bolts from the panel bracket.

5. Carefully lift the sunroof from the vehicle.

To install:

6. Inspect the sunroof liner clips and replace as necessary.

7. Install the sunroof in reverse order of removal. Adjust the sunroof such that the panel is level with the sunroof seal and not more than ³⁄₃₂ inches (2mm) above the roof of the vehicle.

MOTOR REPLACEMENT

➡**If the sunroof motor fails, the sunroof can be closed by removing the slotted plug between the sun visors and using the tool provided in the tool kit to manually wind the sunroof shut.**

1. Remove the front headliner to access the motor.

2. Detach the motor electrical connector.

3. Remove the 3 screws holding the motor in place, then remove the motor from the bracket assembly.

4. Installation is the reverse of the removal procedure, making sure to only connect the brown electrical connector; the gray electrical connector is not used.

INTERIOR

Dashboard

REMOVAL & INSTALLATION

CR-V Models

◆ **See Figure 22**

➡**Before disconnecting the battery cable(s) or the radio electrical connectors, make sure to** note the radio security code. Once disconnected, the radio will not function until the code is entered.

✳✳ CAUTION

The models covered by this manual are equipped with a Supplemental Restraint System (SRS), which uses an air bag. Whenever working near any of the SRS components, such as the impact sensors, the air bag module, steering column and instrument panel, disable the SRS, as described in Section 6.

1. Note the radio security code and disconnect the negative battery cable.

2. Disable the Supplemental Restraint System (SRS) as outlined in Section 6.

3. Remove the following components as outlined in this section:
- Glove box
- Driver's side lower dash cover
- Driver's side lower knee bolster
- Lower center console trim (automatic transaxle)
- Center pocket/beverage holder (automatic transaxle)
- Center console (manual transaxle)
- Center dashboard lower cover
- Dashboard center panel
- Driver's side electric switch panel

4. Remove the instrument cluster, as outlined in Section 6.

5. Detach the driver's air bag electrical connector and lower the steering column.

6. Unsnap the driver's side dash cover. Remove the screw in the passenger's lower side cover and unsnap to remove.

7. Detach the dash electrical connectors from the upper portion of the left side under dash fuse/relay panel. Remove the two fasteners, then move the left side under dash fuse/relay panel aside.

8. Disconnect the antenna lead, and disconnect the harness clips.

9. Remove the electrical connector holder from the dashboard frame.

10. Unbolt the control unit/relay bracket from the behind the center of the dash.

11. Remove the 7 dash panel bolts, located as follows:
- 1 bolt at the left side of dash
- 2 bolts at the lower left side of dash
- 2 bolts at the left and right sides of center console
- 2 bolts at the right side of dash at glove box opening.

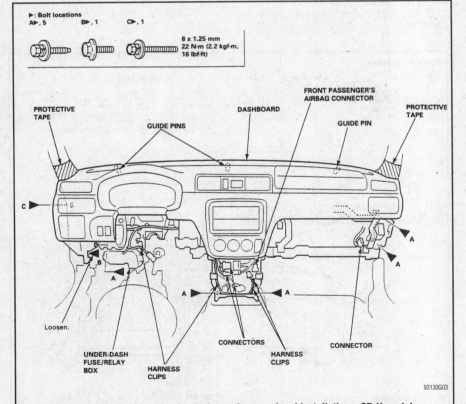

```
▶: Bolt locations
A▶, 5    B▶, 1    C▶, 1
                          8 x 1.25 mm
                          22 N·m (2.2 kgf·m,
                          16 lbf·ft)
```

PROTECTIVE TAPE   GUIDE PINS   DASHBOARD   FRONT PASSENGER'S AIRBAG CONNECTOR   GUIDE PIN   PROTECTIVE TAPE

Loosen.

UNDER-DASH FUSE/RELAY BOX   HARNESS CLIPS   CONNECTORS   HARNESS CLIPS   CONNECTOR

93130G03

Fig. 22 Fastener type and location for dash panel removal and installation—CR-V model shown

12. Cover the lower inside of the windshield trim with protective tape.

13. Verify that all electrical connectors, brackets and clips have been disconnected.

14. Carefully lift and remove the dashboard assembly.

15. Installation is in reverse order of removal, making sure to properly activate the SRS and enter the radio security code.

Odyssey Models

4-CYLINDER ENGINES

▶ See Figure 23

➡Before disconnecting the battery cable(s) or the radio electrical connectors, make sure to note the radio security code. Once disconnected, the radio will not function until the code is entered.

✳✳ CAUTION

The models covered by this manual are equipped with a Supplemental Restraint System (SRS), which uses an air bag. Whenever working near any of the SRS components, such as the impact sensors, the air bag module, steering column and instrument panel, disable the SRS, as described in Section 6.

1. Note the radio security code and disconnect the negative battery cable.

2. Disable the Supplemental Restraint System (SRS) as outlined in Section 6.

3. Remove the following components as outlined in this section:
- Glove box
- Driver's lower dash cover
- Driver's lower knee bolster
- Center console
- Beverage holder
- Center pocket
- Radio/heater control panel
- Dashboard compartment
- Center vent/switch panel

4. Remove the instrument cluster, as outlined in Section 6.

5. Detach the driver's air bag electrical connector and lower the steering column.

6. Unplug the dash electrical connectors from the upper portion of the left side underdash fuse/relay panel, then remove the two fasteners, and move the left side under dash fuse/relay panel aside.

7. Disconnect the antenna lead, and disconnect the harness clips.

8. Remove the electrical connector holder from the dashboard frame.

9. Remove the glove box striker bracket nut.

10. Pull back on the door seals and remove the lower windshield pillar trim.

11. Lift up on the forward portion of the dashboard side upper trim, then slide back to release the hook toward the back of the windshield pillar area.

12. If equipped, detach the radio tweeter electrical connector.

13. Unplug the passenger side air bag electrical connector, then remove the two nuts just above the connector.

14. Remove the 10 dash panel bolts. The bolts are located as follows:
- 2 bolts on the left side of the dash
- 2 bolts at the instrument cluster opening
- 2 bolts each on the left and right sides of center console
- 2 bolts on the right side of dash at glove box opening and windshield pillar

15. Cover the lower inside of the windshield trim with protective tape.

16. Verify that all electrical connectors, brackets and clips have been disconnected.

17. Carefully lift and remove the dashboard assembly.

18. Installation is in reverse order of removal, making sure to properly activate the SRS and enter the radio security code.

V6 ENGINE

▶ See Figure 24

➡Before disconnecting the battery cable(s) or the radio electrical connectors, make sure to note the radio security code. Once disconnected, the radio will not function until the code is entered.

✳✳ CAUTION

The models covered by this manual are equipped with a Supplemental Restraint System (SRS), which uses an air bag. Whenever working near any of the SRS components, such as the impact sensors, the air bag module, steering column and instrument panel, disable the SRS, as described in Section 6.

1. Note the radio security code and disconnect the negative battery cable.

2. Disable the Supplemental Restraint System (SRS) as outlined in Section 6.

3. Remove the following items:
- Dashboard lower cover
- Steering column cover
- Center lower pocket
- Glove box

4. Unsnap the heater lower console side covers.

5. Slide off the front door seal opening trim.

6. Carefully remove the left and right kick panels.

7. Carefully unsnap and remove the inside windshield pillar trim.

▶: Bolt locations, 10

6 x 1.0 mm
9.8 N·m (1.0 kgf·m,
7.2 lbf·ft)

PROTECTIVE TAPE GUIDE PIN GUIDE PINS PROTECTIVE TAPE

DASHBOARD

93130G02

Fig. 23 Fastener location for dash panel removal and installation—4-cylinder Odyssey model shown

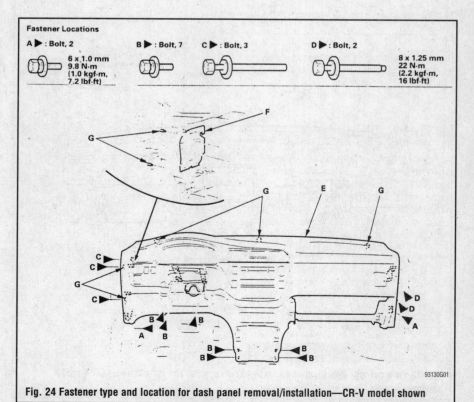

Fastener Locations

A ▶ : Bolt, 2
6 x 1.0 mm
9.8 N·m
(1.0 kgf·m,
7.2 lbf·ft)

B ▶ : Bolt, 7

C ▶ : Bolt, 3

D ▶ : Bolt, 2
8 x 1.25 mm
22 N·m
(2.2 kgf·m,
16 lbf·ft)

93130G01

Fig. 24 Fastener type and location for dash panel removal/installation—CR-V model shown

8. From outside of the driver's door, at the pillar corner, lift the small trim cover, remove the screw and carefully remove the corner trim from the clips.

9. Open the passenger side door, remove the screw from the dash right side panel, and carefully unsnap the panel.

10. Remove the bolt at the bottom of the fuse/relay box and pull out the box.

11. Disconnect the electrical connectors at the left, center and right side of the dash.

12. Using a T-30 Torx® bit, remove the ground bolt on the left side of the lower center dash at the SRS control unit.

13. Disconnect all of the harness and connector clips from under the dash.

14. During removal, make sure to note the location each of the 14 dash mounting bolts, as there are 4 different bolt sizes.

15. Remove the 3 bolts from the left side of the dash, the 3 bolts from the right side of the dash, 1 left side dash bolt, 3 steering column opening bolts, and the 4 center console mounting bolts.

16. Carefully lift the dashboard and release it from the steering hanger beam.

To install:

17. Installation is the reverse of the removal procedure, making sure to perform the following:

a. Use a T30 Torx® bit to install the ground bolt on the left side of the lower center dash at the SRS control unit.

b. Properly enable the SRS, as outlined in Section 6.

c. Enter the radio security code.

Dash Panels, Covers and Vents

REMOVAL & INSTALLATION

CR-V Models

➡ Before disconnecting the battery cable(s) or the radio electrical connectors, make sure to note the radio security code. Once disconnected, the radio will not function until the code is entered.

✳✳ CAUTION

The models covered by this manual are equipped with a Supplemental Restraint System (SRS), which uses an air bag. Whenever working near any of the SRS components, such as the impact sensors, the air bag module, steering column and instrument panel, disable the SRS, as described in Section 6.

Perform the following procedures BEFORE working on the interior components.

1. Note the radio security code and disconnect the negative battery cable.

2. Disable the Supplemental Restraint System (SRS) as outlined in Section 6.

✳✳ CAUTION

Failure to observe the previously stated repair procedures could result in severe physical injury.

GLOVE BOX

▶ See Figure 25

1. Open the glove box and release the two limiting stops from both sides of the glove box.

2. Remove the two Phillips screws that secure the glove box hinges, and remove the glove box.

3. Installation is the reverse of the removal procedure.

Fig. 25 After removing the 2 pressed-in glove box stops, unfasten the hinge screws and remove the glove box—CR-V shown

DRIVER'S SIDE LOWER DASH COVER

▶ See Figure 26

1. Remove the Phillips screws from the lower left and right corners.

2. Carefully pull the panel to release the clips on the upper portion of the panel. There are 3 clips on the left, and one on the right.

3. Installation is the reverse of the removal procedure.

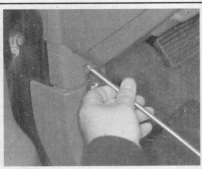

Fig. 26 Remove the lower left and right screws, then carefully release the lower cover from the clips to remove—CR-V model shown

DRIVER'S SIDE LOWER KNEE BOLSTER

1. Remove the driver's lower dash cover.

2. Remove the knee bolster mounting bolts and release the bolster from the hooks to remove.

3. Installation is the reverse of the removal procedure.

LOWER CENTER CONSOLE TRIM (AUTOMATIC TRANSAXLE)

▶ See Figure 27

1. Using a suitable trim panel removal tool, carefully remove the two plastic pressed-in fasteners from the center console lower trim.

2. Carefully pull on the lower part of the trim to release the clips and the trim panel.

3. Installation is the reverse of the removal procedure.

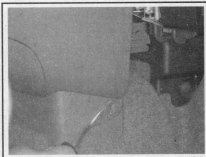

Fig. 27 Use a suitable trim panel removal tool to remove pressed in fasteners—CR-V model shown

CENTER POCKET/BEVERAGE HOLDER (AUTOMATIC TRANSAXLE)

▶ See Figures 28 and 29

1. Remove the lower console cover.

2. Open the center pocket and remove the 6 Phillips screws that mount the center pocket onto the console.

3. Using a small flat-bladed prytool or a suitable small curved pick, pull outward on the hook located on the upper right hand side of the center pocket, while pulling on the box to remove it from the console.

4. Installation is the reverse of the removal procedure.

CENTER CONSOLE (MANUAL TRANSAXLE)

1. Rotate the shift knob counterclockwise to remove it from the shift shaft.

2. Remove the screws from the side of the console and the two just below the center pocket.

Fig. 28 Remove the screws surrounding the center pocket . . .

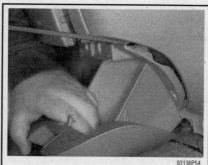

Fig. 29 . . . then, release the hook on the upper right side and remove the pocket— CR-V model shown

3. Remove the center pocket mounting screws.
4. Remove the center pocket, then carefully remove the center console.
5. Installation is the reverse of the removal procedure.

CENTER DASHBOARD LOWER COVER

▶ See Figures 30 and 31

1. Remove the driver's side lower dash cover.
2. Remove the glove box.
3. On automatic transaxle models, remove the center pocket.
4. On manual transaxle models, remove the center console and center pocket.

Fig. 30 The cover is held in place with 3 clips and 4 screws. Two of the screws are visible when the glove box is removed

Fig. 31 The other two screws are located at the bottom and accessible once the lower cover is removed—CR-V model shown

5. Remove the 2 lower and 2 upper Phillips screws from the cover.
6. Carefully pull the left side of the console away from the dash to release the left side clips.
7. Installation is the reverse of the removal procedure.

DASHBOARD CENTER PANEL

▶ See Figures 32 and 33

To dashboard center panel is comprised of the combination radio and heater control assembly. To remove that assembly from the center dash, perform the following:

1. Remove the driver's side lower dash cover.
2. Remove the glove box.
3. On automatic transaxle equipped vehicles, remove the center pocket.
4. On manual transaxle equipped vehicles, remove the center console and upper pocket.
5. Remove the center dash lower cover.
6. Remove the left and right side bolts, that mount the assembly to the dash brackets, with an 8mm wrench or Phillips screwdriver.
7. Once both bolts are removed, carefully pull the combination radio and heater control assembly from the center dash. The assembly is secured with 6 clips and may require a little patience to release it from the console.
8. Once the assembly has been loosened, reach behind it to release the two wire terminals from the heater controls, and the wire terminal and antenna lead from the radio.

Fig. 32 Once the lower cover is moved aside, remove the left and right side fasteners . . .

Fig. 33 . . . then carefully release the dashboard center panel from the clips— CR-V model shown

9. To remove the radio, remove the two bolts on the left and right sides using an 8mm wrench or Phillips screwdriver.
10. Installation is the reverse of the removal procedure.

DRIVER'S SIDE ELECTRIC SWITCH PANEL

1. Remove the driver's side lower dash panel.
2. Carefully push out the switch panel by hand to release it from the retaining clips.
3. Detach the electrical connectors.
4. Installation is the reverse of the removal procedure.

DASH VENTS

The dash vents have small hooks at the top and clips at the bottom.

1. Carefully release the clips at the bottom of the vent.
2. Rock the lower portion of the vent outward, then down to release the upper hooks.
3. If necessary, detach the electrical connector.
4. Remove the vent assembly.
5. Installation is the reverse of the removal procedure.

4-Cylinder Odyssey Models

➡**Before disconnecting the battery cable(s) or the radio electrical connectors, make sure to note the radio security code. Once disconnected, the radio will not function until the code is entered.**

✳✳ CAUTION

The models covered by this manual are equipped with a Supplemental Restraint System (SRS), which uses an air bag. Whenever working near any of the SRS components, such as the impact sensors, the air bag module, steering column and instrument panel, disable the SRS, as described in Section 6.

Perform the following procedures BEFORE working on the interior components.

1. Note the radio security code and disconnect the negative battery cable.
2. Disable the Supplemental Restraint System (SRS) as outlined in Section 6.

✳✳ CAUTION

Failure to observe the previously stated repair procedures could result in severe physical injury.

GLOVE BOX

1. Open the glove box and remove the two screws securing the two limiting stops and remove the stops.
2. Remove the screws that secure the glove box hinges, and remove the glove box.
3. Remove the glove box bracket and damper assembly.
4. Installation is the reverse of the removal procedure.

DRIVER'S LOWER DASH COVER

1. Remove the Phillips screws at top of the change box and the right lower corners.
2. Carefully pull the panel to release the clips on the upper portion of the panel. There are 3 clips on the left side, and one each at either side of the steering column.
3. Disconnect the dash brightness control.
4. Installation is the reverse of the removal procedure.

DRIVER'S LOWER KNEE BOLSTER

1. Remove the driver's lower dash cover.
2. Remove the knee bolster mounting bolts and release the bolster from the hooks to remove.
3. Installation is the reverse of the removal procedure.

CENTER CONSOLE

1. Remove the left side dash lower cover.
2. Remove the glove box stops.
3. Remove the 7 screws mounting the center console.
4. Detach the cigarette lighter electrical connector.
5. If necessary, remove the two screws in the base of the center pocket and remove the pocket.
6. Remove the center console.
7. Rotate the shift knob counterclockwise to remove it from the shift shaft.
8. Installation is the reverse of the removal procedure.

BEVERAGE HOLDER

1. Remove the dashboard lower left cover.
2. Remove the center console.
3. Remove 2 screws from each side of the beverage holder and remove the holder.
4. Installation is the reverse of the removal procedure.

CENTER POCKET

The center pocket is located below the radio and above the center beverage holder.
1. Remove the beverage holder.
2. Remove the bolts from behind the center pocket for the radio bracket.
3. Slide the radio assembly forward, without disconnecting the wiring, then remove the screw at each side of the pocket and remove the pocket.
4. Installation is the reverse of the removal procedure.

RADIO/HEATER CONTROL PANEL

1. Note the radio code and disconnect the negative battery cable.
2. Remove the dash left side lower cover.
3. Remove the center console.
4. Remove the beverage holder.
5. Remove the clip securing the heater outlet duct.
6. Disconnect the air mix control cable.
7. Remove the bolt from either side of the radio mounting bracket.
8. Detach the electrical connectors from the radio and heater unit.
9. Remove the lower rear bolts securing the radio in place and remove the radio.
10. Remove the screws around the bracket to remove the cosmetic panel.

11. Installation is the reverse of the removal procedure.

DASHBOARD COMPARTMENT

1. Open the lid and remove the 4 screws.
2. Detach the clip at the right side of the housing.
3. Remove the compartment.
4. Installation is the reverse of the removal procedure.

CENTER VENT/SWITCH PANEL

1. Remove the instrument panel trim.
2. Remove the dashboard compartment.
3. Remove the two screws from the left and right sides and remove the panel.
4. Detach the electrical connectors as necessary.
5. Installation is the reverse of the removal procedure.

DASH VENTS

The dash vents have small hooks at the top and clips at the bottom.
1. Carefully release the clips at the bottom of the vent.
2. Rock the lower portion of the vent outward, then down to release the upper hooks.
3. If necessary, disconnect the electrical connector.
4. Remove the vent assembly.
5. Installation is the reverse of the removal procedure.

V6 Odyssey Models

➡ Before disconnecting the battery cable(s) or the radio electrical connectors, make sure to note the radio security code. Once disconnected, the radio will not function until the code is entered.

❋❋ CAUTION

The models covered by this manual are equipped with a Supplemental Restraint System (SRS), which uses an air bag. Whenever working near any of the SRS components, such as the impact sensors, the air bag module, steering column and instrument panel, disable the SRS, as described in Section 6.

Perform the following procedures BEFORE working on the interior components.
1. Note the radio security code and disconnect the negative battery cable.
2. Disable the Supplemental Restraint System (SRS) as outlined in Section 6.

❋❋ CAUTION

Failure to observe the previously stated repair procedures could result in severe physical injury.

CENTER LOWER POCKET

1. Remove the center dashboard lower trim pins, then carefully release the trim from the clips.
2. Remove the 6 screws from around the

pocket, then carefully pull along the top of the pocket to releases it from the clips.
3. Detach the electrical connectors for the pocket light, and remove the pocket.
4. Installation is the reverse of the removal procedure.

CENTER LOWER CONSOLE

1. Remove the center lower pocket assembly.
2. Remove the 4 screws securing the console.
3. Carefully pull out the console and detach the accessory socket electrical connector.
4. Remove the console.
5. Installation is the reverse of the removal procedure.

DASHBOARD LOWER COVER

1. Remove the Phillips screw at the lower left corner.
2. Carefully pull the panel to release the clips on the upper and right side portion of the panel.
3. Installation is the reverse of the removal procedure.

DRIVER'S SIDE SWITCH PANEL

1. Carefully pull out the switch panel by hand to release it from the retaining clips.
2. Unplug the electrical connectors.
3. Installation is the reverse of the removal procedure.

DASHBOARD CENTER PANEL

1. Remove the steering column covers.
2. Carefully release the center panel clips by gently pulling the panel from the dash.
3. Once the panel has been removed, detach the electrical connector as necessary.
4. Installation is the reverse of the removal procedure.

GLOVE BOX

1. Open the glove box and release the two limiting stops from both sides of the glove box.
2. Remove the two bolts that secure the glove box hinges, and remove the glove box.
3. Installation is the reverse of the removal procedure.

PASSENGER DASH VENT

1. Carefully release the right side of the vent using a small flat-bladed prytool to press the vent away from the side of the vent opening.
2. Then, release the left side pivot by carefully prying the vent away from the side of the vent opening.
3. Remove the vent assembly.
To install:
4. Make sure the left side pivot bushing is installed in the vent.
5. Install the left pivot portion of the vent first, then press the right pivot into place.

BEVERAGE HOLDER

1. Remove the dashboard.
2. Remove the beverage holder base fasteners.
3. Installation is the reverse of the removal procedure.

Door Panels

REMOVAL & INSTALLATION

CR-V Models

▶ See Figures 34 thru 44

1. Remove the screw from the door handle trim, then slide the handle assembly forward and out to access the lock rod clip. Release the clip, disconnect the door lock switch and remove the door opener handle assembly.

2. Carefully pry at the small opening on the bottom of the speaker grill, and remove the grille.

3. Remove the speaker mounting screws,

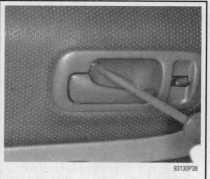

Fig. 34 Remove the screw from the door handle trim

Fig. 35 Remove the screws from the arm rest supports

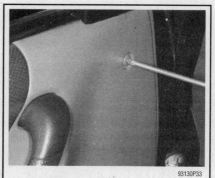

Fig. 36 Remove the center pin from the panel clip, then remove the clip

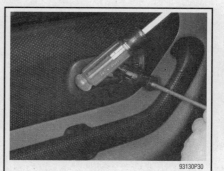

Fig. 37 Slide the handle assembly forward using 2 screwdrivers, one inserted in the housing, the other to tap lightly

Fig. 38 Once the handle slides forward, the retaining hook will release, allowing you to remove the handle

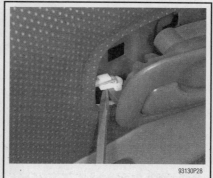

Fig. 39 Push the lock rod clip to release the rod

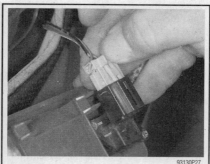

Fig. 40 Unplug the connector from the electric door lock before removing the door handle

Fig. 41 Remove the speaker grille by carefully prying at the small opening at the bottom of the grille

Fig. 42 Remove the speaker, then remove the door panel screws

Fig. 43 Once all the fasteners are removed, use a suitable door panel trim tool to release the door panel clips . . .

Fig. 44 . . . then carefully lift the door panel up and away from the door

detach the electrical connector and remove the speaker.

4. Remove the screws in the armrest.

5. Remove the center from the trim clip at the upper front of the door panel and remove the clip.

6. Using a suitable trim panel removal tool, unsnap the door panel from the door frame.

7. Carefully lift the door panel up and away from the door frame.

8. Installation is the reverse of the removal procedure.

Odyssey Models

4-CYLINDER ENGINES

1. Remove the screw in the door handle trim, slide the handle assembly forward, and out to access the lock rod clip. Release the clip, disconnect the door lock switch and remove the door opener handle assembly.

2. Carefully pry off the cap(s) in the armrest pocket, then remove the screw(s).

3. Carefully pry off the cap under the armrest and remove the screw.

4. Using a suitable trim panel removal tool, unsnap the door panel from the door frame.

5. Unplug the electrical connectors for the power windows, power mirror and courtesy light.

6. Carefully lift the door panel up and away from the door frame.

7. Installation is the reverse of the removal procedure.

V6 ENGINE

1. Remove the screw in the door handle trim, slide the handle assembly forward, and out to access the lock rod clip. Release the clip, disconnect the door lock switch and remove the door opener handle assembly.

2. Carefully unsnap the rear of the speaker grill, lift and pull back to release it and remove the grille.

3. Remove the panel mounting screws located around the perimeter of the speaker.

4. Remove the cap and screw in the pull pocket of the armrest.

5. Slide the pocket back slightly to release the front hook, then lift up, detach the electrical connectors and remove the pocket assembly.

6. Using a suitable trim panel removal tool, unsnap the door panel from the door frame.

7. Carefully lift the door panel up and away from the door frame slightly and disconnect the speaker connector.

8. Installation is the reverse of the removal procedure.

Door Locks

REMOVAL & INSTALLATION

CR-V and 4-Cylinder Odyssey Models

▶ See Figure 45

1. Remove the door panel.
2. Remove the plastic vapor barrier.
3. Remove the lock cylinder and outer door handle.
4. Remove the bolt from the rear window channel guide.

Fig. 45 Use a hand impact driver to loosen and tighten the door lock fasteners

5. Unplug the electrical connectors, wire harness clips and inner handle rod.

6. Remove the latch mounting screws, using a hand impact driver if necessary.

7. Installation is the reverse of the removal procedure.

V6 Odyssey Models

1. Raise the door glass up fully.

2. Remove the door panel, vapor barrier and remove the lock cylinder as outlined in this section.

3. Detach the electrical connector and wire harness clips in the area surrounding the door latch.

4. Remove the access cap above the door latch, and remove the door handle mounting bolts.

5. Pull the outer door handle away from the door and measure the amount of the actuating rod protruding above the clip and write it down for reassembly.

6. Using a diagonal cutting pliers, pry the actuating rod clip from the door handle. Make sure to replace the clip upon reassembly.

7. Remove the interior lock rod protector mounting screw, unsnap and remove the protector.

8. Release the inner handle lock rod from its holder, disconnect the electrical connector for the door latch and release the wiring harness clip from the door.

9. Remove the door latch mounting screws and remove the door latch assembly through the door.

10. Installation is the reverse of the removal procedure, making sure to use a new outside door handle clip installed to the measurement taken during disassembly.

Door Lock Cylinder

REMOVAL & INSTALLATION

CR-V and 4-Cylinder Odyssey Models

1. Remove the door panel.
2. Remove the plastic vapor barrier.
3. Release the lock cylinder rod retainer clip and disconnect the rod.
4. Remove the U-shaped retainer clip, then remove the lock cylinder.
5. On 4-cylinder Odyssey models if necessary, remove the screw holding the lock cylinder switch.
6. Remove the outer door handle retainer bolts, and pull the handle out.

7. Wrap a clean soft shop towel around the handle to protect the door from damage and use a pair of diagonal cutting pliers to gently pry the release rod clip out of the handle. Replace the door handle-to-release rod clip.

8. Installation is the reverse of the removal procedure, making sure to use a new release rod clip.

V6 Odyssey Models

⁜⁜ CAUTION

Wear gloves during these procedures for protection.

1. Raise the door glass.

2. Remove the outside mirror as outlined in this section.

3. Remove the door panel as outlined in this section.

4. Remove the vapor barrier.

5. Remove the rubber window channel from the rear window guide bracket, then remove the bracket bolt and slide the metal guide bracket down and out of the door.

6. Unsnap the lock rod clip from the lock cylinder, remove the rod, then remove the U-clip from the lock cylinder and remove the cylinder.

7. Remove the lock cylinder switch screw and remove the lock cylinder.

8. Installation is the reverse of the removal procedure.

Rear Window/Hatch Lock

REMOVAL & INSTALLATION

CR-V Models

1. Remove the tailgate interior trim panel.
2. Detach the electrical connector.
3. Matchmark the lock-to-tailgate alignment.
4. Remove the latch bolts and remove the latch.
5. Installation is the reverse of the removal procedure.

Odyssey Models

4-CYLINDER ENGINES

1. Remove the rear hatch side and lower trim panels.
2. Remove the lock mounting screws.
3. Slide the lock rod and handle rod clips off, then remove the rods.
4. Detach the electrical connector and remove the lock.
5. Installation is the reverse of the removal procedure.

V6 ENGINE

⁜⁜ CAUTION

Wear gloves for protection.

1. Remove the hatch trim as outlined in this section.

2. Disconnect the cable, cylinder rod, lock rod, and the electrical connector and harness clip.

3. Remove the tailgate latch mounting bolts and

remove the latch enough to disconnect the latch electrical connector.

4. Installation is the reverse of the removal procedure.

Tailgate Lock

REMOVAL & INSTALLATION

CR-V Models

✳✳ WARNING

When opening the tail gate ALWAYS open the window first. When closing the tailgate, close the tailgate, then close the window.

The tailgate door lock works in conjunction with the latch stop. The purpose of the latch stop is to not allow the tailgate to be opened unless the rear window is opened first. When the tailgate key lock is turned, the rear window is unlatched. Once the window is raised, the tailgate door handle that is concealed by the license plate trim can be lifted to open the tailgate. When the window is closed, part of the window frame pushes against the latch stop, preventing the tailgate door handle from moving to open the tailgate latch.

1. Remove the tailgate interior trim panel.
2. Remove the license plate.
3. Remove the license plate trim, by removing the four 8mm nuts and releasing the center clip.
4. Disconnect the door handle lock rod clip at the upper latch stop.
5. Remove the latch stop and tailgate door latch fasteners and move the latch stop and door latch downward.
6. Measure the amount the lock rod protrudes through the latch stop rod clip, and write it down.
7. Using a diagonal cutting pliers, carefully pry the latch rod clip from the latch stop assembly.
8. Installation is the reverse of the removal procedure, making sure to use a new latch stop rod clip installed to the measurement taken during disassembly.

Door Glass and Regulator

REMOVAL & INSTALLATION

CR-V Models and 4-Cylinder Odyssey Models

▶ **See Figures 46, 47, 48 and 49**

1. Remove the door panel, as outlined in this section.
2. Remove the plastic vapor barrier.
3. On 4-cylinder Odyssey models rear door glass, remove the center rear channel bolt and remove the channel.
4. Carefully raise the door glass until the bolts are visible.
5. On 4-cylinder Odyssey models rear door glass perform the following:
   a. Remove the self-tapping screws from the outer triangular trim cover and remove the cover.
   b. Remove the door glass bolts.

c. Carefully lower the glass, then remove the bolts and nut from the rear lower guide channel.
   d. Remove the glass from the rear guide channel.
   e. Apply protective tape around the painted surfaces of the window sash trim.
   f. Tilt the window forward and remove from the window slot.
6. Loosen the bolts, then slide the lower guide forward and remove the window from the guide.
7. Carefully pull the glass out through the window slot. Take care to not drop the glass.
8. To remove the regulator, perform the following:

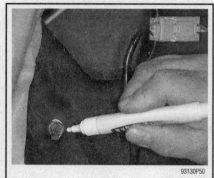
Fig. 46 Always matchmark any fasteners that are mounted through a slotted hole. This bolt is used to adjust the window position

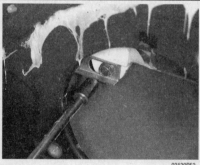
Fig. 47 The window is raised just enough to access the mounting bolts

Fig. 48 Once the window fasteners are loosened, the window can be tilted and lifted out of the door

Fig. 49 Slide the window motor/regulator assembly out of the door

a. Scribe a line around the rear roller guide bolt to mark its original position.
   b. Disconnect the electrical connector and harness clip, then remove the regulator mounting bolts.
   c. Remove the regulator through the hole in the door.
9. Installation is in reverse order of removal. Apply grease to the rollers, guides and sliding surfaces of the regulator. Make sure to install the roller guide with the rectangular hole facing rearward. Check the window operation before installing the door panel and adjust if necessary.

V6 Odyssey Models

1. Remove the door panel as outlined in this section.
2. Remove the fasteners from the door panel pull pocket bracket and remove the bracket.
3. Carefully raise the window glass until the mounting bolts are visible.
4. Remove the window mounting bolts, then carefully remove the window.
5. Installation is the reverse of the removal procedure.

Electric Window Motor

REMOVAL & INSTALLATION

▶ **See Figures 50 and 51**

1. Remove the door panel.
2. Remove the plastic vapor barrier.

Fig. 50 Before removing the electric window motor, matchmark the window regulator to the motor mounting housing

Fig. 51 View of the electric window motor and flanged bolts, once they are removed from the vehicle

3. Remove the door glass.
4. Remove the motor/regulator assembly.
5. On CR-V and 4-cylinder Odyssey models, scribe a line across the sector gear and the regulator before removing the window motor.
6. On V6 Odyssey models, the motor and regulator must be replaced as a unit, the motor cannot be removed separately.
7. Installation is the reverse of the removal procedure, making sure to perform the following:
　a. On CR-V and 4-cylinder Odyssey models, apply grease to the rollers, guides and sliding surfaces of the regulator. Make sure to install the roller guide with the rectangular hole facing rearward. Check the window operation before installing the door panel and adjust if necessary.
　b. On V6 Odyssey models, apply grease to the sliding surface of the regulator. Check the window operation before installing the door panel and adjust as necessary.

Inside Rear View Mirror

REPLACEMENT

CR-V Models

▶ See Figures 52 and 53

1. Carefully pry the cover off using a suitable prytool.
2. Remove the rubber damper from the mirror stalk.

Fig. 52 Avoid damaging the headliner by using a paint stick or ruler to pry against when removing the rear view mirror trim cover

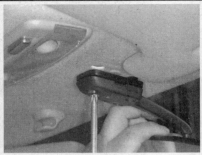

Fig. 53 Unfasten the counter sunk Phillips screws to remove the rear view mirror— CR-V model shown

3. Remove the machine screws from the base and remove the mirror.
4. Installation is the reverse of the removal procedure.

4-Cylinder Odyssey Models

WITHOUT SUNROOF

To remove the rear view mirror on these models, refer to the procedure for CR-V models.

WITH SUNROOF

1. Carefully pry the cover off using a suitable prytool.
2. Loosen the lock bolt by turning it counterclockwise.
3. Remove the mirror by sliding it from the base mounted on the windshield.
4. Installation is the reverse of the removal procedure.

V6 Odyssey Models

1. Carefully slide the rear view mirror down toward the bottom of the windshield and remove it from the mount and tensioning spring.
　To install:
2. Turn the mirror such that the base is at a 90° angle, slide the base of the mirror over the mount and pivot the mirror 90° to secure the mirror in place.

Seats

REMOVAL & INSTALLATION

✳✳ WARNING

When removing the seats, be careful not the damage the covers or tear the seams.

✳✳ CAUTION

Due to the size and weight of a seat, have an assistant on hand to help.

Front

1. On CR-V and 4-cylinder Odyssey models, perform the following:

　a. Slide the seat forward. Remove the seat track end/bolt covers.
　b. Remove the attaching bolts.
2. On V6 Odyssey models, perform the following:
　a. Wear gloves for protection.
　b. Unsnap the front and rear lower seat frame covers.
　c. Remove the attaching bolts.
3. On CR-V and 4-cylinder Odyssey models, perform the following:
　a. Slide the seat rearward.
　b. Remove the seat track end covers.
　c. Remove the attaching bolts.
4. Lift the seat and then detach the seat electrical connectors and wiring harness clips.
5. Carefully remove the seat through the front door.
6. Installation is the reverse of the removal procedure.

Rear

CR-V

1. Remove the lower hinge covers, then remove the bolts.
2. Fold the seat cushion forward, then remove the seat base cover fasteners and the seat base cover.
3. Remove the headrest.
4. If the seat is a tilting seat, tilt the seat slightly, if necessary, remove the seat latch striker.
5. Have an assistant carefully assist in removing the seat through the door opening.
6. Installation is the reverse of the removal procedure.

4-CYLINDER ODYSSEY—SIX PASSENGER MODELS

The second seats on the six passenger model are designed to be easily removable.
1. At the rear base of the seat pull up on both lock release levers while pulling up on the rear of the seat.
2. Pull the seat back slightly, then pivot the seat upward.
3. Remove the seat from the vehicle.

✳✳ CAUTION

Always remove an unfastened seat from the vehicle. Should an accident occur, the seat may become a projectile.

　To install:
4. Hook the front of the seat to the floor and push back on the locks, making sure both the front and the back of the seat are securely fastened before driving.

4-CYLINDER ODYSSEY—SEVEN PASSENGER MODELS

The second seat on the seven passenger model is a bench style seat that can be removed as necessary.
1. Raise the second seat.
2. Remove the bolts at the base of the seat supports.
3. Pull up and remove the seat.
4. Remove the seat from the vehicle.

✳✳ CAUTION

Always remove an unfastened seat from the vehicle. Should an accident occur, the seat may become a projectile.

To install:

5. Install the seat support into the base and install the 10 x 1.25mm bolt and torque to 25 ft. lbs. (34 Nm).

V6 ODYSSEY MODELS

➡The second seat removal procedures are the same for the bucket and bench seats, however due to the weight of the bench seat, an assistant should help with the removal and installation of the seat.

1. Pull up the seat back adjustment lever and fold the seat forward.
2. Pull the lock release lever under the front corner of the seat and lift the rear of the seat.
3. Pull the seat back slightly while pivoting the seat upward to release the front of the seat.

✳✳ CAUTION

Always remove an unfastened seat from the vehicle. Should an accident occur, the seat may become a projectile.

To install:

4. Hook the front of the seat to the floor and push the back into the locks, making sure both the front and the back of the seat are securely fastened before driving.

Power Seat Motor

REMOVAL & INSTALLATION

1. Remove the negative battery cable.
2. Remove the seat.
3. Remove the connector from the power seat motor.
4. Remove the bolts that secure the power seat motor to the seat frame.
5. Remove the seat motor.
6. Installation is the reverse of the removal procedure.

TORQUE SPECIFICATIONS

Components	Ft. Lbs.	Nm
Antenna nut	31-44 inch lbs.	4-5 Nm
Door / hatch / tailgate striker bolts	13 ft. lbs.	18 Nm
Door hinge bolts	22 ft. lbs.	29 Nm
Door latch bolts	48 inch lbs.	6 Nm
Door stop arm bolts	89 inch lbs.	10 Nm
Doorglass-to-regulator, 2.2L/2.3L Odyssey	60 inch lbs.	7 Nm
Doorglass-to-regulator, CR-V, 3.5L V-6 Odyssey	86 inch lbs.	9.8 Nm
Fender retaining screws	89-124 inch lbs.	10-14 Nm
Front seat retaining bolts, CR-V, 10 x 1.25 mm	27 ft. lbs.	37 Nm
Front seat retaining bolts, CR-V, 8x 1.25 mm	16 ft. lbs.	22 Nm
Front seat retaining bolts, Odyssey	25 ft. lbs.	34 Nm
Hood hinge bolts	86 inch lbs.	9.8 Nm
Hood latch bolts	86 inch lbs.	9.8 Nm
Outside mirror retaining bolts, CR-V	48 inch lbs.	6 Nm
Outside mirror retaining bolts, Odyssey	86 inch lbs.	9.8 Nm
Rear bench seat retaining bolts, 2.2L/2.3L Odyssey	25 ft. lbs.	34 Nm
Rear hatch hinge nuts/bolts, Odyssey	16 ft. lbs.	22 Nm
Tailgate hinge bolts, CR-V	19 ft. lbs.	26 Nm

93130C01

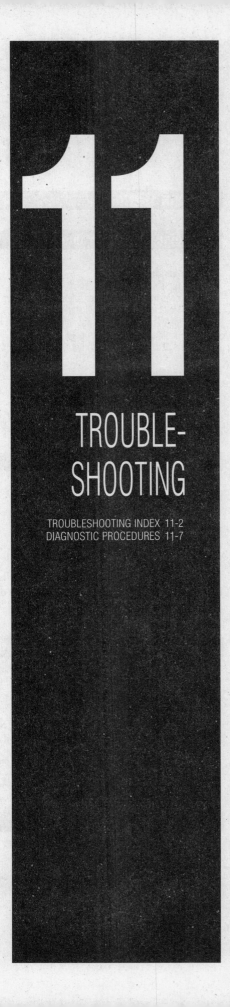

11

TROUBLE-SHOOTING

Condition	Section/Item Number

The following troubleshooting charts are divided into 7 sections covering engine, drive train, brakes, wheels/tires/steering/suspension, electrical accessories, instruments and gauges, and climate control. The first portion (or index) consists of a list of symptoms, along with section and item numbers. After selecting the appropriate condition, refer to the corresponding diagnostic procedure in the second portion's specified location.

INDEX

SECTION 1. ENGINE

A. Engine Starting Problems

Gasoline Engines

Engine turns over, but will not start	1-A, 1
Engine does not turn over when attempting to start	1-A, 2
Engine stalls immediately when started	1-A, 3
Starter motor spins, but does not engage	1-A, 4
Engine is difficult to start when cold	1-A, 5
Engine is difficult to start when hot	1-A, 6

Diesel Engines

Engine turns over but won't start	1-A, 1
Engine does not turn over when attempting to start	1-A, 2
Engine stalls after starting	1-A, 3
Starter motor spins, but does not engage	1-A, 4
Engine is difficult to start	1-A, 5

B. Engine Running Conditions

Gasoline Engines

Engine runs poorly, hesitates	1-B, 1
Engine lacks power	1-B, 2
Engine has poor fuel economy	1-B, 3
Engine runs on (diesels) when turned off	1-B, 4
Engine knocks and pings during heavy acceleration, and on steep hills	1-B, 5
Engine accelerates but vehicle does not gain speed	1-B, 6

Diesel Engines

Engine runs poorly	1-B, 1
Engine lacks power	1-B, 2

C. Engine Noises, Odors and Vibrations

Engine makes a knocking or pinging noise when accelerating	1-C, 1
Starter motor grinds when used	1-C, 2
Engine makes a screeching noise	1-C, 3
Engine makes a growling noise	1-C, 4
Engine makes a ticking or tapping noise	1-C, 5
Engine makes a heavy knocking noise	1-C, 6
Vehicle has a fuel odor when driven	1-C, 7
Vehicle has a rotten egg odor when driven	1-C, 8
Vehicle has a sweet odor when driven	1-C, 9
Engine vibrates when idling	1-C, 10
Engine vibrates during acceleration	1-C, 11

D. Engine Electrical System

Battery goes dead while driving	1-D, 1
Battery goes dead overnight	1-D, 2

E. Engine Cooling System

Engine overheats	1-E, 1
Engine loses coolant	1-E, 2
Engine temperature remains cold when driving	1-E, 3
Engine runs hot	1-E, 4

Condition	Section/Item Number

SECTION 1. ENGINE (continued)

F. Engine Exhaust System

Exhaust rattles at idle speed	1-F, 1
Exhaust system vibrates when driving	1-F, 2
Exhaust system seems too low	1-F, 3
Exhaust seems loud	1-F, 4

SECTION 2. DRIVE TRAIN

A. Automatic Transmission

Transmission shifts erratically	2-A, 1
Transmission will not engage	2-A, 2
Transmission will not downshift during heavy acceleration	2-A, 3

B. Manual Transmission

Transmission grinds going into forward gears while driving	2-B, 1; 2-C, 2
Transmission jumps out of gear	2-B, 2
Transmission difficult to shift	2-B, 3; 2-C, 2
Transmission leaks fluid	2-B, 4

C. Clutch

Clutch slips on hills or during sudden acceleration	2-C, 1
Clutch will not disengage, difficult to shift	2-C, 2
Clutch is noisy when the clutch pedal is pressed	2-C, 3
Clutch pedal extremely difficult to press	2-C, 4
Clutch pedal remains down when pressed	2-C, 5
Clutch chatters when engaging	2-C, 6

D. Differential and Final Drive

Differential makes a low pitched rumbling noise	2-D, 1
Differential makes a howling noise	2-D, 2

E. Transfer Assembly

All Wheel and Four Wheel Drive Vehicles

Leaks fluid from seals or vent after being driven	2-E, 1
Makes excessive noise while driving	2-E, 2
Jumps out of gear	2-E, 3

F. Driveshaft

Rear Wheel, All Wheel and Four Wheel Drive Vehicles

Clunking noise from center of vehicle shifting from forward to reverse	2-F, 1
Excessive vibration from center of vehicle when accelerating	2-F, 2

G. Axles

All Wheel and Four Wheel Drive Vehicles

Front or rear wheel makes a clicking noise	2-G, 1
Front or Rear wheel vibrates with increased speed	2-G, 2

Front Wheel Drive Vehicles

Front wheel makes a clicking noise	2-G, 3
Rear wheel makes a clicking noise	2-G, 4

Condition	Section/Item Number

SECTION 2. DRIVE TRAIN (continued)

Rear Wheel Drive Vehicles

Front or rear wheel makes a clicking noise	2-G, 5
Rear wheel shudders or vibrates	2-G, 6

H. Other Drive Train Conditions

Burning odor from center of vehicle when accelerating	2-H, 1; 2-C, 1; 3-A, 9
Engine accelerates, but vehicle does not gain speed	2-H, 2; 2-C, 1; 3-A, 9

SECTION 3. BRAKE SYSTEM

Brakes pedal pulsates or shimmies when pressed	3-A, 1
Brakes make a squealing noise	3-A, 2
Brakes make a grinding noise	3-A, 3
Vehicle pulls to one side during braking	3-A, 4
Brake pedal feels spongy or has excessive brake pedal travel	3-A, 5
Brake pedal feel is firm, but brakes lack sufficient stopping power or fade	3-A, 6
Vehicle has excessive front end dive or locks rear brakes too easily	3-A, 7
Brake pedal goes to floor when pressed and will not pump up	3-A, 8
Brakes make a burning odor	3-A, 9

SECTION 4. WHEELS, TIRES, STEERING AND SUSPENSION

A. Wheels and Wheel Bearings

All Wheel and Four Wheel Drive Vehicles

Front wheel or wheel bearing loose	4-A, 1
Rear wheel or wheel bearing loose	4-A, 2

Front Wheel Drive Vehicles

Front wheel or wheel bearing loose	4-A, 1
Rear wheel or wheel bearing loose	4-A, 2

Rear Wheel Drive Vehicles

Front wheel or wheel bearing loose	4-A, 1
Rear wheel or wheel bearing loose	4-A, 2

B. Tires

Tires worn on inside tread	4-B, 1
Tires worn on outside tread	4-B, 2
Tires worn unevenly	4-B, 3

C. Steering

Excessive play in steering wheel	4-C, 1
Steering wheel shakes at cruising speeds	4-C, 2
Steering wheel shakes when braking	3-A, 1
Steering wheel becomes stiff when turned	4-C, 4

D. Suspension

Vehicle pulls to one side	4-D, 1
Vehicle is very bouncy over bumps	4-D, 2
Vehicle seems to lean excessively in turns	4-D, 3
Vehicle ride quality seems excessively harsh	4-D, 4
Vehicle seems low or leans to one side	4-D, 5

Condition	Section/Item Number

SECTION 4. WHEELS, TIRES, STEERING AND SUSPENSION (continued)

E. Driving Noises and Vibrations

Noises

Vehicle makes a clicking noise when driven	4-E, 1
Vehicle makes a clunking or knocking noise over bumps	4-E, 2
Vehicle makes a low pitched rumbling noise when driven	4-E, 3
Vehicle makes a squeaking noise over bumps	4-E, 4

Vibrations

Vehicle vibrates when driven	4-E, 5

SECTION 5. ELECTRICAL ACCESSORIES

A. Headlights

One headlight only works on high or low beam	5-A, 1
Headlight does not work on high or low beam	5-A, 2
Headlight(s) very dim	5-A, 3

B. Tail, Running and Side Marker Lights

Tail light, running light or side marker light inoperative	5-B, 1
Tail light, running light or side marker light works intermittently	5-B, 2
Tail light, running light or side marker light very dim	5-B, 3

C. Interior Lights

Interior light inoperative	5-C, 1
Interior light works intermittently	5-C, 2
Interior light very dim	5-C, 3

D. Brake Lights

One brake light inoperative	5-D, 1
Both brake lights inoperative	5-D, 2
One or both brake lights very dim	5-D, 3

E. Warning Lights

Ignition, Battery and Alternator Warning Lights, Check Engine Light, Anti-Lock Braking System (ABS) Light, Brake Warning Light, Oil Pressure Warning Light, and Parking Brake Warning Light

Warning light(s) remains on after the engine is started	5-E, 1
Warning light(s) flickers on and off when driving	5-E, 2
Warning light(s) inoperative with ignition on, and engine not started	5-E, 3

F. Turn Signal and 4-Way Hazard Lights

Turn signals or hazard lights come on, but do not flash	5-F, 1
Turn signals or hazard lights do not function on either side	5-F, 2
Turn signals or hazard lights only work on one side	5-F, 3
One signal light does not work	5-F, 4
Turn signals flash too slowly	5-F, 5
Turn signals flash too fast	5-F, 6
Four-way hazard flasher indicator light inoperative	5-F, 7
Turn signal indicator light(s) do not work in either direction	5-F, 8
One turn signal indicator light does not work	5-F, 9

Condition	Section/Item Number

SECTION 5. ELECTRICAL ACCESSORIES (continued)

G. Horn

Horn does not operate	5-G, 1
Horn has an unusual tone	5-G, 2

H. Windshield Wipers

Windshield wipers do not operate	5-H, 1
Windshield wiper motor makes a humming noise, gets hot or blows fuses	5-H, 2
Windshield wiper motor operates but one or both wipers fail to move	5-H, 3
Windshield wipers will not park	5-H, 4

SECTION 6. INSTRUMENTS AND GAUGES

A. Speedometer (Cable Operated)

Speedometer does not work	6-A, 1
Speedometer needle fluctuates when driving at steady speeds	6-A, 2
Speedometer works intermittently	6-A, 3

B. Speedometer (Electronically Operated)

Speedometer does not work	6-B, 1
Speedometer works intermittently	6-B, 2

C. Fuel, Temperature and Oil Pressure Gauges

Gauge does not register	6-C, 1
Gauge operates erratically	6-C, 2
Gauge operates fully pegged	6-C, 3

SECTION 7. CLIMATE CONTROL

A. Air Conditioner

No air coming from air conditioner vents	7-A, 1
Air conditioner blows warm air	7-A, 2
Water collects on the interior floor when the air conditioner is used	7-A, 3
Air conditioner has a moldy odor when used	7-A, 4

B. Heater

Blower motor does not operate	7-B, 1
Heater blows cool air	7-B, 2
Heater steams the windshield when used	7-B, 3

DIAGNOSTIC PROCEDURES

1. ENGINE

1-A. Engine Starting Problems

Gasoline Engines

1. Engine turns over, but will not start

a. Check fuel level in fuel tank, add fuel if empty.
b. Check battery condition and state of charge. If voltage and load test below specification, charge or replace battery.
c. Check battery terminal and cable condition and tightness. Clean terminals and replace damaged, worn or corroded cables.
d. Check fuel delivery system. If fuel is not reaching the fuel injectors, check for a loose electrical connector or defective fuse, relay or fuel pump and replace as necessary.
e. Engine may have excessive wear or mechanical damage such as low cylinder cranking pressure, a broken camshaft drive system, insufficient valve clearance or bent valves.
f. Check for fuel contamination such as water in the fuel. During winter months, the water may freeze and cause a fuel restriction. Adding a fuel additive may help, however the fuel system may require draining and purging with fresh fuel.
g. Check for ignition system failure. Check for loose or shorted wires or damaged ignition system components. Check the spark plugs for excessive wear or incorrect electrode gap. If the problem is worse in wet weather, check for shorts between the spark plugs and the ignition coils.
h. Check the engine management system for a failed sensor or control module.

2. Engine does not turn over when attempting to start

a. Check the battery state of charge and condition. If the dash lights are not visible or very dim when turning the ignition key on, the battery has either failed internally or discharged, the battery cables are loose, excessively corroded or damaged, or the alternator has failed or internally shorted, discharging the battery. Charge or replace the battery, clean or replace the battery cables, and check the alternator output.
b. Check the operation of the neutral safety switch. On automatic transmission vehicles, try starting the vehicle in both Park and Neutral. On manual transmission vehicles, depress the clutch pedal and attempt to start. On some vehicles, these switches can be adjusted. Make sure the switches or wire connectors are not loose or damaged. Replace or adjust the switches as necessary.
c. Check the starter motor, starter solenoid or relay, and starter motor cables and wires. Check the ground from the engine to the chassis. Make sure the wires are not loose, damaged, or corroded. If battery voltage is present at the starter relay, try using a remote starter to start the vehicle for test purposes only. Replace any damaged or corroded cables, in addition to replacing any failed components.
d. Check the engine for seizure. If the engine has not been started for a long period of time, internal parts such as the rings may have rusted to the cylinder walls. The engine may have suffered internal damage, or could be hydro-locked from ingesting water. Remove the spark plugs and carefully attempt to rotate the engine using a suitable breaker bar and socket on the crankshaft pulley. If the engine is resistant to moving, or moves slightly and then binds, do not force the engine any further before determining the problem.

3. Engine stalls immediately when started

a. Check the ignition switch condition and operation. The electrical contacts in the run position may be worn or damaged. Try restarting the engine with all electrical accessories in the off position. Sometimes turning the key on an off will help in emergency situations, however once the switch has shown signs of failure, it should be replaced as soon as possible.
b. Check for loose, corroded, damaged or shorted wires for the ignition system and repair or replace.
c. Check for manifold vacuum leaks or vacuum hose leakage and repair or replace parts as necessary.
d. Measure the fuel pump delivery volume and pressure. Low fuel pump pressure can also be noticed as a lack of power when accelerating. Make sure the fuel pump lines are not restricted. The fuel pump output is not adjustable and requires fuel pump replacement to repair.
e. Check the engine fuel and ignition management system. Inspect the sensor wiring and electrical connectors. A dirty, loose or damaged sensor or control module wire can simulate a failed component.
f. Check the exhaust system for internal restrictions.

4. Starter motor spins, but does not engage

a. Check the starter motor for a seized or binding pinion gear.
b. Remove the flywheel inspection plate and check for a damaged ring gear.

5. Engine is difficult to start when cold

a. Check the battery condition, battery state of charge and starter motor current draw. Replace the battery if marginal and the starter motor if the current draw is beyond specification.
b. Check the battery cable condition. Clean the battery terminals and replace corroded or damaged cables.
c. Check the fuel system for proper operation. A fuel pump with insufficient fuel pressure or clogged injectors should be replaced.
d. Check the engine's tune-up status. Note the tune-up specifications and check for items such as severely worn spark plugs; adjust or replace as needed. On vehicles with manually adjusted valve clearances, check for tight valves and adjust to specification.
e. Check for a failed coolant temperature sensor, and replace if out of specification.
f. Check the operation of the engine management systems for fuel and ignition; repair or replace failed components as necessary.

6. Engine is difficult to start when hot

a. Check the air filter and air intake system. Replace the air filter if it is dirty or contaminated. Check the fresh air intake system for restrictions or blockage.

b. Check for loose or deteriorated engine grounds and clean, tighten or replace as needed.

c. Check for needed maintenance. Inspect tune-up and service related items such as spark plugs and engine oil condition, and check the operation of the engine fuel and ignition management system.

Diesel Engines

1. Engine turns over but won't start

a. Check engine starting procedure and restart engine.

b. Check the glow plug operation and repair or replace as necessary.

c. Check for air in the fuel system or fuel filter and bleed the air as necessary.

d. Check the fuel delivery system and repair or replace as necessary.

e. Check fuel level and add fuel as needed.

f. Check fuel quality. If the fuel is contaminated, drain and flush the fuel tank.

g. Check engine compression. If compression is below specification, the engine may need to be renewed or replaced.

h. Check the injection pump timing and set to specification.

i. Check the injection pump condition and replace as necessary.

j. Check the fuel nozzle operation and condition or replace as necess-ary.

2. Engine does not turn over when attempting to start

a. Check the battery state of charge and condition. If the dash lights are not visible or very dim when turning the ignition key on, the battery has either failed internally or discharged, the battery cables are loose, excessively corroded or damaged, or the alternator has failed or internally shorted, discharging the battery. Charge or replace the battery, clean or replace the battery cables, and check the alternator output.

b. Check the operation of the neutral safety switch. On automatic transmission vehicles, try starting the vehicle in both Park and Neutral. On manual transmission vehicles, depress the clutch pedal and attempt to start. On some vehicles, these switches can be adjusted. Make sure the switches or wire connectors are not loose or damaged. Replace or adjust the switches as necessary.

c. Check the starter motor, starter solenoid or relay, and starter motor cables and wires. Check the ground from the engine to the chassis. Make sure the wires are not loose, damaged, or corroded. If battery voltage is present at the starter relay, try using a remote starter to start the vehicle for test purposes only. Replace any damaged or corroded cables, in addition to replacing any failed components.

d. Check the engine for seizure. If the engine has not been started for a long period of time, internal parts such as the rings may have rusted to the cylinder walls. The engine may have suffered internal damage, or could be hydro-locked from ingesting water. Remove the injectors and carefully attempt to rotate the engine

using a suitable breaker bar and socket on the crankshaft pulley. If the engine is resistant to moving, or moves slightly and then binds, do not force the engine any further before determining the cause of the problem.

3. Engine stalls after starting

a. Check for a restriction in the fuel return line or the return line check valve and repair as necessary.

b. Check the glow plug operation for turning the glow plugs off too soon and repair as necessary.

c. Check for incorrect injection pump timing and reset to specification.

d. Test the engine fuel pump and replace if the output is below specification.

e. Check for contaminated or incorrect fuel. Completely flush the fuel system and replace with fresh fuel.

f. Test the engine's compression for low compression. If below specification, mechanical repairs are necessary to repair.

g. Check for air in the fuel. Check fuel tank fuel and fill as needed.

h. Check for a failed injection pump. Replace the pump, making sure to properly set the pump timing.

4. Starter motor spins, but does not engage

a. Check the starter motor for a seized or binding pinion gear.

b. Remove the flywheel inspection plate and check for a damaged ring gear.

1-B. Engine Running Conditions

Gasoline Engines

1. Engine runs poorly, hesitates

a. Check the engine ignition system operation and adjust if possible, or replace defective parts.

b. Check for restricted fuel injectors and replace as necessary.

c. Check the fuel pump output and delivery. Inspect fuel lines for restrictions. If the fuel pump pressure is below specification, replace the fuel pump.

d. Check the operation of the engine management system and repair as necessary.

2. Engine lacks power

a. Check the engine's tune-up status. Note the tune-up specifications and check for items such as severely worn spark plugs; adjust or replace as needed. On vehicles with manually adjusted valve clearances, check for tight valves and adjust to specification.

b. Check the air filter and air intake system. Replace the air filter if it is dirty or contaminated. Check the fresh air intake system for restrictions or blockage.

c. Check the operation of the engine fuel and ignition management systems. Check the sensor operation and wiring. Check for low fuel pump pressure and repair or replace components as necessary.

d. Check the throttle linkage adjustments. Check to make sure the linkage is fully opening the throttle. Replace any worn or defective bushings or linkages.

e. Check for a restricted exhaust system. Check for bent or crimped exhaust pipes, or internally restricted mufflers or catalytic converters. Compare inlet and outlet temperatures for the converter or muffler. If the inlet is hot, but outlet cold, the component is restricted.

f. Check for a loose or defective knock sensor. A loose, improperly torqued or defective knock sensor will decrease spark advance and reduce power. Replace defective knock sensors and install using the recommended torque specification.

g. Check for engine mechanical conditions such as low compression, worn piston rings, worn valves, worn camshafts and related parts. An engine which has severe mechanical wear, or has suffered internal mechanical damage must be rebuilt or replaced to restore lost power.

h. Check the engine oil level for being overfilled. Adjust the engine's oil level, or change the engine oil and filter, and top off to the correct level.

i. Check for an intake manifold or vacuum hose leak. Replace leaking gaskets or worn vacuum hoses.

j. Check for dragging brakes and replace or repair as necessary.

k. Check tire air pressure and tire wear. Adjust the pressure to the recommended settings. Check the tire wear for possible alignment problems causing increased rolling resistance, decreased acceleration and increased fuel usage.

l. Check the octane rating of the fuel used during refilling, and use a higher octane rated fuel.

3. Poor fuel economy

a. Inspect the air filter and check for any air restrictions going into the air filter housing. Replace the air filter if it is dirty or contaminated.

b. Check the engine for tune-up and related adjustments. Replace worn ignition parts, check the engine ignition timing and fuel mixture, and set to specifications if possible.

c. Check the tire size, tire wear, alignment and tire pressure. Large tires create more rolling resistance, smaller tires require more engine speed to maintain a vehicle's road speed. Excessive tire wear can be caused by incorrect tire pressure, incorrect wheel alignment or a suspension problem. All of these conditions create increased rolling resistance, causing the engine to work harder to accelerate and maintain a vehicle's speed.

d. Inspect the brakes for binding or excessive drag. A sticking brake caliper, overly adjusted brake shoe, broken brake shoe return spring, or binding parking brake cable or linkage can create a significant drag, brake wear and loss of fuel economy. Check the brake system operation and repair as necessary.

4. Engine runs on (diesels) when turned off

a. Check for idle speed set too high and readjust to specification.

b. Check the operation of the idle control valve, and replace if defective.

c. Check the ignition timing and adjust to recommended settings. Check for defective sensors or related components and replace if defective.

d. Check for a vacuum leak at the intake manifold or vacuum hose and replace defective gaskets or hoses.

e. Check the engine for excessive carbon build-up in the combustion chamber. Use a recommended decarbonizing fuel additive or disassemble the cylinder head to remove the carbon.

f. Check the operation of the engine fuel management system and replace defective sensors or control units.

g. Check the engine operating temperature for overheating and repair as necessary.

5. Engine knocks and pings during heavy acceleration, and on steep hills

a. Check the octane rating of the fuel used during refilling, and use a higher octane rated fuel.

b. Check the ignition timing and adjust to recommended settings. Check for defective sensors or related components and replace if defective.

c. Check the engine for excessive carbon build-up in the combustion chamber. Use a recommended decarbonizing fuel additive or disassemble the cylinder head to remove the carbon.

d. Check the spark plugs for the correct type, electrode gap and heat range. Replace worn or damaged spark plugs. For severe or continuous high speed use, install a spark plug that is one heat range colder.

e. Check the operation of the engine fuel management system and replace defective sensors or control units.

f. Check for a restricted exhaust system. Check for bent or crimped exhaust pipes, or internally restricted mufflers or catalytic converters. Compare inlet and outlet temperatures for the converter or muffler. If the inlet is hot, but outlet cold, the component is restricted.

6. Engine accelerates, but vehicle does not gain speed

a. On manual transmission vehicles, check for causes of a slipping clutch. Refer to the clutch troubleshooting section for additional information.

b. On automatic transmission vehicles, check for a slipping transmission. Check the transmission fluid level and condition. If the fluid level is too high, adjust to the correct level. If the fluid level is low, top off using the recommended fluid type. If the fluid exhibits a burning odor, the transmission has been slipping internally. Changing the fluid and filter may help temporarily, however in this situation a transmission may require overhauling to ensure long-term reliability.

Diesel Engines

1. Engine runs poorly

a. Check the injection pump timing and adjust to specification.

b. Check for air in the fuel lines or leaks, and bleed the air from the fuel system.

c. Check the fuel filter, fuel feed and return lines for a restriction and repair as necessary.

d. Check the fuel for contamination, drain and flush the fuel tank and replenish with fresh fuel.

2. Engine lacks power

a. Inspect the air intake system and air filter for restrictions and, if necessary, replace the air filter.

b. Verify the injection pump timing and reset if out of specification.

c. Check the exhaust for an internal restriction and replace failed parts.

d. Check for a restricted fuel filter and, if restricted, replace the filter.

e. Inspect the fuel filler cap vent . When removing the filler cap, listen for excessive hissing noises indicating a blockage in the fuel filler cap vents. If the filler cap vents are blocked, replace the cap.

f. Check the fuel system for restrictions and repair as necessary.

g. Check for low engine compression and inspect for external leakage at the glow plugs or nozzles. If no external leakage is noted, repair or replace the engine.

ENGINE PERFORMANCE TROUBLESHOOTING HINTS

When troubleshooting an engine running or performance condition, the mechanical condition of the engine should be determined *before* lengthy troubleshooting procedures are performed.

The engine fuel management systems in fuel injected vehicles rely on electronic sensors to provide information to the engine control unit for precise fuel metering. Unlike carburetors, which use the incoming air speed to draw fuel through the fuel metering jets in order to provide a proper fuel-to-air ratio, a fuel injection system provides a specific amount of fuel which is introduced by the fuel injectors into the intake manifold or intake port, based on the information provided by electronic sensors.

The sensors monitor the engine's operating temperature, ambient temperature and the amount of air entering the engine, engine speed and throttle position to provide information to the engine control unit, which, in turn, operates the fuel injectors by electrical pulses. The sensors provide information to the engine control unit using low voltage electrical signals. As a result, an unplugged sensor or a poor electrical contact could cause a poor running condition similar to a failed sensor.

When troubleshooting a fuel related engine condition on fuel injected vehicles, carefully inspect the wiring and electrical connectors to the related components. Make sure the electrical connectors are fully connected, clean and not physically damaged. If necessary, clean the electrical contacts using electrical contact cleaner. The use of cleaning agents not specifically designed for electrical contacts should not be used, as they could leave a surface film or damage the insulation of the wiring.

The engine electrical system provides the necessary electrical power to operate the vehicle's electrical accessories, electronic control units and sensors. Because engine management systems are sensitive to voltage changes, an alternator which over or undercharges could cause engine running problems or component failure. Most alternators utilize internal voltage regulators which cannot be adjusted and must be replaced individually or as a unit with the alternator.

Ignition systems may be controlled by, or linked to, the engine fuel management system. Similar to the fuel injection system, these ignition systems rely on electronic sensors for information to determine the optimum ignition timing for a given engine speed and load. Some ignition systems no longer allow the ignition timing to be adjusted. Feedback from low voltage electrical sensors provide information to the control unit to determine the amount of ignition advance. On these systems, if a failure occurs the failed component must be replaced. Before replacing suspected failed electrical components, carefully inspect the wiring and electrical connectors to the related components. Make sure the electrical connectors are fully connected, clean and not physically damaged. If necessary, clean the electrical contacts using electrical contact cleaner. The use of cleaning agents not specifically designed for electrical contacts should be avoided, as they could leave a surface film or damage the insulation of the wiring.

1-C. Engine Noises, Odors and Vibrations

1. Engine makes a knocking or pinging noise when accelerating

a. Check the octane rating of the fuel being used. Depending on the type of driving or driving conditions, it may be necessary to use a higher octane fuel.

b. Verify the ignition system settings and operation. Improperly adjusted ignition timing or a failed component, such as a knock sensor, may cause the ignition timing to advance excessively or prematurely. Check the ignition system operation and adjust, or replace components as needed.

c. Check the spark plug gap, heat range and condition. If the vehicle is operated in severe operating conditions or at continuous high speeds, use a colder heat range spark plug. Adjust the spark plug gap to the manufacturer's recommended specification and replace worn or damaged spark plugs.

2. Starter motor grinds when used

a. Examine the starter pinion gear and the engine ring gear for damage, and replace damaged parts.

b. Check the starter mounting bolts and housing. If the housing is cracked or damaged replace the starter motor and check the mounting bolts for tightness.

3. Engine makes a screeching noise

a. Check the accessory drive belts for looseness and adjust as necessary.

b. Check the accessory drive belt tensioners for seizing or excessive bearing noises and replace if loose, binding, or excessively noisy.

c. Check for a seizing water pump. The pump may not be leaking; however, the bearing may be faulty or the impeller loose and jammed. Replace the water pump.

4. Engine makes a growling noise

a. Check for a loose or failing water pump. Replace the pump and engine coolant.

b. Check the accessory drive belt tensioners for excessive bearing noises and replace if loose or excessively noisy.

5. Engine makes a ticking or tapping noise

a. On vehicles with hydraulic lash adjusters, check for low or dirty engine oil and top off or replace the engine oil and filter.

b. On vehicles with hydraulic lash adjusters, check for collapsed lifters and replace failed components.

c. On vehicles with hydraulic lash adjusters, check for low oil pressure caused by a restricted oil filter, worn engine oil pump, or oil pressure relief valve.

d. On vehicles with manually adjusted valves, check for excessive valve clearance or worn valve train parts. Adjust the valves to specification or replace worn and defective parts.

e. Check for a loose or improperly tensioned timing belt or timing chain and adjust or replace parts as necessary.

f. Check for a bent or sticking exhaust or intake valve. Remove the engine cylinder head to access and replace.

6. Engine makes a heavy knocking noise

a. Check for a loose crankshaft pulley or flywheel; replace and torque the mounting bolt(s) to specification.

b. Check for a bent connecting rod caused by a hydro-lock condition. Engine disassembly is necessary to inspect for damaged and needed replacement parts.

c. Check for excessive engine rod bearing wear or damage. This condition is also associated with low engine oil pressure and will require engine disassembly to inspect for damaged and needed replacement parts.

7. Vehicle has a fuel odor when driven

a. Check the fuel gauge level. If the fuel gauge registers full, it is possible that the odor is caused by being filled beyond capacity, or some spillage occurred during refueling. The odor should clear after driving an hour, or twenty miles, allowing the vapor canister to purge.

b. Check the fuel filler cap for looseness or seepage. Check the cap tightness and, if loose, properly secure. If seepage is noted, replace the filler cap.

c. Check for loose hose clamps, cracked or damaged fuel delivery and return lines, or leaking components or seals, and replace or repair as necessary.

d. Check the vehicle's fuel economy. If fuel consumption has increased due to a failed component, or if the fuel is not properly ignited due to an ignition related failure, the catalytic converter may become contaminated. This condition may also trigger the check engine warning light. Check the spark plugs for a dark, rich condition or verify the condition by testing the vehicle's emissions. Replace fuel fouled spark plugs, and test and replace failed components as necessary.

8. Vehicle has a rotten egg odor when driven

a. Check for a leaking intake gasket or vacuum leak causing a lean running condition. A lean mixture may result in increased exhaust temperatures, causing the catalytic converter to run hotter than normal. This condition may also trigger the check engine warning light. Check and repair the vacuum leaks as necessary.

b. Check the vehicle's alternator and battery condition. If the alternator is overcharging, the battery electrolyte can be boiled from the battery, and the battery casing may begin to crack, swell or bulge, damaging or shorting the battery internally. If this has occurred, neutralize the battery mounting area with a suitable baking soda and water mixture or equivalent, and replace the alternator or voltage regulator. Inspect, service, and load test the battery, and replace if necessary.

9. Vehicle has a sweet odor when driven

a. Check for an engine coolant leak caused by a seeping radiator cap, loose hose clamp, weeping cooling system seal, gasket or cooling system hose and replace or repair as needed.

b. Check for a coolant leak from the radiator, coolant reservoir, heater control valve or under the dashboard from the heater core, and replace the failed part as necessary.

c. Check the engine's exhaust for white smoke in addition to a sweet odor. The presence of white, steamy smoke with a sweet odor indicates coolant leaking into the combustion chamber. Possible causes include a failed head gasket, cracked engine block or cylinder head. Other symptoms of this condition include a white paste build-up on the inside of the oil filler cap, and softened, deformed or bulging radiator hoses.

10. Engine vibrates when idling

a. Check for loose, collapsed, or damaged engine or transmission mounts and repair or replace as necessary.

b. Check for loose or damaged engine covers or shields and secure or replace as necessary.

11. Engine vibrates during acceleration

a. Check for missing, loose or damaged exhaust system hangers and mounts; replace or repair as necessary.

b. Check the exhaust system routing and fit for adequate clearance or potential rubbing; repair or adjust as necessary.

1-D. Engine Electrical System

1. Battery goes dead while driving

a. Check the battery condition. Replace the battery if the battery will not hold a charge or fails a battery load test. If the battery loses fluid while driving, check for an overcharging condition. If the alternator is overcharging, replace the alternator or voltage regulator. (A voltage regulator is typically built into the alternator, necessitating alternator replacement or overhaul.)

b. Check the battery cable condition. Clean or replace corroded cables and clean the battery terminals.

c. Check the alternator and voltage regulator operation. If the charging system is over or undercharging, replace the alternator or voltage regulator, or both.

d. Inspect the wiring and wire connectors at the alternator for looseness, a missing ground or defective terminal, and repair as necessary.

e. Inspect the alternator drive belt tension, tensioners and condition. Properly tension the drive belt, replace weak or broken tensioners, and replace the drive belt if worn or cracked.

2. Battery goes dead overnight

a. Check the battery condition. Replace the battery if the battery will not hold a charge or fails a battery load test.

b. Check for a voltage draw, such as a trunk light, interior light or glove box light staying on. Check light switch position and operation, and replace if defective.

c. Check the alternator for an internally failed diode, and replace the alternator if defective.

1-E. Engine Cooling System

1. Engine overheats

a. Check the coolant level. Set the heater temperature to full hot and check for internal air pockets, bleed the cooling system and inspect for leakage. Top off the cooling system with the correct coolant mixture.

b. Pressure test the cooling system and radiator cap for leaks. Check for seepage caused by loose hose clamps, failed coolant hoses, and cooling system components such as the heater control valve, heater core, radiator, radiator cap, and water pump. Replace defective parts and fill the cooling system with the recommended coolant mixture.

c. On vehicles with electrically controlled cooling fans, check the cooling fan operation. Check for blown fuses or defective fan motors, temperature sensors and relays, and replace failed components.

d. Check for a coolant leak caused by a failed head gasket, or a porous water jacket casting in the cylinder head or engine block. Replace defective parts as necessary.

e. Check for an internally restricted radiator. Flush the radiator or replace if the blockage is too severe for flushing.

f. Check for a damaged water pump. If coolant circulation is poor, check for a loose water pump impeller. If the impeller is loose, replace the water pump.

2. Engine loses coolant

a. Pressure test the cooling system and radiator cap for leaks. Check for seepage caused by loose hose clamps, failed coolant hoses, and cooling system components such as the heater control valve, heater core, radiator, radiator cap, and water pump. Replace defective parts and fill the cooling system with the recommended coolant mixture.

b. Check for a coolant leak caused by a failed head gasket, or a porous water jacket casting in the cylinder head or engine block. Replace defective parts as necessary.

3. Engine temperature remains cold when driving

a. Check the thermostat operation. Replace the thermostat if it sticks in the open position.

b. On vehicles with electrically controlled cooling fans, check the cooling fan operation. Check for defective temperature sensors and stuck relays, and replace failed components.

c. Check temperature gauge operation if equipped to verify proper operation of the gauge. Check the sensors and wiring for defects, and repair or replace defective components.

4. Engine runs hot

a. Check for an internally restricted radiator. Flush the radiator or replace if the blockage is too severe for flushing.

b. Check for a loose or slipping water pump drive belt. Inspect the drive belt condition. Replace the belt if brittle, cracked or damaged. Check the pulley condition and properly tension the belt.

c. Check the cooling fan operation. Replace defective fan motors, sensors or relays as necessary.

d. Check temperature gauge operation if equipped to verify proper operation of the gauge. Check the sensors and wiring for defects, and repair or replace defective components.

e. Check the coolant level. Set the heater temperature to full hot, check for internal air pockets, bleed the cooling system and inspect for leakage. Top off the cooling system with the correct coolant mixture. Once the engine is cool, recheck the fluid level and top off as needed.

NOTE: The engine cooling system can also be affected by an engine's mechanical condition. A failed head gasket or a porous casting in the engine block or cylinder head could cause a loss of coolant and result in engine overheating.

Some cooling systems rely on electrically driven cooling fans to cool the radiator and use electrical temperature sensors and relays to operate the cooling fan. When diagnosing these systems, check for blown fuses, damaged wires and verify that the electrical connections are fully connected, clean and not physically damaged. If necessary, clean the electrical contacts using electrical contact cleaner. The use of cleaning agents not specifically designed for electrical contacts could leave a film or damage the insulation of the wiring.

1-F. Engine Exhaust System

1. Exhaust rattles at idle speed

a. Check the engine and transmission mounts and replace mounts showing signs of damage or wear.

b. Check the exhaust hangers, brackets and mounts. Replace broken, missing or damaged mounts.

c. Check for internal damage to mufflers and catalytic converters. The broken pieces from the defective component may travel in the direction of the exhaust flow and collect and/or create a blockage in a component other than the one which failed, causing engine running and stalling problems. Another symptom of a restricted exhaust is low engine manifold vacuum. Remove the exhaust system and carefully remove any loose or broken pieces, then replace any failed or damaged parts as necessary.

d. Check the exhaust system clearance, routing and alignment. If the exhaust is making contact with the vehicle in any manner, loosen and reposition the exhaust system.

2. Exhaust system vibrates when driving

a. Check the exhaust hangers, brackets and mounts. Replace broken, missing or damaged mounts.

b. Check the exhaust system clearance, routing and alignment. If the exhaust is making contact with the vehicle in any manner, check for bent or damaged components and replace, then loosen and reposition the exhaust system.

c. Check for internal damage to mufflers and catalytic converters. The broken pieces from the defective component may travel in the direction of the exhaust flow and collect and/or create a blockage in a component other than the one which failed, causing engine running and stalling problems. Another symptom of a restricted exhaust is low engine manifold vacuum. Remove the exhaust system and carefully remove any loose or broken pieces, then replace any failed or damaged parts as necessary.

3. Exhaust system hangs too low

a. Check the exhaust hangers, brackets and mounts. Replace broken, missing or damaged mounts.

b. Check the exhaust routing and alignment. Check and replace bent or damaged components. If the exhaust is not routed properly, loosen and reposition the exhaust system.

4. Exhaust sounds loud

a. Check the system for looseness and leaks. Check the exhaust pipes, clamps, flange bolts and manifold fasteners for tightness. Check and replace any failed gaskets.

b. Check and replace exhaust silencers that have a loss of efficiency due to internally broken baffles or worn packing material.

c. Check for missing mufflers and silencers that have been replaced with straight pipes or with non-original equipment silencers.

NOTE: Exhaust system rattles, vibration and proper alignment should not be overlooked. Excessive vibration caused by collapsed engine mounts, damaged or missing exhaust hangers and misalignment may cause surface cracks and broken welds, creating exhaust leaks or internal damage to exhaust components such as the catalytic converter, creating a restriction to exhaust flow and loss of power.

2. DRIVE TRAIN

2-A. Automatic Transmission

1. Transmission shifts erratically

a. Check and if not within the recommended range, add or remove transmission fluid to obtain the correct fluid level. Always use the recommended fluid type when adding transmission fluid.

b. Check the fluid level condition. If the fluid has become contaminated, fatigued from excessive heat or exhibits a burning odor, change the transmission fluid and filter using the recommended type and amount of fluid. A fluid which exhibits a burning odor indicates that the transmission has been slipping internally and may require future repairs.

c. Check for an improperly installed transmission filter, or missing filter gasket, and repair as necessary.

d. Check for loose or leaking gaskets, pressure lines and fittings, and repair or replace as necessary.

e. Check for loose or disconnected shift and throttle linkages or vacuum hoses, and repair as necessary.

2. Transmission will not engage

a. Check the shift linkage for looseness, wear and proper adjustment, and repair as necessary.

b. Check for a loss of transmission fluid and top off as needed with the recommended fluid.

c. If the transmission does not engage with the shift linkage correctly installed and the proper fluid level, internal damage has likely occurred, requiring transmission removal and disassembly.

3. Transmission will not downshift during heavy acceleration

a. On computer controlled transmissions, check for failed sensors or control units and repair or replace defective components.

b. On vehicles with kickdown linkages or vacuum servos, check for proper linkage adjustment or leaking vacuum hoses or servo units.

NOTE: Many automatic transmissions use an electronic control module, electrical sensors and solenoids to control transmission shifting. When troubleshooting a vehicle with this type of system, be sure the electrical connectors are fully connected, clean and not physically damaged. If necessary, clean the electrical contacts using electrical contact cleaner. The use of cleaning agents not specifically designed for electrical contacts could leave a film or damage the insulation of the wiring.

2-B. Manual Transmission

1. Transmission grinds going into forward gears while driving

a. Check the clutch release system. On clutches with a mechanical or cable linkage, check the adjustment. Adjust the clutch pedal to have 1 inch (25mm) of free-play at the pedal.

b. If the clutch release system is hydraulically operated, check the fluid level and, if low, top off using the recommended type and amount of fluid.

c. Synchronizers worn. Remove transmission and replace synchronizers.

d. Synchronizer sliding sleeve worn. Remove transmission and replace sliding sleeve.

e. Gear engagement dogs worn or damaged. Remove transmission and replace gear.

2. Transmission jumps out of gear

a. Shift shaft detent springs worn. Replace shift detent springs.

b. Synchronizer sliding sleeve worn. Remove transmission and replace sliding sleeve.

c. Gear engagement dogs worn or damaged. Remove transmission and replace gear.

d. Crankshaft thrust bearings worn. Remove engine and crankshaft, and repair as necessary.

3. Transmission difficult to shift

a. Verify the clutch adjustment and, if not properly adjusted, adjust to specification.

b. Synchronizers worn. Remove transmission and replace synchronizers.

c. Pilot bearing seized. Remove transmission and replace pilot bearing.

d. Shift linkage or bushing seized. Disassemble the shift linkage, replace worn or damaged bushings, lubricate and reinstall.

4. Transmission leaks fluid

a. Check the fluid level for an overfilled condition. Adjust the fluid level to specification.

b. Check for a restricted transmission vent or breather tube. Clear the blockage as necessary and check the fluid level. If necessary, top off with the recommended lubricant.

c. Check for a porous casting, leaking seal or gasket. Replace defective parts and top off the fluid level with the recommended lubricant.

2-C. Clutch

1. Clutch slips on hills or during sudden acceleration

a. Check for insufficient clutch pedal free-play. Adjust clutch linkage or cable to allow about 1 inch (25mm) of pedal free-play.

b. Clutch disc worn or severely damaged. Remove engine or transmission and replace clutch disc.

c. Clutch pressure plate is weak. Remove engine or transmission and replace the clutch pressure plate and clutch disc.

d. Clutch pressure plate and/or flywheel incorrectly machined. If the clutch system has been recently replaced and rebuilt, or refurbished parts have been used, it is possible that the machined surfaces decreased the clutch clamping force. Replace defective parts with new replacement parts.

2. Clutch will not disengage, difficult to shift

a. Check the clutch release mechanism. Check for stretched cables, worn linkages or failed clutch hydraulics and replace defective parts. On hydraulically operated clutch release mechanisms, check for air in the hydraulic system and bleed as necessary.

b. Check for a broken, cracked or fatigued clutch release arm or release arm pivot. Replace defective parts and properly lubricate upon assembly.

c. Check for a damaged clutch hub damper or damper spring. The broken parts tend to become lodged between the clutch disc and the pressure plate. Disassemble clutch system and replace failed parts.

d. Check for a seized clutch pilot bearing. Disassemble the clutch assembly and replace the defective parts.

e. Check for a defective clutch disc. Check for warpage or lining thicknesses larger than original equipment.

3. Clutch is noisy when the clutch pedal is pressed

a. Check the clutch pedal stop and pedal free-play adjustment for excessive movement and adjust as necessary.

b. Check for a worn or damaged release bearing. If the noise ceases when the pedal is released, the release bearing should be replaced.

c. Check the engine crankshaft axial play. If the crankshaft thrust bearings are worn or damaged, the crankshaft will move when pressing the clutch pedal. The engine must be disassembled to replace the crankshaft thrust bearings.

4. Clutch pedal extremely difficult to press

a. Check the clutch pedal pivots and linkages for binding. Clean and lubricate linkages.

b. On cable actuated clutch systems, check the cable routing and condition. Replace kinked, frayed, damaged or corroded cables and check cable routing to avoid sharp bends. Check the engine ground strap for poor conductivity. If the ground strap is marginal, the engine could try to ground itself via the clutch cable, causing premature failure.

c. On mechanical linkage clutches, check the linkage for binding or misalignment. Lubricate pivots or linkages and repair as necessary.

d. Check the release bearing guide tube and release fork for a lack of lubrication. Install a smooth coating of high temperature grease to allow smooth movement of the release bearing over the guide tube.

5. Clutch pedal remains down when pressed

a. On mechanical linkage or cable actuated clutches, check for a loose or disconnected link.

b. On hydraulically actuated clutches, check the fluid level and check for a hydraulic leak at the clutch slave or master cylinder, or hydraulic line. Replace failed parts and bleed clutch hydraulic system. If no leakage is noted, the clutch master cylinder may have failed internally. Replace the clutch master cylinder and bleed the clutch hydraulic system.

6. Clutch chatters when engaging

a. Check the engine flywheel for warpage or surface variations and replace or repair as necessary.

b. Check for a warped clutch disc or damaged clutch damper hub. Remove the clutch disc and replace.

c. Check for a loose or damaged clutch pressure plate and replace defective components.

NOTE: The clutch is actuated either by a mechanical linkage, cable or a clutch hydrauiic system. The mechanical linkage and cable systems may require the clutch pedal free-play to be adjusted as the clutch disc wears. A hydraulic clutch system automatically adjusts as the clutch wears and, with the exception of the clutch pedal height, no adjustment is possible.

2-D. Differential and Final Drive

1. Differential makes a low pitched rumbling noise

a. Check fluid level type and amount. Replace the fluid with the recommended type and amount of lubricant.

b. Check the differential bearings for wear or damage. Remove the bearings, inspect the drive and driven gears for wear or damage, and replace components as necessary.

2. Differential makes a howling noise

a. Check fluid level type and amount. Replace the fluid with the recommended type and amount of lubricant.

b. Check the differential drive and driven gears for wear or damage, and replace components as necessary.

2-E. Transfer Assembly

All Wheel and Four Wheel Drive Vehicles

1. Leaks fluid from seals or vent after being driven
a. Fluid level overfilled. Check and adjust transfer case fluid level.
b. Check for a restricted breather or breather tube, clear and check the fluid level and top off as needed.
c. Check seal condition and replace worn, damaged, or defective seals. Check the fluid level and top off as necessary.

2. Makes excessive noise while driving
a. Check the fluid for the correct type of lubricant. Drain and refill using the recommended type and amount of lubricant.
b. Check the fluid level. Top off the fluid using the recommended type and amount of lubricant.
c. If the fluid level and type of lubricant meet specifications, check for internal wear or damage. Remove assembly and disassemble to inspect for worn, damaged, or defective components.

3. Jumps out of gear
a. Stop vehicle and make sure the unit is fully engaged.
b. Check for worn, loose or an improperly adjusted linkage. Replace and/or adjust linkage as necessary.
c. Check for internal wear or damage. Remove assembly and disassemble to inspect for worn, damaged, or defective components.

2-F. Driveshaft

Rear Wheel, All Wheel and Four Wheel Drive Vehicles

1. Clunking noise from center of vehicle shifting from forward to reverse
a. Worn universal joint. Remove driveshaft and replace universal joint.

2. Excessive vibration from center of vehicle when accelerating
a. Worn universal joint. Remove driveshaft and replace universal joint.
b. Driveshaft misaligned. Check for collapsed or damaged engine and transmission mounts, and replace as necessary.
c. Driveshaft bent or out of balance. Replace damaged components and reinstall.
d. Driveshaft out of balance. Remove the driveshaft and have it balanced by a competent professional, or replace the driveshaft assembly.

NOTE: Most driveshafts are linked together by universal joints; however, some manufacturers use Constant Velocity (CV) joints or rubber flex couplers.

2-G. Axles

All Wheel and Four Wheel Drive Vehicles

1. Front or rear wheel makes a clicking noise
a. Check for debris such as a pebble, nail or glass in the tire or tire tread. Carefully remove the debris. Small rocks and pebbles rarely cause a puncture; however, a sharp object should be removed carefully at a facility capable of performing tire repairs.
b. Check for a loose, damaged or worn Constant Velocity (CV) joint and replace if defective.

2. Front or rear wheel vibrates with increased speed
a. Check for a bent rim and replace, if damaged.
b. Check the tires for balance or internal damage and replace if defective.
c. Check for a loose, worn or damaged wheel bearing and replace if defective.
d. Check for a loose, damaged or worn Constant Velocity (CV) joint and replace if defective.

Front Wheel Drive Vehicles

3. Front wheel makes a clicking noise
a. Check for debris such as a pebble, nail or glass in the tire or tire tread. Carefully remove the debris. Small rocks and pebbles rarely cause a puncture; however, a sharp object should be removed carefully at a facility capable of performing tire repairs.
b. Check for a loose, damaged or worn Constant Velocity (CV) joint and replace if defective.

4. Rear wheel makes a clicking noise
a. Check for debris such as a pebble, nail or glass in the tire or tire tread. Carefully remove the debris. Small rocks and pebbles rarely cause a puncture; however, a sharp object should be removed carefully at a facility capable of performing tire repairs.

Rear Wheel Drive Vehicles

5. Front or rear wheel makes a clicking noise
a. Check for debris such as a pebble, nail or glass in the tire or tire tread. Carefully remove the debris. Small rocks and pebbles rarely cause a puncture; however, a sharp object should be removed carefully at a facility capable of performing tire repairs.

6. Rear wheel shudders or vibrates
a. Check for a bent rear wheel or axle assembly and replace defective components.
b. Check for a loose, damaged or worn rear wheel bearing and replace as necessary.

2-H. Other Drive Train Conditions

1. Burning odor from center of vehicle when accelerating
a. Check for a seizing brake hydraulic component such as a brake caliper. Check the caliper piston for surface damage such as rust, and measure for out-of-round wear and caliper-to-piston clearance. For additional information on brake related odors, refer to section 3-A, condition number 9.
b. On vehicles with a manual transmission, check for a slipping clutch. For possible causes and additional information, refer to section 2-C, condition number 1.

c. On vehicles with an automatic transmission, check the fluid level and condition. Top off or change the fluid and filter using the recommended replacement parts, lubricant type and amount. If the odor persists, transmission removal and disassembly will be necessary.

2. Engine accelerates, but vehicle does not gain speed

a. On vehicles with a manual transmission, check for a slipping or damaged clutch. For possible causes and additional information refer to section 2-C, condition number 1.

b. On vehicles with an automatic transmission, check the fluid level and condition. Top off or change the fluid and filter using the recommended replacement parts, lubricant type and amount. If the slipping continues, transmission removal and disassembly will be necessary.

3. BRAKE SYSTEM

3-A. Brake System Troubleshooting

1. Brake pedal pulsates or shimmies when pressed

a. Check wheel lug nut torque and tighten evenly to specification.

b. Check the brake rotor for trueness and thickness variations. Replace the rotor if it is too thin, warped, or if the thickness varies beyond specification. Some rotors can be machined; consult the manufacturer's specifications and recommendations before using a machined brake rotor.

c. Check the brake caliper or caliper bracket mounting bolt torque and inspect for looseness. Torque the mounting bolts and inspect for wear or any looseness, including worn mounting brackets, bushings and sliding pins.

d. Check the wheel bearing for looseness. If the bearing is loose, adjust if possible, otherwise replace the bearing.

2. Brakes make a squealing noise

a. Check the brake rotor for the presence of a ridge on the outer edge; if present, remove the ridge or replace the brake rotor and brake pads.

b. Check for debris in the brake lining material, clean and reinstall.

c. Check the brake linings for wear and replace the brake linings if wear is approaching the lining wear limit.

d. Check the brake linings for glazing. Inspect the brake drum or rotor surface and replace, along with the brake linings, if the surface is not smooth or even.

e. Check the brake pad or shoe mounting areas for a lack of lubricant or the presence of surface rust. Clean and lubricate with a recommended high temperature brake grease.

3. Brakes make a grinding noise

a. Check the brake linings and brake surface areas for severe wear or damage. Replace worn or damaged parts.

b. Check for a seized or partially seized brake causing premature or uneven brake wear, excessive heat and brake rotor or drum damage. Replace defective parts and inspect the wheel bearing condition, which could have been damaged due to excessive heat.

4. Vehicle pulls to one side during braking

a. Check for air in the brake hydraulic system. Inspect the brake hydraulic seals, fluid lines and related components for fluid leaks. Remove the air from the brake system by bleeding the brakes. Be sure to use fresh brake fluid that meets the manufacturer's recommended standards.

b. Check for an internally restricted flexible brake hydraulic hose. Replace the hose and flush the brake system.

c. Check for a seizing brake hydraulic component such as a brake caliper. Check the caliper piston for surface damage such as rust, and measure for out-of-round wear and caliper-to-piston clearance. Overhaul or replace failed parts and flush the brake system.

d. Check the vehicle's alignment and inspect for suspension wear. Replace worn bushings, ball joints and set alignment to the manufacturer's specifications.

e. If the brake system uses drum brakes front or rear, check the brake adjustment. Inspect for seized adjusters and clean or replace, then properly adjust.

5. Brake pedal feels spongy or has excessive travel

a. Check the brake fluid level and condition. If the fluid is contaminated or has not been flushed every two years, clean the master cylinder reservoir, and bleed and flush the brakes using fresh brake fluid that meets the manufacturer's recommended standards.

b. Check for a weak or damaged flexible brake hydraulic hose. Replace the hose and flush the brake system.

c. If the brake system uses drum brakes front or rear, check the brake adjustment. Inspect for seized adjusters and clean or replace, then properly adjust.

6. Brake pedal feel is firm, but brakes lack sufficient stopping power or fade

a. Check the operation of the brake booster and brake booster check valve. Replace worn or failed parts.

b. Check brake linings and brake surface areas for glazing and replace worn or damaged parts.

c. Check for seized hydraulic parts and linkages, and clean or replace as needed.

7. Vehicle has excessive front end dive or locks rear brakes too easily

a. Check for worn, failed or seized brake proportioning valve and replace the valve.

b. Check for a seized, disconnected or missing spring or linkage for the brake proportioning valve. Replace missing parts or repair as necessary.

8. Brake pedal goes to floor when pressed and will not pump up

a. Check the brake hydraulic fluid level and inspect the fluid lines and seals for leakage. Repair or replace leaking components, then bleed and flush the brake system using fresh brake fluid that meets the manufacturer's recommended standards.

b. Check the brake fluid level. Inspect the brake fluid level and brake hydraulic seals. If the fluid level is ok, and the brake hydraulic system is free of hydraulic leaks, replace the brake master cylinder, then bleed and flush the brake system using fresh brake fluid that meets the manufacturer's recommended standards.

9. Brakes produce a burning odor

a. Check for a seizing brake hydraulic component such as a brake caliper. Check the caliper piston for surface damage such as rust, and measure for out-of-round wear and caliper-to-piston clearance. Overhaul or replace failed parts and flush the brake system.

b. Check for an internally restricted flexible brake hydraulic hose. Replace the hose and flush the brake system.

c. Check the parking brake release mechanism, seized linkage or cable, and repair as necessary.

BRAKE PERFORMANCE TROUBLESHOOTING HINTS

Brake vibrations or pulsation can often be diagnosed on a safe and careful test drive. A brake vibration which is felt through the brake pedal while braking, but not felt in the steering wheel, is most likely caused by brake surface variations in the rear brakes. If both the brake pedal and steering wheel vibrate during braking, a surface variation in the front brakes, or both front and rear brakes, is very likely.

A brake pedal that pumps up with repeated use can be caused by air in the brake hydraulic system or, if the vehicle is equipped with rear drum brakes, the brake adjusters may be seized or out of adjustment. A quick test for brake adjustment on vehicles with rear drum brakes is to pump the brake pedal several times with the vehicle's engine not running and the parking brake released. Pump the brake pedal several times and continue to apply pressure to the brake pedal. With pressure being applied to the brake pedal, engage the parking brake. Release the brake pedal and quickly press the brake pedal again. If the brake pedal pumped up, the rear brakes are in need of adjustment. Do not compensate for the rear brake adjustment by adjusting the parking brake, this will cause premature brake lining wear.

To test a vacuum brake booster, pump the brake pedal several times with the vehicle's engine off. Apply pressure to the brake pedal and then start the engine. The brake pedal should move downward about one inch (25mm).

4. WHEELS, TIRES, STEERING AND SUSPENSION

4-A. Wheels and Wheel Bearings

1. Front wheel or wheel bearing loose

All Wheel and Four Wheel Drive Vehicles

a. Torque lug nuts and axle nuts to specification and recheck for looseness.

b. Wheel bearing worn or damaged. Replace wheel bearing.

Front Wheel Drive Vehicles

a. Torque lug nuts and axle nuts to specification and recheck for looseness.

b. Wheel bearing worn or damaged. Replace wheel bearing.

c. Wheel bearing out of adjustment. Adjust wheel bearing to specification; if still loose, replace.

Rear Wheel Drive Vehicles

a. Wheel bearing out of adjustment. Adjust wheel bearing to specification; if still loose, replace.

b. Torque lug nuts to specification and recheck for looseness.

c. Wheel bearing worn or damaged. Replace wheel bearing.

2. Rear wheel or wheel bearing loose

All Wheel and Four Wheel Drive Vehicles

a. Torque lug nuts and axle nuts to specification and recheck for looseness.

b. Wheel bearing worn or damaged. Replace wheel bearing.

Front Wheel Drive Vehicles

a. Wheel bearing out of adjustment. Adjust wheel bearing to specification; if still loose, replace.

b. Torque lug nuts to specification and recheck for looseness.

c. Wheel bearing worn or damaged. Replace wheel bearing.

Rear Wheel Drive Vehicles

a. Torque lug nuts to specification and recheck for looseness.

b. Wheel bearing worn or damaged. Replace wheel bearing.

4-B. Tires

1. Tires worn on inside tread

a. Check alignment for a toed-out condition. Check and set tire pressures and properly adjust the toe.

b. Check for worn, damaged or defective suspension components. Replace defective parts and adjust the alignment.

2. Tires worn on outside tread

a. Check alignment for a toed-in condition. Check and set tire pressures and properly adjust the toe.

b. Check for worn, damaged or defective suspension components. Replace defective parts and adjust the alignment.

3. Tires worn unevenly

a. Check the tire pressure and tire balance. Replace worn or defective tires and check the alignment; adjust if necessary.

b. Check for worn shock absorbers. Replaced failed components, worn or defective tires and check the alignment; adjust if necessary.

c. Check the alignment settings. Check and set tire pressures and properly adjust the alignment to specification.

d. Check for worn, damaged or defective suspension components. Replace defective parts and adjust the alignment to specification.

4-C. Steering

1. Excessive play in steering wheel

a. Check the steering gear free-play adjustment and properly adjust to remove excessive play.
b. Check the steering linkage for worn, damaged or defective parts. Replace failed components and perform a front end alignment.
c. Check for a worn, damaged, or defective steering box, replace the steering gear and check the front end alignment.

2. Steering wheel shakes at cruising speeds

a. Check for a bent front wheel. Replace a damaged wheel and check the tire for possible internal damage.
b. Check for an unevenly worn front tire. Replace the tire, adjust tire pressure and balance.
c. Check the front tires for hidden internal damage. Tires which have encountered large pot holes or suffered other hard blows may have sustained internal damage and should be replaced immediately.
d. Check the front tires for an out-of-balance condition. Remove, spin balance and reinstall. Torque all the wheel bolts or lug nuts to the recommended specification.
e. Check for a loose wheel bearing. If possible, adjust the bearing, or replace the bearing if it is a non-adjustable bearing.

3. Steering wheel shakes when braking

a. Refer to section 3-A, condition number 1.

4. Steering wheel becomes stiff when turned

a. Check the steering wheel free-play adjustment and reset as needed.
b. Check for a damaged steering gear assembly. Replace the steering gear and perform a front end alignment.
c. Check for damaged or seized suspension components. Replace defective components and perform a front end alignment.

4-D. Suspension

1. Vehicle pulls to one side

a. Tire pressure uneven. Adjust tire pressure to recommended settings.
b. Tires worn unevenly. Replace tires and check alignment settings.
c. Alignment out of specification. Align front end and check thrust angle.
d. Check for a dragging brake and repair or replace as necessary.

2. Vehicle is very bouncy over bumps

a. Check for worn or leaking shock absorbers or strut assemblies and replace as necessary.
b. Check for seized shock absorbers or strut assemblies and replace as necessary.

NOTE: When one shock fails, it is recommended to replace front or rear units as pairs.

3. Vehicle leans excessively in turns

a. Check for worn or leaking shock absorbers or strut assemblies and replace as necessary.
b. Check for missing, damaged, or worn stabilizer links or bushings, and replace or install as necessary.

4. Vehicle ride quality seems excessively harsh

a. Check for seized shock absorbers or strut assemblies and replace as necessary.
b. Check for excessively high tire pressures and adjust pressures to vehicle recommendations.

5. Vehicle seems low or leans to one side

a. Check for a damaged, broken or weak spring. Replace defective parts and check for a needed alignment.
b. Check for seized shock absorbers or strut assemblies and replace as necessary.
c. Check for worn or leaking shock absorbers or strut assemblies and replace as necessary.

4-E. Driving Noises and Vibrations

Noises

1. Vehicle makes a clicking noises when driven

a. Check the noise to see if it varies with road speed. Verify if the noise is present when coasting or with steering or throttle input. If the clicking noise frequency changes with road speed and is not affected by steering or throttle input, check the tire treads for a stone, piece of glass, nail or another hard object imbedded into the tire or tire tread. Stones rarely cause a tire puncture and are easily removed. Other objects may create an air leak when removed. Consider having these objects removed immediately at a facility equipped to repair tire punctures.
b. If the clicking noise varies with throttle input and steering, check for a worn Constant Velocity (CV-joint) joint, universal (U-joint) or flex joint.

2. Vehicle makes a clunking or knocking noise over bumps

a. A clunking noise over bumps is most often caused by excessive movement or clearance in a suspension component. Check the suspension for soft, cracked, damaged or worn bushings. Replace the bushings and check the vehicle's alignment.
b. Check for loose suspension mounting bolts. Check the tightness on subframe bolts, pivot bolts and suspension mounting bolts, and torque to specification.
c. Check the vehicle for a loose wheel bearing. Some wheel bearings can be adjusted for looseness, while others must be replaced if loose. Adjust or replace the bearings as recommended by the manufacturer.
d. Check the door latch adjustment. If the door is slightly loose, or the latch adjustment is not centered, the door assembly may create noises over bumps and rough surfaces. Properly adjust the door latches to secure the door.

3. Vehicle makes a low pitched rumbling noise when driven

a. A low pitched rumbling noise is usually caused by a drive train related bearing and is most often associated with a wheel bearing which has been damaged or worn. The damage can be caused by excessive brake temperatures or physical contact with a pot hole or curb. Sometimes the noise will vary when turning. Left hand turns increase the load on the vehicle's right side, and right turns load the left side. A failed front wheel bearing may also cause a slight steering wheel vibration when turning. A bearing which exhibits noise must be replaced.

b. Check the tire condition and balance. An internally damaged tire may cause failure symptoms similar to failed suspension parts. For diagnostic purposes, try a known good set of tires and replace defective tires.

4. Vehicle makes a squeaking noise over bumps

a. Check the vehicle's ball joints for wear, damaged or leaking boots. Replace a ball joint if it is loose, the boot is damaged and leaking, or the ball joint is binding. When replacing suspension parts, check the vehicle for alignment.

b. Check for seized or deteriorated bushings. Replace bushings that are worn or damaged and check the vehicle for alignment.

c. Check for the presence of sway bar or stabilizer bar bushings which wrap around the bar. Inspect the condition of the bushings and replace if worn or damaged. Remove the bushing bracket and apply a thin layer of suspension grease to the area where the bushings wrap around the bar and reinstall the bushing brackets.

Vibrations

5. Vehicle vibrates when driven

a. Check the road surface. Roads which have rough or uneven surfaces may cause unusual vibrations.

b. Check the tire condition and balance. An internally damaged tire may cause failure symptoms similar to failed suspension parts. For diagnostic purposes, try a known good set of tires and replace defective tires immediately.

c. Check for a worn Constant Velocity (CV-joint) joint, universal (U- joint) or flex joint and replace if loose, damaged or binding.

d. Check for a loose, bent, or out-of-balance axle or drive shaft. Replace damaged or failed components.

NOTE: Diagnosing failures related to wheels, tires, steering and the suspension system can often times be accomplished with a careful and thorough test drive. Bearing noises are isolated by noting whether the noises or symptoms vary when turning left or right, or occur while driving a straight line. During a left hand turn, the vehicle's weight shifts to the right, placing more force on the right side bearings, such that if a right side wheel bearing is worn or damaged, the noise or vibration should increase during light-to-heavy acceleration. Conversely, on right hand turns, the vehicle tends to lean to the left, loading the left side bearings.

Knocking noises in the suspension when the vehicle is driven over rough roads, railroad tracks and speed bumps indicate worn suspension components such as bushings, ball joints or tie rod ends, or a worn steering system.

5. ELECTRICAL ACCESSORIES

5-A. Headlights

1. One headlight only works on high or low beam

a. Check for battery voltage at headlight electrical connector. If battery voltage is present, replace the headlight assembly or bulb if available separately. If battery voltage is not present, refer to the headlight wiring diagram to troubleshoot.

2. Headlight does not work on high or low beam

a. Check for battery voltage and ground at headlight electrical connector. If battery voltage is present, check the headlight connector ground terminal for a proper ground. If battery voltage and ground are present at the headlight connector, replace the headlight assembly or bulb if available separately. If battery voltage or ground is not present, refer to the headlight wiring diagram to troubleshoot.

b. Check the headlight switch operation. Replace the switch if the switch is defective or operates intermittently.

3. Headlight(s) very dim

a. Check for battery voltage and ground at headlight electrical connector. If battery voltage is present, trace the ground circuit for the headlamp electrical connector, then clean and repair as necessary.

If the voltage at the headlight electrical connector is significantly less than the voltage at the battery, refer to the headlight wiring diagram to troubleshoot and locate the voltage drop.

5-B. Tail, Running and Side Marker Lights

1. Tail light, running light or side marker light inoperative

a. Check for battery voltage and ground at light's electrical connector. If battery voltage is present, check the bulb socket and electrical connector ground terminal for a proper ground. If battery voltage and ground are present at the light connector, but not in the socket, clean the socket and the ground terminal connector. If battery voltage and ground are present in the bulb socket, replace the bulb. If battery voltage or ground is not present, refer to the wiring diagram to troubleshoot for an open circuit.

b. Check the light switch operation and replace if necessary.

2. Tail light, running light or side marker light works intermittently

a. Check the bulb for a damaged filament, and replace if damaged.

b Check the bulb and bulb socket for corrosion, and clean or replace the bulb and socket.

c. Check for loose, damaged or corroded wires and electrical terminals, and repair as necessary.

d. Check the light switch operation and replace if necessary.

3. Tail light, running light or side marker light very dim

a. Check the bulb and bulb socket for corrosion and clean or replace the bulb and socket.

b. Check for low voltage at the bulb socket positive terminal or a poor ground. If voltage is low, or the ground marginal, trace the wiring to, and check for loose, damaged or corroded wires and electrical terminals; repair as necessary.

c. Check the light switch operation and replace if necessary.

5-C. Interior Lights

1. Interior light inoperative

a. Verify the interior light switch location and position(s), and set the switch in the correct position.

b. Check for battery voltage and ground at the interior light bulb socket. If battery voltage and ground are present, replace the bulb. If voltage is not present, check the interior light fuse for battery voltage. If the fuse is missing, replace the fuse. If the fuse has blown, or if battery voltage is present, refer to the wiring diagram to troubleshoot the cause for an open or shorted circuit. If ground is not present, check the door switch contacts and clean or repair as necessary.

2. Interior light works intermittently

a. Check the bulb for a damaged filament, and replace if damaged.

b. Check the bulb and bulb socket for corrosion, and clean or replace the bulb and socket.

c. Check for loose, damaged or corroded wires and electrical terminals; repair as necessary.

d. Check the door and light switch operation, and replace if necessary.

3. Interior light very dim

a. Check the bulb and bulb socket for corrosion, and clean or replace the bulb and socket.

b. Check for low voltage at the bulb socket positive terminal or a poor ground. If voltage is low, or the ground marginal, trace the wiring to, and check for loose, damaged or corroded wires and electrical terminals; repair as necessary.

c. Check the door and light switch operation, and replace if necessary.

5-D. Brake Lights

1. One brake light inoperative

a. Press the brake pedal and check for battery voltage and ground at the brake light bulb socket. If present, replace the bulb. If either battery voltage or ground is not present, refer to the wiring diagram to troubleshoot.

2. Both brake lights inoperative

a. Press the brake pedal and check for battery voltage and ground at the brake light bulb socket. If present, replace both bulbs. If

battery voltage is not present, check the brake light switch adjustment and adjust as necessary. If the brake light switch is properly adjusted, and battery voltage or the ground is not present at the bulb sockets, or at the bulb electrical connector with the brake pedal pressed, refer to the wiring diagram to troubleshoot the cause of an open circuit.

3. One or both brake lights very dim

a. Press the brake pedal and measure the voltage at the brake light bulb socket. If the measured voltage is close to the battery voltage, check for a poor ground caused by a loose, damaged, or corroded wire, terminal, bulb or bulb socket. If the ground is bolted to a painted surface, it may be necessary to remove the electrical connector and clean the mounting surface, so the connector mounts on bare metal. If battery voltage is low, check for a poor connection caused by either a faulty brake light switch, a loose, damaged, or corroded wire, terminal or electrical connector. Refer to the wiring diagram to troubleshoot the cause of a voltage drop.

5-E. Warning Lights

1. Warning light(s) stay on when the engine is started

Ignition, Battery or Alternator Warning Light

a. Check the alternator output and voltage regulator operation, and replace as necessary.

b. Check the warning light wiring for a shorted wire.

Check Engine Light

a. Check the engine for routine maintenance and tune-up status. Note the engine tune-up specifications and verify the spark plug, air filter and engine oil condition; replace and/or adjust items as necessary.

b. Check the fuel tank for low fuel level, causing an intermittent lean fuel mixture. Top off fuel tank and reset check engine light.

c. Check for a failed or disconnected engine fuel or ignition component, sensor or control unit and repair or replace as necessary.

d. Check the intake manifold and vacuum hoses for air leaks and repair as necessary.

e. Check the engine's mechanical condition for excessive oil consumption.

Anti-Lock Braking System (ABS) Light

a. Check the wheel sensors and sensor rings for debris, and clean as necessary.

b. Check the brake master cylinder for fluid leakage or seal failure and replace as necessary.

c. Check the ABS control unit, pump and proportioning valves for proper operation; replace as necessary.

d. Check the sensor wiring at the wheel sensors and the ABS control unit for a loose or shorted wire, and repair as necessary.

Brake Warning Light

a. Check the brake fluid level and check for possible leakage from the hydraulic lines and seals. Top off brake fluid and repair leakage as necessary.

b. Check the brake linings for wear and replace as necessary.

c. Check for a loose or shorted brake warning light sensor or wire, and replace or repair as necessary.

Oil Pressure Warning Light

a. Stop the engine immediately. Check the engine oil level and oil filter condition, and top off or change the oil as necessary.

b. Check the oil pressure sensor wire for being shorted to ground. Disconnect the wire from the oil pressure sensor and with the ignition in the ON position, but not running, the oil pressure light should not be working. If the light works with the wire disconnected, check the sensor wire for being shorted to ground. Check the wire routing to make sure the wire is not pinched and check for insulation damage. Repair or replace the wire as necessary and recheck before starting the engine.

c. Remove the oil pan and check for a clogged oil pick-up tube screen.

d. Check the oil pressure sensor operation by substituting a known good sensor.

e. Check the oil filter for internal restrictions or leaks, and replace as necessary.

WARNING: If the engine is operated with oil pressure below the manufacturer's specification, severe (and costly) engine damage could occur. Low oil pressure can be caused by excessive internal wear or damage to the engine bearings, oil pressure relief valve, oil pump or oil pump drive mechanism.

Before starting the engine, check for possible causes of rapid oil loss, such as leaking oil lines or a loose, damaged, restricted, or leaking oil filter or oil pressure sensor. If the engine oil level and condition are acceptable, measure the engine's oil pressure using a pressure gauge, or determine the cause for the oil pressure warning light to function when the engine is running, before operating the engine for an extended period of time. Another symptom of operating an engine with low oil pressure is the presence of severe knocking and tapping noises.

Parking Brake Warning Light

a. Check the brake release mechanism and verify the parking brake has been fully released.

b. Check the parking brake light switch for looseness or misalignment.

c. Check for a damaged switch or a loose or shorted brake light switch wire, and replace or repair as necessary.

2. Warning light(s) flickers on and off when driving

Ignition, Battery or Alternator Warning Light

a. Check the alternator output and voltage regulator operation. An intermittent condition may indicate worn brushes, an internal short, or a defective voltage regulator. Replace the alternator or failed component.

b. Check the warning light wiring for a shorted, pinched or damaged wire and repair as necessary.

Check Engine Light

a. Check the engine for required maintenance and tune-up status. Verify engine tune-up specifications, as well as spark plug, air filter and engine oil condition; replace and/or adjust items as necessary.

b. Check the fuel tank for low fuel level causing an intermittent lean fuel mixture. Top off fuel tank and reset check engine light.

c. Check for an intermittent failure or partially disconnected engine fuel and ignition component, sensor or control unit; repair or replace as necessary.

d. Check the intake manifold and vacuum hoses for air leaks, and repair as necessary.

e. Check the warning light wiring for a shorted, pinched or damaged wire and repair as necessary.

Anti-Lock Braking System (ABS) Light

a. Check the wheel sensors and sensor rings for debris, and clean as necessary.

b. Check the brake master cylinder for fluid leakage or seal failure and replace as necessary.

c. Check the ABS control unit, pump and proportioning valves for proper operation, and replace as necessary.

d. Check the sensor wiring at the wheel sensors and the ABS control unit for a loose or shorted wire and repair as necessary.

Brake Warning Light

a. Check the brake fluid level and check for possible leakage from the hydraulic lines and seals. Top off brake fluid and repair leakage as necessary.

b. Check the brake linings for wear and replace as necessary.

c. Check for a loose or shorted brake warning light sensor or wire, and replace or repair as necessary.

Oil Pressure Warning Light

a. Stop the engine immediately. Check the engine oil level and check for a sudden and rapid oil loss, such as a leaking oil line or oil pressure sensor, and repair or replace as necessary.

b. Check the oil pressure sensor operation by substituting a known good sensor.

c. Check the oil pressure sensor wire for being shorted to ground. Disconnect the wire from the oil pressure sensor and with the ignition in the ON position, but not running, the oil pressure light should not be working. If the light works with the wire disconnected, check the sensor wire for being shorted to ground. Check the wire routing to make sure the wire is not pinched and check for insulation damage. Repair or replace the wire as necessary and recheck before starting the engine.

d. Remove the oil pan and check for a clogged oil pick-up tube screen.

Parking Brake Warning Light

a. Check the brake release mechanism and verify the parking brake has been fully released.

b. Check the parking brake light switch for looseness or misalignment.

c. Check for a damaged switch or a loose or shorted brake light switch wire, and replace or repair as necessary.

3. Warning light(s) inoperative with ignition on, and engine not started

a. Check for a defective bulb by installing a known good bulb.

b. Check for a defective wire using the appropriate wiring diagram(s).

c. Check for a defective sending unit by removing and then grounding the wire at the sending unit. If the light comes on with the ignition on when grounding the wire, replace the sending unit.

5-F. Turn Signal and 4-Way Hazard Lights

1. Turn signals or hazard lights come on, but do not flash

a. Check for a defective flasher unit and replace as necessary.

2. Turn signals or hazard lights do not function on either side

a. Check the fuse and replace, if defective.

b. Check the flasher unit by substituting a known good flasher unit.

c. Check the turn signal electrical system for a defective component, open circuit, short circuit or poor ground.

3. Turn signals or hazard lights only work on one side

a. Check for failed bulbs and replace as necessary.

b. Check for poor grounds in both housings and repair as necessary.

4. One signal light does not work

a. Check for a failed bulb and replace as necessary.

b. Check for corrosion in the bulb socket, and clean and repair as necessary.

c. Check for a poor ground at the bulb socket, and clean and repair as necessary.

5. Turn signals flash too slowly

a. Check signal bulb(s) wattage and replace with lower wattage bulb(s).

6. Turn signals flash too fast

a. Check signal bulb(s) wattage and replace with higher wattage bulb(s).

b. Check for installation of the correct flasher unit and replace if incorrect.

7. Four-way hazard flasher indicator light inoperative

a. Verify that the exterior lights are functioning and, if so, replace indicator bulb.

b. Check the operation of the warning flasher switch and replace if defective.

8. Turn signal indicator light(s) do not work in either direction

a. Verify that the exterior lights are functioning and, if so, replace indicator bulb(s).

b. Check for a defective flasher unit by substituting a known good unit.

9. One turn signal indicator light does not work

a. Check for a defective bulb and replace as necessary.

b. Check for a defective flasher unit by substituting a known good unit.

5-G. Horn

1. Horn does not operate

a. Check for a defective fuse and replace as necessary.

b. Check for battery voltage and ground at horn electrical connections when pressing the horn switch. If voltage is present, replace the horn assembly. If voltage or ground is not present, refer to Chassis Electrical coverage for additional troubleshooting techniques and circuit information.

2. Horn has an unusual tone

a. On single horn systems, replace the horn.

b. On dual horn systems, check the operation of the second horn. Dual horn systems have a high and low pitched horn. Unplug one horn at a time and recheck operation. Replace the horn which does not function.

c. Check for debris or condensation build-up in horn and verify the horn positioning. If the horn has a single opening, adjust the opening downward to allow for adequate drainage and to prevent debris build-up.

5-H. Windshield Wipers

1. Windshield wipers do not operate

a. Check fuse and replace as necessary.

b. Check switch operation and repair or replace as necessary.

c. Check for corroded, loose, disconnected or broken wires and clean or repair as necessary.

d. Check the ground circuit for the wiper switch or motor and repair as necessary.

2. Windshield wiper motor makes a humming noise, gets hot or blows fuses

a. Wiper motor damaged internally; replace the wiper motor.

b. Wiper linkage bent, damaged or seized. Repair or replace wiper linkage as necessary.

3. Windshield wiper motor operates, but one or both wipers fail to move

a. Windshield wiper motor linkage loose or disconnected. Repair or replace linkage as necessary.

b. Windshield wiper arms loose on wiper pivots. Secure wiper arm to pivot or replace both the wiper arm and pivot assembly.

4. Windshield wipers will not park

a. Check the wiper switch operation and verify that the switch properly interrupts the power supplied to the wiper motor.

b. If the wiper switch is functioning properly, the wiper motor parking circuit has failed. Replace the wiper motor assembly. Operate the wiper motor at least one time before installing the arms and blades to ensure correct positioning, then recheck using the highest wiper speed on a wet windshield to make sure the arms and blades do not contact the windshield trim.

6. INSTRUMENTS AND GAUGES

6-A. Speedometer (Cable Operated)

1. Speedometer does not work

a. Check and verify that the speedometer cable is properly seated into the speedometer assembly and the speedometer drive gear.

b. Check the speedometer cable for breakage or rounded-off cable ends where the cable seats into the speedometer drive gear and into the speedometer assembly. If damaged, broken or the cable ends are rounded off, replace the cable.

c. Check speedometer drive gear condition and replace as necessary.

d. Install a known good speedometer to test for proper operation. If the substituted speedometer functions properly, replace the speedometer assembly.

2. Speedometer needle fluctuates when driving at steady speeds.

a. Check speedometer cable routing or sheathing for sharp bends or kinks. Route cable to minimize sharp bends or kinks. If the sheathing has been damaged, replace the cable assembly.

b. Check the speedometer cable for adequate lubrication. Remove the cable, inspect for damage, clean, lubricate and reinstall. If the cable has been damaged, replace the cable.

3. Speedometer works intermittently

a. Check the cable and verify that the cable is fully installed and the fasteners are secure.

b. Check the cable ends for wear and rounding, and replace as necessary.

6-B. Speedometer (Electronically Operated)

1. Speedometer does not work

a. Check the speed sensor pickup and replace as necessary.

b. Check the wiring between the speed sensor and the speedometer for corroded terminals, loose connections or broken wires and clean or repair as necessary.

c. Install a known good speedometer to test for proper operation. If the substituted speedometer functions properly, replace the speedometer assembly.

2. Speedometer works intermittently

a. Check the wiring between the speed sensor and the speedometer for corroded terminals, loose connections or broken wires and clean or repair as necessary.

b. Check the speed sensor pickup and replace as necessary.

6-C. Fuel, Temperature and Oil Pressure Gauges

1. Gauge does not register

a. Check for a missing or blown fuse and replace as necessary.

b. Check for an open circuit in the gauge wiring. Repair wiring as necessary.

c. Gauge sending unit defective. Replace gauge sending unit.

d. Gauge or sending unit improperly installed. Verify installation and wiring, and repair as necessary.

2. Gauge operates erratically

a. Check for loose, shorted, damaged or corroded electrical connections or wiring and repair as necessary.

b. Check gauge sending units and replace as necessary.

3. Gauge operates fully pegged

a. Sending unit-to-gauge wire shorted to ground.

b. Sending unit defective; replace sending unit.

c. Gauge or sending unit not properly grounded.

d. Gauge or sending unit improperly installed. Verify installation and wiring, and repair as necessary.

7. CLIMATE CONTROL

7-A. Air Conditioner

1. No air coming from air conditioner vents

a. Check the air conditioner fuse and replace as necessary.

b. Air conditioner system discharged. Have the system evacuated, charged and leak tested by an MVAC certified technician, utilizing approved recovery/recycling equipment. Repair as necessary.

c. Air conditioner low pressure switch defective. Replace switch.

d. Air conditioner fan resistor pack defective. Replace resistor pack.

e. Loose connection, broken wiring or defective air conditioner relay in air conditioning electrical circuit. Repair wiring or replace relay as necessary.

2. Air conditioner blows warm air

a. Air conditioner system is discharged. Have the system evacuated, charged and leak tested by an MVAC certified technician, utilizing approved recovery/recycling equipment. Repair as necessary.

b. Air conditioner compressor clutch not engaging. Check compressor clutch wiring, electrical connections and compressor clutch, and repair or replace as necessary.

3. Water collects on the interior floor when the air conditioner is used

a. Air conditioner evaporator drain hose is blocked. Clear the drain hose where it exits the passenger compartment.

b. Air conditioner evaporator drain hose is disconnected. Secure the drain hose to the evaporator drainage tray under the dashboard.

4. Air conditioner has a moldy odor when used

a. The air conditioner evaporator drain hose is blocked or partially re-stricted, allowing condensation to build up around the evaporator and drainage tray. Clear the drain hose where it exits the passenger compartment.

7-B. Heater

1. Blower motor does not operate

a. Check blower motor fuse and replace as necessary.
b. Check blower motor wiring for loose, damaged or corroded contacts and repair as necessary.
c. Check blower motor switch and resistor pack for open circuits, and repair or replace as necessary.
d. Check blower motor for internal damage and repair or replace as necessary.

2. Heater blows cool air

a. Check the engine coolant level. If the coolant level is low, top off and bleed the air from the cooling system as necessary and check for coolant leaks.
b. Check engine coolant operating temperature. If coolant temperature is below specification, check for a damaged or stuck thermostat.

c. Check the heater control valve operation. Check the heater control valve cable or vacuum hose for proper installation. Move the heater temperature control from hot to cold several times and verify the operation of the heater control valve. With the engine at normal operating temperature and the heater temperature control in the full hot position, carefully feel the heater hose going into and exiting the control valve. If one heater hose is hot and the other is much cooler, replace the control valve.

3. Heater steams the windshield when used

a. Check for a loose cooling system hose clamp or leaking coolant hose near the engine firewall or under the dash area, and repair as necessary.
b. Check for the existence of a sweet odor and fluid dripping from the heater floor vents, indicating a failed or damaged heater core. Pressure test the cooling system with the heater set to the fully warm position and check for fluid leakage from the floor vents. If leakage is verified, remove and replace the heater core assembly.

NOTE: On some vehicles, the dashboard must be disassembled and removed to access the heater core.

GLOSSARY

AIR/FUEL RATIO: The ratio of air-to-gasoline by weight in the fuel mixture drawn into the engine.

AIR INJECTION: One method of reducing harmful exhaust emissions by injecting air into each of the exhaust ports of an engine. The fresh air entering the hot exhaust manifold causes any remaining fuel to be burned before it can exit the tailpipe.

ALTERNATOR: A device used for converting mechanical energy into electrical energy.

AMMETER: An instrument, calibrated in amperes, used to measure the flow of an electrical current in a circuit. Ammeters are always connected in series with the circuit being tested.

AMPERE: The rate of flow of electrical current present when one volt of electrical pressure is applied against one ohm of electrical resistance.

ANALOG COMPUTER: Any microprocessor that uses similar (analogous) electrical signals to make its calculations.

ARMATURE: A laminated, soft iron core wrapped by a wire that converts electrical energy to mechanical energy as in a motor or relay. When rotated in a magnetic field, it changes mechanical energy into electrical energy as in a generator.

ATMOSPHERIC PRESSURE: The pressure on the Earth's surface caused by the weight of the air in the atmosphere. At sea level, this pressure is 14.7 psi at 32°F (101 kPa at 0°C).

ATOMIZATION: The breaking down of a liquid into a fine mist that can be suspended in air.

AXIAL PLAY: Movement parallel to a shaft or bearing bore.

BACKFIRE: The sudden combustion of gases in the intake or exhaust system that results in a loud explosion.

BACKLASH: The clearance or play between two parts, such as meshed gears.

BACKPRESSURE: Restrictions in the exhaust system that slow the exit of exhaust gases from the combustion chamber.

BAKELITE: A heat resistant, plastic insulator material commonly used in printed circuit boards and transistorized components.

BALL BEARING: A bearing made up of hardened inner and outer races between which hardened steel balls roll.

BALLAST RESISTOR: A resistor in the primary ignition circuit that lowers voltage after the engine is started to reduce wear on ignition components.

BEARING: A friction reducing, supportive device usually located between a stationary part and a moving part.

BIMETAL TEMPERATURE SENSOR: Any sensor or switch made of two dissimilar types of metal that bend when heated or cooled due to the different expansion rates of the alloys. These types of sensors usually function as an on/off switch.

BLOWBY: Combustion gases, composed of water vapor and unburned fuel, that leak past the piston rings into the crankcase during normal engine operation. These gases are removed by the PCV system to prevent the buildup of harmful acids in the crankcase.

BRAKE PAD: A brake shoe and lining assembly used with disc brakes.

BRAKE SHOE: The backing for the brake lining. The term is, however, usually applied to the assembly of the brake backing and lining.

BUSHING: A liner, usually removable, for a bearing; an anti-friction liner used in place of a bearing.

CALIPER: A hydraulically activated device in a disc brake system, which is mounted straddling the brake rotor (disc). The caliper contains at least one piston and two brake pads. Hydraulic pressure on the piston(s) forces the pads against the rotor.

CAMSHAFT: A shaft in the engine on which are the lobes (cams) which operate the valves. The camshaft is driven by the crankshaft, via a belt, chain or gears, at one half the crankshaft speed.

CAPACITOR: A device which stores an electrical charge.

CARBON MONOXIDE (CO): A colorless, odorless gas given off as a normal byproduct of combustion. It is poisonous and extremely dangerous in confined areas, building up slowly to toxic levels without warning if adequate ventilation is not available.

CARBURETOR: A device, usually mounted on the intake manifold of an engine, which mixes the air and fuel in the proper proportion to allow even combustion.

CATALYTIC CONVERTER: A device installed in the exhaust system, like a muffler, that converts harmful byproducts of combustion into carbon dioxide and water vapor by means of a heat-producing chemical reaction.

CENTRIFUGAL ADVANCE: A mechanical method of advancing the spark timing by using flyweights in the distributor that react to centrifugal force generated by the distributor shaft rotation.

CHECK VALVE: Any one-way valve installed to permit the flow of air, fuel or vacuum in one direction only.

CHOKE: A device, usually a moveable valve, placed in the intake path of a carburetor to restrict the flow of air.

CIRCUIT: Any unbroken path through which an electrical current can flow. Also used to describe fuel flow in some instances.

CIRCUIT BREAKER: A switch which protects an electrical circuit from overload by opening the circuit when the current flow exceeds a predetermined level. Some circuit breakers must be reset manually, while most reset automatically.

COIL (IGNITION): A transformer in the ignition circuit which steps up the voltage provided to the spark plugs.

COMBINATION MANIFOLD: An assembly which includes both the intake and exhaust manifolds in one casting.

COMBINATION VALVE: A device used in some fuel systems that routes fuel vapors to a charcoal storage canister instead of venting them into the atmosphere. The valve relieves fuel tank pressure and allows fresh air into the tank as the fuel level drops to prevent a vapor lock situation.

COMPRESSION RATIO: The comparison of the total volume of the cylinder and combustion chamber with the piston at BDC and the piston at TDC.

CONDENSER: 1. An electrical device which acts to store an electrical charge, preventing voltage surges. 2. A radiator-like device in the air conditioning system in which refrigerant gas condenses into a liquid, giving off heat.

CONDUCTOR: Any material through which an electrical current can be transmitted easily.

CONTINUITY: Continuous or complete circuit. Can be checked with an ohmmeter.

COUNTERSHAFT: An intermediate shaft which is rotated by a mainshaft and transmits, in turn, that rotation to a working part.

CRANKCASE: The lower part of an engine in which the crankshaft and related parts operate.

CRANKSHAFT: The main driving shaft of an engine which receives reciprocating motion from the pistons and converts it to rotary motion.

CYLINDER: In an engine, the round hole in the engine block in which the piston(s) ride.

CYLINDER BLOCK: The main structural member of an engine in which is found the cylinders, crankshaft and other principal parts.

CYLINDER HEAD: The detachable portion of the engine, usually fastened to the top of the cylinder block and containing all or most of the combustion chambers. On overhead valve engines, it contains the valves and their operating parts. On overhead cam engines, it contains the camshaft as well.

DEAD CENTER: The extreme top or bottom of the piston stroke.

DETONATION: An unwanted explosion of the air/fuel mixture in the combustion chamber caused by excess heat and compression, advanced timing, or an overly lean mixture. Also referred to as "ping".

DIAPHRAGM: A thin, flexible wall separating two cavities, such as in a vacuum advance unit.

DIESELING: A condition in which hot spots in the combustion chamber cause the engine to run on after the key is turned off.

DIFFERENTIAL: A geared assembly which allows the transmission of motion between drive axles, giving one axle the ability to turn faster than the other.

DIODE: An electrical device that will allow current to flow in one direction only.

DISC BRAKE: A hydraulic braking assembly consisting of a brake disc, or rotor, mounted on an axle, and a caliper assembly containing, usually two brake pads which are activated by hydraulic pressure. The pads are forced against the sides of the disc, creating friction which slows the vehicle.

DISTRIBUTOR: A mechanically driven device on an engine which is responsible for electrically firing the spark plug at a predetermined point of the piston stroke.

DOWEL PIN: A pin, inserted in mating holes in two different parts allowing those parts to maintain a fixed relationship.

DRUM BRAKE: A braking system which consists of two brake shoes and one or two wheel cylinders, mounted on a fixed backing plate, and a brake drum, mounted on an axle, which revolves around the assembly.

DWELL: The rate, measured in degrees of shaft rotation, at which an electrical circuit cycles on and off.

ELECTRONIC CONTROL UNIT (ECU): Ignition module, module, amplifier or igniter. See Module for definition.

ELECTRONIC IGNITION: A system in which the timing and firing of the spark plugs is controlled by an electronic control unit, usually called a module. These systems have no points or condenser.

END-PLAY: The measured amount of axial movement in a shaft.

ENGINE: A device that converts heat into mechanical energy.

EXHAUST MANIFOLD: A set of cast passages or pipes which conduct exhaust gases from the engine.

FEELER GAUGE: A blade, usually metal, or precisely predetermined thickness, used to measure the clearance between two parts.

FIRING ORDER: The order in which combustion occurs in the cylinders of an engine. Also the order in which spark is distributed to the plugs by the distributor.

FLOODING: The presence of too much fuel in the intake manifold and combustion chamber which prevents the air/fuel mixture from firing, thereby causing a no-start situation.

FLYWHEEL: A disc shaped part bolted to the rear end of the crankshaft. Around the outer perimeter is affixed the ring gear. The starter drive engages the ring gear, turning the flywheel, which rotates the crankshaft, imparting the initial starting motion to the engine.

FOOT POUND (ft. lbs. or sometimes, ft.lb.): The amount of energy or work needed to raise an item weighing one pound, a distance of one foot.

FUSE: A protective device in a circuit which prevents circuit overload by breaking the circuit when a specific amperage is present. The device is constructed around a strip or wire of a lower amperage rating than the circuit it is designed to protect. When an amperage higher than that stamped on the fuse is present in the circuit, the strip or wire melts, opening the circuit.

GEAR RATIO: The ratio between the number of teeth on meshing gears.

GENERATOR: A device which converts mechanical energy into electrical energy.

HEAT RANGE: The measure of a spark plug's ability to dissipate heat from its firing end. The higher the heat range, the hotter the plug fires.

HUB: The center part of a wheel or gear.

HYDROCARBON (HC): Any chemical compound made up of hydrogen and carbon. A major pollutant formed by the engine as a byproduct of combustion.

HYDROMETER: An instrument used to measure the specific gravity of a solution.

INCH POUND (inch lbs.; sometimes in.lb. or in. lbs.): One twelfth of a foot pound.

INDUCTION: A means of transferring electrical energy in the form of a magnetic field. Principle used in the ignition coil to increase voltage.

INJECTOR: A device which receives metered fuel under relatively low pressure and is activated to inject the fuel into the engine under relatively high pressure at a predetermined time.

INPUT SHAFT: The shaft to which torque is applied, usually carrying the driving gear or gears.

INTAKE MANIFOLD: A casting of passages or pipes used to conduct air or a fuel/air mixture to the cylinders.

JOURNAL: The bearing surface within which a shaft operates.

KEY: A small block usually fitted in a notch between a shaft and a hub to prevent slippage of the two parts.

MANIFOLD: A casting of passages or set of pipes which connect the cylinders to an inlet or outlet source.

MANIFOLD VACUUM: Low pressure in an engine intake manifold formed just below the throttle plates. Manifold vacuum is highest at idle and drops under acceleration.

MASTER CYLINDER: The primary fluid pressurizing device in a hydraulic system. In automotive use, it is found in brake and hydraulic clutch systems and is pedal activated, either directly or, in a power brake system, through the power booster.

MODULE: Electronic control unit, amplifier or igniter of solid state or integrated design which controls the current flow in the ignition primary circuit based on input from the pick-up coil. When the module opens the primary circuit, high secondary voltage is induced in the coil.

NEEDLE BEARING: A bearing which consists of a number (usually a large number) of long, thin rollers.

OHM: (Ω) The unit used to measure the resistance of conductor-to-electrical flow. One ohm is the amount of resistance that limits current flow to one ampere in a circuit with one volt of pressure.

OHMMETER: An instrument used for measuring the resistance, in ohms, in an electrical circuit.

OUTPUT SHAFT: The shaft which transmits torque from a device, such as a transmission.

OVERDRIVE: A gear assembly which produces more shaft revolutions than that transmitted to it.

OVERHEAD CAMSHAFT (OHC): An engine configuration in which the camshaft is mounted on top of the cylinder head and operates the valve either directly or by means of rocker arms.

OVERHEAD VALVE (OHV): An engine configuration in which all of the valves are located in the cylinder head and the camshaft is located in the cylinder block. The camshaft operates the valves via lifters and pushrods.

OXIDES OF NITROGEN (NOx): Chemical compounds of nitrogen produced as a byproduct of combustion. They combine with hydrocarbons to produce smog.

OXYGEN SENSOR: Use with the feedback system to sense the presence of oxygen in the exhaust gas and signal the computer which can reference the voltage signal to an air/fuel ratio.

PINION: The smaller of two meshing gears.

PISTON RING: An open-ended ring with fits into a groove on the outer diameter of the piston. Its chief function is to form a seal between the piston and cylinder wall. Most automotive pistons have three rings: two for compression sealing; one for oil sealing.

PRELOAD: A predetermined load placed on a bearing during assembly or by adjustment.

PRIMARY CIRCUIT: the low voltage side of the ignition system which consists of the ignition switch, ballast resistor or resistance wire, bypass, coil, electronic control unit and pick-up coil as well as the connecting wires and harnesses.

PRESS FIT: The mating of two parts under pressure, due to the inner diameter of one being smaller than the outer diameter of the other, or vice versa; an interference fit.

RACE: The surface on the inner or outer ring of a bearing on which the balls, needles or rollers move.

REGULATOR: A device which maintains the amperage and/or voltage levels of a circuit at predetermined values.

RELAY: A switch which automatically opens and/or closes a circuit.

RESISTANCE: The opposition to the flow of current through a circuit or electrical device, and is measured in ohms. Resistance is equal to the voltage divided by the amperage.

RESISTOR: A device, usually made of wire, which offers a preset amount of resistance in an electrical circuit.

RING GEAR: The name given to a ring-shaped gear attached to a differential case, or affixed to a flywheel or as part of a planetary gear set.

ROLLER BEARING: A bearing made up of hardened inner and outer races between which hardened steel rollers move.

ROTOR: 1. The disc-shaped part of a disc brake assembly, upon which the brake pads bear; also called, brake disc. 2. The device mounted atop the distributor shaft, which passes current to the distributor cap tower contacts.

SECONDARY CIRCUIT: The high voltage side of the ignition system, usually above 20,000 volts. The secondary includes the ignition coil, coil wire, distributor cap and rotor, spark plug wires and spark plugs.

SENDING UNIT: A mechanical, electrical, hydraulic or electro-magnetic device which transmits information to a gauge.

SENSOR: Any device designed to measure engine operating conditions or ambient pressures and temperatures. Usually electronic in nature and designed to send a voltage signal to an on-board computer, some sensors may operate as a simple on/off switch or they may provide a variable voltage signal (like a potentiometer) as conditions or measured parameters change.

SHIM: Spacers of precise, predetermined thickness used between parts to establish a proper working relationship.

SLAVE CYLINDER: In automotive use, a device in the hydraulic clutch system which is activated by hydraulic force, disengaging the clutch.

SOLENOID: A coil used to produce a magnetic field, the effect of which is to produce work.

SPARK PLUG: A device screwed into the combustion chamber of a spark ignition engine. The basic construction is a conductive core inside of a ceramic insulator, mounted in an outer conductive base. An electrical charge from the spark plug wire travels along the conductive core and jumps a preset air gap to a grounding point or points at the end of the conductive base. The resultant spark ignites the fuel/air mixture in the combustion chamber.

SPLINES: Ridges machined or cast onto the outer diameter of a shaft or inner diameter of a bore to enable parts to mate without rotation.

TACHOMETER: A device used to measure the rotary speed of an engine, shaft, gear, etc., usually in rotations per minute.

THERMOSTAT: A valve, located in the cooling system of an engine, which is closed when cold and opens gradually in response to engine heating, controlling the temperature of the coolant and rate of coolant flow.

TOP DEAD CENTER (TDC): The point at which the piston reaches the top of its travel on the compression stroke.

TORQUE: The twisting force applied to an object.

TORQUE CONVERTER: A turbine used to transmit power from a driving member to a driven member via hydraulic action, providing changes in drive ratio and torque. In automotive use, it links the driveplate at the rear of the engine to the automatic transmission.

TRANSDUCER: A device used to change a force into an electrical signal.

TRANSISTOR: A semi-conductor component which can be actuated by a small voltage to perform an electrical switching function.

TUNE-UP: A regular maintenance function, usually associated with the replacement and adjustment of parts and components in the electrical and fuel systems of a vehicle for the purpose of attaining optimum performance.

TURBOCHARGER: An exhaust driven pump which compresses intake air and forces it into the combustion chambers at higher than atmospheric pressures. The increased air pressure allows more fuel to be burned and results in increased horsepower being produced.

VACUUM ADVANCE: A device which advances the ignition timing in response to increased engine vacuum.

VACUUM GAUGE: An instrument used to measure the presence of vacuum in a chamber.

VALVE: A device which control the pressure, direction of flow or rate of flow of a liquid or gas.

VALVE CLEARANCE: The measured gap between the end of the valve stem and the rocker arm, cam lobe or follower that activates the valve.

VISCOSITY: The rating of a liquid's internal resistance to flow.

VOLTMETER: An instrument used for measuring electrical force in units called volts. Voltmeters are always connected parallel with the circuit being tested.

WHEEL CYLINDER: Found in the automotive drum brake assembly, it is a device, actuated by hydraulic pressure, which, through internal pistons, pushes the brake shoes outward against the drums.

MASTER
INDEX